THE MAKING OF
Shinkokinshū

Harvard East Asian Monographs 208

THE MAKING OF
Shinkokinshū

Robert N. Huey

Published by the Harvard University Asia Center
and distributed by Harvard University Press
Cambridge (Massachusetts) and London 2002

© 2002 by the President and Fellows of Harvard College

Printed in the United States of America

The Harvard University Asia Center publishes a monograph series and, in coordination with the Fairbank Center for East Asian Research, the Korea Institute, the Reischauer Institute of Japanese Studies, and other faculties and institutes, administers research projects designed to further scholarly understanding of China, Japan, Vietnam, Korea, and other Asian countries. The Center also sponsors projects addressing multidisciplinary and regional issues in Asia.

Library of Congress Cataloging-in-Publication Data

Huey, Robert N., 1952–
    The making of Shinkokinshū / Robert N. Huey
      p. cm. -- (Harvard East Asian monographs ; 208)
    Includes bibliographical references and index.
    ISBN 0-674-00853-7 (cloth : alk. paper)
      1. Shin kokin wakashū. 2. Waka--History and criticism. 3. Japanese poetry--To 1600--History and criticism. I. Title: Making of Shin kokinshū. II. Title. III. Series.
PL728.29.H84 2002
895.6'12208--dc21

                                                      2001059366

Index by the author

∞ Printed on acid-free paper

Last figure below indicates year of this printing
12 11 10 09 08 07 06 05 04 03 02

In memory of

Marie Hewitt, Dorothy Huey, Jeff Mass,

and Harold Stewart

Fana min to / uweken fito mo / naki yado no / sakura fa kozo no / faru zo sakamasi
Those who helped plant it, / In hopes of seeing its blossoms, /
Are now gone. / Would that the cherry in this garden /
Had bloomed for them in an earlier spring!
—Ōe no Yoshitoki, *Shinkokinshū* 763

kinofu misi / fito mo fakanaku / narinikeri / yo no ma ni tireru / fana ni magafite
Those I saw / Just yesterday / Are now no more /
Like flowers scattered / During the night.
—Jien, *Shūgyokushū* 90

Acknowledgments

In preparing this work, I benefited greatly from the valuable comments of many colleagues. The anonymous reviewers for the Harvard University Asia Center pointed out numerous errors and made several suggestions, both general and specific, for tightening the manuscript. Although I fear the result still falls short of readability, the text is much crisper now, thanks to their efforts. The University of Hawai'i Japan Studies Endowment, funded by a grant from the Japanese government, provided me with several summer grants for time in Japan. These helped immensely and allowed me to gather bibliographic materials and consult with colleagues. Among the latter, I particularly thank Professor Yasuaki Watanabe, of Sophia University, whose stint as my mentor began twenty years ago at a Tōdai seminar conducted by Professor Kubota Jun. Dr. Watanabe was then a graduate student, and I was there on a dissertation research grant. Over the years, both of us moved from late to early Kamakura in our research interests, and in the late stages of this manuscript he provided much useful advice and information. Drs. Alexander Vovin and John Bentley were always helpful in matters relating to texts and historical linguistics.

I also thank John Ziemer, my editor. He was knowledgeable, patient, and perceptive. Many of his queries, from the very beginning, cut right to the heart of the matter, and he has been instrumental in turning a huge mass of information into something readable.

R.N.H.

Contents

	Tables and Figures	xi
	Conventions and Editions	xiii
	Abbreviations	xxi
	Introduction	1
1	The Political Context	17
2	First Steps, Shōji 2 (1200)	50
3	New Faces and a New Wakadokoro, Kennin 1 (1201)	86
4	Go-Toba's Retreat at Minase, Kennin 2 (1202)	142
5	The *Sengohyakuban Uta-awase*	193
6	The Persistence of *Miyabi*, Kennin 3 (1203)	222
7	Diversions and Mourning, Genkyū 1 (1204)	257
8	Preparations Continue, Genkyū 2 (1205)	296
9	Finishing Touches, Ken'ei and Beyond (1206–1208)	333
	Conclusion	381

Appendixes

A	Family Trees and Patronage Charts	387
B	Short Biographies of Principals	391

C	*Shōji ninen Shunzeikyō no waji sōjō*	405
D	Details of the *Sengohyakuban uta-awase*	413
E	Three Poetry Exchanges Between Go-Toba and Jien	419
F	*Shinkokinshū* Time Line	437

Reference Material

Works Cited	445
Index of First Lines	453
Index of Poets	459
Subject Index	463

Tables and Figures

Tables

1	Mikohidari vs. Rokujō, *Sengohyakuban uta-awase*, by judge	198
2	Scores in the Kasuga contest, by team	280
3	*Shinkokinshū* poems from *Saishōshitennō-in shōji waka*	373
D.1	Teams in the *Sengohyakuban uta-awase*	413
D.2	Arrangement of rounds in the *Sengohyakuban uta-awase*	414
D.3	Participants in *Sengohyakuban uta-awase* ranked by number of winning poems	416
D.4	Judgments by judge and faction	417
D.5	Details of judgments in rounds matching Kujō/Mikohidari poets against Tsuchimikado/Rokujō poets	418

Figures

1	Seating arrangement at the Kennin 2 *eigu* poetry contest at Jōnan Temple	152
2	Layout of Wakadokoro for Shunzei's ninetieth-year celebration	247
3	Rokujō family tree through the early 1200s	387
4	Mikohidari family tree through the early 1200s	388
5	Marriage and family ties in Go-Toba's poetry circle	389

Conventions and Editions

As does everyone who deals with premodern Japanese court society, I have faced the problem of rendering into readable English an array of terms and titles and distinctions. Throughout the narrative I continually refer to the palace (with lowercase "p") when speaking of Go-Toba's residence as retired emperor. The whole issue of where emperors and retired emperors resided is problematic; because of frequent fires and the need to remodel, they moved quite often. The biggest dislocation occurred in 1177, when most of the *daidairi*—which John Hall calls "the Great Palace Enclosure"[1]—was destroyed by fire; much of it was never rebuilt. Of course, the matter is further complicated by the retired emperor system (*insei*). From the late Heian through the Kamakura period, it would be fair to say that the true locus of imperial power lay with the senior living retired emperor. As Hall dryly notes in assessing the consequences of the disastrous 1177 fire, "Already, well before the end of the twelfth century, however, the effective political machinery of state had found a way to function independently of the public facilities of the Great Palace Enclosure."[2] Incidentally, it is not simply a matter of *political* power. It is clear that from Shirakawa on, the retired emperor had also become the center of cultural, and especially poetic, activity.[3]

The "palace," then, does not necessarily refer to the Imperial Palace (the *daidairi*), located at the northern end of Suzaku ōji between Ichijō and Nijō avenues. We may just as well consider wherever the senior *in* lived as the *de*

---

1. Hall, "Kyoto as Historical Background," p. 13.
2. Ibid., p. 10.
3. See Huey, "The Medievalization of Poetic Practice."

facto "palace," since that would be the locus of "palace politics," as well as the base for major public poetry events such as 100-poem sequences (*hyakushu*) and imperial anthologies (*chokusenshū*). Thus, the term "palace" (lowercase "p") as used in this study refers to Go-Toba's current residence, wherever it might have been at the time.[4] Even more broadly, I use "palace" to refer to the room or rooms in which Go-Toba (or any relevant imperial personage) held court at any given location. In other words, when Go-Toba and his courtiers were visiting the Minase Villa, and Teika used the expression *sanjō* (*ue ni mairu*) in his diary to mean that he went from his sleeping quarters or some other place at Minase into the room where Go-Toba was or was planning to make an appearance, I might describe Teika as "going to the palace." This seems less awkward than saying "he went into the imperial presence." By contrast, the *daidairi* is called the "Imperial Palace." (In Japanese, the basic distinction is between the *daidairi*, where the sitting emperor lived, and the *sentō*, or *sentō gosho*, where the senior retired emperor resided.)

Another choice I faced involved how to identify people mentioned in diary entries. As tedious as court titles may be to read (not to mention how awkward they are to translate), I believe it is reductive and misleading to call everyone by his or her given name, as if we are all friends or co-workers of long standing. Hierarchy was defining (and confining) in this period, and it is significant that Teika, for example, in the same entry referred to Kujō Yoshitsune as "the Minister of the Left" while calling Fujiwara Masatsune by his given name, even though he was probably more intimate with the former, whose family he served. So in translating diary entries I have generally tried to use the form of identification the writer himself used and have added the personal name in brackets if the writer gave only a title. From time to time I deviate slightly from that rule of thumb, especially when, in my judgment, a string of titles would sound excessively cumbersome. However, for the most part, I have tried to preserve the tone of a *kanbun* diary describing a formal poetic event and, in so doing, keep in the forefront the formal, hierarchical nature of the Heian/Kamakura era court.

Identifications of people raised another issue. The number of people involved in even the short time period dealt with here is quite large, and even the specialist will likely have trouble keeping track of more than the

---

4. Hall ("Kyoto as Historical Background," p. 23) claims that as retired emperor, Go-Toba occupied 18 residences in 23 years, though only three were long-term stays.

best-known names (e.g., Shunzei, Teika, Go-Toba). And although many of the identifications can be found in standard English-language reference sources,[5] and most of the rest can be found in Japanese dictionaries such as those mentioned below, it seemed to me that the reader of this book needed something a little handier. Appendixes A and B contain several family trees and mini-biographies of many of the people mentioned in this book; I pay particular attention to genealogical and group affiliations since marriage relationships and patronage played an important role in the politics and art of this age.

The main aristocratic families in Heian and Kamakura Japan (in this study, the Fujiwara and Minamoto appear most frequently) consisted of many branches, and in some cases the names of the branches became widely used as surnames. I have chosen to use the branch names Rokujō, Kujō, and Asukai as surnames in both the text and the index, although at first appearance, I identify the members of these branch families as Fujiwara, with the branch name in parentheses; for example, Akisuke, Fujiwara (Rokujō). Other branch names, such as Mikohidari (the branch to which Shunzei and Teika belonged) are less commonly encountered in historical sources as the primary form of identification, and for people belonging to these families, I have used Fujiwara or Minamoto generically.

In presenting the romanized versions of poem texts, I have made two choices that call for clarification. First, I have retained the five-line format, both in the romanized version and, in almost all cases, the translation. I am aware of arguments to the contrary, but I remain convinced that the 5-*ku* distinction was a powerful one to traditional waka poet/scholar/critics. Not only do various works refer to it explicitly, but it is also certainly implicit in many of the verbal "tricks" (*kyō*) the poets used, such as syntactical parallelism.[6] Although the notion of *ku* is not exactly the same as the notion

---

5. E.g., Miner et al., *Princeton Companion to Classical Japanese Literature;* or Hisamatsu, *Biographical Dictionary of Japanese Literature.*

6. For example, Fujiwara Kintō (966–1041) begins his treatise *Shinsen zuinō* with these lines: "The form of a poem is 31 syllables (*ji*) in 5 *ku*" (*Uta no arisama sanjūichiji sōjite goku ari;* Hisamatsu and Nishio, *Karonshū nōgakuronshū,* p. 26). And Shunzei (1114–1204), in *Korai fūteishō,* describes a waka poem as "5-7-5-7-7 *ku* in 31 syllables" (ibid., pp. 295–96). In addition, numerous poetry contest judgments make reference to individual *ku,* in some cases even calling them "the second *ku,*" "the fifth *ku*" (*dainiku, daigoku*); see, e.g., Kenshō's judgment for Round 1307 in the *Sengohyakuban uta-awase*). As for the way in which a poem might actually

of "line" in English-language prosody, I feel that using a single- or double-line translation (which seeks to capture the "other" *ku* division—that between the so-called *kami no ku*, or "upper" 5-7-5 section of the poem, and the *shimo no ku*, or "lower" 7-7 section of the poem) obscures the 5-*ku* structure.

Second, in romanizing the texts of poems, I have chosen to reflect certain aspects of the significant phonological changes that Japanese underwent from the Nara through the Heian and into the Kamakura periods. The most significant of these was the collapsing of the eight Nara vowels into five by the Heian period. Also significant was the shift in sound of the consonant now transcribed as "h" in the so-called *ha-gyō*. In Nara Japanese, this was probably aspirated and closer to modern "p," whereas in the Heian period, it was a fricative, closer to modern "f."[7] Furthermore, "f" and "w" began to merge in the Heian period, which is why one often finds in texts of the period different *kana* spelling for certain words.[8] It was also in the mid-

---

use the 5-*ku* structure to strengthen its effect, perhaps the most obvious example is the famous poem sent by the Ise Vestal to Ariwara no Narihira (825–80) after their night of love: *Kimi ya kosi / ware ya yukikemu / omofoezu / yume ka ututu ka / nete ka samete ka*—"Did you come to me? / Did I go to you? / I cannot tell. / Was it dream or reality? / Was I sleeping or awake?" (*KKS* 645; XIII, Love 3; also *Ise monogatari*, Episode 69). The first two *ku* are grammatical parallels: personal pronoun–interrogative particle *ya*–verb indicating an action in the past. The last two *ku* are mathematical in their symmetry: 2-syllable noun (*yume*/dream—night) + interrogative particle *ka* and a 3-syllable noun (*ututu*/reality—day) + interrogative particle *ka* in the fourth *ku*, while the fifth *ku* has a 2-syllable verb (*nete*/sleeping—a night activity associated with "dream") + interrogative particle *ka* and a 3-syllable verb (*samete*/awake—a daytime state) + interrogative particle *ka*. In other words, the five-*ku* structure itself is fully exploited by playing its elements against each other. I will point to other examples in the course of this study. For different views of the function of *ku* in waka, see M. Morris, "Waka and Form, Waka and History"; and Satō, "Lineation of Tanka in English Translation."

7. There is some controversy as to whether the Nara *ha-gyō* consonants were aspirated or fricative and how much they differed from their Heian counterparts (see Martin, *The Japanese Language Through Time*, p. 12, for some of the arguments). I am following Dr. John Bentley's view, conveyed to me in personal communications (5/28/2000, 6/7/2000). In any case, the point is not crucial to this study.

8. For example, the word "big" (*ō[kii]* in modern Hepburn) appears variously as *ofo, owo*, or *oo* in Heian texts. Similarly, *nao* (still) might appear as *nafo* or *nawo*, while *kotowari* (reason; principle) can be found spelled *kotofari* or *kotowari* (in both cases, the second of the pairs is the more recent spelling). In fact, a careful reader of this study may notice this inconsistency in some of my romanizations, since I have followed the received texts unless their editors have pointed to textual lines that offer "correct" variants.

Heian period that the final "n" emerged (which explains why the auxiliary verb *mu* sometimes appears as *-n* and sometimes as *mu* in Heian texts). Such changes as occur in the Kamakura period (most notably, the replacement of "e" with "ye"—a change that begins to reverse itself in the mid-Edo [or should I say mid-Yedo?] period) likely had little impact on the period I am discussing in this study.

If waka were only a written art, these changes would probably not be important to us, other than as a way to account for the occasional odd spellings in old texts. But in fact, even in the Shinkokin era, waka was always recited at public poetry events, in addition to being submitted in written form. It is hard to say when the emphasis shifted. David Bialock argues that Teika was a key figure in the change and asserts that Teika's increasing emphasis on textuality and *honkadori*, and strict rules for it, marked a privileging of text over song.[9] Bialock's point is persuasive, although the tension between oral and written continued for at least another century or so. I would argue, for example, that the Kyōgoku poets' propensity in the early fourteenth century to have *ji-amari* (supernumerary syllables) in their poems, whereas their Nijō rivals shunned the practice, was a throwback to *Kokinshū* times, when the "syllable" count was based on how words *sounded* rather than how they were written. (Thus a line like Narihira's *tabi wo si zo omofu*, which would be written with eight *kana*, was probably pronounced in seven beats because the final "o" in *zo* and the initial "o" in *omofu* were likely collapsed when spoken or, in the case of waka, recited/sung.)

In short, if I were approaching this study from a strictly linguistic point of view, and I wanted to give the modern English reader at least some sense of how a poem actually sounded in its original context, I would probably need to transcribe that poem in one of three different ways (representing Nara, Heian, or Kamakura Japanese) depending on when it was composed. However, as Joshua Mostow has pointed out, reception *is* an issue—all the more so since the Shinkokin poets were so active in appropriating (or troping, as Bialock would have it) their courtly predecessors.[10] We cannot be concerned simply with what the original poem, say a verse from the eighth-century *Man'yōshū*, was, but would do better to ask how it was read/heard

---

9. Bialock, "Voice, Text, and the Question of Poetic Borrowing in Late Classical Japanese Poetry," esp. pp. 211–15.
10. Mostow, *Pictures of the Heart*, pp. 1–8.

by later poets. This is made even more complicated by the inherent conservatism of the genre; traditional readings, and presumably pronunciations, were kept alive in formal performances a lot longer than they probably were in everyday speech. Yet it is doubtful that such fossilized readings were completely true to the original, either. Another problem is that knowledge of *Man'yōshū*, as I shall argue at several points in this book, was fragmentary and often mediated by mid-Heian texts such as the poetry compendium *Kokin waka rokujō*; the result was that the Shinkokin poets were *two* steps from the original.

Because of these considerations, I have decided to transcribe most poems using a system based on Heian Japanese. (In a few cases, where I have no evidence that a given poem was mediated—for example, if it appears in *Man'yōshū* but *not* in *Kokin waka rokujō* or other Heian collections—I will also provide a transcription based on Nara Japanese.)[11] The system I am using was codified (and kindly explained to me) by Dr. John Bentley and was adapted from one first developed by Dr. Gerald Mathias. The *ha-gyō* of the Hepburn system appears as fa-fi-fu-fe-fo; the *ya-gyō* is ya-yu-ye-yo; and the *wa-gyō* consists of wa-wi-we-wo.[12] In addition, the voiced *sa-gyō* is transcribed za-zi-zu-ze-zo, and the voiced *ta-gyō* as da-di-du-de-do. Furthermore, *kana* are transcribed as they appear in the original text (although I have, following modern editors, distinguished between voiced and unvoiced even if the original did not), rather than how they would be romanized today according to the Hepburn system. (For example, the word for "today" is rendered *kefu* rather than *kyō*.) Furthermore, inconsistencies in spelling are preserved, since I have chosen not to second-guess the received texts. Although initially jarring for many of us, this system reveals consonant repetitions that the Hepburn system obscures, and while it does not tell us exactly *how* these things sounded, it puts us closer than Hepburn, which has the effect of flattening

---

11. I have followed Ōno Susumu's *Kogo jiten* for my romanizations of Nara Japanese and distinguish so-called *otsu* vowels by placing an umlaut over them. Following Bentley and Gerald Mathias, however, I have treated the unvoiced *ha-gyō* consonants as aspirated and written them with "p" rather than the "f" used by Ōno. (Bentley and Mathias make further distinctions in their romanization of Nara vowels, but I have opted here for the simpler system Ōno uses.)

12. As noted above, there is evidence that the fricative pronunciation in the *ha-gyō* was giving way in the Heian period and in ordinary speech may have disappeared by the time of *Shinkokinshū*, but I retain it in my transcription of waka, an inherently conservative art.

some of the phonological qualities (perhaps forcing us further toward meaning-centered readings that miss the music).

However, in romanizing proper names (such as the names of poets or the titles of collections, poetry contests, and so on) I have used Hepburn, since that is generally how these would appear in modern reference works (thus *Shinkokinshū* rather than *Shinkokinshifu*). I have also used Hepburn for other cited prose passages (even ones from Heian period works) *except* in certain poetry contest judgments that cite specific lines from a poem, and when I am quoting a word or line from a poem under discussion. In so doing, I am sacrificing consistency for the sake of readability.

Other conventions used in this study are:

In the headnotes to poems, as well as in other discussions, I have capitalized words and phrases that I consider to be formal poetic topics (*dai*) rather than simple descriptions.

For proper name readings (including people or poetic events and titles of works), I have followed Ariyoshi Tamotsu, *Wakabungaku jiten* (Ōfūsha, 1982) unless otherwise noted. For items not found in Ariyoshi, I have turned to Yasuda Motohisa, *Kamakura Muromachi jinmei jiten* (Shinjinbutsu ōraisha, 1985). For the translation of court ranks and titles, I have followed Helen McCullough and William McCullough, *A Tale of Flowering Fortunes* (Stanford, 1980) or Robert Reischauer, *Early Japanese History* (Princeton, 1937), if necessary. In diaries, headnotes, and the like, a person's court title was often used in lieu of his or her proper name, and in such cases, I have treated the titles as proper nouns and have capitalized them.

For basic background information about a given event, I have consulted Ariyoshi, *Wakabungaku jiten*; Inukai Kiyoshi, et al., *Waka daijiten*; and Minegishi Yoshiaki, *Uta-awase no kenkyū*. To reduce the number of footnotes, I have not given specific page references to these sources unless they contain a particular piece of information or line of argument that I wish to highlight; the reader may assume that, unless otherwise noted, basic data about times, dates, participants, and so on come from these sources.

Dates of people appear in the index, and when citing a traditional lunar date, I have indicated, for example, the 26th day of the Third Month of the First Year of Kennin (1201 in the Western calendar) as Kennin 1 (1201)/iii/26, or Kennin 1/iii/26. Intercalary months or days are marked with a preceding asterisk (e.g., "*iv" for the intercalary Fourth Month). When writing dates out, for example in the full title of poetic events, I have capitalized the year and month designations and written the day number in arabic numerals, as above.

In citations from the *Dai Nihon shiryō*, I give the part numbers in roman numerals, followed by a colon, and the volume numbers in arabic numerals (e.g., " *DNS*, iv:5" refers to pt. IV, vol. 5).

There are slight discrepancies in numbering among variant texts of many collections, including *Shinkokinshū*. The poem numbers herein are from *Shinpen kokka taikan*, unless otherwise noted. In citations from *Shinpen kokka taikan*, I give the volume number first, followed by a colon, and then the section number of the relevant collection within that volume; when applicable, I give the poem number within the section, preceded by a "#" sign and then the page number (e.g., 3:131; #1706, p. 680). With *Man'yōshū*, the numbering discrepancy is quite significant, and I also give the old *NKBT* (*Nihon koten bungaku taikei*) number, which corresponds to the old *Kokka taikan* number, in parentheses for poems from that collection.

For citations from *Gunsho ruijū* and *Zoku gunsho ruijū*, I give the old *Gunsho ruijū* fascicle number first, followed by the volume number of the modern printed edition (with sub-volumes, if any, set off by a decimal point, then the page number (e.g., GR 192, 12: 368; ZGR 399, 14.2, 940–54).

Abbreviations

The following abbreviations (from Brower and Miner's *Japanese Court Poetry* [Stanford, 1960] in the case of imperial anthologies) are used for frequently cited collections, works, and journal titles:

DNS	*Dai Nihon shiryō*
GR	*Gunsho ruijū*
GSIS	*Goshūishū*
GSS	*Gosenshū*
HJAS	*Harvard Journal of Asiatic Studies*
IN	*Ienaga nikki*
JJS	*Journal of Japanese Studies*
KKS	*Kokinshū*
KWR	*Kokin waka rokujō*
KYS	*Kin'yōshū*
MN	*Monumenta Nipponica*
MYS	*Man'yōshū*
NKBT	*Nihon koten bungaku taikei*
NKBZ	*Nihon koten bungaku zenshū*
SIS	*Shūishū*
SKKS	*Shinkokinshū*
SKS	*Shikashū*
SNKBT	*Shin Nihon koten bungaku taikei*
SZS	*Senzaishū*
WBJ	*Waka bungaku jiten* (Ariyoshi Tamotsu, ed.)
ZGR	*Zoku gunsho ruijū*

THE MAKING OF
Shinkokinshū

Introduction

In the history of traditional Japanese poetry, generically known as waka, three anthologies are usually regarded as particularly significant: *Man'yōshū* (759), *Kokinshū* (905), and *Shinkokinshū* (1205).[1] In its own time and for at least a century thereafter, *Shinkokinshū* was seen as something of an anomaly—compiled by a committee (instead of by a single poet), and guided firmly by a retired emperor who was later exiled for his failed attempt to overthrow the Kamakura Bakufu. Yet over time, the quality of its poetry overshadowed those political and factional concerns, and in the mid-1950s, when, for example, the Iwanami publishing house decided to canonize traditional Japanese literature in its *Nihon koten bungaku taikei* series, *Shinkokinshū* was chosen, along with *Man'yōshū* and *Kokinshū*, to represent the waka tradition.[2]

Shinkokinshū—its very title, "New *Kokinshū*," announces its program—is, in many ways a neo-classical effort. Reading history backward, scholars have often taken this to be a nostalgia for greatness presumed to have been lost in the Genpei War (1180–85). I would argue, much as Andrew Goble has done

---

1. For example, Fujihira Haruo (*Shinkokin to sono zengo*, p. 3) describes these three anthologies as the "three models" of waka composition. Incidentally, the dates given here are the commonly accepted dates for the compilation of the three collections, although both *Man'yōshū* and *Shinkokinshū* underwent subsequent revision, and the date for the *Kokinshū* is also uncertain.

2. By contrast, earlier series, such as the *Kokumin bunko* (1909–13) and the *Yūhōdō bunko* (1913), included the first eight imperial anthologies (*Kokinshū* through *Shinkokinshū*, collectively known as the *hachidaishū*), and Iwanami's newest venture into the canon, the *Shin Nihon koten bungaku taikei*, will, when completed, include all 21 imperial anthologies.

in regard to Go-Daigo and the Kenmu Restoration of nearly a century later, that the compilers of *Shinkokinshū* saw their collection as a "new" beginning, a revitalization and affirmation of courtly traditions, and not a reaction to loss.[3] It is, after all, a dynamic collection, full of innovative, challenging poetry—not an elegy.[4]

Surely *Shinkokinshū* owes much of its appeal to the richness of its verse. The descriptive approach that characterizes most of its seasonal poetry appeals to the senses while *seeming* to avoid the verbal mannerisms of earlier poetry. And its use of allusive variation (*honkadori*) and the contemplative, philosophical, religious tone that underlies its best poems give it, to the modern reader at least, a weight not present in other collections. Or so the argument often goes.[5] Yet the descriptive approach had been around since Minamoto Tsunenobu (1016–97) and his son Toshiyori (1055–1129) and was the dominant mode for nature poems by the time of *Senzaishū* (1188), the imperial anthology immediately preceding *Shinkokinshū*.[6] Nor had religious concerns been in such short supply. Buddhist and Shinto poems, identified as such, had been part of imperial anthologies since *Goshūishū* (1086), although it was not until *Senzaishū* that they were given their own chapters.[7]

---

3. See Goble, *Kenmu*. Goble's critique of historiography of the Kamakura period (pp. xi-xxi) applies directly and indirectly to the period covered in this book. The situation at the time of *Shinkokinshū* is not exactly analogous, although it is similar. As the word "revolution" in his subtitle implies, Goble does not see Go-Daigo as necessarily reaffirming traditional court values but more as repositioning himself and his followers as a force to contend with in a new age. I would argue that Go-Toba and his court had not yet given up on the old aristocracy and did not perceive the bakufu as Go-Daigo did. Nevertheless, Goble's model is useful for re-evaluating the early Kamakura period.

4. Edward Kamens strikes a fine balance in viewing this age by noting that "Shunzei, Teika, and their patrons, colleagues, and competitors were all very much aware of and deeply drawn into the literary culture that had survived into these [post-Genpei War] times, and they sought to preserve it even as they sought to make it new" (*Utamakura, Allusion, and Intertextuality in Traditional Japanese Poetry*, p. 45). See also Huey, "Warrior Control over the Imperial Anthology," pp. 171–72. The "dispossessed courtier" view, which puts more emphasis on the "preserve" side of the equation, is discussed further in Chapter 1.

5. The clearest articulation of this view is, of course, to be found in Brower and Miner's *Japanese Court Poetry*; many of their arguments are still compelling 40 years later.

6. See Ivo Smits's excellent study of the origins of the descriptive style in waka, *The Pursuit of Loneliness*.

7. For a fuller discussion of this, see Morrell, "The *Shinkokinshū*: 'Poems on Śākyamuni's Teachings (*Shakkyōka*).'"

Allusive variation is one area where *Shinkokinshū* seems truly to have broken ground, and its significance is discussed below in this chapter and throughout this study. However, since allusive variation requires much cross-referencing and explanation, this aspect of medieval poetry is probably the least accessible to the modern reader—and not just the Western reader—it can hardly account for *Shinkokinshū*'s popularity.

One intangible that may make *Shinkokinshū* so esteemed is the sheer range (the term being relative when applied to the product of a tiny, aristocratic society) of its voices, which still somehow seem to harmonize. In fact, one thing the three canonical collections (*Man'yōshū*, *Kokinshū*, and *Shinkokinshū*) have in common—and this puts them in the minority—is that they were *not* the product of a single compiler. Of the twenty-one imperial anthologies (*chokusenshū*), seven were compiled by committee; the rest had been assigned to a single compiler.[8]

Man'yōshū, strictly speaking not an imperial anthology but canonical nonetheless, is often credited to Ōtomo Yakamochi (718–85), yet there is much evidence that he did not work alone and that his edition was extensively revised after his death. In any case, since his own version was an anthology of anthologies, by default it involved many hands. *Kokinshū*, too, the first of the imperial anthologies, although associated primarily with Ki no Tsurayuki (868?–945), was compiled by a committee, whose final selections belied, in a way, some of Tsurayuki's critical comments in his Japanese preface. And although the four imperial collections preceding *Shinkokinshū* (*Goshūishū* [1086], *Kin'yōshū* [1126], *Shikashū* [1151], and *Senzaishū* [1188]) were all products of a solo compiler—indeed, there was a great deal of political maneuvering involved in choosing the compilers—*Shinkokinshū* was compiled by a committee. *Man'yōshū*, *Kokinshū*, and *Shinkokinshū*, then, represented a range of voices yet were directed by one especially talented hand.

There is no question that the process by which *Shinkokinshū* came into existence was strictly guided, even as it tended to be inclusive. Like the other imperial anthologies, *Shinkokinshū* was, in one sense, a public works project, an effort by its sponsor, Retired Emperor Go-Toba (1180–1239, r. 1183–98), to put his stamp on the cultural life of the capital, if not the nation. This is

---

8. *Shūishū* (1006) was also likely compiled by committee, with Retired Emperor Kazan (968–1008, r. 984–86) in charge, but we do not know the details; thus eight anthologies may have been compiled by committee.

especially the case with Go-Toba, who, if we read history backward from his attempt at imperial restoration, the Jōkyū War of 1221, may well have seen *Shinkokinshū* as an important preliminary step in his consolidation of the imperial court.

The first decade of the thirteenth century has often been called the Shinkokin Age, but Kubota Jun, for one, has suggested "the Age of Go-Toba" would be a more apt description.[9] There is no question that Go-Toba was the driving force behind *Shinkokinshū* and indeed the world of waka during this time. He sponsored a staggering number of poetry events in a few short years, clearly with a new imperial anthology in mind. In fact, almost 20 percent of the poems in *Shinkokinshū* came from events Go-Toba sponsored between 1200 and 1207. And he did so by juggling contending political factions (the Kujō branch of the Fujiwara and the Tsuchimikado branch of the Minamoto) as well as poetic ones (the more innovative Mikohidari school and its rival, the older, more traditional Rokujō school).[10] How did he manage this? This book will attempt to demonstrate that process.

As one goes through, week by week, month by month, the poetic calendar of the first few years of the 1200s, one is aided by an array of sources, including but not limited to records of the poetry events themselves. Go-Toba's own voice is relatively rare (aside from his poems, of course—and they are not "his" voice but that of his artistic persona) except as he is quoted or paraphrased by others and in his own treatise, discussed below, which was written after the fact and is a mere ten pages in modern typeset

---

9. Kubota Jun, *Shinkokin wakashū*, 1: 344. Akiko Hirota ("Ex-Emperor Go-Toba," pp. 8–9) uses similar wording and the identical citation to Kubota in the introduction to her dissertation. Hirota's dissertation provides a detailed and sympathetic look at Go-Toba in English. Like Hirota, for convenience sake, I begin using the name Go-Toba here, although he was rarely if ever called that name in his lifetime.

10. It is important to understand the difference between branch family and school. Both the Mikohidari and Rokujō *houses* were branch families of the Fujiwara. By the late 1100s, the two families had developed clearly different views of poetry. Around them arose schools (quite literally, since the family heads were seen as poetic masters, qualified to teach the art to others), which came to be known by the name of the branch family at their center. Thus it is quite possible to be a member of the Mikohidari school, or group, without being a member of the Mikohidari family. Since a large number of courtiers in this age shared the surname Fujiwara, it is not always possible to tell just by surname to which branch a poet belonged, let alone which school he or she favored. See Appendix A for family trees of the Rokujō and Mikohidari houses.

Introduction 5

form. Thus, although he stands at the center of all this activity, by default we must look at him from different perspectives. These sources themselves reveal much not only about the process behind *Shinkokinshū* but also about their own authors and about the way in which waka language and imagery, not to mention larger philosophical visions such as Buddhism and Confucianism, framed how people talked and wrote about their lives.

Among the most important sources for this period is Fujiwara Teika's (1162–1241) *Meigetsuki*, a meticulous *kanbun* (Sino-Japanese) diary loaded with information about all sorts of public and private activities. At every turn, it betrays the prickly, intense personality of its author, a reminder that it is, after all, just one perspective.[11] Yet given that Teika ranks as perhaps the most important single poet in all of waka history, his view certainly matters.

Another is Minamoto Ienaga's (1173?–1234) memoirs, called *Minamoto no Ienaga nikki* (hereafter *Ienaga nikki*), written in *wabun* (Japanese prose). In some ways, it resembles a court lady's diary, with its lyrical descriptions, gossip (this is by no means to suggest that *kanbun* diaries never contained gossip—quite the contrary!), and anecdotes of the years leading up to *Shinkokinshū*.[12] Ienaga was for the most part an uncritical retainer of Go-Toba, but as the Chief Recorder (*kaikō*) for the Wakadokoro (Bureau of Poetry—about which much more below), he had a unique viewpoint and responsibility.

Ienaga admitted that his memory was faulty and that his recordkeeping was weak, which means that we cannot always trust his account. Further-

---

11. There is a related document, called *Meigetsuki shōshutsu*, apparently put together by the poet and scholar Ton'a (1289–1372) in the fourteenth century. It contains bits and pieces of *Meigetsuki*, mostly entries that are waka-related, including some entries not in the extant version of *Meigetsuki* proper. See ZGR 470, 17.1, pp. 247–69. For a careful study of the *Meigetsuki* as a document, see Tsuji, *Fujiwara Teika Meigetsuki no kenkyū*.

Since 1995, motivated by a text in Teika's own hand that was discovered in the Reizei family's Shiguretei library in the 1970s, Gomi Fumihiko and a group called the Meigetsuki kenkyūkai have been studying and writing extensively (first in 1995 in the journal *Bungaku* and then, beginning in the fall of 1996, in their own publication series, called *Meigetsuki kenkyū*) about *Meigetsuki*. Their work will continue to have a huge impact on the field, and I have cited some of it in these pages.

12. For an extensively annotated text of Ienaga's work, which I relied on a great deal in writing this study, see Ishida and Satsukawa, *Minamoto no Ienaga nikki zenchūkai* (hereafter called *Ienaga nikki* and abbreviated *IN*). There is another version, out of print, which I was unable to consult: Minamoto Ienaga nikki kenkyūkai, ed., *Minamoto Ienaga Nikki: kōi, kenkyū, sōsakuin*.

more, he compiled the work some years after the fact, but he presents matters as if he were writing a diary, usually without obvious tense markers.[13] Within a given section, time may be telescoped, compressed, ill-defined, even factually impossible. So, as a piece of chronology, Ienaga's work is not reliable. But as a document of one type of early medieval discourse in Japan, his diary is remarkable and reveals how the language of waka, as well as Buddhist thought, permeated the thirteenth-century mind and manner of expression (at least his mind and that of his implied readers).

Another work is the poet Kamo no Chōmei's (1155–1216) poetic treatise *Mumyōshō*, which also discusses many of the poetic events of this period. Go-Toba himself touches on the same events in his own treatise, *Go-Toba-in onkuden*.[14]

The last part of Fujiwara (Kujō) Kanezane's (1149–1207) *kanbun* diary, *Gyokuyō*, and fragments of *Denki*, the journal kept by his son, Yoshitsune (1169–1206), also give crucial information. These two men stood at the center of court and Bakufu politics, yet, especially in the case of Yoshitsune, they also played a pivotal role in poetry, both as patrons and writers. The diary of another courtier, Fujiwara Nagakane (fl. 1176–1214), a retainer of Kanezane's, is also an important source of information. Called the *Sanchōki*, it exists in generally available form only in *Dai Nihon shiryō*, a multivolume historical compendium that lists important historical events day by day and cites relevant documents as evidence. Large portions of *Sanchōki* are reproduced in this work and provide yet another view of the activities of the age, especially the political ones. In fact, *Dai Nihon shiryō* reproduces other portions of diaries (most notably for this period *Inokuma kanpakuki*, the diary kept by Fujiwara [Konoe] Iezane [1179–1242], who succeeded Yoshitsune as chancel-

---

13. Richard Okada (*Figures of Resistance*, pp. 15–20) reminds us that the notion of "tense" is not exactly relevant to Heian writing. Ienaga's early Kamakura prose is a further illustration of this.

14. Both of these treatises appear in Hisamatsu and Nishio, *Karonshū nōgakuronshū*, the former on pp. 35–98, and the latter (the title of which can also be read *Go-Toba-in gokuden* and *Go-Toba no in gokuden*) on pp. 141–51. For a translation of *Mumyōshō*, see Katō, "The *Mumyōshō* of Kamo no Chōmei and Its Significance in Japanese Literature." See below for a discussion of Robert Brower's translation of Go-Toba's treatise. See also Hare's discussion of Chōmei in his "Reading Kamo no Chōmei."

lor/regent [*kanpaku*][15] when the latter died in 1206) and documents that might otherwise be inaccessible.[16]

Less reliable for factual information but certainly as important for seeing how history is built are the later "histories" (e.g., *Azuma kagami* [ca. 1266], *Masukagami* [late fourteenth c.]) and poetic treatises, such as Ton-a's (1289–1372) *Seiashō*, which tell us how certain events came to be officially viewed. Not to be overlooked is Jien's (1155–1225) *Gukanshō*. Jien, younger brother of Kanezane and thus a member of the Kujō house, wears his ideological and factional biases on his sleeve, and although one must be careful about the rumors and stories he portrays as facts, it is precisely because he is clearly such an interested party that his work is an invaluable document of the age.

Some of this documentation has been previously translated. Among such efforts, Robert Brower's translation of and introduction to Go-Toba's treatise *Go-Toba-in onkuden* stands out. Brower cites many entries from *Meigetsuki* and *Ienaga nikki*, and sketches a preliminary portrait of the age, focusing especially on the rocky relationship between Teika and Go-Toba.

---

15. In the old *ritsuryō* administrative system, the "official" position was *daijō daijin* (or *dajō daijin*), or chancellor. During the Heian period, the position of regent (*sesshō*) came into being, so that the head of the main branch of the Fujiwara, who was often the emperor's grandfather, could have a sanctioned reason for "watching over" an emperor who was still a minor. Even after that emperor came of age, his relationship with his former regent could hardly cease to exist in a Confucian context, and the term *kanpaku*, which amounted to a regent for someone who was no longer a minor, was appropriated from China and institutionalized. The *kanpaku* title was generally granted to the *daijō daijin*, since during the time of the Fujiwara dominance in the first half or so of the Heian period, the two jobs naturally fell to the same person, that is, the head of the main branch of the Fujiwara clan. In this study I will use "regent" for *sesshō*, "chancellor" for *daijō daijin*, and "chancellor/regent" for *kanpaku*.

The initial syllable of the word *sesshō* when combined with the initial syllable of *kanpaku* yielded the term *sekkan*, and the family (*ke*) that supplied people for these positions was known as the *sekkanke*. Through most of the Heian period, only one family, the Fujiwara Northern Branch, was of sufficient rank and power to be called the *sekkanke*, but as will be shown in the next chapter, by the beginning of the Kamakura period it had split into two contending branches (Konoe and Kujō), who jockeyed between themselves for the appointments. (These two families eventually splintered again, with the Takatsukasa branching off from the Konoe, and the Ichijō and Nijō branching off from the Kujō, but this happened in the mid-Kamakura period, beyond the scope of this study.)

16. When citing these below, I give their title and entry information, as well as the *Dai Nihon shiryō* volume and page number.

Despite his tendency to oversimplify the situation, seeing Teika as a cranky, old genius and Go-Toba as a rash, young master, Brower highlights important events and information in his introduction and provides a valuable document with his translation.[17]

Japanese scholarship on this period, beginning almost from the very inception of *Shinkokinshū* itself, has been exhaustive. For example, several early textual lines record who among the selection committee chose which poems; this can be very revealing information when it comes to assessing poetic theories or analyzing factional considerations.[18] More recently, three scholars stand out as particularly thorough: Ariyoshi Tamotsu, Gotō Shigeo, and Kubota Jun.[19] These scholars have been extraordinarily painstaking in establishing the basic "facts" for *Shinkokinshū*, for example, how many poems were collected from which sources, and what contemporary records, mostly Teika's *Meigetsuki*, have to say about the various poetic events. Indeed, it was initially difficult for me to conceive of this book as much more than a translating into English of Kubota's and Ariyoshi's work, since these two have left no stone unturned. In turn, all three of these scholars, as well as Ishida Yoshida and Satsukawa Shūji in their notes to *Ienaga nikki*, refer time and again to the groundbreaking (and elegantly written) work of Kojima Yoshio. His shadow falls on them as theirs does on me.

But as I looked at the events one by one, it became clear that a clear narration of them would be a revelation to students of this period. And if, furthermore, I could, building on Kubota and Ariyoshi, bring in a range of other details—historical context, factional disputes, judgment styles in con-

---

17. Brower, "'Ex-Emperor Go-Toba's Secret Teachings': *Go-Toba no in gokuden*." Note that Brower prefers a different reading of the Japanese title than I use. Other Western scholars have, of course, dealt with this period, and many of their works are cited in this study.

18. Among modern annotated editions of *Shinkokinshū*, for the standard list of compilers' selections, see Kubota Jun, *Shinkokin wakashū*, 2: 332–70. For an exhaustive analysis on this point of every known extant textual line to the date of publication (1968), see Gotō Shigeo, *Shinkokin wakashū no kisōteki kenkyū*, pp. 668–892.

19. The landmark studies from each of these scholars are Ariyoshi Tamotsu, *Shinkokin wakashū no kenkyū: kiban to kōsei*; Gotō Shigeo, *Shinkokin wakashū no kisōteki kenkyū*; and Kubota Jun, *Shinkokin kajin no kenkyū*. Ariyoshi has recently added a supplement to his study: *Shinkokin wakashū no kenkyū: zokuhen*. I did not see a copy until after this manuscript was completed, but most of the new information has to do with texts that have been discovered since the earlier edition, which should not affect most of my argument. More recent scholarship, such as the work of Gomi Fumihiko mentioned above, is discussed in the body of the study.

tests, Go-Toba's ability to mediate—a much fuller picture of the age would emerge.

What I propose to do here, then, is focus on the first few years of the thirteenth century and examine several of the most important—or just plain interesting—events (poetic and non-poetic, public and private) from as many perspectives as are available. The results will not only cast light on the process leading up to *Shinkokinshū* but also reveal much about how people thought and framed their thoughts and how they worked in medieval Japan.

Inevitably in studies of this sort, the first problem one faces is one of parameters. Where does one begin the discussion? If the main focus of this book were *Shinkokinshū* itself, surely Saigyō (1118–90) and the *Roppyakuban uta-awase* (1192–93) would have to figure into the narrative.[20] Indeed, even though he died in 1190, when Go-Toba was only ten, Saigyō cast a very long shadow over *Shinkokinshū* and enjoys the distinction of being the author with the most poems (94) in that collection. And the *Roppyakuban uta-awase*, with its exhaustive judgments by Fujiwara (Mikohidari) Shunzei (1114–1204; Teika's father, whose innovative poetry and self-confident scholarship posed a challenge to the established Rokujō school), stands as a poetic monument and crucial guide to the emergence of a new poetic. But the focus here is not just *Shinkokinshū* per se. It is the early years of Go-Toba's tenure as retired emperor and the poetic world he fostered. So, albeit reluctantly, I leave Saigyō and the *Roppyakuban uta-awase* to another forum. Both deserve an exhaustive study in English.

Go-Toba, at the ripe old age of eighteen, became senior retired emperor (*chisei no kimi*, head of the imperial household and virtual ruler) in 1198 when his son became the Emperor Tsuchimikado (1195–1231, r. 1198–1210). The political situation in Kamakura and in Kyoto (I use the name anachronistically) was very much in ferment, and Go-Toba did not embark on his frenzy of poetry right away. It took him a year or two to get his bearings, while political matters settled somewhat.

Once the Kujō house, headed by Yoshitsune, recovered a certain prominence at court, Go-Toba, who had a hand in that re-establishment, had a powerful ally in artistic matters. This is not to say he ignored the rivals of the Kujō clan, the Tsuchimikado branch of the Minamoto family, which

---

20. Kubota Jun has done precisely this in his *Shinkokin kajin no kenkyū*.

was ascendant for a time in the 1190s and provided Go-Toba the consort who gave birth to the Emperor Tsuchimikado. On the contrary, much of the following narrative revolves around Go-Toba's efforts as mediator. It is not so much that he was attempting to enforce a single artistic vision as that he was attempting to foster a climate conducive to good poetry of whatever style—a cultural consensus that accepted diversity, to put it in terms that would suit our current climate. In any case, Yoshitsune clearly shared Go-Toba's aggressive, forward-looking view of waka, and he had the clout and skill to further it.[21]

Ariyoshi argues essentially that the "Age of Go-Toba" (an expression he does not use, although obviously he accepts the notion) did not begin until the retired sovereign shook himself free of Tsuchimikado and Rokujō control. He asserts that Go-Toba's *kadan* (poetry circle) did not emerge as an independent force until 1200 (Shōji 2), when Go-Toba ordered his first of three sets of 100-poem sequences from the poets around him.[22]

Although I agree with Ariyoshi that the *Shōji ninen in shodo hyakushu* marks the emergence of Go-Toba as the premier poetic sponsor and patron, I think Ariyoshi is missing the point when he casts it in terms of breaking free from Rokujō control. For one thing, many of the events of the next several years were initiated by Rokujō poets or their Tsuchimikado patrons (as Ariyoshi himself chronicles). And for another, as is evident in the most spectacular poetic "event" of the decade, the *Sengohyakuban uta-awase* (Poetry Contest in 1,500 Rounds; about which much more below), Go-Toba was very much a mediator and gave all groups an opportunity to prove their worth. Given his evenhandedness, perhaps the view of *Shinkokinshū* as his creation is somewhat misleading. After all, the Okibon version that he compiled in roughly 1235, while in exile on Oki Island, made some 380 changes in the version produced by Teika and the committee, which implies a significant disagreement with that version of *Shinkokinshū*. History, too, at least for several hundred years, tended to see *Shinkokinshū* as an oddity—Teika's own descendants, the Nijō poets of late Kamakura, left *Shinkokinshū* out of their

---

21. Both Hirota ("Ex-Emperor Go-Toba," pp. 10–17) and Brower ("Ex-Emperor Go-Toba's Secret Teachings," p. 12) argue that although Go-Toba was a strong supporter of innovative styles, he was rather more conventional in his own practice and took a fairly orthodox, courtly stance toward the social role of poetry.

22. Ariyoshi, *Shinkokin wakashū no kenkyū: kiban to kōsei*, pp. 43–44.

"New Sandaishū" canon. For them, *Senzaishū*, *Shinchokusenshū*, and *Shokugosenshū* more properly represented waka's mainstream.[23]

But clearly Go-Toba engineered the poetry events of the early 1200s with an eye to *Shinkokinshū* as their culmination. What was the nature of these events? How, in fact, were waka "published" in this age? Where did the poems that appear in an anthology like *Shinkokinshū* come from? Before we examine specific events, it would be useful to know more about them generically, so that we can better appreciate how Go-Toba made use of the conventions. It was an age when precedent mattered, and Go-Toba, no matter how bold he was, did not ignore precedent. He simply made creative use of it to help him gather contemporary poems for his anthology.

Imperial anthologies inevitably included poems from earlier ages, as well as work from contemporary or near-contemporary poets. The job of the anthologizer (or the committee) was to comb earlier records (not including other imperial anthologies and usually not including *Man'yōshū*, either, at least in theory) for older poems and to sift through such contemporary works as were available. It was in the latter area that Go-Toba's efforts bore fruit.

Many sources, public and private, were available to the compilers of anthologies throughout waka history.[24] Many of the poems came from letters. Over time, individuals or families might maintain a library of sorts of good poems that they either sent or received as part of a letter, or poems they produced for this or that occasion. These collections, called variously "personal collections" (*shikashū*) or "house collections" (*ie no shū*, or *kashū*) became sources for anthologizers when they needed poems from earlier ages. Often, when poems from these kinds of collections were used in public anthologies, the identity of the poet might be protected by marking the poem as "anonymous," especially if it were a love poem. In other cases, the circumstances of the letter and its poem might be explained (perhaps even fictionalized, again to protect someone's identity) in a headnote (*kotobagaki*) preceding the poem.

---

23. Of course, there is an element of family pride involved in this selection, since the three generations, Shunzei, Teika, and Tameie, were the sole compilers, respectively, of these three anthologies, whereas *Shinkokinshū* was a committee effort. Yet that makes the argument more persuasive, since it demonstrates that partisanship *was* an issue for the various factions, though Go-Toba strove to surmount it.

24. Joshua Mostow (*Pictures of the Heart*, pp. 17–19) also touches on some of the following points in a similar discussion.

Obviously, Go-Toba was not in a position to control the production of private poems like this. But in public forums, he could and did have a profound impact. Although poems were usually a part of virtually any public occasion and poems produced on such occasions might well end up being anthologized, by Go-Toba's day there were four types of public events in which the production and/or sharing of poetry played a key role: screen paintings (*byōbue no uta*, or simply *byōbu uta*), 100-poem sequences (*hyakushu uta*), poetry parties or gatherings (*kakai*, or *utakai*), and poetry contests (*uta-awase*). Go-Toba made use of all four activities to generate contemporary poems for *Shinkokinshū*, and the compilers drew from records of earlier activities of similar nature in order to find suitable older poems. Let us examine each of these four areas of poetic performance more closely.

When a new residence was completed, a palace rebuilt, the birthday of an illustrious person celebrated, or when a daughter from a powerful clan such as the Kujō branch of the Fujiwara entered the palace as an imperial consort, screen paintings of landscape scenes were often commissioned. It was common practice to solicit from well-known poets poems to be inscribed on these paintings and to ask an expert calligrapher to do the inscription.[25] Obviously a commission like this would put any poet on his or her mettle since the results were displayed in public on a daily basis. One of the things that makes a screen poem especially interesting is the fact that it is at least once removed from its topic (perhaps even more if the painting on which it is based is itself either of an imagined scene, or of one, such as a landscape in a remote province, that the painter himself could not have directly experienced and might know, ironically, only from other poems); it is therefore a document of poetic convention as much as anything else.[26] From the time of *Kokinshū*, screen painting poems, which were almost inevitably seasonal or

---

25. By Go-Toba's time, screen paintings, *byōbu*, were generally in the Japanese style (*yamato-e*)—pictures of Japanese landscapes, or scenes from stories. These illustrations, by convention, were to be accompanied by Japanese-style poems (*waka*). Obviously the practice of inscribing poems on paintings was appropriated from China, and in fact, in early Heian, when screens were sometimes illustrated with paintings in the Chinese style, or of Chinese scenes, Chinese poems (*kanshi*) were selected to accompany them.

26. Such paintings, and the poetry they inspired, were closely tied in to the concept of *utamakura* (places of poetic renown); see Kamens, *Utamakura*, pp. 168–221. For a brief treatment of screen painting poems in general, see Mostow, *Pictures of the Heart*, pp. 88–90.

nature poems, found their way into imperial anthologies, and *Shinkokinshū* was no different.

Of somewhat more recent vintage than the *byōbu uta* were 100-poem sequences (*hyakushu uta*). First appearing in the late 900s, these sequences were originally private, or at least personal, in nature. The earliest known example is *Yoshitada hyakushu* (ca. 960), attributed to Sone no Yoshitada (fl. 960–1003). Arranged like a mini-anthology, with Seasonal, Love, and Miscellaneous poems, its verses are plaintive in tone, lamenting the author's low station and the unpredictability of life. Later poets sometimes followed this model for their own 100-poem sequences.

However, more than a century later, the 100-poem form began also to have a more public function. In 1105 or 1106, Minamoto Toshiyori arranged to have 100-poem sequences from fourteen to sixteen poets (the exact number is uncertain because some of the texts have been lost) presented to Emperor Horikawa (1079–1107; r. 1086–1107). Each of the 100 poems was assigned a separate topic, and the so-called *Horikawa hyakushu* became a model for centuries. All the participating poets were part of Emperor Horikawa's poetry circle, and the purpose of the event seems to have been simply to generate a large body of public poetry for the sake of it.[27]

It became apparent that this approach could be used to generate poetry for specific purposes, such as imperial anthologies, and in the Sixth Year of the Kyūan era (1150), Retired Emperor Sutoku (1119–64; r. 1123–41) requested 100-poem sequences from fourteen poets, evidently to generate poetry for use in the imperial anthology *Shikashū*, but the poets were slow to produce, and the sequences were not ready in time for that anthology.[28] However, the *Kyūan hyakushu*, as the sequences are called, did become an

---

27. The *Horikawa hyakushu* has a rather complicated textual history. Briefly, it was probably initiated in 1102 or 1103 by Minamoto Toshiyori and formally presented to Emperor Horikawa in 1105 or 1106. It is most famous for having set topics for each of the 100 poems and was almost immediately recognized as a significant poetic event. Indeed, throughout medieval times it was seen as one of the most important poetic events of early medieval Japan. For details, see *WBJ*, pp. 577–78.

28. The *Kyūan hyakushu* were commissioned by Retired Emperor Sutoku in Kyūan 6 (1150) and probably formally presented in 1152, after Shunzei had been requested to classify the poems. The topics for this sequence were much more general than in the Horikawa poems, hence the need to classify (*ruijū*) them, that is, put them in appropriate seasonal and/or narrative order.

important source for the subsequent anthology, *Senzaishū*, and in any case, the precedent was now established that 100-poem sequences might be commissioned whenever an imperial anthology was being planned. As will be seen, Go-Toba used this approach to great effect.

Throughout the history of the court, poetry parties were popular. One of the earliest on record was a plum blossom–viewing party held by Ōtomo Tabito at his Dazaifu residence in 730. Thirty-two of the poems produced on this occasion were included in *Man'yōshū*, and the event illustrates the major elements of a poetry party: drinking, enjoying some seasonal phenomenon, and composing poems.[29] Many entries in *Meigetsuki* describe such activities, and the poetry composed at them was not always serious, as we shall see. On the other hand, such gatherings could also take on a very formal air. During the Heian period some of them became quite elaborate and included music. By the time of Emperor Shirakawa (1053–1129, r. 1072–86), poetry parties at the palace were very structured affairs; they could include topics assigned in advance, formal presentations, and readings, and consequently they were treated with greater seriousness, not unlike that accorded a large-scale, imperially commissioned 100-poem sequence. Again, Go-Toba made use of events like this to encourage poetic output. But more casual parties, too, continued to be held throughout the decade under discussion here, and the poems they produced were also an important source for *Shinkokinshū*.

The most intimidating, and perhaps most important, poetic activity, aside from the imperial anthology itself, was the poetry contest. The basic poetry contest involved dividing a group of poets into two teams, Left and Right, and matching poems from each team, one at a time, in rounds. Most contests were judged (by one master, or rarely, more master poets), with one poem per round being awarded a win (*kachi*) or with a draw (*ji*, or *mochi*) being declared. Reasons for the decision, if recorded, were called *hanshi*. There was considerable variation in how these judgments might be written. Around the early 1200s, and then again in the late Kamakura period, some contests, especially if the poets were from a single faction, were judged jointly by all the participants (*shūgihan*).

---

29. The poems are in *Man'yōshū* Book V, 815–46 (*NKBT* 819–50), and are preceded by a preface in literary Chinese that describes the scene and the party ("the wine cup flew around," it says).

In the early days (900–1100), contests averaged 10 rounds and 5–10 participants. From 1166, they suddenly started getting larger, running 50–60 rounds, with 20 or so poets (even up to 50 or more).[30] This trend toward the massive culminated in the *Roppyakuban uta-awase* (Poetry Contest in 600 Rounds; 1192–93) and the *Sengohyakuban uta-awase* (Poetry Contest in 1,500 Rounds; 1203), the latter of which is discussed at length in this study. Whereas earlier contests had usually been parties of a sort, where the participants gathered at one place and acted together, these last two contests took a number of months to complete and were not like the poetry contests of old since they were essentially constructed on paper.

Yet they were not without precedent, either. As early as Fujiwara Kintō (966–1041), there were poetry contests that consisted of matching poems that had already been written, either by others (*senka-awase*, literally "contest of selected verses") or by oneself (*jika-awase*, literally "contest of one's own verses"). Furthermore, whereas earlier contests had usually been *tōza*, that is, contests in which the topics were given out on the spot and the poems composed (ostensibly) extemporaneously, as the stakes in poetry contests became greater, the practice of posting topics in advance (*kendai*) became more frequent, although *tōza* contests never disappeared altogether.

It is in the area of poetry contests that Go-Toba was most creative. Throughout the decade, he experimented with a number of different permutations of the genre, evidently hoping that by ignoring some of the traditional rules, which usually produced judgments that favored the emperor or the contest's patron or that were too biased in favor of the judge's own faction, he might get not only better poems but also better-articulated standards. This book examines these permutations in detail.

Before looking at how Go-Toba exploited all these poetic performance forms, however, we need to set the stage by going back a decade or so and examining the political brew with which Go-Toba was working. When one understands how volatile the situation was, *Shinkokinshū* seems an even more remarkable achievement.

---

30. See, e.g., the *Kaō ninen jūgatsu kokonoka Sumiyoshi no Yashiro no uta-awase* (The Sumiyoshi Shrine Poetry Contest of the 9th Day, Tenth Month, Second Year of Kaō) of 1170, which totaled 75 rounds.

ONE

The Political Context

"Political context" can be understood on different levels. Although the main body of this chapter is concerned with political events as traditionally defined (wars, power struggles at court, patronage, and so on), one should not overlook the political and ideological implications of the aesthetic choices made by the poets discussed herein.[1] I will begin there.

The Politics of Allusion

It is widely accepted that *honkadori* (borrowing words and phrases from older poems) and *honzetsu* (borrowing words and phrases from earlier prose works) are characteristic rhetorical devices of the Shinkokin style.[2] Shunzei and the Mikohidari school were especially drawn to *The Tale of Genji*, and allusions in their poems to both poetry and prose passages from that work perhaps outnumber those to any other source.[3] No doubt their interest in this important work was genuine, but cultivating the *Genji* connection also had strategic benefits for Shunzei and his successors.

The poetry world in the second half of the Heian period, from Emperor

---

1. Edward Kamens rightly took me to task for failing to do this in my book on Tamekane in his review of my *Kyōgoku Tamekane*.
2. In addition to Brower and Miner's discussion of the subject (see esp. pp. 287–91), see two recent articles that take a compelling look at *honkadori* and intertextuality in the poetry of this period: David Bialock's "Voice, Text, and the Question of Poetic Borrowing in Late Classical Poetry," and Haruo Shirane's "Lyricism and Intertextuality: An Approach to Shunzei's Poetics." Some of the issues raised by these two scholars are addressed later in this book.
3. Teramoto Naohiko devotes over half of his book on Genji reception, *Genji monogatari juyōshi ronkō*, to discussions of the relationship between Mikohidari poets and Genji.

Horikawa in the late eleventh century through Go-Toba in the early thirteenth, was dominated by "professional poets" of low-to-middle rank, poets from families whose function at court consisted largely of teaching and composing poetry.[4] As this study will show, poetry was a form of service for these people. Contemporary sources, for example, speak of Go-Toba's search for ladies-in-waiting with poetic skills. And Teika's descriptions of activities at the Wakadokoro make it clear that the highest-ranking members were rarely present for the day-to-day work, which fell instead on the middle- and lower-ranked poets. Indeed, the *Shinkokinshū* selection committee, which carried out the actual editorial work for the collection (with periodic interference from their superiors), had no member higher than the Fourth Rank, a step below the ministerial and counselor ranks, although still high enough to be allowed into the Emperor's presence.

From the early tenth century and *Kokinshū*, this class of poets had been central to the literary scene, but in the later Heian period, they became more important. After Horikawa, the emperors themselves—perhaps because they were occupied with the increasingly powerful organs of the Retired Emperor's Office (*insei*), and certainly by the mid-twelfth century as they became caught up in the struggles (such as the Hōgen Disturbance of 1156) that culminated in the Genpei War—played a lesser role in literary activities. Leadership was instead assumed by such mid-ranking courtiers as Minamoto Toshiyori and his rival Fujiwara Mototoshi (1060–1142), as well as Fujiwara (Rokujō) Akisue (1055–1123).

Given the modest ranks of these men, their continuing leadership required the patronage of higher-ranking people. From these three poets, Akisue and the Rokujō school emerged as the most powerful literary group, probably because Akisue was initially in service to Emperor Shirakawa, who, after he retired in 1086, continued to exercise influence as the first of the powerful retired emperors (*in*). Charisma, or lack thereof, may also have been a factor. Neither Mototoshi nor Toshiyori reached the same rank as their fathers, which in the tight world of the Heian court was more than likely due to a lack of social skills. Akisue, on the other hand, surpassed his father by one full rank and seemed comfortable with court politics.

---

4. Frequently these families would also specialize in something else. For example, both the Mikohidari and Asukai (another branch of the Fujiwara) houses specialized in waka and *kemari* (kickball).

Among other things, by way of bolstering his credentials as a poetry master, Akisue established his family's primacy in Man'yō studies by sponsoring the court's first formal poetry event centering on Hitomaro veneration (*Hitomaro eigu*), in 1118. Poetry rites for Kakinomoto no Hitomaro (d. ca. 710) were to become, as this study shows, increasingly important to the literary scene over the next century. By the second half of the twelfth century, Akisue's grandson Fujiwara (Rokujō) Kiyosuke (1104–77) and Kiyosuke's adopted brother, the priest Kenshō (1130–1209), had moved to the center of the waka stage with a series of scholarly works on poetry that emphasized, among other things, their special knowledge of *Man'yōshū*.[5] In addition to close connections to the imperial house, the Rokujō poets also enjoyed the patronage of other powerful political figures, including Minamoto (Tsuchimikado) Michichika (1149–1202), whose name figures prominently in later chapters of this book.

Another important political actor who served as a patron of poets was Kujō Kanezane. In his direct service was the talented poet and scholar Fujiwara (Mikohidari) Shunzei, who was struggling to establish his own reputation in the face of Rokujō pre-eminence. Originally part of Retired Emperor Sutoku's poetry circle—in which Kiyosuke played the central leadership role—Shunzei had broken with the Rokujō orthodoxy by the 1170s. Undoubtedly the differences between them in aesthetic matters were real, but so was Shunzei's need to obtain patronage and thus a more secure base from which he and his family could produce and propound their art. Proof of Shunzei's success in this endeavor came in 1183 when Retired Emperor Go-Shirakawa (1127–92; r. 1155–58) commissioned him alone to compile what would become the seventh imperial anthology, *Senzaishū*. That Go-Shirakawa and Shunzei's patron Kanezane were often at odds in court politics makes this commission an even clearer testament to Shunzei's name as a poet.

Senzaishū is seen as the earliest public indication of the direction the Mikohidari school was taking in terms of aesthetics, and the practice of *honkadori* figured prominently in their work, although it was *honkadori* of a rather specific nature. Although Shunzei was fairly generous in his inclusion of Rokujō poets in *Senzaishū*, whatever goodwill may have resulted evaporated within a decade, when Kanezane's son Yoshitsune asked Shunzei to be

---

5. See, e.g., Kiyosuke's *Ōgishō* (1124–1144?), *Waka shōgakushō* (ca. 1168), or Kenshō's *Shūchūshō* (ca. 1186).

the sole judge of the *Roppyakuban uta-awase*, by far the largest public poetry event in decades. In his judgments in this contest, Shunzei began to articulate his *honkadori* aesthetic more clearly, and Rokujō poets fared poorly in the contest. It was here that Shunzei made his famous remark: "To compose poetry without knowing *Genji* is a regrettable thing."[6]

In contrast, in his judgments for this contest, Shunzei evinced less enthusiasm for *Man'yōshū* as an appropriate source for vocabulary, much less allusion. In fact, in one famous round, he dismissed the use of *Man'yō* locution. Unfortunately for his reputation, he revealed his own ignorance in the process. In Round 7 of Love Section 7, Shunzei misread the character for "whale" in a poem by Kenshō as *kuzira*; the correct reading in *Man'yōshū* is *izana*. He also anticipated that Kenshō would cite *Man'yōshū* poem 3874 (NKBT 3852) as the "proof poem" (*shōka*) to justify his use of the archaic term. Shunzei dismissed it as a "nonsense poem" (*kyōka*), unsuitable for use as a precedent for serious waka, and awarded the win to Kenshō's opponent, Jakuren (1139?–1202). Kenshō, in a critique of Shunzei's judgments, the *Roppyakuban chinjō*, published soon after the contest, conclusively proved not only that Shunzei was wrong about the reading of the character but also that he was ignorant of the true proof poem, the "Dead Man at Samine" poem by Hitomaro (MYS 220–22 [NKBT same]), so beloved by Brower and Miner.[7]

The lines were drawn quite clearly. The members of the Rokujō school prized a *Man'yō*-based aesthetic and could call on their considerable scholarship in that area to justify (and mystify) their claims. Shunzei was obviously not as well prepared in that field, and his understanding of *Man'yōshū* was apparently limited to such poems as had been recorded in easier-to-read script during the Heian period through intermediary texts such as *Kokin waka rokujō* (mid-tenth century)—a point explored more fully in subsequent chapters of this study. He needed to establish his own aesthetic and scholarly territory elsewhere. He chose *The Tale of Genji*, which appealed to his

---

6. *Genji mizaru utayomi wa ikon no koto nari.* The comment is found in his judgment for Winter I, Round 13 (Hagitani and Taniyama, *Uta-awaseshū*, p. 442).

7. See ibid., pp. 452–53, for an annotated text of the *Roppyakuban uta-awase* round in question, and p. 543n56 for a summary of Kenshō's argument. The fact that Sengaku (1203–69+), in his *Man'yōshū chūshaku* (1269), the scholarly study that is considered to have resolved the major remaining linguistic issues surrounding *Man'yōshū*, explicates several lines of this poem suggests that it may not have been widely known or understood before his time; See Nihon tosho sentaa, *Man'yōshū sengakushō, Man'yōshū meibutsukō*, p. 61.

contemporaries and his patrons on several levels. Not only was it intrinsically masterful, it also depicted an age untouched by the warfare that swept Japan in the late 1100s and a court uncompromised by power-sharing arrangements such as had resulted from the Genpei War and the rise of Minamoto Yoritomo (1147–99) and his warrior government in Kamakura. In contrast, the Rokujō ideal must have appeared arcane and out of touch within the court, even though the aim of the Rokujō school was to re-energize waka by bringing back some of the less inhibited expressions from pre-Heian times.

Not surprisingly, Shunzei's (and later Teika's) celebration of the mid-Heian court matched Go-Toba's own view (not to mention his eventual restoration program) quite well and garnered his patronage. Shunzei grew more insistent on the primacy of *Genji monogatari* through the next decade and, in a formal letter to Go-Toba, attacked Kiyosuke for being woefully ignorant of the text.[8] So successful was Shunzei in advocating this new, *Genji*-based aesthetic that a little more than ten years later, at the time of the *Sengohyakuban uta-awase*, Kenshō was paying lip service![9]

Along with privileging *Genji*, Shunzei and Teika also established their famous formula "old diction, new spirit" (*kotoba furuki kokoro atarashiki*).[10] By "furuki" they meant the elegant vocabulary of the Heian court, not the occasionally rough figures found in *Man'yōshū*. Eschewing the more rhetorically flashy work of *Kokinshū* poets like Tsurayuki (not to mention the later, self-consciously "novel" work of the Rokujō poets), they preferred instead the poetry of Narihira and Komachi, which was concerned less with technique and more with lyrical effect. Similarly, Murasaki Shikibu's hyperrefined world was presented in an elegant (*yū*) and gentle (*yasashi*) way, which suited the "old diction" part of the equation.[11]

But the Mikohidari vision was not uncritical worshiping of *Genji*. It was careful appropriation of certain moments, scenes, and poems from the

---

8. See Chapter 2, p. 57, for a discussion of this incident in relation to the events surrounding Go-Toba's first commission of a set of 100-poem sequences.

9. Teramoto, *Genji monogatari juyōshi ronkō*, pp. 666–72, notes that Kenshō cited *Genji* in fifteen of the 150 rounds he judged, but Teramoto simply acknowledges the allusions without predicating anything about the act of alluding to *Genji*.

10. See, e.g., Teika's *Kindai shūka* (1209) in Hisamatsu and Nishio, *Karonshū nōgakuronshū*, p. 102.

11. Teramoto, *Genji monogatari juyōshi ronkō*, pp. 30–32, argues this point well.

massive tale. This in itself had hegemonic implications. *The Tale of Genji* was, after all, *prose*—unworthy of canonical veneration in the East Asian cultural context—and it was written by a woman. It required the efforts of a *male poet* (doubly blessed!) to bring it into the canon. Thus even though the entire tale (aside from whatever changes time has wrought through the copying process) has survived, in canonical medieval Japanese aesthetics (including Nō, for example, and pictorial representations), it has largely been those *Genji* moments transmuted by Shunzei and his son Teika that have appeared and reappeared in Japanese literature, art, and performance.[12] Furthermore, by the Muromachi period the so-called Aobyōshibon line of texts, descended from a copy Teika made, had become the standard *Genji* text. Since there is evidence that this textual line differed significantly from others, it becomes clear how successful Shunzei and Teika were at making *Genji* their own preserve.[13]

Other Heian classics, *Ise monogatari* (mid-tenth century) and *Sagoromo monogatari* (ca. 1070), were also considered appropriate sources for allusion. Since Teramoto Naohiko and others have written in detail of what parts of *Genji* and the other classics Shunzei and especially Teika favored, I will not do so here, although I discuss many allusions in the body of this book.[14] Briefly, Shunzei and Teika were attracted, in the case of *Genji*, primarily to portions of the book that relate the death of one or another of the female characters. As for other works, and to some extent *Genji* as well, their eye was on passages that emphasized an extremely aestheticized vision of romance and courtship, especially themes of separation and loss. Successful allusions to such literary moments defined, for Shunzei, *en* (or *yōen*), a kind of

---

12. Anecdotal to be sure, but when the most recent of *Genji*'s "translators," the nun Jakuchō (formerly Setouchi Harumi), spoke at the University of Hawai'i in 1998, she singled out *Genji*'s seduction of Oborozukiyo as one of her favorite scenes in the entire book. This happens to be a scene that Shunzei cited repeatedly in poetry contest judgments (see Teramoto, *Genji monogatari juyōshi ronkō*, pp. 17–18). Teramoto also demonstrates how Teika's view of *Genji* passed to Shōtetsu (1381–1459) and then to Shinkei (1406–75). In an unpublished master's thesis (University of Hawai'i, 1998), John Creamer also connects this view to the Nō dramatist Zenchiku (1405–68).

13. Teramoto, *Genji monogatari juyōshi ronkō*, pp. 661–86, provides persuasive evidence that the text of the *Genji* used by the Rokujō poets differed from the Aobyōshibon. Thus it was probably unfair of Shunzei to taunt them for their "ignorance," although it certainly was a wise move strategically since it enhanced Shunzei's claim to be the arbiter of *Genji*.

14. See esp. ibid., pp. 15–232.

ethereal, elegant beauty, which was to him one of waka's highest goals, as well as *aware* (the sad beauty of something short-lived). In contrast, as Teramoto notes, the goal of those who made reference to *Man'yōshū* poetry was *okashi*, a quality of "charm," and, increasingly in Shunzei's eyes at least, mere "novelty."[15]

Thus the Mikohidari appropriation of *Genji* represented a legitimate aesthetic difference that separated them from the till-then mainstream Rokujō school (and ironically, since members of that school are usually called "innovators," cast the Mikohidari poets in a rather conservative light). At the same time, it gave them a field of mastery that bolstered their claim to patronage from the Heian court, which in Kyoto at least, was still a strong, if somewhat nervous and defensive, presence. The Mikohidari valorization of great moments in the court's cultural past surely went a long way toward securing them political favor. It is somewhat paradoxical that by privileging the work of socially marginal writers (Narihira, Komachi, Murasaki Shikibu) and paying only cursory attention to the mainstream canon (including Tsurayuki and *Kokinshū*), they gained more support from Go-Toba and the powerful Kujō house.

Politics at Court

Although the focus of this book is on poetic events from the first decade of the thirteenth century, one cannot understand the shifting patterns of political and literary patronage in the early 1200s without backing up a decade or more to the founding of the Kamakura Bakufu and the alignment of various courtiers around either Minamoto Yoritomo, the first head of the Bakufu, or Retired Emperor Go-Shirakawa after the Genpei War.

Court politics in Japan often seem to be little more than endless disputes over whose daughter will be named empress, and which son will be named crown prince, and it is hard to break into this chain at any given point and say "This is the beginning of X." Nevertheless, we have to start somewhere, and Retired Emperor Go-Shirakawa provides a recognizable and significant point of reference. His behavior during the Taira ascendancy and the Genpei War might be seen as a politically astute effort to steer the imperial family through uncharted and dangerous waters. But it is just as plausible to see

---

15. Ibid., pp. 19–22.

his actions as quite lacking in the qualities one would expect in a Confucian Son of Heaven. Indeed, during his lifetime, both points of view obtained at court, and the groups that held them eventually crystallized into factions that affected the compilation of the *Shinkokinshū*.[16]

In 1184, Fujiwara (Konoe) Motomichi (1160–1233) was reappointed regent, with the support of Go-Shirakawa himself.[17] As son of Motozane (1143–66), who was in turn Tadamichi's (1097–1164) eldest son and older brother to Kanezane, he was, by traditional definition, the logical successor to his father as clan head.[18]

Yoritomo, however, had his own preferences and suggested, initially with discretion, that Kujō Kanezane was a more appropriate candidate.[19] As the Genpei War wound down and Yoritomo consolidated his position in Kamakura as head of the Bakufu, it became less and less prudent for Go-Shirakawa to ignore his suggestion. Go-Shirakawa's support of Yoritomo's brother, Yoshitsune (1159–89; not to be confused with Kanezane's son, Kujō Yoshitsune, whose name will appear much more frequently in this study), further compromised his position. In the Fourth Month of 1186, the Senior Retired Emperor yielded to Bakufu pressure and persuaded Motomichi to cede his position as head of the *sekkanke* to Kanezane, who had not incidentally supported Yoritomo over Yoshitsune. This is the origin of the split between the Konoe and Kujō branches of the Fujiwara clan.

---

16. Anti-Go-Shirakawa sentiment went back at least as far as the time of the Hōgen Disturbance (1156), when his backers, including Fujiwara Tadamichi (1097–1164; Kujō Kanezane's father), not to mention Taira Kiyomori (1118–81), eliminated the supporters of Retired Emperor Sutoku (Go-Shirakawa's older brother, by the same mother) and assured Go-Shirakawa's ascendancy to the throne. He was the fourth son of Emperor Toba, which in itself probably rankled traditionalists, who would have preferred to see a more orderly father-to-son-to-grandson progression. Interestingly, Go-Toba, too, was the fourth son of an emperor, in his case Takakura, whose first son, Antoku, made a quick if dramatic exit during the last stages of the Genpei War.

17. Motomichi had originally received the appointment in 1180 but had resigned it in 1183 during a minor political skirmish.

18. Fujiwara Tadamichi, fifth-generation descendant of Michinaga, overcame his brother Yorinaga's opposition in the Hōgen Disturbance and helped Go-Shirakawa come to power. In addition to Motozane and Kanezane, Tadamichi also fathered Jien, who figures later in this book.

19. For two other views of this time period, see Hurst, "The Kōbu Polity"; and Mass, "The Early Bakufu and Feudalism."

Initially, Kanezane apparently had difficulty asserting his authority, since his connections with Yoritomo were viewed with suspicion.[20] George Sansom's depiction of Kanezane as a dispassionate statesman struggling to bring court and Bakufu together is a bit naïve, for there is no question that he had ambitions for himself and his family and made use of the marriage politics that his forefathers had exercised so skillfully.[21] Once in position, he tried to consolidate his power. Aoki Kengō draws attention to a passage in *Gyokuyō* in which Kanezane explicitly compared his situation to that of Fujiwara Michinaga (966–1027), who represented the pinnacle of Fujiwara power in the mid-Heian period. And regarding his plans for his daughter, Ninshi, Kanazane says "the main purpose of sending [Ninshi] to court is [for her] to give birth to imperial offspring."[22] Subsequently, in early 1190, Ninshi (later known as Gishūmon-in), formally entered the Palace and, on iv/26, was named Go-Toba's empress (*chūgū*), making Kanezane the emperor's father-in-law and potentially a grandfather to a future emperor—a position Fujiwara leaders were accustomed to, as he himself noted in the *Gyokuyō* entry cited above. He was named chancellor/regent for Go-Toba late in the following year.

Although hardly a puppet of Yoritomo, Kanezane did maintain good relations with him through the early 1190s. As was so often the case, this relationship was cemented through a marriage connection: on Kenkyū 2 (1191)/vi/26, Kanezane's son, Yoshitsune, married the daughter of Fujiwara (Ichijō) Yoshiyasu (1147–97), who was Yoritomo's brother-in-law, and lived for a time in Kamakura before returning to Heian to serve as Yoritomo's liaison with the court. As Uwayokote Masataka notes, Yoshitsune was marrying down, and the liaison does seem to demonstrate an effort on the part of the Kujō house to be accommodating.[23]

---

20. See Mass, *Development of Kamakura Rule*, p. 8, and notes therein for *Gyokuyō* entries from 1191 in which Kanezane complains about his lack of power.

21. Sansom, *A History of Japan to 1334*; see, e.g., p. 319.

22. *Gyokuyō*, Bunji 5 (1189)/xi /28 (3: 574–75). (All *Gyokuyō* citations in this study are from the 1907 Kokusho kankōkai three-volume edition.) See also Aoki, *Fujiwara Yoshitsune zenkashū to sono kenkyū*, pp. 241–42.

23. Yoshiyasu's branch of the Fujiwara had historically not risen above the Third Rank. Yoshiyasu himself only rose to Senior Third and Provisional Middle Councilor (*gonchūagon*), and even this was probably because of Yoritomo's support; see Uwayokote, *Kamakura jidai seijishi kenkyū*, p. 59.

Whatever his relationship with Yoritomo, Kanezane was not entirely sympathetic toward Go-Shirakawa.[24] His obituary for the ex-emperor, who died in 1192, is ambiguous:

13th. Clear. Today, at the hour of the Tiger,[25] the Senior Priestly Retired Emperor passed away at the Nishi no Tōin Palace. He was sixty-six years old. The fourth prince of former Emperor Toba, his mother was Taikenmon-in. He was the father of the two Retired Emperors Nijō and Takakura. He was grandfather to three sovereigns: the late Rokujō Emperor and the two most recent ones.[26] He has ruled the land for over thirty years, since the Hōgen era.[27]

Magnanimous in character, he governed the world with compassion. He was converted to the virtues of Buddhism and [ruled] very much like Liang Wu-ti.[28] It's just that unfortunately he forgot the traditions of Engi and Tenryaku.

He began to show symptoms of illness in the early winter of last year. Things gradually got worse, and he has finally gone on to the next world. Everyone under Heaven grieves, but especially those who have benefited morning and evening from his boundless power. All in the land ache, but especially those who owe their fame and fortune to his limitless patronage.[29]

On the surface, this might appear to be laudatory, or at least standard. But some of Kanezane's word choices suggest a great deal of irony. First, his

---

24. Uwayokote (ibid., pp. 59–60) says that much of the problem between Kanezane and Go-Shirakawa was personal, especially since Kanezane despised Tango no Tsubone, Go-Shirakawa's favorite concubine. He cites some of the unflattering terms Kanezane uses for her in *Gyokuyō*: "the Retired Emperor's pet concubine (*aishō*)" and "a low-class person (*hisen no mono*)." Uwayokote gives the relevant *Gyokuyō* entries as Bunji 1 (1185)/xii/28 (3: 130) and Bunji 3 (1187)/ii/19 (3: 332) for the latter. The second example is even more arch than Uwayokote lets on. In the *kanbun* equivalent of a parenthetical aside Kanezane wrote, "and the Lady Tango (the Retired Emperor's pet concubine; once wife of the late Narifusa; a low-class person, yet he favors her above the others)" and goes on to liken her to Yang Guifei, a comparison meant to suggest her undue influence on the throne.

25. The Hour of the Tiger, the third zodiac sign, fell between 3:00 and 5:00 A.M. Numerologists might remark at all the threes involved here: the *Third* Year of Kenkyū, the *Third* Month, the *13th* day, under the *third* sign of the zodiac. Never mind that he was sixty-six years old!

26. This refers to Antoku and Go-Toba.

27. Most specifically, this refers to the Hōgen Disturbance of 1156, from which Go-Shirakawa emerged victorious; see above. "Ruled the land" is *tenka wo osameru* and means that Go-Shirakawa was the *chisei no kimi*, or chief of the imperial house.

28. The Emperor Wu of Liang (r. 502–49) established the Liang dynasty and sought to rule as a proper Buddhist monarch, using the Buddhist ruler Emperor Asoka as his model. For a brief biographical sketch, see Ch'en, *Buddhism in China*, pp. 124–28.

29. *Gyokuyō*, Kenkyū 3/iii/13 (3: 798).

comparison of Go-Shirakawa to Liang Wu-ti is double-edged, for although Emperor Wu was indeed a vigorous propounder of Buddhism, he proved, at least to Confucian commentators of later ages, to be a rather poor ruler, unable to punish wrongdoing and control those under him, especially in his later years. (Perhaps this is Kanezane's oblique swipe at Tango no Tsubone [?–1216].)

Kanezane's reference to the Engi and Tenryaku eras (roughly the first half of the tenth century) is much less ambiguous. These eras were seen even as early as the eleventh century as a golden age of sorts, in which, from a Confucian standpoint, all the elements of good government worked: laws and historical chronicles were compiled, and high culture, as exemplified by *Kokinshū* and *Gosenshū*, obtained.[30] Saying that someone had forgotten the old ways of Engi and Tenryaku was a fairly standard reproof by Kanezane's time.

But Kanezane's final lines contain the most telling criticism. Structurally, they make two parallel lines. The first half of each line appears to describe people's genuine grief at the passing of the sovereign. However, the second part of each line proceeds to take aim at those who were Go-Shirakawa's favorites. To be sure, the words Kanezane used—what I have translated as "power" and "patronage"—could also be read "virtue" and "charity." But the prefacing of each phrase by the rhetorical *iwanya* (how much more so; especially) suggests irony. Finally, Kanezane's word choices may also be an allusion to lines from a Bo Juyi poem, "I Shall Resign":

With the morning dew, one revels in fame and wealth;
At the evening sun, one grieves for one's descendants.[31]

The implication here—that those left behind will suffer from Go-Shirakawa's excesses—might be seen as quite damning, although the parallel

---

30. See Sansom, *History of Japan to 1334*, p. 149, who cites Ōe Masahira (952–1012) on this point.

31. Saku, *Kanshi taikan*, 4: 1752. The poem is included as part of what came to be called *Hakushi monjū*, a collection of Bo Juyi's works that appeared in many forms throughout the centuries in both China and Japan. References to versions of this collection can be found as far back as early Heian, and there is no question that someone like Kanezane would have been familiar with its content, although I cannot at this time prove whether the particular text of it that he knew included this poem or not. See also Smits, *The Pursuit of Loneliness*, esp. pp. 35–66, and 201–2, for a discussion of what mid- to late Heian poets knew about Chinese poetry and how they chose to use that knowledge.

lines with which Kanezane ended his obituary also echo a parallel pair of rhetorical questions that Bo Juyi asked later in the same poem: "Who does not covet wealth and position? Who does not desire our Lord's favor?"[32]

Whatever Kanezane's feelings toward Go-Shirakawa, his ascendancy rankled not only Motomichi but also a coterie of courtiers who supported Go-Shirakawa and saw no reason for an accommodation with Kamakura. One of those courtiers was Minamoto (Tsuchimikado) Michichika, who figures prominently in this study. An indication of Michichika's relationship with Go-Shirakawa can be found in the fact that the retired emperor sent him to Ise in early 1192 to offer prayers to help alleviate Go-Shirakawa's illness. Selection as an imperial messenger to Ise was a sign of great favor.[33]

Go-Shirakawa's supporters seem to have succeeded in making life unpleasant for Kanezane. As Jeffrey Mass notes, in 1191 he complained of feeling helpless and isolated by the backbiting going on in the palace.[34] Among his nemeses, surely Tango no Tsubone ranked high.[35] Her worldly name was Takashina Eishi. She was originally married to Taira Narifusa, a low-ranking attendant in Go-Shirakawa's court, whose highest rank was Junior Fifth Lower. Caught in Kiyomori's purge of Go-Shirakawa's followers in 1179, Narifusa was exiled to Izu and killed the following year as he tried to escape. In the meantime, Eishi was serving Go-Shirakawa, who had been placed under house arrest and confined to the Toba Palace. It was at this time that she grew close to Go-Shirakawa and eventually became his favorite, with considerable influence over political matters.

She bore Go-Shirakawa a daughter, and for a time there was talk of the child being offered to Go-Toba as his primary consort, but perhaps the mother's extremely low rank prevented that from happening. Besides, as we shall see, there were several other contenders, with powerful backing, for that position. So Tango and Go-Shirakawa settled for the next best thing.

---

32. Uwayokote (*Kamakura jidai seijishi menkyū*, p. 60)—it is not clear whether he sees a Bo Juyi allusion here—also cites the last lines but assesses them as simply an attempt to ridicule the grief of those close to the late retired emperor. Either way, they probably should not be taken at face value.

33. Kenkyū 3 (1192)/i/12. *Rekishi sōran*, 4: p. 85.

34. Mass, *Development of Kamakura Rule*, pp. 7–8, with reference to *Gyokuyō*, Kenkyū 2/vii/17 and Kenkyū 2/xi/15. Given his daughter's success at court at that stage, however, I am less inclined than Mass to take Kanezane's complaints entirely at face value.

35. She was also known as Jōdōji no Nii and Tan no Nii. The following account is largely from Yasuda, *Kamakura Muromachi jinmei jiten*, pp. 368–69.

They contrived to have the daughter given a palace name, an honor usually conferred only on full empresses. In the Sixth Month of 1191 she was named Sen'yōmon-in. Her mother, Tango, was promoted to Junior Second Rank (unthinkably high given her family background), and Minamoto Michichika was named the daughter's *bettō*, that is, the chief administrator for her now-royal household.

Even after Go-Shirakawa's death, Tango no Tsubone wielded considerable influence, placing herself at the center of the anti-Bakufu and anti-Kanezane courtiers. In Kenkyū 7 (1196) she concocted an unusual stratagem to get Kanezane ousted. She produced the young wife of a minor courtier named Tachibana Kanenaka and claimed that the woman was a medium who had been possessed by the ghost of Go-Shirakawa. Through this medium, the late ex-emperor had expressed his displeasure at the way things were going, demanded that changes be made, and ordered that a temple be built to honor him. (This latter request may seem innocent enough, but the temple would have qualified for a tax exemption that would have allowed Tango to generate income from the arrangement; it was clearly a ploy to bring more land under Tango no Tsubone's control).[36] Kanezane, it seems, had both husband and wife exiled, a demonstration of power that tends to dispute Mass's notion that he was hanging by a thread at this stage. (Incredibly, Tango no Tsubone tried an almost identical ploy in 1206, this time appealing to Go-Toba. He would have none of it, either, and her two pawns in this second attempt, a Minamoto Nakakuni and his wife, met the same fate as the first.)[37]

Tango and others derived most of their power from Go-Shirakawa himself, and Kanezane's influence could only increase when Go-Shirakawa died

---

36. From the time of the Taihō Codes (708–12) shrines and temples were allowed to have assigned for their upkeep the income generated from certain lands. This income could not be taxed. Over the centuries, powerful courtiers were able to use their influence in government to increase the amount of temple or shrine land that could be tax-immune. Retired emperors from Shirakawa onward made use of this provision to generate income for the imperial family by setting up temples for themselves when they retired from the throne and then designating tax-exempt land for the support of those temples; see Hurst, *Insei*. Even in death, Go-Shirakawa was seeking to extend this privilege—or so Tango no Tsubone would have people believe.

37. See Mass, *Development of Kamakura Rule*, p. 9. For Jien's version of the story, see Nakajima, *Gukanshō*, pp. 513–18; or, Brown and Ishida's translation, *The Future and the Past*, pp. 168–71.

in 1192 (iii/13). Notably, just four months after Go-Shirakawa's passing, Kanezane persuaded Go-Toba to give Yoritomo the title of Seii Taishōgun, thus recognizing the reality of Kamakura's importance and establishing a formal relationship between court and Bakufu (*not*, as traditionalists would have it, legitimizing a usurper).[38] Kanezane's brother Jien also seems to have benefited from his influence, since Jien was rapidly promoted through the ecclesiastical ranks and made Chief Abbot (*zasu*) of the Tendai sect in Kenkyū 3 (1192)/xi/29, at the age of just twenty-eight, the first person to achieve that post before the age of thirty, and thus young enough to have ruffled a few feathers.[39]

Through the early 1190s, Kanezane maintained his power and influence, and his sons, most notably for our purposes Yoshitsune, made rapid progress through the ranks. Bear in mind that this was not analogous to the Taira Kiyomori depicted in *Tales of the Heike* misusing his newfound influence to benefit his relatives. Kanezane was, after all, head of the Fujiwara *sekkanke* branch (albeit, one of several candidates who might qualify for that position, the line having split). It was only natural that his offspring would rise at court. Indeed, a failure to rise would have been more significant. In 1195 (xi/10—nine days after the future emperor Tsuchimikado's birth), Yoshitsune achieved the office of Palace Minister (*naidaijin*) and was also confirmed in his position as Major Captain of the Left Bodyguards (*sakon'e no taishō*), which placed him at the head of the Emperor's personal Konoe guards.[40]

---

38. It is misleading to characterize, as Ariyoshi (*Shinkokin wakashū no kenkyū: kihan to kōsei*, p. 43) does, the court factions at this time as pro-Bakufu (*shinbakuha*—literally, "the close-to-the-Bakufu faction") and anti-Bakufu (*tōbakuha*—"crushing-the-Bakufu faction"). In my opinion, this gives some of the participants more credit than they deserve. Rather, I see the factions as either practical and cognizant of the larger reality (Ariyoshi's "pro-Bakufu" group) or narrowly focused on local court politics (the "anti-Bakufu" group).

39. *Rekishi sōran*, 4: 93. For a sense of how some reacted to his relative youth, see *DNS*, iv:5, p. 306, *Kakō yōyaku* entry.

40. See *Kugyō bunin*, as quoted in *DNS*, iv:5, pp. 47, 58. Yoshitsune was apparently first appointed to the adjunct position (*kaneru*) of *sakon'e no taishō* on Bunji 5 (1189)/xii/30 and given a regular appointment (*ninzu* or *ninjiru*) on Kenkyū 1 (1190)/vii/18; see Aoki, *Fujiwara Yoshitsune zenkashū to sono kenkyū*, pp. 214, 235. The *taishō* (also read *daishō*) post was generally conferred only on top-ranking aristocracy and usually as an adjunct (*kaneru*) position to someone who was at least a Major Counselor (*dainagon*) or Minister (*daijin*). It was entirely honorary, requiring attendance at various ceremonies but no actual martial duties or skills. See Ōno et al., *Iwanami kogo jiten*, p. 1469. Incidentally, on the same day, Minamoto

Normally, one barometer of relative standing in Heian and Kamakura court politics is sponsorship of poetic activity.[41] Poetry events such as anthologies, contests, and large-scale parties were in a sense the "public works projects" of their day since they required, and in turn exhibited, political and economic resources and influence. One might be able to get a better reading of who was ascendant at court if there had been more poetry events during this period. But the fact is, it was a very quiet time on that score. Although he did commission *Senzaishū*, Go-Shirakawa had never been an especially ardent waka practitioner on a day-to-day basis (he was more interested in *imayō*, "songs in the 'modern style'"),[42] and in any case his death in 1192 removed the logical imperial sponsor for large-scale public activities. No one else appeared to fill the vacuum.

Kanezane had always been an active supporter of waka. He had learned the art under the tutelage of the Rokujō master Fujiwara Kiyosuke, but at the latter's death in 1177, he moved toward Shunzei and gradually, presumably through Yoshitsune's influence, became a supporter of the Mikohidari school of innovators.[43] Although Kanezane had sponsored several notable poetry events in earlier years,[44] through the 1190s, it was Yoshitsune rather

---

(Tsuchimikado) Michichika, the Kujō family's most formidable rival, was promoted to the position Yoshitsune was vacating, Provisional Major Counselor (*gondainagon*).

Both men were the same rank, Senior Second, but Yoshitsune's bloodlines placed him on the faster track, even though he was twenty years younger than Michichika. Still, it is not as if the Kujō ascendancy slowed Michichika's bureaucratic career. In fact, he followed the same track, and the same timing, as his father Masamichi had; both achieved Senior Second Rank and the position of Palace Minister in their fifties.

41. See Huey, "Medievalization of Poetic Practice"; and idem, *Kyōgoku Tamekane* for evidence of the close ties between politics and poetic activity, even into the late Kamakura period.

42. *Imayō* were popular songs—some reworked waka, others of a highly religious nature, and still others singing of the activities of commoners—that enjoyed a particular vogue in the late twelfth and early thirteenth centuries due largely to Retired Emperor Go-Shirakawa's enthusiastic, even fanatical, patronage. He is credited with compiling *Ryōjin hishō* (date unknown), the best-known collection of these songs. See Kim, *Songs to Make the Dust Dance*, pp. xiii–xiv, and 1–45; and for a complete translation of the extant songs, Nakahara, "Songs of *Ryōjin hishō*."

43. *WBJ*, p. 109.

44. Ariyoshi (*WBJ*, p. 47) lists nine poetry contests that Kanezane, as Minister of the Right, sponsored between 1173 and 1179. The first four were judged by Kiyosuke (1104–77). Of the five after Kiyosuke's death, two were judged by Shunzei, one by Kiyosuke's younger brother Shigeie (1128–80), and for two the judges are not known.

than his father who emerged as the primary poetry patron in the family.⁴⁵ We will return to his role presently.

The 1170s had witnessed a lot of poetic activity, some of it, as noted above, sponsored by Kanezane; the Genpei War years naturally saw little of it. Between 1185 and 1190, there was a burst of activity, most of it privately sponsored. For example, in early 1190, Kanezane solicited screen poems for his daughter's apartments in the palace, which brought forth poems from Teika, Takanobu (1142–1205; one of Teika's half-brothers, who will appear again later in this book), Shunzei, Fujiwara (Rokujō) Suetsune (1131–1221; half-brother of Kiyosuke and later a staunch foe of the Mikohidari school), Kanezane, Yoshitsune, and two other lesser-known Fujiwara poets, Sanesada (1139–91) and Sanefusa (1147–1225), who neither allied themselves with any particular poetic school nor were members or retainers of the Kujō house.⁴⁶ Rokujō poets sponsored similar in-house activities. In fact, the only truly "public" event in this period, and by "public" I mean one that brought together members of various families and factions, was the activity surrounding the compilation and final presentation of *Senzaishū*, which was first formally presented to its sponsor, Go-Shirakawa, in 1187 and then revised and presented again the following year. Otherwise, the activities during this time were small-scale and exclusive.

Yet 1192–93 witnessed an event that in its scale and scope pointed to a certain degree of publicly acknowledged political power on the part of its sponsor, Kujō Yoshitsune—the *Roppyakuban uta-awase*.⁴⁷ Perhaps it is significant that the sponsor was Yoshitsune and not his father, Kanezane.

---

45. Incidentally, Yoshitsune's interest in Chinese is evident throughout this period, as the topics for many of the events he sponsored were four-character Chinese topics (*kudai*). He and Jien also collaborated on a 100-round *senka-awase* in which Yoshitsune wrote his poems in the pose of "Nankai gyofu (or 'gyoho')" (Ch. *nanhai yufu*, "the old fisherman in the South China Sea"). Jien posed as "Hokusan shōkyaku" (Ch. *beishan qiaoqie*, "the woodcutter of the Northern Mountains"). This is discussed further in Chapter 5, pp. 204–6. See Aoki, *Fujiwara Yoshitsune zenkashū to sono kenkyū*, pp. 59–65, for Yoshitsune's verses in this contest. A full text of the contest, including both poets' contributions, and the judgments, can be found in Higuchi et al. *Chūsei wakashū*, pp. 82–117. *Sanchōki* also mentions Yoshitsune's sponsoring of many Chinese poetry parties (*shikai*) in the Eighth and Ninth Months of Kenkyū 6 (1195).

46. Aoki, *Fujiwara Yoshitsune zenkashū to sono kenkyū*, p. 235.

47. There is some uncertainty as to its exact dates, but the event seems to have spanned 1192 and 1193, if not also 1194. For various theories, see Kubota Jun, *Shinkokin kajin no kenkyū*, pp. 689–90; Minegishi, *Uta-awase no kenkyū*, pp. 222–25; *WBJ*, p. 705.

Maybe Kanezane had too many enemies to pull it off himself. (As noted above, he had pretty much retired from poetry sponsorship some years before.) Yet it was the Kujō house, nonetheless, that put this event together, and it was on an unprecedented scale, larger and more comprehensive than any single waka occasion in history before it (excepting imperial anthologies, which are by nature quite different).

As noted earlier, this contest deserves much more attention than I can give it here, especially since nine of its participants ended up a decade later on Go-Toba's resuscitated Wakadokoro and thirty-four of its poems were selected for *Shinkokinshū*. But for the purposes of this book, the significance of the event lies in its demonstration of public clout. Yoshitsune was able to bring together members of the two main rival poetic schools—Mikohidari (Ietaka [1158-1237], Jakuren, Takanobu, and Teika) and Rokujō (Ariie [1155-1216], Kenshō, Suetsune, and Tsuneie [1149-1209])—as well as representatives of the ruling elite, including, of course, Yoshitsune himself and his uncle, Jien, for the Kujō house and two other ranking Fujiwara from other houses, Kanemune (1163-1242) and Iefusa (1167-96).[48] And in a move that showed where his own poetic allegiances lay, he asked Shunzei, head of the Mikohidari school, to be the judge.

The fact that Yoshitsune sponsored the contest and not his father gains added significance in light of Kanezane's subsequent fall, which did not have the effect on Yoshitsune's fortunes that one might expect. Maybe Kanezane's withdrawal from sponsorship of poetic events more than a decade earlier (*Gyokuyō* does not even mention any *uta-awase* after Jishō 3 [1179]/x/30, though there are references to *shiika* [Chinese poetry and waka] activities from time to time in the Bunji and Kenkyū eras) tells us all we need to know about his precarious position at court.[49]

---

48. Kanemune rose to the Senior Second Rank in his lifetime and took part in, among other events, the *Sengohyakuban uta-awase*, which is discussed at length in Chapter 6. Iefusa belonged to the Matsudono branch of the Fujiwara, and his father, Motofusa, had served as *sesshō* in the mid-twelfth century before running afoul of Kiyomori. Even in his short life, Iefusa rose to the Junior Second Rank.

49. Kanezane does discuss yet another intriguing poetry event in *Gyokuyō* (pp. 887-88). On Kenkyū 5 (1194)/viii/11, his daughter, the imperial consort Ninshi, sponsored a big poetry party and concert. There was quite a range of participants, including Michichika (then a Middle Counselor), who was put in charge of writing the introduction to the written account of the occasion (assuming that's what *josha* means), and other Rokujō, Mikohidari, Tsuchimikado, and Kujō poets, though mostly lesser names. One suspects that in this case the reason for the wide-ranging participation is not so much Kujō prestige as that it was held at

Given the nature and scale of the event, it could not have been done as a *tōza* contest, in which poems are submitted and judged at one sitting. *Senka-awase* (contests of selected poems) had grown steadily in popularity, and such a format suited Yoshitsune's purpose well. Although the exact chronology for this contest is still debated, it appears that Yoshitsune called for 100-poem sequences, following set topics, from each of the participants in 1192.[50] Teika submitted his in the Eighth Month of 1193, and it is assumed the others did so as well. The poems were then matched in generally random order (by whom is not certain, but one imagines it was Yoshitsune) and presented to the two teams over the course of many evenings at Yoshitsune's home. Team members debated the merits (and demerits, of course) of the night's poems, and after hearing these discussions, Shunzei formulated his judgments. Not everyone showed up every night; it is not even certain that Shunzei, who was eighty at the time, did. Minegishi Yoshiaki speculates that he probably worked from written transcripts.[51]

The results displeased the Rokujō camp and prompted Kenshō to write a detailed rebuttal now known as *Roppyakuban chinjō*. Indeed, the contest is seen as the "coming out," as it were, of the innovative Mikohidari style that was to culminate in *Shinkokinshū*, which pulled, as noted above, 34 poems from this contest (making it the third largest single source for that anthology).[52] But again, for the argument here, the event's significance lies in the facts that it occurred, was sponsored by the Kujō house, and brought together a wide range of views. And given the results, it is fair to say that one alliance—between the Kujō house and the Mikohidari poets—had been established that was to have a major impact on the next ten years or so of waka practice.

---

the palace. Information on how often Kanezane discusses poetry events in *Gyokuyō* is gleaned from Ōae, *Gyokuyō jikō sakuin*.

50. The sources we might normally turn to for more information about this contest, Kanezane's *Gyokuyō* and Teika's *Meigetsuki*, have big gaps during these years, and unfortunately neither has any entries discussing it. The description that follows is based on the account found in Ton'a's *Seiashō* (ca. 1360), as quoted in Minegishi, *Uta-awase no kenkyū*, p. 223. For the full text of *Seiashō*, see Sasaki Nobutsuna, *Nihon kagaku taikei*, 5: 18–122; the passage in question is on p. 99.

51. Minegishi, *Uta-awase no kenkyū*, p. 224.

52. For a detailed analysis of the relationship between this contest and *Shinkokinshū*, see Ariyoshi, *Shinkokin wakashū no kenkyū: kiban to kōsei*, pp. 4–20.

The genesis and development of the other important alliance, that between the Rokujō school of poets and the Tsuchimikado branch of the Minamoto, is less easily documented, since during this entire period there were no poetic events clearly sponsored by Michichika or his family. Like Kanezane, Michichika had been active in the early 1170s, but in the following years his name rarely appeared in poetic events. His connection with the Rokujō school stems from the fact that his poetry teacher was Suetsune, and there is little doubt, as we shall see, that in the next decade he and Suetsune worked together to promote the Rokujō school and undermine its main rival, the Mikohidari group.

One other event is notable, the *Kenkyū rokunen shōgatsu hatsuka minbukyō no ie no uta-awase* (Poetry Contest at the Residence of the Popular Affairs Ministry Chief on the 20th Day, Tenth Month, Sixth Year of Kenkyū [1195].[53] Its sponsor, Fujiwara Tsunefusa (1142?–1200), brought together forty-six poets from both major schools, with Shunzei as judge. Minegishi believes Shunzei favored the Rokujō poets in his judgments and speculates it was either as a result of fallout from the *Roppyakuban uta-awase*, which had created such a stir, or out of pity for the declining Rokujō school, a scenario I find unlikely given the ferocity of his attack on them a few years later.[54] In any case, only two poems from the contest ended up in *Shinkokinshū*.

One has to wonder how someone of Tsunefusa's modest rank and stature could have sponsored such an elaborate event. Hosting forty-six courtiers was no small feat. Scions of great political houses sometimes sponsored poetry contests when they were young and still low-ranking, but their backing is obvious. Tsunefusa's case is more problematic. His father rose only as high as the Fifth Rank, but Tsunefusa seems to have been a very skillful politician. Having gained Go-Shirakawa's confidence in the 1170s, he was named *bettō* for the newly retired Takakura in 1180. Apparently as slippery as his first imperial patron, Go-Shirakawa, he quickly switched sides at the end of the Genpei War and became a trusted friend of the Kamakura Bakufu. The support of Yoritomo is probably what propelled him through court in a manner his father never could have achieved. And, as discussed below, it was about this time, 1195, that Yoritomo was jockeying to marry his daughter to

---

53. Kenkyū 6 (1195)/i/20 was the date. For a text, see GR 189, 12: 283–304.

54. Minegishi, *Uta-awase no kenkyū*, p. 225. The "attack" occurs in a letter called the *Shōji sōjō*, which Shunzei sent to Go-Toba in 1200. It is discussed at length in Chapter 2, pp. 56–58, and translated in Appendix C, pp. 405–12.

Go-Toba. Tsunefusa may have been lending his house and connections to the effort. Inukai maintains that Tsunefusa must have been a hard-working bureaucrat, too, which helps explain his multiple appointments, although it may simply have been the very number of appointments that led Inukai to his conclusion.[55] At the time of this contest, Tsunefusa was Senior Second Rank and held joint posts as Middle Counselor (*chūnagon*) and chief of the Popular Affairs Ministry (*minbukyō*). On his mother's side of the family, he was also Shunzei's nephew, which undoubtedly helped him to be taken seriously in poetry circles.

Gyokuyō (Kenkyū 6/vii/2) has an intriguing reference to Tsunefusa. By the Japanese count, that day was the fortieth anniversary of Emperor Toba's death, and memorial services were held in various places. Kanezane wrote that at the services at Saishō-ji, the person who should normally have acted as officiator (*shōkei*) was himself in mourning for someone else, and so "Minbukyō Tsunefusa was made acting officiator."[56] It is also obvious from other entries in *Gyokuyō* that Tsunefusa was a frequent visitor to Kanezane's residence, if not an outright retainer.[57] So evidently Tsunefusa had friends in high places, and it is likely that one of them actually sponsored this event. If it was Kanezane, he did not show up, however. On the night in question, he was at one of his residences, discussing Tōdai-ji business.[58]

In any case, 1195 also saw two imperial births that would greatly affect the course of events. Kanezane's daughter Ninshi gave birth to the first imperial child (viii/8), a daughter, who became known as Shōshi Naishinnō. Outside the imperial house, the birth of a daughter in a high-ranking family was frequently seen as a boon, since she always stood a chance of becoming an empress, as Ninshi had done. But within the imperial family, princesses (or later-born princes, for that matter) were of little political value. And although Shōshi Naishinnō received all the proper ceremony and was unquestionably accepted into the Palace[59] and Ninshi herself returned with appropriate ceremony after the birth abstinence period was over, little more than a year later Ninshi suddenly left the Palace for good.[60]

---

55. Inukai et al., *Waka daijiten*, p. 696.
56. *Gyokuyō*, 3: 883.
57. For example, the entry for Kenkyū 7 (1196)/iii/2 (*Gyokuyō*, 3: 923–24) describes an elaborate outing to Uji by Kanezane and his entourage, of which Tsunefusa is part.
58. Kenkyū 6 (1195)/i/20; *Gyokuyō*, 3: 901.
59. See *DNS*, iv:5, pp. 15–23, pp. 28–33; sources include *Gyokuyō* and *Sanchōki*.
60. Kenkyū 7 (1196)/xi/23—see *DNS*, iv:5, pp. 299–300, for various accounts of this event.

What is traditionally assumed to have prompted Ninshi's departure was the second imperial birth, that of the future Emperor Tsuchimikado on 1195/xi/1. The mother was Zaishi, Michichika's adopted daughter. This could indeed have posed a threat to the Kujō house.[61] However, one need look no further than Go-Toba himself to see that this turn of events would not necessarily be enough to harm Ninshi's standing at court. As noted above, Go-Toba was the *fourth* son of Emperor Takakura. (Recall, too, that Go-Shirakawa had also been the fourth son.) Given the rather high infant mortality rate and the vagaries of imperial politics, surely neither Ninshi nor her father would have given up and assumed, just one year after his birth, that the new prince had a lock on the throne. The fact that he was not formally named Crown Prince until 1198/i/11, more than a year after Ninshi's departure, suggests that things were not that cut and dried. (The birth of the future Emperor Juntoku in 1197/ix/10 may have clouded the picture, too. In fact, in the long run, it seems Go-Toba was closer to Juntoku than to Tsuchimikado. Michichika may well have had a struggle ensuring that Tsuchimikado got named Crown Prince.)

Jien, Kanezane's brother, thus Ninshi's uncle, gives another explanation in *Gukanshō*. He claims that Yoritomo was seeking to send his own daughter to court and conspiring with Go-Shirakawa's old entourage to do so.[62] He proposes that Michichika, having learned of Yoritomo's intention, had sought to block the move in the first place by marrying a woman known as

---

61. Ariyoshi, *Shinkokin wakashū no kenkyū: kiban to kōsei*, p. 59, espouses this view, saying simply that Ninshi had lost imperial favor, and it also stands behind Kubota Jun's remarks on the subject (*Shinkokin kajin no kenkyū*, p. 674).

62. See Nakajima, *Gukanshō*, pp. 494-95; or Brown and Ishida, *The Future and the Past*, p. 158. Mass (*Development of Kamakura Rule*, pp. 8-9) is inclined to believe this story and cites as supporting evidence two *Azuma Kagami* entries (Kenkyū 6/iii/29 and iv/21) in which Yoritomo is shown acceding to a request by Tango no Tsubone whereby certain *shōen* would pass into the control of her faction—a plan that Mass claims Kanezane had thwarted earlier. Uwayokote (*Kamakura jidai seijishi kenkyū*, p. 15) believes Yoritomo first conceived of sending his daughter to court in Kenkyū 2 (1191) and argues that since Yoritomo was part of the old aristocracy, not the new regional warrior class, this desire to send his daughter to court was natural. He further maintains (pp. 16-18) that the Bakufu was completely established (*kanzen ni taiseika*) with the death of Yoritomo's brother Yoshitsune, and that once established, it proceeded to renew its relationship with the court on its own terms, thus rendering Kanezane "useless" (*muyō*). It is an interesting notion, although much of Jeff Mass's work demonstrates that the Bakufu took many years to find itself institutionally; it is something of a stretch to see Kamakura as dealing with Kyoto on equal (or at least equally confident) terms this early.

Norikane's Daughter, who had, from her marriage to one Nōen, already produced a daughter—the Zaishi referred to above—who would be an appropriate candidate for empress. Michichika formally adopted Zaishi as his own and then sent her to court as Go-Toba's consort.[63]

Although Jien is hardly an objective outsider in the matter—his own official career ended at the same time as Ninshi's withdrawal (and probably for related reasons, about which more presently)—and he cites no evidence, his suggestion of a wide-ranging plot is probably not too far off the mark. The question is, at whom was the plot aimed?

Given subsequent events, it seems likely that getting Ninshi out of the palace was simply the logical consequence of the real purpose, which was to topple Kanezane. And indeed, with frustratingly little warning in the records that now remain to us, both Kanezane and Jien resigned their various offices on xi/25 and 26, just two days after Ninshi left the Palace. Historians call this the *Kenkyū no seihen*, which might be best translated colloquially, as the "Kenkyū Era Shakeup."

Dai Nihon shiryō devotes six pages to Kanezane's resignation, citing the accounts of nine sources.[64] One of these, the *Kugyō bunin*, the official record of court appointments, is naturally terse: "Regent and Junior First Rank Fujiwara Kanezane stepped down from his position on the Eleventh Month, 25th Day, at the age of forty-nine, without offering his written resignation to the Emperor (*mujōhyō no koto*)."

The lack of a formal letter is significant. Normally when one wished to resign, due to illness, for example, one would send a formal letter of resignation to the emperor, who might or might not accept it.[65] For Kanezane to

---

63. Anthropologists might be interested in the defense of Tsuchimikado's (Go-Toba's and Zaishi's prince) legitimacy put forward in the history *Masukagami*. The argument is that Tsuchimikado had a claim to the throne, even though his mother was not the "real" daughter of Michichika, because she was, in any case, of the womb of Michichika's primary wife (*kita no kata*). In other words, the identity of Zaishi's biological father was irrelevant. See Iwasa et al., *Jinnō shōtōki Masukagami*, p. 254.

64. DNS, iv:5, pp. 300–306.

65. Consider a similar case: on Kenkyū 6 (1195), ix/25, Fujiwara Sanefusa attempted to resign from his office, but his request was denied. The *Kugyō bunin* describes his circumstances as follows: "Minister of the Left and Senior Second Rank Fujiwara Sanefusa submitted a letter of resignation to the Emperor on the Ninth Month, 25th Day, at the age of forty-nine, citing recent inauspicious phenomena, but his letter was returned to him." In fact, the act of composing the letter itself was deemed significant. In *Sanchōki*, Fujiwara Nagakane, a retainer of Kanezane and a well-known specialist in Chinese poetry, says that Munenari, a clerk in the

have resigned without a letter, then, implies that either he was leaving unwillingly, or he wished to spare the emperor the necessity of dealing formally with the matter. The next day, however, Jien submitted a letter on Kanezane's behalf and then resigned too, as will be discussed below.[66]

Nagakane, in *Sanchōki*, has quite a bit to say about Kanezane's situation. In an entry dated the 18th, he writes of going to Kanezane's residence, which was buzzing with rumors of Kanezane's imminent resignation. These rumors had apparently been making the rounds for quite a few days. Nagakane was shocked at the suggestion, since he saw Kanezane as a loyal subject of the throne and undeserving of such treatment. On the 19th, he met with Kanezane, who indicated that he understood the seriousness of the situation. When Kanezane resigned, Nagakane expressed great indignation that a man whose line went back many generations, all faithful servants to the throne, should come to such an end. Interestingly enough, in an entry dated the 28th, he specifically dismissed suggestions by other Kujō family retainers that Yoritomo was somehow in on the whole plot. "I cannot believe such a thing," he said and noted that people serve (and by this he presumably means both Kanezane and the Shogun) at the pleasure of the *Emperor*, which could be taken as a rather pointed criticism of Go-Toba.[67] The incident is also treated in *Gukanshō*. Jien charges that Michichika actually demanded Kanezane be exiled, but when Go-Toba asked him for specific charges, he backed down.[68]

The day after Kanezane resigned, Jien followed suit, giving up all his offices and ecclesiastical responsibilities and going into seclusion. Unlike Kanezane, however, Jien did submit a letter to the emperor. Its exact contents have not survived, but it seems to have said that Jien, as younger brother of Kanezane, felt compelled to follow his sibling in resigning his

---

bureaucracy and the one who actually authored Sanefusa's resignation letter, came to Nagakane and bragged about how well-written it was, in formal Chinese, replete with appropriate historical references. See *DNS*, iv:5, p.11.

Judging from events in the preceding weeks, the "inauspicious phenomena" appear to have been extended drought, followed by a typhoon, and an astronomical conjunction of Venus and Mars. See Tōkyō daigaku shiryō hensanjo, *Shiryō sōran*, Kenkyū 6/vii/16; Kenkyū 6/ix/6 and 7; 4: 117–18. (Since a number of illnesses and deaths are mentioned, there may have been an epidemic as well.)

66. *DNS*, iv:5, pp 307, from *Sanchōki*, Kenkyū 7/xii/26.
67. *DNS*, iv:5, pp. 300–302, from *Sanchōki*, Kenkyū 7/xi/18, 19, 25, and 28.
68. *DNS*, iv:5, p. 305; Nakajima, *Gukanshō*, p. 494; and Brown and Ishida, *The Future and the Past*, p. 159.

posts since he relied on his brother for support.[69] Jien's replacement was Shōnin Hōshinnō (or Hosshinnō), one of Go-Shirakawa's sons. In *Gukanshō*, Jien notes—with some satisfaction, one assumes—that the Priest-Prince Shōnin fell ill and died within a year. "People wonder," Jien writes, "if this isn't a sign"—a sign, of course, that Jien had been wronged.[70]

Although it is evident from Nagakane's remarks, not to mention Ninshi's sudden departure from the palace, that something was in the air, there is little indication in other records remaining from 1196 that the Kujō house—or more specifically, Kanezane, Jien, and Ninshi (Yoshitsune, as we shall see, seemed to suffer less)—was about to take a fall. Unfortunately, Kanezane's own diary, *Gyokuyō*, becomes less complete after 1194 and not just for the period of his downfall.[71] One might have expected that after his forced retirement, he would have had more time on his hands to write and a great inclination to set the record straight. But the years from 1196 on are barely covered, and the final entry we have is for the Twelfth Month, 29th day of Shōji 2 (1200), more than a year before he took the tonsure and almost seven years before his death. Did Kanezane censor himself? Did others censor his diary? Were portions simply lost to time? Or was he just too busy to write more than he did? But these questions are putting us ahead of the story. In any case, there is little in the 1196 portions of *Gyokuyō* that indicates trouble.[72] Neither is Teika's *Meigetsuki* of any use here. Its 1196 entries stop at the Seventh Month, and all of 1197 has only a few lines. However, the gaps here are not necessarily significant of anything other than the vagaries of ancient

---

69. *DNS*, iv:5, p. 307; from *Sanchōki*, Kenkyū 7/xi/26.

70. *DNS*, iv:5, p. 306; Nakajima, *Gukanshō*, pp. 494–95.

71. In the standard printed edition used for this book, entries for Bunji 4 (1188), for example, take up 60 pages, and those for Kenkyū 2 (1191) amount to 130 pages and Bunji 3 (1187) to 165. Even the years Kenkyū 3–5 (1192–94) average 30–35 pages each. By comparison, the year in question here, Kenkyū 7 (1196), covers only fourteen pages.

72. The entries for the beginning of the year are lengthy, but concentrate on New Year's visits and ceremonies. The only entry for the Fourth Month is on the first day, and it is just slightly over one line long and seems to end in mid-sentence. In the Fifth Month, there are entries only for the 22nd through the 24th, and these describe a series of Buddhist sermons. There is nothing at all for the Sixth through Ninth Months, or the Twelfth. The sole Tenth Month entry is for the 25th, and talks about an imperial visit to Iwashimizu Shrine. And the only account in the important Eleventh Month covers an imperial visit to Kamo Shrine on the 5th day. Perhaps it is significant that in these last two cases Kanezane says he did not go to the palace, but went straight home after the events. See *Gyokuyō*, Kenkyū 7/x/25, and xi/5; 3: 926–28.

documents and how they survive, since 1191 also has only a few lines, and there are no entries at all for 1194 or 1195, either.

The fact that when pressed by Go-Toba, Michichika had not been able (at least according to Jien) to make any specific charges suggests that there is nothing one can conveniently point to as the cause of Kanezane's trouble. Sansom calls the whole thing a "palace revolution, under Michichika's guidance," which is probably as good a way to describe it as any. But to characterize Michichika and his group as "restorationists," as Sansom also does, seems quite wide of the mark.[73] They were no friends of Kamakura, to be sure, but it was Go-Toba who was the restorationist. To the extent that Michichika supported him vis-à-vis the Bakufu, Michichika might be called one, too. But it seems in light of subsequent events that his main goal was placing his own candidate (and step-grandson), Tsuchimikado, on the throne. (For that matter, Kanezane also sought to become an imperial grandfather, and no one called *him* a restorationist.) Larger issues of Bakufu vs. court were of secondary concern.[74]

All these maneuverings at court—some despite the Kamakura Bakufu, and others even instigated by Yoritomo himself, not to overthrow, but to integrate himself into the old aristocracy—should be enough to put to rest the hoary view that somehow the Genpei War marks the fall of the traditional imperial court, so that literature from this time onward, most notably waka and *Shinkokinshū* in particular, needs to be read against this backdrop. In this view, the neo-classicism of *Shinkokinshū* is an almost pathetic attempt by disempowered courtiers to recapture their past greatness.[75] The activities

---

73. Sansom, *A History of Japan to 1334*, pp. 333–34.

74. I have found support for this view in Uwayokote (*Kamakura jidai seijishi kenkyū*, pp. 17–18). He argues that Kanezane had lost his value to Kamakura as liaison with Kyoto because things had settled down considerably after Go-Shirakawa's death. Thus, he says, Michichika's political defeat of Kanezane is "nothing more than an internal struggle between power factions at court" that for Yoritomo "just wasn't that serious a matter." He adds, "Michichika was never close to the Bakufu, but his real concern was wiping out his political opposition at court, beginning with the Kujō house, and he gave no thought to how it would affect the Bakufu." I think Uwayokote overstates the degree to which Yoritomo had already been co-opted by the court, but his basic assessment here is valid. (See also note 62 to this chapter, p. 37.)

75. In describing this period, Brower and Miner (*Japanese Court Poetry*, p. 235) say, for example, "The imperial Court had been at its zenith in the preceding age, and now was reduced to playing an increasingly impotent role in government." They might be excused this notion, since their *Japanese Court Poetry* predates the work of revisionist institutional historians like Hall, Mass, Nagahara Keiji, and Uwayokote Masataka. But more than thirty years later, we

described in this book make it clear that the courtiers did *not* view themselves as fading into oblivion. The Bakufu was an upstart reality that had to be dealt with, but it did not begin to intrude seriously into the lives of the Heian aristocracy until after the Jōkyū War, and even then, the process was gradual. A century later, retired emperors and courtiers alike were still ignoring the Bakufu as much as possible or using it to further their own, local ends.[76] Nostalgia for the past was a trope for poets no less than for historians and can be found in *Man'yōshū* and *Kokinshū* poems, as well.

On the issue of Kanezane's setback, Sansom makes another statement that deserves closer scrutiny: "Michichika's success brought an end to the supremacy of the Kujō branch of the Fujiwara clan, and Kanezane disappeared from public life. He died in 1207."[77] As we shall see, this was hardly the case. In fact, that is what makes the story all the more compelling, for we can speculate not only why Kanezane and Jien fell, but also why Yoshitsune did not, or at least not as hard.

On Kenkyū 9 (1198)/i/19, after Tsuchimikado had ascended the throne, Yoshitsune resigned his post as *sakon'e no taishō*, but since this post by definition involved personal service to the emperor, it is not surprising that a new emperor might expect a new person in that position (although at the age of three, Tsuchimikado himself probably didn't think much about it). Judging from Teika's account, Yoshitsune was not happy about having to give up the title.[78]

---

find similar sentiments. David Bialock ("Voice, Text, and the Question of Poetic Borrowing," p. 201), for instance, in discussing a poem by, of all people, Yoshitsune, states: "Only a generation before the publication of the *Shinkokinshū* that [imperial] court culture had been devastated by wars and was passing from the domain of fact to a subliminal realm of poetic nostalgia." As will be seen throughout this study, there is little evidence that Yoshitsune viewed himself or his group as "passing into" some sort of marginal realm. Further on, Bialock also collapses pre- and post-Jōkyū War Go-Toba into a single entity, "frustrated in his political ambitions" (ibid., p. 213). He certainly was that after 1221, but at the time of *Shinkokinshū*, and in the events described in this book, one sees a powerful, self-confident ruler who energetically pursues court life as it had been lived for centuries.

76. Jeffrey Mass, and others, now locate the final dominance of the warrior class in the *fourteenth* century; see the essays in Mass, ed., *The Origins of Japan's Medieval World*.

77. Sansom, *A History of Japan to 1334*, p. 334.

78. See *Meigetsuki*, Kenkyū 9/i/8, where Teika describes going to visit Yoshitsune, only to find the gates of his residence locked, with Yoshitsune receiving no visitors. The day before Teika discusses rumors about Yoshitsune's imminent resignation from the *taishō* post, and the implication is that Yoshitsune is in seclusion over the matter (*Meigetsuki*, 1: 50–51).

But within a year, on Shōji 1 (1199)/vii/22, he was promoted to Minister of the Left (*sadaijin*). Uwayokote argues that this promotion (he mistakenly implies it was to Chancellor [*daijō daijin*]) was Michichika's way of getting Yoshitsune out of the way (*tanaage suru*—"kicking him upstairs," or, literally "shelving him") so that Michichika himself could become a minister (which he did, on the same day, as Palace Minister, *naidaijin*).[79] I find this rather strained reasoning. Michichika had no trouble forcing the resignations of Kanezane and Jien, if indeed he had been behind the events. He would not need to go to such elaborate lengths to work around Yoshitsune. Uwayokote asserts that it was Yoshitsune's connection to Yoshiyasu (through marriage to his daughter) that made him less vulnerable to Michichika's machinations, since Michichika had already begun to court Yoshiyasu's Ichijō branch to isolate them from the Kujō. But it seems to me the connection had been just as strong between Kanezane and Yoshiyasu, and I do not see why it could "protect" Yoshitsune but not his father. All in all, I am inclined to think that Yoshitsune was "spared" because his personal qualities and skills appealed to Go-Toba. But more about that presently.[80]

As for immediate repercussions, there is only one other resignation that might have been related, that of Fujiwara Kanefusa (?–1217) from his position as Chancellor on Kenkyū 7 (1196)/xii/9. One of Kanezane's younger brothers, he had been appointed on Kenkyū 2 (1191)/iii/28[81] and rose to Junior First Rank three years later, presumably with Kanezane's backing. To judge from his frequent appearances in *Gyokuyō*, the two were close. It is problematic, however, how much his resignation had to do with Kanezane's downfall, for in the *Gyokuyō* entry for Kenkyū 7/i/17, Kanezane describes a consultation he had with Kanefusa: "The Chancellor came to consult with me and show me his resignation letter to the Emperor. I advised that such a thing should not be done too hastily."[82] In other

---

79. Uwayokote, *Kamakura jidai seijishi kenkyū*, p. 64.

80. In any case, it is not fair to say the Kujō house was destroyed. Not even Kanezane and Jien were entirely discredited. As I discuss in the next chapter, Kanezane made at least two "public" appearances in 1200 and 1201, in poetry events sponsored by Yoshitsune, and of course Jien was soon back in the thick of poetry activities. Incidentally, Kubota Jun, *Shinkokin kajin no kenkyū*, p. 793, supports the view that this promotion marked a resurgence of Kujō fortunes.

81. Tōkyō daigaku shiryō hensanjo, *Shiryō sōran*, 4: 74.

82. Kanefusa uses the term *jōhyō*, often translated as "memorial," but which I have rendered here and elsewhere as "letter of resignation." The editors of *DNS*, iv:5, p. 314, imply by

words, Kanefusa seems to have been planning to resign for nearly a year, if not longer. Unfortunately, we have no clue as to why. It was probably not for health reasons, since Kanezane would not likely have counseled against it in that case, and there is no other indication in the records that he was seriously ill. At any rate, his resignation was accepted without formal reply—itself something of an anomaly, implying that it was, in fact, seen as the natural consequence of Kanezane's troubles, about which the less said the better.[83]

Kanezane himself seems to have slipped gracefully, perhaps even gratefully, into semi-retirement. In the New Year's Day entry of Gyokuyō for Kenkyū 8 (1197), a little more than a month after his resignation, he described himself as doing the proper religious obeisance, in "housecoat rather than court costume."[84] Not that he was entirely without resentment, of course. In several of the entries for the rest of the month, he related what others told him about the various official New Year's ceremonies, which he could no longer attend, and dwelt with apparent relish on slips of etiquette and procedure.[85] And the entry for the 13th Day of the Third Month seems almost tongue-in-cheek: "My wife told me of an auspicious dream she had, in which demons were swept away. I wish I could believe it! I wish I could believe it!"[86] (Three years later, the last entries of Gyokuyō contain these same

---

their cross-reference and gloss that they see this as a letter of resignation, not just a memorial. They cite the Gyokuyō entry in the context of Kanefusa's actual resignation eleven months later. For the original entry, see Gyokuyō, 3: 919.

83. At Kanefusa's urging, Nagakane argued at court that precedent demanded a formal imperial reply (chokutō) to a jōhyō letter of resignation, but despite the lack of precedent for *not* issuing one, none was forthcoming. It is another element in the mystery. See DNS, iv:5, pp. 316–19.

Incidentally, there were at least two prominent Kanefusas in the Heian/Kamakura periods. The earlier one (1001–1069) rose only as high as the Fourth Rank but had a fairly good poetic career (see WBJ, p. 111). The other is the Kanefusa we are discussing here. Unfortunately, Inukai et al., *Waka daijiten*, p. 185, seem to have confused the two. See instead Yasuda, *Kamakura Muromachi jinmei jiten*, p. 498.

84. Gyokuyō, Kenkyū 8/i/1, 3: 929. Actually the term Kanezane uses to describe what he is wearing is *shukubō*, a word I have been unable to find in any dictionary, but its literal translation, "house coat," is probably not too far off in terms of imagery. He is clearly calling attention to the fact that he is now a man of leisure and *outside the court*.

85. Gyokuyō, Kenkyū 8 (1197)/i/1 and 6, 3: 329, for example.

86. Gyokuyō, Kenkyū 8 (1197)/iii/13, 3: 929.

elements: clucking over the ignorance of court ritual shown by Motomichi and others, and entertaining auspicious dreams.[87])

As time goes on, he turns to other pursuits to fill the time court activities used to take up. The entire entry for Kenkyū 8 (1197)/iv/2, for example, is a description of an elaborate astronomical/astrological ritual he sponsored to take advantage of the congruence of the hour, day, month, and year of the Snake, which occurs only once every thirteen years and is an important rite for those born in the year of the Snake, which included his daughter Ninshi, and the current Middle Captain, by which he presumably means Teika, who had held that post for many years.[88] And it is perhaps a relief to know that his retirement was not all tense. In a scene that calls to mind Sei Shōnagon's *Pillow Book*, Kanezane tells of building a snow mountain at his residence and inviting people to enjoy it.[89] It is also clear that Kanezane kept in touch with Yoritomo. As late as the First Month of Kenkyū 9 (1198), he wrote of exchanging letters with Yoritomo, although he did not reveal the contents.[90]

At court, however, Michichika was consolidating his power. The daughter Yoritomo had supposedly hoped to marry into the Palace died on Kenkyū 8 (1197)/vii/14.[91] With her and the Kujō candidate, Ninshi, now out of the way, there was no serious opposition to making Prince Tamehito the Crown Prince. Still, Michichika was playing his hand cautiously. Kenkyū 9 (1198) began inauspiciously, with two days of heavy rain that forced the cancellation of many New Year's events. This was followed by a solar eclipse.[92]

---

87. For example, in the entry for Shōji 2 (1200)/i/1, Kanezane related gaffes that Yoshitsune told him had been committed by Michichika and Motomichi during the New Year's ceremonies. He saw these as signs of *masse* ("the end of the world"; 3: 936.) And in the entry for Shōji 2/xi/13, he described the Gosechi Dances as related to him by Yoshitsune. Apparently the Regent Motomichi sat in the wrong place and thus forced everyone else to move back onto the boards of the veranda. Kanezane quoted Yoshitsune as complaining, "Sitting on [bare] boards, our rear ends (*shiri*) were cold, and it was hard to bear" (ibid., 3: 944).
As far as auspicious dreams, in the entry for Shōji 2/i/9, he related: "Last night my wife had a dream, in which this year, for certain, help would come. She said she felt elated" (ibid., 3: 938).

88. Ibid., 3: 930. Again, three years later many of the same concerns appear. Astronomy/astrology figures in entries for Shōji 2/ii/3 (3: 940) and Shōji 2/x/17 (3: 944).

89. See *Gyokuyō*, Shōji 2/i/19, 3: 939.

90. *Gyokuyō*, Kenkyū 9 (1198)/i/4 and 5, 3: 931-32.

91. *DNS*, iv:5, pp. 447-49.

92. See the entries for Kenkyū 9/i/1, in both *Meigetsuki* (1: 48-49) and *Gyokuyō* (3: 930-31).

On Kenkyū 9 (1198)/i/5, a series of promotions was announced, including that of Michichika to Chief Administrator to the Retired Emperor's Office (*in no bettō*).[93] Since there were no living retired emperors at the time, that could mean only one thing: that Go-Toba was about to step down.

Judging from remarks in *Gyokuyō*, it is obvious that Kanezane knew what was about to happen and was none too pleased. Regarding the promotions, which he naturally considered undeserved, he said: "Is this good government? Of course not!" He was also quite concerned that the whole process was being carried out despite what he calls Kantō's "repeated" objections to having such a young emperor (Tsuchimikado was four at the time; three by the Western count). He raised numerous criticisms of his own on the basis of precedent, but revealed, perhaps, his true concern when he said of Michichika, "By making himself *in no bettō*, won't he have the Emperor and the Retired Emperor in the palm of his hand?"[94] But Kanezane's objections remained between him and his diary, and on the 11th, less than a week later, in a single day Tamehito was named Crown Prince and then immediately ascended the throne as Emperor Tsuchimikado. And to Motomichi's Chancellor title was added that of Regent.

The ill omens that had dogged the New Year's celebrations seemed to cloud Go-Toba's early days as Retired Emperor. There was some sort of disturbance in the street during his progress to the abdication ceremony. The imperial regalia were damaged, and at least one person was killed.[95] And when he arrived at Sumiyoshi during a series of shrine visits that began on Kenkyū 9/i/21, a sudden storm arose.[96] Still, these signs did not seem to

---

93. The move was not a complete surprise. In his diary, Minamoto Ienaga claimed that rumors had been making the rounds since the Twelfth Month of the previous year that Go-Toba was about to abdicate and that the new emperor had already been selected, "through divination," he said, although in fact the only other candidate, Nagahito, had little backing. The winning candidate was the First Prince, Tamehito. See *IN*, p. 20.

94. *Gyokuyō*, Kenkyū 9 (1198)/i/6 and 7, 3: 932.

95. *IN*, pp. 22–24. In their notes, Ishida and Satsukawa cite specific sections of the *Gyokuyō* and *Meigetsuki* entries for this date (Kenkyū 9/i/11).

96. *IN*, p. 27. From its opening lines, it is evident that Ienaga saw his diary as being as much literary as historical. (The notion that literary and historical writing were somehow distinct did not necessarily obtain in traditional East Asian.) When one reads Ienaga's accounts of these omens, even though the street brawl is independently confirmed, one thinks of *Genji monogatari*, its famous carriage quarrel, and the storm at Suma "caused" by the god of Sumiyoshi, which storm itself is reminiscent of a *Tosa Diary* account of a similar event.

prevent Go-Toba from what, in Ienaga's diary at least, appears to be the sort of quest for fun and relaxation not surprising in a young man of not quite eighteen who, like a caged bird set free, has a chance to get away from the political pressures the throne had placed on him. As we shall see, however, although Go-Toba never quite lost his taste for pleasurable activities (banquets, outings, and the like), within a year these activities begin to take on a decidedly ideological shape.

A year into Tsuchimikado's reign, Yoritomo fell ill, took the tonsure, and then died within two days.[97] As noted earlier, some accounts consider Kanezane's downfall to have been in part a result of Yoritomo's betraying him in an effort to marry his own daughter into the Palace. But, as also mentioned above, Kanezane continued to correspond with Yoritomo and noted with distress that the enthronement of Tsuchimikado was carried out without Yoritomo's permission. Thus I suspect he still saw Yoritomo as an important player in the political arena and, given the long personal connection, may have felt a sense of private loss, as well. However, since there are no entries at all in *Gyokuyō* for this entire year, we unfortunately cannot know how he reacted.[98]

Hardly was Yoritomo's body cold when Michichika had himself appointed Major Captain of the Right Bodyguards (*ukon'e no taishō*), in addi-

---

97. Shōji 1 (1199)/i/11 and 13. *DNS*, iv:6, pp. 17–33, gives numerous accounts of Yoritomo's death (from 28 different sources, in fact, although not all are contemporary, and many of the entries have to do with his memorial temple, his grave, and so on). Among the tidbits:
—Iezane in his *Inokuma kanpakuki* says that Yoritomo seems to have caught his illness from drinking water. His information is seven days old (see following note; *DNS*, iv:6, p. 17)
—*Azuma kagami* claims he had been ill since the Twelfth Month of the previous year, which, combined with the courtiers' diary entries first recording the illness in the First Month, makes one think that Kamakura was keeping quiet about the problem, perhaps—and this is hindsight—because the succession was not clear (*DNS*, iv:6, p. 18).
—*Hōryaku kanki* (author unknown), a mid-fourteenth-century history covering the years from Hōgen (1156–59) to Ryakuō (1348–42) and written from a Buddhist perspective (*Nihon koten bungaku daijiten*, 5: 441), relates a "ghost story" that claims Yoritomo's death was caused by the avenging ghosts of his brother Yoshitsune and others whose deaths Yoritomo had caused, most dramatically the child emperor Antoku's. The story itself appears in *DNS*. The text of *Hōryaku kanki* can be found in GR 458, 26: 1–65; the passage in question is on p. 40.

98. Teika mentions Yoritomo's illness and death rather briefly. It is noteworthy that his accounts, like those of Iezane, follow by exactly seven days the actual events, giving us a sense of how long it took news to travel from Kamakura to Kyoto. See *Meigetsuki*, Shōji 1 (1199)/i/18 and 20, 1: 79–80.

tion to his position as Provisional Major Counselor. In fact the appointment came on the 20th, the very day, according to Teika, that news of Yoritomo's death reached Kyoto. When Teika heard on the 20th that Michichika intended to carry out promotion announcements as scheduled, despite Yoritomo's death, he was disgusted and called it immoral. But apparently, according to Teika's entry on the 22nd, Michichika simply pretended he had not heard the news and went ahead with the promotions, feigning surprise on the 22nd, *after* the promotion ceremony has been completed, when he publicly acknowledged Yoritomo's passing. When he ostentatiously went into seclusion the next day, ostensibly for the purpose of mourning Yoritomo, Teika wrote that Michichika "will go to any lengths in his scheming."[99] From this point on, most historians agree that Michichika held the reins at court, and with Yoritomo's succession causing much confusion in Kamakura, he apparently had little *outside* interference.

"Inside" opposition proved to be a different matter. Apparently from the very beginning, Go-Toba had shown an independent, take-charge spirit. Hirota Akiko, drawing on accounts in *Gukanshō* and *Heike Monogatari*, recounts how at age three Go-Toba had impressed Go-Shirakawa with his boldness, thus convincing Go-Shirakawa that he should be the next emperor, although these two sources cannot generally be taken at face value.[100] And although there is little evidence that Go-Toba attempted to go up against the heavyweights (Kanezane and Michichika) who were battling in his name in the 1190s, there is at least a small indication of an ability to use patronage to garner support, an ability that he was to hone in the next decade. The case in point is one Fujiwara (Asukai) Masatsune (1170–1221), who had been in Kamakura since 1189 teaching *kemari* (kickball) to the warriors, but was summoned back to Kyoto by Go-Toba in the Second Month of Kenkyū 8 (1197) and launched on a court and poetic career. In fact, Masatsune became the progenitor of the Asukai branch of the Fujiwara family, a branch that continued to be famous for its *kemari* and poetry skills well into the

---

99. For information about the appointment, see Tōkyō daigaku shiryō hensanjo, *Shiryō sōran*, 4: 145. See also *Meigetsuki*, Shōji 1/i/20 and 22, 1: 80, and Kubota Jun's pithy recounting of the incident in *Shinkokin kajin no kenkyū*, p. 792. As with Yoshitsune's appointment to Major Captain of the Left Bodyguards, described above, this adjunct appointment to *ukon'e no taishō* was appropriate to someone of Michichika's rank and further indicated the likelihood that he would spend time in close physical proximity to the emperor.

100. Hirota, "Ex-Emperor Go-Toba," pp. 42–44.

Muromachi period and throughout maintained close ties to important warrior houses.[101] Not only did Go-Toba recognize and encourage literary talent in this case, but he opened his own lines to Kamakura in the process. And this pattern of literally promoting talent in the arts was one that he would repeat frequently in the coming decade.

So, as we enter the thirteenth century, the Tsuchimikado clan is in apparent control of court politics. However, what the Kujō clan may have lost in political clout is soon compensated by their crucial importance to the literary scene (especially Yoshitsune and Jien), both as poets in their own right and as patrons to Teika and the Mikohidari school. And we will see that their success was achieved with the obvious support of Go-Toba.

---

101. *WBJ*, pp. 586–87, and pp. 11–12 for general background on the Asukai family.

TWO

First Steps, Shōji 2

(1200)

As noted in the preceding chapter, Go-Toba began his "retirement"—such an odd term to use for a seventeen-year-old—by having fun, although it seems he was not without a serious side. An early passage in Ienaga's diary poetically captures these times while also showing why those memoirs, with their obvious concern for the literary over the "factual" and their uncritical adulation of Go-Toba, need to be used carefully:

Sometimes we would go to see the cherry blossoms along mountain paths. At other times we would dip water from pure streams. Or again, we would hunt deer on the moors or go falconing on cold winter mornings. In such ways did we amuse ourselves through the seasons.

But one thing His Majesty would never do is kill any living thing.[1] Although still young, he would summon monks from the twelve schools of Buddhism for lectures and was always reading the sutras himself. Each day he would listen to the sermons without concern as to how long they might turn out to be. In his various devotions, he especially favored the Bodhisattva Jizō and would make offerings to Him every morning. Indeed, the Jizō statue he honored was one for which he himself had performed the formal dedication. And in his own hand he wrote the prayers offered to the Amida triad. I doubt there are any previous examples of comparable piety, even in the sutras themselves. And of course, offering a horse to a shrine was a daily practice for him. Rare was the day that he did not honor in some way the gods and Buddhas. Thus was his bright majesty unmatched.

---

1. Note the apparent contradiction here with the falconing image introduced in the first paragraph.

Be that as it may, even among the many leisure activities we indulged in perpetually, poetry contests and parties were especially common. Although I ought to have recorded each of them, there were so many that I wouldn't know where to begin, and besides, now, so much later, I have forgotten the details of most of them.[2]

The contrast among the paragraphs of this opening produces something akin to bathos. But in them, Ienaga introduces what becomes more or less the main topic of his memoirs: Go-Toba's various leisure activities. The breadth of Go-Toba's interests was daunting to Ienaga, who noted that the retired emperor seemed fascinated by every art and capable of mastering anything he attempted.[3] Even allowing for hyperbole, Go-Toba does seem to have loved diversion. Indeed, his motivation for calling Masatsune back from Kamakura (as mentioned in the preceding chapter) may have been initially as much for Masatsune's *kemari* skills as his poetry; just days after he returned to Kyoto, Go-Toba had him attend a *kemari* match.[4]

Nevertheless, it was not long before Go-Toba seemed to focus on waka as the means by which he would bring together the various elements of the court. To begin with, he was faced with the rivalry between the two political giants, the Tsuchimikado branch of the Minamoto clan, headed by Michichika, and the Kujō house of the Fujiwara clan, with Yoshitsune as its *de facto* head. In addition, the world of poetry was divided into two broad camps—the more established Rokujō house and the newer, and more innovative, Mikohidari—although not all poets were clearly allied with one or the other. Go-Toba's resuscitation of the Kujō house and his playing of it off against its rivals on the field of poetry, whatever the political purposes and consequences, had an enormous impact on the development of waka and ultimately *Shinkokinshū*.

Go-Toba began to restore the reputation of the Kujō house in the First Month of 1200, when he invited Jien to his Palace to perform esoteric Buddhist rites.[5] Thus Jien's forced seclusion, which had lasted since his resigna-

---

2. *IN*, pp. 36–37.
3. *IN*, pp. 34–35. Hirota ("Ex-Emperor Go-Toba," pp. 66–70) also dwells at length on Go-Toba's varied tastes and skills, listing sumo, archery, *imayō*, and *shirabyōshi* dancing among them, and cites appropriate sources for each.
4. *DNS* iv:5, pp. 389–92.
5. *Gyokuyō*, Shōji 2/i/29 and ii/1–6, 3: 940. Teika also notes the event. Since it came on the same day that the court received the news that Kajiwara Kagetoki, pretender to Yoritomo's position, had been hunted down and killed by the Bakufu as a rebel, Teika says: "Infinitely

tion from his ecclesiastical offices in 1196, was lifted. Yoshitsune's status, on the other hand, had always been somewhat more ambiguous, even from the time of Kanezane's fall. Most sources claim that he, too, had gone into seclusion in 1196 (*rōkyo*, which implies staying away from the Palace and one's job), but he did not resign all his posts. (Recall, too, that he was promoted to Minister of the Left in the interim.) And given the frequency with which he provided Kanezane with reports about what had happened at this or that festival or event, he hardly seems to have been entirely shunned.[6] Yet not until the Tenth Month of 1200 does Kanezane write: "Safu [Yoshitsune] has for the first time gone to the Retired Emperor's residence and appeared before His Majesty."[7] This is taken by Ariyoshi to indicate that Yoshitsune's seclusion was now officially over. Yet, as discussed below, he evidently had also been publicly exonerated in the spring of 1200, only to be sent back into seclusion in the Fourth Month; this Tenth Month pardon appears to have marked his permanent return.[8]

In any case, by 1200 Go-Toba had begun to rehabilitate the Kujō house. His motivation is problematic. Perhaps he wanted a counterbalance in court politics. On the other hand, the poetic talents of Jien and Yoshitsune were considerable, and at this point in his retirement, Go-Toba was probably as concerned about that as anything else.

In the preceding chapter it was noted that the last decade of the twelfth century was not one of the more active ones in waka history—somewhat surprising considering the poetic talent alive at the time. The highlight of the decade was, of course, the *Roppyakuban uta-awase*. But toward the last three years, another poetic group arose—to "fill the vacuum," as Ariyoshi puts it[9]—with Shukaku Hosshinnō (1150–1202) at its center. The second son of Go-Shirakawa and full brother of Princess Shikishi (Shikishi Naishinnō; 1152?–1201), Priest-Prince Shukaku had entered the monastery at Ninna-ji at the age of six and had taken the tonsure by the age of ten. By 1195 he was chief ecclesiastical administrator (*sōhōmu*) of Ninna-ji.[10] By the late 1170s he

---

strange are the workings of Heaven. No sooner do the misfortunes of one man reach our ears than this happy news [Jien's invitation] comes" (*Meigetsuki*, Shōji 2/i/29, 1: 137).

6. See, e.g., *Gyokuyō*, Shōji 2/i/1, 3: 936.
7. Ibid., 2/x/14, 3: 944.
8. See *WBJ*, p. 672.
9. Ariyoshi, *Shinkokin wakashū no kenkyū: kiban to kōsei*, p. 21.
10. Kenkyū 6/ii/24. *Shiryō sōran*, 4: 113.

had already shown a great interest in waka and had begun sponsoring monthly activities at Ninna-ji; hence Ariyoshi's sobriquet for the group—the "Ninna-ji *kadan*." But he really came into his own as a poetry patron between 1197 and 1200, when he brought together fellow monks at Ninna-ji with poets of various factions, such as Shunzei, Teika, and Kenshō, for two large poetic events now known as *Shukaku Hosshinnō no ie no gojisshu* (Fifty-Poem Sequences at the Residence of Priest-Prince Shukaku) and *Omuro senka-awase* (Contest of Selected Poems at Omuro). The former was a set of fifty-poem sequences commissioned by Shukaku Hosshinnō from seventeen poets in late 1197; the latter was a sixty-round *senka-awase* made up of poems chosen from the former and completed sometime between 1199 and 1201. Ariyoshi has studied these two events exhaustively and concluded that although the fifty-poem sequences yielded twenty-five poems for *Shinkokinshū*, on the whole, based on the selections and judgments in the *Omuro senka-awase*, the tenor was dictated by the older, conservative Rokujō poets.[11]

One way in which these events were significant is that they drew the lines ever more sharply between the Mikohidari and Rokujō schools, while nevertheless demonstrating that given the right kind of sponsorship, even those bitter rivals could be brought together. They thus provided a springboard for Go-Toba's own sponsorship. One has to wonder, however, how well Go-Toba would have fared as a "mediator" if Shukaku Hosshinnō had lived. Given that Go-Toba generally favored the more progressive Mikohidari style (though his Oki-bon revisions of *Shinkokinshū* do reveal a more conservative approach than, say, Teika's) whereas Priest-Prince Shukaku was close to the Rokujō school, the poetic scene might have remained fragmented. Given that political lines also divided along poetic ones, the consequences for Go-Toba's long-range political plans may have been far-reaching. But then, "if so-and-so had lived" is one of history's great games.

---

11. See Ariyoshi, *Shinkokin wakashū no kenkyū: kiban to kōsei*, pp. 21–41. The crux of his argument is that the poems selected for *Shinkokinshū* from the fifty-poem sequences have little overlap with the poems selected for the *Omuro senka-awase* from those same sequences, and of the five poems that do overlap, only two had been judged winners in the *Omuro senka-awase*, the other three being draws. He adduces other evidence as well (i.e., that Rokujō poets fared far better in the Omuro contest judgments than Mikohidari poets, etc.), but the above is sufficient to make the point. Ironically, Shunzei is listed as the judge for the *Omuro senka-awase*, though Ariyoshi feels he was probably doing little more than recording discussions dominated by conservative factions.

For a time, Yoshitsune, too, attempted to sponsor "umbrella" events and hosted several contests in the Second and Intercalary Second months of 1200 with both Mikohidari and Rokujō poets. At one of them, a contest on the 25th day of the Second Month, Kanezane even took part, although under a pseudonym. Still, the fact that he made an appearance, with the dean of the Rokujō family, Kenshō, in attendance, is significant.[12] At another, *Yoshitsune no ie no nijūban uta-awase* (Poetry Contest in Twenty Rounds at the Residence of Yoshitsune; held on *ii/1), Yoshitsune invited Rokujō Suetsune to judge. Teika took exception to his shabby treatment in the contest at the hands of his rival and vowed in a formal, and evidently intemperate, letter never again to participate in any contest judged by "a charlatan poet like Suetsune." This further polarized the situation, and in the Fourth Month, Suetsune succeeded in having Yoshitsune forced into seclusion again by holding the Kujō house responsible for the behavior of one of its retainers, Teika.[13] This put an end to Yoshitsune's sponsorship for a while.

The very mention of any possible "long-range political plans" in Go-Toba's growing involvement in the poetry scene itself raises questions. There is great temptation to read history backward, to explain earlier events on the basis of their later effects rather than their preceding causes. This has been especially insidious in the study of medieval Japanese history, which was traditionally read backward from the Tokugawa period.[14] We need to

---

12. Kanezane also "appeared" the following year as a participant in the *Sanbyakurokujūban uta-awase* (Poetry Contest in 360 Rounds) of 1201/iii/20, also sponsored by Yoshitsune, although this seems to have been a *senka-awase* and he may not actually have showed up in any public forum. The contest is discussed in more detail below.

13. This sequence of events is described in Ariyoshi, *Shinkokin wakashū no kenkyū: kiban to kōsei*, pp. 62–63, apparently reconstructed from *Meigetsuki*. The two contests I discuss are described in *Meigetsuki*, Shōji 2 (1200)/ii/25 and *ii/1, 1: 144 and 145, respectively. In fact, this section of the diary describes a number of poetry events at Yoshitsune's. And although the letter itself is not recorded, Teika discussed it (this is where he used the phrase "charlatan poet like Suetsune") and related Suetsune's reaction and Yoshitsune's subsequent punishment in the entries for Shōji 2/iv/6 and 9, 1: 157–58.

Surely one of the most frustrating things about diaries like this is their selective lack of detail. We may learn what everyone wore and where everyone sat at a banquet, but we will never know exactly what Suetsune said to persuade Go-Toba to turn once again against Yoshitsune. All Teika said (iv/9) is: "Chikamasa's and Suetsune's slanderous charges [*zangen*, a word one finds time and again in medieval diaries in connection with palace politics] were given credence."

14. Jeffrey Mass, in several of his books, makes this point tellingly with regard to the establishment of the Kamakura Bakufu; see, e.g., *The Kamakura Bakufu*, pp. 7–8. He notes it is

be careful when examining Go-Toba's actions that we do not assume too much about his activities in the early 1200s, when he was barely twenty, based on his later involvement in the Jōkyū War of 1221 and the frankly restorationist vision it represented. In other words, it is probably a mistake to view all his activities from the time of his abdication as pointing inexorably toward a restoration movement as such. Clearly the idea developed over time, but I do not believe the evidence is there to say he had any long-range plans in 1200.

Indeed, Go-Toba's first major poetic event did not start off as the initial step in a grand scheme to unify the court and restore traditional imperial prerogatives. On the contrary, he seemed almost to be following Shukaku Hosshinnō's lead, because the event, which came to be known as *Shōji ninen in shodo hyakushu* (The Retired Emperor's First Set of 100-Poem Sequences, from the Second Year of the Shōji Era; often called by the shorter title *Shodo hyakushu*), was originally conceived and proposed to Go-Toba by the conservative Michichika of the Tsuchimikado house and Suetsune and Tsuneie of the Rokujō school.

Their idea was to commission sets of 100-poem sequences from older— "establishment," if you will—poets, which by definition (and presumably design) would have excluded young innovators like Teika and Ietaka. Ariyoshi gives the original list as Shunzei, Jakuren, Takanobu, and Jien (representing the Mikohidari/Kujō axis), and Suetsune, Tsuneie, Sanefusa, and Shōren (lay name Minamoto Moromitsu; 1130?–1203?), who represented the Rokujō/Tsuchimikado axis.[15] It would be impossible to improve on the ac-

---

not just a matter of how Western historians have viewed Japan. For example, the *Azuma kagami* accounts, which for centuries were accepted as definitive, themselves do the same thing, projecting into earlier times institutions that did not, in fact, come into existence until later. (The *shugō* office as an agent of the Kamakura Bakufu is one of his examples.)

15. Ariyoshi, *Shinkokin wakashū no kenkyū: kiban to kōsei*, p. 74. This list seems to be a deduction on Ariyoshi's part. He cites no written document (such as the initial formal order from Go-Toba) but apparently has reconstructed this from evidence in *Meigetsuki*, remarks in Shunzei's *Shōji sōjō*, extant texts of the final products of the commission, and other unidentified sources. The only flaw I can find in his reasoning involves one of his arguments for the eventual breakdown of the project. He asserts that the term "old" (*rō* or *oitaru*, which appears in the vii/18 *Meigetsuki* entry, and in Shunzei's *Shōji sōjō* as a delimiting factor for the initial 100-poem sequence commission) is, by definition, forty or older. He cites as evidence the 1201 *Rōnyaku gojisshu uta-awase* (Fifty-Poem Contest Between Old and Young, which I discuss below), in which he claims forty is the dividing line between the two teams (Ariyoshi, *Shinkokin wakashū no kenkyū: kiban to kōsei*, p. 70). But Tadayoshi, a member of the "Old" team in that

count Ariyoshi gives of the sequence of events surrounding this commission, and I will simply summarize them here.[16]

Teika's *Meigetsuki* provides the bulk of the evidence regarding the event's genesis, the earliest indication being the entry for Shōji 2 (1200)/vii/15, in which Teika says he was told by his friend Fujiwara Kintsune (1171–1244) that Go-Toba had commissioned 100-poem sequences from some poets, but that Teika had not been selected as one of them. Kintsune agreed to argue Teika's case to Go-Toba.[17] Three days later, Teika related what he had subsequently heard from Kintsune:

Shōji 2/vii/18.... At first His Majesty seemed inclined to accept the notion [of my participation], but because of Michichika's demands, it has all of a sudden turned around. Kintsune says it [the sequence commission] is now to be limited just to older poets, those who have mastered old and new styles. I've never heard of limiting such things only to older poets. That biased Suetsune must be behind it all. It's just a scheme to keep me from participating. Suetsune, Tsuneie, and the others are all from that house [i.e., the Rokujō group].[18]

Teika felt that the Rokujō faction, hiding behind an "age limit," was in fact attempting to deny more innovative poets a voice. Since this was the first major poetic event sponsored by the newly retired emperor, such a precedent worried him. At this stage Shunzei decided to intervene.[19] As we have seen from his role in Shukaku Hosshinnō's *Omuro senka-awase*, Shunzei had catholic tastes in poetry and could be conciliatory in public poetry activities when asked to perform the role of judge. This was his reputation at least from the time of *Senzaishū*. But he was also probably the most accomplished critic in the history of Japanese poetry. He recognized the genius of

---

contest, was only 38 by the Japanese count (37 by the Western), one year *younger* than Teika at the time of the *Shōji ninen in shodo hyakushu*. Then, as now, I think "old" was not so much a measurable age as a mind set, and the issue for Suetsune was one's sympathies with the styles of the past, not how many years one had lived on this planet.

16. Ariyoshi, *Shinkokin wakashū no kenkyū: kiban to kōsei*, pp. 52–78. Kubota Jun (*Shinkokin kajin no kenkyū*, pp. 793–94), too, except for a quibble over the true identity of one of the participants—the otherwise unknown Nobuhiro (see note 25 to this chapter, p. 58)—accepts Ariyoshi's account as definitive and moves on from there to concentrate on individual poets.

17. At this point in time, Teika had been banned from the palace and could not make the plea himself. That ban is a story in itself and is taken up below.

18. *Meigetsuki*, 1: 161.

19. Based on relevant *Meigetsuki* entries, Ariyoshi (*Shinkokin wakashū no kenkyū: kiban to kōsei*, p. 54) says Shunzei's letter must have been presented between vii/26 and viii/8.

his second son.[20] Add to that an obvious paternal affection (we will see more examples of this throughout this study), and Shunzei felt compelled, even at the age of 87, to write a direct appeal to Go-Toba on behalf of his son. The result is a surprisingly blunt, forceful document now most commonly known as the *Shōji sōjō*. It is a fascinating look into the world of waka and the workings of Shunzei's mind (see Appendix C, pp. 405-12, of this study for a complete translation).

The letter first cites illustrious examples of 100-poem sequences from the past (such as the *Horikawa hyakushu*) that included poets in their thirties, thus ridiculing the notion that an age limit was appropriate in such an event. Shunzei then went after two of his rivals, Fujiwara Norinaga (1109-1178?) and Rokujō Kiyosuke, who, as Shunzei's contemporaries in earlier years, had borne the brunt of his disdain. He cited their lack of learning and ineptitude at properly classifying waka and especially lamented their unfamiliarity with *Genji monogatari* ("Norinaga mo Kiyosuke mo *Genji* wo misorawazu")[21] and their ignorance of the works of Bo Juyi.[22] The letter includes an attack on Rokujō Akisuke's (1090-1155) *Shikashū* and Kiyosuke's private collection, *Shokushikashū*. Shunzei was thus suggesting that Go-Toba ought not to be taking advice on poetic matters from their heir, Suetsune, whom Shunzei also criticized directly. Shunzei then recommended that Go-Toba add Teika, Ietaka, and Fujiwara Takafusa (1148-1209) to the list[23] and ended the letter with a poem, whose full significance will become clear below:

---

20. Teika was not Shunzei's first son. That was Nariie (1155-1220), who had the same mother as Teika but not the same talent. Nariie had an utterly undistinguished poetic career, and it is clear that in terms of the family vocation of poetry, Shunzei treated Teika as his true heir. In fact, a century later, Kyōgoku Tamekane, himself not descended from the first son, used the Nariie/Teika example as precedent for arguing that talent, not birth order, should dictate family headship in the Mikohidari house; see Huey, *Kyōgoku Tamekane*, p. 166.

21. Hisamatsu, ed., *Karonshū I*, p. 273. One is reminded of Shunzei's remark, cited in Chapter 1, p. 20, in one of his judgments for the *Roppyakuban uta-awase*.

22. Bo Juyi's works, in more or less complete form, had been known in Japan since the time of Emperor Ninmyō (r. 833-50), and were referred to as the *Hakushi monjū*. Shunzei simply calls it *Monjū* here: "Mashite, Monjū to mōsu bun mo misorawade" (Hisamatsu, ed., *Karonshū I*, pp. 273-74).

23. Fujiwara Ietaka, who had a marriage connection to Shunzei through Jakuren, was very close to the Mikohidari group and became one of its top poets. Go-Toba admired him greatly. Fujiwara Takafusa was of a branch line of the Rokujō family (his great-great-grandfather had been Akisue [1055-1123], the progenitor of the Rokujō line) but did not seem to be a strict partisan of the Rokujō style of poetry.

Waka no ura no	The crane which cries
asibe wo sasite	As it heads toward the reeds
naku tadu mo	By Poetry Bay—
nado ka kumowi ni	Why can it not return
kaferazarubeki.	To that place beyond the clouds?[24]

From entries for the 9th and 10th of the Eighth Month in *Meigetsuki*, it is evident that Shunzei's letter had the desired effect, and over Michichika's repeated objections, Go-Toba expanded his commission to include all three of the poets Shunzei had recommended. At this point Go-Toba may also have added Fujiwara Tadayoshi (1164-1225), a Rokujō poet, to the list, although it is possible Tadayoshi had been part of the original group. In any case, Go-Toba carefully maintained a balance of schools in these first two invitations.

Go-Toba apparently expanded the commission yet again on viii/15, this time adding several court ladies, as Shunzei had suggested, as well as himself, his older brother Koreakira Shinnō (1179-1221), Michichika, and several others, again being careful to preserve the balance. The final group is listed as twenty-three (one name, Nobuhiro, appears to be spurious, and there are several theories as to his true identity):[25] Go-Toba, Koreakira Shinnō, Shikishi Naishinnō, Shukaku Hosshinnō, Yoshitsune, Michichika, Jien, Tadayoshi, Takafusa, Suetsune, Tsuneie, Shunzei, Takanobu, Teika, Ietaka, Fujiwara Norimitsu (1154-1215), Jakuren, Moromitsu (under his priestly name Shōren), Sanefusa, Sanuki (1141?-1217?), Kojijū (fl. 1161-1203), Tango (1113?-1208?; also known as Gishūmon-in no Tango, and not to be confused with Tangō no Tsubone, Go-Shirakawa's favorite), and Nobuhiro. The alle-

---

24. Shunzei is alluding to the following poem by Yamabe Akahito (fl. 724-34; *MYS* 924; *NKBT* 919, and *KWR* 4353): *Waka no ura ni / sifo mitikureba / kata wo nami / asibe wo sasite / tadu nakiwataru*—"At Waka Bay / As the tide comes flooding in / Till tide pools disappear, / Heading toward the reeds, / Cranes fly crying overhead." Another allusion to this poem (and issues pertaining to its use as a *honka*) is discussed in Chapter 9, pp. 357-58.

25. Leaving aside the particulars here, Ariyoshi, *Shinkokin wakashū no kenkyū: kiban to kōsei*, pp. 76-78, argues that the sequence attributed to Nobuhiro (whoever he was—and Ariyoshi does not address that question) was probably added much later (Muromachi period or after) to one of the textual lines. Kubota Jun (*Shinkokin kajin no kenkyū*, pp. 793-94) believes it is a pseudonym, probably for Jien or possibly Yoshitsune.

There is a Nobuhiro mentioned a year later in *Meigetsuki*, Kennin 1 (1201)/xii/2, 1: 227, in attendance at a poetry contest, but he is an officer in the Saemon guards and the Nobuhiro listed as a participant in this 100-poem sequence is called a Middle Counselor. Besides, the *Meigetsuki* Nobuhiro is not participating in the contest but simply standing in attendance.

giances of these various poets can be summarized as follows (omitting Nobuhiro, and assuming Go-Toba was neutral, although from his poetry one surmises his heart was with the Mikohidari school in literary matters at least):

Rokujō/Tsuchimikado: Koreakira Shinnō, Shukaku Hosshinnō, Michichika, Tadayoshi, Takafusa, Suetsune, Tsuneie, Norimitsu, Moromitsu (Shōren), Sanefusa, and Kojijū

Mikohidari/Kujō: Shikishi Naishinnō, Yoshitsune, Jien, Shunzei, Takanobu, Teika, Ietaka, Jakuren, Sanuki, and Tango

What had started out as a modest activity at the behest of Suetsune had turned into a large, public event. Although the various political and poetic factions pressured him at different times, as Go-Toba expanded the scope of his commission, he preserved a balance among contending groups at each step of the way. Yet as we shall see, the winners turned out to be the Kujō house and the Mikohidari school.

In the midst of all this, the human cycle of birth and death rolled on, with little noticeable effect on the debates over who would be asked to submit poems. Perhaps the most dramatic turn was the death, on viii/4, of Michichika's wife, Noriko, mother of Go-Toba's consort Shōmeimon-in (Zaishi) and thus grandmother of Emperor Tsuchimikado. The official mourning included suspension of court duties (*haichō*, generally called only for the death of an imperial parent or a solar eclipse). Yet less than a week later, Michichika is depicted as strenuously opposing Shunzei's proposal to add three names to the 100-poem sequence commission.[26]

Similarly, Yoshitsune's main wife had died in childbirth on vii/13. Yet within a month Yoshitsune would be asked to participate in this large-scale public poetry event. Kubota notes that there is barely a hint of sorrow over his wife's death in the poems he submitted, seventeen of which (second only to Shikishi Naishinnō's twenty-five) ended up in *Shinkokinshū*. Kubota sees him as thus rising to the importance of the public occasion, which certainly challenges the notion that great waka necessarily had to be a spontaneous and occasional lyrical expression.[27] If we accept the argument that Kane-

---

26. *Meigetsuki*, Shōji 2/viii/10, 1: 164. It is uncertain whether Michichika was actually there since Teika says Michitomo spoke on his behalf, but present or not, his mind was clearly on this matter.

27. Kubota Jun, *Shinkokin kajin no kenkyū: kihan to kōsei*, pp. 812–22. In this entire section, pp. 793–834, Kubota examines the circumstances and poems of most of the major contribu-

zane's Tenth Month *Gyokuyō* entry, cited above, does in fact mark Yoshitsune's return to public life, it does not seem too much of a stretch to think that his success in this commission had something to do with it.

On the other end of the spectrum, Ienaga describes Go-Toba sponsoring a poetry party even as prayers are being said for his wife's labor (the child was born on ix/11).[28] Prayers and services for her safe delivery had been commenced on viii/16.[29] As a result, Ienaga wrote, Go-Toba was not partying as much as he had been (*nan no miasobi mo nashi*—this is in stark contrast to the previous entries, which are filled with descriptions of banquets, outings, and such). But, he continued, there *were* poetry events from time to time (*saredo uta no koto wa tokidoki haberi*).

One is reminded by this just how important poetry was, not just the literary product but also the *act* of making it and the social and political ramifications of creating an opportunity for it to occur. Birth and death might be celebrated, mourned, and/or prayed over, but poetic activity (and I am referring not to micro-activity such as private poems of mourning or consolation, which would have been an assumed part of major turns in the life cycle, but to macro-activities such as contests and public sequences) continued through it all.

Returning to the event itself, for Teika, getting the commission meant he faced the sort of situation described by the old saw "Be careful what you wish for; you may get it." Success in this endeavor was extremely important to him as a poet and as a courtier; so important, in fact, that he went to Kitano Shrine to pray.[30] Many years earlier, in 1185, he had been banned from the palace after an argument with another courtier, one Minamoto Masayuki,

---

tors to the sequence in great detail, linking their work to events in their lives or finding allusions to earlier poetry and prose (both Chinese and Japanese). It is Kubota at his best.

28. *IN*, pp. 40–41.

29. Ishida and Satsukawa only mention prayer services on viii/19, but Go-Toba had also commissioned dances at Iwashimizu on the viii/16 for the same purpose; see *Rekishi sōran*, 4: 165.

30. *Meigetsuki*, Shōji 2 (1200)/viii/13, 1: 165. Teika indicated that he went to Kitano Shrine on this day to offer thanks that his previous petition had been fulfilled. Unfortunately, I can find no reference to that previous visit in any entry between vii/15, when Teika first mentioned the 100-poem sequence commission, and this date. He made numerous references to temple visits but did not identify them as being specifically related to the poetry commission as this one is. I discuss the relationship between poetry and the Shinto *kami* further in Chapter 8, esp. pp. 301–4.

during which Teika grabbed a torch and hit Masayuki with it. After a letter and poem of apology by Shunzei a year later, Teika was pardoned by then-Emperor Go-Toba and allowed to return to the palace. Obviously Shunzei was making reference to this earlier exchange at the end of his *Shōji sōjō* as cited above.

Shunzei's poem a year after the original offense:

Asitadu no	The year drew to a close
kumodi mayofisi	With the reed-dwelling crane
tosi kurete	Still wandering on cloud paths.
kasumi wo safe ya	Now will spring mists, too,
fedate fatubeki	Be allowed to block its way?

Fujiwara Sadanaga (1149–1195) was asked to reply on behalf of the Palace:

Asitadu fa	The reed-dwelling crane
kasumi wo wakete	Parts spring mists
kaferu nari	And now returns,
mayofisi kumowi	The clouds through which it wandered
kefu ya faruran	From today are cleared.

Shunzei wondered how much longer the crane, Teika, must be left outside the Palace. *Kumowi*—literally the "cloud dwelling," that is, the Palace—is suggested by *kumodi*, "path through the clouds," which generally refers to a bird in flight. In this case, the notion is that a bird in flight would be able to ascend into the cloud-dwelling, as Teika should be allowed to ascend to the Palace. The ban went into effect the year before, and now with spring, must he still stay away? On behalf of the Emperor, Sadanaga replied that both the way and Teika's reputation (the verb *faru*, "to clear," can also be used in the sense of "clearing one's name") were now clear, and Teika was allowed to return to the Palace.[31]

---

31. For the torch incident and Ienaga's account of it, see *IN*, pp. 43–50, which forms the basis for my discussion above. Kanezane's version appears in *Gyokuyō*, Bunji 1/xi/25, 3: 118. Shunzei's poem appealing for clemency and the reply from Fujiwara Sadanaga on behalf of the Palace are also found, with explanatory headnotes, in *Senzaishū* (XVII, Miscellaneous 2), 1158 and 1159. The initial cause of the argument is not known. Unfortunately, the extant *Meigetsuki* does not cover this period at all.

Ishida and Satsukawa also reproduce the letter of appeal accompanying Shunzei's poem (*IN*, p. 50) in which Shunzei essentially argued "youthful indiscretion" on Teika's part and suggested that the year-long ban had been sufficient. One wonders how often Shunzei must have had to do things like this, since Teika seems to have been prickly, to say the least. In an

However, when Tsuchimikado became emperor, the permission was withdrawn, presumably because of Teika's close ties with the Kujō house. Go-Toba's invitation to participate in the 100-poem sequence suggested that once again Teika could return to favor.

So it is not surprising that Teika labored hard and painfully at this commission, as various entries in *Meigetsuki* show. On viii/15, he wrote, "I am really struggling with the poems. I did not go out today." On viii/23, the day before the poems were to be submitted, he visited Shunzei for help. Shunzei assured him the poems he had written so far were fine. Shunzei himself had finished the 100-poem sequence, but Teika had only done twenty poems. During this time he was also kept busy critiquing the poems of others, such as those of Yoshitsune and Sanuki (viii/24).[32]

Teika did manage to complete his poems on time, though the formal presentation was actually a day later than planned. Quite a few poets, according to Ariyoshi's reading of events, did not finish in time.[33] In any case, Teika's efforts paid off, much as Yoshitsune's seem to have. Among the poems in the *jukkai* (Personal Grievances) section was an appeal for clemency to Go-Toba. Making reference to the poem Shunzei had sent more than fifteen years before on Teika's behalf, Teika wrote:

Kimi ga yo ni	This reed-dwelling crane
kasumi wo wakesi	Who during His Majesty's reign
asitadu no	Once parted the mists—
sara ni safabe ni	Must it still remain by the marsh,
ne wo ya nakubeki	Calling plaintively?

---

essay entitled "Fujiwara Teika no ijōsei" (literally, "Fujiwara Teika's abnormality," first published in 1959), Ishida Yoshisada attempts to explore Teika's psychology and notes the possibility that he may have been epileptic. There is more than a touch of "Freudian psychology meets traditional Japanese scholarship" in the piece—which should serve to remind us how trendy literary theory can be—but it does raise important issues, and psychological and physiological factors undoubtedly accounted for the extremity of some of Teika's behavior. The article is reproduced in Ishida, *Shinkokin sekai to chūsei bungaku*, 1: 54–70.

32. These *Meigetsuki* entries are presented and glossed in Ariyoshi, *Shinkokin wakashū no kenkyū: kiban to kōsei*, pp. 55–56, and I have followed Ariyoshi's interpretation.

33. Ibid., pp. 56–58. Support for Ariyoshi's view may be found in *Ienaga nikki*. In an entry that is generally assumed to refer to the year 1200, Ienaga says that Go-Toba is impatient at the slow response to his commission on the part of some of the poets. But the remarks are not wholly reliable since Ienaga says the commission was made in the spring, an indication that he may be confusing it with the third round of 100-poem sequences requested the following year; see *IN*, pp. 36–39.

Go-Toba, deeply moved, promptly permitted Teika to return to the Palace. Ienaga noted, "Truly, those who devote themselves to the way of poetry cannot but gain His Majesty's favor."[34]

For his part, Teika was beside himself with joy, recognizing how important this was to him as a court poet.[35] I am inclined to agree with Ariyoshi that his success in this event moved him toward the center of Go-Toba's *kadan*.[36] Kubota takes a somewhat different view and notes the wide variety of styles represented in Teika's sequence. He says that "it is from this point that Teika's multifaceted genius becomes more and more evident" and offers two main reasons for Teika's success in this endeavor: one, the reviving fortunes of the Kujō house, and two, that by nature a 100-poem sequence is a less stressful event than, say, a contest, especially one like the *Roppyakuban uta-awase* where the topics were explicit. These conditions, Kubota argues, allowed Teika to compose more freely.[37] The problem with Kubota's first reason is that if anything this is the very poetic event that helped revive the fortunes of the Kujō house (as Kubota himself notes in his discussion of Yoshitsune cited above). There is something of a chicken-and-egg relationship here that makes Kubota's rationale hard to justify. As for his second argument, the *Meigetsuki* entries cited above hardly portray a relaxed Teika, calmly composing his 100 poems. Although Kubota's assessment of Teika's genius in these poems is on the mark, his evaluation of the overall context is less astute.

Not all the poets invited to participate were as conscientious as Teika in meeting the deadline. One might argue that probably they did not have as much at stake as Teika did, but one of the stragglers was Yoshitsune, who clearly did have. Throughout the Ninth Month, several references in *Meigetsuki* indicate that both Yoshitsune and Tango, who was in the service of the Kujō family, had not yet completed their commission, since they repeatedly asked Teika and/or Shunzei for advice.[38] There is some question as to when Yoshitsune actually submitted his sequence, and some of the poets

---

34. The incident is noted in *IN*, pp. 43–44, with lengthy notations, commentary, and supporting documentation from Ishida and Satsukawa, on pp. 44–50.
35. *Meigetsuki*, Shōji 2/viii/26, 1: 167.
36. Ariyoshi, *Shinkokin wakashū no kenkyū: kiban to kōsei*, p. 57.
37. Kubota Jun, *Shinkokin kajin no kenkyū*, pp. 800–801.
38. Again, Ariyoshi, *Shinkokin wakashū no kenkyū: kiban to kōsei*, provides all the references from *Meigetsuki*, pp. 57–58. The entries in question are Shōji 2 (1200)/ix/5, 9, 10, 11, and 21; see *Meigetsuki*, 1: 169–73, for the full entries.

may never have finished.[39] But the details of who completed the sequence on time is tangential to this study.[40]

The *Shōji ninen in shodo hyakushu* was significant on several levels. First, it marked the public rehabilitation of Jien, Yoshitsune, and Teika and pushed them more openly toward the center of the waka world. Second, its initiation by the conservative Rokujō school and its political backer Michichika and the original plan to include only a few older poets demonstrate that, in the beginning at least, Go-Toba apparently had no grand political scheme in mind. However, the Retired Emperor's quick response to Shunzei's appeal and his subsequent widening of participation suggest that he immediately saw the potential of such an event, if for nothing other than a future imperial anthology. (And of course it did, in fact, become an important source of poetry for *Shinkokinshū*.) Further, his standing up so directly to Michichika surely marks his move toward what would become a fiercely independent stance in poetry and politics.

Thus the "winners," as I noted above, were members of the Mikohidari/Kujō group. Not only were several members of this group restored to the public limelight, but their poems fared much better in *Shinkokinshū* several years later. Of the seventy-nine poems from this event in *Shinkokinshū*, sixty-seven were by Mikohidari partisans.[41] It might be argued that since the *Shinkokinshū* selection committee was weighted toward the Mikohidari school, the fact that Mikohidari poets in this contest fared so well is to be expected and not worth pointing out. The counterargument would be that the process that led to their eventual dominance in the *Shinkokinshū* selection began

---

39. Curiously, with regard to when Yoshitsune submitted his poems, Kubota (*Shinkokin kajin no kenkyū*, p. 813) says, "According to *Meigetsuki*, it seems he [Yoshitsune] completed his composition by the 5th day of the Ninth Month." However, this contradicts the above-noted entries from Teika's diary (see previous note). Kubota gives no indication why he thinks the later entries in the Ninth Month do not contradict this. Ariyoshi (*Shinkokin wakashū no kenkyū: kiban to kōsei*, p. 58) cites the *Meigetsuki* entry for ix/27 as proof that Yoshitsune submitted his poems on *that* day.

40. Ariyoshi's final conclusions as to who was commissioned when, and who submitted their poems when, appear in a chart on p. 75 of his *Shinkokin wakashū no kenkyū: kiban to kōsei*. Several poets apparently never finished at all, as far as we know.

41. For a breakdown, see Ariyoshi, *Shinkokin wakashū no kenkyū: kiban to kōsei*, p. 80. Shikishi Naishinnō ended up the runaway winner in the *Shinkokinshū* sweepstakes with twenty-five poems, although presumably this is partly because this was the last big event she participated in before she died, which meant if the *Shinkokinshū* selection committee wanted to honor her work, her poems here would have provided the most recent examples.

with their success here, which is precisely why they commemorated this event by including so many of its works.

Apparently Go-Toba was beginning to realize poetic activities could be a powerful tool in organizing a community. He next proceeded to solicit 100-poem sequences from a group that included several decidedly minor poets.[42] The participants included Go-Toba, Jien, Norimitsu, Masatsune, Minamoto Tomochika (fl. 1200–1262), Fujiwara Nobuzane (1177–1265; known as Takazane at the time of this event), Ienaga, Chōmei, Kamo no Sueyasu (fl. 1200–1237), Kunaikyō (1185?–1205?), and Echizen (?–1248?). People like Nobuzane/Takazene and Sueyasu, who at best could only have expected to appear as lesser lights in a large-scale *tōza* (impromptu) poetry contest, were now being asked by the Retired Emperor to submit 100 poems for the public record. This event, generally known as the *Shōji ninen in dainido hyakushu* (The Retired Emperor's Second Set of 100-Poem Sequences, from the Second Year of the Shōji Era) is usually dismissed by scholars as minor, since only nine of its poems ended up in *Shinkokinshū*.[43] However, I think there was more involved here than just throwing a bone to some mediocre poets. Teika's struggle to be included in the first round demonstrates that participation was seen as an honor, and Go-Toba's extension of an invitation to lesser poetic lights has to be understood as part of a political effort to solidify support.

In this event, too, Go-Toba strove for balance, only this time of a different sort. Along with Go-Toba, of the contributors to the first event, only Jien (representing the Kujō line), and Norimitsu (a Rokujō partisan) participated in the second. Perhaps these two were invited to create a sense of continuity and an aura of seniority, Jien being forty-five and Norimitsu forty-seven. Among the other participants, Kunaikyō and Tomochika were brother and sister (Tomochika was the older, but their dates are uncertain), offspring of Moromitsu, a Rokujō partisan. But Kunaikyō, especially, was independent in her poetic approach, as was the other court lady represented, Echizen. Nobuzane was Rokujō in terms of training but was at this stage a virtual unknown. Ienaga had no particular poetic affiliations and, like Kunai-

---

42. There is no extant documentary evidence with which to chart the course of this commission, but indications are that the call for poems was made between the Tenth and the Twelfth Months of Shōji 2 (1200); see *WBJ*, p. 321.

43. *SKKS* 680 (VI, Winter), by Jien, may possibly have been from the sequence he submitted on this occasion, which would make the total in *Shinkokinshū* ten. For the *Shinkokinshū* numbers for the selected poems, see Ariyoshi, *Shinkokin wakashū no kenkyū: kiban to kōsei*, p. 538.

kyō, owed his political career to Go-Toba himself. Both Sueyasu and Chōmei (of *Hōjōki* fame) came from Shintō families, again with no strong poetic or political allegiances. And Masatsune, as discussed in the preceding chapter, came from (or, more precisely, founded) the Asukai branch of the Fujiwara family, which specialized in *kemari* and *waka*. So Go-Toba maintained "balance" in this case not through equal representation from the dominant groups but by gathering a diverse range of poets. And in the context of the *Shodo hyakushu*, it is clear that Go-Toba was trying to enlist a wider range of poetic styles, perhaps to send the message that *waka* need not be thought of as either a Rokujō or a Mikohidari preserve.

So modest in rank were many of these *Dainido hyakushu* participants in the rarified world of the court that we do not know their exact dates in many cases. But to the extent we can surmise, Tomochika, Nobuzane, Ienaga, Sueyasu, and Kunaikyō were in their teens or twenties, Masatsune was thirty, and Chōmei forty-five. Echizen is virtually unknown except for her appearance in poetry events of this period, but since she seems to have begun her career in Go-Toba's service, she was probably in her twenties too.[44] In other words, it was an overwhelmingly youthful group, in every way the opposite of what Suetsune had had in mind at the time of the *Shodo hyakushu*.

However unknown many of these people may have been at the time of their invitation to the *Dainido hyakushu*, this event proved to be a coming out for them in the world of *waka*. Tomochika, Ienaga, Chōmei, and Masatsune would all end up serving in the Wakadokoro (about which more below), and Masatsune was added to the *Shinkokinshū* selection committee as well. Kunaikyō and Echizen became regulars at poetry events throughout this period. The others either faded away or had middling careers in a later, less stellar age. So another of Go-Toba's purposes here was to find and foster new talent, something I discussed above in relation to his recall of Masatsune from Kamakura.

But again, was this part of a master plan to restore the court to its former glory? Or did Go-Toba just want to add a little zest to his retirement? After all, he was still just twenty. Ienaga's memoirs shed some light on this question. One section, dated Kennin 1 (1201), is worth quoting at length:[45]

---

44. *IN*, p. 67.
45. Dates in *Ienaga nikki* are tentative, and as is clear in this cited section, Ienaga's narrative roams a bit in time. For example, according to Teika, Shunzei no Musume did not enter

Shōji 2

His Majesty would often lament that there were not many women poets around these days. There were a few court ladies who could be called poets left from earlier times. Infukumon-in no Daisuke had died the year before. And Sanuki, Mikawa no Naishi, and Tango no Shōshō had all grown quite old, turned their attention to the next world, and withdrawn to live in retreat here and there. They had all given up poetry, and when summoned occasionally by the Palace to compose would, I hear, complain among themselves that such things were a hindrance to the *nenbutsu*. But apart from these women I had heard of no others.

Still, since poetry is something a person with feelings cannot really avoid, I thought there must be someone suitable. But how would such a person ever come to our attention? A high-born lady would be too modest to put herself forward like that. On the other hand, there might be many of lower rank who would be too intimidated to stand out. How could we learn about them? Thus, from time to time, I would hear His Majesty say with regret that once these elderly ladies passed away the day of the woman poet would be past.

About the time this whole thing had become a little tiresome to listen to, one day I had occasion to be with a woman whom I had grown close to. I picked up what appeared to be some writings and took a peek. On the paper were some poems written in a woman's hand. When I asked about it, she said it was from a lady named Echizen, who was in the service of Shichijō no In.[46]

I took the poems to His Majesty, who must have found them to his liking, for he gave orders to find out where the lady lived. So I left the palace to inquire after her, and discovered she was the daughter of Ōnakatomi Kinchika.[47] Having learned that she thus came from a long and distinguished [poetic] lineage, I passed the information on to His Majesty. He sent Lord Norimitsu to fetch her in a carriage, and it seems she was soon in Go-Toba's service.

Toward the end of the poems I had seen before there was one which read:

Sazona ge ni	Ah, it's true
kore mo yosinaki	These poems are simply
susami kana	Pointless diversion,
tare ka afare wo	For who will see their poignance
kakete sinoban	And fall in love with me?

Go-Toba's service until Kennin 2 (1202)/vii/13 (*Meigetsuki*, 1: 271). For the passage cited here, including extensive notes by Ishida and Satsukawa, see *IN*, pp. 63–72.

46. Shichijō no In, or simply Shichijō-In (1157–1228), born Fujiwara Shokushi, was Go-Toba's birth mother.

47. Kinchika was a descendant of Ōnakatomi Yorimoto (886–958), one of the original Thirty-Six Poetic Sages and highly respected poet of the tenth century. Kinchika himself does not appear to have excelled at verse, however.

This is the one that had particularly caught His Majesty's eye. He ordered all of us to compose poems using the central theme of this one as our topic, so those of us in his service set about writing our verses. Since none of them was significant enough to single out, I did not record any of them. Thinking he would like to test her poetic mettle, His Majesty had summoned her to the palace. This was toward the end of autumn.[48] And it was at this time that, when ordered by Go-Toba to compose a poem that suits this season, she replied with "cleaving storm winds / the belling of a stag."[49]

Kunaikyō, too, came into service soon after this. She was the daughter of Moromitsu. From a long line of poets, she was said to be especially talented. And following that, Shunzei no Musume offered her poetry skills to His Majesty. Although she seems to have spent her budding years shaded from society, soon His Majesty evidently found her competitiveness when she was asked to compose poems a bit unsettling.[50] Nevertheless, since hers was a talent that could not be overlooked, Go-Toba naturally felt it would be a pity to let her waste away somewhere.

Also, in the service of Hachijō-in[51] was a lady named Takakura-dono.[52] Someone brought to Go-Toba's attention the following poem by her:

Kumorekasi	Please, cloud over, moon!
nagamuru karani	Oh, the sadness that I feel
kanasiki fa	Just from gazing at you
tuki ni oboyuru	And there, the face
fito no omokage	Of the one I love ...[53]

Once Go-Toba had heard this poem, she, too, was regularly invited to submit her work.

There was also the lady known as Dainagon-dono,[54] in the service of Shichijō no

---

48. This is a kind of flashback, since before he quotes the poem, Ienaga has already said that Go-Toba had brought Echizen into his service.

49. The rest of this poem is no longer extant (or at least it is not listed in any of the volumes of *Shinpen kokka taikan*), although Ienaga's implication here is that it is a verse for which Echizen became widely known.

50. There are several textual problems in this sentence, and I have more or less followed Ishida and Satsukawa's suggestions (*IN*, p. 70).

51. Hachijō-in (1137–1211) was the third daughter of Emperor Toba and had been a nun for several decades.

52. Generally known as Hachijō-in no Takakura (dates uncertain, 1177?–1237?), she has seven poems in *Shinkokinshū*.

53. *SKKS* XIV (Love 4), 1270.

54. Shichijō no In no Dainagon (dates uncertain) has three poems in *Shinkokinshū*. Ienaga proceeds to relate just about all we know about her.

In. She was the daughter of Middle Councilor Sanetsuna.[55] Being a high-born lady, she probably felt reluctant to put herself forward, but assured that someone from such a poetic lineage need not feel uncomfortable, she heeded His Majesty's summons and appeared at poetry events from time to time.[56] Her mother was Mikawa no Naishi.[57] Yet despite the poetic pedigree on both sides of her family, somehow the promise was not fulfilled in her.

Thus did His Majesty gather around him young men and women poets in great numbers. Since by day they would attend to official business at their palace or bureau posts, it was by night that they would take part in the constant stream of poetry contests and parties that were held. They would find hidden corners of the palace here and there and busily plot their strategies.[58]

Several points of note emerge from this passage. First, politics aside, Go-Toba was hardly uninterested in the opposite sex. By this time he had already fathered four children that we know of, and it seems obvious that he wanted a change of scenery from the older women who had dominated his poetic world. It is equally obvious, however, that physical charms were not the issue so much as poetic skill. Ienaga's aside that Shichijō no In no Dainagon did not live up to her hereditary promise hints at Go-Toba's own disappointment. Yet skill without appropriate reserve is somewhat off-putting to him, as the remarks about Shunzei no Musume (1171–1252?) reveal.[59]

It is curious that no mention is made in this section of Shikishi Naishinnō, who died in early 1201, the purported date of this passage. She certainly had a significant impact on the poetic scene. However, all the other women discussed here were ladies-in-waiting, whose service to Go-Toba or emperors before him would not necessarily be limited to matters literary.

---

55. Fujiwara Sanetsuna (1128–80), who was represented in *Senzaishū*, hence Ienaga's subsequent remark about poetic lineage. I am following Ishida and Satsukawa's suggestion that there is a misprint in the memoirs, and this refers to *Sane*tsuna, not *Mune*tsuna.

56. The final phrase, "at poetry events from time to time," is my interpolation, but the original is so elliptical that it needed something to achieve coherence in English.

57. Nijō-in no Naishi Mikawa (dates uncertain, 1135?–1200?), daughter of Fujiwara Tamenari, wife of Sanetsuna, and active poet in the service of Emperor Nijō.

58. The point of this last sentence was that many of the contests and parties were *kendai*, that is, the topics for the event were posted in advance. Thus the ever-competitive young palace poets would plan and practice beforehand.

59. As far as poetic skills go, in his poetic treatise *Mumyōshō*, Kamo no Chōmei writes of Kunaikyō and Shunzei no Musume that "these two were talents who could face the greats of the past without embarrassment" (Hisamatsu and Nishio, eds., *Karonshū nōgakuronshū*, p. 78).

Shikishi Naishinnō, a princess by birth and half-sister (same father, different mother) of Go-Toba's own father, Emperor Takakura, would not fall into this category and perhaps was not seen, then, as being a "woman poet" (*onna no utayomi* is the phrase Ienaga used throughout this passage) but as forming a category of her own.

In fact, this period, like virtually any other in waka history, shows the ambivalence of the literary world in aristocratic Japan toward women poets, that is, poets whose gender is female, regardless of their rank (I leave to others the question of whether Shikishi Naishinnō transcended "woman" by virtue of her rank).[60] Are the women mentioned by Ienaga here more than just accessories for the palace? One might at first argue that they were, given that Ienaga and others take their *poetic* skills seriously and take pains to describe them.[61] Yet theirs is also clearly seen as a gentle, polite art, much like piano playing nowadays, one that would make these women "nice to have around." As we shall see in Chapter 5, the notion that women somehow compose a different kind of waka—not any less valuable *as waka* perhaps, but different—is well established by this time; Shunzei, for one, made reference to the idea in one of his judgments for the *Sengohyakuban uta-awase*.[62]

---

60. Several recent studies have attempted to tackle this area. Much of the work, such as Michele Marra's "The Buddhist Mythmaking of Defilement" and Joni Koehn's "Gender and Narrativity in Japanese Literature," revolves around theoretical issues such as mythologizing, image construction, and the like, and this is certainly an important view. But I also hope that more hard-core, practical information is brought forth as time goes on. Monographs like Edward Kamens's on Daisaiin Senshi, or Hiroaki Satō's on Shikishi Naishinnō, which give factual information about the circumstances in which these women lived their lives and composed their poetry, help us reconstruct their social position and their roles. Some excellent work has been done in Japan on this point, including Amino Yoshihiko's *Chūsei no hinin to yūjo*, especially Part 2, "Chūsei no josei to yūjo," pp. 181–259. Amino includes extensive notes and references for anyone who wishes to pursue the topic.

61. In *Mumyōshō*, for example, Chōmei describes in compelling detail the different approaches to formal composition taken by Shunzei no Musume (who withdraws from everyone, pores over old poetry collections, then puts them away, and starts writing) and Kunaikyō (who spreads an array of books before her to consult as she works). His tone is one of admiration, not condescension, although he does suggest (and quotes her own father on this) that Kunaikyō's excessive devotion to poetry is what ruined her health and caused her early demise; see Hisamatsu and Nishio, eds., *Karonshū nōgakuronshū*, pp. 76–77. As noted above, Shunzei argued in support of these young talents in his *Shōji sōjō*.

62. See Chapter 5, p. 201, the discussion for Round 218. Of course Tsurayuki had already suggested it, too, in his *kana* preface to *Kokinshū* where, in discussing the work of Ono no Komachi, he wrote: "[Her poetry] is moving, but lacks strength.... It is like a highborn lady who is vaguely unwell. Its lack of strength surely stems from its being woman's poetry" (*Aware*

No matter how much praise these women received from their male contemporaries and how often they were invited to take part as poets in important poetic events, not one of them was asked to judge a contest or serve in the Wakadokoro, let alone on the *Shinkokinshū* selection committee. It is not till the end of the Kamakura period, in the Kyōgoku group, that women begin to be taken seriously as critics and scholars of waka as well as creators of it, and even then public records of them pursuing such activities are scarce.[63]

Women were not the only beneficiaries of Go-Toba's efforts to foster poetic talent. The passage from Ienaga's memoirs makes it clear that Go-Toba brought new men into the palace, too. His goal, then, was not just to attract mates for himself but to create a more youthful, energetic salon. But, in his Confucian mode, Ienaga was careful to note that this was not a frivolous, pleasure-centered world. Everyone attended to affairs of state by day. Still, what Ienaga portrayed in this portion of his memoirs was a Go-Toba intent on patronizing all the arts, especially poetry. As he put it, in an entry a few pages earlier than the one cited above, "These days . . . I can't count the number of poets who have been invited to the palace to share in His Majesty's favor."[64] He goes on to describe two specific cases—men this time—Jakuren and Tomochika (Kunaikyō's brother):

> The Priest Jakuren, for example, had renounced this world and set himself up in a hut outside the capital. For some years he had been wearing the moss-colored robes of the clergy and dedicating all his efforts to the next life. But then His Majesty called him to court and, treating him like other courtiers, awarded him land rights at Akashi Bay, in Harima province. Soon he was active and flourishing in this world again!
>
> And then there was Tomochika, whose father, Moromitsu, had been Provisional Administrator of the Capital Right Sector before taking the tonsure. Tomochika was living a quiet, undistinguished life out near Ninna-ji Temple when Go-Toba summoned him to court service. At length he was made an officer of the palace

---

naru yō nite, tsuyokarazu . . . Yoki ōna nayameru tokoro aru ni nitari. Tsuyokaranu wa ōna no uta nareba narubeshi; Ozawa, ed., *Kokin wakashū*, p. 59).

63. I am thinking specifically of the active organizing role Eifukumon-in took in poetic activities and the status Kyōgoku Tameko seemed to have had as a teacher (helping her brother Tamekane tutor their imperial patrons) and critic. Although her editorial contribution to *Gyokuyōshū* is alluded to by Emperor Hanazono in his diary, it was behind the scenes. However, in *Fushimi-in nijūban uta-awase*, she was publicly acknowledged for her critical acumen—a rare instance indeed. For more information, see Huey, *Kyōgoku Tamekane*, pp. 22–23, 57; and idem, "Fushimi-in Nijūban Uta-awase," pp. 169–70, 181.

64. *IN*, p. 50.

guard, and it was not surprising to learn that his father, by then retired to religion, shed tears of joy.⁶⁵

Ienaga noted that Tomochika should not have fallen so low in the world, given his family background.⁶⁶ In other words, as he did with Yoshitsune, Go-Toba was helping to revive the fortunes of a family fallen on hard times. (Jakuren's case was a little different. Even after taking the tonsure, he had continued to be very active in poetry circles, participating in, among many other events, the *Roppyakuban uta-awase* and Shukaku Hosshinnō's fifty-poem sequences of the late 1190s. What Go-Toba did, then was bring him back into secular life, too, although Jakuren did not renounce his vows.) So we can identify a number of new faces in the palace, brought in by Go-Toba specifically for their poetic skills. The Retired Emperor proceeded to provide them with public outlets for their work. One such outlet was the *Shōji ninen in dainido hyakushu*, in which Echizen, Kunaikyō, Masatsune, and Tomochika, among the people described by Ienaga above, participated.

With these two sets of 100-poem sequences, Go-Toba had begun to forge a very large *kadan*. Even the first commission alone, with twenty-two names (not counting the mysterious Nobuhiro) was much larger than the two sets of famous, public 100-poem sequences that can be seen as its precedents: the *Horikawa hyakushu* (ca. 1105, with fourteen to sixteen participants) and the *Kyūan hyakushu* (ca. 1150, with fourteen). When the eight new names on Go-Toba's second commission are added, the resulting thirty poets represent a *kadan* unprecedented in size, scope, and range.

Furthermore, the *Kyūan hyakushu* had been intended to provide poems for the sixth imperial anthology, *Shikashū* (1151), but it was not completed in time to have much of an impact on that collection. However, nearly one-tenth of the subsequent imperial anthology, *Senzaishū* (compiled by Shunzei and completed in 1188), comes from this event. The *Kyūan hyakushu*, then, as noted in the Introduction to this study, established the convention that in order to generate contemporary materials to choose from, an imperial an-

---

65. *IN*, pp. 50–52.
66. As grandson of a Minister of the Left and son of a Major Counselor (*dainagon*), Tomochika's father, Moromitsu, should not have ended up as a lowly city administrator of the Senior Fifth Rank Lower, but he was the adopted son of the politically ambitious Fujiwara Yorinaga (1120–56), who had backed the losing side (and died in the process) in the Hōgen Disturbance of 1156. This is probably the reason why Moromitsu failed to advance at court.

thology would be preceded by a call for 100-poem sequences from important poets. Thus, Go-Toba's sponsoring of such a set of sequences, whatever else it did in terms of helping him build a large and active salon (and political base?), also implied an intention to commission an imperial anthology in the near future.

Although the planning and wrangling over these events occurred in the palace, the creative acts themselves were individual and private (except to the extent that poets consulted each other, as noted above). But Ienaga also repeatedly refers to parties and contests within the palace itself, and several of them have left their mark on waka history. Most notable were three contests held by Go-Toba in quick succession at the end of the Ninth Month and early in the Tenth Month. The first is known as *Shōji ninen sentō jūnin uta-awase* (Ten-Person Poetry Contest in the Retired Emperor's Palace in the Second Year of Shōji). It was evidently a *kendai* contest, with ten poems solicited from each participant on ix/12, the resulting 100 poems being worked into a contest format (by Go-Toba?) of fifty rounds, formally presented between ix/27 and x/5. Teika is listed in the *Gunsho ruijū* text as judge, but there is much uncertainty about this.[67]

The guest list consisted predominantly of Mikohidari partisans, with only Tadayoshi and Michichika representing Rokujō interests and Go-Toba and Masatsune belonging formally to neither side. The others were Yoshitsune, Takanobu, Teika, Ietaka, Jien, and Jakuren. There were no teams per se, since the poems were matched in an order that did not follow any team breakdown. Thus, the poems by any given poet might appear sometimes on the Left and other times on the Right, and not every poet ended up compet-

---

67. See Minegishi, *Uta-awase no kenkyū*, pp. 226–27; Gotō Shigeo, *Shinkokin wakashū no kisōteki kenkyū*, pp. 41–42; and *WBJ*, p. 322. The dates are reconstructed by Ariyoshi, his argument being that the date given in the extant GR text (190), which is ix/12, is the date of the commission not the completion, since Teika mentions only the request for poems on that date in *Meigetsuki* (1: 171). (Incidentally, Kanezane mentions Yoshitsune's being asked to submit poems on x/12; see *Gyokuyō*, 3: 944, although that would seem to be for a different purpose.) As for who judged this contest, *DNS*, iv:6, p. 682, says Shunzei (without citing any evidence), and Ariyoshi quotes several scholarly opinions suggesting combinations involving Go-Toba himself, Michichika, Yoshitsune, and Shunzei. Taniyama Shigeru (*Shinkokin jidai no uta-awase to kadan*, pp. 339–45) speculates, largely on the basis of the poor win/loss records for the highest-ranking participants (and some other evidence involving one of the textual lines), that Go-Toba, Yoshitsune, and Michichika judged the contest together. A version of the text for this contest also appears in *Shinpen kokka taikan*, 5:181, pp. 350–53.

ing once with every other poet, although all ten poems by each poet appeared.[68] I am unable to discern a pattern in the matchups, but I assume that whoever made them must have had something in mind. Since the poems of the Left won twenty times out of fifty (with fourteen wins for the Right and sixteen draws), one possibility is that the organizer placed what he believed to be the winning poems on the Left and wanted to test his own standards against the judge (or judges), but this is pure speculation.

Several points of note do emerge from this contest. First, two of the poems ended up in *Shinkokinshū*.[69] Second, the two "politicians," Michichika and Yoshitsune, fared extremely poorly in the judgments. Neither won a single round.[70] This has led some scholars to speculate that these two must have been co-judges for the contest, although I find it difficult to imagine these two cooperating on such a project.[71] I think Michichika's losses are explained more easily by the fact that he simply was not a good poet by the standards of the day. Ienaga implies that people at court generally had a low opinion of Michichika's literary output, however much they may have appreciated him as an organizer of poetic events.[72] And the judgments in this contest can be quite scathing toward him, as in Round 36, with the topic Snow at Dawn:

Left, Tadayoshi, Win

    Fima siramu
    mado no akegata
    nagamureba
    yokogumo sayuru
    mine no fatuyuki

    Its gaps whiten
    As I gaze through the window
    At breaking dawn—
    Trailing clouds freeze
    First snow upon the peaks.

Right, Michichika

    Asato akete
    tofoti no sato wo
    nagamureba
    yuki no sita ni zo
    tori mo naku naru

    Opening the door,
    At dawn, as I gaze across
    To the distant village
    There, beneath the snow,
    Birds, too, are singing.

---

68. To give just one example, Teika's poems were put up against Go-Toba's three times out of ten, but he was never once pitted against Takanobu or Michichika.

69. Masatsune's Right entry in Round 14 is *SKKS* 145 (II, Spring 2), and Jien's Left entry in Round 4 is *SKKS* 1891 (XIX, Shinto Poems). Both poems won their rounds in the contest.

70. Michichika loses eight and draws two, whereas Yoshitsune loses five and draws five.

71. See note 67 to this chapter, p. 73.

72. *IN*, p. 85.

Judgment: The Left poem is excellent. The Right poem, with its "distant village," speaks of "gazing," yet then there is the line "birds, too, are singing," which produces a marked dissonance between the upper and lower parts of the poem.[73]

Michichika is faulted for writing about two senses, the visual and the auditory, instead of concentrating on just one. This lack of focus creates a sense of disharmony. All the other judgments against Michichika's losing poems are similarly explicit in criticizing particular aspects of his poems.[74] On the other hand, the judgments against Yoshitsune tend to be brief and confined to remarks such as "has nothing to recommend it" (*saseru koto nashi*) or "is ordinary" (*tsune no koto ni haberi*).[75] As we will see in other contests, these are the kinds of phrases a judge often uses to dismiss his own work, and none of them appears in the judgments against Michichika. I am inclined to think, then, that Yoshitsune may well have had a hand in judging this contest, although my guess is that Michichika did not. Of course, if that is the case, we cannot rule out partisanship as a factor in Michichika's poor showing, although poems such as that quoted above do seem to show the kinds of faults one might expect in a beginner. And *if* partisanship hurt Michichika, it certainly did not affect Tadayoshi, a non-Mikohidari poet who, with six wins, no losses, and four draws, was the most successful in the contest. All in all, although this was certainly not the most important poetic event of the period, it has historical value because it is the earliest palace event sponsored by Go-Toba as Retired Emperor of which we have a full record, and it was probably quite typical of the many contests and parties Ienaga referred to.

One other aspect of this contest is worth extra note. The device of soliciting poems and then reworking them into contest form—a kind of *senka-awase*—seems to have had great appeal for Go-Toba. He was to use it repeatedly throughout the next few years, indeed for the rest of his life.[76] The practice would reach its most impressive proportions in the *Sengohyakuban uta-awase*, discussed at length in Chapter 5. Of course, Go-Toba did not invent the procedure, but he used it remarkably often. It is not always clear

---

73. GR 190, 12: 320. See also *Shinpen kokka taikan*, 5:181, p. 352.
74. See, e.g., Rounds 6, 15, 18, 24, 30, 33, and 44.
75. See, e.g., Rounds 14, 17, and 23.
76. A famous example from his later years is the *Teika Karyū ryōkyō senka-awase*, a contest of selected poems between Teika and Ietaka ("Karyū" being the Sinified reading of "Ietaka") that Go-Toba put together between 1236 and 1239, during his Oki exile.

that he himself was the one who reorganized the poems even if he was the sponsor of the event. In any case, his preference for the routine accords well with his synthetic approach to poetry throughout the early 1200s: take a broad group of poets and a wide range of poems and then rework them into a new whole that transcends its parts. This seemed aimed at de-emphasizing schools and individuals and creating a cultural consensus (which brings us back to the long-range political implications of Go-Toba's efforts).

On the 30th day of the Ninth Month of 1200, Go-Toba sponsored another contest, now known as *Shōji ninen kugatsu sanjūnichi nijūyoban uta-awase* (Poetry Contest in Twenty-four Rounds on the 30th Day of the Ninth Month, Second Year of Shōji), with Shunzei as the judge.[77] This was a *tōza* contest in twenty-four rounds, with sixteen poets. Minegishi Yoshiaki's characterization of this event as "a gathering of eminent poets" (*yūmeikajin o atsume*) is misleading.[78] Of the sixteen who took part, at least three were in their twenties, another three in their thirties (by Western count).[79] Another way to look at it is that six of them had been represented in the *Shōji ninen in shodo hyakushu*, but four of them in the *Shōji ninen in dainido hyakushu*, the "lesser" of the two *hyakushu*. (These numbers exclude Go-Toba and Nori-

---

77. The text for this contest can be found in *Katsuranomiyabon sōsho*, 14: 241–54 (roman numbers), reprinted in *Shinpen kokka taikan*, 5:179, pp. 347–49. Gotō Shigeo (*Shinkokin wakashū no kisōteki kenkyū*, pp. 43–44) refers to it as the *Shōji ninen kugatsu sanjūnichi in no tōza uta-awase*.

78. Minegishi, *Uta-awase no kenkyū*, p. 227, entry #54. Regardless of whether one takes *yūmei* to mean "famous" or "accomplished" here, it is not quite right under the circumstances.

79. The participants were Go-Toba, Michichika, Tadayoshi, Shunzei, Kintsune, Michitomo, Teika, Masatsune, Norimitsu, Tomochika, Takanobu, Sagami, Sanuki, Takanori, Nobuzane (called Takazane in this contest), and Chōmei. Of those whose age can be established, aside from Go-Toba, Kintsune, Michitomo, and Nobuzane were in their twenties (Tomochika probably was, too). Tadayoshi, Teika, and Masatsune were in their thirties. (Takanori was Nobuzane's elder brother—both sons of Takanobu—but his dates are unknown. Nobuzane was twenty-three at the time, and Takanori was probably in his late twenties or early thirties, although since his father was fifty-eight, he might even have been forty or so.)

The other mystery in this group is Sagami, not to be confused with the famous late Heian poet of the same name, whose approximate dates were 1000?–1061?. No court lady by this name appears in any other contest in this period, and none of the "Sagami" poems in *Shinkokinshū* seems to be by anyone other than the earlier Sagami (though #1079 is the only one without a source listed—all the rest but one are from *Sagamishū* and the other one is from *Norinagashū*). In fact, Teika's account of this event does not mention her by name, though it does specifically mention Sanuki and the other fourteen. Perhaps "Sagami" was a pseudonym.

mitsu, who took part in both.) Of the remainder, Takanori and Sagami did not have a big impact on waka of this age, and the other two, Kintsune and Minamoto (Tsuchimikado) Michitomo (1171–1227), would within a year or two certainly have qualified as *yūmeikajin*.[80] In other words, it was a mixed group, not only in age, skill, and rank, but also in terms of political and poetic affiliations.

There were eight rounds for each of three topics, for a total of twenty-four rounds. The extant text fails to record the poets for the Right team in two of the rounds, but otherwise we can pretty much see the shape of the matchups, which were in no fixed order, with some poets appearing on both teams.

Teika described the contest in some detail, and because it provides an insight into how these events were conducted, I quote his description at length:[81]

It was early afternoon and I was about to leave when I received a letter from the Daifu Fujiwara Chikamasa [1145–1210] saying that I was to appear before His Majesty this evening. The official invitation stated: "You are to present yourself at the West Central Gate." This was something I could not even have dreamed of happening not so long ago![82] I accepted with humility. He also said Shunzei would be going, too. At dusk, I went to the Sanjō Residence and after nightfall we went off together to Go-Toba's palace.[83] They had us enter at the West Central Gate.

The Captain Michitomo was already in attendance at the gathering. Raising the lattice shutters, we passed through the sliding door and went behind His Majesty's curtains to have an audience with him. We were able to speak freely. We remained next to him for a while.

Then Kintsune was beckoned to join, and he had a quiet audience with His Majesty. They were subsequently joined by Michichika. Then, in response to Go-Toba's request, Shunzei went and sat before him for a time; His Majesty having the blinds opened (so that they could speak face to face).

---

80. See previous note.
81. This passage is from *Meigetsuki shōshutsu*. The first line or so of this entry is identical with the last line or so in the Shōji 2 (1200)/ix/30 entry of our extant version of *Meigetsuki* (1: 175). The *Meigetsuki shōshutsu* entry seems to be picking up where the other left off. Here and there in the text one finds parenthetical asides, possibly textual variants, which were presumably added by Ton'a, who is supposed to have selected and edited these passages from some text, or texts, of the *Meigetsuki*. I have included them in parentheses.
82. Recall that just a month or so before this Go-Toba had restored Teika's palace privileges. See above.
83. The Sanjō Residence was Shunzei's home.

Along the wide north eaves a curtain was hung, running from east to west, to make places for the lords. Michichika, Shunzei, Kintsune, and Michitomo sat here.[84] Behind them, along the veranda, another curtain was hung, to make places for the attendant courtiers.[85] Takanobu, myself, Norimitsu, Masatsune, Takanori (who said he had been summoned tonight), Tomochika (Moromitsu's son), and Takazane took our places there. Below the eaves to the east, at the base of the veranda another curtain was hung. Chōmei sat alone here.[86] To the left front of the room there was a vase of altar flowers. (It was said the offering poem had been selected by His Majesty.) Sanuki arrived by carriage and went to attend His Majesty directly at the north end of the room.

At His Majesty's command, Shunzei posed the topics and provided commentary on each one: Promises under the Moon of Many Autumns, Tinted Maples Leaves Seen at Evening Dusk, and Hearing the Belling of a Deer at Daybreak.[87]

---

84. Strictly speaking, the term *kugyō*, what I have translated as "lords," refers to people of the Third Rank and above, holding offices of Consultant (*sangi*), Counselor (*nagon*), or Minister (*daijin*, or *otodo*). At this time, Michitomo was only Fourth Rank and a lieutenant in the guards (*chūjō*), but as Michichika's son there was little doubt that he would continue to rise in rank, and he would in this context be considered *kugyō*.

85. Here the term is *jishin*. A less specific term than *kugyō*, it refers to attendants who serve their lord directly. In this context, it obviously means courtiers of lesser rank than the first group but still of the aristocracy. The overall aristocratic scheme of the Heian/Kamakura imperial court was that lords (*kugyō*) served the sovereign and the attendants (*jishin*) served the lords, the word "served" having a broad range of meanings beyond simply attending to physical needs. In a later chapter we will a discuss a poetry contest based on this lord/attendant distinction. For more information on Heian court structure, see Hurst, "The Structure of the Heian Court."

86. *Migiri* is the term here, and it has a range of meanings, referring generically to the garden, for example, or more specifically to the graveled area below the eaves that separates the garden from the foundation of the building, or even the steps leading up from that point. In any case, Chōmei, who was the lowest-ranking member of the group, was placed noticeably off to one side. Although he was later to have his problems with Go-Toba (see *IN*, pp. 104–14), at this stage Go-Toba was trying to bring him back into the poetry scene, and his poor seating was certainly due only to rank.

87. The topics were four-character compound topics (a form of *musubidai* called *shijidai*), that is, each was made up of four Chinese characters and introduced a multi-layered topic in terms of scene, imagery, and theme. As such, they were rather difficult, and this is probably why Shunzei provided a commentary on them. Indeed, the first one is very dense, the word *chigiri* (which I have provisionally rendered as "promises") actually covers a wide range of meanings, from pledges of love to (by extension) sexual relations to "connections; ties" (that elusive word *en*, which suggests bonds from a previous life) to karmic fate. Judging from the poems actually produced under this topic, most of which were "sovereign-praising," it would appear that the word in this case implies the special *en* that is possessed by the imperial family and allows them to reign over countless autumns. An example would be Sagami's winning

These were also sent to Tadayoshi by imperial messenger (one of His Majesty's personal guards, I understand).[88] Some time passed while he was preparing his poems.

After Tadayoshi's poems arrived, the rest of us handed forward our poems in order (not everyone actually went forward). The Minister Michichika placed them on a stand, and then they were gathered up and offered to His Majesty. Off in a quiet corner they were then matched in contest rounds.[89] They were then brought back (these were the first set of poems, the ones on the Moon, which were returned after they had been copied). The Finance Minister, acting as reader [*kōji*], recited the poems to His Majesty. Go-Toba instructed that there should be discussion on each poem, but the lower-ranking participants were not allowed to speak.[90] Michichika summarized the discussions; then Shunzei decided upon the placings.

Then the second set of poems was brought forward, and after the discussion of them was completed, I was summoned from my seat to go before His Majesty, in front of the lords. He had the lamp brought closer (since the lamplight was weak, he ordered Ienaga to add more oil to it) and Shunzei asked me to copy the text down. In my mortification, I could hardly write a single word. I felt embarrassed and re-

---

4th Round, Right entry: *Kimi ga fen / titose no aki no / tomo tote ya / nodokeku sumeru / yofa no tukikage*—"Is it as a friend / For the thousand autumns / Through which His Majesty will pass / That it shines serenely clear / Moon's light at midnight?"

Likely, too, these topics were from some Chinese poem or treatise, and this may also have been why Shunzei talked about them and perhaps discussed their implications in the original context. I was unable to find appropriate lines among the poems in *Wakan rōeishū*, but there were many other Chinese works to choose from.

88. Apparently Tadayoshi was being allowed to participate in absentia. Perhaps he was ill or otherwise occupied, although generally Go-Toba seems to have been strict about participation. The following year, when Tomochika left such a gathering early, Go-Toba was quite piqued and made him spend the entire next day alone in the Wakadokoro as a kind of penance; see *IN*, pp. 59–61.

89. The word is *ketsuban*, which means to take poems already composed and put them in a poetry contest format. Unfortunately, Teika does not say who did this, and the honorific he uses is vague enough to apply to just about anyone there of higher rank than himself. Since the last specified subject was Michichika, he would be my guess.

90. Teika's use of the character *kaku* (each; every) is ambiguous here. He could be saying "Although Go-Toba decreed that each of us should express our views, the lower-ranking participants [which would include Teika] were not allowed to speak." This would be in keeping with Teika's firm belief that his opinion mattered in all poetic forums. Indeed, the word he uses for "lower-ranking" is *gerō*, which is practically like "servant," and one wonders if he is being sarcastic ("No one cares what we peons have to say"). And this interpretation would also be consonant with the tension between Michichika and Teika that we have already seen at the time of the *Shodo hyakushu*.

sentful.[91] As soon as I finished copying, I withdrew to my place toward the back. After a servant returned the poems to the poets and then gathered them up again, Michichika once more recited the poems to His Majesty and then returned to his seat.

My poems tonight were unpolished and sparked considerable discussion. Two of them lost, and one was a draw. I was rather ashamed in front of the others.[92]

However detailed the discussions of the poems may have been (according to Teika), the judgments are terse, picking at most a single phrase and saying things like "it sounds good" or "it is excellent." In other words, if part of the purpose of the contest was to introduce newer poets to the ways of the *uta-awase*, most of that education was kept out of the public record. As he often—although not always—did, Shunzei steered a politically careful course in this contest.[93] He diplomatically judged all three of his own poems as losers, a tack judges often took. And to Michichika, the premier politician (aside from Go-Toba) in the group, he awarded two wins and one loss, the two wins being against Shunzei himself and Teika. This is probably Michichika's best showing in a contest![94] Teika seemed depressed by his poor

---

91. This might seem a strange set of emotions for Teika to experience—mortification, embarrassment, and resentment—but there are probably several reasons for it. There must have been a certain amount of awe on Teika's part at being asked into such close proximity with Go-Toba, who had only recently "pardoned" him. To compound it, his father made him copy texts in front of the Retired Emperor (calligraphy itself being such an important skill, Teika must have been nervous about doing it while Go-Toba watched), and, as we will see a few lines later, Teika's own poems in the contest fared rather poorly. Finally, he had poor eyesight and was probably worried about misreading something. I believe this is why Teika uses terms like *shūshō* (what I have rendered "mortification," but which might just as well be called "agitation"), *haji*, and *urami* rather than words like *kashikoki* (awe-inspiring), *osore* (fearful), or *medetashi* (a splendor that one is lucky to be privy to) that one more often finds in a description of someone entering an imperial presence.

92. *Meigetsuki shōshutsu*, Shōji 2 (1200)/ix/30, ZGR 470, 17.1: 248.

93. The two extremes would be the *Omuro senka-awase*—assuming Shunzei did, in fact, judge it—and the *Roppyakuban uta-awase*. In the former, Shunzei seems to have responded to the political nature of the occasion and rendered safe judgments favoring the sponsors, whereas in the latter he wrote freely and produced what many consider the most important contest judgments in the history of waka. He was capable of doing both in a single event, as he did in the *Sengohyakuban uta-awase*, sometimes backing off and throwing a bone to the opposition, other times offering penetrating critical insight. This is what makes him in my mind an even more compelling figure than Teika.

94. In the case of the match between himself, on the Right, and Michichika on the Left (Topic 2, Round 3), Shunzei all but admitted that he was fudging when he wrote: "The poem on the Left sounds good. The poem on the Right is by the judge. The phrase 'can be heard

showing, but since the judge was his own father, his journal entry does not contain the kind of vitriol he often spewed at other contest judges who slighted him.

Minegishi notes, apparently with some surprise, that "despite the fact that Shunzei wrote the judgments, this contest has remained relatively unknown, perhaps because of the scarcity of texts."[95] More likely this is because the poems and the judgments are forgettable. The event is important more for extra-literary reasons: its breadth of representation, the obvious attempt on Go-Toba's part to sponsor new poets, and the public rehabilitation of Teika.

A third contest at the palace, on the 1st day of the Tenth Month, like the second one on ix/30, bore a similar relation to the *Sentō jūnin uta-awase* as the *Dainido hyakushu* bore to the *Shodo hyakushu*. That is, whereas the latter included generally top-line poets, the former seemed to be a forum for lesser lights. This contest, called *Shōji ninen jūgatsu tsuitachi uta-awase* (Poetry Contest on the 1st Day of the Tenth Month, Second Year of Shōji), brought together twelve poets in eighteen rounds.[96] The cast was largely low-ranking poets of no known partisan connections, including Tomochika (whose new lease on life is chronicled above) and Ietaka's son Takasuke (although, as noted below, he may not have actually taken part), rounded out by Jien (or possibly Yoshitsune), Go-Toba, Teika, and Chōmei. The mix of seasoned veterans and new faces is about the same as in the ix/30 event, although it is mostly a different group.[97]

---

deep into the tinted maple leaves' [from Michichika's poem] is superior, so I award it a Win." This is the only time where he identifies himself as the author of one of the poems, which in my view is like saying, "Well, since I wrote this poem and I'm the judge, I have to disqualify it, but I wouldn't otherwise"; see *Katsuranomiyabon sōsho*, 14: 246; or *Shinpen kokka taikan*, 5:179, pp. 348–49.

95. Minegishi, *Uta-awase no kenkyū*, p. 227.

96. ZGR 409, 15: 242–46. Another version, based on this text, can be found in *Shinpen kokka taikan*, 5:180, pp. 349–50.

97. The teams were: Left—Kintsune, Yasusue (fl. 1200–1221), Yasunari (Jien), Tomochika, Teika, Munenaga (11??–1225); Right—Norimitsu, Takasuke, Nyōbō (Go-Toba), Minamoto Suekage (dates unknown), Chōmei, Kinkage (dates unknown).

Sasaki Takahiro ("Go-Toba In kadan seiritsuki ni okeru ichimondai") argues that the poems attributed to Ietaka's son Takasuke in this contest were really written by Masatsune, that the name *Munenaga* is a miscopy for *Ienaga*, and that Yasunari was a pseudonym for some well-known and influential person, probably Yoshitsune (Ariyoshi evidently thinks it is Jien). Sasaki's arguments are well made, although he admits he cannot account for why the deception (Masatsune ghost-writing for Takasuke) occurred. Even if it is true, none of this really

Although the teams were set, the matchups were not; that is, a particular poet did not necessarily go up against the same opponent on the other team each time.[98] The extant text says the contest was *tōza* and judged by the group (*shūgihan*), with the remarks being written up by Teika. In *Meigetsuki*, Teika himself, however, implies that he is the one who suggested the outlines of the judgments, which presumably, then, became the basis for discussion. He also says Go-Toba encouraged everyone to speak freely, which suggests that the contest was in part a seminar for the neophytes, who could learn from Teika, Jien, and other of the senior members.[99] The veterans did not fare especially well in the placings, with only two wins among the twelve poems the four of them submitted, although the matchups put them against each other more often than not, which would skew the results. And of course raw placings do not tell the whole story, especially in the case of draws, which could happen because both poems were equally good or because they were equally bad. The big winner in the contest was Munenaga, elder brother of Masatsune, but not as well known in poetry circles, with three wins. Otherwise the placings were fairly evenly distributed.

As with the *Dainido hyakushu*, this contest gave neophytes the opportunity to take part in a public poetry event in the palace and compete with the best. And as with the *Dainido hyakushu*, some of the poets in this contest went on to make a name for themselves. Munenaga disappeared from sight, but Kintsune and Yasusue (fl. 1200–1221), for example, were invited to a much bigger and more important *hyakushu* commission the following year, the event that would eventually become the *Sengohyakuban uta-awase*. So contests like these were a kind of farm league, from which the best could rise.

This contest also demonstrated Go-Toba's intention to bring Jien and Teika into prominence in the poetic world. At first glance, matching them with such an unknown group might appear to be an insult. But if you look on the contest as a seminar—and the detailed judgments could certainly be seen as useful guidelines for newcomers—then Teika, Jien, and to some

---

affects my discussion, except that there would be two fewer "unknowns" in the group than I have described. My assumption about Ariyoshi's opinion comes from the fact that in *WBJ* (p. 322) he lists Jien as a participant, although in his earlier *Shinkokin wakashū no kenkyū: kiban to kōsei* (p. 551), he lists Yasunari, but not Jien.

98. In fact, due to the small scale, not every poet competed against every counterpart on the other team, and in three cases, a single poet was matched twice to the same opponent.

99. *Meigetsuki*, Shōji 2 (1200)/x/1, 1: 175.

extent Chōmei were being honored by the invitation, since Go-Toba set them up as mentors. In particular, Teika's prominent role in this event and his participation in the two previously discussed contests demonstrate how quickly and thoroughly he had been rehabilitated and brought from the edge to the center of the poetic stage. Less than two months had passed since Go-Toba had allowed him to return to the palace.

Go-Toba was not the only sponsor of poetic activities during this period. Ariyoshi lists seventy-six waka events of all types for the year Shōji 2 alone.[100] Of course, many of these are small or private affairs, for example, a Chinese verse party at Yoshitsune's house, and the list includes references to Teika's reviewing someone else's poems before they submit them for the *Shōji ninen in shodo hyakushu* or an exchange of letter/poems between two people. But there were also bigger events of a public nature.

For a time, Michichika seemed intent on making himself the center of poetic activities by sponsoring monthly *eigu* meetings at his home.[101] *Eigu* originally meant to honor the portrait of a deceased saint or deity. By late Heian, however, it had acquired the more specific meaning of honoring a portrait of Hitomaro as the "sage of waka" and inevitably included poetic composition as part of the rite. The earliest recorded event of this nature was in 1118, sponsored by Fujiwara Akisue at his home. Perhaps through the Rokujō connection, Michichika became an ardent sponsor of the practice, and by early 1200 was holding *eigu* meetings every month at his home. He expected every important poet to attend. Indeed, Teika grouses about this in *Meigetsuki*. But in his obituary for Michichika, Ienaga says that occasionally Go-Toba would also show up on the quiet to these contests, which implies that he, too, considered them worthwhile.[102] There is also reference to a poetry contest Michichika held at his home on the 26th day of the Twelfth

---

100. Ariyoshi, *Shinkokin wakashū no kenkyū: kiban to kōsei*, pp. 548–52; this is part of a longer time line—which he calls "Time Line of Waka-Related Activities in the Shinkokin Period" ("Shinkokin jidai wakakankei nenpyō")—stretching from 1190 through 1209 (pp. 542–65). He lists every event he can trace from various sources (including diary references, headnotes in later anthologies, etc.), regardless of whether it has left a text behind. It is an invaluable listing.

101. For a closer look at four *eigu* events from this period (all of which are also treated in this study), see Taniyama, *Shinkokin jidai no uta-awase to kadan*, pp. 348–451. Taniyama gives background information and a collated text for these contests. For a discussion of Michichika's involvement in these *eigu* events and a list of those that occurred during the period covered in this study, see ibid., pp. 258–360.

102. *IN*, p. 85.

Month of Shōji 2, from which two poems were taken for *Shinkokinshū*.[103] There is no question from the above-cited *Ienaga nikki* obituary that Michichika was an ardent fan of waka, if somewhat less than a skillful practitioner. When we consider, too, his involvement in the initial stages of the *Shōji ninen in shodo hyakushu*, it seems fair to say that he was trying hard to put his mark on the waka world.

As noted above, Yoshitsune, too, had seemed eager to stake a claim, with several contests in early 1200, before he ran into another round of political problems. His rehabilitation later in the year may have led him to attempt another large-scale event known as the *Sanbyakurokujūban uta-awase* (Poetry Contest in 360 Rounds).[104] A great deal of doubt and controversy surrounds the details of this event. There is little agreement as to when it was held, or even that Yoshitsune was its sponsor. In any case, it was a *senka-awase*—I am partial to Ariyoshi's characterization of it as a "contest on paper"[105]—in which selected poems from thirty-six poets (Kintō's *Sanjūrokuninsen* [Selections from 36 Poets] of 1009? was the model) were put in a contest format of 360 rounds, with no judgments and no fixed order or representation in terms of teams. Although the preface of the extant text is dated Shōji 2 (1200)/viii/26, since there is a 160-poem overlap with the *Shōji ninen in shodo hyakushu* and a 10-plus poem overlap with the *Shingū senka-awase* of the following year (an event discussed in more detail in the next chapter), it is difficult to put an exact date to this activity.

In terms of numbers of poems represented, the "contest" was dominated by the heavyweights in what will soon become clearly Go-Toba's *kadan*. Go-Toba himself, Yoshitsune, Jien, Shunzei, and Shikishi Naishinnō had thirty-nine poems each. Teika and Jakuren had thirty-six poems each, and Ietaka thirty-five. The Rokujō partisan Tadayoshi and his patron, Michichika, were only slightly less represented, with thirty-three and thirty poems, respectively. But especially striking is that Kanezane was represented by thirty-three poems, and he is not hidden behind a pseudonym but is clearly identified in the text as Zenkanpaku (or Saki no Kanpaku, "The Former Chancellor/Regent"). Although there is some debate over who organized this contest (the two major theories point to Yoshitsune and his partisans or

---

103. Ariyoshi, *Shinkokin wakashū no kenkyū: kiban to kōsei*, p. 538.
104. For the texts for this contest, see ZGR 409, 15.1: 198–241; and *Shinpen kokka taikan*, 5:183, pp. 363–79 (based on a copy made in 1206 and held by the Tenri Library).
105. *WBJ*, p. 285.

to someone from the Rokujō school), I think the distribution of representation, especially the prominent presence (his first poem appears as the Left entry in Round 2) of Kanezane, points to Yoshitsune as the sponsor. And even if the text was not completed until the following year, as Ariyoshi argues, it is another clear indication that the Kujō house was on the rise again.

In the end, whether or not Yoshitsune was responsible for the *Sanbyakurokujūban uta-awase*, there is little doubt that he and Michichika saw themselves as important patrons of poetry. There is also little doubt from the events described in this chapter that Go-Toba was beginning to see himself in that light, too. The following year saw him start to bring all the elements together under his control, which is the subject of the next chapter.

THREE

New Faces and a New Wakadokoro, Kennin 1 (1201)

Go-Toba quickly followed up on the groundwork he had laid in 1200 by sponsoring an ever-increasing array of poetry events that not only consolidated the poetic scene itself but also firmly established him at the center of it. And his actions made it clearer and clearer that he was intending to commission an imperial anthology in the near future.

The year began with a New Year's poetry party at Go-Toba's palace on the 7th of the First Month, but details are sketchy, and it need not detain us.[1] The more significant event from the standpoint of waka history was the death, on 1/25, of Shikishi Naishinnō. Teika was very close to her—recall that she turned to him for help in the *Shōji ninen in shodo hyakushu*—and a number of his diary entries in Shōji 2 (1200) describe her increasingly serious illness and his frequent visits to her. In fact, there has been speculation since early on that he and the princess may have been lovers, although I doubt they were.[2] Swollen legs and what may well have been breast cancer seem to

---

1. Ariyoshi, *Shinkokin wakashū no kenkyū: kiban to kōsei*, p. 552. *Meigetsuki* has no entries for the first two and a half months of the year, but we know from various private collections such as Teika's *Shūi gusō* (1216, with later additions) that Teika was at this party.

2. I am indebted to DNS, which lays out all the relevant *Meigetsuki* entries, along with references to other sources, as well, iv:6, pp. 900–907. The dates, all from Shōji 2, that contain entries related to her illness (followed by the page number where the passage appears in the

have been the important symptoms, and various medications and prayers were tried to help her. According to Teika, she appeared to rally at the end of the year, but then since *Meigetsuki* itself is blank until the Third Month of the following year, we have no details of her final days.[3] Ienaga best captured the poetic pathos—the *aware*, if you will—of her death in a passage written one year after her death:

The death of Zensaiin [Shikishi Naishinnō] left all at a loss for words. As more and more die, the Way of Poetry declines; so one feels one must try all the harder.[4]

A year before her death, at the time of the 100-poem sequences,[5] she had com-

---

Meigetsuki text, vol. 1) are ii/30 (p. 144); *ii/24 (p. 150); iii/ 6 (p. 151); ix/9 (p. 170); then a series of entries in the Twelfth Month that chronicle the ever-worsening condition, xii/1, 5, 8, 10–15, 18, 19, 26, and 28 (pp. 193–200). Since the symptoms described in the earlier entries are not always the same as those in the later ones, it may be that she suffered several different illnesses throughout the year. But clearly by the Twelfth Month she had entered her final decline.

Ishida Yoshisada (*Shinkokin sekai to chūsei bungaku*, 1: 157) says some twenty *Meigetsuki* entries between Shōji 1/v/1 and Shōji 2/xii/28 touch on Princess Shikishi's illness. He nevertheless rejects the gossip that subsequently appeared in medieval writings that Teika and Shikishi Naishinnō were lovers—a notion also dismissed by Fujihira Haruo (*Shinkokin to sono zengo*, pp. 384–86) for much the same reason: that it was a socially inconceivable match.

3. Ishida (*Shinkokin sekai to chūsei bungaku*, 2: 18–19) argues, admittedly with no objective evidence, that the "blank" (*kūhaku*) two and a half months is because Teika was too overcome with emotion to write about anything. This seems untenable. First, Teika writes all the way up to the 29th of the Twelfth Month of Shōji 2 (the omission of the last day is not significant, since he frequently skipped days at a time), and since the first few weeks of the New Year were important to diarists, one would expect him to keep on writing; even if we accept Ishida's notion, Shikishi Naishinnō did not die until the 25th, and in his last entries for the previous month, Teika depicts her as rallying. So grief can certainly not account for the gap during the first three weeks of the month, the period *before* she died. As for the remainder of the gap, Teika wrote in lengthy detail about his father Shunzei's final illness and death. It stretches the imagination to think that he could remain sufficiently detached in *that* case but not in the case of Princess Shikishi, especially considering that from all accounts he and Shunzei were very close. I am inclined to think, then, that the "blank," like so many others in *Meigetsuki* and *Gyokuyō*, is accidental, or at least not due to an excess of grief on Teika's part.

4. For the purposes of annotation, Ishida and Satsukawa have divided Ienaga's memoirs into small sections that are not always discrete. The citation translated here, though contiguous in Ienaga's narrative, actually covers two and a half of Ishida/Satsukawa's sections (Sections 15–17). Since Ienaga's reminiscences here represent a lyrical arc, I am ignoring Ishida/Satsukawa's divisions and section headings, which are editorial anyway. The expression "as more and more die," in the first paragraph, refers to the death of Jakuren, which Ienaga had just been discussing. See *IN*, pp. 75–78.

5. This refers to the *Shōji ninen in shodo hyakushu* described in the preceding chapter.

posed "Do not forget me / Even you, plum tree by the eaves!"[6] And when, the following year, the tree at her Ōidono residence bloomed as if in sympathy, I could not help saying to myself "This year, at least . . . ."[7]

It was about the 20th of the Third Month a year ago that His Majesty, deciding there should be a *kemari* match, came to this villa accompanied by his court. The cherry blossoms had piled up so deep as to obscure the outlines of the garden, and here and there the wisteria flowers entwined in the pine branches, and the yellow roses along the fence were just beginning to peep out. Fine fragrances vied with the scent of the flowers, and altar incense wafted from the chapel, not to be outdone.[8] I felt that this was the way the dwelling of someone who has renounced the secular world should look, so elegant did the place seem to me. At the timeworn eaves, ferns and day lilies grew in green profusion, which left an even more pleasing effect than if it had been newly decorated. The *kemari* match began, and such was the atmosphere that even though the place was full of people, one could only see them in silhouette, and there was no one watching the action from makeshift screens in the garden.[9] As the day drew to a close, the sound of a hand bell from deep inside the villa, and the

---

6. The entire poem is: *Nagameturu / kefu fa mukasi ni / narinutomo / nokiba no ume fa / ware wo wasuru na*—"Though today / Through which I gaze out, lost in thought / May become the past / Do not forget me / You, plum tree by the eaves!" In this version of Ienaga's diary, the final particle in line 4 has changed from "fa" to "mo," which I have rendered as "even" in the translation of his memoirs. The "fa" is a bit more forlorn, a contrastive particle suggesting "people may forget me, but *you*, at least, plum tree (on which I am gazing now) must not." This poem, with "fa" intact, appears as *SKKS* 52 (Book I, Spring 1).

7. Reference to a well-known *Kokinshū* poem by Kamitsuke no Mineo (fl. 835–91?) lamenting the death of Fujiwara Mototsune (836–91), whose remains were laid to rest in Fukakusa: *Fukakusa no / nobe no sakura si / kokoro araba / kotosi bakari fa / sumizome ni sake*—"You, cherries by the fields / In Fukakusa / If you have feelings / Then this year, at least, / Bloom in dark mourning!" (*KKS* 832, XVI, Laments). This is an archetypal *Kokin*-style poem, lyrical, directly addressing a natural phenomenon as though it were human, but aware of the contrast between the seasonal cycle that is inevitable, immutable, and the human life cycle, which seems arbitrary and impermanent.

8. The "fine fragrances" presumably come from the incense people used to scent their robes.

9. This passage is elliptical, but I have tried to avoid an explanatory translation here, although I have interpolated "even though" and "only (see them)" in an effort to create a grammatical sentence. Ishida and Satsukawa suggest that in the last phrase of the sentence, Ienaga is contrasting this situation to the one that would normally obtain at a palace *kemari* match, where people would be watching from makeshift *tatejitomi*, temporary screen enclosures made by interlocking small strips of wood with the lattice-work of a wall or fence, which allowed an "overflow" crowd to see the game from outside without being visible to others. What I have translated as "such was the atmosphere," Ishida and Satsukawa gloss as "so refined were the surroundings," or words to that effect.

ring of the evening bell when struck—they seem hardly to have been produced by human hand—had a lonely, spiritual dignity.[10]

Now, when not so many months or years had passed, how sad it was to see this villa empty, without its mistress. I felt I could not stop my tears.

These days as I come and go from the Kyōgoku Palace, not by horse or carriage anymore, but on foot, I walk past the Ōidono villa.[11] And when I look in through crumbling gaps in the wattle fence, there I see wormwood brush overtaking the eaves, and a clump of plume grass triumphant. Then, when I reach the nearby Kyōgoku Palace, polished and bright like a jeweled mirror, I am deeply struck by the contrast.[12]

In this brilliant sketch, in addition to providing a mini-seminar in waka vocabulary, Ienaga created, presumably as a kind of offering to the soul of Princess Shikishi, a microcosmic Buddhist paradise.

First, he suspends time. Although strictly speaking, these are memoirs, the ambiguity of tense markers in classical Japanese makes Ienaga's narrative seem more like a journal of events that have just occurred. Beyond that, however, Ienaga deliberately plays with time in this passage. The opening lines move from present to past to the future of the past (that is, to the present again—he stands in the present and says of the past "who would have thought a year from then that such-and-such would happen?"); this movement is repeated at least twice. In waka, this progression gets played out in the terms *mukashi* (past), *ima* (present), and *yukusue* (future) and sets up an infinite continuum.[13] And waka discourse is further employed in the spring

---

10. The adjective Ienaga uses here, *tōtoki* (*tautoki*), implies, among other things, the dignity and awe inherent in something sacred.

11. As will be discussed later, Go-Toba moved to the Kyōgoku Palace in Kennin 2 (1202), Tenth Month. Since this was close to Ienaga's home, he walked to work after that.

12. For another translation of part of this passage, one that differs in detail from mine, see Hiroaki Satō, *String of Beads*, pp. 6–7. Satō says the *kemari* match took place in Kenkyū 8 (1197)/iii/16, although he does not cite a source for this. Kanezane mentioned a *kemari* match at Princess Shikishi's Ōidono in a *Gyokuyō* entry for that date (*Gyokuyō*, 3: 929).

13. Although the poem was written a century after Ienaga's memoirs, Emperor Fushimi's Left entry in Round 21 of *Kingyoku uta-awase* illustrates the point dramatically: *Mukasi ima / yukusuwe kakete / omofiidenu / koyofi fitoyo no / tuki no afare ni*—"The past, and now, / And on to what will come— / These are brought to mind / By the sad and lovely moon / Of this one night alone"; see Huey, "The Kingyoku Poetry Contest," p. 316. Since my translation, a new, annotated version of that contest has been published in Japanese: Higuchi et al., eds., *Chūsei wakashū: Kamakurahen*, pp. 371–91. Round 21 appears on p. 378.

This temporal notion can also be expressed in terms of yesterday (*kinō* [*kinofu*]), today (*kyō* [*kefu*]), and tomorrow (*asu*), as in KKS 933 (XVIII, Miscellaneous 2), Anonymous: *Yo no*

imagery, as well as the reference to "timeworn eaves" and, more tellingly, the mention of ferns (*shinobugusa*—literally, "grasses of longing") and daylilies (*wasuregusa*—literally, "grasses of forgetfulness"), since the puns on these plant names are conventionally used in waka to describe lost love or the loss of a loved one. There are also two allusive variations, one to Shikishi Naishinnō's own poem and the other to a venerable *Kokinshū* verse. This serves to sanctify the event in literary terms, just as what follows will sanctify it in religious ones.

Next Ienaga creates a celestial garden replete with jewel-flowers of varying hues, ethereal fragrances, and music, which he himself says is as if not produced by humans (*hito no suru ka to dani oboete*—literally, "one wondered if it was made by humans"). All these are marks of Amida's Western Paradise.[14] It is an overwhelming vision, only temporary for those left behind; but comfort is offered in the implicit notion that Shikishi Naishinnō is now in the true Western Paradise, of which this was just a transformed vision.

It is a rebirth she has "earned," since in addition to their symbolic significance as musical instruments in the Pure Land, the bells Ienaga refers to—a *suzu*, or small hand-rung bell, and a *kane*, a larger bell rung by striking it with a mallet and probably located in the Buddhist prayer chapel alluded to earlier in the passage—are both associated with Buddhist ceremonies. Here they suggest that the occupant of the villa, Princess Shikishi, was concerned less with the trappings of this world, represented by the *kemari* match, than with salvation in the next. While others play, she quietly retreats to her devotions.[15] Toward the end of his sketch, Ienaga returns to the present and contrasts the sad, neglected state of the Ōidono garden (which he this time

---

naka fa / nani ka tune naru / Asukagafa / kinofu no futi zo / kefu fa se ni naru—"In this world of ours / What, then, is the norm? / For in the Asuka, River of Tomorrow / Yesterday's deep pools / Become today's shallows!"

14. Jeweled bells hang from nets, six times a day the air is perfumed by a shower of lotus petals, the trees there have the leaves, flowers, and fruits of the Seven Jewels. These are some of the descriptions of the Western Paradise from *The Larger Sutra on Amitāyus*; see Inagaki and Stewart, *The Three Pure Land Sutras*, pp. 258–67. Ienaga's more immediate source for this vision of the Western Paradise may have been Genshin's *Ōjōyōshū*.

15. The use of a *kemari* match as a figure for the secular world, or more specifically the Heian court, can also be found in the first *Wakana* ("New Herbs, Part One," in Seidensticker, pp. 581–84) chapter of *The Tale of Genji*, when Genji watches the younger generation, lords and retainers (the former blessed, according to Murasaki Shikibu's narrator, with natural talent and elegance, the latter rough and tumble), play a match in front of the Third Princess's quarters.

describes with autumn images, wormwood and plume grass, to balance the spring scene he had depicted before, and to complete the Spring and Autumn cycle, a Chinese figure that represents the "march of time") to the polished, jewel-like beauty of the Kyōgoku Palace. His choice of jewel and mirror images suggests the imperial line, to which Shikishi Naishinnō belonged, and Shinto. It is quite a performance, and although this discussion has taken us temporarily from the progression of poetic events that is the main topic of this book, it demonstrates the layers of culture (waka convention, Buddhism, Shinto, the figures of crumbling fence and neglected villa) that go into the literary creations I am chronicling.

As noted earlier, however, the cycle of birth and death seem to have had minimal impact on Go-Toba's poetic pursuits. The retired sovereign was soon (ii/8, not even two weeks after Shikishi Naishinnō's death) sponsoring another gathering, this time, to be sure, a fairly quiet, in-house affair. Now known as *Kennin gannen nigatsu yōka jisshu waka* (Ten Poems on the 8th Day, Second Month, First Year of Kennin), the event took place in his palace and involved twenty of Go-Toba's close retainers, including Masatsune, Michitomo, Tomochika, and Ienaga. The poets submitted one poem on each of ten topics, for a total of 200 poems. None was ever selected for *Shinkokinshū*, and on the whole it was not a literary landmark, but it shows how incessant such activities had become. The next few years would see several major figures die, but the poetry gatherings would continue, with hardly a missed beat. In a way, then, *Shinkokinshū* itself became the monument for those lost along the way.

A week or so later Go-Toba put together a larger, more comprehensive contest, one that was to have significant impact on *Shinkokinshū*. As evidenced by the three contests Go-Toba had held in the fall of the previous year, the Retired Emperor was experimenting with contest configurations. He had come to prefer some form of selected-verse contests (*senka-awase*), even if the poems themselves were composed on the spot (*tōza*). He also liked to bring together diverse poets, and given the high placings of some of the more obscure poets in the events late in the year 1200, he may have been satisfied that this was one way to improve the overall quality of poetic output.

His next project combined these elements and revealed a sense of humor as well, for the contest bears the designation *Rōnyaku gojisshu uta-awase* (Fifty-Poem Contest Between Old and Young). The title is undoubtedly, considering that neither was invited to participate, a swipe at Michichika and Suetsune, who had made such an issue of age the year before at the time of the *Shodo hyakushu*.[16] "Old," as in that earlier case, seems to have meant late thirties or above, and this time it includes Teika.[17] The seniors made up the Left team, and their juniors the Right. The participants and their ages (by the Japanese count) are:

Left: Tadayoshi (38), Jien (47), Teika (40), Ietaka (44), Jakuren (60?)

Right: Go-Toba (22), Yoshitsune (33), Kunaikyō (20?), Echizen (?), Masatsune (32)

With the exception of Tadayoshi, the Left team were Mikohidari poets, whereas the Right has only one representative from that axis, Kujō Yoshitsune, although it is fair to say that the Right team poets also represented a new, innovative approach to waka.[18] In fact, this team arrangement poses many ironies. Here is the Mikohidari school being characterized as "old"! Recall that just one year before, at the time of the *Shōji ninen in shodo hyakushu*,

---

16. Texts for the *Rōnyaku* contest can be found in GR 191, 12: 323–47; and *Shinpen kokka taikan*, 5:184, pp. 379–89.

17. Gotō Shigeo (*Shinkokin wakashū no kisōteki kenkyū*, p. 59) notes that in an *eigu* contest at Michichika's on Shōji 2 (1200)/xi/8, the teams were also divided along age lines, with Teika being "young" in that case (yet only five months separate these two events). In fact, Teika discusses Michichika's event in *Meigetsuki*. He is displeased at the team divisions and the implication (undoubtedly a follow-up on the controversy a few months earlier at the time of the *Shodo hyakushu*) that he is not mature as a poet. He says: "On this evening, the teams were divided into Old and Young, and I was placed with the Young. Surely this makes no sense, but I was told that forty was the demarcation, although if that's true, then why is it that Ietaka was placed on the Young team, too?" (Teika was thirty-nine by the Japanese count, and Ietaka was forty-three.) See *Meigetsuki*, Shōji 2/xi/9, 1: 184–85. Interestingly, Teika mentioned that the Young team scored more wins in this contest, too.

18. There is some difference of opinion as to how closely Tadayoshi associated himself with either the Mikohidari or Rokujō schools. Since his mother was the daughter of Rokujō Akisuke, which would make Kenshō his adoptive uncle, he had blood ties to the Rokujō house. He was also half-brother to Motomichi, who had allied himself with Michichika against Kanezane and succeeded the latter as Regent. Thus Ariyoshi (*Shinkokin wakashū no kenkyū: kiban to kōsei*, p. 94), for example, considers him a Rokujō partisan. Gotō Shigeo (*Shinkokin wakashū no kisōteki kenkyū*, p. 47), on the other hand, takes a narrower view of what it means to be a Rokujō; evidently for him it is the name itself that counts, which is probably what leads him to state that there was no Rokujō representation in this contest. My own view is that since Tadayoshi did not participate in any other prominently Mikohidari event besides this one, and since he was not present at Shunzei's ninetieth year celebration, he probably was seen as more or less a Rokujō partisan.

Teika and Ietaka were scorned by the Rokujō side as too young, too immature, not well enough versed in the traditional styles to warrant inclusion in the sequence. Now, suddenly, they are the "establishment," and furthermore, they take a beating in this contest, especially Teika.

Although the records are not absolutely clear, the group probably first met on ii/12 to submit their 50-poem sequences, which must have been solicited earlier.[19] The topics were extremely general: ten poems each on Spring, Summer, Autumn, Winter, and Miscellaneous. Someone, presumably the sponsor, Go-Toba, took the sequences and arranged them into a contest of 250 rounds, using a set formula (in contrast to the more casual arrangement found in the late-1200 contests discussed in the preceding chapter). The Left entries were fixed in the order Tadayoshi, Jien, Teika, Ietaka, and Jakuren (this matched their rank order), so that, for example, Tadayoshi's poems were the Left entries for Round 1, 6, 11, and so on to the end, and Jien's were Round 2, 7, 12, and so on. The Right team, however, was cycled continuously as below (the designation in parentheses stands for the poet's initial position within his/her team as listed at the beginning of the contest text; for example, L1 means First poet on Left team):

---

19. This is the sort of information *Meigetsuki* would certainly have recorded, which makes the fact that the journal is missing the first two and a half months of Kennin 1 all the more unfortunate. Ariyoshi (*Shinkokin wakashū no kenkyū: kiban to kōsei*, p. 552) claims that *Meigetsuki* talks about a 50-poem sequence commissioned by Go-Toba on ii/5, and he identifies this as related to the *Rōnyaku gojisshu uta-awase*, but nothing like this appears in either the Kokusho kankōkai *Meigetsuki* or *Meigetsuki shōshutsu*. Ienaga Kaori ("Kennin gannen no Go-Toba In kadan") cites from a fragment of the *Meigetsuki* in the Ninna-ji library, dated the 30th day of the First Month. It makes reference to a 50-poem sequence, which she argues is the basis for the *Rōnyaku* contest. She goes on to note, citing Kubota Jun, that there was what turned out to be a "dry run" of the contest on the 9th day of the Second Month.

Aside from this, the other indication that this contest started out as a set of 50-poem sequences is the fact that thirty of the thirty-three poems from the *Rōnyaku* contest selected for *Shinkokinshū* bear, in that anthology, headnotes that identify them as being from a 50-poem sequence submitted to Go-Toba. (The exceptions are two poems by Tadayoshi, #234 and #1476, identified by their headnotes as from a *100*-poem sequence submitted to Go-Toba, headnotes that Minemura Fumihito [*Shinkokin wakashū* (1974), pp. 100, 443] simply dismisses as incorrect, and #1805, by Kunaikyō, which bears no headnote, but is from Round 207 of the contest.)

It is, incidentally, interesting that the *Shinkokinshū* headnotes identify these poems as from a sequence rather than from a contest. In other cases, for example, the *Sengohyakuban uta-awase*, which resembles the *Rōnyaku* in many ways, the *Shinkokinshū* headnotes identify the contest, not the sequence from which it was constructed, as the source.

Round 1—Tadayoshi (L1) vs. Go-Toba (R1)
Round 2—Jien (L2) vs. Yoshitsune (R2)
Round 3—Teika (L3) vs. Kunaikyō (R3)
Round 4—Ietaka (L4) vs. Echizen (R4)
Round 5—Jakuren (L5) vs. Masatsune (R5)

Then,

Round 6—L1 vs. R2	Round 16—L1 vs. R4
Round 7—L2 vs. R3	Round 17—L2 vs. R5
Round 8—L3 vs. R4	Round 18—L3 vs. R1
Round 9—L4 vs. R5	Round 19—L4 vs. R2
Round 10—L5 vs. R1	Round 20—L5 vs. R3
Round 11—L1 vs. R3	Round 21—L1 vs. R5
Round 12—L2 vs. R4	Round 22—L2 vs. R1
Round 13—L3 vs. R5	Round 23—L3 vs. R2
Round 14—L4 vs. R1	Round 24—L4 vs. R3
Round 15—L5 vs. R2	Round 25—L5 vs. R4

With Round 26 the cycle starts again and continues until Round 250 is completed. In fact, it is so regular that I believe the attribution of the Right poem in Round 232 to Echizen in the *Gunsho ruijū* and *Shinpen kokka taikan* texts must be wrong, since it would have been Kunaikyō's turn. (Making this correction also solves the problem of why, in these two texts, Kunaikyō has only 49 poems, and Echizen has 51, whereas everyone else has 50.) This pattern allows each poet to compete with every other poet, and although it is technically a *senka-awase*, it is arbitrary enough to permit true competition. The focus is on the poems rather than on the selector's criteria, and this makes it a much different sort of *senka-awase* than what we saw in the late-1200 contests. Apparently the system suited Go-Toba's purposes well, for he would turn to it again in the *Sengohyakuban uta-awase*.[20]

---

20. Selection practices themselves would make an interesting study. In this contest, for example, if we had the original 50-poem sequences, we could see if Go-Toba respected the poets' own order of poems or whether he juggled them a bit within their broader topical categories. For the late-1200 contests, it is a bit more complicated, since the matchings seem random. We can extract the poems, put them back into sequences, and then line them up in an attempt to discover what criteria Go-Toba might have used in matching them the way he did

Once the matchups were set, the group met again on the 16th and the 18th to discuss the matches and render, or hear someone render, judgment. Unfortunately, we do not know who the judge was. There are no *hanshi* (written explanations of the judge's decision). It is unfortunate that the judge's name and reasoning are missing since the final standings are somewhat surprising. The placings can be summarized as follows.

The Right team—the Young—were overwhelming winners *as a team*. Although because of textual variants there is some question as to the judgment for several rounds, my count shows the Left team winning 66 rounds (27 percent), the Right team winning 121 rounds (48 percent), and 63 rounds (25 percent) ending in a draw. Since in most contests there is a more even distribution of these three categories, the lopsidedness itself is noteworthy. Moreover, it is the neophyte team that scores so well, at the expense of the so-called masters, particularly Teika.[21] Of the Left team, only Jien manages a virtually even distribution of wins, losses, and ties (17–16–17, respectively). The others have significantly more losses than wins or ties.

(associated vocabulary, for example), but we still would not know in some cases if our reconstructed sequences matched the order of the poets' original sequences.

The problem is that the many of the original sequences are no longer extant, although a few have survived. For example, Yoshitsune's collection of his own work, called *Akishino gesseishū*, has come through the ages intact. It is a collection of 1,661 poems from eleven fixed sequences, including the 100-poem sequence he submitted for the *Sengohyakuban uta-awase* (called the *In daisando hyakushu*) and the 50-poem sequence he composed for the *Rōnyaku gojisshu uta-awase* (which bears the heading *In mudai gojisshu*—"Fifty Poems Without Topic for the Retired Emperor"). In both these cases, the order of the sequence poems is the same as the order in which the poems appear in the final contest. There are slight variations in wording here and there, probably attributable to copyists rather than to revision by the contest organizer. For a text of the sequences, see Aoki, *Fujiwara Yoshitsune zenkashū to sono kenkyū*, pp. 77–86.

In the extant version of Teika's 100-poem sequence for the *Sengohyakuban uta-awase*, one again finds a few slight variations in wording, but otherwise the poems appear in the same order as they do in the contest (see Wakashi kenkyūkai, *Shikashū taisei*, vol. 4, Chūsei II, pp. 95–97). In any case, this should be a fruitful avenue to pursue, especially if one wanted to learn more about the process of sequencing in *Shinkokinshū*.

21. In fact, Teika places next to the bottom, with only eleven wins out of fifty entries, tied with Jakuren. Tadayoshi only manages ten wins, and Ietaka and Jien fare a little better with seventeen (still only about a third of the rounds). In terms of outright losses, Teika fares the worst in all the contest, with thirty-one. And even though Tadayoshi and Jakuren managed a winning record against at least one opponent (Echizen in both cases), Teika has a losing record against all five of the Right team. Once more, as much as one might wish to see what Teika said about this in his diary, it is also part of the "lost months."

However, not all the Right poets were successful. The two women, Kunaikyō and Echizen, fared worse than Ietaka and Jien of the Left team and only slightly better than Teika, Jakuren, and Tadayoshi.[22] Perhaps not surprisingly given their status, Go-Toba (36 wins) and Yoshitsune (34 wins) were the big winners. Indeed, their combined presence on one team skews the final result considerably since the social realities of the age made it unthinkable that an imperial personage could have a losing score in a contest even if s/he used a pseudonym. Yoshitsune's status also virtually guaranteed a strong showing. But what most commentators find more significant is that Masatsune won half his rounds, and essentially split the other half between losses and ties. Clearly this contest marks his coming of age just as the events toward the end of the previous year (1200) had marked Teika's.

Without any written *hanshi* we are at a loss to fully explain the final placings. There are some clues, however, in the thirty-three poems that were selected from this contest for *Shinkokinshū*. Ariyoshi has studied them exhaustively, showing whose poems were selected, which selectors designated them, and what their *Shinkokinshū* numbers are. He then discusses some of the implications of these selections, although he occasionally just cites a statistic without evaluation.[23]

For example, Ariyoshi notes that for Tadayoshi this contest was especially important since two of his five *Shinkokinshū* poems came from here, although (as noted above) they bear different headnotes than the others from this contest, and there is no record of which selectors chose them. However, he does not elaborate, although what he has to say about Masatsune's situation (about which more below) may provide a clue. He reminds us that Go-Toba had the final say on what went into *Shinkokinshū*, even in its early stages (that is, not taking into account his massive revisions at the time of his Oki exile).[24] Perhaps the selected poems in *Shinkokinshū* were Go-Toba's

---

22. Assuming that Round 232 is Kunaikyō, not Echizen, Kunaikyō had thirteen wins, sixteen losses, and twenty-one ties, whereas Echizen had thirteen wins, twenty-seven losses, and ten ties. By comparison, Teika had eleven wins, thirty-one losses, and eight ties; Jakuren had eleven wins, twenty-four losses, and fifteen ties; and Tadayoshi had ten wins, twenty-eight losses, and twelve ties.

23. Ariyoshi, *Shinkokin wakashū no kenkyū: kiban to kōsei*, pp. 92–96. Kubota Jun, *Shinkokin kajin no kenkyū*, p. 835, can do little more than summarize Ariyoshi's findings.

24. Ariyoshi, *Shinkokin wakashū no kenkyū: kiban to kōsei*, p. 96. Ariyoshi is in turn citing the work of Kojima Yoshio. The passage he refers to appears to be Kojima, *Shinkokin wakashū no kenkyū*, pp. 7–8. Unfortunately, Ariyoshi does not specify the page number in the Kojima

choice, part of a desire to continue to patronize non-Mikohidari poets. After all, Go-Toba asked Tadayoshi to be a judge for the *Sengohyakuban uta-awase*, and clearly he had some confidence in him.

In poetry, as in politics, Go-Toba seemed increasingly intent on maintaining a balance among various factions so that no single one would emerge as too powerful. This explains (to the satisfaction of many historians, incidentally) his rehabilitation of the Kujō house to help check the power of Michichika and the Konoe branch of the Fujiwara. The principle applies just as clearly to poetry, where time and again (and we have already seen examples of this in 1200, in both the 100-poem sequences and the contests in the autumn and winter) he brings in new players, revives old ones, and balances their participation. This continues through his sponsorship of *Shinkokinshū* itself, as we shall see and is most dramatically evident in *Sengohyakuban uta-awase*. It is this sense of a need for balance that may have prompted him at the time of *Shinkokinshū* to "help" Tadayoshi, who had the worst score in the *Rōnyaku* contest.

One point that Ariyoshi finds especially significant is that in seven (or as many as nine, depending on the textual line) of the thirty-three *Shinkokinshū* selections from this contest, Masatsune is the sole selector, a rate not equaled in any other source for *Shinkokinshū*.[25] In other words, Masatsune, more than any other compiler, found poems from this contest worthy of inclusion in *Shinkokinshū*, a fact that implies that Masatsune himself recognized how pivotal the event was for his own career as a poet.

Ariyoshi extrapolates from this that since Go-Toba had final say in the *Shinkokinshū* selections and since Masatsune was allowed so many single

---

study, nor a date for the *Meigetsuki* entry that he also cites. But he need not have looked so far for such an idea, since Ienaga states the situation with the *Shinkokinshū* text clearly in *Ienaga nikki*: "After the five selectors had presented their choices, Go-Toba looked each one over very carefully, marking this or that among them as acceptable. He then had Left Konoe Guards Inspector Kiyonori make a clean copy, which he inspected again before finally ordering a third copy" (*IN*, p. 211). The selection committee was down to five members after the death of Jakuren.

25. By comparison, Ietaka and Teika have only three sole selections each; all the rest of the poems were designated by more than one person. Incidentally, Masatsune was especially generous to Jien—five of his sole selections (of Jien's eight selected poems) were of Jien poems. Ariyoshi offers no further commentary, and neither can I. It is a conspicuous statistic, one that can hardly be seen as chance, as Ariyoshi notes (p. 96), but was it friendship? a political debt?

selections, he and Go-Toba must have had similar taste in poetry. I think this is greatly overstating the case. It may simply be that Go-Toba was throwing Masatsune a bone here, supporting him the way he supported Tadayoshi, to counterbalance the dominance of the Mikohidari poets. There is no question, however, that Go-Toba had increasing confidence in Masatsune, who became more and more active in the poetic scene over the next few years and was chosen as one of the *Shinkokinshū* compilers. This contest seems to mark his emergence as an important player.

Another issue regarding subsequent selections for *Shinkokinshū* is that five of the thirty-three poems selected actually *lost* their rounds in this contest. Without knowing who the judge was or why a judgment was made, it is difficult to conclude too much from this other than that it does suggest differences in standards. Since the criteria for contests and for imperial anthologies are by their nature different, one would expect a certain amount of variation. What is a good poem in one environment may be inappropriate in another.[26] Ariyoshi tries to explain this ratio by saying that "issues of rank and status were part of the consideration"; he notes that the losing poet in these five cases was of lower rank than the winning poet.[27] Of course, that analysis is difficult to defend statistically since in order for it to be conclusive, one would have to show that in virtually all cases lower-ranking poets lost to higher-ranking ones, which simply was not the case.[28] If Ariyoshi's premise is untenable—and I believe it is, except for cases involving Go-Toba—then his conclusion that these five exceptions can be explained away by that premise does not stand. I reiterate my contention that the exceptions *are* significant, not so much for this contest in particular but as general evidence

---

26. Huey, *Kyōgoku Tamekane*, pp. 77–79.
27. Ariyoshi, *Shinkokin wakashū no kenkyū: kiban to kōsei*, p. 94.
28. True, two of Masatsune's losing efforts ended up in *Shinkokinshū* (Rounds 192 and 242, which became *SKKS* 652 and 940, respectively). However, so did one of his winning ones. In fact, every possible combination obtained: Masatsune's poem lost and did not end up in *Shinkokinshū* (Rounds 17, 67, and 217), Masatsune tied and did not end up in *Shinkokinshū* (Round 117), Masatsune tied, but his poem *did* end up in *Shinkokinshū* (Round 42, *SKKS* 94), Masatsune won, but his poem did not end up in *Shinkokinshū* (Rounds 92 and 142), and Masatsune won, and his poem ended up in *Shinkokinshū* (Round 167, *SKKS* 610). It is difficult to find a pattern here, let alone one that shows the pre-eminence of a higher-ranking poet in the final standings. For that matter, Masatsune's record against Tadayoshi, who technically was the highest-ranking member of the Left Team, also speaks against the notion of status automatically leading to success in the standings, since Masatsune won seven, lost two, and tied one.

that contest poems and imperial anthology poems followed different standards.

This is further underscored by the fact that the overall success of a given poet in the contest did not necessarily translate into inclusion in *Shinkokinshū*. Go-Toba and Yoshitsune were the big winners in the contest, but none of Go-Toba's poems were selected for *Shinkokinshū* (this is much stronger evidence for how status can skew contest results than Ariyoshi's argument above), whereas Yoshitsune had only four poems chosen for the anthology, only half the number of Jien, even though Yoshitsune had twice as many wins in this contest. And as noted earlier, Masatsune, while only third in the number of total wins in the contest, "won" the *Shinkokinshū* sweepstakes as far as this contest goes, with nine of his poems making their way into that collection.

Kubota draws attention to another important element of the *Rōnyaku* contest.[29] It is the debut in a large public setting for two of Go-Toba's young female protegées, Echizen and Kunaikyō, who in terms of scores fare reasonably well. Of the late-1200 contests, only the *Shōji ninen kugatsu sanjūnichi nijūyoban uta-awase* included women—Sanuki (who was 58) and the mysterious Sagami. The younger generation of women poets, which Ienaga had fretted might never appear, did, and for the next few years they were represented in every major contest and gathering.

In sum, the *Rōnyaku gojisshu uta-awase* was significant for a number of reasons beyond its direct impact on *Shinkokinshū* as a source of poetry. That Michichika and Suetsune—indeed the Rokujō group as a whole—were missing gives a strong hint of the direction in which Go-Toba's poetics were heading.[30] Although he continued to provide the Tsuchimikado/Rokujō group opportunities to compose in public settings, he did not sponsor any exclusive events for them that might be seen as a balance for this one. The names in this contest were to dominate the poetic scene for the next five years; indeed, six of them would be appointed to the Wakadokoro (over half its final membership), and four were to be named *Shinkokinshū* compilers (out of the six on that committee). Another indication of the Retired Em-

---

29. Kubota Jun, *Shinkokin kajin no kenkyū*, p. 835.
30. Ariyoshi (*Shinkokin wakashū no kenkyū: kiban to kōsei*, p. 96) argues that this contest marks Go-Toba's emergence from Michichika's shadow, but it was not the first time the Retired Emperor had omitted Michichika. He was also missing from the *Shōji ninen jūgatsu tsuitachi* contest.

peror's sympathies is his re-appointment in the midst of the preparations for the *Rōnyaku* contest, on the 19th of the Second Month to be exact, of Jien as Chief Abbot of the Tendai sect (*Tendai zasu*) when Abbot Benga died.

Furthermore, the manner in which Go-Toba constructed the contest indicated that he was experimenting with ways to ensure a high level of competition and thus a better product, as it were. The artificial selection process of the late-1200 contests gave way to the "invisible hand" of a mathematical formula that allowed the widest range of styles to meet head on. Ironically, he was promoting competition while trying to bring together various factions. In any case, over the next several years we will see him continue to try new permutations of the contest format, presumably in an attempt to eliminate biases like the one that granted him and Yoshitsune so many victories in this contest or the predilection, say, of a judge from the Rokujō school to award a Rokujō poet the win.

As I have noted several times, the cycle of birth and death seemed to have little effect on Go-Toba's incessant sponsorship of poetic activities, and evidence bears that out. Yet it was not as if he did nothing else. As mentioned above, Ienaga described him as extremely energetic in the pursuit of fun. *Meigetsuki*, too, describes some of the things Go-Toba might do on a day when waka was not the main event. The entry for Kennin 1 (1201)/iii/21 provides an amusing glimpse.[31]

The afternoon began when Go-Toba and a few courtiers, including Teika, moved to the fishing pavilion (*tsuridono*) next to the pond in the garden. There Go-Toba decided to divide the group into two teams of five, one representing Eguchi, the other Kanzaki, two river areas near Osaka Bay where courtesans (and itinerant entertainers, for that matter) had gathered for centuries to lure customers from among the people sailing up and down the river.[32] Go-Toba's men then recited in contest form popular songs

---

31. *Meigetsuki*, 1: 201–2.

32. People sailing down the Katsura and Yodo Rivers from Kyoto to Osaka would pass by these areas—strictly speaking, Eguchi was the place where the Yodo and Kanzaki rivers met—hence they were a suitable place for this sort of activity. Eguchi is famous as the site of a poetic exchange between Saigyō and one of these courtesans (*SKKS* 978–79), an exchange that later inspired the Nō play *Eguchi*, in which that courtesan reveals her true form as the Bodhisattva Fūgen. A similar legend had a courtesan from Kanzaki manifesting as Kannon.

Given the tone of the party Teika describes, however, it seems likely that what the men are comparing are not the Bodhisattvas but the relative charms of courtesans from these two areas. Nevertheless, the religious association with Eguchi and Kanzaki was well established

(*imayō*) representing their respective areas. Afterward they went back indoors. But an hour or so later Go-Toba had some of his men demonstrate their horse-riding skills. This was followed in the evening by dancing by some of the courtiers and then by "professional" *shirabyōshi* (white-suited) dancers, all accompanied by court gossip.[33] All was not politics and waka.

Indeed, the party resumed the following day, the 22nd, when in the afternoon Go-Toba and several of his courtiers met again at the fishing pavilion, this time for games of *go* and *shōgi*. Then some female singers were summoned to perform popular songs.[34] This was followed by more horse riding, after which the party broke up. At this point, Teika turned to a discussion of a request from Go-Toba for some poems; the Retired Emperor had by no means forgotten his devotion to the "high arts."

It appears that Go-Toba was about to try yet another approach to the poetry contest, and this one was to have intriguing results. The outcome, now called the *Shingū senka-awase*, was roughly a week in the making.[35]

---

by this time, even in the *imayō* tradition, so that also may have figured in this impromptu contest. Teika does not say. For a discussion of all these elements as they relate to Eguchi and Kanzaki, see Marra, *Representations of Power*, pp. 88–95. For a more detailed look at these courtesans, how they plied their trade, and their relation to the *imayō* tradition, see Kim, "The Female Entertainment Tradition in Medieval Japan," pp. 205-16, and her section on *asobi* in *Songs to Make the Dust Dance*, pp. 7-13. See also Amino, *Chūsei no hinin to yūjo*, pp. 197-231; and Goodwin, "Shadows of Transgression."

33. *Shirabyōshi* dancers were itinerant entertainers with marginal connections to religious institutions (as was so often the case with entertainers in medieval Japan). They specialized in singing and dancing to *imayō*, wearing men's white robes. Groups like this often performed in front of the nobility, and not just at festivals, although these particular dancers are apparently "left over" from a festival held at Iwashimizu Shrine the day before. Readers of *Tales of the Heike* will remember how Kiyomori loses his head over first one, then another, *shirabyōshi* dancer who had come to perform at his home.

34. Here, Teika called the singers *yūjo* (also read *asobime*), which often was just a generic term for the kind of itinerant female entertainers, like the *shirabyōshi* described above, who would sing and dance for customers and for the aristocracy. Although the *shirabyōshi* specialized in *imayō*, the *yūjo* Teika mentioned here were singing *yōkyoku* (accidentally homophonous with the term used for Nō drama singing, but a much different style of song), a decidedly *zoku* (to use Konishi's terminology) form of entertainment, as indeed was *imayō*.

35. The two accessible printed texts for this are GR 191, 12: 347–353, and *Shinpen kokka taikan*, 5:186, pp. 391–94. There are slight differences between them, notably regarding attributions for two rounds. In the GR version, no poet is identified for Round 16, Left, and Round 20, Right, whereas the *Shinpen kokka taiken* attributes the former to Michitomo and the latter to Echizen. My own deduction, based on the *Meigetsuki* account (specifically, how many poems by which poets were selected for the final contest [Kennin 1/ii/28] and the process of

Ienaga Kaori argues that it was intended as an offering to the gods for their protection of Go-Toba's burgeoning "poetry circle."[36] Sometime toward the end of the Third Month—the first mention in *Meigetsuki* is this entry for the 22nd, although the request seems to have been made a day or two earlier—Go-Toba commissioned from twenty-six poets one poem on each of ten four-character compound topics, for a total of ten poems per poet, 260 poems in all. Go-Toba expected them to be submitted to him by the 28th. The twenty-six poets comprised a wide range, including representatives from the Mikohidari and Rokujō schools, as well as members of the powerful patron houses, Kujō and Tsuchimikado.[37]

The details of the next stage of the process come from *Meigetsuki*, the entry for Kennin 1/iii/28.[38] On the 28th, Go-Toba then brought together ten of these poets—presumably the most important ones—and divided them

---

elimination, is that the poet for Round 16, Left, must have been Michichika, not Michitomo, and my following discussion makes that assumption.

36. Ienaga, "Kennin gannen no Go-Toba In kadan," pp. 58–61.

37. The poets were Left: Yoshitsune, Michichika, Fujiwara Kintsugu (1175–1227), Shakua (Shunzei), Echizen, Takanobu, Michitomo, Ariie, Yasusue, Ietaka, Jakuren, Chōmei, Sueyasu; and Right: Go-Toba, Jien, Tadayoshi, Kanemune, Kintsune, Norimitsu, Kunaikyō, Sanuki, Tango, Teika, Masatsune, Tomochika, and Ienaga.

The topics when taken together represented the major groupings of Seasonal, Love, and Miscellaneous poems that characterize virtually every collection of waka. Because complex, compound topics like these became something of a feature of poetic practice in this age, it is worthwhile to list the ten here. The topics, followed in parentheses by the category they represent, were (I have tried to follow the original syntax, hence a certain awkwardness, and the words in caps are literal renderings of each of the four characters): through Breaks in the Mist, Trees in the Distance (Spring); During a Journey, Seeing Flowers (Spring); After Rain, a Cuckoo Sings (Summer); Beneath the Pine Tree, enjoying the Cool of Evening (Summer); at a Mountain Hut, the Autumn Moon (Autumn); Over the Lake, Evening Fog rises (Autumn); Storm winds Blow, withering Plants with their Chill (Winter); Snow Resembling White Clouds (Winter); Lovers Meet Once, then Do Not Meet Again (Love—the Japanese is read *aute awanu koi* [see the judgment for Round 36], literally "love which meets then meets not," which is virtually impossible to render into comprehensible English without some syntactic shuffling, but which means, in the context of waka, lovers who got a chance to meet once but have been prevented from meeting again, either due to circumstances, or more often, the man's fickleness. It is thus a "Waiting Woman" topic); and Felicitations as Expressed by Reference to the Gods (Miscellaneous). Again, for the last topic, I have had to change the syntax a bit, from its original *Jingi ni yosuru iwai*, literally, "Felicitations using Gods as the poetic vehicle or central image."

38. Ariyoshi, *Shinkokin wakashū no kenkyū: kiban to kōsei*, pp. 97–100, provides a synopsis of Teika's various comments about this event, but he leaves a few details out. My account, although indebted to his outline, seeks to fill in the gaps.

into Left and Right "work groups." Each work group then began sifting through the poems of its team. (Apparently, Go-Toba had already divided the twenty-six poets into two teams beforehand and sorted the poems accordingly. Aside from Go-Toba himself, who headed both work groups, the work groups were subsets of these teams, that is, the Left work group looked only at poems from the Left team.) The Left group consisted of Go-Toba, Yoshitsune, Michichika, Jakuren, and Ietaka, and the Right group was made up of Go-Toba, Jien, Norimitsu, Teika, and Masatsune. With the exception of Michichika on the Left and Masatsune on the Right (again, not counting Go-Toba himself), this was a predominantly Mikohidari/Kujō gathering.

For their first run-through, since Go-Toba had removed all the names from the poems, they were being evaluated "blind"; that is, the evaluators did not know whose poems were whose. (We know from the *Meigetsuki* entry for the 27th that Teika had seen Jakuren's poems, and vice versa, before they were submitted, and they would have recognized each other's entries, but Go-Toba put them on separate teams, and at this stage of the proceedings it would not have mattered.) According to Teika, in the Right work group, the poems were read through and the group made initial selections, after which they were read through again. Only those poems that made it through the second reading passed on to the next stage. There were thirty-eight of them. These thirty-eight were read through again, only this time the poet's name was given. It was discovered that there was a disproportionately large number of poems from Go-Toba (*gyosei hanahada ōshi*), the rest being unequally distributed among the remaining poets. In fact, no poems by Tadayoshi and Kanemune had been selected, and "His Majesty decreed, 'There should be (at least) one poem from each poet, and you may eliminate some of mine since it does not look right for me to have so many.'"[39] After some discussion, they narrowed the number of poems to thirty-six. Although poems in each of the ten topics were selected, no effort was made to cover the topics systematically. Since the Left team followed similar procedures, in the final "contest" matchups, the poems in any given round did not necessarily share the same topic.

Go-Toba, Jien, and Teika led the Right team in terms of numbers of poems selected for the final contest (seven, six, and five poems, respectively). Although Teika does not describe the deliberations of the Left team (they occurred in another part of the building), we can deduce the results based on

---

39. *Meigetsuki*, Kennin 1 (1201)/iii/28, 1: 204.

the final contest text. Yoshitsune and Michichika had the most poems selected, with seven each, followed by Michitomo and Jakuren with four each. So if Go-Toba had hoped the "blind" format would lessen the influence of social status on the final outcome, he was wrong. The politically powerful were overwhelmingly favored going into the second phase of the event, the contest itself. Teika was the only modestly ranked exception, and if we consider his showings in contests over the previous year or so, this was a big step forward for him, perhaps the earliest indication that his skills were beginning to overshadow his low rank and propensity to rub people the wrong way.

For the contest itself, Teika again provided the details, in his *Meigetsuki* entry for Kennin 1 (1201)/iii/29. He even made a little drawing of the seating arrangement.[40] Shunzei was asked to judge the contest, and Teika was chosen to write down the discussions (*hyōjō*), dissenting opinions (*nanchin*), and judgment for each poem, although as far as the discussions went, he admitted: "I only wrote down in outline what the Left and Right teams had to say; I did not go into the details."[41] The poems were read aloud by the two readers (Ietaka for the Left and Masatsune for the Right) and then discussed and judged before the names of the poets were revealed to the assembly. (Since the members of each team's working group presumably recognized the authors of their team's selections, the procedure was not entirely blind.) The formality with which, according to Teika's description, the proceedings broke up, suggests that this was seen as quite a serious event.

Teika expressed mixed feelings about his own performance. He noted that five of his ten poems made the first cut, and was proud, as well as

---

40. From the drawing and his remarks in the diary, it does not seem that every one of the original poets was present at this final reading. The only ones mentioned specifically are Go-Toba, Teika himself, Shunzei, Masatsune, Ietaka, Jien, Yoshitsune, Michichika, Jakuren, Norimitsu, Kintsune, and Michitomo—in other words, the work groups plus Shunzei, Kintsune, and Michitomo. Since *Meigetsuki*, like most diaries of its type, tends to be exhaustive when listing participants in an event of this nature (recall Teika's description of the *Shōji ninen kugatsu sanjūnichi nijūyoban uta-awase* in the preceding chapter), I am inclined to think that the remainder of the twenty-six poets simply were not present, although I suspect that one or two of the ladies-in-waiting may have been there. (Incidentally, it is possible that the drawing was added by a later copyist, based on what the text describes.)

41. *Meigetsuki*, 1: 204. In truth, what Teika did choose to record is in most cases rather terse and not especially useful for evaluating the standards applied. *Hyōjō* (or *hyōtei*) is the term usually used to describe the process of group discussion and judgment that occurs in many poetry contests, especially, although not exclusively, those that are *shūgihan* ("group judged").

moved, that Go-Toba praised two of his poems specifically and stated that no poems could better them. (These were the poems for Round 17 and 33, both against Michichika.) But he noted with some bitterness that the judge (his own father, Shunzei) differed with the Retired Emperor over one of the poems and awarded the Win to Michichika.[42] In what amounts to a parenthetical aside, he says in the diary: "Despite the fact that His Majesty was of the opinion that my poem should win, the judge awarded the Win to the Left, so I ended up losing. The Left poem was by the Palace Minister [Michichika], so there was nothing one could do." Although this was supposedly a "blind" judgment, made without Shunzei knowing who the respective poets were, the implication is very clear that Shunzei awarded the judgment on the basis of rank, although what Teika does not mention is that his Round 17 entry—the other poem that Go-Toba had singled out for praise—was given a Win over the same Michichika.[43] So it was, in fact, a split decision. Overall, Teika won two, lost two, and tied one.

But the final Win/Loss records did, in truth, generally favor those of higher rank.[44] Of course, raw scores tell only part of the story. It could make a difference—as suggested in Teika's situation above—who one's opponent was. Even if the contest itself was "blind," someone made the initial matchups after the two work groups had completed their selections on the 28th. Teika does not give us this information in his diary. It is possible that the matchups were random, although Go-Toba's appearance in the first round, customary for the sponsor, argues against that. On the other hand, the rounds, even within the same topic, do not appear to have been arranged in

---

42. This was Round 33, and Teika's reduction of the discussion and judgment in the text of the contest (not in the diary) is pithy indeed: "The judge said, 'Left and Right have spoken eloquently, but still the Left poem is the better one'" (*Hanja iu, sau yoroshiku kikoyuredo, nao hidari wa masaru narubeshi*. It could also be interpreted as "The judge said, 'Both Left and Right poems sound nice"; GR 191, 12: 352). Although Shunzei's remarks might be taken as lukewarm, a few years later, all five of the surviving *Shinkokinshū* selection committee, including Teika, chose Michichika's poem for inclusion in *Shinkokinshū*. And despite Go-Toba's glowing words of praise, Teika's poem does not appear in *Shinkokinshū*.

43. The judgment here is even more laconic than the one quoted above: "The judge said, 'I declare Right the Winner'" (GR 191, 12: 350).

44. Go-Toba won five and tied two; Yoshitsune won four, lost one, and tied two; and Jien won three, lost one, and tied two. Michichika, however, did not fare so well. He won two, lost two, and tied three. His son Michitomo actually compiled better statistics, with three Wins and one Loss. The only other poet with at least four poems in the final contest, Jakuren, ended with three Ties and one Loss.

rank order, which was another standard approach. Yet what points most strongly to some sort of guiding hand is that some rounds match poems on different topics even when it would have been numerically possible to match poems of the same topic from each team. As Teika had implied in his diary, because the two teams had made their selections independently of each other, the final results did not balance in terms of topic. So there were bound to be some rounds that matched poems on different topics. But this happened more than was necessary from a mathematical point of view, an indication that the poems were matched with some other purpose in mind. Again, just what this purpose might be is beyond the scope of this book, although a close study of topics, vocabulary, and so on might yield some interesting evidence.

Another issue to consider is which poems from this event ended up in *Shinkokinshū*. A total of nine were selected from this contest; three of these had tied their round, but none had lost.[45] Two of the Tie cases are contained in a single round, Round 32, in which, according to the written judgment, both participants and judge agreed that Jakuren and Tango had submitted equally superb poems. The other Tie case involves one of Kintsune's two *Shinkokinshū* poems, #72. It is his entry for Round 2, against Yoshitsune. The discussion and final judgment indicate that a Tie was awarded because both poems contained weak points, rather than because they were equally good. This raises the question of why such a poem would be selected for an imperial anthology. Ariyoshi rationalizes that it was because the particular section of *Shinkokinshū* in which it appears needed a "green willow" poem with the kind of vocabulary Kintsune uses here. The argument fails simply because Ariyoshi does not prove that this poem by Kintsune is the only possible one the compilers could have found to fill that position, but at least he entertains the notion that selection for an imperial anthology might involve criteria other than the sheer intrinsic worth of a poem, a position that I argue elsewhere in this study and one that becomes even more manifest in the last stages of the *Shinkokinshū* compilation, as discussed in later chapters. The notion is also implicit and explicit in the "association and progression argument" put forward by Konishi Jin'ichi, who posits a narrative-like structure for *Shinkokinshū* and other collections, something that would explain

---

45. Kintsune had two chosen, and Yoshitsune, Michichika, Michitomo, Jakuren, Sanuki, Tango, and Masatsune had one each.

why a "green willow poem" (whether or not it was Kintsune's) was needed at a particular point in the collection.[46]

There are also a few rounds (14, 29, and 31) in which the winning poems, even if chosen for positive reasons (rather than because the opposing poem had this or that fault), were not later included in *Shinkokinshū*.[47] Teika's entry in Round 17, which so impressed Go-Toba, might be considered one such example. Ariyoshi feels compelled to explain why poems that Go-Toba praised so highly were not selected for *Shinkokinshū*.[48] I am not sure this needs to be seen as such a contradiction. First, Go-Toba was still very young and, compared with many of the others in events like this, inexperienced in poetry activities. It is not surprising that his tastes would not always match those of, say, Shunzei. And that he did not, until the Oki-bon at least, insist

---

46. Ariyoshi, *Shinkokin wakashū no kenkyū: kiban to kōsei*, pp. 103–5. Ariyoshi's argument rests in part on the fact that this is one poem for whom no selectors' names are given. Such poems are generally thought to have been added (mostly by Go-Toba, it is assumed) after the time of the initial selection, which is believed to have been completed around the Fourth Month of 1203, and before the Ienaga copy of 1216 on which most modern texts of *Shinkokinshū* are based. Many of these and later interim changes are taken to be editorial and aimed at achieving the "progression and association" for which the collection is now so famous. See Appendix F, pp. 437–41, for a time line of the process by which *Shinkokinshū* was compiled.

For views on standards for inclusion in imperial anthologies, see Huey, *Kyōgoku Tamekane*, pp. 77–79. For the "association and progression" theory, see Konishi, "Association and Progression"; or Brower and Miner's restatement in *Japanese Court Poetry*, pp. 319–29.

Joshua Mostow (*Pictures of the Heart*, pp. 48–51) raises a tentative challenge to the notion of association and progression or at least to the idea that there were explicit rules consciously applied when creating (or reading) sequences. Although his point is well-taken (and overdue), perhaps the inclusion of Kintsune's mediocre poem (by the standards of the *Shingū* contest) in *Shinkokinshū* in a context where it clearly does match the flow of the poems around it comes close to being the kind of "historical evidence to suggest that these techniques were explicitly recognized" (p. 51) that Mostow claims is *lacking*. (*Shinkokinshū* poems 68 through 75 all deal with willows. Of the poems surrounding Kintsune's, poem 70 features Yoshino River / old willows / and springtime air; poem 71 features storm winds / riverbank / willows / weaving / and waves; Kintsune's poem 72 mentions river rapids / the Mutsuda Pool [on the Yoshino River] / willows / misting spring; poem 73 features spring breezes / gaps in the mist / willow branches, abandoning the river location; while poem 74 mentions gaps in clouds / spring willows / Mt. Katsuragi / and spring breezes.)

47. In Round 14, both sides agreed that Tango's Right poem was superior to Kintsugu's Left entry, and Shunzei concurred. In Round 31, again Shunzei and both teams agreed that Jien's poem on the Right was better than Chōmei's. In Round 29, the group overrode Shunzei's modesty and insisted he award his own Left poem the Win over Kunaikyō's effort.

48. Ariyoshi, *Shinkokin wakashū no kenkyū: kiban to kōsei*, pp. 100, 105–7.

on the imperial prerogative over the contents of Shinkokinshū is to his credit and speaks to his genuine desire to forge an artistic consensus. Much is made of his hand in editing Shinkokinshū, but given the careful groundwork he laid over several years—indeed, this is the very subject of this book—I do not believe he tried to make the project purely a matter of personal whim.

One may agree with Ariyoshi's overall assessment that because of overlap between the major participants in this contest and the Wakadokoro membership as well as the Shinkokinshū selection committee, this contest is important for understanding the Shinkokinshū aesthetic. But one need not gloss over—as I feel Ariyoshi does—the anomalies in trying to prove the relationship between these two poetic events. It is enough to see Shingū senka-awase, like Rōnyaku gojisshu uta-awase before it, as another step toward defining and refining some of the standards that would eventually apply to Shinkokinshū selection. And for that the Shingū contest is in some ways more useful than the earlier one, since it includes the judgments and at least a taste of the arguments. It is also clear that the center of poetic activities had shifted away from Yoshitsune and Michichika and toward Go-Toba. Evidence of that came as early as the Shodo hyakushu of the previous year, when Go-Toba stepped in and took charge of the project, even though it had initially been proposed by Michichika and Suetsune. But with this contest Go-Toba was asserting ever firmer control.

Another piece of evidence comes from the month after the Shingū senka-awase. As mentioned above, for several years, Michichika had been holding monthly eigu contests, ostensibly in honor of Hitomaro. His last one was on Kennin 1 (1201)/iii/16, just before the Shingū senka-awase. Called, among other designations, Kennin gannen sangatsu jūrokunichi eigu uta-awase (Eigu Poetry Contest on the 16th Day, Third Month, First Year of Kennin), it involved six topics, sixty rounds, and twenty poets, including Go-Toba, Shunzei, Jien, Teika, Jakuren, Ietaka, Takanobu, Tomochika, Norimistu, Kunaikyō, and Echizen.[49] Michichika seemed able to accept a strong Mikohidari presence, although, significantly, Yoshitsune was not there.[50] Accord-

---

49. A text can be found in Shinpen kokka taikan, 5:185, pp. 389–91. See also Taniyama, Shinkokin jidai no uta-awase to kadan, pp. 353–55, 403–19.

50. There is one pseudonymous poet whose identity has been lost to history. S/he is only represented in the extant text as "Shinsan," which might be short for "new Sangi," that is, "recently appointed Consultant." Whoever it was emerged with an excellent record (four Wins, against Teika, Ariie, Ietaka, and Jakuren; one Loss, against Shunzei; and one unmarked round, against Jien). Two notable absences were Yoshitsune, of course, and Masatsune, either

ing to Teika in *Meigetsuki*, the poets used pseudonyms, and the poems were discussed and apparently judged by the group (*shūgihan*), although extant texts only show Win or Tie marks.[51] Teika could not resist criticizing slips in precedent and decorum that he saw in the procedures. (Recall that Yoshitsune also did this when he described court events to Kanezane after the latter had been relieved of his duties.) Although two poems from this contest were later selected for *Shinkokinshū*, and it does contain interesting work, it is most significant for our purposes in that it is the last time Michichika sponsored an *eigu* event (although ironically it is the oldest extant text of such an event from this period).

Perhaps Go-Toba was annoyed by the lingering partisanship implicit in Yoshitsune's absence (if, indeed, Yoshitsune was not there), or perhaps he felt that such an event should become a public one (Teika comments that although Michichika's last contest had been a "private affair," it was conducted as if it were in the palace).[52] In any case, in the following month, the Retired Emperor appropriated sponsorship of the *eigu* contests, leaving the custom itself intact, and in so doing he took yet another step toward consolidating poetic activities under his control. On iv/30, he moved the location of the *eigu* event to his Toba palace, hosting twenty-two poets (whose identities were hidden during the judging) in thirty-three rounds, which were judged by the group. Since the arrangements themselves, then, were pretty much the same

---

of whom might have compiled such a record. It is possible, then, that Yoshitsune was actually there, although scholars have not established who this poet actually was. Another possibility is Fujiwara Kintsune, who was active in contests during this period, and who had just recently been appointed Consultant, according to the *Kugyō bunin*. His name is not otherwise listed as a participant in this contest, but with ten poems in *Shinkokinshū*, he was a respected poet who could have scored well in a contest like this. Taniyama (*Shinkokin jidai no uta-awase to kadan*, p. 355) thinks it might have been Shunzei no Musume, although he gives no reason. It is true that at a New Year's gathering the following year (before the new appointments had come out), her husband, Michitomo, is listed as a "new Sangi." So if she is using her husband's title as a kind of nickname—not an unthinkable occurrence—then Shinsan could be Shunzei no Musume, who would also be capable of winning so many rounds. If it was Shunzei no Musume, this contest would have marked her debut.

51. Kennin 1 (1201)/iii/16, 1: 200–201. In fact this is the first entry after the nearly three-month gap mentioned above.

52. Ibid. I do not believe Teika's remark is meant as a criticism, a suggestion that Michichika was putting on airs the way a Kiyomori might have done. I see it as simply an observation; after all, since Go-Toba was present in a formal capacity (*rinkō* is the term Teika uses), it was appropriate to treat the occasion with proper ceremony, which is why Teika finds fault elsewhere in the proceedings.

as Michichika had followed the month before (although Yoshitsune was included in this one), this event was not one in which Go-Toba was experimenting. Called *Kennin gannen shigatsu sanjūnichi Tobadono eigu uta-awase* (Eigu Poetry Contest at the Toba Palace on the 30th Day, Fourth Month, First Year of Kennin), it need not detain us here.[53] Its importance is that it represents another step in Go-Toba's effort to move the center of cultural activity, and as we will see below, it is just an interim step, for he was about to create a new, "permanent" home for *eigu* contests and other poetic activities.

Some time in the Sixth Month—Teika first mentions it in his entry for the 6th day[54]—before establishing that new center, Go-Toba called for a third round of 100-poem sequences, which has come to be called the *Go-Toba-in daisando hyakushu* (Retired Emperor Go-Toba's Third Set of 100-Poem Sequences). It is a rather misleading designation, since it implies a relationship with the two sets of 100-poem sequences solicited the previous year. In fact, presumably that title—a convention used by literary historians apparently from quite early on[55] and not something affixed to the original poem sequences—misled scholars for centuries, because the important relationship of these poem sequences is not with the sequences of Shōji 2, but with the *Sengohyakuban uta-awase* of the following year or so. It was not until 1934 that the connection between the latter two was established, definitively, by Ishida Yoshisada.[56] Thus, the details of this event will be discussed in re-

---

53. See *Shinpen kokka taikan*, 5:187, pp. 394–95, for a text. The participants were Go-Toba, Tadayoshi, Yoshitsune, Ietaka, Michitomo, Masatsune, Kojijū, Moromitsu (now using his priestly name of Shōren), Ariie, Yasusue, Kunaikyō, Teika, Michichika, Shunzei, Kintsugu, Echizen, Takanobu, Kanemune, Jien, Jakuren, Tomochika, and Ienaga. See also Taniyama, *Shinkokin jidai no uta-awase to kadan*, pp. 355–56, 419–27.

54. *Meigetsuki shōshutsu*, Kennin 1/vi/6; ZGR 470, 17.1: 250.

55. However, in Yoshitsune's house collection, *Akishino gesseishū*, the 100 poems he submitted at this time are designated as his second (*dainido*) set, rather than the third, because for him it was only the second time, the *Shodo hyakushu* being the first (see Aoki, *Fujiwara Yoshitsune senkashū to son kenkyū*, p. 21). This further underscores the point that any designation for the sequences Go-Toba requested at this time is a convention. From the standpoint of literary history, the true import of this third set of 100 poems is not revealed until the results appear in contest form as *Sengohyakuban uta-awase*.

56. The essay is reproduced in a collection of Ishida's writings: *Shinkokin sekai to chūsei bungaku*, 1: 303–7. According to this book (p. 504), the original appeared in a journal known as *Mizugame*, 1934, no. 12. Other elements of Ishida's argument are discussed below. I am not entirely sure that no one had seen the connection before Ishida. In the ZGR text of *Meigetsuki shōshutsu* (ZGR 470, 17.1: 250), a marginal note on Teika's Kennin 1/vi/6 entry about the 100-poem sequence clearly relates it to the *Sengohyakuban uta-awase*. It is hard to tell whether the

lation to the *Sengohyakuban uta-awase*. It is introduced now only to illustrate the quickening pace of Go-Toba's preparations for *Shinkokinshū*.

It is in the Seventh Month that he made his most dramatic move to date by re-establishing the Wakadokoro (Bureau of Japanese Poetry), a quasi-government agency that had lain dormant since the mid-900s, when it had been established by Emperor Murakami as the locus for selecting poems for the second imperial anthology, *Gosenshū* (951). Indeed, because of the Wakadokoro's earlier associations, Go-Toba was making it clear (if it was not so already) simply by virtue of reviving this office that he intended eventually to sponsor an imperial anthology himself. In Murakami's time, five poets had been appointed to the Wakadokoro, and offices had been set up in the so-called Pear Jar Room (the Nashitsubo, nicknamed for the potted pear tree that stood in its garden, but actually an annex in the inner Imperial Palace grounds more formally known as the Shōyōsha). This in turn became a nickname for the group.[57] For his part, Go-Toba initially called on a larger number of poets.

There are several contemporary accounts of Go-Toba's commission, some of which are examined below. But the outline is simple. On Kennin 1 (1201)/vii/27, Go-Toba issued an edict establishing the Wakadokoro in an annex of his Nijō Palace and appointing eleven members (*yoriudo*) to serve there. The eleven—and by now their names should be familiar—were Yoshitsune, Michichika, Jien, Shunzei, Michitomo, Ariie, Teika, Ietaka, Masatsune, Tomochika, and Jakuren.[58] Deaths and replacements changed

---

note is Ton'a's, or the editor of *Zokugunsho ruijū*. Even if the latter, the ZGR came out first in Meiji 45, and the edition I refer to was published in 1931, a few years before Ishida's article.

This event also illustrates why Mass (*Kamakura Bakufu*, pp. 225-26) warns against relying too blindly on *Dai Nihon shiryō* or *Shiryō sōran*. The latter, clearly misinterpreting the evidence it cites from *Meigetsuki*, *Ienaga nikki*, and so on, flatly states that "the *Sengohyakuban uta-awase* took place at the Nijō Palace sometime during the Sixth Month" (4: 174).

57. The five, known as the "Nashitsubo no Gonin" (the "Pear Jar Five"), were Kiyowara Motosuke (908-90), Ōnakatomi Yoshinobu (921-91), Minamoto Shitagō (911-83), Ki no Tokibumi (fl. 951-77), and Sakanoue no Mochiki (d. 980).

58. The office itself was located in an annex called the Hiro Gosho. As Gotō Shigeo notes (*Shinkokin wakashū no kisōteki kenkyū*, pp. 26-27), the Nijō palace was destroyed by fire in 1201, and the Wakadokoro was moved to Go-Toba's temporary palace at Kyōgoku for a time. But it was back in its newly rebuilt Nijō quarters by the end of 1203. Here and elsewhere in his discussion of the Wakadokoro and the identity of its members, Gotō relies heavily (as do Ishida and Satsukawa indirectly when they cite, in *IN*, p. 57, this passage from Gotō) on Kojima's *Shinkokin wakashū no kenkyū, zokuhen*, pp. 6-10.

this a bit over the next few years. Takanobu (a Mikohidari partisan), Chōmei (an independent), and Fujiwara Hideyoshi (1184–1240)[59] eventually replaced Jakuren, Shunzei, and Michichika.[60]

On the 5th of the following month, according to *Meigetsuki*, Minamoto Ienaga was chosen by the group to serve as Chief Recorder (*kaikō*).[61] Although at least half the Wakadokoro members were either Mikohidari poets (Shunzei, Teika, Ietaka, and Jakuren) or members of their patron family, the Kujō (Yoshitsune and Jien), Go-Toba clearly had an eye to providing some balance. Representing the competing patron house, Tsuchimikado, were Michichika and Michitomo. Masatsune would be considered an independent, and Ariie, by birth and training a Rokujō, from early on seems to have been closer to the Mikohidari group. Tomochika was something of a cipher in terms of poetic allegiance, although his father, Moromitsu, was closely aligned with the Rokujō school.

Perhaps not surprisingly, others interpret this lineup differently. What I have characterized as an "eye to providing some balance," Gotō Shigeo, for example, argues is evidence that "Mikohidari influence was overwhelming."[62]

---

59. Our extant text of *Ienaga nikki* gives his name in *kana* as Hideyoshi, the reading also used by Kojima, Minemura, and others in their editions of *Shinkokinshū*; I am following this reading, even though Ariyoshi, *WBJ*, prefers Hidetō. Hideyoshi is more commonly known to history by his priestly name of Nyogan, which he acquired upon taking the tonsure after the Jōkyū Disturbance. He was originally one of Michichika's retainers but entered Go-Toba's service when he was sixteen.

60. There has been controversy in the past as to the exact membership of the Wakadokoro, since there is some discrepancy among the sources (see the citation from Ienaga's memoirs below for the most obvious one). Gotō Shigeo (*Shinkokin wakashū no kisōteki kenkyū*, pp. 31–34) reviews the issues and argues for a final list of names, which I have followed (again, much of Gotō's argument is derived from Kojima, *Shinkokin wakashū no kenkyū, zokuhen*, pp. 9–10.)

61. *Meigetsuki*, Kennin 1 (1201)/viii/5, 1: 207. If *Ienaga nikki* is any indication, they may have made a poor choice if recordkeeping was their goal. As fascinating as the document is, it contains numerous errors, and what is worse, time and again Ienaga remarked in describing some poetry event or important occasion things like, "I know I was supposed to write the poems down, but I forgot." It is an endearing stance, perhaps, but for record-conscious waka poets, it must have been rather frustrating. On the other hand, *Ienaga nikki* is, as I stated earlier, a set of memoirs rather than a true journal (even though at times he speaks in the present tense, or uses terms like "this year" or "last year," which suggest that he was working from a journal in writing the memoirs). Perhaps he kept meticulous formal records that simply got lost over time.

62. Gotō Shigeo, *Shinkokin wakashū no kisōteki kenkyū*, p. 38.

It is true that there is no full-fledged Rokujō representation, but then, there were not that many full-fledged Rokujō poets left. At this time, the most important Rokujō poets would probably be Tadayoshi, Yasusue, Kanemune, Kojijū (a lady-in-waiting who is just beginning to come into her own as a poet at this time), Suetsune, and Kenshō. The first four, especially Tadayoshi, appear in many of the events of this period, although it is certainly significant that Suetsune and Kenshō, the most senior members, seem to have been completely ignored. Suetsune had not been heard from since the *Shodo hyakushu* of the year before, when he had tried to block Teika's participation. And Kenshō was even less in evidence. Both of them had reputations for being disputatious, and one might be tempted to argue that Go-Toba was leaving them out of things because of that, but since Jakuren and certainly Teika, even Shunzei, had all squared off against their opposition more than once, it seems highly unlikely that a confrontational personality alone could have been the disqualifying factor here. It does seem safe to say that Go-Toba had pretty much written off the conservative wing, if you will, of the Rokujō school.

But that did not spell total victory for Mikohidari poetics. The scene had evolved to the point that it could no longer be seen as a simple dichotomy, Mikohidari versus Rokujō. Go-Toba could easily have followed precedent and appointed only five people to the Wakadokoro, and given the depth of Mikohidari/Kujō talent, he need not have included anyone else at all. Yoshitsune, Shunzei, Teika, Jakuren, and Ietaka (not to mention Jien or Takanobu, who was appointed later) would have given him an outstanding talent pool. It is the fact that he expanded the number and filled the extra positions with non-Mikohidari (which is not to say necessarily anti-Mikohidari) poets that leads me to characterize his actions as an attempt to provide balance. In other words, rather than saying "half the members were Mikohidari poets," I am pointing out that half the members were not. I believe the pattern that Go-Toba followed, a pattern that first began with the *Shodo hyakushu* and continued through the *Shinkokinshū* selection and subsequent revision process (although most dramatically demonstrated, perhaps, in *Sengohyakuban uta-awase*), is one of inclusion. Even though *Shinkokinshū* may have favored the new over the old, the innovative over the conservative, it was not necessarily a Mikohidari document, as can be seen by comparing it with Shunzei's *Senzaishū*, which preceded it, and Teika's *Shinchokusenshū*, which followed it.[63] And this

---

63. This also explains why, as mentioned earlier, the mainstream Nijō branch of the Mikohidari house omitted *Shinkokinshū* from its "New Sandaishū" canon a century later.

is true because Go-Toba strove for balance, not a balance so much of new and old so much as this new and that new.

Teika first mentioned the new Wakadokoro on vii/26 when he received a letter from one Nagafusa,[64] who told him that Go-Toba planned to inaugurate the Wakadokoro on the following day. The letter also informed him that he was to be one of the *yoriudo* and was to act as Reader for the poetry party to celebrate the event. "I must say it was an unexpected honor for me to be given such an opportunity at this time," Teika wrote. (The same entry lists the names of the eleven *yoriudo*, according to the rumors Teika had heard.)[65]

At poetry parties and contests, the poets would place their poems on a stand near the front of the assembly. The Recorder (*dokushi*) would pick them up one by one, check them, and then hand them to the Reader (*kōji*), whose job it was to chant them formally for the gathering. The *dokushi* was expected to correct any mistakes the *kōji* might make in reading. The Reader's position was generally reserved for someone thought to have a broad scholarly knowledge of waka. Voiced and unvoiced consonants were not marked in the script of the day, and a knowledgeable Reader was expected to recognize the appropriate distinctions based on context and his grasp of traditional waka diction.[66] So Teika's honor was twofold: he was both a *yoriudo* and the Reader at the first Wakadokoro event. The phrase "at this time" can be better understood by recalling that just a little more than a year earlier Michichika and Suetsune, on the occasion of the *Shodo hyakushu*, had argued that Teika's understanding of waka traditions was too shallow for him to take part in the sequences. Now Retired Emperor Go-Toba was publicly expressing his opinion to the contrary.

The next day, Teika met Yoshitsune at the latter's residence, and the two proceeded to the Nijō Palace, "when it was dark enough to need torches" (a

---

64. He is only referred to by title—Middle Controller of the Right (*u no chūben*)—in the diary. In the *Meigetsuki shōshutsu* text, which except for some marginal notes is identical to the main *Meigetsuki* text for this entry, Ton'a (or the editors of ZGR—it is not always clear who is responsible for the marginalia in that series) tentatively identified him as Nagakane, but I am following Kubota Jun (*Shinkokin kajin no kenkyū*, p. 890) who says he is Nagafusa. In either case, he is a minor figure.

65. *Meigetsuki*, Kennin 1/vii/26, 1: 206.

66. Brower and Miner (*Japanese Court Poetry*, pp. 250–52) describe, with as much tongue in cheek as they can manage, the consequences that ensue when the scholar/pedant Fujiwara Mototoshi (1060–1142) misinterprets *tatsu* (dragon) as *tazu* (crane) at one contest. In traditional orthography, both words were written the same way.

standard expression for nightfall). Teika described the gathering in some detail, but his stilted language does not make for gripping reading, and I turn once again to Ienaga's version of the events:

In this the first year of Kennin, the Wakadokoro was initiated. To house it, the Hiro Gosho annex of the Nijō had been rebuilt. Recessed floor boards were put down for the width of two *ken* to mark off the area where the upper-ranking nobles would sit. Sheet board was laid down for those of lower rank. And appointed as *yoriudo* were:[67]

The Chancellor and Minister of the Left[68]
The Palace Minister, Michi[69]
Lord Ariie
Lord Michitomo
Ietaka
Lord Teika
Tomochika
Masatsune
Newly ordained Monk Jakuren
Newly ordained Monk Shakua[70]

Ienaga lists only ten names here and omits Jien, whose name appears on Teika's list of people he had heard would be named. This has kept scholars thrashing about for centuries since, as Kojima, Gotō, and Ishida and Satsu-

---

67. Since the following list has been an important element in the debate over just who the appointees were, I am giving it as Ienaga's text gives it; some members identified by title only, some by title and name, and some by name only. Where needed, I have supplied further information in the notes.

68. *Sesshō sadaijin* is what Ienaga says. This almost certainly refers to Yoshitsune, although he did not actually become *sesshō* until the following year. The *sesshō* at the time the Wakadokoro was established was Motomichi, who had no name at all as a poet. Still, this is one of the discrepancies that has caused confusion over the years. I suspect part of the problem was that Ienaga was writing *memoirs* (thus he used an anachronistic title for Yoshitsune), but the traditional tendency in Japan has been to read anything called a *nikki* as if it were a factual, contemporary *journal*. Thus some scholars assumed the title was contemporary with the date of the event Ienaga was depicting rather than contemporary with the date when he wrote the account.

69. Minamoto *Michichika*.

70. Shakua was Shunzei's priestly name and is the designation under which he appears in most of the events in this period, although for convenience I generally call him Shunzei, except in situations like this one. What I have translated "newly ordained Monk" is *shami*, though both Jakuren and Shunzei had in fact taken the tonsure more than two decades earlier.

kawa all note, Ienaga was, after all, the Chief Recorder for the Wakadokoro and was unlikely to make a mistake about such things. Yet Ienaga's memoirs are full of gaps like this precisely because they are memoirs, and scholars now more or less agree with the conclusion reached by Kojima that Teika's list is the correct one, and Jien was, in fact, one of the original Wakadokoro appointees.[71] But to continue with Ienaga's account:

When I was made Chief Recorder, this is the poem I offered at the first meeting I attended:

Mosiogusa	The store of briny seaweed
kaku tomo tukizi	Gathered for salt is inexhaustible;
kimi ga yo no	So, too, the poems I gather—
kazu ni yomioku	Composed in numbers, like waves on
Waka no uranami	Poetry Bay
	As great as the years of His Majesty's reign.[72]

Properly clad in formal court robes, I wrote and presented this poem to His Majesty in the prescribed manner when I arrived at the Wakadokoro.

Initially, these [the above-listed] were the appointees. But later Lord Takanobu and the lower-ranking gentlemen Kamo no Chōmei and Fujiwara Hideyoshi were also designated to serve.

Some people suggested that there were two or three others who should be appointed as well, and so Yoshitsune and Shunzei were asked by His Majesty what they thought. Although they agreed that all the names that had been mentioned deserved to be invited, for some reason Go-Toba never issued the order.

The poem that Lord Takanobu offered when he made his first appearance at the Wakadokoro:

Uresiku mo	Overjoyed am I
Waka no urakaze	As among the cranes who've come
nodoka nite	For countless reigns to Poetry Bay,

---

71. Kojima, *Shinkokin wakashū no kenkyū, zokuhen*, pp. 8–9. Subsequent scholars like Gotō, Ishida and Satsukawa, Ariyoshi, and others either repeat Kojima's argument or take it as a given.

72. To preserve the pivot, I have translated *kaku* as "gather," although in the first instance, with the seaweed, it means "to rake up," and in the second instance, with the poems, it means "to write." In both cases, however, the implication is "to gather." This figure—writing down and collecting poems as one might rake up and collect seaweed to extract its salt—is used in the prefaces to both *Goshūishū* and *Senzaishū*, a further indication that the Wakadokoro's main charge was related to the eventual production of another imperial anthology.

tiyo femu tadu no	With its gentle breezes,
kazu ni irinuru	I now take my place.

And the poem Kamo no Chōmei brought:

Waga kimi no	Perhaps because it wishes
tiyo wo fen toya	To share the countless years
Akitusima ni	Of our monarch's reign
kayofisomeken	The fisherman's boat has begun to ply
ama no turibune[73]	The waters of His Land.

And the poem Fujiwara Hideyoshi brought:

Tumoriyuku	Accumulating
kagiri mo siranu	Beyond limit the waves
kimi ga yo ni	That roll into Poetry Bay
yorodu yo kakete	For a thousand generations
Waka no uranami[74]	Under our monarch's reign.

One by one the appointees would assemble at the Wakadokoro and sign in.[75] At

---

73. The exact reading of the word in line three is open to some dispute among historical linguists, although it is a standard epithet for Japan. In Nara times, it was read Akidusima, but by the Heian period it seems to have moved to Akitusima and is subsequently (exactly when is not clear, but the earliest *locus classicus* given by the *Kokugo daijiten* and by Ōno Susumu in his *Kogo jiten* dates to the Muromachi period) corrupted to Akitusu (giving the final character its *on*-reading rather than treating it as *ateji*). *Shinpen kokka taikan* indexes the line as "Akitusima ni," and I have followed their lead, even if "Akitusu ni" scans better (although, of course, *ji-amari* is not unthinkable here).

74. Ishida and Satsukawa's text reads *urakaze* (breezes off the bay), but two other textual lines give *uranami* (waves in the bay), which makes more sense with the verb *kakeru* (here, "to roll onto"; "adhere"), and with the verb *tumoru* (to pile up), which works better with a countable noun like waves rather than an uncountable one like wind.

75. There is some doubt as to how to interpret *chakutō shite*. Its main meaning, which Ishida and Satsukawa apply here, is to record one's name in the register as one reports for duty—the time clock of courtly Japan. But during the Kamakura period there emerged a form of poem sequence known as *chakutō waka*, in which a group of poets would come every day for 100 days to a set place and submit a poem on that day's topic. Interestingly enough, the *Meigetsuki* citation Ishida and Satsukawa use to support their reading (Kennin 1/viii/5) is the very one Ōno Susumu gives as the *locus classicus* for *chakutō waka*. The *Meigetsuki* entry says: "There was some discussion about the suggestion by Michitomo and Tomochika that the Wakadokoro run on the *chakutō* system. His Majesty agreed with the idea, and it was so ordered." Either view of the word's meaning would work here, but several things lead me to believe it simply means to sign a work register. First, Ienaga goes on to say below that each poet kept track of his attendance, and they competed with each other as to who showed up the most often. Since a poetry *chakutō* by definition would require each one to be present every

the end of each month, they would present the Retired Emperor with a report of their attendance for that month, competing with each other as to who showed up the most often.[76] In snow, under the moon or flowers—through the seasons—they would come, even when there were no formal functions called, and when the Retired Emperor himself was not there, they would frequently practice composing and reciting to themselves, so the Wakadokoro had the effect of preventing the Way of Poetry from falling into decline.[77]

It became a place for experimenting with poetry.[78] Once, more than twenty people were summoned. Chancellor and Minister of the Left Yoshitsune and Palace Minister Michichika were in attendance, seated toward the eaves at the eastern end. The rest were seated in the main room facing east, which was treated as the head of the room. From behind the imperial blinds, His Majesty sent out ten topics for poems. Since everyone present wrote on these ten topics, I did not copy any of the poems down myself. Undoubtedly some among these poets stood out and were later asked back to compose again.

The appointees came all the time to the Wakadokoro, and there were constant poetry gatherings, but I did not record them. Still, I know that I ought to have written down, if only in outline, at least such poems among them that impressed people, but I was overwhelmed with other public duties and private business of my own and did not do so. Later, when people ask about the poems, I shall doubtless regret not

---

day, competing for attendance records would be moot. Second, the word is used only one other time in *Meigetsuki* for the next hundred days, and that is in the entry for viii/7 in which Teika simply wrote that Go-Toba formally announced that the *chakutō* system would be used. Other than that, Teika made no mention of things one might expect to hear about, for example, the topic for the day or, more important, the banquet at the end of the 100 days, when the final sequence would be formally submitted, if we are to judge from later examples. So I do not think this could be seen as the earliest example of *chakutō waka*, although it is entirely possible that when the appointees registered each time they came they also added a poem to the register.

76. If, as discussed in the previous note, *chakutō* includes the submission of a poem each time, then perhaps they were competing over who could come up with the best poems. The text would allow either interpretation.

77. As Ishida and Satsukawa note, this last sentence is less than transparent. I have more or less followed their gloss (*IN*, pp. 58–59) with some emendation. The main point seems to be that the poets would gather frequently and even without supervision or the pressure of a formal occasion would practice, a custom that could only help the cause of poetry in general.

78. The following section presents a few problems. If Ienaga is referring to a specific event, as he seems to be, there is no other record of it. As Ishida and Satsukawa (*IN*, p. 59) point out, the general description (twenty-some poets, ten topics) fits the *Hachigatsu jūgoya utakai*, but since Ienaga describes that event in detail in the very next section of the diary, they do not believe it is the one discussed here. Furthermore, several of the sentences are extremely elliptical. I have departed somewhat from the gloss given by Ishida and Satsukawa.

keeping records, and such records as others kept have surely gotten lost in the interim and would be difficult to retrieve, so it has all come to naught. And unfortunately even what I did commit to memory has faded away.[79]

Ienaga's description of the physical layout of the Wakadokoro is not precise. Teika's *Meigetsuki* entry for viii/27 includes a drawing that we can use to supplement Ienaga's remarks.[80] Teika's illustration shows an area six *ken* by two *ken*, which seems to be just that part of the Hiro Gosho annex assigned to the Wakadokoro and not the whole annex itself. A *ken* is the distance between two pillars as used in traditional *shinden* architecture and amounts to about six feet; so the dimensions of the area were roughly twelve by thirty-six feet.

The east side of the room was reserved for Go-Toba and high-ranking courtiers (*tenjōbito*), who sat in descending rank from north to south in the room. This is the area Ienaga describes as having "recessed floor boards" (*ochiitashiki*). Another section, about one *ken* by two (or roughly six by twelve feet) was set aside for "those of lower rank." Both Teika and Ienaga used the term *jige*, which generally referred to people of the Sixth Rank and below, who were not allowed into the inner palace, but it could also include—as it did here—"low-ranked nobles" (*jige no kandachime*), who were of the Fifth Rank but still not allowed into the Emperor's immediate presence. No one among the original *yoriudo* fell into this category, which Teika notes in his diary, but since space was set aside for them from the very beginning, it suggests that Go-Toba had a few more appointees in mind, perhaps as alternates. And, in fact, of the three replacement appointments mentioned above, Chōmei and Hideyoshi were *jige*.

What is important in Ienaga's account is not so much his description of physical things as the atmosphere. The appointees treat their position as a real job, signing a work register and keeping monthly attendance sheets. This must in large part have been a result of Go-Toba's leadership. But beyond that, they were very competitive, not just vying with each other for Go-Toba's favor (although that clearly is one reason for their zeal) but also seizing the opportunity to work on their poetry. As mentioned above, elsewhere in his memoirs, Ienaga depicted everyone in Go-Toba's court behav-

---

79. *IN*, pp. 52–58.
80. The drawing, incidentally, is reproduced in Gotō Shigeo, *Shinkokinshū wakashū no kisōteki kenkyū*, p. 26; Ishida's notes in *IN*, p. 57; Ton'a's reduction *Meigetsuki shōshutsu* (p. 252); and probably elsewhere.

ing like this in matters of poetry.[81] Other sources, such as *Meigetsuki*, confirm that the number of poetic events was quite high, although no one captured the sense of urgency and rivalry quite as vividly as Ienaga. The Wakadokoro seems, then, to have become a microcosm, a distillation of this devotion to waka, and as such it provided ideal conditions for Go-Toba's next step, which was to commission an anthology.

Before moving on to that next step, I would like to draw attention once more to the tenuous nature of Ienaga's memoirs as a *factual* historical document. The lengthy disclaimer with which he ended this section—similar disclaimers appear elsewhere—unfortunately seems quite accurate. Despite his unanimous selection as Chief Recorder, he appears not to have kept good records. To some degree, his apology is probably a pose. It is, after all, a *wabun* diary, and as such it may be seen as part of a line going back to *Tosa nikki*, whose author more than once said things like "There may have been other poems, too, but I neglected to write them down." Yet it is also probably true; Ienaga did not write much down and forgot a lot afterward. He did not even correctly identify the original appointees, having overlooked Jien, although he may be forgiven that because he was not named Chief Recorder until a week or so after the initial appointments. This delay may also explain why he included the "joining poems" only of those *yoriudo* who came after him. So when we turn to *Ienaga nikki*, it is generally not for hard facts. But it does convey the mood of the times in a way that a *kanbun* diary rarely does, and its anecdotes and character sketches—one can see a bit of Sei Shōnagon or *setsuwa* in some of them—give life to a world centuries old.[82] And the figures he used (some from waka, some from Confucianism, some from Buddhism) tell a lot about the intertext of medieval Japan.

With the establishment of the Wakadokoro, Go-Toba created in his palace a physical and psychological center for waka activities. Subsequently virtually every public poetry event was under the auspices of the Wakadokoro, and most of them took place there. Michichika and Yoshitsune were eclipsed as sponsors once and for all; Go-Toba had in just over a year

---

81. See Chapter 2, note 45, and pp. 66–69.

82. I am not suggesting that Chinese as a language is incapable of expressing mood, emotion, and so on. I have already cited many entries from Teika's *Meigetsuki* and Kanezane's *Gyokuyō* that are alive with irony, anger, or frustration. However, since Chinese was not the native language of these courtiers, and because as a genre the *kanbun* diary was seen more than anything else as a record of precedent, I think it is fair to say that Ienaga's *wabun* text is in a different category.

succeeded in bringing virtually all public waka activity under his management. I would have said "under his control," but "control" seems—just barely—too strong a word here, because in the end, he could not really "control" the poetry itself, only the public forums in which it was disseminated. In any case, he immediately put the new office to good use.

On the 3rd of the Eighth Month, even before Ienaga had joined, Go-Toba sponsored an *eigu* contest, confirming that henceforth the Wakadokoro would be the locus for these events. Known as *Kennin gannen hachigatsu mikka eigu uta-awase* (*Eigu* Contest on the 3rd Day, Eighth Month, First Year of Kennin), it was a large-scale affair, with thirty-six poets and 108 rounds (six topics, eighteen rounds each). Four of the topics were compound Seasonal ones (Morning Dew at the First of Autumn; Autumn Winds along the Barrier Road; Hearing a Deer under Moonlight during a Journey; and Insects at the Old Capital), and the other two were relatively simple, two-character Love topics (First Love, and Long-lasting Love).

The matchups and order were fixed, that is, the same two poets met in the same order throughout the contest, for a total of six matchups for each pair. Shunzei was the judge. Although Teika's *Meigetsuki* makes it clear that the assembly discussed each round before the judgment was rendered, only the judgment mark itself was recorded.[83] Artistically it was not the most important occasion of the period, although two of its poems did end up in *Shinkokinshū*. But as with so many of the events that took place in 1200–1201, it is significant in that it represents another permutation of the waka gathering. For one thing, the team divisions were such that most of the high-ranking participants, including Go-Toba, Yoshitsune, Michichika, Jien, and Tadayoshi were on the Left. Teika was the leader of the Right team, and his modest rank of Senior Fourth Lower made him (along with three others at that level) the highest-ranking member of the team except for one Norisue, who was Junior Third Rank.[84]

In fact, all in all it was a mixed group, ranging from the Retired Emperor down to one of his personal guards, who was of the Senior Sixth Rank Upper, barely qualified, in the strict hierarchy of the day, to be in such company.

---

83. The *Shinpen kokka taikan* text (5:188, pp. 395–400) is identical to the one found in GR 192, and both are noticeably corrupt. Large portions of the poems in the last section have been lost, and thirteen of the rounds have no judgment marks.

84. Teika acknowledged that it was an honor for him as a poet to be matched against Go-Toba; see *Meigetsuki*, Kennin 1/viii/3, 1: 207.

There were seven members of the clergy (including Jien, Jakuren, Shunzei, and Minamoto Moromitsu appearing under his ordained name of Shōren), and five ladies-in-waiting (Kojijū, Sanuki, Tango, Echizen, and Kunaikyō). Not counting them, there were eleven poets of the Fifth or Sixth Rank. Go-Toba's decision to set aside a special area of the Wakadokoro for people of lower rank starts to make sense.

As discussed above, Go-Toba was evidently growing impatient with arrangements that gave consideration to rank over talent in contest judgments; thus, the team set-up in this contest, with all the high-ranking participants on one team, seems odd, even though it is one he was to try again in an even more structured way a few years later. But if he was hoping the participants would ignore rank in their considerations, he must have been disappointed, because the Left team outscored the Right nearly two to one, largely because its first four members, Go-Toba, Yoshitsune, Michichika, and Jien, collectively scored twenty wins, no losses, and three ties against their opponents.[85] Considering that their opponents were Teika, Masatsune, Jakuren, and Ariie, respectively, these are impressive numbers, to say the least. Leaving out the rounds these four participated in results in a much more even distribution of wins and losses—statistical evidence, if not proof, that rank did matter here.[86]

Of course, it is no news that rank affected contest judgments. But for Go-Toba to load one side so heavily is quite unusual (although not unique) and may have been some sort of experiment. Given, however, that it was the opening event in the new Wakadokoro and therefore an important social occasion, it seems inevitable that status would play a significant role. Teika provides evidence of this when he says he left as soon as he could because he felt constrained by the atmosphere.[87] Furthermore, Shunzei was not the sort

---

85. The numbers should add up to twenty-four (four poets, six rounds each), but Topic 4, Round 3—Michichika vs. Jakuren—is one of the thirteen rounds without a judgment mark and hence Michichika's win record is incomplete.

86. Seven of the Left team members were Fourth, Fifth, or Sixth Rank, and by that far down on the list, they were matched with poets of roughly equivalent ranks on the Right. It is only the top third of the draw that is skewed in terms of rank, and that is also where the scores are most lopsided. The fact that twelve of the remaining eighty-four rounds have no judgment marks does make it impossible to reach any final statistical conclusions, but extrapolating from what happened in the other matchups between the same two opponents, wins and losses were probably evenly distributed.

87. *Meigetsuki*, Kennin 1/viii/3, 1: 207.

of judge to break with precedent at such a time and would likely follow a conservative line in his decisions. Thus, it is hard to guess what Go-Toba may have had in mind, although the hierarchical team division does seem to be of a piece with the *Rōnyaku* contest, as well as the *Keishō jishin no uta-awase*, which is explored in Chapter 9 (see pp. 352–62).

With regard to the correlation between rank and results in this contest, one anomaly stands out. Tadayoshi, Senior Second Rank and a Major Counselor (*dainagon*, thus unquestionably one of the "elite"), fared poorly against his opponent, the court lady Echizen.[88] This provides fairly clear evidence that he was not thought to be the most talented of Go-Toba's group. Losing to Echizen itself was no shame; she was highly skilled and respected. But in a contest where rank appears to be a defining quality, one would have expected him to do much better.

Not all was parties and contests, however. Go-Toba also saw the Wakadokoro as a means by which to educate and train. In the *Meigetsuki* entry for viii/7, Teika wrote that in order to give budding poets practice in composing on topics (*dai'ei*), Go-Toba had posed three topics to some thirty poets and given them two days to produce. He had also asked Yoshitsune to go through *Gosenshū* and *Shūishū*, considered essential parts of the waka canon, and select 100 poems, presumably so that Go-Toba could then sequence them and use them as a model for poetry students.

The next major Wakadokoro event occurred shortly thereafter, and this one had a considerable impact on *Shinkokinshū*. Called *Kennin gannen hachigatsu jūgoya senka-awase* (Contest of Selected Poems on the Night of the 15th, Eighth Month, First Year of Kennin), preparations for it began several days in advance. Teika claimed to have completed his poems on the 13th, although he does not say when the order was issued.[89] Evidently composing his verses was something of an ordeal: "During this time, I put my heart and soul into these poems. But they did not reach a high level of artistry, and I am ashamed of them."[90]

It is clear from subsequent events that Go-Toba had asked twenty-five poets to submit ten poems each, one poem on each of ten four-character

---

88. Tadayoshi won one round, lost three, and tied one; the other is unmarked.
89. In the *Meigetsuki shōshutsu*, the date of this entry is given as the 12th rather than the 13th (the date given in the received text of *Meigetsuki*), but the contents of the entry are the same. Ariyoshi, *Shinkokin wakashū no kenkyū: kiban to kōsei*, p. 554, gives the 12th.
90. *Meigetsuki*, Kennin 1/viii/13, 1: 208.

topics, all of which were related to the moon, as was appropriate for an event scheduled for the 15th, the night of the full moon. The usual suspects were rounded up, with a few twists. For example, Ietaka did not participate. He had also not been present at the contest on the 3rd, presumably because he was in mourning for his father, Mitsutaka, who had died on the 1st day of the month.[91] And again, there was no major Rokujō representation, although Michichika and Michitomo stood in for the patron Tsuchimikado house, and Tadayoshi, Yasusue, and Kojijū had been trained in the Rokujō style. On the other hand, a new face appeared: Shunzei no Musume. This was the first public event for her, although certainly not the last.[92] And as will be seen below, she made a splash. She joined Kunaikyō, Echizen, Tango, Kojijū, and Sanuki—a mix of younger and older court women who frequently participated in events of this period.

As with the *Shingū senka-awase*, Go-Toba's idea was to solicit poems from a number of poets and then select some of them and match them in a contest to be judged by the group. On the 14th, in a process very similar to the one used for the *Shingū* contest, he invited roughly ten poets to his palace, divided them into Right and Left work groups, and had them select poems from among those their own team members had submitted. He had already divided up the teams; the Right team was the more diverse in terms of affiliations, both political and poetic.[93] Teika described the process followed by the Right work group: "I was the Reader, the Abbot [Jien] and the Palace Minister [Michichika] were Discussants, with Masatsune and Tomochika also assigned to our group. We chose thirty poems."[94] (Jien, Masatsune, and Teika worked together in the Right group for the *Shingū* contest.) Since he

---

91. Ietaka dropped out of sight for quite some time. Teika did not mention him again until the entry for xii/2, discussed later in this chapter, and even then he was not present for the poetry gathering itself. He did not appear again in a poetry event until a contest on Kennin 2 (1202)/ii/10 (see *Meigetsuki* entry for that date) and in the *Santai waka* in the Third Month of Kennin 2 (1202).

92. This is the first extant event in which she is clearly identified, although as discussed above, she may have participated at the *Kennin gannen sangatsu jūrokunichi eigu uta-awase* several months earlier.

93. The teams were Left: Go-Toba, Yoshitsune, Shakua (Shunzei), Shunzei no Musume, Kunaikyō, Echizen, Tango, Ariie, Jakuren, Ienaga, Chōmei, Hideyoshi; and Right: Michichika, Jien, Tadayoshi, Kintsune, Kojijū, Sanuki, Takanobu, Teika, Michitomo, Yasusue, Masatsune, Tomochika, Kinkage.

94. *Meigetsuki*, Kennin 1/viii/14, 1: 208. With thirteen poets on the Right team, this means the Right work group had 130 poems to work with, from which they selected thirty.

did not indicate that the selections were blind, as they had been in the *Shingū senka-awase*, presumably they were not.

Although Teika does not discuss the deliberations of the Left group in detail, it appears from what he says that at least Go-Toba, Yoshitsune, and Jakuren took part. (Likely there were also two others.) The Left team apparently produced better work this time around, because in the initial selection for their side fifty poems were chosen (out of only twelve poets, as compared to the thirteen on the Right team—the absence of Ietaka may account for the disparity). Go-Toba consequently ordered the Right work group to choose an additional twenty poems to even out the numbers. According to Teika, Michichika was the primary beneficiary of this order; in the end eight of his ten poems were selected for the final contest, but only after he pushed them forward himself.[95]

As with the *Shingū senka-awase*, which this contest so closely resembles, at least one poem by every poet who submitted the requested ten poems was selected for the final contest. But some were more favored than others. As already stated, Michichika (Right) led his group with eight poems. Go-Toba and Yoshitsune on the Left and Jien on the Right had seven poems each. They were followed closely by Shunzei no Musume and Kunaikyō (both Left) and Masatsune (Right) with six poems and Shunzei (Left) and Tomochika (Right) with five apiece.

Ariyoshi provides a thorough analysis of the disposition of poems in this event, from which several points emerge.[96] Although Go-Toba directed the selection process to yield an equivalent number of poems from the Right and Left teams, the final score of the contest was overwhelmingly in favor of the Left team, with thirty-six wins, to only six for the Right team (leaving eight ties).[97] Unlike the contest on the 3rd, the reason for such a lopsided score is not readily attributable to rank. The teams were more evenly divided this time. The Left team might have had a slight edge in talent and rank (led by Go-Toba and Yoshitsune), but not enough that such a score would be a

---

95. Ibid. As noted elsewhere, Ienaga also commented on Michichika's propensity toward self-promotion and remarked it did not endear him to others.

96. Ariyoshi (*Shinkokin wakashū no kenkyū: kiban to kōsei*, pp. 110–12) gives a detailed breakdown of which poems (by which poets, on which topics) passed the initial selection process, what the contest scores were, and which poems were eventually anthologized in *Shinkokinshū*. He does not, however, talk about particular matchups, something I discuss below.

97. In the GR 192 text, Round 28 is unmarked, but the *hanshi* says it is a Tie, and I have treated it as such in my calculations. Apparently Ariyoshi has, too, judging from his numbers.

given. In fact, even though the teams were far more unequal socially in the contest on the 3rd, the final outcome was much closer. So Go-Toba was perhaps finally coming closer to his wish: a contest in which the poems were judged on merit rather than extra-literary considerations. Of course, to accept that view one would have to overlook the fact that Go-Toba won six of his seven rounds (he lost one round, to Jien), and Yoshitsune garnered five Wins and two Ties. Both of them met a wide range of opponents, not all of them the toughest. Their status probably had some impact on their scores.

But if we look at some of the remaining matchups and results, as well as the judgments (which reflect the discussions), it does seem that merit played an important part. Perhaps the first indication of this is that Shunzei was not as diffident about his own work in this contest as he had been in others. Of five poems entered, he won two (against Michichika and Masatsune), lost two (both against Jien), and tied with Kojijū. Still, in his judgment for Round 8, one of his two Wins, he at least attempted to maintain a facade of modesty: "The judge awarded the Win to the Right, However both the Left and Right teams insisted the Left poem was especially good and should be awarded the Win."[98]

Two of the court ladies earned excellent records. Shunzei no Musume, in her formal debut, compiled four Wins and two Ties, with two of her Wins against heavyweights Jien and Teika. In two of her Wins (Round 10 against Tomochika and Round 50 against Teika), the judgment draws attention to particular phrases in her poems as being especially skillful, a comment that suggests part of her success lay in a fresh approach to language. In contrast, Tomochika's losing poem in Round 10 is criticized for using a phrase that "we hear a lot these days."[99] Kunaikyō also had an outstanding record: four Wins and two Ties, her most prestigious opponents being Jien and Michichika. And as with Shunzei no Musume, her innovative use of language seems to have been the key; her Wins against Jien and Michichika were credited in the judgments to "striking" (*mi ni shimite*, Round 13, against Jien) or "exceedingly charming" (*kagirinaku okashi*) turns of phrase.

Perhaps the biggest surprise on the Left team was Kamo no Chōmei. Most famous, of course, for his essay *Hōjōki*, the exemplar of hermit literature in Japan, he was also an accomplished waka poet and critic (his *Mumyōshō* explicates the poetics of his master, Shun'e [1113–91]). Yet even though

---

98. GR 192, 12: 367.
99. Ibid., p. 368.

Go-Toba favored him with an appointment to the Wakadokoro, he did not fare quite as well as others in Go-Toba's group in the contests and events of the age (including *Shinkokinshū*, where he had fewer poems selected than poets like Masatsune, Shunzei no Musume, Kunaikyō, and Michitomo, not to mention the masters like Teika, Ietaka, Jakuren, and so on). But in this contest he stood out, winning all four of his rounds, against Kojijū, Sanuki, Tomochika, and Teika. Once again, in two of the four rounds, it was a turn of phrase that caught the judge's attention. One round, number 29 against Tomochika, evidently touched off a spirited debate centering (as near as we can tell from Teika's reduction of the discussion) around the fact that Chōmei did not actually mention the topic word in his poem. His teammates defended him by saying that the synonym he used was indistinguishable in "feeling" from the topic word, and Shunzei agreed, also praising the poem's overall impact (*sama*—one of those elusive critical terms that means essentially how the parts of a poem work together to convey the essential feeling). The topic was "Old Temple under a Lingering Moon":

Left, Kamo no Chōmei, Win

Fatuseyama	At Mount Hatsuse
kane no fibiki ni	When echoes from a temple bell
odorokeba	Awaken me,
sumikeru tuki no	There, a clear moon
irigata no sora	Near setting in the sky!

Right, Tomochika

Kore ya kono	So this must be
nokoru fikari no	That lingering light
kage naran	Of which they speak,
Takano no yama no	Moon at dawn
ariake no tuki	Over Mount Takano.[100]

Judgment: People said, "'echoes from a temple bell' (kane no fibiki) and a 'moon near setting' (irigata no tuki) are both late night images. How do they address the Lingering Moon topic?" But someone argued, "In the lines 'a traveler journeys beneath the lingering moon,'[101] the reference is clearly to a lingering moon at dawn. Dawn moon, lingering moon—they amount to the

---

100. "Takano no yama" is the *kun* reading of Kōya-san, location of a Shingon temple complex founded by Kōbō Daishi.

101. This is a line from *Wakan rōeishū*, #416 (Ōsone and Horiuchi, eds., *Wakan rōeishū*, p. 160).

same thing as far as topic goes." The judge concluded that moreover, since the elements of the Left poem work well together, it should be awarded the Win.[102]

At first glance, one wonders why the Right Team would argue against Chōmei's use of the bell image, when in the very next round one of their own, Jien, used it also in conjunction with a dawn moon and won. But Chōmei's usage is a *honzetsu*, an allusive variation on a passage from the Kiritsubo chapter of *Genji* that clearly takes place at night rather than near dawn, hence the Right team's argument.[103] Teika did not say who made the counterargument, which cites lines from a poem in *Wakan rōeishū*, but one doubts it was Shunzei, who presumably would have given more credence to a *Genji* reference than to a *Wakan rōeishū* one.

Tomochika's poem, though not a *honkadori* in the generally accepted sense, is at least intertextual, in that it employs a set of images associated by this time with Mount Kōya and Kōbō Daishi. The "lingering light" (*nokoru fikari*) may refer to Kōbō Daishi himself, who remains in eternal *samadhi* "beneath the moss" at the Oku-no-in; the "moon at dawn" (*ariake no tuki*) points to the tradition that Kōbō Daishi will one day return as the Maitreya Buddha.[104] This figure can also be seen in *Senzaishū* 1236 (XIX, Buddhist Poems)[105] by Jakuren several decades earlier, which follows the headnote "Composed during a pilgrimage to Kōya":

---

102. GR 192, 12: 370.

103. The *Genji* context is the visit of Myōbu, on behalf of the grieving emperor, to the mother of the recently deceased Kiritsubo. The lines in question, "the moon crossed pure and clear through the sky toward its setting" (*tsuki wa irigata no sora kiyou sumiwatareru ni*—*Genji monogatari I*, NKBT 14, p. 38), appear in Seidensticker in the following passage: "The moon was sinking over the hills, the air was crystal clear, the wind was cool, and the songs of the insects among the autumn grasses would by themselves have brought tears" (Seidensticker, *Tale of Genji*, p. 10). A few paragraphs later, we read that even after the moon set it was still "one or two in the morning" (p. 12). It is clearly, as the Right team insisted, "late at night" and therefore inappropriate to the topic. This passage in *Genji* was frequently alluded to by Shunzei and others in his circle (see Teramoto, *Genji monogatari juyōshi ronkō*, pp. 35, 198ff), and so Chōmei's allusion would have been readily recognized.

104. See Katano and Matsuno, eds., *Senzai wakashū*, p. 375. I am indebted to Arthur Thornhill for pointing this out to me.

105. Robert Morrell ("The *Shinkokinshū*," p. 282) notes that the chapter title *shakkyōka* or *shakkyō no uta* is more accurately rendered "Poems on Śākyamuni's Teachings," and the genre is to be distinguished from "amorphous" poems that deal with basic Buddhist notions such as the fleeting nature of the world. However, in this study, mostly for brevity and convenience, I have rendered the title as simply "Buddhist Poems."

Akatuki no	While I await daybreak
Takano no yama ni	On Mount Takano
matu fodo ya	Even here beneath the moss,
koke no sita nimo	Lingering moon at dawn!
ariake no tuki	

In any case, both Chōmei's and Tomochika's poems in the contest have an obvious religious subtext befitting the topic. Chōmei wrote of "awakening" to a "clear moon" at a temple, which hints at enlightenment to the truth of the Dharma; Tomochika alluded to Kōbō Daishi's immanence (and imminence, for that matter) as an agent of enlightenment. However, when all the arguments are made, it was *sama*, which certainly includes *manner* of expression, that won the round.

One begins to see a constant here. New use of language, even at the expense of traditional approaches to one of waka's most sacred elements, topic, is to be rewarded, although it is not freshness or novelty per se but phraseology that stands out as striking, emotional, or lovely. Round 13, between Kunaikyō and Jien, illustrates this clearly and also reveals a distinction between what was seen as innovation in Go-Toba's time and what might have been seen as innovative a century later among the Kyōgoku poets, who themselves were considered groundbreakers. As with the *Shingū senka-awase*, because of the way the final poems were selected, the topics in a given round might not necessarily match, and that was the case with this round. Kunaikyō's topic was "Fulling Cloth by the Moon's Light," and Jien's was "Wind through Pines Beneath the Moon":

Left, Kunaikyō, Win

Madoromade	I cannot sleep.
nagame yo tote no	As if in play it invites me
susami kana	To have a look—
asa no sagoromo	The rhythmic fulling of hempen robes
tuki ni utu kowe	Under tonight's moon!

Right, the Former Abbot (Jien)

Aki fa tuki	Autumn is moon;
tuki sumu yofa fa	And as the moon clears, deep in
matu no kaze	the night
ika ni nagamete	Wind through pines!
ika ni sinobamu	The more I take all this in,
	The more I am filled with longing!

Judgment: Although the Right poem, with its wind in the pines, is excellent, the lines "as if in play it invites me / to have a look" and "the rhythmic fulling of hempen robes / under tonight's moon" were considered striking, and the Left poem was awarded the Win.[106]

A century later, the Kyōgoku poets might have favored Jien's effort because of its unusual, forceful structure, although they never selected it for their anthologies. It features a poetic preface (*jo*) based on sound repetition ("aki fa tuki / tuki sumu") rather than on a pivot (*kakekotoba*), a technique popular among the Kanpyō era poets (for example, Ariwara no Narihira) which enjoyed a revival under Kyōgoku Tamekane. And its last two lines are a grammatical parallel, which was also found frequently in poems from the Kyōgoku school. Yet here these elements go unremarked, one way or the other. It is Kunaikyō's evocative phrasing that carries the round.

It is hard to understand how the Right team ended up with such a lackluster record. Part of the problem may have been Michichika. When the Right team was asked to select twenty more poems, he lobbied hard for his own work, and as the highest-ranking member of his work group, he had the clout to prevail. But in the larger group, the judgments went overwhelmingly against him. He managed just two Wins against five Losses and one Tie.[107]

Round 23 is especially interesting because it sheds light on the proper use of allusion (*honkadori*) and also gives us a sense of what in Michichika's work made it seem mediocre to his contemporaries. In it, Michichika was faulted because he attempted to make an allusion to an ancient poem but did not develop it. The topic for both him and Tango was "Moon Shining Brightly over the Lake" (the topic is Chinese, of course, but in this case the "lake" is Lake Biwa):

---

106. GR 192, 12: 368.

107. The judgments involving his work are a mixed lot. He won one round (Round 4, against Ariie) because Shunzei thought his poem better (although the group was less enchanted), and won the other (Round 22, against Hideyoshi) because his opponent's poem has a glaring fault. In three rounds, his poems lost because his opponents' poems were seen as simply better (Round 8, against Shunzei; Round 18, against Kunaikyō; and Round 34, against Ariie, wherein Shunzei at least credits Michichika's poem with "some sense of *yūgen*" [*yūgen no koto ni omoiyorite haberedo*]). In two cases (Round 23, against Tango; Round 45, against Yoshitsune) he lost because of faults in his poems. And he tied with Shunzei no Musume (Round 33) because neither poem had anything to recommend it.

Left, Tango, Win

    Yo mo sugara   Throughout the night
    ura kogu fune fa   Boats that row along the shore
    ato mo nasi   Leave no wake behind,
    tuki zo nokoreru   But the moon at least lingers
    Siga no karasaki   Here at Shiga's Karasaki Point.

Right, the Palace Minister (Michichika)

    Yo mo sugara   Since all night long
    Fira no yamakaze   Mountain wind off Hirayama
    umi fukeba   Blows across the lake,
    tuki moteyosuru   They bring along with them
    Siga no sazanami   the moon
                                        These lapping waves at Shiga.

Judgment: In the lines "blows across the lake" there is a reference to the past, but there is nothing fresh about it (kodai naru sama ni haberedomo, medurashiki tokoro na[shi]); so the Left is awarded the Win.[108]

Michichika was citing lines from a *Man'yōshū* poem (*Firayamakaze no umi fukeba* refers to wind on Lake Biwa and appears in MYS 1719 [NKBT 1715]), but the reference seems superfluous since the foundation poem is describing how the wind ruffles the sleeves of fisherfolk on the lake, an image that is unrelated to the topic and adds nothing tonally to Michichika's verse.[109] The message here is that a reference to an old poem must result in something new. It is not enough to be didactic. (Personally, however, regardless of the "failed" allusion, I like Michichika's figure of the moon lapping in on the waves.)

The fact that Michichika makes this particular allusion provides an opportunity to see how the average poet learned about foundation poems. Due to the complexities of the *Man'yōgana* code, much of *Man'yōshū* was inaccessible to even educated courtiers during most of the Heian period, although the Pear Jar Five did some pioneering *Man'yō* scholarship. To the extent that

---

108. GR 192, 12: 369.
109. The *Man'yōshū* poem, which may well have come to Michichika through *Kokin waka rokujō* (#440, with the second and third lines given as *itayamakaze no / utifukeba*) reads: *Sasanami no / Firayamakaze no / umi fukeba / turi suru ama no / sode kaferu miyu*—"Since mountain winds / From wave-lapping Hirayama / Blow across the lake / One can see the stirring / Of sleeves of the fisherfolk."

people knew *Man'yō* poems, it was usually through some mediating collection like *Kokin waka rokujō*.[110] But toward the end of the Heian period, interest and scholarship in *Man'yōshū* began to pick up. Shunzei, Kenshō, and Rokujō Kiyosuke are among the well-known poet/critics who wrote treatises or glosses about the ancient collection or included poems directly from it in their didactic collections.[111] As noted elsewhere in this study, Shunzei's knowledge of *Man'yōshū* was spottier than that of his Rokujō rivals, who as a family specialized in studying the collection.

In any case, the poem Michichika alludes to here appears in at least five such works extant during his lifetime, including *Kokin waka rokujō*.[112] Since most of them were by Rokujō scholars, perhaps Michichika was trying to

---

110. *Kokin waka rokujō* is a categorized collection of over 4,500 poems from the *Man'yō* through *Gosenshū* eras. Although there is uncertainty about the exact circumstances surrounding its creation, the prevailing opinion now (see *WBJ*, pp. 212–13) is that it was done around 980 and that Kaneakira Shinnō (914–87) and Minamoto Shitagō, who was one of the Pear Jar Five, were mainly responsible, although an earlier compilation date, with Tsurayuki as the compiler, has also been put forward. The collection was used in subsequent centuries as a source of verses for imperial anthologies. Its relationship to *Man'yōshū* is painstakingly charted in Nakanishi, *Kokin rokujō no Man'yōka*.

John Bentley has done some interesting work attempting to trace the relationship between *Man'yōshū* and *Kokin waka rokujō*. A summary of some of his findings appears in Bentley, "The Creation of Hitomaro, a Poetic Sage," pp. 154–56. He argues that another collection, no longer extant but referred to in old sources as *Man'yōshūshō* (Selections from *Man'yōshū*) stands between *Man'yōshū* and *Kokin waka rokujō* and had an impact on other Heian works, such as *Ise monogatari*, as well. In any case, over half the *Man'yōshū* poems in *Shinkokinshū* appear in *Kokin waka rokujō*; see Tsugita, "Tamekane no bungaku no mondaiten," pp. 15–20.

111. By "didactic collections," I refer to collections of poems put together by a poetry master for his students to study. Some of these collections still have their marginalia, but most do not. One assumes that the master gave oral instruction as well. A simple example but perhaps the best known of these would be *Kindai shūka*, selected by Teika to instruct the young and poetically untutored Shogun Sanetomo. This was eventually reworked into what we now know as the *Hyakunin isshu* (literally, "one poem each from 100 poets"). The didactic collections I refer to below are much larger, but most are also aimed at amateurs. See also Mostow, *Pictures of the Heart*, pp. 23–28. He prefers the term "exemplary collections."

112. Among the works citing this poem are *Waka ichijishō* (1153, with later emendations) and *Waka shogakushō* (1169), by Kiyosuke, and *Waka iroha* (1198) by Jōkaku (1147–1236). As their titles suggest, these were primers. (Loose translations of the titles would be "The Essentials of Waka," "Elementary Waka," and "The ABCs of Waka," respectively.) For the text and the poem in question, see *Shinpen kokka taikan*, 5:248, #1155, p. 809, for *Waka ichijishō*; 5:296, #100, p. 1017, for *Waka shogakushō*; and 5:302, #80, p. 1055, for *Waka iroha*. At least two other contemporary works also cite the poem.

dazzle the assembly with "house knowledge," although Shunzei recognized the reference. At any rate, it was no scholarly feat for Michichika to allude to such a poem, which makes his inability to pull off a graceful allusion all the more embarrassing for him.

Jien had the best record on the Right team. He was given a very tough draw, facing Go-Toba, Yoshitsune, Shunzei (twice), Shunzei no Musume, Kunaikyō, and Jakuren. Still, he managed three wins, including one against Go-Toba. Traditionally, imperial poets never lost in contests; the worst they could do was tie. Even when they used pseudonyms (*nyobō*, a word meaning simply "court lady," was the usual moniker for an imperial participant regardless of gender), it was always obvious who they were. Rarely does one find an imperial poet losing a round, although from this period on it becomes less and less unthinkable.[113] Jien's other two wins were both against Shunzei, although since Shunzei was the judge and since Jien's family were his patrons, something other than quality may have been behind the decisions.

Personal considerations may have had an effect on Teika's final record, too. As fierce as Shunzei might have been in defending Teika to Go-Toba, he tended to be hard on his son in contests. We have already seen examples of this in earlier contests, and it seems to have happened here as well. Teika managed to win only one of his four matches, against mixed competition.[114] However, this record could not have been solely the result of an effort on Shunzei's part to avoid the appearance of bias toward his son. After all, only four of Teika's poems were selected for the competition in the first place, and the final judgments were made after a group discussion. This contest stands as further evidence that at this stage Teika's potential may have been recognized but not necessarily appreciated. Likewise, Masatsune, whom Kubota and Ariyoshi pegged as Go-Toba's favorite on the basis of his performance in the *Rōnyaku gojisshu uta-awase*, did not do so well here. Although six of his poems made the first cut, none of them won.[115]

---

113. In other contests during these years, Go-Toba lost five times in the *Rōnyaku gojisshu uta-awase* (twice to Teika, twice to Ietaka, and once to Jien) and five out of ten times in the *Shōji ninen sentō jūnin uta-awase* contest. However, in the mammoth *Sengohyakuban uta-awase* he lost only one round out of 100 (not counting the ten times he judged his own rounds and gave himself the loss).

114. Teika managed a win only against Hideyoshi; he lost to Go-Toba, Chōmei, and Shunzei no Musume.

115. Masatsune ended up with three ties and three losses, although he did face difficult opponents: Go-Toba, Tango, Shunzei, Yoshitsune, Shunzei no Musume, and Echizen.

Ienaga relates an odd anecdote about the evening of the contest. Apparently, in the middle of the proceedings, Tomochika suddenly left without explanation. Go-Toba was upset both because he missed Tomochika's company and because Tomochika did not offer a satisfactory explanation for his sudden disappearance. The next morning, Go-Toba summoned him to the palace and demanded that he spend the next twenty-four hours alone in the Wakadokoro. That night, the 16th, the moon shone even more brightly than it had the night before. Tomochika sent a poem of contrition to Ienaga, who passed it on to Go-Toba. The poem, which prompted an imperial pardon:

Kuma mo naku	Even more
na ni ofu aki no	Than last night's renowned
sora yori mo	Perfect sky of autumn,
omofiide aru	The moon tonight fills me
yofa no tuki kana	With memories, regrets.[116]

This unusual punishment shows how central the Wakadokoro itself, not to mention the poetic activities that went on there, had become to Go-Toba's vision.

In sum, the *Kennin gannen hachigatsu jūgoya senka-awase* is another valuable look into the poetic activities of Go-Toba's emerging circle. Like the *Shingū* contest, which it so resembles, it was the result of a collective selection and judgment process that ensured high standards and reflected Go-Toba's efforts to build a consensus. In the enclosed world of courtly Japan, everyone probably knew each other's styles so well that whether the initial selections were "blind," as in the Shingū contest, or open, as in this one, seems to have made little difference. Although the team scores differed markedly between the two contests, the proportion of poems each contributed to *Shinkokinshū* was almost the same (nine out of seventy-two for the *Shingū senka-awase* and thirteen out of a hundred for the *Kennin gannen hachigatsu jūgoya senka-awase*). Go-Toba was apparently beginning to find ways to maximize quality and minimize politics, although he continued to experiment.

Not quite a month later, Go-Toba sponsored another *eigu* contest at the Wakadokoro. Known as *Kennin gannen kugatsu jūsannichi wakadokoro eigu uta-awase* (Eigu Poetry Contest at the Wakadokoro on the 13th Day, Ninth Month, First Year of Kennin), it contributed no poems to *Shinkokinshū*. In contrast to the earlier *eigu* contest, the eighteen participants in this one, aside

---

116. *IN*, pp. 59-61.

from Go-Toba himself, were either court ladies or low-ranking courtiers ranging from the Fifth to the Seventh ranks. Rank and talent did not necessarily reflect each other. The group included some excellent poets: Kunaikyō, Echizen, Masatsune, and Chōmei among them. It was a surprisingly modest group in terms of status, but another indication that Go-Toba saw waka as, among other things, a valuable tool for building an artistic, and presumably political, community. It also reiterated his desire to make the Wakadokoro the center of the world of waka.[117]

Around this time a more important event, now known as the *Sentō kudai gojisshu* (Fifty Poems on Chinese Verse Topics, at the Retired Emperor's Palace), occurred. The exact chronology is uncertain. Although Teika was involved, the extant text of *Meigetsuki* makes no mention of the event. Ariyoshi reviews the arguments and concludes that it must have occurred between the Ninth and Twelfth Months of Kennin 1.[118] Apparently Go-Toba set topics and solicited fifty poems each from six poets: himself, Yoshitsune, Jien, Shunzei no Musume, Kunaikyō, and Teika. The topics were the same

---

117. For a text of the contest, see *Shinpen kokka taikan*, 5:190, pp. 403-4. There are judgment marks, but no judgments. The text is not very clean, with missing words, names, and judgment marks, but it seems to have been another of Go-Toba's variant approaches, with many of the poets switching teams, and Go-Toba himself not starting until Round Three, the opening Left position being given to Fujiwara Norimitsu, a mere Senior Assistant Governor-General of the Dazaifu (*Dazaifu no daini*), thus no more than the lowest rungs of the Fourth Rank at the time. (Norimitsu eventually rose to the Junior Second Rank, quite a jump considering he was already fifty-seven years old at the time of this contest. One would assume that some sort of extraordinary service to Go-Toba was behind this, although Norimitsu's father, Norikane, had been Junior Third Rank and a well-known scholar and poet.) See also Taniyama, *Shinkokin jidai no uta-awase to kadan*, pp. 356, 428-35; he refers to this as the *Kennin gannen kugatsu jūsanya wakadokoro eigu uta-awase*.

118. Ariyoshi, *Shinkokin wakashū no kenkyū: kiban to kōsei*, pp. 116-21. Ariyoshi relies largely on an article by Higuchi Yoshimaro to which I unfortunately do not have access: "Kennin gannen sentō kudai gojisshu to sono seiritsu." What little evidence there is about the process of this event comes from brief headnote references in private collections like Teika's *Shūi gusō*. Since these references range from the Ninth to the Twelfth Months, it may be inferred that an invitation was issued (presumably by Go-Toba) and the various poets completed their task at different times.

The only generally available text of the event is ZGR 399, 14.2: 940-54. Unfortunately, however, it does not show the markings (*gatten*), which greatly decreases its usefulness. *Gatten* refers to the practice in which a poetry master reviews a selection of poems and indicates with a kind of inverted checkmark in the right margin those of superior quality. The figures I cite below are from Ariyoshi (and presumably also from Higuchi), who had access to other texts that show the *gatten*.

as those used in the *Shingū senka-awase* and *Hachigatsu jūgoya senka-awase* and presumably thus represented Go-Toba's standard. The Retired Emperor then had an overlapping group of six poets mark the poems and identify outstanding ones (a process known as *gatten*). This group consisted of Go-Toba, Yoshitsune, Jien, Shunzei, Teika, and Jakuren. Both poets and judges constituted a high-powered group, what we *now* see as the very center of the Shinkokin period. Yet there is some difference between what this group selected and what the *Shinkokinshū* compilers chose.

In all, nearly half the poems (148 out of 300) received a mark from one or more of the judges. Two poems, one by Kunaikyō and one by Shunzei no Musume, were marked by all six. Kunaikyō's poem was also selected for *Shinkokinshū*. The topic is "Moon after Rain":

Tuki wo nafo	I suppose they are
maturan monoka	Still awaiting the moon,
murasame no	Those in the village beyond
fareyuku kumo no	The clouds that have cleared away here
suwe no satobito	After the passing autumn shower.[119]

Because of textual variants, it is not clear which of Shunzei no Musume's poems received six marks, but of the two of her poems from this event selected for *Shinkokinshū*, the following received at least four marks and was placed at the head of Love II at the insistence of Go-Toba. The topic is "Love Conveyed by the image of Clouds":

Sitamoe ni	Surely I will die,
omofikienan	Consumed by flames of longing
keburi dani	Burning inside me.
ato naki kumo no	The aimlessly drifting cloud that is
fate zo kanasiki	my smoke
	Might at least bring sadness to him.[120]

On the whole, what ended up in *Shinkokinshū* from this event was a mixed bag. For example, although Kunaikyō got the fourth highest score in the

---

119. *SKKS* 423 (IV, Autumn 1); *Sentō kudai gojisshu*, *ZGR* 399, 14.2: 947.
120. *SKKS* 1081 (XII, Love 2); *Sentō kudai gojisshu*, *ZGR* 399, 14.2: 952. Teika records that Go-Toba ordered the compilers to place one of Shunzei no Musume's poems at the head of the second Love book, though he does not say whether Go-Toba specifically requested this one. See *Meigetsuki*, Genkyū 2 (1205)/iii/2, 1: 410. I was led to this reference by a note in Kojima, *Shinkokin wakashū no kenkyū*, p. 240.

Sentō kudai gojisshu markings (nineteen of her fifty poems were marked, putting her well behind Yoshitsune, Go-Toba, and Jien), she had the largest number of poems selected for *Shinkokinshū* (four of the twelve selected from this event were hers). On the other hand, Teika scored the lowest in the markings and none of his poems were selected for *Shinkokinshū*, yet his choices (that is, the poems he chose to mark at this event) seem to have carried the most weight from one event to the next.[121]

In trying to rationalize why there is a gap between the standards of the two events, Ariyoshi and Higuchi suggest that the *Shinkokinshū* compilers may not have had access to the records of this event in time to give it a thorough evaluation.[122] But they are making the assumption that the group involved in the *Sentō kudai gojisshu* should somehow be seen as the standard bearers (or standard setters) for poetry of the time and that *Shinkokinshū* would or should necessarily reflect their tastes. Given what we have seen of the events in 1201 alone, where the cast of characters shifted frequently and the method of generating, matching, and judging poems changed just as often, it is clear that only one person can truly be seen as setting the rules, and that is Go-Toba. It is largely after the fact that we have come to see the others as important players. Moreover, as I have argued repeatedly, standards applied to an imperial anthology are not necessarily the same as those applied to other kinds of poetic activity. This event provides more evidence for this thesis: at least five of the twelve poems selected from *Sentō kudai gojisshu* for *Shinkokinshū* received marks from Teika during the contest but were not selected by him for *Shinkokinshū*.

In sum, the process behind the *Sentō kudai gojisshu* shows yet another attempt by Go-Toba to generate high-quality work, and it is fascinating to study. Still, uncertainty remains about the actual procedures and timing (even the sponsorship—it might just as well have been organized by Yoshi-

---

121. Ten of the twelve poems selected from this gathering for *Shinkokinshū* had received a mark from Teika, compared to nine from Yoshitsune, seven from Go-Toba, down to three from Jakuren. Of course, he was the only one of the group (except Jakuren, who died before *Shinkokinshū* was completed) who was both a judge for this event and a compiler for *Shinkokinshū*.

122. Ariyoshi, *Shinkokin wakashū no kenkyū: kiban to kōsei*, pp. 120–21. Higuchi's argument, which Ariyoshi is citing (see note 118, p. 135, to this chapter), is that it was Teika who compiled the record of the event for his own use in selecting poems for *Shinkokinshū*, a thesis that makes sense but cannot be proven.

tsune). Nor did it become one of the most important sources of works for *Shinkokinshū*.

On the 3rd day of the Eleventh Month, Go-Toba finally revealed his hand and announced the commissioning of a new imperial anthology. *Meigetsuki* is surprisingly terse on the matter; the entire entry simply says: "According to a letter of instruction from the Middle Controller of the Left (*sa no chūben*, Fujiwara Nagafusa), 'a collection of waka from ancient times to the present is to be compiled.' He said the order is going to the members (*yoriudo*) of the Wakadokoro."[123]

Ienaga recalls the event with somewhat more flourish:

> Thus (did poetic activity) become an integral part of court life. Of course, both good and bad poems were being produced in ever greater numbers. And there were undoubtedly many ancient poems that earlier anthologizers had overlooked. Perhaps to bring order to the situation, His Majesty ordered six poets to apply themselves wholeheartedly to the task of compiling a new collection. The six were:
>
> Lord Michitomo, Lord Ariie, Lord Teika, Ietaka, Masatsune, the monk Jakuren
>
> These poets accepted the commission and, each striving to outdo the other, moved mountains and rivers to find good poetry. Now, it was not a foregone conclusion that everything they selected would end up being included in the anthology. Every poem would have to pass His Majesty's inspection, and all who considered themselves poets were astir, praying to the Gods and Buddhas that their work would be accepted.[124]

Jakuren died before the collection was completed, and his name is not listed as one of the compilers in the actual *Shinkokinshū* preface. His death is discussed in more detail below.

Ishida and Satsukawa provide some behind-the-scenes information about how Go-Toba arrived at this selection committee. They cite a letter from Teika's son, Tameie (1198–1275), to Masatsune's son, Norisada (d. 1266), in which Tameie discussed what was apparently family lore about the process of choosing the committee and alleged that:

1. Michichika lobbied to have himself named a compiler, but on the grounds that someone of ministerial level had never served in such a capacity before, he was denied. His son, Michitomo, was chosen instead;

---

123. *Meigetsuki*, Kennin 1/xi/3, 1: 221.
124. *IN*, pp. 72–75.

2. From the Rokujō family, both Suetsune and Tsuneie also requested to be included, but since neither was very talented and there was not much basis to choose between them, Ariie was named as the Rokujō representative;
3. Although Masatsune was young (only thirty-two) and of low rank, Go-Toba selected him because he was talented and came from a long line of poets himself.[125]

In any case, as laconic as Teika was about discussing the commission in the first place, he also made no further mention of the project for the rest of the year. He seems to have had little time to think about it. During part of the time, he was suffering from a severe cold (xi/13–21), and then he had the rehearsals and performances for the Gosechi celebration (xi/21–23?). Next he went on retreat to pray for a promotion, and the rest of the palace seems to have been preoccupied with illness and yearend activities. Teika did mention what appears to have been a small poetry contest on xi/23, but the entry is cut off, and the contest is otherwise unknown.[126]

In the entry for xii/2, Teika relates an unsettling story. About 7:00 P.M., a group had gathered with Go-Toba for an *eigu* contest. Teika lists Yoshitsune, Michichika, and a middling group of participants (Michitomo, Tomochika, Ariie, etc.). "Between the fourth and fifth rounds, a fire broke out in the capital." Michichika and Kintsune left immediately to tend to their property. Go-Toba sent people out to investigate, and the report came back that the home of Teika's father-in-law, Fujiwara Sanemune, had burned down, as had Kintsune's, and the fire was spreading. Teika noted almost dryly that the contestants submitted the rest of their poems and then left one by one.[127] Unfortunately, neither the poems nor several aristocratic mansions survived the night.

The year ended with one final contest, called the *Jūnigatsu nijūhachinichi Iwashimizu no Yashiro no uta-awase* (Poetry Contest at the Iwashimizu Shrine

---

125. IN, p. 74, supplementary note 2. Ishida and Satsukawa believe that the letter is authentic and that its contents accurately reflect what happened. Although there is no corroborating evidence, the process Tameie describes does fit with the other things we know about the time and the people, even allowing for flattery as Tameie addresses Masatsune's son.

126. The *Meigetsuki* text is rather corrupt toward the end of Kennin 1, and there is much uncertainty about whether the dates given are for the Eleventh Month or the Twelfth. The entries that seem to cover these months appear in *Meigetsuki*, 1: 221–32.

127. *Meigetsuki*, Kennin 1/xii/2, 1: 227.

on the 28th Day of the Twelfth Month). The extant texts are incomplete, and Teika provided few details. Thirty poets took part, including many of the major figures (Teika, Shunzei, Kunaikyō, Michichika), but just as many were not there (Yoshitsune, Masatsune, Ietaka). Only one poem from this event was selected for *Shinkokinshū*.

Thus ended Kennin 1. It was a pivotal year for waka. Go-Toba had gradually strengthened his grip on the poetry scene and, in so doing, had undermined Michichika's authority both in the literary world and, indirectly, in the political realm. Yoshitsune's increasing importance as Go-Toba's poetic ally went hand in hand with his rehabilitation as a politician.

In addition, a new, innovative group of poets was beginning to emerge. Teika was finally coming into his own, although his success as a poet had not yet translated into political gain. He was passed over for promotion at the end of the year; this prompted one of several similar tirades in *Meigetsuki*. He had gone to Hie Shrine to pray:

8th Day.[128] The skies were quite dark today, and toward late afternoon a light rain began to fall. After nightfall, it rained quite heavily for a while. I received word from the capital of the Promotion Roster announced on the 22nd. Oh, how it grieves me! To be denied His Majesty's favor yet again just compounds my shame. Even if I were favored, deep in my heart I believe I probably don't deserve it, but to be denied favor completely! Lately I have been performing my duties perfunctorily and have interacted with others without any enthusiasm. I feel nothing but shame and disgrace. I thought that I might withdraw completely from court life for a while, but then I thought of my son (Tameie) and decided that for his sake I would continue to bear the court's censure and perform to the best of my limited abilities. If I can survive, I cling to the hope that when he becomes an adult, we can change places.[129] Until then, I will try to serve at court patiently.[130]

In addition, Go-Toba also brought Kunaikyō, Shunzei no Musume, and Asukai Masatsune onto the stage, with prominent roles. Raising the for-

---

128. Most scholars agree this must be a misprint, probably for "28th day," since the promotion roster was not announced until the 22nd. In fact, as noted above, the chronology in *Meigetsuki* for the Eleventh and Twelfth months is quite confused and unreliable, although most entries are clear enough to be of some value.

129. Tameie was four by the Japanese count. The text is missing characters here. The first part of the sentence says "If I live, I await his becoming an adult," followed by the characters *sōten* (or *aikorobu*) which can mean "to revolve around each other; to change places with each other," then some missing characters. I am interpolating the meaning.

130. *Meigetsuki*, Kennin 1/xii/8, 1: 229.

tunes of some while checking those of others like Michichika seemed part of a larger strategy. Experimenting with poetry contests and parties, Go-Toba began to amass a body of poetry that could be drawn on for the imperial anthology that he ordered toward the end of the year. At the same time, he had, through poetry activities, begun to impose a unity at court. But the process was by no means complete.

FOUR

Go-Toba's Retreat at Minase, Kennin 2 (1202)

The second year of the Kennin era (1202) began with a poetry party at the Wakadokoro on the 13th day. The party had been announced and three topics set the day before. Teika described the meeting in detail in *Meigetsuki*. Although not the most compelling passage in his diary, it is exemplary, and worth citing in part to show how form could easily take precedence over content on an occasion like this:

[Earlier in the day, Teika had gone to Kujō Kanezane's residence to pay his respects during services for Kanezane's late wife. From there he went directly to Go-Toba's palace.] I arrived at the Retired Emperor's Palace late in the afternoon. No one was around, and so I talked with some priests until dark, when they left. People were beginning to arrive. At about 9:00 in the evening His Majesty entered the Wakadokoro.[1] The Palace Minister Michichika had Lord Nagafusa summon the poets, and we took our seats. The higher-ranking courtiers (*kugyō*) sat, as always, at the upper end of the room. The inner circle, as at the palace, included the Palace Minister Michichika, the Reizei Middle Counselor Takafusa, and the Ōmiya Consultant-Middle Captain Kintsune, all wearing hunting costume. Along the outer edge of the seating area were the Rokujō Middle Counselor Kintsugu, the Horikawa Middle Counselor Kanemune (who was wearing formal court robes, and who held his baton

---

1. As an indication of how relative notions of time and punctuality can be, Teika wrote in the previous entry that the poetry gathering was to begin at the Hour of the Monkey (between 3:00 and 5:00 P.M.), and indeed he showed up at that time. But Go-Toba does not enter the Wakadokoro until the Hour of the Boar (between 9:00 and 11:00 P.M.). See *Meigetsuki*, Kennin 2/i/13, 1: 238.

and bowed formally whenever he went forward to the poem stand or returned to his seat), the Senior Assistant Governor-General Norimitsu, the New Consultant–Middle Captain Michitomo (he and Norimitsu were in ordinary dress). The lesser courtiers (*tenjōbito*) were seated at the lower end of the room. Lord Ariie and myself were closest to the front. Then came Masatsune and Tomochika.

When Tomochika entered, the Palace Minister Michichika ordered him to quickly bring his poems up; so he came forward from his seat and did so (as ordered). One by one the lower-ranking participants came forward and laid their poems down. Next to the poem stand was a round cushion. When all the poems had been brought forward, I was summoned to the front, and I dutifully approached. The Palace Minister Michichika leaned forward and grabbed four or five poem cards. I took the ones that remained and placed them in front of the stand. When signaled, the New Consultant Michitomo came up to the stand and stacked the poem cards and then Michichika placed them one by one on the poem stand.

I began reciting the poems aloud, going in name order through the ranks. I read each person's three poems before moving on to the next participant: officer of the Left Military Guards Hideyoshi, Kamo no Chōmei, Nakahara Muneyasu, Assistant to the Imperial Stables Ienaga, Lieutenant of the Left Military Guards Tomochika, Provisional Lesser Captain of the Left Bodyguards Masatsune, Teika, Lord Ariie, Lord Takanobu (who was not present, but sent his poems), Lord Michitomo, the Minamoto Middle Captain of the Right Bodyguards (Lord Michiteru, who was not present, but sent his poems), the Fujiwara Senior Assistant Governor-General [Norimitsu], the Fujiwara Middle Captain of the Left Bodyguards (Lord Kintsune), the Fujiwara Provisional Middle Counselor (Lord Kanemune), the Fujiwara Provisional Middle Counselor (Lord Kintsugu), the Fujiwara Former Middle Counselor [Takafusa], and the Provisional Major Counselor (Lord Tadayoshi—I mumbled the word "Provisional").[2] There were also three lady's poems (on "eggshell" paper).[3] After I finished reciting the poems, I rose and returned to my seat.

The New Consultant–Middle Captain Michitomo then approached the Retired Emperor's seat and removed all the courtiers' poems. The Palace Minister placed

---

2. The last part of this list is garbled in terms of titles, but apparently Teika, whose eyesight was bad, could not tell whether the character was *tō* (short for Fujiwara) or *gon* ("provisional") and mumbled it in the hope that no one would notice. I am indebted to Professor Yasuaki Watanabe for this interpretation. It is also possible that someone else was reading the names and poems, and Teika had trouble copying everything down because that person mumbled.

3. The next two phrases are garbled. I read them as something like "Then, after arranging his own poems, the Palace Minister [Michichika]. . . . [He mumbled the last part]." Apparently Teika could not hear what Michichika said and copied down what appears now as a nonsense word.

His Majesty's poems on the stand, and Michitomo recited them. After they were chanted, the participants left one by one, beginning with those of lowest rank.[4]

The formality of the occasion is striking. Teika said not a word about the quality of the poems, although usually at such gatherings he at least critiqued his own work and cited some of the better poems. Here the issue was the form of the event itself, not the poetry it generated, and his critical observations were directed toward missteps in decorum (mispronunciations, Michichika's rudely grabbing the poems off the stand rather than getting up and carefully handling them, and so on).

There were also some noteworthy absences. Neither Yoshitsune nor Jien was there. This would almost certainly be due to the recent death of Kanezane's wife (Yoshitsune's mother and Jien's sister-in-law).[5] Jakuren was also missing, as was Ietaka, who had not appeared at a poetry gathering since the first meeting of the Wakadokoro five months earlier. Nor were the two ranking members of the Rokujō house, Suetsune (who had taken the tonsure the month before) and Kenshō, present. It had now been well over a year since they had been invited to any of Go-Toba's poetry activities, as far as extant records show. Also, no ladies are mentioned by name, although at least one presented poems.[6] The headnote to one of Echizen's *Shinkokinshū* poems says it is from a Wakadokoro event, and Ariyoshi believes the event to be this one.[7] Not all modern editions of *Shinkokinshū* agree, however, but

---

4. *Meigetsuki*, Kennin 2 (1202)/i/13, 1: 238. The comments in brackets are mine, whereas those in parentheses are in the original text, either written by Teika himself or added by later copyists. Professor Yasuaki Watanabe provided some useful guidance through this difficult passage.

5. Kanezane, deeply affected by her death, took the tonsure on i/27, the 49th day after her passing. Hōnen (1133–1212), famous founder of the Pure Land (Jōdo) sect, performed the ceremony. See *Meigetsuki*, Kennin 2/i/27, 1: 241–42.

6. In fact, the text is quite ambiguous at that point. It simply says there are three sheets (*sanmai*) of women's poems. Since each poet was to submit three poems, I am assuming each submitted three cards (*sanmai*), which would suggest only one woman presented poems. But it is possible that each poet wrote all three poems on one page, in which case three cards would suggest three women. Kunaikyō, Shunzei no Musume, and Echizen are the women mentioned most frequently in poetry events around this time. As noted below, there is evidence that Echizen was present, but I cannot be sure about the other two. Shunzei no Musume's private collection makes no mention of this event in any of its headnotes, and Kunaikyō has no extant private collection against which to check.

7. The poem is *SKKS* 24 (I; Spring). Ariyoshi, *Shinkokin wakashū no kenkyū: kiban to kōsei*, p. 539.

there is a good chance that at least Echizen took part.[8] As for the formalities, Teika himself compared the seating arrangement to that followed in the palace. Clearly this was a court ceremony more than a literary event, although it is notably built around the presentation of poems.

A somewhat more literary occasion came up a few weeks later, on the 10th day of the Second Month, although since it was apparently an *eigu* contest at the Wakadokoro, there was ample ceremony on this occasion, as well. No text survives, and in contrast to the New Year's gathering, Teika's description of this contest is perfunctory. He simply lists the participants (*without* titles) and gives the basic seating arrangements.[9] In fact, he did not even identify it as an *eigu* contest, although Masatsune's and Go-Toba's private collections do.[10]

With this *eigu* gathering, Ietaka and Jakuren returned to the poetic scene. Indeed, this was the first poetic event for Ietaka since the Wakadokoro opening ceremonies. Jien and Shunzei were also present, but Yoshitsune was not. Although the Tsuchimikado house was represented by Michichika and Michitomo, there was no one from the Rokujō house, and only Ariie to represent that school (although Ariie was a token practitioner of the Rokujō style at best). Teika mentions the topics and the fact that he was asked to be the Reader (*kōji*). According to him, the judgment discussions took a long time (*shōbu hyōtei hanahada hisashi*), but it may only have seemed that way to him, since he complained that he was suffering from a cold. Three poems from this contest appear in *Shinkokinshū*.[11]

Neither of these two events stands out in terms of format, but Go-Toba was soon to try yet another, much more unusual, approach in his effort to

---

8. For example, Minemura (*Shinkokin wakashū*, 1974, p. 45) glosses the Wakadokoro event referred to in that headnote as one that took place in the Sixth Month of Kennin 2, although neither *Meigetsuki* nor Ariyoshi list any *utakai* for that month. He repeats this contention in a later edition of the collection (Shōgakukan, 1983, 1: 41). An earlier (1953) edition also made the same assertion; see Ogami, *Shinkokin wakashū*, 1: 45.

On the other hand, in their respective editions of *Shinkokinshū*, Kojima (p. 51), Kubota Jun (2: 333), and Tanaka and Akase (p. 26) take this headnote as referring to the gathering on Kennin 2/i/13.

9. *Meigetsuki*, Kennin 2 (1202)/ii/10, 1: 242.

10. *SKKS* 1094 (XII, Love 2), by Masatsune, bears the headnote "From a poetry contest at the Wakadokoro . . . ," but the headnote to this same poem in his private collection calls it an "eigu uta-awase"; see Wakashi kenkyūkai, *Shikashū taisei*, 3: 435.

11. *SKKS* 18 (I, Spring 1), by Go-Toba; 1094 (XII, Love 2), by Masatsune; and 1609 (XVII, Miscellaneous 2), by Ietaka.

generate high-quality poetry for *Shinkokinshū*. In this exercise, the so-called *Santai waka* (literally, "waka in three styles/modes/configurations"), Go-Toba invited several poets to submit six poems, two in each of three styles.[12] Both Kamo no Chōmei's *Mumyōshō* and Teika's *Meigetsuki* contain descriptions of the proceedings. Since the former is a kind of essay in *wabun* and the latter a journal in *kanbun*, the accounts differ somewhat.

Chōmei wrote:

Back when I was in daily service at court, His Majesty [Go-Toba] held one poetry event that was quite out of the ordinary. "Compose six poems with different configurations," he ordered. "I want one Spring and one Summer poem, each to be expansive and grand (*futoku ōki*), an Autumn and a Winter poem, each of which is spare and withered (*hosoku karabi*), and one Love and one Travel poem of evocative charm (*en ni yasashi*). If you cannot do as I request, please clearly tell me your reasons, for I wish to see what is your understanding of poetic configurations (*sama*)."

It being a rather intimidating charge, some who were asked declined. As for those with no deep understanding of such things, they were not even invited in the first place. Thus, appropriately enough, the final group in this gathering included His Lordship Yoshitsune, the Grand Prelate Jien, Teika, Ietaka, Jakuren, and myself—just six.[13]

Chōmei is obviously, and justifiably, proud to be included in such a group, for which, socially speaking, he was no match.[14] This is further illustrated by the one anecdote he relates in connection with the gathering. After citing the poems he entered, he related the following:

Among the categories, I had composed quite a few spring poems. I showed them to the priest Jakuren and asked his advice. He said the poem about Mount Takama was good, and that it deserved a marking, so that is the one I submitted.[15] When we

---

12. For a thorough treatment of the event, with particular emphasis on the poems and the approaches of the respective poets, see Bundy, "*Santai Waka*."

13. Hisamatsu and Nishio, *Karonshū nōgakuronshū*, pp. 77–78. My spin on this passage differs slightly from Bundy, "*Santai Waka*," Part 1, pp. 197–98, but I am indebted to her translations of *sama* ("configuration"), *futoku ōki* ("expansive grandeur"), and *en ni yasashi* ("evocative loveliness").

14. Recall that at the Shōji 2 (1200)/ix/30 event, Chōmei had had to sit outside the hall.

15. The poem is: *Kumo sasofu / amatu farukaze / kaworu nari / Takama no yama no / fanazakari kamo*—"Heaven's springtime breeze / Which summons up the clouds / Is fragrant now— / Surely on Mount Takama / Are the cherries in full bloom!" The phrase "deserves a marking" refers to the practice of *gatten*, described in the previous chapter with reference to the *Sentō kudai gojisshu*.

gathered to have the poems recited, I was surprised to hear that Jakuren's spring poem employed exactly the same "flowers on Mount Takama" image as mine. It had never occurred to him to tell me to change mine because it was too similar to his. Rather, he judged my verse on its merits, and for that I was deeply grateful. The truth is, I have never been praised by people as being particularly sensitive, but here was evidence that in my chosen field, at least, I was being given some credit.

Chōmei then contrasts Jakuren's exemplary behavior to that of an unnamed poet who at an earlier contest had seen one of Chōmei's entries beforehand and had demanded: "Your poem is too much like mine. Change it!" "I could not refuse, so had to change mine on the spot at the contest," laments Chōmei.[16]

Chōmei was of very low rank and not in a position to assert his artistic rights vis-à-vis virtually any of the other poets at court. That is why he was so grateful to Jakuren for showing him respect as a fellow poet. This is as close to egalitarian as the aristocratic Heian court probably ever got, and it is clear from the evidence that this was a tone Go-Toba was deliberately trying to set. The Retired Emperor's sponsorship of the *Shōji ninen in dainido hyakushu* and the *eigu* contest of Kennin 1/ix/13—both of which brought together little-known poets of low rank with some of the masters—as well as his provisions for seating for *jige* (low-ranked courtiers) in the Wakadokoro, point to a sustained effort to bring a wider range of people into his cultural realm. Of course, this sort of thing is relative. Even the lowest-ranking participant in one of Go-Toba's gatherings was still an aristocrat. Nevertheless, his efforts are in marked contrast to earlier practices.

Chōmei's account suggests that Go-Toba gave the poets some time to prepare. But Teika's version, in *Meigetsuki*, implies that they only had two days' warning. On the 20th day of the Third Month, he wrote: "I was asked to come to the Minister Yoshitsune's residence, but as I was feeling ill, I did not go. Late in the afternoon, I was sent some topics by His Majesty and told to be prepared to present poems on them the day after tomorrow."[17] There is nothing to indicate that he found the task onerous, and indeed, there is no mention at all of the poems in the entry for the next day. However, on the day of the gathering, he had more to say:

---

16. Hisamatsu and Nishio, *Karonshū nōgakuronshū*, pp. 78–79.
17. *Meigetsuki*, Kennin 2 (1202)/iii/20, 1: 249.

I was summoned yet again to the Minister Yoshitsune's residence and spent the day going back and forth. At nightfall, the Minister and I went to the Retired Emperor's place. Tonight we were to submit our six poems. (The Retired Emperor had ordered us to compose them in three styles, which was extremely difficult to manage.)

Around ten at night, His Majesty entered the Wakadokoro. At his summons, I came forward and presented him the poems. Again, at his order, I proceeded to recite them aloud as the Minister Yoshitsune handed them to me one by one.

Those responding to His Majesty's invitation were Chōmei, Ietaka, Teika, Jakuren, the Abbot Jien, and the Minister Yoshitsune. The Retired Emperor also submitted six poems. Ariie and Masatsune had also been asked to participate but did not come, pleading illness. No one else took part.

Tonight, all the poems submitted were of high quality. Afterward, there was an extemporaneous poetry party that Sueyoshi was also invited to join. The topic was "Springs Draws to a Close." Again I was ordered to be the Reader. Afterward, His Majesty retired.

The [six] poems were configured as follows: Spring and Summer were grand and expansive (*ōki ni futoki*), the Autumn and Winter poems were withered (*karabi*) (that is to say, spare and chill [*yasesugoki*]), while the Love and Travel poems were in the style of evocative charm (*entai*).[18]

Although he had refrained from saying so earlier in his diary, Teika obviously found the challenge daunting, too. The reason that Ariie and Masatsune did not participate is unclear. Teika (or some later copyist) wrote in a parenthetical aside that they claimed to be *rō* (*itawari*), which might be charitably understood as "indisposed" (the interpretation Ariyoshi gives it),[19] but it might also mean they found the task overwhelming, which would accord with Chōmei's account. The illness excuse is at least plausible since *Meigetsuki* entries throughout the Third Month mention a number of people being sick, including Teika himself just two days before the event (see above). Furthermore, neither Masatsune nor Ariie appear in other entries around this time, even though at least two entries later in the same week involve large-scale court gatherings in which Teika lists numbers of participants.[20] So they may well have been too ill to participate.

It is also significant that for the third time in a row, Teika was asked to be the Reader, an important role entrusted to someone thought to know the

---

18. Ibid. As elsewhere, the material in brackets is my explanation, and the information in parentheses is there in the text.
19. *WBJ*, p. 274.
20. *Meigetsuki*, Kennin 2/iii/23–29, 1: 249–55.

waka tradition well. His move toward the center of Go-Toba's group had been gradual over the previous two years, but now it seems the Retired Emperor was beginning to see him as Shunzei's true heir.

Five of the forty-two poems produced for *Santai waka* were included in *Shinkokinshū*, two from Ietaka, and one each from Jien, Jakuren, and Teika. Not surprisingly, only one of the five was in the "expansive and grand" mode. The two other modes were represented by two poems each.[21] Perhaps more interesting is who among the *Shinkokinshū* compilers selected these poems. It appears that Masatsune had a hand in selecting all five poems (the only compiler whose name appears as selector for all five). Depending on the text, it seems that the participants (Teika, Ietaka, and Jakuren took part in the *Santai waka* and also the *Shinkokinshū* selection, although Jakuren died before the selections were complete) avoided recommending poems from this event except perhaps in one or two cases.[22] Indeed, even though Teika called the works at this gathering "of high quality," he apparently only recommended one of them, Ietaka's Travel poem (*SKKS* 981), for *Shinkokinshū*. Since the compilers were elsewhere not shy about recommending their own work or works from gatherings at which they had been present, this gap invites speculation, even more so since the process of producing the poems was evidently difficult for the participants. But hard evidence is too slim for definitive answers. Perhaps the poems seemed too mannered or too bound by condition—useful as an exercise but not spontaneous enough to have *kokoro*. But the event itself stands as an important experiment in form. One cannot help being struck by Go-Toba's focus and commitment to exploring poetry and its production, especially considering that he was still only twenty-one years old by the Western count. And one must admire those who rose to the

---

21. Bundy ("*Santai Waka*," Part 1) discusses quite extensively the three modes (and tries to account for why Teika and Chōmei used somewhat different wording for them) and how they fit into more traditional categorizations. The "expansive and grand" mode fits most closely with the traditional designation of *take*, an elevated tone that is not unknown in *Shinkokinshū* poetry but cannot be called the dominant style.

22. Gotō Shigeo's (*Shinkokin wakashū no kisōteki kenkyū*, pp. 670–890) extremely thorough analysis of all extant texts shows that it is impossible to be certain on this issue. Gotō's chart, which maps every known text, is frustrating at times, since little of a definitive nature can be drawn from it. For example, for *SKKS* 891, some textual lines list Ariie, Teika, and Masatsune as selectors, whereas others substitute Ietaka for Masatsune. Some list no selectors at all for this poem. I have based my remarks on the preponderance of evidence in this case.

challenge, most of all, perhaps, Chōmei, who stood proudly, representing the ideals of his late mentor Shun'e.

The Fourth and Fifth Months were rather quiet from a poetic standpoint. In fact, the next significant poetry gathering did not occur until the 26th day of the Fifth Month, when Go-Toba sponsored an *eigu* contest at Jōnan Temple on the grounds of his Toba residence to the south of the capital.[23] It was a large-scale event in terms of participants—twenty-six in all, including Go-Toba himself (using the pseudonym of Chikasada), Yoshitsune, Michichika, Jien, Shunzei, Michitomo, Teika, Ietaka, Kunaikyō, Shunzei no Musume, Echizen, Chōmei, Jakuren, and others—virtually all of the circle Go-Toba had so carefully built. Even the Rokujō house was represented, by Ariie and Yasusue, the latter the adopted son and nephew of Suetsune.[24]

Once again, *Meigetsuki* provides a contemporary account, complete with illustration. The contest was first announced on the 12th, with Ienaga distributing the topics. Originally set for the 18th, a postponement was announced on that day, but Teika gave no reason for it. Finally, the 26th arrived:

26th Day. Clear. Early in the morning I hurried back to my Kujō residence. I had received orders from the Minister Yoshitsune: "Since there is to be a poetry contest tonight, I want you to come to my place before evening. In fact, come straight away." So I went....

As the sun was going down, the Minister and I went to the Toba palace. We

---

23. A text for the contest can be found in GR 192, 12: 373–77; and *Shinpen kokka taikan*, 5:192, pp. 406–7.

24. The entire list: Go-Toba, Yoshitsune, Michichika, Jien, Tadayoshi, Takafusa, Kintsugu, Kintsune, Michiteru, Shunzei, Shunzei no Musume, Takanobu, Ienaga, Kanemune, Michitomo, Kunaikyō, Hakushi, Echizen, Ariie, Teika, Yasusue, Ietaka, Tomochika, Jakuren, Chōmei, and Hideyoshi. The identity of Hakushi is unknown, although like Kunaikyō and Echizen "she" is given the title *nyōbō* in the list of participants. Since the characters used to write it mean something like "Count/Uncle Senile," it is obviously a nickname, but for whom is not known, and the *nyōbō* title, if used with a pseudonym, could conceal gender as easily as reveal it. Ariyoshi, Kubota, and Gotō do not include the name in their respective indexes.

That Chikasada was a pseudonym for Go-Toba in this contest is proven by the fact that *SKKS* 1271 (XIV, Love 4), identified as Go-Toba's, appears in this contest in Round 2 of the Love topics under the name Chikasada, where it won. (He also uses the same pseudonym in the *Minase tsuridono rokushu uta-awase* a few weeks later. See below.) The *Shinkokinshū* headnote says it is from a 100-poem sequence, but Minemura (*Shinkokin wakashū* [NKBZ], p. 386) states flatly that this is an error. The poem also appears as #1582 in Go-Toba's personal collection, the *Go-Toba-in gyoshū*, where it is identified as being from this *eigu* contest (*Shinpen kokka taikan*, 4:18, p. 142).

arrived after dark. We were told His Majesty was at the Jōnan Temple. After a good while, about 9:00 P.M., His Majesty had the sliding doors taken down to double the size of the room. He was sitting at the northernmost end of the room. To his east [along the north wall] was hung the Hitomaro portrait, with the altar placed in front of it and torches for light. The nobles were then summoned, and we entered: the Minister of the Left Yoshitsune, the Palace Minister Michichika, the Abbot Jien, the noblemen [kyō] Takafusa, Kintsugu, and Kanemune, Lord [ason] Michitomo, Takanobu, Ariie, myself, Ietaka, Jakuren, and Tomochika. At His Majesty's command, Lord Michitomo offered the ceremonial wine to the portrait. Tomochika then took away the flask. The Retired Emperor asked me to be the Reader (kōji), and Palace Minister Michichika to be the Recorder (dokushi). (This must have caused the Minister of the Left, Yoshitsune, considerable pain. Surely there is no precedent for such a thing. Still, as unseemly as it was, I could only do as I was told.[25] Ietaka appeared in mourning clothes.)

Following custom, I read out the three topics and then the judgment marks were assigned after a group discussion (shūgi hyōtei). Since everyone seemed reluctant to commit [to an opinion], this took a very long time. After I had read all three fascicles and then read out the final marks, I retired from the gathering. As soon as His Majesty went back to the palace, everyone vied for the exit.[26]

Teika speaks of a group judgment, but the extant text gives only the final marks and none of the arguments. There are some unusual aspects in the way the contest was conducted. Although the matchups stay the same throughout, the rounds in which each pair appears might change from topic to topic, with no discernible order. Also, the lead-off poet on the Left team, by custom the highest-ranking member of the group, was actually Michichika, the *third*-ranking member of his team (after Go-Toba and Yoshitsune). Even in contests in which the imperial sponsor participated under a pseudonym, it was customary for that sponsor to begin the first round, Left position. But here, Go-Toba does not appear until Round 3. Truer to form is the fact that Michichika did win in the initial Left position, and Go-Toba won his rounds (at least two out of three, the third being unmarked in the extant text).

The team configurations are also lopsided. The highest-ranking member of the Right team was Kanemune, a Provisional Middle Counselor. Go-

---

25. By rank, Yoshitsune should have been chosen over Michichika to be Recorder. Teika is caught in the middle, since his loyalty, and friendship, belong to the Kujō house.
26. *Meigetsuki*, Kennin 2/v/26, 1: 262.

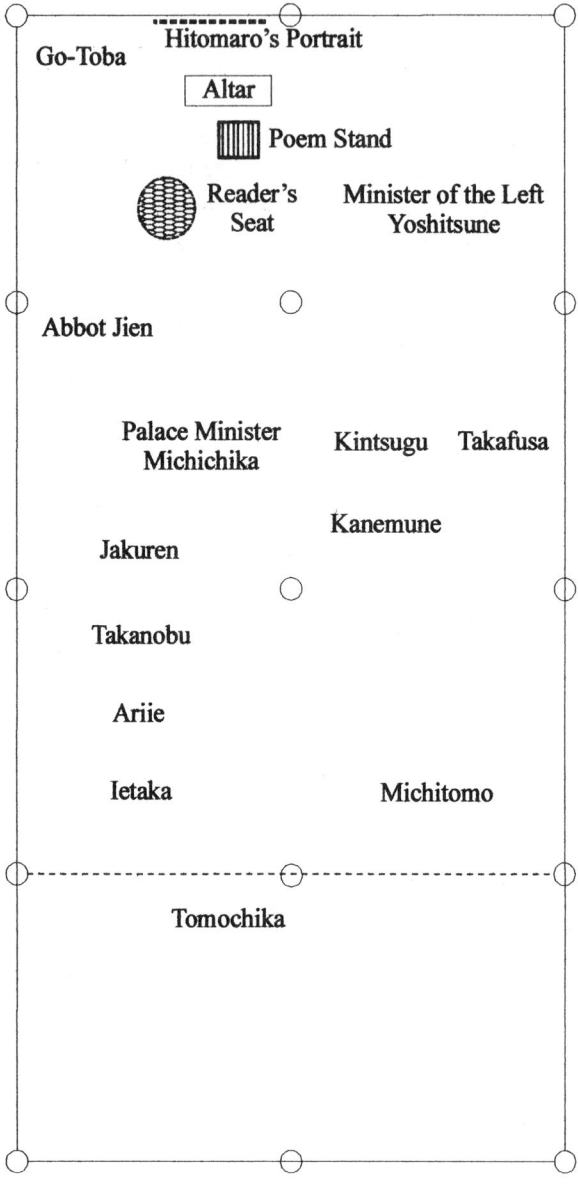

Fig. 1 Seating arrangement at the Kennin 2 (1202)/v/26 *eigu* contest at Jōnan Temple (from *Meigetsuki*, 1: 263; not all participants were shown in the original diagram).

Toba, Minister of the Left Yoshitsune, Palace Minister Michichika, the Abbot Jien, and the Provisional Grand Counselor Tadayoshi all outrank him on the Left team, whose next two members, Takafusa and Kintsugu, are also Middle Counselors. We have seen this sort of arrangement before in the *Rōnyaku gojisshu uta-awase*. In terms of talent, however, the teams are more evenly split. Yet the score was grossly one-sided. Of thirty-nine rounds, the Left team won twenty-one, the Right team only won once. Fourteen rounds ended in a Tie, and three of the rounds are unmarked. Without the judgment discussions, however, it is impossible to know what lay behind this score. My own guess is that given the formality of the occasion, rank was an important factor. Teika remarked at the length of the discussions; perhaps when people found it difficult to decide, they took the safe route and chose on the basis of rank.

In any case, four of the seventy-eight poems presented at this gathering ended up in *Shinkokinshū*. Interestingly, all four of them are from the Love rounds (specifically, the topic "Lovers Meet Once, then Do Not Meet Again," *aute awanu koi*). It is from one of these, *SKKS* 1271 (XIV, Love 4), that we know the name Chikasada in the contest text was a pseudonym, since the *Shinkokinshū* identifies Go-Toba as the poet. The other three were written by relatively low-ranked poets, who tied their rounds. Of these, two come from a single round, the eighth round of the Love topic, although they appear in separate books of *Shinkokinshū*. They are from Shunzei no Musume on the Left and Jakuren on the Right:

Left, Shunzei no Musume

    Yume ka to yo   They must have been dreams:
    misi omokage mo   That face of yours I saw,
    tigirisi mo   Those promises you made—
    wasurezunagara   For although I cannot forget them,
    ututu naraneba[27]   There's no substance to them now.

Right, Jakuren

    Sato fa arenu   My home is desolate;
    munasiki toko no   And even through my empty bed
    atari made   They blow—

---

27. *SKKS* 1390 (XV, Love 5) with the headnote: "On the topic of Lovers Meet Once then Do Not Meet Again, from a poetry contest at the Wakadokoro."

mi fa narafasi no	Hopeless, I am used to them,
akikaze zo fuku[28]	These winds of autumn.

Presumably the Tie was assigned because the group could not decide between two excellent poems. Yet they are quite different. Shunzei no Musume relied on careful verbal structure, with parallels in lines two and three and a speculative inversion reminiscent of the pre-Kanpyō style of poets like Narihira. The images in the poem, if they can be called that, are deliberately vague ones: *yume* (dream) and *omokage*, the recollected vision of someone, usually a loved one. The poem's effect, then, rests largely on its grammar and the subtle interrelationships among its vocabulary items: from dream (*yume*) to recollected visual impression (*omokage*) to substantial reality (*ututu*), which reverses the actual order in which these came to her (something made possible by syntactic features of the Japanese language upon which many waka depend, namely: inversion; the fact that modifiers precede what they modify; and the fact that predicates come at the end of a clause so that we do not know until the last two *morae* that reality [*ututu*] is being negated).

Jakuren's poem is more figurative, more elusive grammatically. The images are concrete: home (*sato*, often taken too literally as "village"), bed (*toko*), the speaker's physical being (*mi*), and the penetrating autumn winds (*akikaze*). The effect of the poem is achieved by the movement of the wind from home to bed to self, a wind that blows all the colder because the speaker, the Waiting Woman, is alone and desolate, like her home. Like Shunzei no Musume, Jakuren makes use of inversion, but whereas her poem contrasts *yume* in the first line with *ututu* in the last, his first and last lines act as outer coverings of the inner poem, as description of the external scene: "my home is desolate because the autumn wind is blowing on it." Jakuren's poem is also an allusive variation on a *Shūishū* poem with similar theme, which would have given it added depth for his contemporaries.[29]

These two poems give a sense of how wide Go-Toba's stylistic net was thrown, and how little room there would have been in his world for blind devotion to a particular style. Indeed, neither of them has the features considered most characteristic of the *Shinkokin* style: a string of nouns connected

---

28. *SKKS* 1312 (XIV, Love 4), with headnote: "On the topic Lovers Meet Once then Do Not Meet Again, when there was a poetry contest at the Wakadokoro."

29. SIS 901 (XIV, Love 4), Anonymous: *Tamakura no / sukima no kaze mo / samukariki / mi fa narafasi no / mono nizo arikeru*—"The wind that blew / Through cracks nearby my pillow / Once felt cold. / Now I realize that one / Grows accustomed to such things."

by the particle *no*, and a noun-ending in the last line (*taigendome*). (These features are discussed in more detail below.) No wonder Go-Toba had begun to exclude the doctrinaire Rokujō poets like Suetsune and Kenshō, who doubtless would have found fault with both these poems.

The *Meigetsuki* entry, which describes the aftermath of the event, ends on a personal note, giving unexpected insight into Teika and the toll his role as poetry master has taken on him:

This evening [after the contest] people told me I would have to make a new clean copy of my poems from the *Santai waka* this past spring. It appears that the original sustained water damage.[30] I informed Kanenaga and Kiyonori that since I could no longer see well enough by torchlight, I would make my copy the next day and send it along. I then took my leave. My old eyes just are not up to it anymore. I returned with Minister Yoshitsune. My whole body was exhausted and aching, in extreme pain. It was because I had had to sit formally in front of His Majesty for so long. I really ought to have returned home, but since I had no oxen, I stayed at the Kujō place instead. I could not be with my little son [Tameie] that night and felt like the parent crane deprived of its child.[31]

But evidence was forthcoming that Teika's devotion to waka was not lost on Go-Toba. Although Teika consistently scored relatively poorly in the various poetry contests we have examined, he was also selected time and again to be the Reader at these events, a position of great honor because it presupposed a knowledge of waka and its tradition. But shortly after the *eigu* contest in the Fifth Month, on yet another imperial excursion—this time to Minase—Go-Toba favored Teika with an even greater honor by participating with him in a one-on-one event that has come to be known as the *Minase tsuridono rokushu uta-awase* (Six-Verse Poetry Contest at the Minase Villa Fishing Pavilion).

Go-Toba had established a retreat at Minase several years earlier and had found it an extremely congenial spot for excursions. *Masukagami* describes how Go-Toba first found the place:

His Majesty had the Toba and Shirakawa palaces repaired and spent most of his time at one or the other, but he also had built, at a place called Minase, a villa so wonderful it is difficult to put into words. He would go there from time to time and

---

30. Perhaps this explains why the Summer poem Chōmei recorded in *Mumyōshō* differs from the one that appears in the extant text for *Santai waka*. For the differences, see Bundy, "Santai Waka," Part 1, pp. 206–7.

31. *Meigetsuki*, Kennin 2/v/26, 1: 262–63.

would conduct, under the spring flowers or autumn leaves, entertainments as the spirit moved him, causing quite a stir in society.

It seems that the distant view of the river was especially lovely, and in the Genkyū era, on the occasion of a contest of Chinese verse and Japanese poems, he composed the following:

Miwataseba	As I gaze out
yamamoto kasumu	Over the Minase River, misted
Minasegafa	At this mountain's base
yufube fa aki to	I wonder why one ever thought
nani omofikemu[32]	That "evenings are for autumn."

The thatched galleries and corridors of the villa spread out over the area in a manner most charming. The layout of the rocks around the waterfall that cascaded from the mountain in front of the villa, the way branches of the small garden pines were entwined among the trees that grew in the deep moss on the mountainside— all this truly bespoke the mist-shrouded dwelling of the ageless sage ruler.[33]

Go-Toba apparently found the site especially conducive to poetry, and many of his frequent visits there generated poetry records.[34] Go-Toba also seems to have had other reasons for choosing the Minase site, reasons that laudatory histories such as *Masukagami* were less likely to reveal. The Minase River empties into the Yodo River, which in turn empties into Osaka Bay at Eguchi, an area famous for prostitution and other forms of popular entertainment.[35] Since, according to *Meigetsuki*, visits to Minase involved *yūjo*

---

32. This poem appears as *SKKS* 36 (I, Spring 1), with the headnote: "Composed on the topic of Spring Scenery along the River, when his courtiers were having a contest between Chinese- and Japanese-style verse" (*shiika-awase*). The occasion was the *Genkyū shiika-awase* of Genkyū 2 (1205)/vi/15, which is discussed in Chapter 8.

For several interpretations of this poem, see Huey, review of Steven Carter, *The Road to Komatsubara*, pp. 361–62. Essentially I argue that Go-Toba's poem is, among other readings, a dialogue with Sei Shōnagon, who in the opening lines of her *Pillow Book* declares "Autumn is evening" (*aki fa yufugure*).

33. Iwasa et al., *Jinnō shōtōki Masukagami*, pp. 253–54. In the last sentence, the *Masukagami* writer (traditionally supposed to be Nijō Yoshimoto, although with little evidence) is playing on the original meaning of the word *sentō*, used generically in Japan to describe the palace of a Retired Emperor. Its literal meaning is "(Taoist) sage's cave-dwelling," which is a flattering comparison for Go-Toba. (One is reminded that Ienaga, too, remarked on Go-Toba's serious commitment to spiritual matters. See the opening section of Chapter 2.)

34. For example, *DNS* records nine visits for the year Kennin 2 alone (*DNS*, iv:7, pp. 16–37).

35. See the discussion of the *Meigetsuki* entry for Kennin 1 (1201)/iii/21, in Chapter 3, pp. 100–101.

(professional female entertainers) as often as waka, one may surmise that the Minase Villa was Go-Toba's "party palace." *Masukagami* makes much of the Minase Villa's rustic beauty and lovely natural surroundings, but presumably its proximity to the pleasure areas of Kanzaki and Eguchi was an equally compelling reason for Go-Toba's frequent visits.

On the 28th of the Fifth Month, Go-Toba went to the Minase Villa, taking along various courtiers, including Michichika and Teika. Teika seemed less than charmed by the summons. In his *Meigetsuki* entry for the date, he complained, with characteristic hyperbole, about the weather, the loneliness, and the forced separation from his wife and child. Once again he lamented his inability to advance at court:

I try to encourage myself, but to no avail. I work as hard as I can, but grow old, still poor. I'm sick and have nothing to my name and feel in my heart that there is no more I can do. Now here I am—having abandoned wife and child and left my home—lying in misery in these dilapidated lodgings. The rain leaks into my sleeping quarters all night, and I am helpless to stop it. So insubstantial my life! Will I never know a day of happiness? How sad!

Yuku fotaru	O, departing firefly,
nare mo yami nifa	You, too, are burning brighter
moemasaru	In the darkness.
ko wo omofu namida	Could you also know the pain of tears
afare siru yafa	From longing for one's child?[36]

Although his manner of expression may be somewhat exaggerated, the concerns Teika aired here—his frustration over his career, his desire to spend more time with his family—appear in entry after entry in *Meigetsuki*, and one may assume that they are genuine. His remarks about the weather were more literal. Over the next few days it rained heavily and frequently, and the resulting floods kept Go-Toba from returning to Kyoto. The imperial stay was extended on the 2nd of the Sixth Month and then again on the 8th. Go-Toba did not return to the capital until the 13th. (Teika went back once to check on his house but had to return to Minase.)

However, Teika's gloom did not seem to pass to Go-Toba. As we have seen before, Go-Toba's outings were anything but boring, and he made the best of this one as well, at least twice going boating as much to gawk, it

---

36. *Meigetsuki*, Kennin 2/v/28, 1: 263–64. For a somewhat different approach to the prose portion of this passage, see Brower, "Ex-Emperor Go-Toba's Secret Teachings," p. 18. He takes it much more at face value than I do.

seems, as to survey the damage to his realm. He also repeatedly enjoyed performances by *yūjo* and *shirabyōshi* dancers. Teika remarked that the former, from Eguchi, were especially upset at the flooding, presumably because Eguchi's location at the mouth of the Yodo River made it vulnerable. Go-Toba also managed a side-trip to Uji for some hunting.[37] Teika was a reluctant participant in these activities, at least to hear him tell it, and he often retired early, pleading illness.

But poetry was never far from Go-Toba's mind. Suddenly, on the 3rd Day of the Sixth Month, he sent Ienaga to Teika's room to deliver a charge: compose six poems, one on each of six topics posed by Go-Toba: Summer Moon on the River; Watching Fireflies by the Sea; Wind through Pines at a Mountain Hut; First Love; Hidden Love; Abiding Love. Teika was not given much time; Ienaga came by later that day to pick up the poems. Interestingly, Teika says he had Michichika look the poems over.[38] Teika learned that evening that Go-Toba was taking a bit more time with his verses. Two days later, Go-Toba had his six poems sent to Teika, who was enthusiastic enough about them to write them down in his diary, something he did not do with his own verses in this case.[39]

Nothing more was said, and Teika may have thought that was the end of it, for he seems to have been surprised when, on the 15th, after they had returned to Kyoto, Go-Toba sent him the twelve poems rearranged into a contest form, with judgments by the retired emperor himself. "This is an honor far greater than I deserve," Teika told the imperial messenger. This "contest" is known as the *Minase tsuridono rokushu uta-awase*. The poems and judgments are a special opportunity to look at the complex artistic relationship between Teika and Go-Toba through the latter's eyes. The second round, with its four-character compound topic (*musubidai*) on a seasonal motif, demonstrates the persistent influence of *The Tale of Genji* on medieval waka. The sixth round topic, "Abiding Love" (*hisashiki koi*, literally "long-lasting love"), might better be rendered "Unrequited Love," since that was the traditional essence (*hon'i*) of the topic.

---

37. *Meigetsuki*, Kennin 2/v/29 to vi/13, 1: 264–67.
38. Ibid., vi/3, 1: 264–65.
39. Ibid., vi/5, 1: 265. The extant text of *Meigetsuki* is damaged here, and only one of Go-Toba's poems appears in full, but as will be seen below, a full text of both Teika's and Go-Toba's six poems has survived in another form.

Round 2: *Watching Fireflies by the Sea*

Left, Teika

<blockquote>

Suma no ura	Here at Suma's shore
mosifo no makura	With briny seaweed as my pillow—
tobu fotaru	O, flitting fireflies,
karine no yumedi	Let people know how wretched I am,
wabu to tugekose[40]	Caught on a dream path, as geese call overhead.

</blockquote>

Right, Chikasada (Go-Toba)

<blockquote>

Tu no kuni ya	Here in Ashiya village,
Asiya no sato ni	In the province of Tsu—
tobu fotaru	O, flitting fireflies,
taga sumu kata no	Who once resided at this place
ama no isaribi[41]	That you mark like fisherman's flares?

</blockquote>

Judgment: The Left poem arouses memories of Middle Counselor Yukihira's lines about brine-dripping seaweed at the Suma shore and is very effective for that.[42] Further, it recalls the lines of the old poem "Pass along a message to the geese / that autumn winds now blow!"[43] Its final lines are particularly graceful. As for the Right poem, its diction is not especially striking, and the opening lines are not what one might have wished, so the Left Wins.

---

40. The *Shinpen kokka taikan* version of this poem (7:193, p. 408) has a *ya* at the end of the first line and gives the last line as *wabu to kotafeyo*, which would tie it more closely to the Yukihira poem. But the *Gunsho ruijū* version, which I have used here, accords better with the rest of the judgment (GR 192, 12: 378), for without this last line, the reference to the *Gosenshū* poem, discussed below, would not be clear. The judgments in the two versions are virtually identical.

Unfortunately, *Kokka taikan* gives no information on the textual variations in this contest, and it is not clear why the editors chose one text over another. *Meigetsuki* is little help in this matter. To begin with, Teika cites only Go-Toba's poems, and the copy has been damaged around this entry so that the text of the poems has not come down in full. What has survived has at least one copyist's error, which leads one to suspect others.

41. The *Shinpen kokka taikan* text gives the fourth line as *taga sumu ato no*, "the ruins of whose home." This could also work, but I am following the *Gunsho ruijū* text for the sake of consistency here. *Meigetsuki* also gives the line as *taga sumu kata*, although as discussed in the previous note, the diary copy is poor at this point.

42. Go-Toba is referring to KKS 962 (XVIII, Miscellaneous 2) by Ariwara no Yukihira: *Wakuraba ni / tofu fito araba / Suma no ura ni / mosifo taretutu / wabu to kotafeyo*—"If, by chance, / Anyone should ask, / Just say this: / That on the shores of Suma / Dripping brine, I suffer."

43. These lines are from GSS 252 (V, Autumn 1), by Ariwara no Narihira. The entire poem is: *Yuku fotaru / kumo no ufe made / inubeku fa / akikaze fuku to / kari ni tugekose*— "Departing fireflies / If you indeed can go off / Beyond the clouds / Let the geese know / That autumn winds now blow!"

Round 6: Abiding Love
Left, Teika

Iku yo fenu	For countless ages,
Sodefuruyama no	Like the holy fence surrounding
midugaki ni	Sleeve-waving Mountain,
koenu omofi no	I shall ever stretch sacred ropes
sime wo kaketutu[44]	To consecrate my unsurpassed love.

Right, Chikasada (Go-Toba)

Omofitutu	My longing, longing
fenikeru tosi no	Throughout these many years—
kafi ya naki	Has it been to no avail?
tada aramasi no	All I have left is my desire,
yufugure no sora[45]	Empty like this evening sky.

Judgment: The Right poem has nothing particular to recommend it, but neither does it have any faults. Perhaps this one round could be a Win for the Right.

In the second round, Teika's reference to Yukihira's poem may have had a hidden message. As noted above, Teika had, in an earlier entry in *Meigetsuki* during this same outing to Minase, vented his frustration about his lack of progress at court. The occasion of Yukihira's poem, according to its headnote in *Kokinshū*, was a self-imposed exile for some unspecified "incident." This has long been taken as one of Murasaki Shikibu's inspirations for the Suma chapter of *The Tale of Genji*, and the allusion could not have been missed by Teika's contemporaries. Perhaps Teika is suggesting that he feels a bit like Yukihira, hovering on the margins.

Go-Toba's likening of fireflies' lights to the torches fishermen use to attract fish is not a new one, although it is appropriate to the Suma locale (Suma being not far from Ashiya). He probably has Genji (or Yukihira, or both) in mind when he wonders who used to live there.

Maybe due to his desire to win at least one round, Go-Toba chose, in the sixth round, to overlook Teika's allusive variation on an old *Man'yōshū* poem attributed to Hitomaro:

---

44. The *Gunsho ruijū* text gives the last two lines as *taenu omofi no / sime wo kaketu to* ("intending to consecrate / my abiding love").

45. The *Gunsho ruijū* and *Shinpen kokka taikan* texts are the same. *Meigetsuki* gives a slightly different wording, probably due to miscopying; see *Meigetsuki*, Kennin 2/v/5, 1: 265.

Wotomera ga	You, who flutter your sleeves
Sodefuruyama no	Like the maidens at Sleeve-waving
midugaki no	Mountain,
fisasiki toki yu	With its sacred fence
omofiki ware fa	That has stood so long–
	So long have I yearned for you![46]

Or perhaps he felt that even with the clever allusion the poem lacked depth, or at least was not as good as his verse. His poem, too, contains an allusion:

Omofitutu	My longing, longing
fenikeru tosi wo	Throughout these many years
sirube nite	Is now a part of me.
narenuru mono fa	How given to routine
kokoro narikeri	Is the human heart![47]

Go-Toba's allusion is more subtle than Teika's in that Go-Toba turns the original poem in a new direction. Whereas the *Gosenshū* poet has come to wear his/her longing like a comfortable robe, Go-Toba's speaker is driven to despair. As evening—that loneliest of times for waka love—approaches, he is reminded by a cruel pun (*sora* meaning both "sky" and "empty") that his love remains unfulfilled. In fact, Go-Toba's high assessment of his own poem was shared by Teika, who wrote in *Meigetsuki*: "This [poem] is a surpassing representation of the topic."[48] It was the only poem from this contest that was selected for inclusion in *Shinkokinshū*; Teika was one of the selectors.[49]

The Minase Villa is also associated with three related poetry events in the autumn of Kennin 2, the last significant ones of 1202. But before then, the ebb and flow of life had brought changes to Go-Toba's poetry circle.

On the 7th Day of the Seventh Month, Jien resigned as Tendai Chief Abbot. It is not entirely clear why he resigned—even he fails to give a reason

---

46. MYS 504 (NKBT 501), from "Three Poems by Kakinomoto Ason Hitomaro." Also appears as #2419 (NKBT 2415), with slightly different wording. As with many *Man'yōshū* poems, this may have been known primarily through *Kokin waka rokujō* (#2549), where it appears with somewhat different wording, although the lines Teika borrows are the same in all three versions.
47. GSS 1021 (XIV, Love 6), Anonymous; Topic Unknown.
48. *Meigetsuki*, Kennin 2/vi/5, 1: 165.
49. SKKS 1033 (XI, Love 1). For information on the selectors, see Gotō Shigeo, *Shinkokin wakashū no kisōteki kenkyū*, p. 785.

in *Gukanshō*—although from Teika's reaction in *Meigetsuki*, and from surrounding events, it may have been to protest growing corruption in the priesthood as well as for personal reasons.[50] It did not seem to have any adverse effect on him politically or socially, and he was reappointed to the position several years later.[51]

On the 13th Day of the Seventh Month, Shunzei no Musume formally entered service in Go-Toba's court. She had married Minamoto Michitomo in 1190, and they had two children, but the marriage had apparently dissolved by this time. *Meigetsuki* describes the occasion of Shunzei no Musume's entry into court in some detail, from which a portion is cited here:

> This evening our lady [Shunzei no Musume] is entering the Retired Emperor's court for the first time. This event has been sheer madness from start to finish. When the Saishō Chūjō [Michitomo, her husband] had moved in with a new, politically connected wife and let his first wife's house fall into ruin,[52] the Retired Emperor summoned Shunzei no Musume to join him because of her great skill in po-

---

50. On the 3rd of the Seventh Month, one of Jien's nephews, whom Jien had taken on as a disciple, abruptly disappeared from the temple to which he had been assigned. Teika wrote there had been problems between the two men; see *Meigetsuki*, Kennin 2/vii/3 and 8, 1: 269–70.

For *Meigetsuki* readings for the Seventh Month, I have been aided by Gomi et al., "Meigetsuki, Kennin ninen shichigatsu o yomu." This article provides a careful, annotated reading of *Meigetsuki* entries for each day of the month, by members of the Meigetsuki kenkyūkai. Each entry includes a collated text (based on the text in Teika's hand uncovered among the Shiguretei library holdings of the Reizei family), a *kundoku* reading (a "Japanized" reading of the *kanbun*), followed by a modern Japanese gloss, and notes. The section covering the entries mentioned above was written by Ogami Yōsuke.

51. See DNS, iv:7, pp. 482–90; and *Meigetsuki*, Kennin 2/vii/8–13, 1: 270–71. None of the secondary sources I consulted gave this resignation more than passing attention, if that. Most simply noted that Jien was appointed to the position of Tendai Abbot a total of four times. The first resignation (see Chapter 1) was significant politically, since it coincided with the temporary setback of the Kujō house, but the later resignations are barely mentioned.

In the chronological portion of *Gukanshō*, Jien mentioned his resignation, but as Brown and Ishida remark, he gave no reason for it, although he did give reasons for the resignations of other Tendai Abbots in the same time frame. See Nakajima, *Gukanshō*, p. 169; and Brown and Ishida, *The Future and the Past*, p. 340, who also remark on the fact the Jien remained silent about his reasons for resigning.

52. This new wife, whom Michitomo married in 1199, was a daughter of the Priest Nōen, named Azechi no Tsubone Nobuko (Shinshi). Another of Nōen's daughters, Zaishi, had been adopted by Michichika (Michitomo's father) and had become Go-Toba's main wife after Kanezane's daughter, Ninshi, had left the palace in 1196 (see Chapter 1, p. 37). A less charitable observer might suggest that the Tsuchimikado clan was attempting to make up for its lack of poetic talent by forging complex and confining familial ties with Go-Toba.

etry. Could it be that Michitomo had been planning this all along from the time that he formally married his new wife? To get rid of one's principal wife and move in with that court lady seems devilish indeed, and not very honorable. Yet he says he visited Shunzei no Musume just two days ago, and that he has discussed this with father.

And so I went to Shunzei no Musume's house [to escort her]. This lady had been especially loved by her mother and had never been left to her own devices. After that, Michitomo made all her decisions for her. Then the Palace Minister Michichika recommended her to His Majesty at the request of the Retired Priest Shunzei. Now she has already been allowed to wear the forbidden colors, truly a great honor![53]

Teika seems to have had a mixed reaction to the situation. He did not like the idea that his "sister" appears to have been thrown over, yet the evidence is that Michitomo had orchestrated the whole thing carefully and given Shunzei no Musume a graceful option. Even Michitomo's father, Michichika, helps out. Ienaga Kaori argues that this was not a divorce, just a separation, and later entries in *Meigetsuki* bear this out.[54]

A week later the court was saddened by the news of Jakuren's death.[55] Of course, Teika describes this turn in *Meigetsuki*, although his reaction seems rather restrained. Everyone had gone to the Minase Villa:

20th. Weather clear. Around noon I went to Go-Toba's palace. The Middle Controller of the Left, Nagafusa, told me "The Shōsuke Nyūdō Jakuren has passed away. His son [Shōkan], the Abbot of Tennōji, sent word to the Naifu [Michichika]. Hadn't you heard?" On hearing this, I immediately took my leave, since under the circumstances I was dressed inappropriately. Although one should not be surprised by transience in this insubstantial world, it was difficult to suppress the feelings of deep sorrow that this news occasioned in me. We had been close since childhood and had remained so for many years. And in the realm of waka, was there

---

53. *Meigetsuki*, Kennin 2/vii/13, 1: 271. Imagawa's (*Meigetsukishō*, p. 123) gloss was helpful for part of this passage. Even more useful, however, was Ienaga Kaori's reading in Gomi et al., "*Meigetsuki*, Kennin ninen shichigatsu o yomu," pp. 10–12, 27.

54. Ienaga Kaori in Gomi et al., "*Meigetsuki*, Kennin ninen shichigatsu o yomu," p. 27. Two years later, when Shunzei was on his deathbed, Shunzei no Musume and Michitomo showed up together to pay him a visit. Teika noted, "For some time now, the two have supposedly been living apart, but to see them together again reminds me of earlier times" (*Meigetsuki*, Genkyū 1/xi/27, 1: 390). This is discussed further in Chapter 7, p. 290.

55. Although Teika announced the death in his entry for the 20th, for various reasons, scholars assume that Jakuren must actually have died from one day to one week earlier. See Gomi et al., "*Meigetsuki*, Kennin ninen shichigatsu o yomu," pp. 28–29.

anyone his equal? He was truly a wondrous talent. And now he has gone on to the next world. For the way of poetry, it is regrettable; for me personally, it is very sad. Ienaga told me that I should not wait until the mourning period was over, but should hurry back to His Majesty without concern for the taboo. After nightfall, the mourning was formally concluded on the banks of the Minase River in a service conducted by one of Haremitsu's disciples.[56]

The rest of this and the next three entries are taken up almost entirely by Teika's discussion of the latest round of promotions—he was once again passed over—and an imperial hunting outing. No further mention of Jakuren.[57] It is hard to know what to make of Teika's terseness here. As noted earlier, *Meigetsuki* contains no explicit mention of Shikishi Naishinnō's death even though Teika and the princess were very close. However, that gap was likely a historical accident.[58] Teika spoke much more freely about Shunzei's death, as we shall see below.

Ienaga also mentioned Jakuren's death, and with a little more flair, although some of the difference may stem from the fact that Ienaga was writing *wabun*:

Before we knew it, one year passed as the [*Shinkokinshū* compilers] worked earnestly gathering poems. In the following autumn, the monk Jakuren fell ill and presently passed away. Of course, such is the way of the world, and perhaps it was his time to go, but one wonders how he must have felt as he faced death, having received the honor of an imperial appointment but being unable to fulfill his duties before he died.

His Majesty was profoundly saddened, as was readily apparent from his appearance. Likewise, words fail me when I try to describe how those who, like him, had embraced the world of poetry grieved with one another. Among them in particular were his fellow members of the Wakadokoro, who were sunk in the deepest tears of mourning and took the loss more personally than anyone else.

Since at that time we were all at the Minase Villa with His Majesty, we were not able to attend the funeral services for Jakuren, alas! When Teika heard of Jakuren's death, he sent the following poem to Masatsune:

---

56. *Meigetsuki*, Kennin 2/vii/20, 1: 272–73. The Haremitsu mentioned here is presumably the same one who appears in the *Gukanshō* passage describing Kujō Yoshitsune's death, where he is characterized as a Master Astrologist (*tenmon hakase*—an official post in the Bureau of Yin-Yang, or Bureau of Divination, as some translations have it). See Nakajima, *Gukanshō*, pp. 509, 512; and Brown and Ishida, *The Future and the Past*, pp. 166–67 (where his name is read Harumitsu). See also Chapter 9, pp. 336–37, of this study.

57. *Meigetsuki*, Kennin 2/vii/20–23, 1, 272–73.

58. See Chapter 3, pp. 86–91.

Tamakifaru	I cannot follow
yo no kotofari fa	The workings of
tadorarezu	This soul-spent world.
nawo uramesiki	How resentful I feel now
Sumiyosi no kami	Toward the God of Sumiyoshi[59]

Masatsune's reply:

Wakaredi wo	What else is there to do
uramite mo mata	But feel resentment
ikaga sen	At this separation—
kakaru ukiyo ni	For we live in such a sad, uncertain world
Sumiyosi no kami	Subject to the God of Sumiyoshi?

Indeed, one has to wonder why the God of Sumiyoshi discarded Jakuren. I, too, felt resentment and could not stop my tears.

And just the year before, the death of Shikishi Naishinnō had brought grief too difficult to describe! As more and more died like this, the future of poetry looked dim, and I felt my own responsibility all the more keenly.[60]

We may surmise that in the meantime the *Shinkokinshū* selection committee has been carrying out its charge. It appears that in the early stages each compiler worked on his own, culling old collections for good poems. In a *Meigetsuki* entry for the 13th day of the Eighth Month, Teika wrote: "Since the day before yesterday, my right eye has been extremely swollen. It must be due to eyestrain from my work selecting poems. For two days, I tried to report for duty, but since yesterday evening it has swollen shut, and I did not go out today."[61]

---

59. What I have rendered "soul-spent" is the pillow word *tamakifaru*, which is of uncertain meaning. The most common speculation is that the *tama* element is from the word for "soul" and the *kifaru* is a verb meaning "break into bits" or "reach its limits." How it came to be associated with words like *inoti* (one's allotted life span) and *yo* (this world; phenomenal reality) is unclear.

The God of Sumiyoshi was seen as a patron deity for waka, hence Teika's resentment, since Sumiyoshi should have been watching out for Jakuren. There is also an ironic pun on the *sumi* in Sumiyoshi, since it is also a form of the verb meaning "to live."

60. *IN*, pp. 75–78. It is at this point that Ienaga begins his "obituary" for Princess Shikishi, quoted in Chapter 3 above. He treats time as fluid indeed.

61. *Meigetsuki*, Kennin 2 (1202)/viii/13, 1: 276. I am indebted to Ishida and Satsukawa (*IN*, p. 213), for drawing my attention to the importance of this reference. For a detailed reading of all the *Meigetsuki* entries for the Eighth Month, see Gomi et al., "*Meigetsuki* Kennin ninen hachigatsu o yomu."

On the 10th of the Ninth Month, Go-Toba returned to the Minase Villa, where he initiated an important poetry contest that, along with its two permutations, would be the last important poetry activity of the year. Strictly speaking, there was only one submission of poetry, but the poems were then reconfigured into three separate *senka-awase*, and judged differently; so each is considered a distinct "event."[62]

As usual, one starts with *Meigetsuki* to learn about the sequence of activities, which began toward the end of the previous month. In the entry for the 29th of the Eighth Month, Teika mentioned that Go-Toba sent him fifteen topics for poems, but he gave no other details. He completed the poems the next day and sent them back to Go-Toba.[63] (Although Teika did not know it at the time, eight others submitted poems to Go-Toba: Yoshitsune, Jien, Kintsugu, Ariie, Shunzei no Musume, Kunaikyō, Ietaka, and Masatsune. The Retired Emperor also composed poems on these topics.) On the 9th of the Ninth Month, the courtiers learned that Go-Toba intended to leave for Minase the following day, and Teika was informed through an intermediary that Go-Toba was going to hold a poetry contest at Minase on the 13th and wished Shunzei to come. Teika expressed concern since the elderly poet was suffering from some sort of respiratory illness. Teika traveled with the others to Minase on the 10th, but Shunzei did not arrive until about sundown on the 12th, after a difficult journey by boat and palanquin.[64]

Teika's description of the events of the following evening, when the contest occurred, are worth quoting at length:

13th Day. The morning skies gradually cleared; clouds and fog completely dissipated. At nightfall, the moon shone pure and bright. I went to the main villa at midmorning.[65] Most everyone was dressed in formal hunting costume; it seems that the Minister of the Left Yoshitsune was due to arrive soon. After noon, I changed into hunting costume myself and joined the others in waiting eagerly for the Minister's arrival. He was to be housed in the quarters normally occupied by the entertainers.[66]

---

62. Much of the following is indebted to Ariyoshi, *Shinkokin wakashū no kenkyū: kabin to kōsei*. On pp. 123–26 he excerpts all the *Meigetsuki* entries related to the *Minasedono koi jūgoshu uta-awase*, and on pp. 126–48 he provides an exhaustive evaluation of the known textual lines.

63. *Meigetsuki*, Kennin 2/vii/29, 30, 1: 278–79.

64. *Meigetsuki*, Kennin 2/ix/9, 10, 12, 1: 280; and *Inokuma kanpakuki*, Kennin 2/ix/9 (DNS, iv:7, p. 546).

65. Teika says it was the Hour of the Snake, about 10:00 A.M. at this time of year.

66. "Entertainers" here is *yūjo*, literally "play girls," female entertainers, such as the *shirabyōshi* dancers, who would be brought into the homes of the aristocracy to perform. As discussed

Some time passed, and finally, around mid-afternoon, the Minister's party arrived.[67] The Abbot Jien was the first to appear. Then came the Minister's carriage, accompanied by Lords Ariie and Sukeie.[68] They went directly to His Majesty's rooms.

Then orders came that Shunzei was to present himself immediately to His Majesty. I quickly relayed the message to him. Shortly after father came, His Majesty Go-Toba entered the room. A poetry contest of fifteen love poems was announced. As usual, I was the Reader. Lords Ariie and Masatsune were in attendance upon the Retired Emperor. Aside from the participants, the Palace Minister Michichika was also present. Deliberations on the poems lasted until well after nightfall.

After the contest was completed, His Majesty posed topics for extemporaneous composition. I was suffering discomfort due to some moxa treatments[69] and did not compose with any noteworthy skill. The topics were "Autumn Storm Beneath the Moon," "Autumn Moon Upon the Water," and "Deer Cries under a Lingering Moon." After everyone had finished composing their poems, I was once again asked to act as Reader. Then we composed acrostic poems on the syllables zi-u-sa-mu-ya, for "thirteenth night."[70] And again I acted as the Reader after the poems were completed. And finally we composed with the hidden topic "Minasegawa."[71] And again I was the Reader. When all this was over, His Majesty withdrew to his rooms and everyone else left.[72]

One can only imagine how exhausting this evening must have been. This entry and many others like it in *Meigetsuki* support Ienaga's depiction of Go-

---

above, they were almost always in attendance at Minase when Go-Toba went there. The fact that the Minase Villa had special quarters for them (ones nice enough to accommodate the Prime Minister at that!) indicates how often they must have been brought in for visits.

67. Teika says the early Hour of the Monkey, at this time of year between 3 and 4 P.M.

68. Fujiwara Sukeie (1177–1224+) was named Wakadokoro Bettō (chief administrator) in 1204, and eventually rose to the Junior Third Rank in 1218, before taking the tonsure in 1224, after which nothing is known of him. He does not figure in Go-Toba's poetry circle.

69. I am assuming that *shaji*, which does not appear in any standard dictionary, including Morohashi's *Daikanwa jiten*, is a mistake or alternative for *kyūji*, meaning moxa, which makes sense in the context.

70. These were standard *oriku*, in which a five-syllable word is broken into its constituent syllables, which are then placed in order at the head of each line of a five-line tanka. In this case, the word is *jūsanya* (meaning "thirteenth night" of the lunar month) the syllables for which were zi-u-sa-mu-ya in the traditional spelling.

71. In a "hidden topic" (*kakushidai*) composition, a word or phrase was "buried" in a poem so that its constituent syllables formed parts of other contiguous words. The resulting poem referred to or pointed at the hidden topic without stating it overtly. An example in English might be if one were to use the word "apple" as a hidden topic in the following lines: "'Take off your *cap, please*,' said Bill Tell, as he took aim."

72. *Meigetsuki*, Kennin 2/ix/13, 1: 280.

Toba as almost fanatically devoted to poetry and literary play. In fact, in such evenings as these, in which one activity followed quickly on another, one can see *suki*, the pursuit of elegant pleasures that became intimately linked with the composition of poetry.[73]

The feature contest of the evening, now known as *Minasedono koi jūgoshu uta-awase* (Poetry Contest of Fifteen Love Verses at the Minase Villa) survives in several textual lines. Since it was also reconfigured as two separate *senka-awase*, as discussed below, there is some doubt as to how the event unfolded.[74] From the *Meigetsuki* we know that the poems were prepared in advance, and we can guess that Go-Toba matched them before the night of the 13th. Present on the night of the 13th were Go-Toba, Yoshitsune, Jien, Kintsugu, Ariie, Shunzei, Teika, Masatsune, and Michichika. Of these nine, neither Shunzei nor Michichika had submitted poems for the contest. The purpose of the gathering on the 13th was evidently to discuss the poems and provide Shunzei with opinions upon which he could base his judgments. In fact, a notation in the standard text says that judgment marks were decided on the night of the 13th, but the judgment comments were added later. Three other poets, Shunzei no Musume, Kunaikyō, and Ietaka, appear in the extant texts of the contest, but there is no evidence that they were present for the discussion on the 13th.[75]

This was not a true *tōza* contest, then. The matchups by round did not follow a strict order, nor were the teams fixed. Only Go-Toba and Masatsune appeared on the same team throughout; the former, under the pseudonym Chikasada, is always on the Left, and the latter on the Right. The other poets moved between the teams from round to round in no fixed order,

---

73. As we saw in Chapter 3, pp. 100–101, Go-Toba is described as sponsoring an all-day "play" session involving horseback riding, *shirabyōshi* dancers, and mock song contests comparing the virtues of prostitutes from Kanzaki and Eguchi; the pursuits surrounding waka composition were not always exclusively elegant, but they inevitably involved connoisseurship.

74. Ariyoshi (*Shinkokin wakashū no kenkyū: kiban to kōsei*, pp. 126–46) lists twenty-three separate extant texts and details all the variants among them. The more recent Chūsei uta-awase kenkyūkai, *Chūsei uta-awase denbon shomoku* (pp. 68–72), catalogs a staggering sixty-nine texts. In my discussion I am following the collated version found in the *Shinpen kokka taikan*, 5:194, pp. 408–14.

75. Ariyoshi (*Shinkokin wakashū no kenkyū: kiban to kōsei*, p. 125) makes a solid argument that they were not, though the details are not necessary here. His view, repeated in such places as Murao Sei'ichi's essay on the *Minase koi jūgoban uta-awase* in vol. 6 of Ōsone Shōsuke et al., eds., *Kenkyū shiryō Nihon koten bungaku* (pp. 336–37), is now widely accepted.

although rank seems to have been one important consideration, since Yoshitsune, Jien, and Kintsugu appear predominantly on the Left team, and the low-ranking Ariie, Teika, and Ietaka appear in roughly comparable proportions on the Right team.[76] The two court ladies, Shunzei no Musume and Kunaikyō, appear seven times on the Left, and eight on the Right.

Go-Toba—assuming it was he who prepared the matchups—presumably had other principles in mind, too, when he paired the poems. Sometimes the matches fit in obvious ways, through the use of similar words or phrases for example (in Round 7, for instance, both poets use variants of the word *amari*, which is noted in the judgment), but at other times the reason for the pairing is not so clear. Since the Left team won nearly twice as many rounds as the Right (forty-one to twenty-one, with thirteen Ties), it might be that Go-Toba placed the poems he considered better on the Left as a way to test his own judgment against the group's and Shunzei's. However, as noted above, since the politically powerful Go-Toba, Yoshitsune, and Jien were on the Left Team in forty of the forty-five rounds in which they competed, the contest was weighted toward the Left team in any case. Their Win:Loss records—fourteen to one for Go-Toba, ten to five for Yoshitsune, and nine to three (with three Ties) for Jien—tend to confirm the importance of social status in the final judgments.

The quality of the poetry is high, and the judgments provide a good look at the poetics of some of Go-Toba's group. Fifteen (10 percent) of the poems from this contest ended up in *Shinkokinshū*.[77] Following are two representative rounds:

Round 13: Autumn Love

Left, Shunzei no Musume, Tie

    Nakiwataru   Even the tears of geese
    kumowi no kari no   As they fly, crying,
    namida safe   Beyond the clouds
    tuyu oku sode no   Fall as dew on these sleeves
    yofa no katasiki   Which I spread tonight as lonely bedding.

---

76. Yoshitsune, Jien, and Kintsugu appeared on the Left team in thirteen, twelve, and eleven of the fifteen rounds, respectively. Ariie and Teika each appeared on the Right team eleven times; Ietaka thirteen times.

77. See Ariyoshi, *Shinkokin wakashū no kenkyū: zokuhen*, pp. 254–66, for a discussion of all fifteen of these poems and how they fared in the contest.

Right, Masatsune

Nagamesi ya	How I have gazed upon it,
kokorodukusi no	With a heart grown weary,
aki no tuki	This autumn moon,
tuyu no kagoto mo	My reproaches insubstantial like the dew
sode fukaki koro	Now deep as tears upon my sleeves!

Judgment: The effect of the lines "even the tears of wild geese beyond the clouds" (kumowi no kari no namida safe) in the Left poem is fine, yet the last lines of the Right poem, "My reproaches insubstantial like the dew now deep as tears upon my sleeves" (tuyu no kagoto mo sode fukaki koro) are also very lovely; so this must be considered a Tie.

Round 21: Love at Daybreak

Left, Ietaka, Win

Wasurezu yo	I do not forget,
ima fa no kokoro	My heart in turmoil
Tukubane no	For your promised visit—
mine no arasi ni	Above the storm-lashed peak of Tsukuba
ariake no tuki	Lingering moon at dawn…

Right, Masatsune

Namida safe	So even my tears
sigi no fanegaki	Are now beyond counting,
kaki mo afezu	Like the beating of a snipe's wings—
kimi ga konu yo no	Sky before the dawning
akatuki no sora	Of a night when you did not come…

Judgment: In the Left poem, the lines "my heart in turmoil for your promised visit" (ima fa no kokoro tukubane no) convey much feeling. In the Right poem, the lines "beyond counting, like the beating of a snipe's wings" (sigi no fanegaki kaki mo afezu) call to mind the poem "I mark off the nights / when you do not come" and are outstanding.[78] *However, the lines "above the storm-lashed peak of Tsukuba / lingering moon at dawn" (mine no arasi ni ariake no tuki) are even better.*

Syntactically, all four poems feature a pattern that, although not unique to the Shinkokin era, became particularly prominent from that time. I am referring to the stringing together of three or more nouns, using the case

---

78. As the judgment notes, Masatsune's poem alludes to an anonymous *Kokinshū* poem, (#761; XV, Love 5): *Akatuki no / sigi no fanegaki / momofagaki / kimi ga konu yo fa / ware zo kazu kaku*—"The snipe beats its wings / Beats them a hundred times and more / Just before dawn / I mark off the nights / When you do not come."

particle *no* in between each.[79] For convenience, I will call this the "x-no-y-no-z pattern." Unfortunately, English usage generally demands that the order of the images be reversed in translation, which considerably dilutes its effect. The device is often, although not always, used to lead the reader's focus from wide to narrow (as in Ietaka's *Tukubane no mine no arasi*, literally, "storm on the peak of Tsukubane"), large to small (as in Shunzei no Musume's *kumowi no kari no namida*, literally, "tears of geese beyond the clouds"), general to particular, and so on.[80] (Not incidentally, both Ietaka's and Shunzei no Musume's phrases were specifically cited in the judgments.) Given the emphasis on nouns in the descriptive approach, such syntax might seem inevitable, yet adjectives or verbs in their attributive form might just as easily work as connectors for nouns. However, the neutral case particle "no" demands virtually no attention at all, thus assuring the focus remains on the noun images. The poet's challenge then becomes how best and most imaginatively to juxtapose these nouns. Although this stringing together of nouns can be found practically throughout waka history, it became particularly marked from the late twelfth century and was associated more with Mikohidari and other progressive poets than with their Rokujō counterparts.

Another noteworthy feature of these *Minasedono* contest poems is that all four of them end with a substantive in the last line (a device known as *taigendome*). Again, this is not unknown in earlier poetry, but statistically, it becomes far more frequent from the late 1100s. A simple comparison will illustrate this. In the *Kyūan gannen rokugatsu jūhachinichi uemon no kami Ienari no ie no uta-awase* (Poetry Contest at the Residence of Commander of the Right Guards Ienari on the 18th Day, Sixth Month, First Year of Kyūan [1149]), a gathering of predominantly Rokujō poets, judged by Akisuke, only three of the thirty-three poems (10 percent) in the contest end with a substantive. A somewhat higher percentage can be found in the *Nin'an ninen hachigatsu taikō taigōgū no suke Tsunemori no ie no uta-awase* (Poetry Contest at the Residence of Assistant to the Empress Dowager Tsunemori in the Eighth Month, Second Year of Nin'an [1167]), again a mostly Rokujō event, where the proportion is

---

79. Kunaikyō's *tuki wo nafo* poem from *Sentō kudai gojisshu*, translated in Chapter 3, is another example of the points discussed below.

80. Using apostrophes in English can be misleading, since the *no* is not always simply a possessive, but also functions as a delimiter or qualifier. For example, *kumowi no kari* is better thought of as "geese that are [in] the cloud-place," rather than "cloud-place's geese." Brower and Miner, *Japanese Court Poetry*, pp. 278–85, discuss this feature, although they inaccurately characterize the "no" as a "possessive particle."

thirteen of sixty poems (22 percent), although none of the twelve Love poems in this contest ends with a substantive. By contrast, in a mixed Rokujō/Mikohidari event, with Shunzei as the judge, the *Jishū sannen jūgatsu jūhachinichi udaijin Kanezane no ie no uta-awase* (Poetry Contest at the Residence of Minister of the Right Kanezane on the 18th Day, Tenth Month, Third Year of Jishū [1179]), thirteen of the thirty poems (43 percent) had substantive endings, although again, this feature is not found among the eight Love poems in the contest.[81] However, in the *Minasedono koi jūgoban uta-awase*, largely a Mikohidari / Go-Toba group, judged by Shunzei, 53 of the 150 poems ended with substantives (35 percent), and, of course, these were *all* Love poems.

It is fair to say, then, that *taigendome* is something of a trademark of the *Shinkokin* style. It seems a logical outcome of the descriptive style, leaving the reader with a concrete image that itself may be familiar but has been redefined by the lines that precede it. The technique also fits with the neo-classicism that characterizes the age. As noted earlier, Heian classics such as *The Tale of Genji* and *The Pillow Book* rose to new prominence due to the efforts of Shunzei and Teika. In the famous opening passage of *The Pillow Book*, Sei Shōnagon used a device that might be called *taigenSome*, that is, she *began* (*someru*) each section with a substantive in isolation (each of the four seasons, and the time of day most appropriate to it from a poetic standpoint) and then proceeded to qualify and modify it. *Faru fa akebono* (spring is dawn), she asserted; for autumn, *aki fa yufugure* ("autumn is evening"). It is no accident that so many of the *taigendome* of the *Shinkokin* era are *faru no akebono* or *aki no yufugure*.

In line with this neo-classicism, Shunzei no Musume's poem contains a *Genji* reference: *kumowi no kari* (wild geese beyond the clouds)—a phrase prominently featured in *Genji* (one character derives her name from it), yet not canonized in imperial anthologies until Teika's *Shinchokusenshū* (1235). In his own work, Teika "sanctified" many of Murasaki Shikibu's poetic phrases—in effect codifying his father's belief that a knowledge of *Genji* was crucial for poets.[82]

Even if the story ended here, we would have a valuable document for understanding the emerging *Shinkokin* style. But there is more. Perhaps in an attempt to remove rank consideration as a factor (although Go-Toba,

---

81. I have calculated these statistics using the versions of these contests found in Hagitani and Taniyama, *Uta-awaseshū*, pp. 360–427.

82. See Chapter 1, "The Politics of Allusion," pp. 17–23.

Yoshitsune, and Jien still fared best both in terms of how many of their verses were selected and how they scored), about two weeks after the contest, Go-Toba took thirty of the verses and rematched them into a shorter, fifteen-round contest, which he then judged himself and evidently intended to offer at the Wakamiya Shrine at Kasuga. This shorter contest, now known as *Kennin ninen kugatsu nijūrokunichi Wakamiya senka-awase* (Contest of Selected Poems for the Wakamiya Shrine on the 26th Day, Ninth Month, Second Year of Kennin), was subsequently judged yet again, apparently by Shunzei, and offered to the Sakuranomiya Shrine. The history of this text, called the *Minase Sakuranomiya jūgoban uta-awase* (Poetry Contest in Fifteen Rounds for the Minase Sakuranomiya Shrine), is obscure. Ariyoshi's view is that Go-Toba sent Shunzei the *Wakamiya senka-awase* for his comments and that Shunzei's slightly revised judgments (*tsuihan*) form the *Minase Sakuranomiya jūgoban uta-awase*. In fact, in many cases the wording of the judgments is virtually identical, and the differences between the two are negligible. Ariyoshi painstakingly reviews the textual variants (several texts have emerged since he wrote his analysis), and even at one point seems to want to say that Teika, not Shunzei, was responsible for the *Sakuranomiya* judgments; ultimately, however, his conclusions are tentative.[83]

In any case, the result is that for some of the poems in the original *Minasedono koi jūgoshu uta-awase* we have three different judgments. We can also look at which of these poems were selected for *Shinkokinshū*. This gives us even more insight into the poetic values of Go-Toba's group. The poems from two rounds of the original *Minasedono* contest can serve as examples:

Round 20: Winter Love

Left, Shunzei no Musume, Win

Kayofikosi	The grasses on the path
yado no mitisiba	That he once took to my house
karegare ni	Are withered, untouched

---

83. Ariyoshi, *Shinkokin wakashū no kenkyū: kiban to kōsei*, pp. 154–77. I do not wish to slight Ariyoshi's exhaustive analysis, which is an impressive piece of detective work, but many of the small differences one finds between the texts of the *Wakamiya* and *Sakuranomiya* versions might just as easily be explained by the vagaries of copying practices through the centuries, and only two or three of them shed any light on how Go-Toba's poetic standards might be diverging from the Mikohidari style. For a list of all known texts of the *Wakamiya* and *Sakuranomiya* contests as of 1991, see Chūsei uta-awase kenkyūkai, *Chūsei uta-awase denbon shomoku*, pp. 72–75.

ato naki simo no	By his footprints now gone.
musuboforetutu	A frost is crystallizing there.

Right, Teika

Toko no simo	The frost on my bed,
makura no kofori	The ice on my pillow,
kiewabinu	I despair that they will ever melt,
musubi mo okanu	For they are fixed steadfast in a way
fito no tigiri ni	My lover's promises never were.

Judgment: The Left poem is very nice in feeling and in overall effect. And the lines in the Right poem, too, "toko no simo makura no kofori" and "musubi mo okanu" are excellent. However, since the Left poem is also nice, it was awarded the Win.

In the *Wakamiya* and *Sakuranomiya senka-awase*, Shunzei no Musume's poem appears on the Right in Round 4, against a poem on Autumn Love by Ietaka that had also won its round in the *Minase* contest. The judgment given below is that found in the *Wakamiya* contest:

Left, Ietaka, Win

Omofiiru	Deeply in love.
mi fa Fukakusa no	Am I no more than autumn dew
aki no tuyu	On Fukakusa's deep grasses,
tanomesi suwe ya	Subject in the end, despite my trust,
kogarasi no kaze[84]	To the withering blast of a cold wind?

Right, Shunzei no Musume

Kayofikosi	The grasses on the path
yado no mitisiba	That he once took to my house
karegare ni	Are withered, untouched
ato naki simo no	By his footprints now gone,
musuboforetutu	A frost is crystallizing there.

Judgment: Although both Left and Right poems have a nice configuration, the Left's "subject in the end, despite my trust / to the withering blast" is lonelier.

The *Sakuranomiya* judgment begins slightly differently ("Both Left and

---

84. Ietaka's poem is Round 15, Right, in the *Minase* contest, where the first line is given as *omofiiduru* (to recall) in the standard text. The *Minase* judgment quotes with admiration the lines *mi fa Fukakusa no / aki no tuyu* (the allusive lines, in others words), and *tanomesi suwe ya / kogarasi no kaze*, the final substantive.

Right poems have a truly lovely configuration"), but ends the same way. There may be significance in the word change from "nice" (*yoroshi*) to "lovely" (*omoshiroshi*), the former being as common and innocuous in these judgments as its equivalent "nice" is in modern American English. But overall, the evaluation of this round seems the same in the *Sakuranomiya* and *Wakamiya* versions of the contest.

Both poems contain allusions, a common feature of *Shinkokinshū* style. Ietaka's, in fact, alludes to two sources. The first is to a poem by Michitsuna's Mother in *Kagerō nikki*, and the second is to a famous poem about Fukakusa by Narihira, which appears in both *Ise monogatari* and *Kokinshū*. Shunzei no Musume's poem borrows from a verse in the Heian romance tale *Sagoromo monogatari*.[85]

"Niceness" is what gave Shunzei no Musume's poem the Win against Teika in the *Minase* contest. She uses assonance (*karegare ni* and *ato naki simo no*) to give the poem rhythm, and her image of delicate frost—even something so delicate as frost!—untouched by footprints suggests the fragile psychological state (as well as the precarious social position) of the Waiting Woman. Teika's poem, on the other hand, opens with waka's version of a parallel couplet (*toko no simo / makura no kofori*, literally "bed's frost / pillow's ice") that points back to a technique favored by Ariwara no Narihira and

---

85. The poem by Michitsuna's Mother, composed when she was left behind by her siblings after the mourning period for her father had passed, reads: *Fukakusa no / yado ni narinuru / yado moru to / tomareru tuyu no / tanomosigenasa*—"Dew left behind / Lodged in the lodgings / Surrounded by deep grasses / Not something to rely on!" (Suzuki et al., *Tosa nikki, Kagerō nikki, Izumi shikibu nikki, Sarashina nikki*, p. 329).

The Narihira poem, purportedly sent by the poet to a woman he was leaving behind in Fukakusa (lit., "deep grasses") when he moved to the capital, can be found in *Ise monogatari*, Episode 123, and KKS 971 (XVIII, Misc. 2): *Tosi wo fete / sumikosi sato wo / idete inaba / itodo Fukakusa / no toya narinamu*—"If I were to leave / This village of Fukakusa / Where I've lived through many years / How much deeper, then, / Its grasses would become!" Shunzei no Musume's reference to *Sagoromo monogatari* is a poem by the hero, longing for a lover who has disappeared: *Tadunubeki / kusa no fara safe / simogarete / tare ni tofamasi / mitisiba no tuyu*—"Although I should visit / Even the grassy plains / Are now withered by frost. / Whom can I ask about her? / The dew upon the roadside grasses?" (*Shinpen kokka taikan*, 5:424, #45, or see Mitani and Sekine, *Sagoromo monogatari*, p. 119). This poem was highly thought of in medieval times, appearing in Teika's *Monogatari nihyakuban uta-awase* (Contest in Two Hundred Rounds of Poems from Romance Tales, ca. 1206), as well as in *Shōtetsu monogatari* (1448?), among other places.

poets of that era and draws approval in the judgment. Why, in the end, one poem was chosen over the other is not clear, unfortunately.[86]

In any case, Shunzei no Musume's "niceness" is not enough against Ietaka's poem. "Loneliness," a specific emotion appropriate to Ietaka's topic of Love in Autumn, prevails. This accords with the commonly held view that *sabishisa* (loneliness), or tonal depth in general, was an important aesthetic concept to the *Shinkokinshū* poets.[87] In addition, only Ietaka's poem exhibits the syntactical features discussed above, namely, the x-no-y-no-z modification pattern and *taigendome*, both of which were noted implicitly in the original winning judgment from the *Minasedono* contest.

All three poems were selected for *Shinkokinshū*.[88] The selection committee, however, was not unanimous in these choices. Shunzei no Musume's poem was selected by Ariie, Teika, Ietaka, and Masatsune, Ietaka's by Ariie and Masatsune, and Teika's only by Michitomo, the one surviving compiler who had had no connection to the *Minase* contest.[89] Since Go-Toba did not excise these poems from the Oki-bon, we may assume he approved of them. Shunzei no Musume's and Ietaka's poems appear in a six-poem sequence of poems from the *Minase* contest that straddles Love Books Four and Five. Ariyoshi rightly comments that this was a privileged position and surely drew attention to these works.[90] Teika's poem is placed less prominently, eleven poems from the end of the second Love book. However, it is placed right after a poem by Shunzei no Musume that appears as the Right entry in Round 1 of the *Minase* contest (and the Left entry for Round 1 of the *Wakamiya* and *Sakuranomiya* contests).[91] Clearly their diction, their depth, and their use of allusion were seen as exemplary by the compilers.

Round 75 of the *Minase koi jūgoban uta-awase* provides another example:

---

86. Teika's poem was also selected for the *Wakamiya*/*Sakuranomiya* contests. It was put in Round 5 against a poem by Kunaikyō, which itself had "lost" its round in the *Minase* contest. In the *Wakamiya* and *Sakuranomiya* contests, the two poems tied.

87. It is hard to improve on the discussion in Brower and Miner, *Japanese Court Poetry*, pp. 231–33ff.

88. The *Shinkokinshū* numbers are 1335 (XV, Love 5) for Shunzei no Musume's poem, 1137 (XII, Love 2) for Teika's, and 1337 (XV, Love 5) for Ietaka's.

89. Gotō Shigeo, *Shikokin wakashū no kisoteki kenkyū*, pp. 797, 820.

90. Ariyoshi, *Shinkokin wakashū no kenkyū: kiban to kōsei*, p. 180.

91. In fact, only two of the *Shinkokinshū* poems (1101 and 1108, both by Yoshitsune) from the *Minase Love* contest are isolated in *Shinkokinshū*. The rest are adjacent to one or more poems from the *Minase* event.

Round 75: Love as expressed through the Wind
Left, Teika

    Sirotafe no On our white mulberry sleeves
    sode no wakare ni That now part
    tuyu otite Dew tears fall,
    mi ni simu iro no Dyeing them a deeper hue—
    akikaze zo fuku How piercing the autumn wind
        that blows!

Right, Masatsune, Win

    Ima fa tada Now, as once again
    konu yo amata ni Another night deepens
    sayo fukete Without him coming,
    matazi to omofu ni I resolve to wait no longer—
    matukaze no kowe But, oh, the sigh of wind
        through pines!

Judgment: In the Left poem, the lines "mi ni simu iro no akikaze zo fuku" (Dyeing them a deeper hue—How piercing the autumn wind that blows!) are not displeasing. In the Right poem, the phrase "matazi to omofu ni matukaze no kowe" (I resolve to wait no longer—But, oh, the song of wind through pines!) is truly lovely; so it was selected as the winner.

What happens to these poems in the *Wakamiya* and *Sakuranomiya* contests suggests that Go-Toba did not agree with the judgment rendered by the group at the *Minase* sitting. Teika's poem is matched in Round 14 of the *Wakamiya* contest with a poem on the same topic (Love as expressed through the Wind) by Kunaikyō, a poem that had won its round in the *Minase* contest:

Left, Kunaikyō, Tie

    Kiku ya ikani Do you hear it?
    ufa no sora naru Even the wind in uncertain skies
    kaze dani mo Now, by habit,
    matu ni oto suru Sighs "Await his visit!"
    narafi ari tofa[92] As it rustles pines.

---

92. Kunaikyō's poem appears as the Left poem in Round 71 of the *Minase* contest, where it wins over a poem by Ariie. The judgment describes Kunaikyō's poem as "nicer from start to finish in both diction and feeling" (*kokoro kotoba shijū nao yoroshiku haberu*).

Right, Teika

    Sirotafe no   On our white mulberry sleeves
    sode no wakare ni   That now part
    tuyu otite   Dew tears fall,
    mi ni simu iro no   Dyeing them a deeper hue—
    akikaze zo fuku   How piercing the autumn wind
                                                   that blows!

Judgment: Both the Left and Right poems are especially nice. The Left poem draws a correlation between the empty, uncertain sky and the lonely bed of one who faces dawn having waited in vain for a lover all night, whereas the Right poem speaks of dew tears fallen on sleeves of parting. It is difficult to choose between them.

The *Sakuranomiya* judgment for this round contains somewhat different wording (it includes a reference to the word *akikaze*, "autumn wind," in Teika's poem) but comes to the same conclusion.[93] Go-Toba's selection of a "losing" poem by Teika and his awarding that poem a Tie in his *senka-awase* implies that he had a higher opinion of it than had Shunzei or the group on the night of the 15th. Furthermore, he drew attention to different lines ("*sode no wakare ni [okeru] tuyu*") than Shunzei did in the *Koi jūgoban uta-awase* ("*mi ni simu iro no akikaze zo fuku*"). Go-Toba was emphasizing the sense of the poem, and Shunzei was focusing on the diction. That *akikaze* is reintroduced into the judgment of the *Sakuranomiya* contest suggests that Shunzei—if he was indeed the judge of the *Sakuranomiya* event—was reasserting what he thought to be the important element of the poem. Regardless, Go-Toba's high opinion of Teika's poem was further demonstrated by his insistence that it be placed at the head (*maki no tō*) of the fifth Love book in *Shinkokinshū*.[94]

---

93. The wording is so close and yet so different that one wonders, given the bewildering textual history of the two works, whether it is not a matter of copying errors. The *Sakuranomiya* judgment makes more sense and fits the actual wording of the poems better. Transcribed (in Hepburn), the two judgments read:

(*Wakamiya*): *Hidari migi tomo ni koto ni yoroshiku haberi. Hidari wa matsu yo mo nakute akenanzuru toko wo, uwa no sora ni yosoe, migi wa sode no wakare ni okeru tsuyu wo kakotsu. Yorite izure mo sadamegatashi.*

(*Sakuranomiya*): *Hidari migi tomo ni yoroshiku haberi. Hidari wa matsu yo munashiku akenamu to suru koto o, sora ni uree, migi wa sode no wakare ni okeru tsuyu o akikaze ni kakotsu ni yorite, izure masareru tomo sadamegatashi.*

94. *Meigetsuki*, Genkyū 2 (1205), iii/2, 1: 410. Teika records that Go-Toba, feeling that too many of the books in *Shinkokinshū* used works from deceased poets as their opening poems, ordered that verses by Ietaka, Shunzei no Musume, and Teika be placed at the beginning of

Go-Toba seems to have been less impressed with Masatsune's winning poem from the *Koi no jūgoshu* contest, though he did like it enough to include it in his reworking of the original contest. In the *Wakamiya* contest he rematched it with one of Jien's winning poems from the *Koi no jūgoshu* contest (Round 39, Left), and gave the nod to Jien's effort again, although neither poem was selected for *Shinkokinshū*.[95] Jien's work reads:

Yamakage ya	Mountain shadows,
yamadori no wo no	Like the tail of the mountain pheasant
nagaki yo wo	Grown longer,
ware fitori kamo	How long these nights I spend alone,
akasikanetutu	Hardly able to last till dawn![96]

This poem is discussed in more detail below.

Kunaikyō's poem, however, garnered more favorable attention. In the original contest, it was the Left poem for Round 71, where it won; the judgment praised it for perfectly combining feeling (*kokoro*) and diction (*kotoba*). In the rematch, it gained only a Tie, but for positive, rather than negative, reasons, and it was selected for *Shinkokinshū* (1199; XIII, Love 3).

These four poems (Teika's *sirotafe no*, Masatsune's *ima fa tada*, Kunaikyō's *kiku ya ikani*, and Jien's *yamakage ya*), set against one another or other poems, allow us a look into the poetic approaches that too often get lumped into the single designation "*Shinkokin* style." The different judgments demonstrate a range of taste within the group, and furthermore, although all four of these poets were key members of Go-Toba's circle, and two of them were *Shinkokinshū* compilers, their poetry could be quite different.

---

the second Autumn book, the second Love book, and the fifth Love book, respectively. The entry does not specify *which* of those poets' poems should be used, but given the tight editorial control Go-Toba was obviously exercising at this stage, he surely either selected, or approved, the poems himself. Gotō (*Shinkokin wakashū no kisōteki kenkyū*, p. 820) credits Ietaka and Masatsune with choosing Teika's poem for inclusion in *Shinkokinshū* in the first place.

95. Masatsune's poem, however, was selected more than two centuries later for the final imperial anthology, *Shinshokukokinshū* (#1227; XIII, Love 3).

96. The last three lines of the extant *Wakamiya* version are slightly different: *nagaki yo ni / ware fitori kafa / okiakasitutu* (These long nights / shall I alone / lie awake till dawn?). In the extant *Sakuranomiya* text, the wording of the poem is the same as in the *Minase* contest. The version found in these two texts is closer to the Hitomaro poem that is its *honka*. That allusion is discussed more fully in the main body of this study.

To help with the following discussion, the four poems are repeated here, with their respective records in the *Minase koi jūgoya uta-awase* and the *Wakamiya* and *Sakuranomiya senka-awase*, as well as their *Shinkokinshū* number if relevant:

Teika (Minase 75, Left, Loss; Wakamiya 14, Right, Tie; SKKS 1336)

Sirotafe no	On our white mulberry sleeves
sode no wakare ni	That now part
tuyu otite	Dew tears fall,
mi ni simu iro no	Dyeing them a deeper hue—
akikaze zo fuku	How piercing the autumn wind that blows!

Kunaikyō (Minase 71, Left, Win; Wakamiya 14, Left, Tie; SKKS 1199)

Kiku ya ikani	Do you hear it?
ufa no sora naru	Even the wind in uncertain skies
kaze dani mo	Now, by habit,
matu ni oto suru	Sighs "Await his visit!"
narafi ari tofa	As it rustles pines.

Masatsune (Minase 75, Right, Win; Wakamiya 13, Right, Loss; not selected for SKKS)

Ima fa tada	Now, as once again
konu yo amata ni	Another night deepens
sayo fukete	Without him coming,
matazi to omofu ni	I resolve to wait no longer—
matukaze no kowe	But, oh, the sigh of wind through pines!

Jien (Minase 15, Left, Win; Wakamiya 13, Left, Win; not selected for SKKS)

Yamakage ya	Mountain shadows,
yamadori no wo no	Like the tail of the mountain pheasant
nagaki yo wo	Grown longer,
ware fitori kamo	How long these nights I spend alone,
akasikanetutu	Hardly able to last till dawn!

Teika's poem relies on complexity, both in the fact that it alludes to two other poems, and in the way it uses implication to suggest layers of description. The allusions are:

Sirotafe no	Regrettable it is
sode no wakare fa	That our white mulberry sleeves
wosikedomo	Now must part,

omofimidarete	Yet, my thoughts in disarray,
yurusituru kamo	I let my lover go.[97]
Fukikureba	Now that it's come blowing,
mi nimo simikeru	And pierced me to the core,
akikaze wo	This autumn wind,
iro naki mono to	I've come to think of it
omofikeru kana	As something lacking charm.[98]

What Teika borrowed from those two poems is the sense of regret at parting and the cruelty of the cold autumn wind. But why should the wind be perceived as "lacking charm" (*iro naki*), when in other poems it is a moving image of autumn? Because it implies that the departing lover in Teika's poem may not come back. Grammatically, Teika's wind has *iro* (whereas Tomonori's does not—*iro naki* meaning "without *iro*"), but Teika is using the word *iro*, one of waka's most elusive terms, in a different way, by saying that it has a nature (*iro*), but its nature is such as to pierce one to the core, which brings him back to the sense of Tomonori's poem. By juxtaposing these two allusions, Teika's speaker is left more forlorn and less comfortably resigned to her fate than the speaker of the *Man'yōshū* poem. This notion of abandonment is underscored by the pun on *aki* (meaning both "autumn" and "to grow tired of [someone]") which suggests the speaker's fear that her lover has grown tired of her and will not return. In other words, the autumn wind is a wind of abandonment, which makes it blow all the colder to her.[99]

Teika was also playing with the words he chose. The sleeves of the departing lover are covered with dawn's dew; those of the speaker left behind are wet from a dew of tears. This association of dew and tears is standard in Love and Autumn waka, and if this were all there were to Teika's poem, there would not be much to recommend it. But Teika also plays on the "white" (*siro*) and "hue" (*iro*) because "white" (*siro*) is itself a "color" (*iro*).[100]

---

97. MYS 3196 (NKBT 3182); Anon.; from a group of poems on "The Sadness of Parting." This is one of the few *Man'yōshū* poems cited in this study that does not appear in any mediating collection such as *Kokin waka rokujō*.

98. KWR 423; attributed to Ki no Tomonori.

99. In this, I take strong exception to the interpretation of this poem given by Kubota Shōichirō et al., *Waka kanshō jiten*, pp. 143-44. They see the speaker as a wife, saddened by the departure of her husband in the morning (the couple living apart as was the courtly custom), but they do not see any suggestion that the husband's feelings may be fading.

100. One might be tempted to note that *siro* and *iro* "rhyme." However, in pre-Heian, the "o" vowels in these two words were distinct. Although the two vowels had collapsed into one

Further, another color lies behind Teika's words. That is the red tears of blood (a hoary Chinese conceit) shed by the speaker, who has been abandoned. And "red" and "white" are an associated pair of "colors" (*iro*) in traditional East Asian aesthetics. Presumably it is the complex combination of allusions, diction, and forlornness (the *sabishisa* mentioned above) that excited Go-Toba's enthusiasm for this poem.

Masatsune's poem is less complex and relies on the traditional waka notion that nature and human emotions are at odds. It is often mistakenly held that classical Japanese literature viewed human beings and nature as existing in harmony. In fact, more often than not, waka poets emphasized the fact the two were out of synch. Nature is regular, cyclical, infinite, and runs according to *kotowari* (Chinese *li*—the governing principle of the universe, what might be called the East Asian equivalent of Aristotelean logic or of the Positivist "laws of nature"). A human being, on the other hand, is finite and unpredictable and subject to the limitations of *inochi*, one's allotted life span, which was colored from the Heian era on with the Buddhist notion of karma. Illustrations of this are too numerous to mention here, but two clear examples are the very first poem of *Kokinshū*, which speaks to the tension between the natural, lunar cycle and the manmade calendar (*koyomi*), and this anonymous poem (KKS 97):[101]

Faru goto ni	Though each spring
fana no sakari fa	It is for certain
arinamedo	That the flowers will bloom full,
afimimu koto fa	Yet to see them once again
inoti narikeri	Is surely a matter of fate!

In the same vein would be the many laments that speak of a flowering plant or tree that the deceased would have enjoyed seeing in bloom.[102]

---

by Teika's time, the distinction was still preserved here and there in orthography, and it would be difficult to say with assurance that Teika's audience would have perceived a "rhyme," especially since the notion itself was foreign to waka prosody.

101. The first poem in *Kokinshū*, by Ariwara no Motokata (fl. 890–905): *Tosi no uti ni / faru fa kinikeri / fitotose wo / kozo to ya ifamu / kotosi to ya ifamu*—"Spring has come / While it's still the old year— / As for this one year, then, / Shall we say it is last year? / Or shall we say it is this year?"

102. See, e.g., SKKS 763 (VIII, Laments), by Ōe no Yoshitoki (fl. 992–1009): *Fana min to / uweken fito mo / naki yado no / sakura fa kozo no / faru zo sakamasi*—"He who planted it, / In hopes of seeing its blossoms, / Is now gone. / Would that the cherry in his garden / Had bloomed in spring last year!"

But Masatsune also showed an ability to manipulate the language skillfully. He breathed new life into the hoary pun on *matu* (meaning "pine tree" and "to wait") by playing it off the negative presumptive form of the verb *matu*, namely *matazi* ("I will not wait"), reinforcing further the tension between the human being, who "wills," and nature, which "is." Whatever the intention of the Waiting Woman speaker, nature's counsel, brought by the wind, is to wait, since that is the "natural" thing to do in the courtly vision of love.

Masatsune also made an effective allusion to a poem attributed to Hitomaro:

Tanometutu	Again, again I've expected you,
konu yo amata ni	But since so many are the nights
narinureba	When you do not come,
matazi to omofu zo	I've resolved to wait no longer—
matu ni masareru	Finding that better than the wait.[103]

As with any "good" allusion, this one varies the original while borrowing an important element of it for emotional power. Both speakers have been stood up repeatedly, but their reactions are quite different. Hitomaro's is unwilling to let herself be trapped into passivity by her faithless lover; Masatsune's is left listening wistfully to the wind, aware of the irony discussed above between nature and human feelings, but still waiting.

Kunaikyō's poem (which makes no clear allusions) also plays with the *matu* pun, and the notion that nature and human inclinations are not in accord. To the speaker—the Waiting Woman—all the evidence indicates that she has been abandoned. The expression *ufa no sora* literally means the upper skies (the upper atmosphere, where clouds can be seen blown along by a wind that one may not feel at ground level), but it also brings to mind the term *ufaki*, unfaithfulness in love. The wind visits (an imperfect pun on *oto suru* yields *otoduru*, "to visit; to send news") the pines (*matu*), causing them to "make the sound" (*oto suru*), "Await (*matu*) him!" but her lover does not visit her. The final irony, which again underscores the *difference* between human and natural affairs, is that the wind's visit is habitual (*narafi*)—regular and dependable, so unlike the visit of a lover.

---

103. *SIS* 848 (XIII, Love 3), no topic, attributed to Hitomaro. The poem also appears as *Wakan rōeishū* 788, again attributed to Hitomaro.

Jien's poem ("Yamakage ya") appeared as the Left verse in Round 39 of the *Minasedono koi jūgoshu uta-awase*, where it was matched with a different poem by Masatsune and declared the winner because of its "lofty" (*takaku*) tone. In the *Wakamiya* contest, the judge (Go-Toba, presumably) noted that both Jien and Masatsune were alluding to poems by Hitomaro (or at least traditionally attributed to him), but again favored Jien's work because it is "lofty" (*taketakaku*).[104]

What gives it that lofty tone? The easiest answer is to say it is because Jien alludes to a *Man'yō*-era poem. But then, Masatsune did, too; association with the *Man'yō* era does not per se guarantee "loftiness." The poem to which Jien referred is one of Hitomaro's best known, probably because of its connection to the *Hyakunin isshu*:

Asibiki no	In foot-weary hills
yamadori no wo no	Mountain pheasants' tails,
sidari wo no	Their tails, trailing long,
naganagasi yo wo	Long is this night—
fitori kamo nemu	Must I sleep through it alone?[105]

Aside from theme and topic, these two poems share a stylistic feature that may be one key to the notion of *take* (loftiness). They are dominated by the vowels "a" "o" and "i" to the exclusion of all others save a lone "e" and "u" at the very end of Hitomaro's last line, and one "e" in the first line, then an "e-u-" sequence in the very last word of Jien's poem. (In its original form, Hitomaro's poem contained two kinds of "o" and two kinds of "i," and the assonance would not have been as pronounced as in Jien's day. Still, the paucity of "e" and "u" obtains in either age.)[106] Such vowel distribution is mark-

---

104. See note 96 to this chapter, p. 179.

105. *MYS* 2813 (*NKBT* 2802, left note), alternative version, and *SIS* 778 (XIII, Love 3). As with so many of the *Man'yōshū* poems that appear in *Shūishū*, this one survived in readable form, with a slightly different last line, in the *Kokin waka rokujō* (#924). In fact, this poem is listed, in various forms, in at least seventeen sources in *Shinpen kokka taikan*.

106. Scholars have identified two types of "i" vowels and two types of "o" vowels in Nara-period Japanese, which they have labeled *kō*-type (or Type A) and *otsu*-type (or Type B). (There is also a *kō-otsu* distinction between "e" vowels, but it is not relevant to the discussion here.) What the vowels actually sounded like is not important here, but the fact that they differed is. The distinction is believed to have gradually collapsed into the present-day five vowels during the Heian period. See Martin, *The Japanese Language Through Time*, pp. 43–52.

In actuality, only one of the "i" vowels in the *MYS* version of Hitomaro's poem is of the *otsu* type; all the rest are the *kō* type. The "o" vowels are more evenly mixed between *kō* and

edly different from the normal distribution in prose, or even waka, and gives both poems a marked rhythm, with the exceptional vowels serving to highlight the punch line, as it were, of a speaker sleeping alone.[107]

It is difficult to pin down what else might contribute to a sense of loftiness in either poem. *Taketakashi* (loftiness) is one of several poetic styles identified and discussed by poet-scholars from the mid-Heian period. Nevertheless, modern scholars can give only vague definitions for it.[108] Brower and Miner take a stab. Their glossary definition for *taketakashi* includes the following: ". . . Considered particularly appropriate for solemn occasions calling for a decorum of the auspicious. Tended to treat large subjects from nature with simple description or direct declaration and often used archaic diction to enhance the effect of noble forthrightness and superiority to mundane concerns."[109] However, unless one understands what is meant by "a decorum of the auspicious" and "noble forthrightness" (as opposed, one wonders, to "ignoble forthrightness" or "noble evasiveness"!), this is not an entirely helpful definition.

More useful are the twenty-one example poems of the "lofty style" found in *Teika jittei*, a collection of 286 poems illustrating the "ten styles" (*jittei*) that Teika discussed in his treatise *Maigetsushō*.[110] The tendency now is to see *Maigetsushō* as genuine, but *Teika jittei* as the work of someone else.[111] All

---

otsu types, although since in the second and fifth *ku*, most of them are *otsu*, and in the fourth *ku*, they are both *kō* type, there is still considerable assonance.

Incidentally, the "i" in the "ki" element of the word *asifiki* is of the *otsu* type, and in Hitomaro's day was distinct from the verb *fiku* that meant "pull," "drag." More likely, it meant "cramp," suggesting the cramping of one's legs as one climbed the mountains, although by the Heian period it is hard to know if the average poet understood this. "Foot-weary" is sufficiently ambiguous to cover either reading. It also appears that during some of the Heian period, the *asi* component was misread (because of accent differences, in this case, not vowel distinctions) as the word for "reeds," so the expression *asibiki* was taken to mean "reed-pulling." (See Ōno, *Kogo jiten*, entry for *asibiki no* [page numbers vary according to edition]).

107. For details on the issue of vowel distribution, see my *Kyōgoku Tamekane*, pp. 106–11.
108. Typical is the discussion found in *NKBZ*, which does little more than tell who used the term and when but does not really attempt a definition. See Hashimoto et al., *Karonshū*, p. 621. Bundy ("*Santai Waka*," Part 1, pp. 208–12) struggles with the term and reviews how various critics such as Shun'e, Go-Toba, and Shunzei handled it. Of course, no clear conclusion can be drawn, although she apparently sees unadorned (and sometimes archaic) diction and elevated tone as two elements the various poets seem to agree on.
109. Brower and Miner, *Japanese Court Poetry*, p. 511.
110. Sasaki Nobutsuna, *Nihon kagaku taikei*, 4: 365–66.
111. For a summary of the arguments, see *WBJ*, pp. 462, 579–80.

but one of the example poems in *Teika jittei* are from *Shinkokinshū* or collections preceding it (in fact, 80 percent are from *Shinkokinshū*), and the one exception, a poem from *Gyokuyōshū*, is by Shikishi Naishinnō and was probably accessible to Teika or his contemporaries; hence, even if *Teika jittei* is a forgery, it probably reflects an early or mid-Kamakura view of what Teika meant by his ten styles.

In any case, a few common elements can be found in these poems. Virtually all contain one or more of the following: mountains, moon, clouds, wind, or rain. The majority of the poems also describe an autumn night scene. Only two of the *Teika jittei* examples mention spring flowers. One of the twenty-one is clearly a Love poem, and several others suggest a Waiting Woman speaker (which runs slightly counter to Brower and Miner's notion that *taketakaki* poems are usually nature poems), and at least seven have an explicit or implicit religious connotation.

As for diction, some of the *Teika jittei* example poems use archaic diction (as Jien does), part of Brower and Miner's definition, but most do not. Nor are they uniformly declarative, and although most are, in fact, descriptive, that may be as much because almost all of them are from *Shinkokinshū*, an era when descriptiveness was a feature of many kinds of poems. It would appear, then, that diction is less important than an upward-facing, nighttime scene (building on Brower and Miner's "large subjects from nature") in defining *taketakashi*. In this case, Jien's poem, depicting a mountain scene at night, fits in with much of this profile, only it has no particular religious subtext.

Jien's poem also contains a somewhat slyer allusion:

Fototogisu	However brief
naku ya Satuki no	The Fifth Month night
mizikayo mo	And the cuckoo's song,
fitori si nureba	Since I lie here alone,
akasikanetu mo	I can hardly last till dawn![112]

This foundation poem does not fit the *taketakashi* style, but its relative lightness gives a nice twist to Jien's variation, although there is no indication in the judgments that this was a consideration in the evaluation of this poem.

---

112. Almost as ubiquitous as the above-cited Hitomaro *Asibiki no* poem, this appears as *MYS* 1985 (*NKBT* 1981, with second line *kinaku satuki no*), *SIS* 125 (II, Summer; Topic unknown; Anonymous), *KWR* 2699, and *Wakan rōeishū* 154 (where it is attributed to Hitomaro).

The *Minasedono koi jūgoshu uta-awase* and its companion contests were the last major poetry events of the year, but they provide an excellent example of Go-Toba's experimenting with permutations of the poetry contest format to generate poetry and then subject it to wide-ranging evaluation. Although as the poems cited above show, no single style was dominant, a poetic consensus seems to be present, one that valued certain syntax patterns (x-no-y-no-z, *taigendome*), noun-heavy description, allusion, and depth. Beyond that, the group seemed also to prize complex wordplay (Kunaikyō's twisting of *oto suru* and *matu* back into itself, for example) and the inversion or even subversion of older waka figures (as in Teika's play on *iro naki* and the autumn wind).

Life (and death) proceeded outside the world of poetry. When Go-Toba returned to the capital, it was to take up residence in the newly refurbished Kyōgoku Palace.[113] The new palace was built on land belonging to Minamoto Muneyori (1154–1203), who along with his son-in-law Minamoto Michiteru (1187–1248) oversaw the project. As a reward, Go-Toba promoted Michiteru to Junior Second Rank, an especially high honor for someone outside the *sekkanke*. Michiteru was the son of Go-Toba's wet nurse and Minamoto Michichika, which helps to explain the unusual promotion. In fact, it suggests that even at this late date, Go-Toba continued to be concerned with maintaining the balance between the Tsuchimikado and Kujō houses.[114]

More detailed information about the move comes from *Inokuma kanpakuki*, Fujiwara Iezane's journal. Iezane reported that originally the move had been planned for the 11th of the Tenth Month, but had been delayed because Michichika was ill. But on the 14th, he was much involved in discussions about what to name the new palace, and in the end his opinion, Kyōgokudono, prevailed. By the 19th he had apparently recovered somewhat but still was unable to participate in all the proceedings. The departure ceremonies at the old Nijō Palace were interrupted by a strong earthquake—a portent it

---

113. This is the new palace Ienaga describes in his obituary for Shikishi Naishinnō, as recorded in the opening pages of Chapter 3.

114. *IN*, pp. 80–83. Ishida and Satsukawa's notes to this section also quote from other court sources regarding the move into the new palace. *Meigetsuki* has no entries for the Tenth Month. What made Michiteru's promotion unusual was that in terms of office, he was just a *chūjō* (Middle Captain) at the time, normally a Junior Fourth Rank position. Thus, it was an enormous jump.

turned out (although Iezane does not take it as such). Otherwise, the ceremonies, recorded by several sources in great detail, proceeded smoothly.[115]

Festivities connected with the move continued into the next day. Ienaga tells what transpired:

> There were even more diversions than usual. Everyone wanted to get involved, among them, most of all, the Minister Michichika. He took charge and organized a number of entertainments. Perhaps he was overwhelmed by his son's good fortune at being promoted to the Second Rank, for about six o'clock that evening, after the day's activities were over, he went home and that night passed away like a fleeting dream.[116]

As noted above, *Meigetsuki* lacks entries for the Tenth Month, and we do not know what Teika thought, although we may guess, given his close relationship to the Kujō house and the buffoonish portrait he painted of Michichika, that he was less than devastated.[117]

The other sources, such as *Inokuma kanpakuki*, are quite dry in their announcement of the death and aftermath.[118] Iezane was more concerned with what the proper mourning procedures and clothing should be for the emperor since Michichika was the Tsuchimikado Emperor's maternal grandfather. However, when one considers the earthquake that jarred Go-Toba's move the day before, it is interesting to note that Iezane's weather heading (a standard feature of the *kanbun* diary) says that there was thunder and lightning on the day of Michichika's death, but he drew no conclusions from that. None of the obituaries in *Dai Nihon shiryō*, save two (about which more below), does more than announce Michichika's "sudden death" (*junshi*). There are not even standard laments on the passing of a great statesman. The exceptions are found in Jien's and Ienaga's accounts. Jien's, from his *Gukanshō*, is, not surprisingly given the relationship between his clan and Michichika's, rather arch, suggesting that the death was some sort of karmic or divine retribution.[119]

---

115. See *DNS*, iv:7, pp. 565–95 for a plethora of descriptions, including Iezane's, as well as a record of the religious ceremonies accompanying the move.

116. *IN*, pp. 83–84.

117. See the description of the Wakadokoro contest that opens this chapter for Teika's observation of Michichika's ineptitude on formal occasions.

118. Various discussions of Michichika's death, including *Inokuma kanpakuki* entries, can be found in *DNS*, iv:7, pp. 597–603.

119. After describing in the previous passage some of Michichika's political machinations, he then noted that Michichika died on the 21st day of the Tenth Month, and that people

Ienaga was by far the most charitable. Maybe it was his magnanimous nature, maybe the deference he felt due to the great disparity in rank (it was unlikely to have been clan solidarity since Ienaga was from an entirely different branch of the Minamoto), but he treated Michichika's death with the same respect and (at least conventional) emotion as he treated most others that he recorded.

> There was no one to match him in terms of influence in the world. Naturally the Retired Emperor and the Palace, and even commoners and peasants, were as children who had lost their mother, and all raised cries of lamentation. Since he was the grandfather of the current Emperor, the highest mourning was declared, and Palace concerts and banquets were prohibited. All the noble lords and courtiers, deeply affected by everything that was going on around them, mourned, too.

Yet Ienaga was also aware that Michichika had not been universally admired while alive, however much people may have publicly mourned him in death.

> The world mourned as it would, but it seemed that I was the only one concerned that the Way of Poetry might be adversely affected by this death. Ah, how he would throw himself into poetry contests and parties! Even in contests where the submissions were pseudonymous, he would argue vigorously in favor of his own poems. People thought it quite odd, and would nudge each other quietly when he did so. But he just put his whole heart into poetry.
> The Hitomaro memorials used to be held at the Minister's mansion, and from time to time the Retired Emperor would come on the quiet and offer his poems. When he did so, the Minister would speak with pride about what an honor it was for him. The Hitomaro memorials have since been moved to the Wakadokoro.[120]

Aware that others found Michichika's approach to poetry distasteful, Ienaga nevertheless tried to put a good face on it by concentrating on the Minister's enthusiasm for the art. It is a very diplomatic performance. There is no denying, however, that by this time, Michichika had been pushed to the margins of Go-Toba's poetic world, although as will be seen in the next chapter, he had been given one last, major honor before his death (yet even that had originated some time earlier, when he still had significant clout).

As some waned, however, others waxed. Just a month after Michichika's death, Teika was finally rewarded with the promotion to *chūjō* (Middle Cap-

---

thought the suddenness of it "strange" (*Junshi no tei nari. Fukashigi no koto to hito mo omoerikeri*). See Nakajima, *Gukanshō*, pp. 503–4; and Brown and Ishida, *The Future and the Past*, p. 163.

120. *IN*, pp. 83–86.

tain) that he had awaited impatiently for thirteen years, proof that Teika's poetic skill and his constant service at Go-Toba's poetry events (service that was rarely awarded with high scores in the contests) had finally and fully eclipsed the 1185 torch incident.[121] According to Ienaga, the promotion finally came as a result of Shunzei's efforts:

> In hopes of obtaining a promotion to *chūjō* for his son, Lord Teika, the monk Shunzei sent this poem to His Majesty:
>
> | Ozasafara | This dew that awaits |
> |---|---|
> | kaze matu tuyu no | The wind across fields of bamboo grass |
> | kieyarade | Still does not fade— |
> | kono fitofusi wo | Perhaps because it worries |
> | omofioku kana | For that one stalk, its child.[122] |
>
> Shunzei was quite ill at the time, and there was some doubt as to how much longer he would live. Possibly because it was too early for the autumn appointments, His Majesty did not reply to the request. Some time passed, and thinking that the autumn appointments would be made soon, Shunzei no Musume reminded Go-Toba of the poem. His Majesty then replied:
>
> | Ozasafara | As for that one stalk |
> |---|---|
> | kafaranu iro no | As yet unchanged in hue |
> | fitofusi mo | In the fields of bamboo grass, |
> | kaze matu tuyu ni | Can the dew that awaits the wind |
> | e yafa turenaki. | Be made to wait still longer? |
>
> And at the next round of promotions, Teika was made a *chūjō*.[123]

Shunzei, ill and approaching death, about to fade like the dew, could not let go as long as his son's fate was uncertain. With a pun on *ko* ("this" and "child") in line four, he likened Teika to a stalk of bamboo grass. Go-Toba, noting that until now the stalk had not changed colors (that is, Teika had not received a promotion that would allow him to change the color of his robes—it also implies Go-Toba's recognition of Teika's loyalty), assured Shunzei that he would not have to wait much longer (*tsurenaki* suggests the cruelty of a lover who does not visit) since it is now autumn (the time of the

---

121. See Chapter 2, pp. 60–61, for the story of Teika hitting someone with a torch. Teika had been a *shōshō* since 1189, and although he had risen in rank from Junior Fourth Rank Lower to Senior Fourth Rank Lower during that time, his office title had remained unchanged.

122. The poem was later selected for *Shinkokinshū* (1822; XVIII, Miscellaneous 2).

123. *IN*, pp. 98–100.

second round of annual appointments at court), which should naturally bring about a change in the color of the leaves.

Although *Meigetsuki* has no entries for the Intercalary Tenth Month, the extant text does include what appears to be a note of gratitude written by Teika and found on the back of a fragment of paper. In it, Teika spoke floridly of his joy at having finally been promoted after long service and added this poem:

Tatinoboru	Try to imagine
tadu no kokoro fa	The feelings of this crane
omofiyare	As he now soars!
kafi aru miyo no	Acclaim in His Majesty's reign
Waka no uranami	For waves raised on Poetry Bay![124]

Clearly, Teika saw his accomplishments in poetry as the reason for the promotion.[125] (Takanobu had used the same imagery of crane and Poetry Bay when he had been appointed to the Wakadokoro the previous year, and in 1186, Shunzei, in appealing to Go-Toba for leniency, had likened Teika to a lonely, "reed-dwelling crane" not permitted to soar "above the clouds.")[126]

Ienaga tells us that from this point on, Go-Toba began to show greater favor to Teika and his family. In the following year, Teika's older brother, Nariie, was promoted to the Third Rank, and Nariie's son was made *jijū* (Gentleman-in-Waiting). Go-Toba also enjoyed a visit from Teika's son, later known as Tameie, who, although just five years old (six by the Asian count), showed a precocious ability for verse. Go-Toba was so impressed that he presented the child with a poem. (This incident is recounted in more detail in Chapter 6.) This undermines Brower and Miner's assertion that Tameie's later conservatism was due to the fact that he was essentially inept and uncomfortable with poetry.[127] Soon after, Teika's daughter, who also showed poetic promise, came to serve in Go-Toba's court.[128]

Thus Michichika's death and Teika's promotion (however insignificant his rank and office still were compared with the members of the main Fuji-

---

124. *Meigetsuki*, 1: 281.
125. Kubota Jun (*Shinkokin kajin no kenkyū*) draws attention to a *Meigetsuki* entry of several months earlier (Kennin 2/vii/24, 1: 274), in which Teika spoke enviously of a promotion just gained by Ariie that Teika also viewed as directly connected to Ariie's poetic activities.
126. See Chapters 3 and 2, respectively, for these references.
127. Brower and Miner, *Japanese Court Poetry*, pp. 342–48.
128. *IN*, pp. 101–4.

wara house) marked a clear shift in Go-Toba's poetry circle away from the Tsuchimikado/Rokujō axis and toward the Mikohidari school and its innovative allies. This shift is also seen in the makeup of the *Minasedono koi jūgoban uta-awase*. An important event for *Shinkokinshū* given the number of its poems selected for that anthology, there were no orthodox Rokujō or Tsuchimikado poets involved.[129] By the end of 1202, then, the outlines of Go-Toba's poetic consensus—as exemplified in the poets and poems of the *Minasedono* contest—were becoming clear: younger, innovative (not to mention largely reliant on Go-Toba himself for their position!).

---

129. Ariie was of Rokujō lineage but was much more comfortable with this group, and Kunaikyō's father had been close to the Rokujō poets in his younger years, but Kunaikyō herself was in service to Go-Toba and not a Rokujō poet in terms of style.

FIVE

The 'Sengohyakuban Uta-awase'

One event in this decade looms as large as *Shinkokinshū* itself, and because of its complexity, it defies any attempt to hammer it into a narrative that heretofore has been chronological. Consequently, I have chosen to treat this event, commonly referred to as the *Sengohyakuban uta-awase* (Poetry Contest in 1,500 Rounds), in a chapter of its own. Again, my approach is essentially chronological, although the story spans several of the other chapter headings in this book.

Through political appointments and, as we have seen, a bewildering number of poetry events, Go-Toba had slowly been bringing the world of waka under his control. Although factions still existed (the Tsuchimikado/Rokujō group on one side and the Kujō/Mikohidari group on the other), Go-Toba had managed to put himself at the center of poetic activity, forcing poets to share the field with their fiercest rivals if they wanted to participate in literary activities. Not since Emperor Shirakawa nearly a century earlier had poetry seen such a magnetic force. It is easy to forget that Go-Toba was in just his early twenties.

In the preceding chapters, I have described many of the poetry events that marked Go-Toba's literary scheme. The event discussed in this chapter is more complex by far and began with a series of *hyakushu* solicited by Go-Toba. The first two, called *Shōji ninen in shodo hyakushu* and *Shōji ninen in dainido hyakushu*, are discussed at length in Chapter 2. Initially they were simply what their name implies—poetry sequences that suggested Go-Toba's intent to compile an imperial anthology. But the factionalism that surrounded them and their success in eliciting good poems must have made Go-Toba see further potential for the medium.

It is the third series of *hyakushu* that are the subject of this chapter. This group of poems has come down to us as the *Sengohyakuban uta-awase*. As the largest contest ever, in which all the major factions of the day are represented, and as the single most important source of poetry for *Shinkokinshū* (90 out of that collection's 2,000 poems), it holds an important place in waka history.

Sengohyakuban uta-awase differed in several ways from traditional contests. In the sixth month of 1201, following up on the two *hyakushu* of the previous year, Go-Toba ordered a third series of 100-poem sequences. This is referred to in some private collections as the *Go-Toba-in daisando hyakushu* (The Retired Emperor Go-Toba's Third Set of 100-Poem Sequences). This time he cast his net very wide. Thirty poets were invited to submit their work (see Appendix D, pp. 413–18, for the participants, their affiliations, final scores, and other data). A careful balance was struck among poets from the Rokujō and Mikohidari schools, as well as their respective patron houses, the Tsuchimikado and Kujō. The imperial family was represented by Go-Toba himself, and his older stepbrother, Koreakira Shinnō. The family trees in Appendix A, pp. 387–89, show the relationships among the participants. It is striking how interrelated people were; yet it is also clear that the factions follow familial lines. Interesting, too, is the way in which Go-Toba stands at the center, not only as a patron of poetry but also as the nexus of a complex web of service and marriage.

During the ensuing year, Go-Toba (whether he had help is unknown) rearranged these thirty 100-poem sequences into the form of a poetry contest, with 1,500 rounds and a total of 3,000 poems. Then he chose ten judges and sent each of them a different set of 150 rounds. The ten were Go-Toba himself, then Shunzei, Yoshitsune, Jien, and Teika from the Kujō/Mikohidari group, as well as Michichika, Tadayoshi, Suetsune, Moromitsu, and Kenshō from the Tsuchimikado/Rokujō axis.

If Teika's *Meigetsuki* is accurate, Go-Toba was apparently somewhat secretive about what he was up to: "Kennin 2 (1202)/ix/6. Clear weather... It isn't something widely known yet, but Lord Nagafusa came by and presented me with two fascicles, with orders from Go-Toba that I was to judge the poems therein. It was from the 100-poem sequences of last year. They say there are ten judges, but I don't know who the others are."[1] In fact, in terms of their poetic allegiances, the judges were as carefully balanced as the original participants had been. Eight of the ten had themselves submitted

---

1. *Meigetsuki*, 1: 279.

poems; the other two, Fujiwara Suetsune and Minamoto Moromitsu, were Rokujō partisans. As noted toward the end of the preceding chapter, one judge, Michichika, died in 1202 (x/21), and since his judgments are not recorded in the extant text of the contest, we can date the final form of the contest as some time after that. Ariyoshi Tamotsu, who has studied this contest more than any other contemporary scholar, assumes early 1203 for final completion, but since there was no banquet or formal presentation, we cannot be sure.[2]

What Go-Toba masterminded was an ingenious production. Not only did he bring all the factions under one umbrella, but to minimize partisanship (surely one of the aims of his secrecy, too) he divided the teams so that Tsuchimikado family members, normally patrons for the Rokujō poets, were for the most part teamed with Mikohidari poets, whereas the Kujō patrons ended up with the Rokujō team. It is a tribute to his careful preparation that not a single formal protest was filed. When we consider that even Shunzei had filed a protest over the *Shōji ninen in shodo hyakushu*, this alone speaks to Go-Toba's accomplishment. It is worth noting again that he was only in his early twenties and dealing with some combative characters.

It is obvious, too, that Go-Toba saw this as a dry run for *Shinkokinshū*. All eleven of the poets he had appointed to the Wakadokoro and the six compilers of *Shinkokinshū* took part in this contest, something that cannot be said of any other poetic event in these active years. Furthermore, through the contest, he generated a huge store of poetry and had the benefit of top-rate judging with which to evaluate it.

The contest that Go-Toba produced was quite orderly. The participants on each team are listed and appear, in descending order of rank (a standard arrangement), with an imperial personage at the head of each team (Go-Toba on the Left and Prince Koreakira on the Right). The original *hyakushu* commission called for poems on the following subjects (the number of each to be written is shown in parentheses): Spring (20), Summer (15), Autumn (20), Winter (15), Congratulatory (5), Love (15), and Miscellaneous (10). In the final contest, each of these categories was represented in the same proportions, times fifteen, which was the number of poets on each team. As Appendix D shows, the matches followed a fixed, mathematical order so that everyone on one team was matched at least six times against each mem-

---

2. Ariyoshi, *Sengohyakuban uta-awase no kōhon to sono kenkyū* (hereafter *Sengohyakuban uta-awase*), pp. 2–3.

ber of the opposing team. Each judge was put in charge of a contiguous set of 150 rounds.

As reading matter, the *Sengohyakuban uta-awase* can be tedious. There is little movement since so many poems in a row are on such general topics. Go-Toba, constrained by the elaborate pattern noted above, basically matched the sequences as he received them and could not have had much leeway in applying any integrative principles. Whatever integration individual poets achieved in their own sequences was generally lost in the larger scheme, although as noted below, at least one judge, Moromitsu, noticed the original sequencing as he judged his rounds.[3]

More interesting, and certainly more significant, are the judgments. Not only do they represent the range of opinion at a crucial juncture in waka history, but they were executed in a variety of forms. Seven of the judges wrote standard *hanshi*, ranging from Tadayoshi's generally short comments to Shunzei's characteristically discursive discussions, remarkably lucid and exhaustive for someone who was 88. Kujō Yoshitsune wrote his judgments as *kanshi* (Chinese verse), some of which can be quite difficult to interpret. Jien wrote his as *hanka* (that is, in tanka form), as did Go-Toba, although the latter's were additionally *oriku* (acrostics), with the initial character of each line of his judgment poem spelling out his decision.

Before taking a look at a few of the poems and judgments, let us review some of the results of the contest itself. The final score, adjusted for the fact that the poems Michichika was to have judged were left unmarked due to his death, was: Left, 32 percent Win; Right, 37 percent Win; with a Tie

---

3. The private collections of several of the poets contain the original sequences as submitted for the *Go-Toba-in daisando hyakushu*. We can crosscheck these with the order in which the poems appear in the *Sengohyakuban uta-awase*. For example, in Yoshitsune's case, there is no difference in the poem order and only a few slight differences in wording between the poems he submitted for the *hyakushu* and the verses as they appear in the final contest (more likely, given the textual history of the *Sengohyakuban uta-awase*, these are copyists' variations rather than emendations by Go-Toba). See Aoki, *Fujiwara Yoshitsune zenkashū to sono kenkyū*, pp. 77–83, for Yoshitsune's original *hyakushu*.

There is slightly more variation between Teika's original *hyakushu* and his poems as they appear in the *Sengohyakuban uta-awase*—in at least two cases, the order of pairs of poems is switched, and there are differences in wording in the poems themselves—but again, this may as easily be due to copyists over time. (For Teika's original *hyakushu*, see Wakashi kenkyūkai, *Shikashū taisei* [Chūsei II], 4: 95–97.) If these two cases are typical, it does not appear Go-Toba exercised much, if any, editorial control over the poems themselves before matching them for the contest.

awarded in the remaining 31 percent. Go-Toba was the runaway winner (66 of his 100 poems were awarded a Win), with Shunzei second (49/100). (See Appendix D for a complete breakdown for each poet.) Mikohidari poets and their patrons the Kujō, significantly outscored their Rokujō rivals. Indeed, the lowest scorer was Kenshō, arch-conservative standard-bearer for the Rokujō style and himself one of the judges. This victory by the Mikohidari school is significant since Go-Toba had been just as careful to balance factions among the judges as among the poets themselves. Of course, had Michichika lived to complete his judgments, the results might have been closer, although he would have needed to render exclusively partisan judgments to have achieved anything close to parity for his group.

If one of Go-Toba's hopes for this contest was that his careful orchestration of it would minimize the effects of partisanship, he must have been quite pleased. The distribution of the judges' scores among the various factions shows surprising uniformity. Only Kenshō displays consistent bias, awarding a higher number of Wins than the other judges to the Tsuchimikado and Rokujō poets. Surprisingly, Shunzei and Teika also give more Wins to those two groups than do the other judges.[4]

Evaluating these numbers can be quite tricky, since rank often played a part in the final decision, and some judges tended to award themselves a Loss more than did others. However, if we eliminate the patron poets (that is, those belonging to the Kujō or Tsuchimikado families, plus Go-Toba and Prince Koreakira), and look at the records compiled by the "rank-and-file" Mikohidari and Rokujō poets, we still see a clear victory for the former group. Even taking into account the fact that there were a slightly larger number of Mikohidari poets in the contest, every judge except Kenshō overwhelmingly favored Mikohidari poets in head-to-head matchups with Rokujō poets. Again, it is especially noteworthy that Shunzei and Teika were more evenhanded than most of the other judges (see Table 1).

When the Mikohidari poets are considered along with their Kujō patrons, the proportion of judgments in favor of the two groups is roughly the same as above. All the judges give this alliance a much higher number of wins, except Kenshō, who gave more or less equal numbers of Wins to this

---

4. For example, Kenshō gave Wins to Tsuchimikado/Rokujō poets in thirty-four of his rounds, and Shunzei and Teika awarded Wins to this group in twenty-eight each. In contrast, the rest of the judges ranged from twenty to twenty-six Wins.

Table 1
Mikohidari Vs. Rokujō, *Sengohyakuban Uta-Awase*, by Judge

Judge	Mikohidari Wins over Rokujō	Rokujō Wins over Mikohidari
Tadayoshi	12	3
Shunzei	10	6
Michichika	—	—
Yoshitsune	15	1
Go-Toba	12	3
Teika	11	7
Suetsune	10	4
Moromitsu	11	1
Kenshō	10	8
Jien	10	3
TOTAL	101	36

faction and the Rokujō/Tsuchimikado group. Kenshō was also the most opinionated of the judges, awarding only 36 Ties in 150 rounds. (The other judges range from 42 to 50 Ties, with Shunzei awarding the 50.)

These statistics can be read several ways. Perhaps they indicate the judges' sincere desire to avoid partisanship and please their patron, Go-Toba. Perhaps they show that the Mikohidari style was indeed seen as superior by this time, even by the Rokujō school. But surely one reason is that much of the factionalism was, in fact, purely political, and there was more agreement on aesthetic issues than the various camps would admit. These were, after all, serious poets. A good poem is a good poem and can transcend rules or styles.

From the standpoint of patronage, the most important numbers in Table 1 are those for Go-Toba, who not only favored Mikohidari poets 4-to-1 over Rokujō poets, but also favored the Mikohidari/Kujō faction overall by 4-to-1 in his judgments. Since he was the final patron, this contest marks unambiguously the emergence of the Mikohidari approach as his preference.

One way to get a better sense of the varying poetic and judgment styles is to look at one or two rounds from each judge.[5] The first judge was Fujiwara

---

5. Unless otherwise noted, I am citing from Ariyoshi, *Sengohyakuban uta-awase*, annotated only for textual variants. More complete annotations for seventy-eight of the 1,500 rounds can be found in Hagitani and Taniyama, *Uta-awaseshū*, pp. 477–518. I refer to this edition where appropriate.

(Rokujō) Tadayoshi, who was responsible for Rounds 1–150, Spring I and II. At the time of this event, he was of the Senior Second Rank and a Major Counselor (*dainaigon*), which made him the third highest-ranking member of his team (after Prince Koreakira and Michichika). Tadayoshi was related by blood and training to the Rokujō school, but in this contest his judgments favored the Kujō and Mikohidari camps even more than Shunzei's and Teika's did. Tadayoshi seems to have been out of his league here; in fact, his impact on waka was, in the long run, minimal. His prose *hanshi* are generally short and emphasize a fault or make an impressionistic judgment such as "sounds nice."

Round 120, in Spring II, provides an interesting example because it is a classic confrontation between the Rokujō and Mikohidari schools:

Left, Kenshō

Ume ga ka wo	The scent of plums
yofa no arasi no	If not enticed along by storm winds
sasofazuba	Through the night,
neya no itama wo	How else would it seep through
ikade moramasi	The walls, into my room?

Right, Shunzei no Musume, Win

Kaze kayofu	Carried by the wind
nezame no sode no	To my wakened sleeves
fana no ka ni	The scent of blossoms
kaworu makura no	Which now perfumes my pillow
faru no yo no yume	In this dream on a spring night.

Judgment: Although both Left and Right treat the topic of Blossom Scent nicely, the poem on the Right is a little better, and I award it a Win.[6]

This is a clear-cut stylistic clash. Kenshō, the Rokujō school's most conservative member, used the dated . . . *ba* . . . *masi* construction ("if . . . would"—commonly found in poems from the time of *Kokinshū*, three centuries earlier) in a rather conventional and tortured poem. There is little depth to the poem, little in it to suggest the state of mind of the speaker. It functions on the level of clever aesthetic enjoyment. In the traditional view, this was entirely appropriate in poems composed for public occasions (*hare no uta*), but at a time when poet/readers were beginning to expect more emotional and psychological depth in poetry, it stands out as rather bland.

---

6. Ariyoshi, *Sengohyakuban uta-awase*, pp. 55–56.

On the other hand, in her poem, which was eventually selected for *Shinkokinshū* (*SKKS* 112; II, Spring 2), Shunzei no Musume displayed two of the Mikohidari school's stylistic trademarks: *taigendome* (ending a poem with a substantive) and, in this case, two strings of noun modifiers connected by the case particle *no* (*nezame no sode no fana no ka*, literally "the scent of blossoms on my lying-awake sleeve," and *makura no faru no yo no yume*, literally "dream on my pillow on a night in spring"), the "x-no-y-no-z" pattern done one better and doubled.[7] This produces a poem of considerable depth, in which the scent of blossoms pervades, or even triggers, a dream—or is it the other way around?—and the speaker's state of forlorn longing is subtly but unmistakably conveyed. Although Tadayoshi was a member of the Rokujō camp, he could not help seeing a difference, even if only a "little" one.

The next two books, Spring III and IV, Rounds 151–300, were judged by Shunzei, head of the Mikohidari house. The leading waka theoretician and judge of his, or perhaps any, day, Shunzei was catholic enough in his tastes and apparently even-tempered enough (not counting, perhaps, his rather intemperate *Shōji sōjō*, as discussed in Chapter 2) to fit in almost any poetic activity, although he represented an innovative approach to waka overall. In the *Sengohyakuban uta-awase* his judgments are discursive and generally focus on *honkadori* (allusive variation). He occasionally raised some of the traditional faults (for example, *in*, that is, the use of identical mora in customarily proscribed positions), but usually only to discount them as criteria, the same tack he took in his major poetic treatise, *Korai fūteishō*.[8]

Virtually all of Shunzei's judgments have something of interest in them, but a few seem particularly noteworthy. For example, in Round 210 he ap-

---

7. Kenshō's poem also features what appears to be an x-no-y-no-z sequence (*yofa no arasi no*, literally "night's storm"), but the second *no* is a subject marker, not a qualifier, and it is followed by a verb. Shunzei no Musume's two strings differ slightly from each other. The first is what I would call a "chain modifier," that is, x modifies y, y modifies z, and z modifies q, like links in a chain. In the second, x modifies q, and the string y-z also modifies q (thus it is a "pillow dream" as well as a "spring night's dream"). Analogizing from the notion of "stacked relative clauses," Professor John Haig (pers. comm.) offers the term "stacked modifier" to describe this latter phenomenon, in which the modifiers all collectively modify the noun at the end. One of the enjoyable challenges of reading waka (or Japanese literature in general) is trying to figure out which modification pattern one is encountering—and of course, the fact that a pattern can be read either way is precisely what provides the depth the *Shinkokin* poets were looking for.

8. *Korai fūteishō* was first completed in 1197 and revised in 1201; it is thus immediately relevant to the poetic scene surrounding the *Sengohyakuban uta-awase* and *Shinkokinshū*.

pears to be throwing a bone to the arch-conservative Kenshō by awarding a Win to his mediocre poem. This spirit of diplomacy may be why Shunzei ruffled fewer feathers than his descendants.

In Round 218 we find, according to Shunzei, examples of *en*, an important aesthetic concept that I have translated as "charm" but that includes a sense of depth and nostalgia. In this round, Shunzei awards a Tie to two poems by ladies-in-waiting:

Left, Sanuki, Tie

> Teri mo sezu
> kumo mo kakaranu
> faru no yo no
> tuki fa nifa koso
> siduka narikere

> Neither shining brightly
> Nor obscured by clouds
> On this spring night,
> Moonlight in the garden
> Is now tranquil.

Right, Shunzei no Musume

> Kage kiyoki
> fana no tokoro fa
> ariake no
> tuki mo enarazu
> sumeru sora kana

> Its light flawless
> On the flowers
> This moon at dawn
> Shines glorious
> In a crystalline sky.

Judgment: Although the Left poem skillfully captures the feeling of tranquility in a garden in which the moon shines dim and indistinct, the Right poem shows a glorious moon at dawn over blossoms. We see a charm (en) in both these verses that is just what we would expect of a woman's poem.[9]

Even assuming there is an identifiable "woman's poem,"[10] if Shunzei is our guide, it is certainly not a narrow category. On the surface, these two poems could hardly be more different. Sanuki depicts a dimly lit courtly scene worthy of *Genji*, whereas Shunzei no Musume celebrates—with powerful words like *kiyoki* ("pure," and, when used with words having to do with light, "undimmed" or "unsullied"), *enarazu* (much like modern "unbelievable; incredible" in their colloquial sense), and *sumeru* (to clear away)—a distinctly lit scene. What ties them together, according to Shunzei, is *en* (charm), which often implies subtle allusion to earlier poetry.

---

9. Ariyoshi, *Sengohyakuban uta-awase*, p. 106–7.
10. A well-known example of this idea appears in Tsurayuki's *kana* preface to *Kokinshū*, when he says of Ono no Komachi's poetry: "Its lack of strength surely stems from its being woman's poetry" (see Ozawa, *Kokin wakashū*, p. 59).

Sanuki, both in syntactical features (parallel opening couplets) and in topic, alludes to a poem by Ōe no Chisato (fl. 894–903) that also caught the attention of the *Shinkokinshū* compilers:

Teri mo sezu	It neither shines,
kumori mo fatenu	Nor yet is clouded over
faru no yo no	On this spring night—
oborodukuyo ni	Truly nothing can compare
siku mono zo naki[11]	To this mist-enfolded moon.

Whereas Chisato's poem looks upward, Sanuki's view is focused on the garden. Her speaker, and her audience, would have known both Chisato's poem and the lines by Bo Juyi lines that inspired it, and there was no need to look at the moon itself or at least to linger on it. The skillful use of allusion allowed her to set a scene and then provide, in effect, a sequel, one appropriate to the physical circumstances a court lady usually found herself in. As with so many poems with a moonlit garden scene, there is a hint of longing, of the Waiting Woman here.

Shunzei no Musume made reference to a laudatory verse by Minamoto no Arihito (1103–47), composed on the occasion of an imperial progress to Shirakawa to see the cherry blossoms and found in both *Ima kagami* (1170?) and Shunzei's *Senzaishū*:[12]

Kage kiyoki	The reflection flawless,
fana no kagami to	Appearing like a mirror
miyuru kana	For the flowers,
nodoka ni sumeru	Calm and crystalline,
Sirakafa no midu	The water of Shirakawa River.[13]

Shunzei no Musume borrowed the grandeur of that earlier court occasion to elevate her more intimate, moonlit scene. Blossom-viewing (*hanami*) need not be a large-scale social event. Enjoying such a scene as this after a night of love has its own charm (*en*).

Rounds 451–600 (Summer III, Autumn I) were assigned to Kujō Yoshitsune. As we have seen, Yoshitsune was politically eclipsed by Michichika

---

11. SKKS 55 (I, Spring 1); originally in *Chisatoshū*, 72, with the topic given as a line from a Bo Juyi poem: "Not bright, nor dark, a hazy moon."

12. *Ima kagami*, attributed to Fujiwara Tametsune (d. 1187?—better known by his priestly name Jakuchō), was a historical narrative (*rekishi monogatari*) covering the years 1025–1170.

13. SZS 44 (I, Spring 1).

for a time in the 1190s, but he and his descendants, with Go-Toba's help, reasserted the clan's political dominance and were the Mikohidari house's most important patrons. It is interesting that Go-Toba placed Michichika (who was assigned Rounds 301–450) and Yoshitsune back-to-back as judges, inviting comparison, although Michichika's death prevented that.

Yoshitsune wrote his judgments as four-line *zekku* (Ch. *jueju*, a verse form popular from late Six Dynasties through Tang). Of the two variants of *zekku* (five-character lines and seven-character lines), Yoshitsune used the seven-syllable *zekku*, with rhymes at the ends of lines one, two, and four. In his first judgment, for Round 451, he explained this unusual choice by citing *kudai waka* (waka based on Chinese verse) as precedent. He specifically noted as models Sugawara Michizane's (845–903) *Shinsen Man'yōshū* (893, with posthumous additions in 913) and Ōe no Chisato's *Kudai waka* (894). He argued that since the poetic languages of both waka and Chinese verse have common features, their joint appearance in such a context was not inappropriate.[14]

Although acknowledging certain thematic debts that waka owes to China, scholars in years past (most typically Keene, Brower, and Miner) have dwelt on the *differences* between the two types of poetry.[15] Yet, this emphasis on the distinctiveness of each art is surely a lingering ghost of the *kokugakusha*. In fact, one need look no further than the *Wakan rōeishū* to see that Japanese were quite comfortable moving back and forth between the two genres. As both Robert Borgen and David Pollack have shown, many Japanese literati strove for an accommodation, if not a synthesis, between Chinese and Japanese modes of expression.[16] More recently, Ivo Smits has demonstrated that this close relationship with *kanshi* led directly to the development of the descriptive style of nature poetry so closely associated with *Shinkokinshū*.[17]

Yoshitsune was very much of this mind. His reputation as both a patron and a practitioner of Chinese verse was well established by this time. And he

---

14. Ariyoshi, *Sengohyakuban uta-awase*, pp. 201–2.

15. See Keene, *Anthology of Japanese Literature*, p. 21; and Brower and Miner, *Japanese Court Poetry*, pp. 427–28, for this view.

16. See Borgen, *Sugawara no Michizane and the Early Heian Court*; and Pollack, *Fracture of Meaning*. Borgen, for example, argues that even into early Heian, facility with certain aspects of Chinese culture was simply a given. In his monograph on the scholar/poet/statesman Sugawara no Michizane (845–903), Borgen attempts, in his own words, to portray "a Michizane who wears his Chinese garb comfortably" (p. xviii of Preface to 1994 ed.).

17. Smits, *The Pursuit of Loneliness*.

ran counter to the tendency to see Japanese waka and Chinese *shi* as distinct, if not oppositional, for, as in this case, he often sought to find common ground between the two arts. Between 1199 and his death early in 1206, we have records of his involvement in at least twenty-five literary events related to Chinese verse, and at least half of these included both Chinese and Japanese verse. He and his father, Kanezane, sponsored many Chinese poetry events at their home, especially in the first two or three years of the decade.[18] Among the important waka poets of the day, only Teika and Ariie regularly joined him in Chinese composition, although in the waka segments of the *shiika* (Chinese and Japanese verse) events sponsored or planned by Yoshitsune, at some point or other most of the names mentioned frequently in this study appear.

Yoshitsune also made efforts to bring Chinese motifs into his "ordinary" waka. For example, when he and Jien (or Jichin, as he was called at this time) composed 100-poem sequences with the intention of then arranging them as a poetry contest, he took the persona of Nankai Gyofu (Ch. Nanhai yufu, the Old Fisherman in the Southern Sea), and Jien was Hokusan Shōkyaku (Ch. Beishan qiaoqie, the Woodcutter of the Northern Mountains).[19] In another 100-poem sequence, he adopted the persona of Saitō Inshi (Ch. Xidong yinshi, the Hermit of the Western Cave).[20] The pose of Taoist sage to the contrary, the verses he composed in these sequences were by no means consciously "Chinesy." Indeed, among the Miscellaneous poems in the latter sequence, we find this almost chauvinistic wedding of waka with Japanese geography (and *kami*):

---

18. Aoki, *Fujiwara Yoshitsune zenkashū to sono kenkyū*, pp. 265–73.

19. Known as *Yoshitsune Jichin hyakuban uta-awase* (Poetry Contest in 100 Rounds Between Yoshitsune and Jichin), and also referred to as *Nankaigyofu hokuzanshōkyaku hyakuban uta-awase* (Poetry Contest in 100 Rounds Between the Old Fisherman in the Southern Sea and the Woodcutter of the Northern Mountains), texts of the contest can be found in Taga, ed., *Kōhon shūgyokushū*, pp. 183–209; and Higuchi et al., *Chūsei wakashū*, pp. 82–117. Yoshitsune's 100-poem sequence for this contest, under the heading *Nankaigyofu hyakushu*, can also be found in Aoki, *Fujiwara Yoshitsune zenkashū to sono kenkyū*, pp. 59–65.

20. See Aoki, *Fujiwara Yoshitsune zenkashū to sono kenkyū*, pp. 65–71. In a personal communication, Professor David McCraw indicated to me that there is no single well-known *locus classicus* for these two characters (the old fisherman and the woodcutter), but that they represent more or less generic Taoist sages, who can be found here and there throughout ancient writings, which is how they seem to be treated in Morohashi's *Dai kanwa jiten*.

Sikisima ya	When we trace
Yamato koto no fa	The language of Yamato
tadunureba	In this land of Shikishima,
kami no miyo yori	It emerges in the age of the gods
Idumo yafegaki	And the Eightfold Fence at Izumo.[21]

The expression *sikisima ya* was a pillow word (*makurakotoba*) for Yamato as well as a name for Japan itself. Further, in the preface of *Senzaishū*, *sikisima no miti* (the Way of Shikishima) appears as a synonym for "waka."[22] The reference in the final line of Yoshitsune's work is to a poem attributed to Susanoo no Mikoto, brother of Amaterasu. It is first recorded in *Kojiki* and, in traditional waka lore, was considered the earliest example of the tanka poetry form:

Yagumo tatu	Eightfold clouds arise
Idumo yafegaki	At Izumo—an eightfold fence
tumagome ni	To shelter my wife
yafegaki tukuru	I'll build an eightfold fence
sono yafegaki wo	Ah, that eightfold fence![23]

Furthermore, the first spring poem of the Hermit of the Western Cave sequence makes an allusion not to Bo Juyi or any Taoist sage, but to Murasaki Shikibu's *Genji*:

Fuyu no yume no	In this dawn,
odorokifaturu	Which fully wakens me
akebono ni	From a winter dream,
faru no ututu no	I can now see
madu miyuru kana	The first realities of spring.[24]

The figure of being awakened from a winter dream comes from the end of the "Asagao" chapter, when Genji is suddenly awakened by a dream of the

---

21. Aoki, *Fujiwara Yoshitsune zenkashū to sono kenkyū*, p. 70.

22. Kubota and Matsuno, *Senzai wakashū*, p. 62.

23. Kurano and Takeda, *Kojiki Norito*, p. 89. Among the works citing or referring to this poem as the earliest of all waka are the *kana* preface to *Kokinshū*, as well as Minamoto Toshiyori's *Toshiyori zuinō* (between 1111 and 1113?), and Shunzei's *Korai fūteishō*. Some texts spell the first word as *yakumo*.

24. Aoki, *Fujiwara Yoshitsune zenkashū to sono kenkyū*, p. 65.

late Fujitsubo.[25] It is a painful, poignant scene as Murasaki tries to comfort him, even though she guesses that the object of his dream had been the one woman he loves more than her. This puts a plaintive spin on Yoshitsune's variation, a seasonal poem hinting that, after all, for the hermit it might have been better to stay asleep.

For his judgments in the *Sengohyakuban uta-awase*, Yoshitsune divides the four lines of the *zekku*, using the first two lines to judge odd-numbered rounds, and the concluding two lines to judge the following even-numbered rounds. Although it is not a form that can reveal much about Yoshitsune's poetics, Taniyama points out that the terms *en* and *yūgen* (and variants) appear often enough to suggest their importance in Yoshitsune's aesthetic world.[26] In this context, *en* can be thought of as a pretty, charming, elegant, light beauty that is hazy, indistinct, even covered up, and therefore triggers the poet's desire or longing. As noted above in the discussion of Shunzei's judgments, it is often used in *uta-awase* judgments to describe poems that have successfully used *honkadori* or *honzetsu* to add depth. In waka, *yūgen* refers to fathomless depths, suggestive beauty, and unworldly or lonely natural scenes.[27]

Because Yoshitsune's *zekku* judgments are divided, we need to look at two rounds to see their full effect. Following are Rounds 525 and 526, the last round of the Summer poems and the first round of the Autumn ones:

Round 525

Left, Kenshō, Tie

Suzusisa wo	First, as wind
nara no fa kaze ni	Through oak tree leaves
sakidatete	It brings forth coolness;
Sinobi no mori ni	Perhaps autumn has come
aki ya kinuran	To this hidden forest of Shinobi.

---

25. The poem, which is also discussed at the end of Chapter 9, is *Tokete nenu / nezame sabisiki / fuyu no yo ni / musuboforeturu / yume no mizikasa*—"Restless sleep shattered, / And now awake / This lonely winter night— / How brief the dream / That had crystallized!" (Yamagishi, ed., *Genji Monogatari* 2, NKBT 15, p. 270).

26. Hagitani and Taniyama, *Uta-awaseshū*, p. 488n3.

27. For a detailed discussion of the notion of *yūgen* in waka, see Cranston, "Mystery and Depth in Japanese Court Poetry."

Right, Kanemune

    Ukikoto no   Sad it is, but if today
    minaduki faturu   Is the day that ends
    kefu naraba   The Sixth Month,
    asu ya misogi no   Tomorrow we shall see a sign
    sirusi wo mo min   Of change in the sacred trees.

Judgment: No mistakes, no faults, no zest / Winner, loser, hard to choose the best

Round 526

Left, Go-Toba, Tie

    Kaze no oto ni   From the sound of wind
    aki fa kefu yori   I know that autumn has come
    Tatutayama   To Mount Tatsuta
    yofa ni ya natu no   Is it that deep in the night,
    fitori koyuran   Alone, I left summer behind?

Right, Shunzei

    Sifodi yori   Is it because Fall has come
    aki ya taturan   From across the sea lanes
    akegata fa   That as dawn breaks
    kowe kafaru nari   Its voice has changed—
    Suma no urakaze   The wind on Suma's coast?

Judgment: How is it that this old poetry master / At age ninety still serves his lord without rest?[28]

    The judgments themselves do not, in fact, say much as far as poetics goes. Yoshitsune was obviously not enamored of either poem in Round 525; in this case "Tie" indicates two equally mediocre poems. Kenshō's poem uses the speculative *ramu* ending in a way that any Heian court poet might. His image of the hidden *forest* of Shinobi is unusual—indeed, there is some question as to whether it should even be seen as an *utamakura*, since this poem is only one of three (all contemporaneous) listed in the *Utamakura nayose* under this heading.[29] But there are numerous other examples of Shinobi no X

---

28. Ariyoshi, *Sengohyakuban uta-awase*, pp. 229–31.
29. Yoshida et al., *Utamakura nayose*, 5: 19. There are other entries for Shinobi no Oka (The Hill of Shinobi), and both places are identified as located in Musashi province. Along the Japan Sea coast, there is also a Shinobu no Mori, which is also used with the same pun on "hidden."

place-names, and the wordplay itself, on the word "hidden," is common (although more often in spring poems, referring to the cuckoo singing unseen).

Kanemune's poem relies on a subtle wordplay. On the last day of the Sixth Month, the court would perform a purification (*misogi*) ceremony to mark the seasonal change. But Kanemune speaks, instead, of the other *misogi*, trees whose wood was used to make shrine or palace buildings and furnishings. He wonders if tomorrow, the day after the summer-ending purification ceremonies (*misogi*), the sacred trees (*misogi*) will look any different. It is clever but not profound.

However, Round 526 presents a more interesting situation. Normally Go-Toba would be expected to win this round, because he is a former emperor and because his is the first Left poem in the section.[30] By awarding a Tie, Yoshitsune seems to be paying tribute to his teacher Shunzei as much as to Shunzei's poem.

Retired Emperor Go-Toba assigned himself the next section, Rounds 601–750 (Autumn II, III). Mastermind of the *Sengohyakuban uta-awase* and a talented poet and organizer, he nonetheless seems to have been a bit daunted by the occasion. *Masukagami* describes the situation:

Prior to *Shinkokinshū*, His Majesty conducted the Poetry Contest in 1,500 Rounds, for which only the best were chosen, with the poetic geniuses of the age rendering their judgments. Go-Toba added himself to the body of judges but modestly noted that he was not really advanced enough to belong in such company. Indeed, he declined to write any explanation for his judgments, choosing instead to mark the good and bad by means of simple verses, which were, in truth, not without charm themselves.[31]

In the text of the contest, Go-Toba began his first judgment with a *wabun* (Japanese) disclaimer. This is in marked contrast to the *kanbun* explanation provided by Yoshitsune in the previous set of judgments:

---

30. As implied by the section cited from *Meigetsuki* in which Teika first mentioned receiving the judgment commission for this contest, the individual judges did not know what the final form of the contest would be. Most apparently treated the books in their sections as discrete contests and, following custom, awarded a Win to the first poem of the Left, which was always by Go-Toba. The clear exceptions to this are Yoshitsune's Round 526, a Tie, Rounds 601 and 751 (the beginning of Autumn III and Autumn IV, respectively, judged by Go-Toba himself), Round 826, a Tie (judged by Teika, it is the first round of Winter I), and Round 1276, a Tie (judged by Kenshō, the first round of Love III).

31. Iwasa et al., eds., *Jinnō shōtōki Masukagami*, p. 256.

I have taken the *hyakushu* submitted to me and arranged them into a twenty-fascicle poetry contest and have asked certain people to judge the good and the bad in two fascicles each. Now it is my section, and I could get by with just putting a Win or Lose mark on each round. I am not sure what I could say about faults [i.e., I'm not sure what kind of *hanshi* I could write]. Still, if I just put a single character after Left or Right, surely it would be a waste. Therefore, where one would normally place a judgment explanation alongside the poems, I have written tanka and have included in them as acrostics my Win or Lose judgments at the head of each line of the judgment poem.[32]

As with Yoshitsune's *zekku*, this is not the most enlightening form of judgment, especially since few of Go-Toba's judgment verses comment on the poems he is judging. Most of his *hanka* are simply independent poems, with the acrostic providing the only judgment information. One example, Round 714 (Autumn III):

Left, Kojijū

<blockquote>

Kuraki yo no	Though it be a road
yami ni mayofan	On which one might get lost
miti nite mo	In the darkness of night,
koyofi no tuki ya	Long should we remember
omofiidubeki	The moon on this night.

</blockquote>

Right, Michitomo, Win

<blockquote>

Fukakusa no	In Fukakusa Village
sato no tukikage	The loneliness of the moonlight
sabisisa mo	Is as ever,
sumikosi mama no	So, too, since I have lived here,
nobe no akikaze	Autumn wind upon the moors.

</blockquote>

Judgment

<blockquote>

Mine no tuki	*Moonlight over peaks*
Kiyoki ifama ni	*Has come to rest, pure*
Yadori kite	*Among the crags,*
Sazanami koforu	*At Sazanami, ripples freeze*
Siga no yama no wi	*In the mountain wells of Shiga.*[33]

</blockquote>

As shown, the judgment acrostic spells out *migi ya sasi* (literally, "I indicate the Right"—*ki* and *gi* were not distinguished orthographically at this time), but its contents bear no apparent relation to either competing poem.

---

32. Ariyoshi, *Sengohyakuban uta-awase*, p. 260.
33. Ibid., p. 304.

Since both of the contest poems allude to well-known works,[34] it was not *honkadori* that attracted Go-Toba to one rather than the other. Although Michitomo's Tsuchimikado clan were patrons of the Rokujō poets, his entry features two devices favored by the more innovative poets of this era: the x-no-y-no-z modification pattern (twice!) and a substantive final (*taigendome*). Presumably Go-Toba found this diction more to his taste. In any case, Michitomo's poem was subsequently included in *Shinkokinshū* (374; IV, Autumn 1).

Rounds 751–900 (Autumn IV, Winter I) were assigned to Teika, who was coming into his own as a poetic force. Most of his judgments here were written in *wabun*, although a few are in *kanbun*. From time to time he discussed rules for *honkadori*, taking roughly the same position he took in *Kindai shūka* regarding the number of syllables one may borrow and so on. Although in scoring he was more generous than most of the other judges toward the Tsuchimikado and Rokujō poets, he was not as diplomatic as his father in some of his comments and was especially sharp in his attacks on Kenshō, dean of the Rokujō school.

His judgment for Round 898 is of note for those interested in the Kyōgoku style. He awards the Win to Ietaka's poem (which is, incidentally, about hail, a favorite Kyōgoku topic) because "the scene feels as if it is before our very eyes and is truly fine" (*[sono] keshiki me no mae ni mukaeru kokoro shite makoto ni okashiku koso miehaberumere*). This type of judgment, emphasizing the importance of creating a scene in the mind's eye of the audience, also appears in Kyōgoku contests of the early 1300s.[35]

But Round 752 (Autumn IV) gives a better overall sense of Teika's approach:

---

34. The Left poem takes as its *honka* Izumi Shikibu's famous *Kuraki yori / kuraki miti ni zo / irinubeki / faruka ni terase / yama no fa no tuki*—"Out of darkness / Into a darkened path / I must now enter / Illuminate the far reaches / Moon over mountain's ridge!" (*SIS* 1342 [XX, Laments]). The Right poem alludes to *KKS* 971 (XVIII, Miscellaneous 2), Ariwara no Narihira: *Tosi wo fete / sumikosi sato wo / idete inaba / itodo Fukakusa / no to ya narinamu*—"If I were to leave / This village of Fukakusa / Where I've lived through many years / How much deeper, then, / Its grasses would become!"

35. In Round 4 of the *Fushimi-in nijūban uta-awase*, Tamekane's entry, on early winter rains, is awarded the Win in part because "it seems as if we can see before us the beating of early winter rains in the evening sky" (*shigure uchitaru yū no sora ima mo miru kokochi shite*; Fukuda and Inoue, eds., *Chūsei uta-awaseshū to kenkyū*, 1: 72). For a translation of this contest, see Huey, "Fushimi-in nijūban uta-awase."

Left, Yoshitsune, Tie

 Aki fa nafo   Even as I resent
 kuzu no urakaze   Autumn winds that still blow
 uramite mo   Showing arrowroot's under-leaves
 tofazu karenisi   I still long for one departed
 fito zo kofisiki   Who visits not this withered place.

Right, Shunzei no Musume

 Tofu fito mo   Autumn has come,
 arasi fukisofu   When storms blow ever harder,
 aki fa kite   But no one visits me
 ko no fa ni udumu   Through the grassy path to
 yado no mitisiba   my hut
             Now buried by fallen leaves.

Judgment: Both poems have pushed beyond the pathos of autumn and entered into the feelings of one in love. In the poem on the Left, the speaker resents the wind that blows the arrowroot leaves about and longs for one who has departed from the withered scene. In the poem on the Right, the speaker now thinks fondly of the traces of a visitor, traces that are now buried by leaves blown in a storm. Both poems are deeply dyed by tears and early winter rains (sigure) and colored with the sadness of autumn loneliness, and it is difficult to choose between them.[36]

 Both poems make allusions, the Left to a poem in *Shikashū*, by Fujiwara Mototoshi (264; VIII, Love 2):

 Asadifu ni   Tangled weeds,
 kesa oku tuyu no   Withered by the cold of
 samukeku ni   morning dew
 karenisi fito no   Settled on them—
 nazo ya kofisiki   Why do I so long for
             The one now gone away?

 The Right poem refers to a verse from the "Hahakigi" (Broom Tree) chapter of *The Tale of Genji*, spoken by Yūgao to Tō no Chūjō when he visits her after a long absence and insists that he treasures her as he would a beautiful wild carnation:

 Utifarafu   Even the sleeve
 sode mo tuyukeki   That would stroke the wild carnation
 tokonatu ni   Seems wet with dew—

---

36. Ariyoshi, *Sengohyakuban uta-awase*, pp. 319–20.

arasi fukisofu	Tired of this tryst, as autumn comes,
aki fa kinikeri	When storms blow ever harder...[37]

Both the poems alluded to are Love poems, which is the point of Teika's judgment. The issue of seasonal poems overlapping with the love category is essential. Taniyama considers it one of the noteworthy features of *Shinkokinshū* and adds that Teika's stand is similar to that in his *Eiga no taigai* in which he stated flatly that for allusions, one should "borrow vocabulary from Seasonal poems when composing Love and Miscellaneous verse and borrow vocabulary from Love and Miscellaneous poems when one is composing Seasonal verse."[38] Given the use of Love poems—or more specifically, the courtly love affair as traced through the love poetry of the imperial anthologies—as a basis for prose, there is ample indication here of waka's narrative function, since Teika seems to be arguing that a poem is better if it participates somehow in narration. Teika's argument also suggests that the extremely subjective view of nature found in *Kokinshū* seasonal poetry has not disappeared but simply taken a new form. In any case, one's reading of virtually any waka from this time onward is enhanced if one keeps Teika's notion in mind.

In his *kanbun* judgment for the Round 771 matchup between Fujiwara Sueyoshi and the Mikohidari partisan Ietaka, Teika sharply attacked the diction of Sueyoshi's poem while focusing on more ethereal qualities when he praised Ietaka's:

Left, Sueyoshi

Iza ikani	Hey! No matter how much
miyama no oku ni	You may have waned
siworete mo	Over distant mountains,
kokoro siritaki	I want to know what you are feeling,
aki no yo no tuki	Moon of this autumn night.

Right, Ietaka, Win

Yo ya fukuru	Night deepens.
kumowi faruka ni	Beyond far-off clouds
naku kari mo	The call of a wild goose

---

37. Yamagishi, ed., *Genji monogatari* 1, NKBT 14, p. 79. See also Seidensticker, *The Tale of Genji*, 1: 33.

38. Hagitani and Taniyama, *Uta-awaseshū*, p. 555. The relevant section in *Eiga no taigai* can be found in Hashimoto et al., *Karonshū*, p. 493. In the latter, Teika's advice is aimed at helping the poet avoid mere imitation of the ancient poem s/he is alluding to.

| fitotu ni narinu | Becomes one with it— |
| koromo utu kowe | The sound of cloth being fulled. |

Judgment: *The expression "I want to know" (siritaki) is something we hear in common speech, but has such diction ever been used in poetry? And that first line does not sound very nice.*[39] *In the Right poem, the tones of the fulling block and the calls of geese from beyond the clouds late at night work together to create a dimly lit scene infused with a feeling of depth.*[40]

Teika's distaste for the colloquial in poetry shows a conservative stance toward diction, which was inherited by his Nijō successors a century later. His criticism of Sueyoshi's choice of words is similar to the Nijō denunciation of the Kyōgoku style. The writer of the anonymous tract *Kaen renjo no kotogaki* (Poetic Garden Particulars, Jointly Signed; 1315) attacks a number of *Gyokuyōshū* poems for using unpoetic diction. Even one of Teika's own poems—a decidedly odd verse about an ox plodding along on a hot day, raising dust—is criticized as "shocking to the ear." The writer wryly noted that genius does guarantee that all of one's poems are perfect and that it is the anthologizer's responsibility to "separate the gold from the sand."[41] At least that later Nijō partisan had precedent in Teika himself for a traditional approach to poetic diction.

On the other hand, this judgment also shows Teika's preference for poems with "depth" (*yūgen*, here simply called *yū*). What gives Ietaka's poem added depth is the subtle reference to Kumoinokari's plaintive remark, overheard by Yūgiri late at night, in "The Maiden" chapter of *The Tale of Genji*. She and Yūgiri have been prevented from seeing each other, but unbeknownst to her, he is in the next room, intensely longing to be with her. He realizes with a mixture of frustration and satisfaction that she, too, longs for him when he hears her, lying awake, say to herself as she catches the plain-

---

39. Teika uses the expression *hatsu no itsumoji*, literally "the first five characters," a common phrase in contest judgments when referring to the first line of a poem. In fact, each of the lines has a designation in traditional criticism; this demonstrates quite clearly that waka poets and critics did see what we call "lines," or *ku* if you will, as basic elements of a poem.

40. Ariyoshi, *Sengohyakuban uta-awase*, p. 331.

41. Teika's poem: *Yukinayamu / usi no ayumi ni / tatu tiri no / kaze safe atuki / natu no woguruma*—"As it plods along / Underneath the ox's hooves / Dust swirls / In a breeze that itself blows hot / Round the small cart in summer." The problem with Teika's poem is as much topic as diction, but in another poem from *Gyokuyōshū* cited in this tract, his use of the word "rainbow" (*nizi*) prompted mock outrage in the writer, who claimed it was inappropriate because one cannot find that word in any other imperial anthology (Sasaki Nobutsuna, *Nihon kagaku taikei*, 4: 100–101; the entire tract is on pp. 97–107).

tive call of a wild goose: "The wild goose beyond the clouds, is it like me?" (*kumoi no kari mo waga goto ya*).[42] Thus, again, a seasonal poem is enhanced by suggesting, through allusion, a love subtext.

The next judge was Fujiwara (Rokujō) Suetsune, also known by his priestly name, Renkei. He was assigned Rounds 901–1050 (Winter II, III). The son of Rokujō Akisuke, Suetsune was quite conservative and tended in this contest to write long, discursive judgments focusing on the traditional faults and/or vocabulary issues. In one judgment (Round 1023), however, he discouraged pedantry in poetry by noting that a *honkadori* is useless if one takes such an obscure part of the poem that the *honka* is not recognizable. More typical, however, was his judgment for Round 959:

Left, Tomochika

    Faru aki no   Spring and autumn views
    nagame fa yuki ni   Have been covered deeply
    tumorikeri   With the snow—
    fana to tuki to wo   Seen now as flowers or moonlight
    Miyosino no sato   At a village in lovely Yoshino.

Right, Michichika, Win

    Tukifatesi   Deep sadness of an autumn
    aki no afare fa   That has run its course
    akatuki no   Still lingers
    sigure no oto ni   In the sound of early winter rains
    nafo nokorikeri   Beating at daybreak.

Judgment: The Left poem has identical syllables at the head of its upper and lower sections [faru, fana] *which, I have to say, sounds terrible. Furthermore, are not "views" and "seen" the same thing? As for the Right poem, its "deep sadness of an autumn run its course yet lingering in the sound of early winter rains" truly soothes the spirit, and I award the Win to the Right.*[43]

Tomochika's poem is more interesting than Suetsune implied. Its parallelism (spring and autumn—flowers and moon) might have appealed to the Kyōgoku poets. And what Suetsune regarded as a fault is verbal underscoring of the parallel that makes it more effective. Still, Suetsune's conservatism prevailed, especially in a poetry contest.

---

    42. From "The Maiden" (*Otome*) chapter, in Yamagishi, *Genji monogatari* 2, NKBT 15, p. 298; and Seidensticker, *The Tale of Genji*, p. 371.
    43. Ariyoshi, *Sengohyakuban uta-awase*, pp. 429–30.

Rounds 1051–200 (Congratulatory; Love I) were judged by Minamoto Moromitsu. Father of Tomochika and Kunaikyō, who also participated in this contest, Moromitsu rose only to Fifth Rank. Although allied to the Rokujō school, his judgments here are not noticeably partisan. Not surprisingly, given his low rank, he was quite generous in his judgments of the two ministers, Yoshitsune and Michichika. Both win six of the ten rounds in which their works appear. But when rank was not a consideration, he gave Teika high scores and Kenshō, the ultimate Rokujō poet, low ones. In fact, in one-on-one matchups between Mikohidari and Rokujō poets, Moromitsu's decisions in favor of the former are the most lopsided of the ten judges (see Table 1 above and Appendix D, pp. 417–18). Apparently he was more liberal than his background would indicate. In fact, some of his judgments do take issue with traditional practices. In Round 1122, for example, he noted that an expression used by one of the poets had been censured in the famous *Kanpaku sadaijin Yorimichi uta-awase* (Poetry Contest Sponsored by Chancellor/Regent and Minister of the Left Yorimichi) of 1035 (often cited in poetry contest judgments as a model) but concluded: "That was quite a long time ago, and I wonder if we still need be concerned with such things."[44] On the other hand, at least twice in the Love section (Rounds 1128 and 1193), he argued that Love poems in a poetry contest ought to be more subtle than in other forums.[45]

Moromitsu's judgments are often brief and impressionistic, using words like *okashi* and *yoroshi* (nice, fine), although he did expound at length a number of times. He was not a faultfinder, but occasionally he singled out lines that sounded odd to him. For example, he slyly tweaked the pedantic Kenshō (whose own judgments in this contest tend toward dry recitation of precedent) in Round 1170 by saying of Kenshō's entry, "I know there is precedent for the expression *yoru no itoma* (leisure time at night), but I still find it vulgar (*zoku*)."[46] He tends to like clever *kyō* (the device or trick a poet uses to capture the essence of the topic). In at least five rounds (1093, 1105, 1111, 1158, and 1184), successful *kyō* are the deciding factor. One of these rounds deserves special attention. In Round 1111, there is evidence that Moromitsu, at least, remained conscious of the fact that this contest was

---

44. Ibid., p. 512.
45. Ibid., pp. 515, 547.
46. Ibid., p. 535. At least one precedent appears as MYS 4479 (NKBT 4455) and KWR 3861.

made up of individual sequences, even while he judged it as a contest. In fact, it was the sequencing trick (*kyō*) he saw in Go-Toba's work that prompted him to award Go-Toba a Win, as if in reward not only for this one round but also for the device Go-Toba used throughout the section:

Left, Go-Toba, Win

> Yorodu yo to As if for ten thousand years
> Mikumano no ura no The "beach brocade" lilies grow
> famayufu no In layers along the shore
> kasanete mo nafo At sacred Kumano, yet
> tukisezarubesi Still they cannot be depleted.

Right, Ienaga

> Kimi ga yo fa The years of my lord's reign,
> futaba no matu no Surpass one thousand,
> tiyo wo fete Like needles of the bifold pine,
> kozuwe no kaze wo Such that wind through its branches
> kumo ni kiku made Is heard even beyond the clouds.

*Judgment: In the Left poem, the lines "grow in layers [. . .] yet still they cannot be depleted" seem to me far beyond the ordinary. I felt as I read the poem that somehow I had seen several times before the notion "as if for ten thousand ages" (*yorodu yo to mi*). And, indeed, when I looked back through the section, I found that His Majesty had begun each of his poems with that same line and had further treated each of the four seasons in turn. It was quite a striking device (*kyō*). The Right poem is also skillfully composed, but in the end I award the Win to the Left.*[47]

Go-Toba's poem is an allusive variation on a Hitomaro poem, and as with the best allusions of his day, it uses a poem from a different category, in this case a Love verse:

> Mikumano no By lovely Kumano
> ura no famayufu Along the shore grow "beach brocade"
> momofe nasu   lilies,
> kokoro fa omofedo One hundred layers deep—
> tada ni afanu kamo Like the feelings for you in my heart,
>   Though I might never meet you.[48]

---

47. Ariyoshi, *Sengohyakuban uta-awase*, p. 507.
48. MYS 499 (NKBT 496). Several variations appear in both *Man'yōshū* and *Kokin waka rokujō* (see, e.g., *Shinpen kokka taikan*, 2:4, #1937), and it is impossible to say which version Go-Toba had in mind. *Famayufu* (Hepburn *hamayū*) is crinum, a variety of amaryllis, with large,

Moromitsu also favored other poems that reach back toward or successfully allude to *Man'yōshū* verse (e.g., Rounds 1065, 1131, and 1189). His favorite aesthetic concept seems to be *nabiyaka* (having gentle, graceful beauty), a word that appears numerous times in his judgments, as in Round 1193:

Left, Sanuki, Win

    Utifafete   All along, completely
    kurusiki mono fa   Hiding my love from public view—
    fitome nomi   How knotty it has been,
    Sinobu no ura no   Like rope used by fisherfolk
    ama no takunafa[49]   At Shinobu's hidden shore!

Right, Ietaka

    Karakoromo   Chinese robes, cords tied—
    fi mo yufugure no   Daytime sky already takes
    sora no iro   The color of evening.
    kumoraba kumore   If you're going to cloud over, cloud over,
    matu fito mo nasi   For the one I await is not here.

Judgment: The Left poem expresses itself gently. Besides, although the Right poem is lovely, I wonder if it is not better in a poetry contest to express the feeling of the Love topic a bit more subtly. Thus, the Left poem wins.[50]

Drawing from an earlier poem, Sanuki uses *engo* (associative vocabulary) related to rope to make her statement.[51] In addition to the explicit "rope" (*takunafa*), she puns on *kuru* (to haul or reel in) in the adjective *kurusiki* (which I have rendered "knotty") and *fitome* (its primary meaning here being "public view," but *me* also means the knots in a fishing net). These figures help shift attention from the speaker of the poem so that she does not seem so self-absorbed; hence Moromitsu's comment that the poem "expresses itself gently."

---

lily-like flowers. Since it grows in great layers along the shore, it got the nickname "beach brocade."

49. Also *SKKS* 1096 (XII, Love 2).

50. Ariyoshi, *Sengohyakuban uta-awase*, p. 546–47.

51. *GSIS* 960 (XVI, Miscellaneous 2), sent by Tsuchimikado Mikushigedono (d. 1026; a lady-in-waiting to the Retired Emperor Sanjō's Empress Kenshi) to Prince Koichijō-in (994–1051) when he had been away for a long time: *Kokoro etu / ama no takunafa / utifafete / kuru wo kurusi to / omofunarubesi*—"I realize now / As for fisherfolk the endless / Drawing in of rope is painful / So, too, for you / Must have been those visits to me."

Ietaka also uses *engo*, in this case clothing figures, and a *makurakotoba*, as well. *Karakoromo*, literally "Chinese robes," sometimes, in fact, meant robes imported from China. But it was often used in waka in the more general sense of clothing cut, dyed, or embroidered in a foreign (Chinese) style or even to indicate an especially lovely robe. It is also considered a *makurakotoba*, that is, a fixed epithet, followed by other clothing-related words such as the verb *tatsu* (*tatu*; "stitch") or the noun *himo* (*fimo*; "string; cord"). However, since it almost inevitably appears as such in poems of love, longing, and separation, it might better be thought of as a fixed synecdoche that stands in for either one of the lovers. Here, Ietaka followed it with the expression *fi mo yufugure* (day to evening), in which is embedded the pun *fimo yufu* (tie a cord). I read this as the speaker, the Waiting Woman, referring to herself, dressed up and waiting for her lover to come. The connection with *fimo yufu* and love/separation is found in numerous poems back to *Man'yōshū* and is thought to reflect a folk practice of two lovers who are going to be separated tying a knot in a cord to symbolize their steadfast commitment.[52] Perhaps because it focuses so clearly on the speaker herself, Moromitsu found it lacking in the subtlety he preferred in formal occasions such as poetry contests.

In what Taniyama believes was deliberate irony, Go-Toba assigned the next section, Rounds 1201–350 (Love II, III) to the cranky monk Kenshō (1130?–1209?), the Rokujō school's most conservative spokesman.[53] Not surprisingly, Kenshō was especially hard on the Mikohidari poets. His judgments are long, often citing several *honka* in their entirety; indeed, his scholarly, even pedantic, tone reminds one of Mototoshi a century earlier. Round 1234 is typical:

Left, Kintsugu

Ikade ware	This transferred scent,
sinobi ni naruru	Of which I've grown secretly fond,
uturika no	How might I take it
taenu nifofi wo	And add its insistent fragrance
sode ni kasanen	Again and again to my sleeves?

---

52. An example would be this envoy (*hanka*) to a long poem (*chōka*) on parting: *Wagimoko ga / yufitesi fimo wo / tokame yamo / taeba tayu tomo / tada ni afu made ni*—"The cord tied / By my sweetheart, / Would I ever untie it? / Not till we meet again, / Though if it breaks, it breaks" (*MYS* 1793 [*NKBT* 1789]; also appears as *KWR* 3353, attributed to Hitomaro, with the fourth line reading *taeba tayu toya*).

53. Hagitani and Taniyama, *Uta-awaseshū*, p. 318.

Right, Michitomo, Win

Akatuki no	As day now breaks,
toko fa kusaba no	Perhaps our bed should take
na ni nare ya	The name grass-mat,
tuyu ni wakare no	For tears of parting
namida okuran[54]	Settle there as dew.

Judgment: In the poem on the Left, the word uturika *(transferred scent) in the upper section and the word* nifofi *(fragrance) in the lower section are synonyms and thus a violation (*yamafi*). It is true that in the* Rokujō sadaijin no ie no uta-awase *the poem* Waga yado no / fanatatibana no / nifofi nifa / fitori nuru yo mo / uturika zo suru *(The fragrance / Of orange blossoms / In my garden / Is a transferred scent to me / Even on this night when I sleep alone) was awarded a Win, and this might be advanced as evidence that a poem can win even with such a violation.[55] However, since the judgment in that contest does not set forth detailed reasons, it is rather vague. Perhaps it was because the other poem was utterly bad, even worse than this one with its fault. It is difficult to know what the judge had in mind. The Right poem refers to* Fitori nuru / toko fa kusaba ni / aranedomo / aki kuru yofi fa / tuyukekarikeri *(Though this bed / On which I lie, alone, / Is not a grass mat / On this night as Autumn nears, / It's covered now with dew!).[56] Due to the violation, the Left poem loses.*

This is characteristic of Kenshō's "scholarship." However, he apparently overlooked, for example, KKS 876, which uses both *uturika* and *nifofi*. On the other hand, perhaps this simply reflected the different standards for poetry contests and imperial anthologies. What was acceptable in one was not always acceptable in the other.[57]

---

54. Reading *(w)okuran* as *okuran*, "to settle."

55. This appears to be what is now known as *Tō no chūjō Minamoto Akifusa no ie no uta-awase*, sponsored by Minamoto Akifusa in 1056. In the extant text, this poem, with the last two lines quite different from those Kenshō quoted, appears as the poem of the Right, Round 9, Orange Blossoms, by Chikamoto (otherwise unknown). The last lines read *ka wo tadunetutu / konu fito zo naki*—"all who come inquire / repeatedly after its scent"; this seems a little awkward here and suggests textual corruption. Kenshō's quote may well be more accurate. The round is marked Tie, and there is no *hanshi*. For a text of the contest, under the designation *Tō no chūjō Akifusa no uta-awase*, see Hagitani, *Heianchō uta-awase taisei*, 4: 1109–16; Chikamoto's poem appears on p. 1116.

56. KKS 188 (IV, Autumn I), Anonymous.

57. There are numerous examples in *Sengohyakuban uta-awase* of winning poems being passed over in favor of losing ones for inclusion in later imperial anthologies. To cite just a few from this contest (omitting examples involving Go-Toba, or the judge in question, since the judgments in such cases are suspect), with the judge's name in parentheses: Rounds 72 (Tadayoshi), 195 (Shunzei), 713 (Go-Toba), 879 (Teika), 963 (Suetsune), 1066 (Moromitsu),

For the Right poem, Kenshō merely quoted the source poem but did not identify it as being from *Kokinshū*. Evidently, he saw *Kokinshū* as virtually common knowledge, memorized by all poets so that specific identification is unnecessary. Interestingly enough, *KKS* 188 is an Autumn poem, which lends support to Teika's stance regarding the blurring of lines between Love and Nature poetry. Although Kenshō usually mentioned something about a *honkadori* when he drew attention to it (whether it was a good or bad allusion), in this case he did not. He did not even use the word "refers," which I have added for clarity. Since he ended the judgment calling a Loss rather than a Win, this would seem to be a lesser-of-the-two-evils round.

The final section, Rounds 1351–500 (Miscellaneous I, II), was given to Jien for judgment. Allied with the innovative Mikohidari school, he was second to Saigyō in number of poems in *Shinkokinshū* (92). For the *Sengohyakuban uta-awase*, he wrote his judgments as tanka but, unlike Go-Toba, did not use acrostics. His *hanka* (literally, "judgment poems") almost always integrate one or more images from judged poems. Round 1424 provides a good illustration:

Left, Tomochika, Win

    Kusa no ifo   A grass hut—
    tadunesi ato mo   All traces of visitors
    furifatete   Are now past memories,
    arasi zo samuki   Storm winds are cold
    Afusaka no seki   Here at Ōsaka Barrier.

Right, Tadayoshi

    Tuki yosuru   On this moonlit night
    Akasi no nami wo   I make of Akashi's bright waves
    makura nite   A pillow—
    miyako no yume ni   My dreams of the capital
    Suma no sekimori   Checked by Suma's Barrier guards.

Judgment

    Yume fa Suma mo   Dreams at Suma,
    tuki yosuru nami mo   Waves on a moonlit night,
    iza ikani   Are fine,
    tadune mo siten   But surely one must pay a call
    Semimaru ga ato   On memories of Semimaru's past.

The Left wins.

1219 (Kenshō), and 1399 (Jien). In other words, every judge except Yoshitsune was second-guessed by history.

The form of judgment is frustratingly terse. Both poems are *honzetsu*, that is, allusions to prose (or, alternatively, legend). The Left poem calls to mind Semimaru, the blind prince, at his lonely Ōsaka Barrier hut; the Right poem refers to Genji's exile. It is impossible to tell why Jien preferred one over the other. From the wording, it does not appear that he based his judgment on technical considerations. And he had no reason for partisanship since both poets were allied with the Rokujō school. Perhaps it is simply that Semimaru, assumed in Jien's age to be a real person and a fallen prince at that, evoked more pity (*aware*) than the fictional Genji.[58]

The *Sengohyakuban uta-awase* is easily the most important document of its time for displaying the range of practices and aesthetic notions that surrounded waka in the early 1200s. In this it surpasses even *Shinkokinshū* itself, which in the end is the vision of a largely Mikohidari committee under the firm hand of Go-Toba. In the *Sengohyakuban uta-awase*, on the other hand, the judges and poets are allowed to speak for themselves. Each section deserves a far more thorough reading than this chapter has been able to provide. The result would be a much fuller picture of the age.

---

58. For a thorough look at Semimaru as he was read in medieval Japan, see Matisoff, *The Legend of Semimaru*.

SIX

The Persistence of 'Miyabi,' Kennin 3 (1203)

Aside from the *Sengohyakuban uta-awase*, which was probably completed around this time, the Third Year of Kennin, 1203, was rather quiet from the standpoint of poetry production. Texts survive for only two events, both of which are discussed below, although *Meigetsuki* makes reference to a few other poetic activities. However, several other events occurred that help give a fuller picture of Go-Toba's literary circle and the people who inhabited it. Among other things, the year marked Shunzei's ninetieth birthday. Go-Toba celebrated the occasion with an appropriately elaborate, yet poignant, party at the Wakadokoro toward the end of the year. However, there are other moments to look at before turning to that affair.

The year opened with a large party at the Kyōgoku Palace on the 15th of the First Month. Go-Toba had relocated to this Minamoto family villa late in 1202 after his palace at Nijō had burned down (see Chapter 4), and this party was the "housewarming." Like any proper gathering, it included poetry, although neither Teika nor Ienaga recorded any of it.[1] According to Teika, the Wakadokoro itself was relocated to this new palace soon after this party.[2]

In mid-spring, there was flower-viewing, which, of course, would hardly have been unusual, except this particular excursion was carefully reported by

---

1. A congratulatory poem by Yoshitsune, however, did make it into *Shinkokinshū* (735; VII, Felicitations).
2. *Meigetsuki*, Kennin 3/ii/4, 1: 292.

both Teika and Ienaga, whose accounts demonstrate clearly that the elegant courtly outing, filled with flowers and poems, was not entirely a thing of the past.[3]

On the 24th of the Second Month, members of the Wakadokoro and their friends suddenly decided to go and see the cherry blossoms at the palace before all the flowers could scatter. The company included Teika, Ienaga, Masatsune, Tomochika, and Kamo no Chōmei, as well as several lesser-known companions.[4] At the palace, it appears that others had the same idea, for throngs of monks and court ladies were walking about. The poets seemed unhappy to have to share the experience; both Ienaga and Teika are contemptuous in their description of the court ladies they encounter. Ienaga calls them "affected"; Teika is even less charitable, dismissing them as "lady fools" (*kyōjo*).[5] Worse, the other sightseers recognized the group as members of the Wakadokoro and felt compelled to show off their own literary talents by bringing poems over to them for their comment. Ienaga described his discomfort at being noticed by the crowds of people, who whispered and nodded to each other as if to gather their courage before coming forward with their verses. Teika, naturally, was even more blunt in his distaste: "Lady fools dumped their worthless poems on us; people stared at us as though we were a show." Apparently, the price of fame does not change over the centuries, although the objects of public adulation might. (Would poets ever get such attention today?)

Eventually, people left them alone, and the Wakadokoro group sat at the edge of the south veranda of the palace and began to compose *renga* as well as *waka*, one by one. Teika later recalled that Ienaga provided saké to smooth the proceedings. According to Ienaga:

We broke off branches of cherry, and attached our poems to them. Teika, still a Lieutenant, wrote:

---

3. My account here relies on ibid., 3/ii/24–25, 1: 297; and *IN*, pp. 168–79 (including both Ienaga's text and Ishida and Satsukawa's extensive notes).

4. In *Shūi gusō*, Teika also mentioned Ietaka, but his name does not appear in either Ienaga's account of this excursion or Teika's account in *Meigetsuki*.

5. The characters Teika uses, *kyōjo*, literally mean "mad woman," and when applied, for example, to Nō plays, refer to a woman who is insane or at least temporarily "dysfunctional." Imagawa (*Meigetsukishō*, p. 132) glosses it here as meaning *tawabure asobu onna*, which would suggest a woman of the entertainer class who specializes in clever repartee. However, I have been unable to confirm that definition in any dictionary.

Tosi wo fete	Years have passed
miyuki ni naresi	And I've grown used to serving my Lord
fana no kage	Under these snow-like flowers,
furiyuku mi wo mo	And they must pity me, too,
afare to ya omofu	Now falling into old age.[6]

My brother, the priest Saiei, had been invited along with us. He composed:

Kozuwe nifa	On the branches here
nafo ofouti no	At the palace they still abound,
yamazakura	Blossoms of the mountain cherry.
kaze mo ada nifa	It seems that the wind dares not
omofazarikeri	Treat these flowers with disdain.

Since everyone in the group agreed that these were especially fine verses, I made a point to write them down. As we were about to leave, some ladies came up to us and said, "Please break off a branch of blossoms for us. The palace guards don't recognize us and would get mad if we did it ourselves." Nakahara no Muneyasu did so and attached a poem:

Ore to ifaba	If you tell me to break some off,
ito mo kasikosi	I do so with utmost respect—
sakurabana	These cherry blossoms.
akanu nifofi wo	But make sure their ineffable scent
sode ni makase yo	Also suffuses your sleeves.[7]

The ladies sent a verse in reply but, alas!, I have forgotten it. As the waxing moon rose brightly, we left the palace grounds and headed home.[8] All of us must have had in mind the line "Is it easy to leave?" and the blossoms, as if expressing their resentment at our taking leave, streamed down.[9] As we approached the Moon Flower Gate (Gekkamon), one of our number began to play on the reed pipes, and I took

---

6. *SKKS* 1455 (XVI, Miscellaneous 1).

7. *IN*, p. 171, specifies two *honka* for this poem, but citing them here would not enrich our reading of this clever, but not especially profound verse.

8. Ienaga wrote "the Tenth night moon of the Third Month," but either his memory was faulty (his diary is full of this kind of mistake) or he was taking poetic license. Teika's *Meigetsuki* date of ii/24 is probably correct.

9. They recall lines from a poem by Ōshikōchi no Mitsune (fl. 894–925) on the "End of Spring" that appears as the last spring poem in *Kokinshū*: *Kefu nomi to / faru wo omofanu / toki dani mo / tatu koto yasuki / fana no kage kafa*—"Even if today / We did not believe it to be / The end of spring / Would it be easy to leave behind / The sheltering image of these flowers?" (*KKS* 134, [II, Spring 2]). The word *kage* carries an enormous range of meanings, including "image," "vision," "silhouette," "light," "shade," and "shelter." Since a simple one-to-one translation is especially tricky and misleading here, I have gone with "sheltering image," which even still is limiting.

up a flute and played along with him. Captain Masatsune joined in on the reed flute, and we walked through the Kenshūmon gate and then left the outer palace compound by the Taikenmon gate, returning home with shared sweet memories.[10]

One is immediately struck by the old-fashioned elegance of the occasion. It demonstrates clearly how Heian *miyabi* has given way to a kind of studied *fūryū*, or pursuit of elegance as a pastime. The many descriptions of such moments in both *Ienaga nikki* and *Meigetsuki* show how persistent court values were. Second, one sees how close the members of the Wakadokoro had become, even spending much of their free time together. They had also achieved a fair degree of fame *as poets*, at least in aristocratic circles, to the point where they felt constrained—an indication that poetry truly had become a profession at which a few excelled and made their name.

Teika's poem, too, is interesting. He did not quote it in the *Meigetsuki* entry for this outing, but he included it (with slightly different wording) in his private collection *Shūi gusō*, saying simply that it was composed when Ietaka, Masatsune, and others invited him to join them in a palace flower-viewing excursion. However, its "true" nature as a poem lamenting his languishing official career—he had been serving in the Konoe guards for fourteen years—was obvious to his contemporaries. When the poem was added to *Shinkokinshū*, it was accompanied by a much more revealing headnote: "Composed when the poet had been serving in the Konoe guards for a long time and accompanied some of His Majesty's gentlemen to a flower-viewing at the palace." Despite the fact that the verse might be seen as an indirect criticism of him, Go-Toba was quite taken by it, not only permitting its inclusion in *Shinkokinshū*, but also quoting it and commenting on it in his *Go-Toba-in onkuden*, praising the gentleness with which Teika conveyed his dissatisfaction and the "matchless quality" of his manner of expression.[11] On ceremonial occasions, the Left Konoe Guards (Sakon'efu), in which Teika served, would line up by the palace cherry tree outside the main Audience Hall (Shishinden). That tree thus became known as the "Sakon Cherry." This was one of the things Teika suggested with the lines "serving my Lord under these flowers." At the time of this anecdote, Teika and his companions were admiring the palace cherry blossoms on their own time, as it were,

---

10. *IN*, pp. 168–69.
11. Sasaki Nobutsuna, *Nihon kagaku taikei*, 3: 5–6. I am indebted to *IN*, pp. 172–73; and Brower's translation of Go-Toba's treatise ("Ex-Emperor Go-Toba's Secret Teachings," p. 39) for drawing my attention to these various cross-references.

but Teika seized the opportunity to show the parallel. He also made a subtle pun on "snow" ("mi*yuki*") "falling" ("*furi*yuku"), which participates in two venerable poetic conceits: the confusion of blossoms with snow and the implication that one's hair has grown "snowy" with age.

When Go-Toba heard of the excursion, he summoned Ienaga upon his return to Go-Toba's residence later that evening and asked who had composed memorable poems. Ienaga told him of Teika's poem, and the Retired Emperor chuckled, saying he wished he had been invited along. Go-Toba then decided he would go to the palace himself the next day to see the flowers and dispatched messengers to others to accompany him.

Go-Toba and his companions left the next day for the palace, at about noon. Although the arrangements had supposedly been made in secret, there was a crush of carriages and horses belonging to those who apparently wanted to see the action. Seeing the throng, Ienaga was reminded of a Chinese verse from *Wakan rōeishū* about how "fleet carriages raise dust along Ninth Avenue" as they race to see the flowers at the imperial gardens.[12] Ienaga continues the story:

> We entered the palace grounds through the Taikenmon gate. So impatient was His Majesty that the short road we had to travel seemed very long indeed, and even the footsteps of the attendants sounded rushed. Seeing the royal procession, a group of palace ladies were not surprisingly thrown into a stir. The Retired Emperor sent me to hold them back for a while. I went over to them and conveyed His Majesty's wishes by reciting as the opening of a poem: "Flowers though you be / Please stay back awhile / Here among the trees" (*fana nagara / sibasi na tiri so / ko no moto wo*). One of them handed me a globeflower she had been holding and capped the poem: "And what will it avail us / To remain here silently?" (*ifade fa ari to / kafi ya nakaran*).

Ever the faithful attendant, Ienaga's elegant verse to the ladies reflected Go-Toba's wishes on two levels. On the surface, it was a graceful way to ask the women to stay away from the imperial party. At the same time, it represented Go-Toba's request to the cherry blossoms he was in such a hurry to view: "Please stay long enough on the branches that I might see you." Ishida and Satsukawa have difficulty interpreting the ladies' reply. They gloss it as essentially, "it is a rare treat for us that His Majesty has come here to view the blossoms; how could we not go over and make formal greeting?"[13] But

---

12. *Wakan rōeishū* 115 (Part One; Spring).
13. *IN*, p. 175.

the key seems to be the globeflower (*yamabuki*). I believe their verse refers to this anonymous *Kokinshū* poem:

Yamabuki fa	O, globeflowers,
aya na na saki so	Do not bloom needlessly,
fana mimu to	For my lord, who planted you,
uwekemu kimi ga	Hoping to see you bloom,
koyofi konaku ni	Will not be visiting tonight.[14]

In other words, "you are asking us not to show ourselves, as the ancient poet asked the globeflowers not to bloom, but unlike that poem, today our lord is, in fact, coming to see the flowers, so why should we remain silent?"

Or they may be referring to another *Kokinshū* poem, this one by Sosei (fl. 896–909):

Yamabuki no	You, wearing a robe
fanairokoromo	The color of globeflower,
nusi ya tare	Who are you?
tofedo kotafezu	Though I ask, you do not reply.
kutinasi ni site	You must be a silent gardenia.[15]

In this case, their gesture and verse hint that, unlike the lady in the poem, they would be more than willing to tell the sovereign their names.

In any case, there was still more for Ienaga to tell:

After that, the Retired Emperor gathered his retinue closer to him under the flowers, and complaining that there were hardly any blossoms left, he produced inkstone and paper and ordered everyone to compose poems, dividing up the paper among us. Someone broke off a branch from one of the trees and used it to fashion a poem stand on which everyone placed their finished poems. His Majesty's poem:

Amatukaze	Heavenly winds,
sibasi fukitodi yo	Blow awhile and block their passage
fanazakura	Through the clouds,
yuki to tirimagafu	These cherry blossoms
kumo no kayofidi	Fluttering down like snow.

---

14. KKS 123 (II, Spring 2). Since *naku ni* can also be concessive ("although/while something is not the case"), this poem might also be read as "do not bloom needlessly until my lover gets here" (as in the modern *nai uchi ni*), or "do not bloom as long as my lover is not here."

15. KKS 1012 (XIX, Miscellaneous Forms, *Haikaika* section).

When we were to return, His Majesty had some of the fallen flowers gathered up and placed on the lid of his inkstone box, which he sent, along with a poem, to the Regent Yoshitsune:

Kefu dani mo	Only just today
nifa wo sakari to	The flowers in the garden bloomed
uturu fana	Full, then scattered—
kiezu fa ari tomo	Though they do not melt
yuki ka tomo miyo.[16]	Please look on them as snow.[17]

His Majesty entrusted this poem and the flowers to someone, who set out for the Regent's Sanjō villa. I accompanied him. Apparently Yoshitsune was about to set out to pay a call on the Retired Emperor, for his outriders and bodyguards were all lined up in the garden. We made our way through them and stated our business to Lord Nakasuke, who conveyed our message to the Regent. Lord Yoshitsune came out and took our gift and poem with his own hands, then composed this reply:

Sasofarenu	Were these left behind
fito no tame to ya	For the one uninvited,
nokoriken	These white snow flower petals
asu yori saki no	From the day before tomorrow?[18]
fana no sirayuki	

All three poems in this passage, especially the exchange between Go-Toba and Yoshitsune, rely on allusion for their full effect. The first poem, by Go-Toba, which Teika thought highly enough of to quote in the *Meigetsuki* entry for this date, alludes to a poem composed by Henjō (816–90) as he watched a Gosechi dancer:

Amatukaze	Heavenly winds
kumo no kayofidi	Blow, and block her passage
fukitodi yo	Through the clouds,
wotome no sugata	For I wish to detain for a while
sibasi todomemu.	This maiden's dancing figure![19]

---

16. The textual line Ishida and Satsukawa are following gives the last line of the poem as *yuki to kamo miyo*, a remotely possible reading that they themselves believe to be a miscopy. I have "corrected" the line so that it conforms to the poem as it appears in *Shinkokinshū* and in Yoshitsune's house collection *Akishino gesseishū*.

17. SKKS 135 (II, Spring Two), with a headnote briefly describing the circumstances as Ienaga has recounted them.

18. SKKS 136 (II, Spring 2).

19. KKS 872 (XVII, Miscellaneous 1). Among Henjō's sixteen poems in *Kokinshū*, this is one of three that appears under his lay name, Yoshimine no Munesada.

Henjō's heavenly dancing maiden becomes in Go-Toba's poem a whirl of snow-white cherry petals, reversing the more common comparison of woman to flower (a comparison seen earlier in the episode when Ienaga addressed the court ladies and asked them to stay behind).

The exchange between Go-Toba and Yoshitsune is considerably more complex. Although the allusions were obviously not obscure in their day, the translator now can only fall back on explanations to fill out the picture. To begin with, Go-Toba's poem alludes to a *Kin'yōshū* verse about a garden being in "full bloom" with fallen petals.[20] More important, however, both Go-Toba and Yoshitsune share an allusion to a poem by Narihira, but that poem (and the allusion here) cannot be fully appreciated outside its own larger context. It is part of a poetic exchange between an anonymous lady and Narihira, which appears in *Ise monogatari* and *Kokinshū*. After a long absence, Narihira has finally come to visit the lady just when the cherry blossoms are in full bloom. The lady slyly recites:

Atanari to	They may have a reputation
na ni koso tatere	For falling too easily
sakurabana	These cherry blossoms,
tosi ni marenaru	Yet, see, they have awaited
fito mo matikeri.	One hardly seen for months!

True to *his* reputation, Narihira quickly turns the accusation against the lady with his reply:

Kefu kozu fa	Had I not come today,
asu fa yuki tozo	Tomorrow they'd be gone,
furinamasi	Fallen like snow,
kiezu fa aritomo	Yet, though they do not melt,
fana to mimasi ya	Should I see them as my flowers?[21]

Go-Toba plays with Narihira's use of time words. Whereas Narihira says that the blossoms will fall as snow tomorrow, Go-Toba says that even today they are already as snow. Borrowing the Love context of the original exchange, he worries that if Yoshitsune sees the petals as flowers, he will feel that Go-Toba's heart is fickle, just as Narihira suggested that the lady was

---

20. KYS 58 (I, Spring): *Kesa mireba / yoru no arasi ni / tirifatete / niwa koro fana no / sakari narikeri*—"As I look this morning / After last night's stormy winds / Scattered all the petals / It is now the garden / That is in full bloom!"

21. The exchange can be found in *Ise monogatari*, Episode 17; and KKS 62–63 (I, Spring 1).

no longer "his flower." By inviting Yoshitsune to see the petals as snow—and snow that does not melt, at that!—Go-Toba is asking him to overlook the fact that he had not been invited on the outing and not to take that oversight as an indication of waning friendship. Yoshitsune adroitly accepts the apology by saying, in effect, "Flowers? What flowers? I only see this snow, which fell, as you said, today (literally, "tomorrow's yesterday"), not tomorrow as the old poem would have it. How kind of you to save some for me." Yet, he also inserts a couple of barbs, too, first by reminding Go-Toba in the first line of his reply that he had been "uninvited" and second by wondering (the auxiliary verb *kemu* introduces some doubt) why this "snow" has not melted away; the implication is that, after all, Go-Toba is as fickle as the actual blossoms.

Although *Meigetsuki* also has an entry for this excursion on the 25th, it is rather perfunctory. Teika even seemed a little miffed to be pulled away from his books when he received Go-Toba's summons to join the excursion. He mentioned that he heard later about the exchange of poems between Go-Toba and Yoshitsune, but apparently he had already left the party before it occurred. Although he described the workings of the poetry party itself (who sat where, and so on), he cited no poems from it and instead complained that "we were ordered to come up with our poems quickly; there was no time for deep reflection." Overall, his somewhat crabby account, especially of the second day of the cherry blossom celebration, contrasts sharply with Ienaga's lyrical, waka- and Go-Toba–centered vision of *fūryū*. The difference in focus between Ienaga's view and Teika's delineates clearly the differing purposes of these two works, *Ienaga nikki* and *Meigetsuki*, yet it also demonstrates how well the two can be used together to deepen our understanding of events.

Anecdotes like this and character sketches are a feature of Ienaga's writings. In another entry in *Ienaga nikki*, dated in the extant text as Kennin 3 (1203) but with no internal evidence to prove that date definitively, Ienaga wrote about Kamo no Chōmei. He was not entirely sympathetic to Chōmei, and his account sheds interesting light on this poet and lute (*biwa*) aficionado, who is perhaps Japan's most famous recluse. Once again Ienaga managed to reveal more facets of a character than popular tradition has chosen to remember:

When one has a talent, no matter how small, and one devotes oneself wholeheartedly to developing it, one may attract the attention of his lord. Such was the case with Kamo no Chōmei, who despite His Majesty Go-Toba's patronage, was unable to achieve his dream.[22] I wonder if this wasn't because of something in a previous life. After his father died, Chōmei stopped attending to the family shrine and went into seclusion. But because of his skill in poetry, he was soon being invited to Go-Toba's palace and before long was appointed as a member (*yoriudo*) of the Wakadokoro. Thereafter, he took part in even the most ordinary poetry events and virtually never left the palace, being in constant service to His Majesty.

About the time His Majesty was looking for a way to appropriately reward Chōmei for his service, the post of Shrine Assistant (*negi*) opened up at Kawai Shrine. Everyone assumed that this time His Majesty would appoint Chōmei to the position. Even before Chōmei could petition for the job, it appeared that His Majesty was inclined to favor him, and when Chōmei secretly got word of this, he was overcome and shed tears of joy.

However, when Sukekane, the Chief Attendant at Kamo Shrine, heard what was afoot, he protested: "When appointing shrine officials, rank is not to be disregarded. I am of the Senior Fifth Rank Lower, as is my son, Sukeyori.[23] To be sure, Chōmei is older than my son, but perhaps because he felt useless, he has hardly done any work at the shrine. By comparison, although Sukeyori is young enough to be Chōmei's son, he has devotedly served the shrine day and night—far more so than Chōmei. Surely the deity of the shrine has taken notice of this.[24] Besides, even if my son had not served the shrine so faithfully, how could Your Majesty ignore the fact that I, his father, have as my own avocation prayed ceaselessly for the welfare of the imperial family and the nation? Furthermore, the eldest son of a Chief Attendant should not have to come after an outsider, and that is a principle not limited to this shrine." Thus did he plead his case in grand terms, claiming he was transmitting the will of the gods.

Against this, Chōmei could not make much argument. He could only hope that His Majesty would take into account his services in the field of poetry, for which he had been summoned to court in the first place. However, Go-Toba agonized over the propriety of ignoring rank-order in any bureaucratic appointment, much less one involving a shrine, and in the end he decided it was best to follow the will of the gods. He formally granted Sukekane's request.

Subsequently, His Majesty designated a branch shrine of Kamo, known as the Ura Shrine, as one under imperial control, and he assigned the office of Assistant to it with the beneficent intention of appointing Chōmei to that newly created post.

---

22. Chōmei's father had been Chief Attendant to the Kamo Shrine, but Chōmei did not succeed him in that post. His dream was to obtain a suitable shrine position.
23. Chōmei was without formal office at this time, and the highest court rank he ever achieved was Junior Fifth Rank, Lower.
24. The text is corrupt here, and I am following Ishida and Satsukawa.

His Majesty went out of his way to grant Chōmei his wish of a shrine appointment, and one would have thought that Chōmei would be delighted to be appointed to a shrine that had been elevated by His Majesty into a full branch of the Kamo Shrine and thus a place that could share in that great shrine's glory. Yet, Chōmei continued to complain loudly that he had not been granted the appointment he really wanted, and I thought he was acting irrationally.

Chōmei then went into seclusion, which I felt was rather unusual. After some time, there suddenly came to the palace fifteen poems from Chōmei, although he still did not reveal where he was living. Among them was this verse:

Sumiwabinu	It's painful now to live here
ge ni ya miyama no	Truly, deep in the mountains,
maki no fa ni	Where, through the cedar leaves
kumoru to ifisi	I should be able to see
tuki wo mirubeki	That moon I once called obscured.

The poem was a reference to one Chōmei had composed at his debut poetry contest, a verse that His Majesty had praised highly. The topic had been Moon Deep in the Mountains:

Yo mo sugara	All night through, alone,
fitori miyama no	Deep in the mountains, I've watched
maki no fa ni	As, through the cypress leaves,
kumoru mo sumeru	At first obscured, now shining bright
ariake no tuki.[25]	The moon appears toward dawn.

Surely Chōmei had this earlier poem in mind when he composed the lines "truly, deep in the mountains" (*ge ni ya miyama*), and people commented among themselves at how sensitive he must be. Yet I recalled how earlier he had been willing to destroy his own career out of sheer stubbornness. I heard that after that incident, he had taken the tonsure and moved to Ōhara to live a religious life. All in all, he seemed to be given over to extremes. Yet, perhaps it was that he had been drawn to the religious path by some connection in a previous life and thereby made some sense out of this illusory dream-world of ours.

At about this time, His Majesty said to me, "Chōmei used to have a lute [*biwa*] called 'Tenarai' [lit., 'learn by playing']. Find out what happened to it." So I went off to Ōhara to convey the imperial inquiry. Chōmei entrusted the instrument to a messenger to present to the Retired Emperor, and on the plectrum he wrote these poems:

---

25. This poem also appears in *Shinkokinshū* (1521, XVI, Miscellaneous 1), and as the Left and winning entry in Round 35 of the *Kennin gannen hachigatsu jūgoya senka-awase* (1201/viii/15). Ienaga has mistakenly remembered the topic, which was actually *Dawn Moon Deep in the Mountains*. See Chapter 3, pp. 123–34, for more information on this contest.

Kakusitutu	I'm hidden away,
mine no arasi no	And now it is only the sound
oto nomi ya	Of storms around the peak
tufi ni waga mi wo	That in the end
fanarezarubeki	Will be my companion here.
Farafubeki	Since dew tears lie
koke no sode nimo	Upon the monk's mossy sleeves
tuyu si areba	That should have wiped it clean,
tumoreru tiri fa	I present it as it is
ima mo sanagara	Covered thick with dust.

When His Majesty saw these, he ordered me to reply, which I did as follows:

Kore wo miru	Seeing this lute
sode nimo fukaki	My sleeves, too, now deep
tuyu si areba	With dew tears—
farafanu tiri fa	The dust you left uncleaned
nafo mo sanagara	Shall stay just as it is.
Yama fukaku	Though I may complain
irinisi fito wo	About the one who has
kakotitemo	hidden away
nakaba no tuki wo	Deep in the mountains,
katami tofa min	At least this half-moon lute
	I shall look upon as a keepsake.[26]

Later I had a chance meeting with Chōmei. He was frail and wasted, so much so that I hardly recognized him.

He said to me, "If I had not been so bitter about that worldly setback, I might never have ended up ridding myself of attachment to this illusory existence. This was the true favor His Majesty bestowed upon me," and dampened the sleeves of his monk's robes with tears.

"Yet there is still one thing that prevents me from completely freeing myself. It's this," and he pulled out of a sutra cover the lute plectrum on which I had earlier sent my two reply poems on behalf of Go-Toba. "No matter what, I shall take this with me to my grave, and we two can turn to dust together."

I felt it was a pity that he could not let go of that one thing into which he had poured so much of his heart in life, even if it stood as a hindrance to his salvation.[27]

---

26. Because of two half-moon shaped holes (actually, they are closer to a crescent shape) on its sound board, the *biwa* was also called a *nakaba no tsuki* (half-moon).

27. *IN*, pp. 104–14.

To return to dateable events in the Third Year of Kennin, early in the Second Month, the Wakadokoro was relocated after the fire at the Nijō Palace. Perhaps this explains why we have almost no record of Wakadokoro events until the Sixth Month.[28] Teika evidently used some of this hiatus for personal matters. On the 1st Day of the Third Month, he took his young son, Tameie, to the palace to meet Go-Toba for the first time. He described the moment in *Meigetsuki*:

About dawn, the rain stopped for a while, but later it started to fall again. . . . Around mid-morning, I took the child with me to have an audience with the Retired Emperor. A summons had come from His Majesty through his lady Etchū no Naishi. Surely we could not refuse an imperial command. . . . We were brought before His Majesty, who presented my son with a poem. We then withdrew. I was overwhelmed with joy and could not stop my tears. Then His Majesty ordered that gifts be given to us. We accepted them humbly and left the palace.[29]

Teika does not cite the poem, but Ienaga recorded it:

Sumiyosi no	At Sumiyoshi
kami mo afare to	The god should be moved
ife no kaze	By the talent of your family,
nafo mo fukikose	Let him continue to send breezes,
Waka no uranami	Raising waves on Poetry Bay.[30]

Judging from entries in *Meigetsuki*, Teika also seems to have been busy selecting poems for *Shinkokinshū* during the early months of the year. On the 7th day of the Third Month, Ienaga informed him that Go-Toba wanted a clean copy of the poems Teika had selected by the time he returned from a royal pilgrimage to Kumano.[31] Teika worried that the text was in a terribly disorganized state at that time, but he accepted the charge.[32] However, he was plagued by kidney stones for the next week or so and spent much of the

---

28. See the *Meigetsuki* entry for Kennin 3/ii/4, 1: 292, for the move to the Wakadokoro's new quarters, and ii/23, ibid., 1: 296–97, for one of the few poetry contests mentioned in the first half of the year.

29. Ibid., 3/iii/1, 1: 298.

30. *IN*, p. 101.

31. Go-Toba makes nearly as many visits to Kumano as he does to Minase, but for very different reasons. For the importance of his religious pilgrimages to Kumano, see Hirota, "Ex-Emperor Go-Toba," p. 75, and the Japanese sources she cites.

32. *Meigetsuki*, Kennin 3/iii/7, 1: 299.

time "flat on his back," to use his own words.[33] He was presumably able to get back to his duties after that, and on the 29th, he went to Kitano Shrine to pray for the poem collection.[34]

On the 11th of the Fourth Month, Ienaga sent word that Teika's selections should be ready for presentation to Go-Toba by the 20th. Teika showed Ienaga what he had completed but noted that in the past twenty days he had done nothing day and night but read old poems.[35] He must have set himself to the task, because for the next eight days there are no entries in *Meigetsuki*. But the pressure was on. When he learned that Minamoto Michitomo was to show his selections to Go-Toba on the 19th, he stayed up all night working on his own. Finally, on the 20th, after again working through the night, Teika completed the copy—"just in time," he says—and around noon took it to the Palace for Go-Toba's inspection. Unfortunately, he gave no more detail, and we do not know how the meeting went or what was discussed. Since it would be another year before Go-Toba ordered the next stage of the process, classification of the poems, most scholars assume that once he took possession of the various compilers' selections, he spent some months reworking them to suit his own tastes. And this is what Ienaga implies in his entry for the *Shinkokinshū* banquet, which is discussed in Chapter 8.[36]

At last, in the Sixth Month, came the first major poetry event of the year, at least as far as extant records show. It was an *eigu* contest, held at the Wakadokoro, and is known as the *Kennin sannen rokugatsu jūrokunichi Wakadokoro eigu uta-awase* (Eigu Poetry Contest at the Wakadokoro on the 16th Day, Sixth Month, Third Year of Kennin). As usual, most of our knowledge of this contest comes from *Meigetsuki*.[37] On the 10th, Teika wrote that Ienaga had sent him the topics for an *eigu* contest to be held after Go-

---

33. See entries for Kennin 3/iii/9, 10, 11, 15, and 16, in ibid., 1: 299–300. On the 15th, he went to Hie Shrine, presumably to pray for his recovery, and indeed, that night he began to pass stones, but lamented, "I understand this illness can last for many years." (Imagawa, *Meigetsukishō*, p. 134, interprets this line as meaning "people say one dies of this disease within a few years. How depressing!") The next day's entry is even pithier: "Weather clear, then rainy. Tonight I again passed a great many stones. Afterward my spirits felt considerably lifted." There is no further mention of the condition for the rest of the month.

34. *Meigetsuki*, Kennin 3/iii/29, 1: 301.

35. The information in this paragraph comes from ibid., Kennin 3/iv/11–20, 1: 302.

36. See below, Chapter 8 (Genkyū 2); and *IN*, p. 211.

37. *Meigetsuki*, Kennin 3/vi/10, 15, 16, 1: 308–9. For background and a text, see Taniyama, *Shinkokin jidai no uta-awase to kadan*, pp. 357–60, 436–51.

Toba returned from a visit to Kasuga. On the 15th, Teika reported that the contest had been postponed one day. But on the 16th, Teika seemed disinclined to attend. His wife had been ill through the night, and Teika himself was in poor health. But Ienaga sent him two or three messages telling him that he must pull himself together and attend. Finally, in the evening, he went to the Wakadokoro.

The contest itself was much like any other, although larger, and Teika's description is detailed but dry. Despite Teika's lack of enthusiasm for the event—perhaps the health problems that would send him to Arima later in the month were already sapping his energy—clearly this was an important poetry occasion, since there were thirty-six participants, with many from the *Sengohyakuban uta-awase* (Yoshitsune, Jien, Tadayoshi, Shunzei, Shunzei no Musume, Kunaikyō, and so on), and others, like Kamo no Chōmei. A notable absence was Ietaka. He had also been absent from the Kyōgoku Palace housewarming party due to illness, which Teika noted in his description of that event, although in his account of the contest in the Sixth Month he did not make a point of it.[38]

An exchange of poems between Shunzei and Ietaka that occurred in the Sixth Month of 1203 may shed light on Ietaka's situation. It is recorded, with a headnote and what appears to be a later editor's explanatory note (which I have placed in parentheses), in Ietaka's house collection, *Minishū*:

In the Sixth Month of Kennin 3, when I was faced with a sorrowful event, I received this from the Lay Priest Shunzei ([Ietaka's] father died in Kennin 1; then his mother in Kennin 3):[39]

Fudigoromo	Though I believed
nugisi fa kinofu to	That only yesterday you had
omofisi wo	Removed your mourning weeds,
mata yafa sode wo	How could it be that once again
nafo siboruramu	Your sleeves are drenched?

My reply:

Kagiri araba	If such sorrows knew bounds,
mata mo ya nufamu	Would I ever have to sew another set

---

38. *Meigetsuki*, Kennin 3/i/15, 1: 288. In the middle of the list of participants, where Ietaka's name would ordinarily have appeared, Teika noted: "Ietaka was ill, and did not come."

39. *Minishū* was compiled in 1245 by Kujō Motoie (1203–80; one of Yoshitsune's sons), according to the notes of Ietaka. The explanatory note (which I have placed in parentheses) following the headnote was probably written either by Motoie or by some later copyist.

fudigoromo	Of mourning weeds?
tofu ni namida no	Your inquiry brings tears;
fate zo sirarenu	I know not when they'll cease.[40]

Although illness may have kept Ietaka from court earlier in the year, apparently it was his mother's death that now prevented him from participating in this contest.

The extant texts for the contest have judgment marks but no judgment explanations (*hanshi*), and none of the poems from this event was included in *Shinkokinshū*.[41] This might be a sign of the mediocre quality of the output that evening. However, since very few poems from any event in 1203 ended up in *Shinkokinshū*, it is more likely that once Go-Toba had received the draft copy of collected poems from the various compilers, the books were closed on *Shinkokinshū*—at least for the time being.[42]

The matchups and even the teams were unfixed for this contest. There were three 4-character topics, all related to late summer, each of which ran for eighteen rounds; hence everyone competed three times, once for each topic. For a change, it might be interesting to look at a round between the two *lowest*-ranking poets, instead of something by others more widely cited in this book. The last matchup in the contest was between Ienaga, who was Senior Sixth Rank, Lower, at the time, and one Taira Kagemitsu, who served in the Retired Emperor's bodyguards (*mushadokoro*), equivalent to the Sixth Rank, but outside the traditional bureaucracy. The topic was "Hearing Cicadas After a Rain":

Left, Ienaga, Win

Murasame no	After a passing shower,
mada finu tuyu ni	In dampness not yet dried,
naku semi no	Keening cicadas,
namida ya itodo	Their tears even deeper
mori no sitakage	In forests' dark recesses.

---

40. *Minishū* #3135–36 (*Shinpen kokka taikan*, 3:132, p. 785). My attention was drawn to this exchange by Yamazaki, "Fujiwara Ietaka," p. 85.

41. The text I have used is from *Shinpen kokka taikan*, 5:198, pp. 514–16.

42. In fact, none of the four *Shinkokinshū* poems (99, 226, 261, and 735, the latter from the Kyōgoku Palace "open house" in the First Month) that derive from events in 1203 appears on any selection list in Gotō, *Shinkokin wakashū no kisōteki kenkyū*, pp. 682, 696, 700, 751. This absence implies that all must have been added after the first draft, presumably by Go-Toba himself.

Right, Kagemitsu

Yufudati fa	After an evening shower
farenuru noki no	Has cleared away
kozuwe yori	From branches by the eaves,
fibiku nagori no	Reverberations left behind:
semi no kowegowe	The shrill trill of cicadas.[43]

No "*ba . . . masi*" structures here (see Chapter 5, p. 199). Both poems feature the *taigendome* that is one of the hallmarks of the *Shinkokinshū* style (Kagemitsu's also makes use of the x-no-y-no-z modification pattern), and both are descriptive on the surface but suggesting emotional depth beneath. Both are dark and monochromatic. Even the lesser lights in Go-Toba's circle have learned the new style. This may speak even more clearly than the *Sengohyakuban uta-awase* of an emerging poetic consensus.

The next important event was somewhat smaller, but still featured most of the eminent names, except Ietaka and Teika. Called *Kennin sannen shichigatsu jūgonichi Hachiman Wakamiya senka-awase* (Contest of Selected Poems from the Hachiman Wakamiya Shrine on the 15th Day, Seventh Month, Third Year of Kennin), it was held, as its name implies, at the Wakamiya shrine, itself part of the Iwashimizu Hachiman Shrine located to the southeast of the city.

That Teika's name is missing from this contest is difficult to explain. True, he was very busy at about this time. Late the previous month, he had gone to Arima Hot Springs, staying there until the 10th of the Seventh Month to enjoy both the baths and the scenery. And he took his time on the way back to the capital, as the *Meigetsuki* entry for the 10th shows:

Weather clear. At daybreak, I set out for the capital, intending to visit Tennōji along the way. From my palanquin I viewed the passing hills and fields. Early in the afternoon, I arrived at an inn in Kanzaki, and after resting there for a while I left by boat at about 4:00 P.M. At nightfall, we reached Eguchi. I disembarked and lay down for a time. (The inn was that of the *yūjo* Sanmi. From there I went to Shitennōji.) I learned that his Majesty had left [Kumano] yesterday [to return to the capital]. This evening, the moon shone bright and clear.[44]

From the hot springs at Arima to the teahouses of Kanzaki and

---

43. *Shinpen kokka taikan*, 5:198, p. 516.
44. *Meigetsuki*, Kennin 3/vii/10, 1: 310. See also the entries for the 7th and 8th, ibid., for Teika's activities at Arima.

Eguchi—small wonder Teika was in no hurry to return to the capital! In fairness to Teika, from the entry for the 11th, we learn that the purpose of his trip had been to find relief from his health problems, presumably through the waters at Arima and prayers to the Yakushi ("Healing Buddha") at Shitennōji. We need not concern ourselves with what role the *yūjo* may have played in this cure. Besides, it was common for pilgrims on the way to Shitennōji from the capital to stop at Eguchi. In addition, Teika, as compiler of *Shinkokinshū*, must surely have had in mind Saigyō's poetic exchange with the Lady of Eguchi as he wrote this entry.[45]

Still, this does not explain why Teika was not at the contest on the 15th, since he was back in the capital by then. In truth, there is a great deal of uncertainty about this contest. To begin with, it is a *senka-awase*, a contest of selected poems, which means that no one needed to be present at the shrine except the selector himself, Go-Toba. Furthermore, historical records give different dates for the contest.[46] Perhaps, as had been the case with the *Minasedono* contest the year before, Go-Toba held a public poetry event and then used the poems from that occasion to generate a *senka-awase*. If the initial poetry party had been held on the 5th, as Go-Toba's house collection says, then Teika could not have been there because he was in Arima at the time. Then, on his way to Kumano (Teika and other sources say he left the capital on the 9th),[47] Go-Toba stopped at Hachiman and put the contest together and offered it on the 15th. However, there is no corroborating evidence for this scenario.[48]

---

45. *SKKS* 978–79 (X, Travel). The courtesan who replied to Saigyō's poem was named Tae, and she appears frequently in *Meigetsuki*. Perhaps because of her skill as a poet, she was in great demand whenever Go-Toba or his group brought in *yūjo* to entertain them.

Imamura Mieko has argued that "Teika was not fond of disporting himself with *shirabyōshi* and *yūjo*, and refused to sleep with them" (in Gomi et al., "*Meigetsuki*, Kennin ninen shichigatsu o yomu," p. 15). She bases this on his remarks in several *Meigetsuki* entries, including ones for Kennin 2 (1202)/vii/19 and Genkyū 1 (1204)/i/20. In both entries, Teika wrote that he has been ordered to put a performer up for the night during an imperial outing, but that he deliberately kept his distance at bedtime.

46. Go-Toba's house collection says it was on the 5th of the month, and at least one extant copy dates it as the 19th of the Ninth Month. Most extant copies, from the Edo period, give the 15th of the Seventh Month if they date it at all (see Chūsei uta-awase kenkūkai, *Chūsei uta-awase denbon shomoku*, pp. 76–77).

47. See the Arima entry from *Meigetsuki*, cited in note 44 to this chapter; and *DNS*, iv:7, pp. 856–57.

48. Yoshitsune's entries in this contest also appear in his house collection, but their headnotes simply describe them as being from among six poems submitted at the *Hachiman Wa-*

Another mystery is who wrote the judgments. The bulk of scholarly opinion is that it was judged by Shunzei, then eighty-nine years old (by the Western count), and was the last contest he judged. The fact that Shunzei's poems lost three of their four rounds (and tied the other) would lend weight to this theory. So, too, does the fact that there are many similar expressions in both these judgments and the ones Shunzei wrote for the *Sengohyakuban uta-awase* (for example, *yoroshiku haberi* [is nice] and *okashiku miehaberi* [shows charm], among others). With a few exceptions, the judgments themselves are not particularly penetrating, but if Shunzei is responsible for them, it is a remarkable feat given his physical deterioration at the time of his ninetieth-year (by the Japanese count) party a few months later.

There are six 3-character topics for the contest, all of which center on nature. Since the contest was a *senka-awase*, the "teams" were not set, nor were all the poets equally represented.[49] In terms of Wins, the higher-ranking poets easily came out on top.

The first-round judgment contains some interesting remarks about judging practices:

Round 1: First Winds of Autumn

Left, Go-Toba, Win

Wagimoko ga	My loved one's sleeves,
sode fukikafesu	Blown inside out
akikaze no	By autumn winds,
mada uranarenu	To which she's unaccustomed—
namida tofuramu	Perhaps that's why her tears come forth.

Right, Kintsune

Karakoromo	Chinese robes—
susono no kaze ya	Is it that autumn winds have risen
tatinuran	Around nearby mountain's hem,

---

kamiya Contest sponsored by the Retired Emperor and give no details about the process (Aoki, *Fujiwara Yoshitsune zenkashū to sono kenkyū*, pp. 108, 144–45, 148).

49. Go-Toba, Shunzei, and Shunzei no Musume appear in four rounds each; Yoshitsune and Jien have poems in three rounds. The remaining ten poets are represented by just one or two poems each. The poet of the Right in the last round is not marked. The topics were First Winds of Autumn (Rounds 1 and 2), Path through the Fields under the Moon (Rounds 3 and 4), Fog in the Ancient Capital (Rounds 5 and 6), Geese by the Sea (Rounds 7–9), Nightfall on a Journey (Rounds 10–12), and Pines by a Mountain Hut (Rounds 13–15).

sode ni sakidatu	That on my sleeves first glistens
aki no siratuyu[50]	White dew of autumn?

Judgment: In the Left poem, the lines "to which she's unaccustomed / perhaps that's why her tears come forth" are charming both in their manner of expression and in their feeling. In the Right poem, the line "that on my sleeves first glistens" similarly shows in its feeling and expression a profound ethereal beauty (en). As a general rule, in poetry contests, a Win is awarded to the Left in the first round, or, if the Right poem is a little stronger, a Tie may be given. But I am not thinking of that practice here. Not only is the Right Poem just slightly weaker, but the Left poem shows great charm. So, I award the Win to the Left, but not because of traditional practice.

Both poems have antecedents, although the allusions are not especially subtle and do not follow Teika's advice about using a poem from a different category in making an allusion. In fact, modern scholars often refer to these kinds of verses as "reference" (*sankō*) poems; that is, they bear an obvious referential relationship but come from collections too recent or otherwise do not fit Teika's or Shunzei's notions of appropriate "foundation poems" (*honka*). Only for the Left poem is the reference poem compelling enough to note here:

Wagimoko ga	My loved one's robe—
koromo no suso wo	Its hem blown inside out
fukikafesi	How touching,
uramedurasiki	How lovely it is,
aki no fatukaze	In first winds of autumn.[51]

As noted elsewhere in this book, by this time, the practice of automatically awarding a Win to the Left poem in the first round had started to relax. The judgment here acknowledges that there was now an institutionalized way out, that is, a Tie. What is interesting is that the judge felt compelled to

---

50. For this contest I am citing the text in *Shinpen kokka taikan*, 5:199, pp. 517–18. The *Gunsho ruijū* text (GR 193, 12: 395–98) has a few small variations.

51. KWR 130, by Ōshikōchi no Mitsune. It also appears in the *Mitsuneshū*, in *Shinpen kokka taikan* #458, 3:12, p. 37. Interesting enough, the Right poem's reference is to the anonymous poem immediately preceding this in our current text of *Kokin waka rokujō*, KWR 129, almost as if Kintsune and Go-Toba had collaborated. However, given the way this context was put together, as well as the fact that the textual history of *Kokin waka rokujō* is so convoluted that the two reference poems may not have been next to each other in the text available in Teika's day, this juxtaposition may not mean much. The anonymous poem: *Fatuaki no / sora ni kiritatu / karakoromo / sode no tuyukeki / asaborake kana*—"In earliest autumn / Mists arise, stitched across the sky— / My Chinese robe / Its sleeves damp with dew / At dawn."

draw attention to the traditional practice to make sure the reader recognized he was breaking from it. What the judge did *not* address, however, is another of the unwritten rules of poetry contests—that of automatically awarding a Win to an imperial poem. That issue would have been too delicate to broach when the sponsor of the contest was a Retired Emperor.

Since none of the poems from this contest was selected for *Shinkokinshū*, there is no need to dwell further on it. The Seventh and Eighth Months also saw Yoshitsune sponsoring two rather elaborate *shiika* (Chinese and Japanese verse) events. At the first, on the 27th of the Seventh Month, only a handful of poets familiar to us from the waka scene were there, including Yoshitsune, of course, and Teika, Tomoie, Ariie, and Yasusue.[52] The rest of the participants were *kanshi* specialists.[53] At the other, on the 1st of the Eighth Month, waka poets and poetry played a larger role, and Jien, Teika, Ietaka (out of mourning now), Tomochika, Masatsune, and Yasusue took part. They began by discussing the merits of the Chinese poetry composed at the party on the 27th, then followed with a *shiika-awase*, with the "specialists" composing in their own respective genres.[54] As Ivo Smits has argued with regard to the late tenth and mid-eleventh centuries, this kind of cross-fertilization surely had a strong impact on waka,[55] and in fact, one poem from the second of the two parties was included in *Shinkokinshū*. The poem is by Ariie, and its topic is "By the Water, it is Cooler than Autumn."

Suzusisa fa	For coolness
aki ya kaferite	Autumn might be shamed—
Fatusegafa	The Hatsuse River,
Furukafa no be no	Along the banks of its Furu tributary
sugi no sitakage	In ancient cedar grove's recesses.[56]

Unfortunately, we do not have the Chinese verse Ariie's poem competed against, but Ariie, in any case, showed clearly how a Chinese topic could be

---

52. Fujiwara (Rokujō) Tomoie (1182–1258) was just coming on to the poetry scene in the early 1200s. Although a Rokujō, by the Genkyū era he had grown closer to Teika; twelve poems by him appear in Teika's *Shinchokusenshū*, although he has only one poem in *Shinkokinshū*. He eventually rose to the Senior Third Rank and took the tonsure in 1238. Since his priestly name, Rensei, is used in the standard text for this contest, we know that text postdates the actual contest by at least several decades.
53. *Meigetsuki*, Kennin 3/vii/27, 1: 314.
54. Ibid., Kennin 3/viii/1, 1: 314.
55. Smits, *The Pursuit of Loneliness*, pp. 96–99 and elsewhere.
56. *SKKS* 261 (III, Summer).

turned into waka, could be "naturalized," as it were. Not only is the placename close to the heart of ancient Yamato, but the verse itself alludes to an anonymous *sedōka* from KKS (1009; XIX, Miscellaneous Forms) and contains two well-placed pivot words (the "fatsu" in Hatsuse was taken as homophonous for *fadu*, "to be shamed," and the "furu" in Furukawa, also suggest that the cedar tress are *furu[ki]*, "ancient"). The conceit was inspired by a Chinese model, but the execution is appropriate to waka. In addition, with its *taigendome* and x-no-y-no-z syntax, it bears the marks of the *Shinkokinshū* style (and reminds us of Ienaga's cicada poem above).

Less than a week after the second *kanshi* party, Go-Toba began planning a celebration for Shunzei's ninetieth birthday. Shunzei's ninetieth-year party is a rich story, and there are several accounts of it, including one in *Meigetsuki*, which contains background entries but nothing, surprisingly, for the day itself. A segment of *Kenreimon-in ukyō no daibushū* (The Poetic Memoirs of Lady Daibu) covers it. In addition, Yoshitsune kept a *kanbun* account of the actual party, known as *Shunzeikyō kujū no gaki* (Record of Lord Shunzei's Ninetieth Celebration). Throughout his description, Yoshitsune purposefully noted precedents for this or that aspect of the ceremony and in general seemed aware that his account would be the formal record of the event. Finally, there is a passage in *Ienaga nikki* that, although lengthy, still does not give us a full picture by itself.[57] We begin with Ienaga:

This year Shunzei reached his ninetieth year. That someone so skilled in the Way of Poetry should live this long in the world is truly a marvelous thing, unmatched in past or future. Until just last year, Shunzei was attending every poetry event in full vigor, but since the beginning of this year his deteriorating health has prevented him from participating anymore. Nevertheless, His Majesty, wishing to bestow on Shunzei the highest of honors, and using as historical justification the party Emperor Kōkō held at the Jijūden hall in the palace in honor of the Hanayama Bishop Henjō [in 885], gave orders that a celebration be held at the Wakadokoro for Shunzei. It was to be on the 23rd of the Eleventh Month, and His Majesty ordered screen-painting poems (*byōbu no uta*) for the occasion.[58]

---

57. For a text of *Kenreimon-in ukyō no daibushū*, see Hisamatsu et al., eds., *Heian Kamakura shikashū*, pp. 413–511; and the excellent translation by Phillip Harries, *The Poetic Memoirs of Lady Daibu*, pp. 279–81. For Yoshitsune's *Shunzeikyō kujū no gaki*, see GR 529 (29: 719–20).

58. *IN*, p. 122. In his account of the event, Yoshitsune cited several other precedents in addition to the Henjō affair, which was in celebration of his seventieth year (*Shunzeikyō kujū no gaki*, GR 529, 29: 719).

Apparently, Go-Toba began to make his plans early. Yoshitsune tells us that originally "this celebration was supposed to have been held on the 13th night of the Ninth Month, but due to some civil disturbances involving monks from Mount Hiei, it was postponed."[59] From the late Heian period, Mount Hiei had been plagued by a series of disputes between the "scholarly monks" (*gakushō*, or *gakuto*) and the monks whose main duties involved temple maintenance (*dōshu*). The latter became militarized over time and formed the nucleus of the "warrior monks" (*sōhei*).[60] In addition to the obvious class conflict, the particular problem at this time, as it so often was, involved who would be named Chief Abbot of the Tendai Sect (*Tendai zasu*). By a show of force in the capital on the 28th day of the Eighth Month, the "scholarly monk" faction was able to coerce the court into accepting the resignation of the current abbot, Shinsei, and selecting their candidate in his place. The custodial faction took up arms and barricaded themselves in, which prompted the court to send troops to rout them. In skirmishes in the first half of the Tenth Month, the custodial monks were finally defeated, at some cost of life. Subsequently (x/28), however, Shinsei was reinstated as Chief Abbot. These activities kept the court busy and put Shunzei's celebration on the back burner.[61]

Events in Kamakura may also have contributed to the delay, for it was in the Ninth Month that the late Yoritomo's ailing eldest son, Yoriie, was involved in a failed assassination plot against the Hōjō that ensured his marginalization from power until his death from illness the following year. On the 7th day of the Ninth Month, his younger brother, who subsequently was given the name we know him by today, Sanetomo, was nominated Shogun, after erroneous reports arrived in Kyoto that Yoriie had died. Under the circumstances, it seems safe to assume that people in Kamakura deliberately sent the false death announcement to gain the Court's confirmation for the new Shogun, who was, in fact, more to the liking of both the Hōjō and Kyoto than the volatile Yoriie had been.[62]

---

59. *Shunzeikyō kujū no gaki*, GR 529, 29: 719.

60. For a discussion of the relative functions of *gakutō* and *dōshū* in Tōdai-ji, which can be seen as similar to the situation on Mount Hiei, see Piggott, "Hierarchy and Economics in Early Medieval Tōdaiji," pp. 48–49. For a broader account of the phenomenon of militarized clergy, see Friday, *Hired Swords*.

61. See DNS, iv:7, pp. 890–93, 935–39, 951–52, for various accounts of the events, including a number of entries from *Meigetsuki*.

62. DNS, iv:7, pp. 893–904, 908–11. The matter-of-fact tone of the various diary entries (including *Meigetsuki*) announcing Yoriie's death suggest that the court took the report at face

But, as noted above, Go-Toba's plans had begun before these events. On the 6th Day of the Eighth Month, Teika was informed in a formal message from Go-Toba that there was to be a celebration in the Wakadokoro in honor of Shunzei's ninetieth year and that Teika was to compose screen-painting poems.[63] In the entry on the 14th, he elaborated:

Last night, I received another reminder from His Majesty that the screen poems for the ninetieth-year celebration were supposed to be submitted today. However, preparations surrounding the *hōjōe* caused a delay.[64] I received a summons from His Lordship, Yoshitsune, and I went to see him in the late afternoon. He showed me the poems he had composed for the celebration and in turn had a look at mine. The poets for this occasion were Chikasada (Go-Toba), His Lordship (Yoshitsune), the Bishop Jien, Lord Ariie, Teika, Masatsune, Sanuki, Tango, Kunaikyō, and Shunzei no Musume. The selections are to be made tomorrow, and I am expected to attend.[65]

The next day, the 15th, proved to be busy. It began with festivities surrounding the *hōjōe* at Iwashimizu Hachiman shrine. Teika described the various activities at length, including the elaborate procession itself and the ceremony at the shrine, which involved dancing and at least sixteen *sumo* matches. A considerable discussion about what precedent to follow ensued when the Prime Minister caused a delay in the procession by not showing up on time. All this lasted into the evening, but the day was not yet done. Teika and many of the participants then went to the Kyōgoku Palace, where they finally made the selections for the screen painting poems. But the indefatigable Go-Toba pressed on and set a topic for impromptu poetry composition, in this case an acrostic (*oriku*) built on the phrase *aki no tuki* (autumn moon). Each poet was to produce five poems using this acrostic. These were presented formally, as at any palace poetry event, and Teika was asked to be the Reader. Not surprisingly, Teika stayed home the following day![66]

---

value and had no reason to doubt its authenticity. Since they were clearly aware of the assassination plot (as evidenced by various diary entries), they might have suspected that Yoriie's "death" was not due to "illness," but they had little reason to doubt he had died.

63. *Meigetsuki*, Kennin 3/viii/6, 1: 315.

64. *Hōjōe*, which Ivan Morris (*World of the Shining Prince*, p. 176) calls "the Liberation," refers to the ritual setting free of animals that was conducted at shrines and temples—most notably for the imperial court, the Iwashimizu Hachiman Shrine—on the 15th day of the Eighth Month.

65. *Meigetsuki*, Kennin 3/viii/14, 1: 316.

66. Ibid., Kennin 3/viii/15, 16, 1: 317–18.

As for the selection process for the screen poems for Shunzei's celebration, Ienaga wrote:

> Each poet was asked to submit poems on twelve topics; then His Majesty summoned all the poets together, and they selected one poem for each topic. A master painter was summoned, and after the meanings of each of the selected poems had been explained to him, he was asked to paint appropriate screens. The Regent Yoshitsune was requested to inscribe the poems on the screen.[67]

Since the twelve topics represented the months of the year, there were three topics for each season. The paintings, then, must have depicted the various aspects of each season. Ienaga cites the selected poems, including one by Fujiwara Tadatsune (1173–1229), who does not appear on Teika's list of invited poets.[68] Yoshitsune was diffident about being asked to inscribe the poems. It is not evident in Ienaga's collapsed account in his memoirs, but apparently the request did not come until the day of the party, three months later:

> Today His Majesty asked me to write the poems on the screens. Although I requested that he ask someone else to do it, he stated that the screens would be kept in the palace for many years to come and that I should be the one to inscribe the poems. So I complied. Since the screens themselves were late in arriving, I was not able to copy the poems onto them until after nightfall.[69]

During the afternoon of the 23rd (Eleventh Month), Yoshitsune made his way to the Wakadokoro at the Kyōgoku Palace. He left a detailed description of the layout of the room (see Fig. 2 for my reconstruction).

Following are excerpts from Yoshitsune's sketch. Parenthetical sections appear as asides or marginalia in the extant printed text; bracketed sections contain information I have added for clarity. Throughout the passage, Yoshitsune refers to Shunzei by his priestly name, Shakua:

---

67. *IN*, p. 125.
68. Three poems by Fujiwara Tadatsune, who eventually rose to the office of Minister of the Left (and whose mother was one of Taira Kiyomori's daughters—which apparently did not hamper his career), appear in *Shinkokinshū*, but he was a rather quiet member of Go-Toba's group.
69. *Shunzeikyō kujū no gaki*, GR 529, 29: 719.

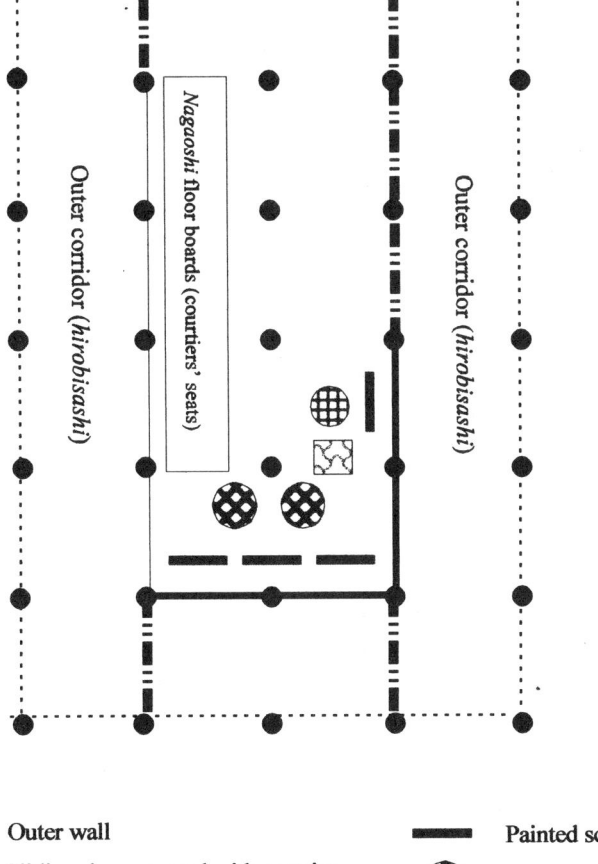

Fig. 2 Layout of Wakadokoro for Shunzei's ninetieth-year celebration (source: "Shunzeikyō kujū no gaki," by Kujō Yoshitsune, GR 529).

The Wakadokoro is some thirty-six feet long, in six sections.[70] . . . The southernmost section was divided from the rest by sliding doors on which hung curtains of state. Before them stood three of the new, four-foot-high painted screens. In front of them were set out two fine rush cushions covered with brocade. This was where His Majesty was to sit. Curtains were also hung on the sliding doors along the east wall of the second and third sections. In front of the curtains in the third section, the fourth painted screen was placed, and a mat with Korean-style edging was put down. On top of the mat was set a cushion brocaded in the Eastern Capital style.[71] Shakua was to be seated there.[72] At the second section, in front of Shakua's seat, a set of monk's robes was laid out. (The stole was white with a raised figured pattern. On it a poem had been stitched in purple thread. The poem had been composed by the lady Kunaikyō. Beside the stole were a coat, skirt, and trousers, embroidered in an arabesque pattern. The lining was plain, with red figuring embroidered on it.)[73] The items were placed in a gold lacquered [*makie*] clothing box and set on a stand. Numerous precedents dictated that they should be set on a cabinet, although since that was inconvenient in this case, boards were used instead. Next to this were a pair of straw sandals,[74] and to the north of it, a "dove staff" made of silver.[75] The staff was fashioned to look like a stalk of bamboo with a dove perched on its top, and to it was affixed a "branch" with two "leaves," on which a poem was written. This poem had been composed by Lord Ariie. Beginning at the second section from the south, matting with Korean-style edging was spread on top of the *nageshi* along the west wall.[76] This was where the nobles [*kuge*] were seated, in descending rank-order from south to north. (Shakua sat across from them on the eastern side.)[77] Along the last

---

70. What I am calling "sections" are *ken*, or the roughly six-foot gap between pillars in the *shinden* architectural style.

71. I will spare the reader the details, but the two items, the mat and the cushion, were reserved for high nobility. For more information, see *Kōjien* under *kōrai(bashi)* for the mat, and *tōkyōki (no shitone)* for the cushion.

72. The marginal note here seems to say "to the southwest was his main wife," but it may just be saying something about a line of people (there is the character for *tsuma*) facing west and seated (in rank-order) from south to north.

73. Admittedly, my strength is not court clothing, and so this section is tentative. In any case, this marginal note must presumably have been Yoshitsune's own.

74. A character is missing from the text here, but given the character that precedes it, the word must almost certainly be *waragutsu* (*waraji*), or "straw sandals."

75. *Hatozue* is a cane or staff, the head of which is decorated with a dove design; it was considered auspicious for an elderly person.

76. *Nageshi* were the wooden boards set between pillars along the floor and the ceiling to divide a room. Since the lower ones were raised slightly off the level of the floor, it seems mats were laid on them in this case to "smooth out" the area.

77. There is a character missing from this marginal note, but the meaning seems to be clear.

three sections of the east wall, the two sections of the north wall, and the sixth section of the west wall, all the curtains of state had been rolled up. There were no mats on the outer corridors along the east and west sides of the hall.[78]

Yoshitsune continues:

After everyone had gathered outside, His Majesty made his entrance. He, too, was wearing a court cap and formal robes. I then took my seat. Lord Nagafusa summoned all the nobles, who took their places in rank-order, from the Prime Minister on down. Next, I formally inquired about His Majesty's health. Then Shakua was summoned by Lord Nagafusa. Aided by his sons, Lord Nariie and Lord Teika, he was brought into the hall. (He was wearing monk's robes, with a plain white stole. The Former Abbot Jien had helped in the preparations.)[79] He took his seat.

After a much briefer, but similar, description of the Wakadokoro layout, Ienaga adds some drama to the story:

After some delay, the Lay Priest [Shunzei] was helped into the hall by his sons Lords Nariie and Teika. He was astonishingly bent with age and frail. It was painful to look at. I was deeply moved to think that he had held on to life so long, as if awaiting this very occasion. Since he was unable to climb the platform and just lay there flat on the floor, his two sons had to help him up onto his cushion. I don't believe I can ever forget the image of him slumped over on his cushion in his monk's robes. In front of him were placed the gifts of monk's stole and staff. The poem on the stole was by Kunaikyō, and the one on the staff by Ariie. These two presumably received the commission because they came from families with a long poetic pedigree.

    The poem on the stole:

        Nagarafete   To have lived so long—
        kesa ya uresiki   How happy you must be this morn!
        oi no nami   Wear this stole,
        yatiyo wo kakete   And may your years roll on like waves
        kimi ni tukafeyo   As you serve your Lord eight
                                                             thousand reigns.

    The poem with the staff:

        Momotose no   As you approach that slope
        tikaduku saka ni   Of one hundred years
        tukisomete   Use now this staff,

---

78. The "outer corridor" is the *hirobisashi*, a kind of marginal room, under the eaves, between the veranda and the main hall.
79. Presumably Yoshitsune's marginalia.

>   ima yukusuwe mo   For I wish you to continue
>   kakare to zo omofu[80]   Ever further down the road!

The first poem was stitched on the stole in purple thread, and the second was stitched, again in purple thread, on the bag that went with the staff.[81]

Kunaikyō's poem is the subject of a famous anecdote in *Kenreimon-in ukyō no daibushū*. In Kunaikyō's original version, the speaker of the poem was Shunzei, expressing his gratitude to Go-Toba for the honor of the party and the gift. Although she felt it was inappropriate, Lady Daibu embroidered the poem, but when Go-Toba saw it, he ordered her to change two syllables so that the speaker of the poem became Go-Toba himself congratulating Shunzei on his long life.[82]

Frail as Shunzei was, Go-Toba seemed prepared to entertain him to within an inch of his life. Once he was seated, a meal was served with great formality. Historians of Kamakura period meal service might find Yoshitsune's detailed enumeration of the various trays on which the food was served of interest, but such is well beyond the scope of this study. Once the meal was done, however, it was time for a concert. This is of greater concern here since, as Ienaga notes, the musicians were also well known for their poetic skills.[83] They included Kintsugu, Kanemune, and Masatsune, all of whom had participated in the *Sengohyakuban uta-awase*. When the music was over, both instruments and dishes were cleared away, and the assembly prepared for what had to be the highlight of an evening honoring Shunzei: poetry.

Again, Yoshitsune's account dwells on the process and the order in which things are done, following precedent. Suffice it to say, the poems were sub-

---

80. The poems are transcribed slightly differently in Yoshitsune's account. The final line of Kunaikyō's is given as *kimi ni tukaferu* (which would take away the sense of command rendered by the English word "may" in the fourth line of the translation), and the first line of Ariie's is given as *momotose ni* (which, if it is not simply a miscopy, would result in the "of" in the second line of the translation being changed to "for") (*Shunzeikyō kujū no gaki*, GR 529, 29: 720).

81. *IN*, pp. 131–32.

82. For a complete translation of this anecdote, see Harries, *The Poetic Memoirs of Lady Daibu*, pp. 278–81. Kunaikyō's original poem read: *Nagarafete / kesa zo uresiki / oi no nami / yatiyo wo kakete / kimi ni tukafemu*—"For having lived so long / A gift, this stole—How pleased I am this morning! / And like my waves of years / Rising for eight thousand generations / May I wear it as I serve my lord."

83. *IN*, p. 136.

mitted and intoned aloud one by one in a ritualistic (and presumably quite drawn out) manner. Ariie performed the important role of *kōji* (reader), and as in contests and events described in earlier chapters, poems from the ladies-in-waiting were submitted and read last. Yoshitsune recorded none of these verses; Ienaga provided the texts of twenty-five of them, one from each guest, it seems.[84]

At last, poor Shunzei was able to leave. Ienaga left this description of the aftermath:

The festivities drew to a close, and around dawn people left one by one. The monk's robes and staff were sent to Shunzei the next morning. Hideyoshi was His Majesty's messenger. Shunzei offered the following poems to His Majesty:

Kono tuwe fa	This staff
waga nifa arazu	Is not for me alone,
waga kimi no	But also for my Lord,
yaso yorodu yo no	To lead him over the peaks
mine no tame nari	Of eight hundred, no ten thousand, reigns.

Kimi ga yo fa	May my Lord's reign last as
koke no ifafo ya	Long as it takes to wear down
nadefaten	A moss-covered boulder
sora yori orosu	By brushing it with the sleeve
fagoromo no sode	Of this feathered robe from heaven![85]

---

84. According to Ienaga, the guest list was Go-Toba, Fujiwara Sukemune, Shunzei himself, then in descending order of rank, Yoshitsune, the Prime Minister Yorimune, Grand Counselor Michisuke, Provisional Grand Counselor Takafusa, Middle Counselor Kanemune, Provisional Middle Counselor Kintsune, Provisional Middle Counselor Norimitsu, Lieutenant of the Right Guards Michiteru, Consultant Michitomo, Senior Third Rank Tsuneie, Junior Third Rank Nariie (Shunzei's eldest son), Lord Ariie, Lord Sadaie (Teika), Lord Tsunemichi, Lord Yorifusa, Masatsune, Tomochika, Ienaga, Kamo no Chōmei, and Hideyoshi. Unfortunately, he did not record the women's poems, although assuming that those who submitted poems for the screen paintings were also guests at the party, Sanuki, Kunaikyō, Tango, and Shunzei no Musume were present. Lady Daibu wrote that she watched from another room, but presumably she was not among those who formally submitted poems (although she did send Shunzei a verse the next day).

85. Shunzei's poem makes references to two earlier Felicitation poems, one from *Kokinshū* (343, VII, Felicitations—poet and topic unknown), and one from *Shūishū* (#299 [V, Felicitations]), each of which in turns makes reference to figures of time from Chinese/Buddhist legends. The former refers to the legend (from the Tang period collection of Chinese stories by Duan Chengshi known as *Yūyō zasso*, C. *Youyang zazu* [ca. 860]) that a pebble locked away in

I was ordered to reply on behalf of His Majesty:

Yaso yorodu	That staff, from the peak
tukinu kumowi no	Beyond the clouds of eight hundred,
mine no tuwe	No, ten thousand reigns and more—
nafo sakayukan	May it help you ever climb, in glory,
miti no tame nari	Up the path of poetry.
Nadefaten	Like countless strokes
koke no ifafo wo	Upon the moss-covered boulder,
tamesi nite	Wearing it down,
tiyo mo kasane yo	May you live a thousand years
ama no fagoromo	Clad in your heavenly robe!

A moment like this is a rare blessing, indeed—rare in the past and rare for years to come. Even the heavens cooperated, clearing for the day. The harsh autumn winds, too, died down, so that near dawn the 23rd night moon shone lovely and clear, like the sounds of the music from the concert. All in all, an extraordinary and precious evening.[86]

Of the many poems composed in connection with this celebration—the screen-painting poems as well as the verses produced during the party—two were selected for *Shinkokinshū*. Both were among the poems submitted for the screens, although neither was selected for inscription. One, by Go-Toba, describes the screen painting depicting cherry blossoms in bloom on a mountainside and became the head poem (*maki no tō*) of the second spring book in *Shinkokinshū*:

Sakura saku	On distant mountains
tofoyamadori no	Where cherries bloom, trailing branches
sidari wo no	Like a pheasant's tail, long,
naganagasi fi mo	Long is this spring day,
akanu iro kana	Its beauty never tiring.[87]

Go-Toba celebrated Shunzei's long and productive life with a lush image of long-trailing flowers on a languid spring day, the flowers themselves being

---

a Buddhist temple for eons eventually turns into a moss-covered stone, and the latter refers to one sutra's (*Bosatsu yōraku hongōkyō*) definition of a *kalpa*, one part of which involves the length of time it would take to wear down a huge boulder by brushing it once every three years with a feather.

86. *IN*, pp. 146–47.
87. *SKKS* 99 (II, Spring 2).

figures for Shunzei's many poems. Furthermore, the poem is an allusion to the love verse attributed to Hitomaro cited above:

Asibiki no	In foot-weary hills
yamadori no wo no	Mountain pheasants' tails,
sidari wo no	Their tails, trailing long,
naganagasi yo wo	Long is this night—
fitori kamo nemu	Must I sleep through it alone?

Needless to say, this should not be taken as evidence that Go-Toba and Shunzei were lovers. As Teika argued, in making allusions, it is best to take lines from a Love poem when one is composing a Nature poem, and vice versa. This ensures better resonance and depth. With this allusion, Go-Toba did, to be sure, imply the depth of his feelings for the poetic master, but the canon is full of poems that use Love figures to express feelings of closeness that may not necessarily be romantic or sexual. Even so, I certainly do not want to imply that members of the same sex would never send conventional Love poems to each other with the intention of expressing genuine sexual or romantic interest. I am simply arguing that since the aristocracy turned to conventional Love poetry figures to express many types of love (types that we distinguish today in our own culture, but which medieval Japanese might not have drawn so distinctly), we would need other evidence to understand the nature of a given relationship fully.

In any case, Go-Toba's allusion also implies that Shunzei can be spoken of in the same breath as the great poetic sage, Hitomaro. (Never mind that Hitomaro might not have composed the poem attributed to him here.)[88]

The other poem to appear in *Shinkokinshū* was by Yoshitsune:

Woyamada ni	Around Oyamada fields
fiku simenafa no	A sacred rope fence
utifafete	Has been stretched full, and long—

---

88. In a series of seminar projects in the fall of 1996, several graduate students at the University of Hawai'i (James Baskind, John Bentley, John Creamer, Katherine Wakayama, and Rokuo Tanaka) demonstrated the provisionality of authorship when it comes to Heian-period attributions to *Man'yō* poets. Poets like Hitomaro, Akahito, and Yakamochi underwent a process of revision much like that which produced *Ise monogatari* out of Narihira's oeuvre. As a result, these *Man'yō* poets were turned into Heian lovers, if one is to judge by the poems attributed to them in Heian collections. Bentley explores the process with regards to Hitomaro in "The Creation of Hitomaro, a Poetic Sage."

kuti ya sinuran	Could it now have rotted
samidare no koro	Under endless early summer rains?[89]

This poem may have skillfully captured the scene as well as the tension between something man-made (the sacred rope) and the truly infinite, Nature (in the form of early summer rains), that is the hallmark of great waka from the *Kokinshū* on. However, despite its images of things long and drawn out (like Shunzei's life?), its central figure of a "rotted rope" seems oddly inauspicious in a verse celebrating the master's age. Even modern commentators are not quite sure what to do with Yoshitsune's poem. Minemura Fumihito comments that "perhaps its image of long-falling early summer rains, as lengthy as the sacred rope, is implicit felicitation for a long life," but he hardly seems sure. And Kubota Utsuho argues that the wording and imagery must have been responses to some element in the screen painting to which it referred, and that the fact that it was a "sacred rope" at least added some sense of auspiciousness, although he concedes that in later treatises such expressions as "rotted" would have been avoided in congratulatory poems.[90]

In addition, as further proof that context is everything in waka, consider that these two poems were good enough for *Shinkokinshū* but deemed unsuitable for the screen paintings themselves, even though their placement in *Shinkokinshū* (among the seasonal poems rather than in the Felicitations book) suggests that they were seen primarily as nature poems. Would that we had records of the discussions involved in the selections of these poems for the imperial anthology as well as for the screens, but the best that can be done here is to cite the poems that were selected over these two for the screen-painting inscriptions. On the topic of (spring) Flowers, Ariie's was chosen, and on Early Summer Rains, Masatsune's was preferred:

Kefu made fa	Until today they've bloomed,
kozuwe nagara no	Mountain cherries on tree branches
yamazakura	At Mount Nagara,
asu fa yuki to zo	But tomorrow they'll fall as snow—
fana no furusato.	Flowers over this ancient capital.

—Lord Ariie

---

89. *SKKS* 226 (III, Summer).

90. Minemura, *Shinkokin wakashū* (1974), p. 98; Kubota Utsuho, *Shinkokin wakashū*, 1: 175. Kubota Jun (*Shinkokin wakashū*, p. 92) offers no comment.

Kame no wo no	At Tortoise Mountain
taki no siratama	Waterfalls' jewel droplets
tiyo no kazu	Countless as a thousand reigns,
ifane ni amaru	Splash profusely on the rocks
samidare no sora.	Under skies of early summer rain.[91]

—Masatsune

Both these poems elegantly celebrate Shunzei's long life, Ariie's through a lush, nostalgic scene of great beauty and Masatsune's through more standard auspicious vocabulary (Tortoise Mountain [Kameyama, at the Ōi River across from Arashiyama, site of Emperor Saga's detached palace], a thousand reigns) and an allusion to a poem by Ki no Koreoka in the Felicitations book of *Kokinshū*.[92] Without knowing the exact nature of the discussions surrounding the selection of poems for the screens, it is difficult to know why these two poems ended up being selected for the screens and the other two were chosen for *Shinkokinshū*.

Lady Daibu mentioned exchanging congratulatory poems with Shunzei the day after the party.[93] There must have been many other such exchanges in succeeding days, although considering Shunzei's physical condition as described by Ienaga, one imagines that Teika or others were actually fielding the poems and writing the replies. In any case, the celebration was a well-deserved tribute to the man who had as profound an impact on poetry in Japan as any other single person. However, one wonders how much he was able to enjoy the tribute. He was to die a year later after a lingering illness.

No less frail than human life—as Kamo no Chōmei would remind us—were the dwellings of those humans, and in the Twelfth Month, just one year after an earlier fire had damaged it, the Nijō Palace burned once again.

---

91. *IN*, p. 123.

92. *Kame no wo no / yama no ifane wo / tomete oturu / taki no siratama / tiyo no kazu kamo*—"Tumbling through the rocks / At Tortoise Mountain / A cascading waterfall / Its jewel droplets numerous / Like a thousand reigns" (*KKS* 350 [VII, Felicitations]). In both Koreoka's and Masatsune's poems, *siratama* is almost certainly to be taken as "pearl." However, I have changed the translation to "jewel droplets" to avoid resonance with the brand name of a toothpaste—a situation encountered from time to time by translators, and one which underscores Bakhtin's notion that words have a culturally and socially conditioned life of their own that the writer cannot control.

93. Harries, *The Poetic Memoirs of Lady Daibu*, p. 281.

Go-Toba had returned to it less than two weeks before the celebration for Shunzei (which was held at the Kyōgoku Palace since the Wakadokoro had not yet moved back to the Nijō Palace), and now he was forced to move again. However, as the year drew to a close, Go-Toba's poetry circle, at least, was firmly in place, and plans for the *Shinkokinshū* were proceeding apace.

SEVEN

Diversions and Mourning, Genkyū 1 (1204)

The first half of Genkyū 1 (1204) appears surprisingly quiet in extant records. (Initially the year was designated Kennin 4, but the reign name was changed to Genkyū on ii/20.) There were still some loose ends in Kamakura after Yoriie's "retirement" and Sanetomo's appointment as Shogun, but nothing dramatic. On the national scene, the biggest news was a Taira uprising in Ise in the Second Month, which was quickly put down.[1] But none of this should have been enough to put poetry activity on hold. Yet there were even fewer events than in the first half of the previous year.

Later in the year, *Shinkokinshū* preparations would take center stage, but otherwise poetry appears to have been just an incidental part of other entertainments. Go-Toba evidently felt that he had gathered enough material for *Shinkokinshū* and so saw no need to sponsor any large-scale events. Eventually it became clear, however, that he was not satisfied with the poems he had to work with.

Affairs within the imperial court seemed very much under Go-Toba's control, and the Kujō house had fully recovered its position. In poetry and government, Yoshitsune had become indispensable, and in the round of New Year's appointments, he was promoted to the Junior First Rank, and on several occasions, Jien performed religious rites with Go-Toba in attendance.[2] Teika, however, was less favored. When appointments and promo-

---

1. *DNS*, iv:8, pp. 42–43.
2. See, e.g., *DNS*, iv:8, entries for Genkyū 1 (Kennin 4) ii/8, vi/13, x/1, and xii/1.

tions were announced on iv/12, he was again passed over and in response went into seclusion for several weeks.[3]

Teika's splenetic reaction to this slight is worth looking at.[4] After examining the new appointment roster, he copied it into his journal, adding pithy marginal comments below some of the names. What I have called a "roster" (*kikigaki*) was more than just a list; it also included justifications for the various honors bestowed. Teika's swipes were apparently reactions to some of the official reasons given. In several cases he pointed to family connections as the reason behind the promotion, but in a few instances he was even blunter. For example, his reaction to one Moritsune's promotion to captain: "I'm surprised to see him called an expert in Confucianism; he's basically a no-talent nobody of low birth." And of another man's promotion to the Junior Fourth Rank, Lower, he commented: "It used to be that people like him would never have achieved such a rank. I guess in these corrupt times, it is the ones without talent who are rewarded." As a group, he derides them as "nobodies, self-serving idiots, and boors lacking talent and manners." He went on to complain:

Such low-ranking types should never be allowed to pass their superiors. Nor does it make sense that mediocre men, just because they are of good family, can move ahead. Appointments to the guards these days go to virtual commoners. That such people should even hope for these positions is unforgivable. Take Kanesada and Moritsune. They have no special abilities. They cannot even write Chinese. They were simply promoted because they possess knowledge of a trade.

He then criticized several other appointments that were based, he felt, on familial claims and nothing else. The rest of the evening he commiserated with a friend, who himself was presumably passed over.

Unfortunately, this petulance robs us of a look at some of Go-Toba's leisure activities, for during Teika's seclusion, Go-Toba spent nearly two months at the Toba Palace south of Kyoto. As we have seen in the preceding chapters, Teika would normally have been invited to join Go-Toba in his leisure activities. Even earlier in 1204, for example, Teika traveled to Minase several times, albeit grudgingly, in the middle of the First Month, at Go-Toba's invitation. The entertainments included horse-racing and *shira-*

---

3. *Meigetsuki*, Genkyū 1/iv/12, 1: 365. See also subsequent entries through v/22, when Teika finally emerged from his self-imposed retreat.

4. The following account is from ibid., 1/iv/13, 1: 365–66.

byōshi dancers and lasted until the 10th of the following month.[5] Less than two weeks later, Go-Toba returned to Minase again, but this time just for a few days, and he used the villa only as a stopover during the main purpose of the trip—a pilgrimage to Shitennōji.[6] During Go-Toba's long stay at the Toba Palace, which lasted from iv/23 to vi/29, Teika was obliged to appear despite his "seclusion," but he was not a gracious guest. He returned home as often as possible, and his diary entries about activities at the Toba Palace are laconic in the extreme; he often said little more than that he went there and that everything was as usual ("same old same old" might be the closest American English equivalent to his *koto goto ni rei no gotosi*).[7] Even the entry covering the Gosechi dances (v/5)—normally an event Teika described at length—is only three lines long. In contrast, during the same time period, he described many of his own activities at much more characteristic length, as if he were getting even with Go-Toba by neglecting him in the journal.[8]

Fortunately, by the Seventh Month, when Go-Toba spent a week at Uji, Teika was back to his more loquacious self, and his records of the Uji activities provide valuable evidence of Go-Toba's energetic pursuit of *furyū*. The impetus for the excursion appears to have been a serious illness that plagued Go-Toba from the end of the Sixth Month. Teika first mentioned the illness on vi/23, and for the following week it remained serious. Courtiers gathered daily at the palace as prayers were offered and medical treatments essayed. Finally, on the first day of the Seventh Month, the symptoms began to abate.[9]

Perhaps to speed his recovery, Go-Toba decided to visit Uji for a few days, but his schedule there was not very relaxing.[10] On the 10th, Teika (although he complained of an upset stomach) and others went up early so as to prepare for Go-Toba's arrival. The host, Yoshitsune (Byōdō-in at Uji was his family's temple), had even constructed a temporary villa for the Retired

---

5. DNS, iv:8, pp. 24–25, cites from a number of *Meigetsuki* entries about this trip (i/19–22, 26–29, and ii/3, 7, and 10). For full entries, see *Meigetsuki*, 1: 357–58.

6. *Meigetsuki*, Genkyū 1/ii/23–27, 1: 360–61.

7. Ibid., 1/iv/26, 1: 367.

8. The entries for ibid., v/9 and 27, 1: 368–69, e.g., are detailed accounts of religious services.

9. DNS, iv:8, pp. 159–63 (including an abridged *Meigetsuki* entry for vi/23 and complete entries for vi/27–29 and vii/1, for which, see also *Meigetsuki*, 1: 373–74).

10. Abbreviated *Meigetsuki* entries for this visit appear in DNS, iv:8, pp. 169–72. See *Meigetsuki*, 1: 374–75, for the full entries.

Emperor.[11] Twice Go-Toba went hunting while there, and on the 11th he enjoyed horseback archery, apparently as a participant. On the 14th, he even went for a swim in the Uji River. Teika elaborated: "Today the weather was fine. His Majesty went upriver to bathe (as he had done on the 10th). People took off their clothes and paraded across the garden in front of the Byōdō-in. Then there was nude, bareback horseriding. I secretly watched as they presented themselves in formation to His Majesty, and I was shocked."[12] On the 15th, after a formal visit to Byōdō-in, which Teika described quite reverently, Go-Toba watched another round of horseback archery and then returned to the capital around sundown. This is how a man in his mid-twenties recovers from a life-threatening illness! More than once, Teika was unable to keep up and skipped the afternoon and evening activities.

But such an excursion required a more traditional conclusion. On the following night, the 16th, back at the capital, Go-Toba summoned the Uji guests to a poetry party at the Wakadokoro to put the final touches on the trip. Teika's description of the event is dry and linear:

16th. Weather fine. At about 10:00 in the morning, I donned formal wear and trousers and went to Minister Yoshitsune's home. About noon, we then made our way to the palace. An hour or so later, His Majesty made an appearance. One by one, in response to his summons, we came forward and presented our poems. As usual, His Majesty requested that I serve as Reader (*kōji*). The poem stand was said to have been made using a bit of wood from the ruined supports of the old Nagara Bridge. The wood had been presented to His Majesty. Today was the first time it had been put on display in the Wakadokoro. After we finished reciting our poems, we all left the room. I went to change into hunting costume, and after Go-Toba withdrew, I left the Kyōgoku Palace.[13]

---

11. *Meigetsuki*, Genkyū 1/vii/10, 1: 374.

12. Ibid., 1/vii/14, 1: 375. Hirota (*Ex-Emperor Go-Toba*, p. 76) interprets this passage differently, paraphrasing it: "Go-Toba, for example, made a visit of several days to Yoshitsune's villa in Uji one summer. He swam in the river and rode a horse in the garden of the Byōdōin temple one day." I disagree with this reading because there are no honorifics in the passage that would cover the horseriding, which must have been done by other people, although obviously for Go-Toba's enjoyment. Besides, it is clear these activities were performed naked (*hadaka*—although just what this means varies from culture to culture), and I have a hard time imagining Go-Toba running around unclothed in front of his subjects. Kamens's (*Utamakura*, p. 135) reading of this passage is much closer to my own.

13. *Meigetsuki*, Genkyū 1/vii/16, 1: 375.

By contrast, Ienaga's narrative of this event, and indeed the Uji visit that preceded it, is textured and anything but linear. He built his tale around the piece of wood from the Nagara Bridge. The Nagara Bridge was famous in poetry because its name could be punned upon (through the verb *nagaraeru*, which means "survive") to suggest something long-lived—an irony that all in the story were aware of since by Ienaga's time, the bridge was long gone. As he did with the *kemari* party at Shikishi Naishinnō's villa (see Chapter 3), Ienaga recast the story in language rich with waka connotations. Since he was relating the events as a kind of memoir about which his recollections were somewhat vague, time markers are meaningless. Even his opening statement—"I can't be sure, but I think it was one year before"—is elusive. One year before what? Presumably he was referring to the previous entry, but it, too, is undatable, although it is thought to have been 1203. But "one year before" 1203 would be 1202, and scholars cannot pin down any likely events from that year. Only part of his story can be dated with assurance, and that is by reference to the *Meigetsuki* entry cited above. The rest probably occurred in mid-1203, to follow the speculation offered by Ishida and Satsukawa.[14] But in its own way, Ienaga's narrative provides every bit as much information as Teika's and is worth citing in full:[15]

I can't be sure, but I think it was one year before. On his way to offer thanks at Sumiyoshi for a successful pilgrimage to Kumano, His Majesty had occasion to stop at lodgings at Nagara. It was near sunset, and since he was to depart that night by boat, people were bustling around in a hurry, concentrating on getting the vessel ready. His Highness watched the goings-on with great interest and was quite moved by the beauty of the place. Stretching off as far as the eye could see was a clean beach along which grew a line of pine trees, deep green. The wind howled as it whipped by, and from time to time autumn showers passed through. It was a place unsurpassed, which stirred memories in one who had spent many days on a traveler's grass pillow.

The clattering of horses' hooves as they clopped along, coming and going over the Watanobe Bridge, and the voices of people calling back and forth from the boats raised quite a din, but His Majesty was simply transfixed by the view before him, and said to himself, "So this is where the ancient Nagara Bridge crossed! The only thing left is its name. How I wish I could see even just a ruined bit of it." But some around him just laughed, wondering where anyone would find such a thing.

---

14. *IN*, p. 116.
15. See Kamens, *Utamakura*, pp. 116–36, for another perspective on this incident and the Uji visit.

Captain Masatsune, who was in attendance on Go-Toba at the time, said, "I know where there's a piece from one of the supports to that bridge." His Majesty insisted that Masatsune present him the fragment as soon as we all got back to the capital. People wondered, however, that if it was just a chunk of decayed wood, what proof could be offered to Go-Toba that it was indeed a fragment of the Nagara Bridge. Here was the story Masatsune told: "The item I'm talking about has been for years in the possession of a palace guardsman named Morifusa, who was originally from this area. It seems that one of his ancestors had been rowing along the river here in a flimsy boat when the boat struck something and got stuck. Someone got out and dove into the water to see what was obstructing them, and he came to the surface with this fragment. Upon examining it closely, they discovered that it had an iron core, and looked to be part of a bridge support. They concluded that it had to be a piece of the ancient Nagara Bridge, and so it was kept in the family down to this day."

Some two or three days after His Majesty returned to the capital, Masatsune presented him with the bridge fragment, and added this poem:

Kore zo kono	Here it is! Just this,
mukasi Nagara no	This bit of pillar as it always was
fasibasira	From that ancient Nagara Bridge.
kimi ga tame to ya	Perhaps it was for Your Majesty
kutinokoriken	That it still remains, though in decay.

The Retired Emperor ordered me to reply:

Kore made mo	That it should last
miti aru miyo no	In the estuary's depths
fukaki e ni	Till this reign which honors poetry
nokoru mo siruki	Is truly an auspicious sign—
fasibasira kana	This bit of pillar from that bridge![16]

The bridge fragment was made into a poem stand for the Wakadokoro, and the first time it was put on display was at the poetry party following the imperial visit to Uji.

For that visit, a villa had been constructed next to the river across from one of the fishing weirs so that the water could flow around the weir and directly into the villa's garden. His Majesty stayed there for just five days. It was the beginning of autumn, and the wind whistled sharply through ripened ears of rice and the pine trees.

---

16. Kamens (ibid., p. 129), presumably following *IN* (p. 118), interprets *miti aru miyo* as "righteousness of his rule," and there is precedent for such a reading in waka (see Ōno Susumu et al., *Kogo jiten*, entry for *michi*). However, I am more inclined to think Ienaga is referring, at least by pun, to that other *michi* that was so important to this group: the "way" of poetry.

Emerging from the fog came voices of the people of Makinoshima as they called out to each other on boats. These combined with the distant clatter of footsteps as people crossed the bridge made us feel melancholy as we passed our days here as travelers in an unfamiliar place. It was then that I came to appreciate the resolve of that ancient poet who dwelled here, "hidden away in a hut at Mount Uji, a world others call sad."[17]

Delighted that His Majesty did not have to leave soon "the rocky shores of Koyurugi," our host, Lord Yoshitsune, decided there should be some proper refreshments to serve with the saké, and he seemed prepared to even harvest seaweed from those "rocky shores" if necessary.[18] Everything he presented was done with meticulous care and matchless beauty.

It was at the poetry party following this excursion that His Majesty first put on display, fashioned into a poem stand, the aforementioned fragment from the Nagara Bridge. Among the poems at that party was this one by Lord Yoshitsune, presumably making reference to the fact that the poem stand contained a piece of the Nagara Bridge:

Koyofi simo	Only tonight
Yasoudigafa ni	Is it possible to see
sumu tuki wo	The bright, clear moon
Nagara no fasi no	Over the Uji River (of eight
ufe ni miru kana	thousand clans)
	As if from the Nagara Bridge!

How one might have wished to stay forever there with the Maiden at Uji Bridge, but His Majesty had to return to the capital. Yet we all felt rushed, and His Majesty himself showed a longing to stay behind even as he left.[19]

Once again, by simply telling a story, Ienaga provided us with a tour of the medieval worldview, and its literary and aesthetic notions, and he crafted a subtle narrative in the bargain.

To begin with, Ienaga worked in an elusive time frame. As noted frequently in this study, part of this vagueness stems from the fact that the "journal" is really a set of memoirs written some years after the fact and with

---

17. Ienaga is referring to a well-known poem by Kisen Hōshi (fl. 840), which appears in *Kokinshū* and was later picked up by Teika in his *Kindai shūka* (progenitor of the *Hyakunin isshu* sequence): *Wa ga ifo fa / miyako no tatumi / sika zo sumu / yo wo udiyama to / fito fa ifuramu*— "My rude hut lies / To the southeast of the capital / And here I live / In this place, Mount Uji / A world others call sad" (*KKS* 983 [XVIII, Miscellaneous 2]).

18. Ienaga's punning use of the pillow word *koyurugi no iso(gu)* (hurrying to the rocky shores of Koyurugi) is analyzed below.

19. *IN*, pp. 114–22.

incomplete records. It is difficult to tell whether Ienaga turned this into a pose—"I cannot clearly recall," or "I neglected to write it down"—in order to cover himself or adopted it as a deliberate device (after all, *The Tale of Genji* starts with an equally vague time marker). In any case, the effect is to remove the account from the realm of what Miner would call the "natural diary" and force the reader to concentrate on the unfolding of the event itself.[20] Here, as in the Princess Shikishi anecdote, Ienaga moved backward and forward in time, beginning with an event in the unspecified past, bringing it up to a dateable event—a poetry party at the Wakadokoro—and then slipping back to describe the events leading up to the poetry party. This contrasts sharply with Teika's linear account.

More important, Ienaga places at the center of his narrative a small fragment of half-rotted wood. Flaubert might have approved. But this piece of wood is special, because it has a poetic pedigree (although are we ever really convinced?). Its poetic connection rests on an irony, for it is alleged to be a fragment from one of the pillars of the Nagara Bridge, which once spanned the Yodo River. The word "nagara" implies something long-lived, but even by *Kokinshū* times the bridge was long gone, as implied in this anonymous poem:

Yo no naka ni	In this world
furinuru mono fa	Two things that grow old
Tu no kuni no	Are the Nagara Bridge
Nagara no fasi to	In the province of Tsu
ware to narikeri	And, it seems, myself![21]

Go-Toba visits the place where the bridge once stood and is so taken by the scene that he longs for a memento of it. On the face of it, it seems like an impossible request, and yet Masatsune—and surely it is for efforts like this that Go-Toba came to hold him in such esteem—claims to be able to get his hands on a fragment of the bridge. After relating a feasible, but by no means leak-proof, account of how the piece of wood had survived (*nagaraete*) all these years, Masatsune presents Go-Toba with a chunk of wood and metal, which Go-Toba then has tailored into a poem stand for the Wakadokoro.

---

20. Earl Miner's (*Japanese Poetic Diaries*, pp. 3–55) discussion of "art" versus "natural" diaries (which he describes on p. 6 as "the day-to-day jottings of events as they more-or-less actually occurred"—Teika's *Meigetsuki* would fall into this category) still stands as an excellent treatise on the functions of the diary in Japanese literature.

21. *KKS* 890 (XVII, Miscellaneous 1).

But when does Go-Toba choose to display the new poem stand first? At the poetry party following his visit to Uji. Why? Because the two places are associated with bridges! The Uji Bridge was every bit as famous as the Nagara span among poets. In fact, the two are paired in a sequence of love poems in *Kokinshū*, the first by an unknown poet, the second by Sakanoue no Korenori (fl. 908–28):

Wasuraruru	Sad I am, forgotten.
mi wo Udibasi no	It's as though the Uji Bridge had been cut
naka taete	In the middle—
fito mo kayofanu	No one comes or goes,
tosi zo fenikeru	And the years just pass me by.
Afu koto wo	Since we last met
Nagara no fasi no	Much time has flowed away,
nagarafete	As long as the Nagara Bridge,
kofiwataru ma ni	Yet my love has spanned that gap
tosi zo fenikeru	As the years just pass me by.[22]

The notions of time and lost love suffuse both poems, and Ienaga picked up on these notions when he described the places themselves. Furthermore, he underlined the links between the two seemingly disparate areas—a link hallowed by *Kokinshū* itself—by subtly constructing his descriptions in a parallel manner. The time for both is autumn. (We may think of the Seventh Month, the month in which the Uji excursion took place, as the height of summer in Japan, but in the lunar calendar it was the first month of autumn, and Ienaga identified it as such. Recall, too, that it is the time of Tanabata, when the celestial Cowherd is allowed to cross the River of Heaven [*ama no kawa*—what we call the Milky Way] to visit his lover, the Weaver Maid.) Compare what Ienaga says about Nagara:

Stretching off as far as the eye could see was a clean beach along which grew a line of *pine trees*, deep green. The *wind howled as it whipped by*, and from time to time autumn showers passed through. It was a place unsurpassed, which *stirred memories in one who had spent many days on a traveler's grass pillow.*

The *clattering of horses' hooves as they clopped along, coming and going over the Watanobe Bridge*, and the *voices of people calling back and forth from the boats* raised quite a din.

with what he says about Uji:

---

22. KKS 825–26 (XV, Love 5).

It was the beginning of autumn, and the *wind whistled sharply* through ripened ears of rice and the *pine trees*. Emerging from the fog came *voices of the people of Makinoshima as they called out to each other on boats*. These combined with *the distant clatter of footsteps as people crossed the bridge* made *us feel melancholy as we passed our days here as travelers in an unfamiliar place*.

I have marked in italics the overlapping elements—wind, pine trees, clattering of horses / people as they cross the bridge, disembodied voices calling to each other on boats, and how all these images stir nostalgia in the heart of a traveler. In addition, within the narrative, both scenes immediately make the observer (Go-Toba at Nagara and Ienaga at Uji) recall an old poem. And in this way, Ienaga drew the two parts of his anecdote together, with waka as (forgive me!) the bridge.

But Ienaga had more tricks up his sleeve. First, there is the passage in the Uji excursion in which he talked of Yoshitsune's preparations. In this section, Ienaga worked an elaborate pun on the word *iso* ("rock," as in the kinds of rock formations found along the seashore). First, Yoshitsune is glad that Go-Toba is not in a hurry (*ISOgu*) to leave. Ienage prefaced the word *isogu* with a pillow word, Koyurugi, the name of a beach in Kanagawa prefecture, which was connected to the word *iso* (and consequently other words beginning with the syllables *iso*) because of its rocky shore. More subtly, he was playing off Kisen's lines in the previous sentence, *yo wo udi(yama)* (people call the world sad), for a well-known instance of the Koyurugi/*iso* combination is a poem from the *Komachishū*:

Mitinoku fa	The far north, Michinoku,
yo wo Ukisima mo	With its floating Uki Isle,
ari to ifu wo	Is a world others call sad, and yet,
seki Koyurugi no	I'm in no hurry to cross its barrier
isogazaranamu	And head back to the shores of Koyurugi.[23]

As in Kisen's poem, the poet here puns on the "u" (meaning "sad") of a place-name, and this seems to be the connection in Ienaga's mind: first Ienaga recalled Kisen's Uji poem because he was at Uji and then he recalled the pun on "u" (*yo wo udi[yama] to ifu*—"people call the world sad"), which reminds him of the *Komachishū* poem employing a similar pun (*yo wo ukisima mo ari to ifu*), which in turn suggests the *koyurugi iso(gu)* (hurrying to the

---

23. *Komachishū* #77, *Shinpen kokka taikan*, 3:5, p. 22.

shores of Koyurugi) locution. This kind of multilayered allusion became an important technique in medieval renga.

To bring his anecdote to a close on a suitable note of longing for the ethereal, the unobtainable, the poetic, Ienaga made reference to the Maiden at Uji Bridge. The Maiden at Uji Bridge (Uji no Hashihime) may originally have been a guardian deity, but by the time of *Kokinshū* she seems to have been transformed into the other kind of woman that frequented bridges in ancient Japan, the professional. (Such ladies appeared even earlier in Japanese poetry, as in Takahashi Mushimaro's [fl. 732] poem about a "maiden walking alone on the great bridge of Kawachi."[24] This issue is discussed further in Chapter 9.) This is the reading suggested here by Ishida and Satsukawa.[25] Given how often *yūjo* are mentioned in connection with Go-Toba's activities at satellite villas such as Minase (although none appears in Teika's account of this Uji trip), it is not a far-fetched interpretation.

The anonymous *Kokinshū* poet wrote:

Samusiro ni	Tonight again
koromo katasiki	Does she spread her robe on half
koyofi mo ya	Of the straw mat laid down
ware wo maturamu	And await my return,
Udi no fasifime	The Maiden at Uji Bridge?[26]

In Ienaga's own time, Teika alluded to this poem:

Samusiro ya	Ah, the straw mat laid down
matu yo no aki no	And through this night of waiting
kaze fukete	The autumn wind deepens
tuki wo katasiku	While moonlight covers half the bed
Udi no fasifime	Of the Maiden at Uji Bridge.[27]

True, some commentators such as Minemura Fumihito wish to see Teika's Maiden as the guardian deity of the Uji Bridge waiting for the male deity,[28] but whether she be a prostitute, a wife,[29] or a goddess, the ethereal image of

---

24. *MYS* 1746–47 (*NKBT* 1742–43).
25. *IN*, p. 121.
26. *KKS* 689 (XIV, Love 4).
27. *SKKS* 420 (IV, Autumn 1).
28. Minemura, *Shinkokin wakashū* (1974), p. 148.
29. Ozawa, *Kokin wakashū*, p. 275.

the lady waiting alone at Uji Bridge under the moonlight for her lover is the one that charmed Ienaga. And it brings his story to a fitting close.

Apparently the Uji visit revived Go-Toba completely, for shortly afterward, he ordered the *Shinkokinshū* compilers to begin the process of classifying (*burui*) the poems they had collected into relevant categories (Spring, Love, Felicitations, and so on). In a series of entries beginning on vii/22, Teika mentioned the process, although many of the entries contain other information—the world did not stop for *Shinkokinshū*.[30] Some examples:

Genkyū 1/vii/22. Weather fine. Around dark there were heavy rains and a light snow. Today we were ordered to go to the Wakadokoro in order to start classifying the poems for the collection, for which there had already been a preliminary session two days earlier. So I dutifully went. However, new demands were being made by the monks on Mount Hiei, and Minister Yoshitsune was ordered to hurry and meet with the Emperor. We left for the palace together late in the afternoon. I did not return home until well after sundown.

Genkyū 1/vii/23. Weather fine. I was left behind to continue the classification of the poems and so did not accompany His Majesty to Minase. However, I did visit Ienaga and Kiyonori, who told me everyone else had gone, and His Majesty himself left in the mid-afternoon.

Genkyū 1/vii/27. Weather fine. Ienaga returned from Minase last night; so when he sent me a message today, I went straight away to the Wakadokoro. There I met with Hideyoshi, Ariie, Masatsune, and Ienaga.[31] We opened the boxes containing the poems and began the process of classifying them. Masatsune kept notes. By working extremely hard, we were able to complete the two Spring books, and in the evening, we left. But before doing so, Ienaga poured us all some saké and served melon. Then each of us, in rank-order, starting with Hideyoshi, made offerings to the portrait of Hitomaro. Tonight, none of the group went back to join the Retired Emperor at Minase.

Genkyū 1/vii/28. Weather fine. Early in the morning I went to Minister Yoshitsune's residence. . . . [After leaving there] I went to the Wakadokoro. It was the

---

30. Gotō Shigeo (*Shinkokin wakashū no kisōteki kenkyū*, pp. 86–89) cites excerpts from all the important *Meigetsuki* entries describing the classification process.

31. Teika used only titles here; I got the names from Imagawa, *Meigetsukishō*, p. 153. However, Imagawa identifies the one Teika calls *dairi* (an officer in the Kebishi guards) as Michitomo. In a personal communication, Watanabe Yasuaki argued that this must refer to Hideyoshi, one of the Wakadokoro members, who also served in the Kebishi guards. I am following Watanabe's suggestion here.

same people as yesterday, except Ietaka also joined us there. (Masatsune came very late.) Hideyoshi produced two boxes that had the titles of imperial anthologies inscribed on them.[32] In one box—a compartmented meal box—there was melon, and in the other—made of porcelain—there was saké and the like. There was also some ice. Hideyoshi shaved off bits of the ice with his own sword. The whole process was quite fascinating.[33] Although there were men around who could do this for us, Hideyoshi insisted on showing his ice-shaving skills. He then wrapped the ice in a white napkin and struck it with his left hand to crush it. Hideyoshi performed this as if he did it all the time. We each partook of the treat. Today we finished classifying the Summer poems, and wrote up the Tanabata poems, as well. After putting everything away, we left. Tonight I went to the Crown Prince's residence and assisted in a meal service there.[34]

Unfortunately, there is no other information about Go-Toba's Minase excursion. It seems like an odd time to leave the capital. (He did not return until the 5th of the next month.)[35] To begin with, it was one of his appointments that had triggered the new demands from the Hiei monks, and furthermore, he had just ordered the Wakadokoro members to start classifying poems for *Shinkokinshū*. Considering how active he was in the collection, I would not have expected him to leave town for two weeks at such an important juncture.

We can also see here that although the Wakadokoro members worked hard in spurts, they also took time off to enjoy themselves. They seemed almost carefree without the boss in town. With the imperial anthology titles inscribed on the lunch boxes, this would appear to be a "theme" meal, at which Hideyoshi shows that poetry is not his only talent. In the next chapter, we will see more examples of such elegant feasting.

The *Meigetsuki* entries for the 5th, 6th, and 7th days of the Eighth Month show the toll the young Retired Emperor's energy (not to mention the changeable autumn weather) was taking on his older subjects:

Genkyū 1/viii/5. Weather fine, though from mid-afternoon it began to grow dark. Recently it has been as hot as mid-summer. I hear the Retired Emperor returned today, and so in the late afternoon I went to the Kyōgoku Palace to receive my orders.

---

32. Here, too, I am following Watanabe rather than Imagawa in identifying *dairi* as Hideyoshi.
33. Imagawa takes one of the characters in this phrase as *koshi* (palanquin), which makes no sense here. The Kokusho Kankōkai text reads it as *kyō* (something that interests one), which fits the circumstances much better.
34. *Meigetsuki*, 1: 376. I am grateful to Watanabe for assistance in puzzling out this passage.
35. Ibid., Genkyū 1/viii/5, 1: 377.

Genkyū 1/viii/6. Windy, rainy, and very cool. I did not go out today. I understand that His Majesty made a visit to the Upper Kamo Shrine and that everyone caught a cold.

Genkyū 1/viii/7. Weather fine. In mid-morning I went to Minister Yoshitsune's place, and together we went to see the Retired Emperor. Although His Majesty had ordered everyone to work on the poem classifications yesterday, it seems that they had all stayed away, claiming they were sick. In mid-afternoon, His Majesty withdrew, and I went home. Minister Yoshitsune had already taken his leave.

Meanwhile, imperial messengers were reporting all sorts of things to the throne: the Hayumaya affair, the problem with the monks on Mount Hiei, the appointment of Princess Reishi as Kamo High Priestess, and so on.[36] But I was a man of leisure, staying at home, sleeping late. What a pleasure it was, I can tell you! About this time, I had gotten a hold of draft copies of the *Zuozhuan*, and day and night I spent trying to pull the text together, using the drafts to reconstruct missing chapters and parts of the text that had decayed.[37]

These entries, especially the last one, remind us how interwoven the worlds of art and politics were. Teika was clearly not cut out for the latter, a fact that may explain his slow progress through the ranks. Yet his close ties to the Kujō house compelled him to attend many meetings he would probably rather have missed. On the 7th day, almost as if he were envious that his colleagues had escaped a day's work at the Wakadokoro by what appears to be what we would now call a "sick-out," Teika defiantly took the afternoon off. But the activity he chose to fill his leisure time reminds us that one of his family's avocations was the maintenance of a good library of classics. Shunzei and Teika collated and copied numerous texts in their lifetimes, both Japanese and, judging from this passage, Chinese, and were responsible for saving many pieces that might otherwise have been lost or transmitted only in fragments.[38]

---

36. See ibid., 1/vi/23, 1: 372–73, for details. The "Hayumaya affair" seems to refer to some sort of dispute involving Hayumaya-shō, an estate over which the Kujō house was proprietor (*ryōke*), although I can find no details. For background on the estate (Teika used somewhat different characters to write it, but I believe it to be the same place), see the entry for *Hayumaya-shō* in Kokushi daijiten henshū iinkai, *Kokushi daijiten*, 11: 695.

37. The *Zuozhuan* (literally, "Zuo's Commentary") was considered the standard commentary on the *Spring and Autumn Annals*. It was traditionally believed to have been written by Zuo Qiuming, a contemporary of Confucius, but now is thought to be a fourth century B.C. work.

38. Although secreted away for centuries at a stretch, Teika's copies of, among other works, *Kokinshū*, *Ise monogatari*, and *Genji monogatari* have long been considered the most important old copies of those classics.

Teika needed his rest, for on the next day, the 8th, Go-Toba formally moved into his new palace at Itsutsuji. The ceremony was elaborate, and Teika was obliged to attend.[39] A week later, the Retired Emperor held the first poetry event for the Wakadokoro in its new quarters, a poetry party on the occasion of the full moon. It was a rather select group, consisting as near as we can tell from Teika's account, of the Wakadokoro members (those still alive or healthy enough to attend) and a few other high-ranking courtiers, including the former Prime Minister Fujiwara Yorizane (1155–1225). Yoshitsune acted as master of ceremonies and coordinated the presentation of formal poems (five from each participant). Yorizane's verse ended up in *Shinkokinshū*.[40] Then, impromptu verse was ordered. Teika seems startled: "An inkstone was set out, and in a flash the Minister Yoshitsune posed the topic. Everyone was to compose one verse, and we each left after submitting ours."[41]

Classification of poems for *Shinkokinshū* continued, and Teika referred to it twice more in the Eighth Month, although without details of the committee's progress.[42] Sometime in the Ninth Month, however, Teika came down with an illness that was to plague him for over a month. At one point, it must have been quite serious, since the *Meigetsuki* entries from the 25th of the Ninth Month through the end of the Tenth Month are noticeably sparse, and virtually every entry mentions his illness.[43] However, he was not as explicit about the symptoms as he had been earlier about his kidney stones. He wrote only about having a cough. The end of the entry for ix/24 points to the toll ill-health was taking on him:

After I returned home, I felt worse than ever. . . . These days they are meeting every day to classify poems, but since there's nothing at all I can do to relieve my symptoms, I have stayed away. I am not interested in anything anymore. It's useless to see anybody. I don't even care about poetry. I've just been utterly listless these past days. My shame just grows deeper.[44]

The entry for the last day of the month is even bleaker. It simply says: "It

---

39. Teika described it in great detail in the entry for Genkyū 1/viii/8, 1: 377–78.
40. *SKKS* 426 (IV, Autumn 1).
41. *Meigetsuki*, Genkyū 1/viii/15, 1: 378.
42. Ibid., 1/viii/24, 29, 1: 381.
43. In fact, there are no entries at all for ix/25–29, and x/1–5, 7, 9–14.
44. *Meigetsuki*, Genkyū 1/ix/24, 1: 383.

rained all day. My illness persists, and here it is already the end of autumn."[45] The Tenth Month brought no relief.

Things were no better for Go-Toba, who suffered a personal loss in the same month—the so-called Godless Month. His favorite concubine, Owari, died, and once again, Ienaga's treatment of her death and Go-Toba's mourning provides a lesson in courtly medieval Japanese discourse. Little is known about Owari save that she was a *kōi*, a concubine of middling rank, in Go-Toba's court. That this was the position of Kiritsubo, Genji's mother, was not lost on Ienaga. After giving birth to an imperial prince (Go-Toba's sixth, seventh, or eighth)[46] in the 7th month of 1205, she fell ill, declined, and died. In a passage reminiscent of *The Tale of Genji*, Ienaga describes how Go-Toba fussed over Owari when she became ill and before she left the palace (before her final decline). Indeed, for a long time Go-Toba would not let her leave. Although the passage is quite short, "plot" and even some phraseology so closely overlap the "Kiritsubo" chapter of *Genji* that coincidence can hardly account for it.[47] From Shunzei's writings in late Heian and early Kamakura, it is obvious that *Genji* was already canonical to waka poets by the early 1200s. As to why Ienaga might allude to Genji in this fashion, I will speculate presently.

Go-Toba, sunk in brooding, decided suddenly to go to the Minase Villa.[48] Ienaga commented that the Tenth Month, early winter, weather

---

45. Ibid., 1/ix/30, 1: 383.

46. There is dispute on this point, which is not important to this study. The child's given name was Tomohito, his priestly name was Dōkaku, and he was eventually named the Chief Abbot of the Tendai Sect (Tendai zasu) in 1247. See *IN*, pp. 157–58.

47. See *IN*, pp. 156–167. The passage most reminiscent of *Genji* appears on p. 156. In their chapters in *The Distant Isle*, both Janet Goff ("Nō and Its Antecedents") and Thomas Hare ("A Separate Piece") discuss the complexity of classical allusion (Hare calls it "appropriation") in medieval writing. Hare discusses how *Genji* allusions might take the form of obvious thematic references or less obvious, scattered, unidentified quotations. Goff writes: "The duplication of *Genji* materials in a wide variety of art forms, for instance, suggests that apparently obscure allusions were part of a common body of knowledge that would have been recognized by audiences familiar with other genres" (p. 174). These observations are also pertinent to Ienaga's use of *Genji* material.

48. Perhaps because he was too preoccupied with his own health problems to care, or perhaps because Go-Toba was quite secretive about the events, Teika had little to say. His depiction of the whole matter comes down to less than two lines in *Meigetsuki* (1: 383): "Genkyū 1/x/19—Weather fine. The Priestly Retired Emperor has gone to Minase. According to reports, the Lady Owari, who was greatly favored by His Majesty and who was truly a fine

(cold wind, *sigure*-tears, and the like) suited Go-Toba's mood. At Minase, he just moped around, talked about the brevity of this life, and cried. At this point Go-Toba entered into an extended poetic exchange with Jien, recently returned to his position as Chief Abbot of the Tendai sect. Go-Toba sent Jien ten poems that expressed his sadness. In a variation on the dialogue poems of the Heian period, Jien's ten reply poems recast the same imagery into religious form. The exchange appears in its entirety in Appendix E (pp. 419–36); here I give only the first set of poems:

Go-Toba's Poem

    Nani to naku   Hoping somehow
    nagusamu ya tote   That I might find solace
    kitaredomo   I came here, and yet
    sigure zo masaru   Winter rain teardrops fall
    fuyu no yamazato   Harder in this mountain village.

Jien's Reply Poem

    Toni kakuni   Though this way or that
    nagusamade simo   You find no solace,
    ikaga sen   What can you do?
    munasiki sora no   It's a lonely mountain village
    fuyu no yamazato   Under an uncertain winter sky.

When Go-Toba returned to Kyoto, he still could not shake his sadness according to Ienaga. The *Genji* connection re-emerges as Ienaga notes (again with a nod to Murasaki Shikibu's wording) that the new prince (Owari's son) was brought to the palace, but instead of finding solace in the "keepsake" (*wasuregatami*), Go-Toba found him a painful reminder.[49] And here might lie one explanation for Ienaga's use of the *Genji* motif. Like *honkadori* in waka, allusion was supposed to be more than mere imitation. One was expected to put new wine in those old bottles. By introducing the Kiritsubo story, Ienaga could in shorthand tell the knowledgeable reader how serious Go-Toba's feelings toward Owari were, and by "twisting" the outcome, he made Go-Toba's attachment even more painfully clear.

One interesting thing about the poetry exchange is that several of Go-Toba's poems (for example, the fourth through seventh of his poems in the

---

companion, has passed away. It seems that His Majesty wishes to avoid the palace for awhile, so has gone elsewhere."
49. *IN*, p. 166.

exchange) hint at the Waiting Woman figure—a Love motif. None of the Lament poems in *Kokinshū* and only two in *Shinkokinshū* do this—in fact, few of them even mention tears on sleeves. The more standard figure is the smoke from the funeral pyre. But this Love subtext reminds us of the sexual dimension of Go-Toba's attachment to Owari and adds poignancy to the physical loss in a way that calls to mind Hitomaro, whose laments for Prince Kawashima, Princess Asuka, and an unnamed lady from the province of Kibi also highlight the loss of sexual intimacy, albeit more explicitly than Go-Toba does.[50] It also disappears from the poems he exchanged with Jien a year later. Ienaga subsequently described the one-year memorial services Go-Toba held for Owari at Minase, and also recorded a second set of poetic exchanges between Go-Toba and Jien following those services.[51] These are discussed in the next chapter.

While at Minase, it appears that Go-Toba held an impromptu poetry contest, which he himself judged and then offered to the Iwashimizu Wakamiya Shrine.[52] Consonant with the circumstances, it was a small-scale event, with only ten participants. None of the stellar cast was there, although the participants did include Ienaga, Yorizane (Prime Minister, First Rank, and of the Nakayama/Rokujō house—Go-Toba was still concerned about keeping a political balance in his court, however close he was to the

---

50. Take, for example, these lines by Hitomaro: "Since he no longer lies with her / his smooth-skinned body like a great sword / how desolate must be her bed / through the pitch black night" (*nikihipadasura wo / turugitati / mï ni sopënureba / nubatama nö / yodökö mo aruramu*—from the lament on the death of Prince Kawashima, *MYS* 194–95), or "when you lay with him / like river-weed tendrils / swaying to and fro" (*köyaseba / kapamo nö götöku / nabikapisi*—from the lament on the death of Princess Asuka, *MYS* 196–98), or "her husband, still young as fresh grass / who would lie next to her / his body like a great sword / how lonely must he be now! / how full of longing when he goes to bed" (*turugitati / mï ni sopënekemu / wakakusa nö / sönö tumanöko pa / sabusimi ka / ömöpite neramu*—from the lament on the death of an *uneme* from Tsu in Kibi province, *MYS* 217–19). (The *Shinpen kokka taikan* and NKBT numbers are the same for these poems.) For more elegant, if looser, translations of these poems, see the Nippon gakujitsu shinkōkai translation of *Man'yōshū*, pp. 36–38, 44–45. The final polish to these collaborative translations was presumably added by Ralph Hodgson, who, because his name does not appear on the title page, rarely gets enough credit, although Keene does clearly acknowledge him in his foreword to the 1965 edition.

51. *IN*, pp. 228–38.

52. Called by Ariyoshi the *Genkyū gannen jūgatsu nijūkunichi Iwashimizu Wakamiya tōza uta-awase* and presumably held on the 29th day of the Tenth Month, it is the contest Ienaga was referring to when he talked about Go-Toba citing Shunzei in one of his judgments (see below in this chapter). *IN*, pp. 151, 155.

Kujō house)—and a few of the new voices in Go-Toba's poetic coterie, most notably a lady named Go-Toba-In no Shimotsuke (also known as Shinano). The latter is discussed more fully in the next chapter. The choice of topics reflected both the season and Go-Toba's mood: the Beginning of Winter, Early Winter Rains (*sigure*), and Fields in the Cold.

Go-Toba stayed at Minase for less than two weeks and returned to the Itsutsuji palace on the 1st of the Eleventh Month.[53] Apparently he was still not satisfied with the pool of poems for *Shinkokinshū*, for he proceeded to arrange an elaborate contest reminiscent of the *Rōnyaku gojisshu uta-awase* and the *Shingū senka-awase* of early 1201, in which the purpose clearly had been to marshal the best talent and subject the output to close scrutiny. The fourteen poems from this 45-round contest selected for *Shinkokinshū* make it the fifth most important source of poems for that collection.

Teika first mentioned this contest, known as the *Kasuga no Yashiro no uta-awase* (Poetry Contest for Kasuga Shrine), in his *Meigetsuki* entry for xi/9 when, after a long day at the Wakadokoro with Ariie, adding and taking out Go-Toba's poems from the verses already classified (presumably at Go-Toba's request), he received a message in the evening: "The Kasuga poetry contest will be tomorrow. It is to be judged by the group. You should come at mid-morning." He was less than enthusiastic: "Every day I get pressed into service! I'm physically exhausted. I don't know how much more I can stand."[54]

Nevertheless, he had no choice, and he dutifully attended the following day. Despite the importance of the event, his account of the activities is spare and lacking in the kind of detail he provided for the earlier contests mentioned above:

Genkyū 1/xi/10. . . . We were then summoned into the Wakadokoro. I was again asked to be Reader (*kōji*) and was also charged with marking which poems won their rounds and writing down the judgment remarks according to form. I took up the brush rather halfheartedly.[55] After the discussions were completed for the forty-five rounds, I withdrew to write everything up.

However, immediately following, we were assigned, impromptu, to write three poems on three topics. By this time, they had brought out lamps. The poems were set into rounds blind, that is, with the names of the poets for each poem hidden. Af-

---

53. *Meigetsuki*, Genkyū 1/xi/2, 1: 384.
54. Ibid., 1/xi/9, 1: 387).
55. Teika's poor eyesight may be one reason that he was so diffident about being made to keep the contest records.

ter we had presented these to His Majesty, I was again summoned before him. He asked me to look over the poems and affix judgment marks to them. He was in a good humor and quite taken by the proceedings. He let his feelings of admiration be known in formal letters of praise (*migyōsho*) to Michitomo, Ariie, Yasusue, Masatsune, and Tango.[56] Truly these are times when one can exhibit one's powers as a poet and be rewarded. It was quite late when His Majesty retired and we could all relax.[57]

It is unfortunate that Teika was so laconic in writing about this contest, but clearly his heart was not in it. He did not even mention his own poems, good or bad, and, in fact, none of them was subsequently selected for *Shinkokinshū*, although one did win its round in the Kasuga contest.

The contest was large in terms of number of participants—thirty poets in two teams of fifteen, and each poet submitted a total of three poems. Although virtually all the old names were there (including Shunzei, although it is possible that he submitted his poems in absentia, a practice we have seen in other contests like this), there are a number of new faces, too. Even as *Shinkokinshū* neared completion, Go-Toba never ceased searching for new talent. In an interesting twist, Ienaga focused his attention on the lesser-known poets. Following are excerpts from his account of the contest, which begins with a characteristic chronological error (Michichika's death in Kennin 2 [1202] preceded the contest by *two* years, not one):

After the death of the Minister Michichika, there were no poetry contests or such events for some time.[58] But in the winter of the year after his passing [*sic*], there was a contest called the Kasuga Shrine Poetry Contest. This contest pitted poets of the same caliber against each other; the rounds were set up so that poets who were thought by people to be worthy of each other were matched. Thus even more so than usual, everyone was determined not to lose in this event. For this contest, only a few of the poems submitted were from poets who were considered masters. On the other

---

56. A *migyōsho* is not necessarily a letter of praise, although in this case that is its purpose. It can be any kind of order, instruction, or comment issued from a higher authority to those below. The term took on a more specific meaning in the Kamakura Bakufu, but in the Heian and early Kamakura court, it was a more or less generic term.

57. *Meigetsuki*, Genkyū 1/xi/10, 1: 387.

58. Although there were, in fact, several fairly large public poetry events, it is true that none of them was especially important to *Shinkokinshū*. According to Ariyoshi (*Shinkokin wakashū no kenkyū: kiban to kōsei*, p. 540), only six *Shinkokinshū* poems came out of contests or events conducted during the two-year period between Michichika's death and the Kasuga contest.

hand, for one Hōribe Narimochi, it was the first time he had ever participated in such an event. He was the grandson of Narinaka and the son of Masanaka.[59] Word was that he was a skillful poet from a long line of skillful poets. Among the poems he submitted for the contest was this one, on the topic of Fallen Leaves:

Fuyu no kite	Winter has come,
yama mo arafa ni	The mountainside is bare
ko no fa furi	The leaves all fallen—
nokoru matu safe	Even the pine which remains
mine ni sabisiki	Stands lonely upon the peak.[60]

Now this contest was held at the Wakadokoro, and it was judged by the group. But when this poem was recited, His Majesty insisted on repeating it several times, and it was clear he felt it was well written. The morning after the contest, as His Majesty was going over the records from the night before, he again took notice of Narimochi's poem and ordered that a formal letter of praise (*migyōsho*) be drawn up. So I wrote the letter and sent it to Narimochi. Instead of sending a formal "receipt letter" (*ukebumi*), Narimochi came straight to the palace all excited. As I stood at the East Gate to greet him, he pulled out the Retired Emperor's letter of praise and tried to express his joy, but words failed him and he ended in tears.

There were several other poets who received letters of praise from Go-Toba. Perhaps because of the strict pairings in the contest, a large number of excellent poems was produced:

Major Captain of the Right Tadatsune, on the topic of Moon at Dawn

Kumo wo nomi	It was only the clouds
turaki mono tote	That were cruel, or so I thought—
akasu yo no	But now as night grows light,
tuki yo kozuwe ni	O moon, you've fallen among branches
otikata no yama	On the distant mountainside.[61]

---

59. The characters used to write Narimochi's name look as though they should be read "Narishige" (and, in fact, that is the way he appears in Ariyoshi's *Wakabungaku jiten*), but later in the passage, Ienaga (or the copyist) wrote the name in *kana*, and it appears as "Narimochi," which is the reading Minemura and Kojima also use in their editions of *Shinkokinshū*. Although his dates are not certain, they are believed to be 1180 to 1254. His sister, Go-Toba-In no Shimotsuke (more commonly known as Shinano), was married to Ienaga. His grandfather, Narinaka, had a total of thirty poems in various imperial anthologies. The Hōribe clan were hereditary shrine attendants (*negi*) at Hie Shrine, in Ōtsu, at the foot of Mount Hiei on the Lake Biwa side.

60. *SKKS* 565 (VI, Winter). I suspect Go-Toba was so moved by this poem because he saw himself as the lonely pine and the recently deceased Owari as the fallen leaves.

61. *SKKS* 1546 (XVI, Miscellaneous 1).

Lord Ariie, Wind in the Pines

    Warenagara
    omofu ka mono wo
    to bakari ni
    sode ni sigururu
    nifa no matukaze

    Even I?
    Even I can have such longings?
    Such longings as this?
    On my sleeves tear-rain falls,
    While in the garden, wind in the pines.[62]

Lord Ietaka, Wind in the Pines

    Kasugayama
    tani no umoregi
    kutinutomo
    kimi ni tugekose
    mine no matukaze

    In a valley on Mount Kasuga,
    I lie, a buried bit of wood,
    Now decayed—
    Please pass this on to my lord,
    Wind through pines on the peak![63]

Lord Yasusue, Moon at Dawn

    Iriyarade
    yo wo osimu tuki no
    yasurafi ni
    fonobono akuru
    yama no fa zo uki

    Not yet setting,
    The moon, reluctant to leave night
    Hesitates, and yet
    How sad that the mountain ridge
    Slowly brightens toward dawn.[64]

Masatsune, Fallen Leaves

    Uturiyuku
    kumo ni arasi no
    oto sunari
    tiru ka masaki no
    Kaduraki no yama

    In clouds rolling past
    One hears distinctly
    The sounds of a storm—
    Is it that spindle tree leaves
    Are scattering on Mount Kazuraki?[65]

Lady Tango, Wind in the Pines

    Nani to naku
    kikeba namida zo
    koborekeru

    For no reason
    When I hear it, the tears
    Just start flowing—

---

62. *SKKS* 1636 (XVII, Miscellaneous 2).
63. *SKKS* 1793 (XVIII, Miscellaneous 3). Ietaka was 47 at this time, and still only Junior Fourth Rank, Lower. He used Mount Kasuga to suggest his lineage (Kasuga Shrine being the family shrine for the Fujiwara clan) and lamented because he had not shared the Fujiwara glory.
64. *SKKS* 1547 (XVI, Miscellaneous 1).
65. *SKKS* 561 (VI, Winter). The central "trick" (*kyō*) of this poem is a pun, lost in translation, on *masaki no kadura* (spindle tree) and Mount *Kaduraki* (Kazuraki in Hepburn romanization).

koke no tamoto ni	Wind through pines as it visits
kayofu matukaze	The hem of my mossy robes.[66]

All of the poets received letters of praise from His Majesty congratulating them on their fine poems.

But returning to Narimochi, since this was his first time submitting poems in such a formal event, that alone would have been cause for joy, but on top of that to receive a formal letter from the Senior Retired Emperor was truly an honor. Ten or so days later, Narimochi came again to the palace, and he told me how waking or sleeping, he could not get over the distinction he had won.... He told me again that he did not even know the right words to express how he felt at receiving an imperial letter, and he took the letter out of a brocade bag he kept it in and showed it to me. Indeed, the feelings must have been all the greater for someone like him who came from a long line of poets and who so loved the art.[67]

In addition to earning letters of praise, the poems cited above were also among the fourteen poems from this contest that were selected for *Shinkokinshū* (all but Yasusue's employ that characteristic *Shinkokin* device, the substantive final), and all won their respective rounds. Ienaga's list of poets who received letters differs from Teika's. Teika mentioned Michitomo, Ariie, Yasusue, Masatsune, and Tango, and Ienaga Narimochi, Tadatsune, Ariie, Ietaka, Yasusue, Masatsune, and Tango.

What do the contest records tell us about this event?[68] To begin with, it involved thirty poets, fifteen on each team. There were three topics, for a total of forty-five rounds. As Ienaga noted, the poets were matched in terms of skill, although this is somewhat misleading in that the teams were also more or less set up in rank-order, which precluded some truly competitive match-ups. Unlike some of the earlier, more experimental contests, the order of the teams was fixed throughout, and the same two poets were matched in each round. Considering the quality of the output, this rather traditional arrangement ended up producing as good a result as had some of the more

---

66. *SKKS* 1794 (XVIII, Miscellaneous 3). Tango had become a nun two years earlier, hence the reference to her "mossy robes."

67. *IN*, pp. 87–95. I am following Ishida's and Satsukawa's suggestion for the interpretation of the last sentence of this passage, since the text is corrupt there. The section itself continues, but the last part is an anecdote unrelated to the Kasuga contest.

68. The only complete extant text appears in both the *Katsuranomiyabon sōsho*, 14: 273–95, and *Shinpen kokka taikan*, 5:202, pp. 520–23.

Table 2
Scores in the Kasuga Contest, by Team

Left	Win/Loss/Tie	Right	Win/Loss/Tie
Go-Toba	2/0/1	Yoshitsune	0/2/1
Jien	2/0/1	Shakua (Shunzei)	0/2/1
Tadayoshi	0/2/1	Lady Tango	2/0/1
Tadatsune	2/0/1	Yoshihira	0/2/1
Michiteru	1/2/0	Kintsune	2/1/0
Michitomo	1/1/1	Ariie	1/1/1
Lady Takakura	1/1/1	Lady Dainagon	1/1/1
Shunzei no Musume	0/0/3	Lady Kunaikyō	0/0/3
Lady Echizen	0/2/1	Lady Shimotsuke	2/0/1
Teika	1/1/1	Ietaka	1/1/1
Yasusue	3/0/0	Iehira	0/3/0
Masatsune	2/1/0	Tomochika	1/2/0
Tadasada	2/1/0	Narimochi	1/2/0
Narikiyo	0/0/3	Ienaga	0/0/3
Yukiyoshi	0/3/0	Hideyoshi	3/0/0

elaborate setups such as the *Shingū* contest. (See Table 2 for the Kasuga contest teams and their records.)[69]

The team scores are fairly close, with seventeen wins for the Left team as opposed to fourteen wins for the Right. As it is, rank may have played some role in that, since Go-Toba was likely to be favored in any close decision, as would Jien over his opponent, Shunzei. Otherwise, the matchups seemed fair.

In fact, several pairs stand out, especially Shunzei no Musume versus Kunaikyō (in the Eighth Round of each topic) and Teika versus Ietaka (in

---

69. In this contest the win-loss records are appended as part of the extant contest text (unlike most other contests in this study). Poets who have not been identified elsewhere: Fujiwara Tadasada (d. 1256; son of Kanemune, his mother was Rokujō Shigeie's daughter; has one poem in *Shinkokinshū*); Fujiwara Narikiyo (dates uncertain; two poems in *Shinkokinshū*); Fujiwara Yukiyoshi (1179–1250+; this contest was his debut, but he became very active from this time; his father was a noted calligrapher, and Yukiyoshi provided the clean copy of *Shinchokusenshū* when it was formally presented in 1235; has one poem in *Shinkokinshū*); Lady Shimotsuke (i.e., Go-Toba-In no Shimotsuke; dates uncertain but alive in 1251; daughter of Hōribe Masanaka and sister of Narimochi; became wife of Ienaga in 1204; this was her debut; has two poems in *Shinkokinshū*); Fujiwara Iehira (dates uncertain; son of Tsuneie; has two poems in *Shinkokinshū*). See Ariyoshi, *Waka bungaku jiten*; and Minemura, *Shinkokin wakashū* (1974), pp. 602–24.

the Tenth Round of each topic). We do not know if the parties saw themselves as rivals, but history, as well as their contemporaries, it seems, appears to have perceived them at least as complementary (if not competitive) pairs. Kamo no Chōmei compared the working styles of the two ladies, who were seen as equal in terms of talent, in one section of *Mumyōshō*.[70] And during his Oki exile, Go-Toba put together a *senka-awase* of poems by Teika and Ietaka called the *Teika Karyū ryōkyō senka-awase* (Contest of Selected Poems from Lords Teika and Ietaka). However, here the group managed a diplomatic outcome by awarding Ties in all rounds between the two women and splitting the decisions in the case of the two men.

Two examples will illustrate these pairings and showcase the differing approaches to poetry. First is this round between Shunzei no Musume and Kunaikyō:

Round 8: Fallen Leaves

Left, Shunzei no Musume, Tie

Tuki zo moru	Moon leaks in
oto fa sigururu	With early winter rains that patter
itama yori	Through gaps in the roof
ko no fa furisiku	And a layer of fallen leaves spreads
toko no samusiro	On the narrow mat that is my bed.

Right, Kunaikyō

Tirimagafu	Scattered in confusion
momidi fa nifa no	Across the garden, maple leaves
Karanisiki	Form a Chinese brocade,
siki mo sadamezu	The folds of its drapery disarrayed
fuku arasi kana	In the blowing storm winds.

Judgment: The sleeping mat in the Left poem and the Chinese brocade in the Right poem are both lovely; so a Tie is awarded.

There is an almost geometric precision to the structure of Shunzei no Musume's poem: a noun heading each line; the first, second, and fourth lines in grammatical parallel (noun/particle/verb; noun/particle/verb); a downward motion from moon to clouds to roof to bed that conforms to both the moonlight (shining down) and the falling of rain and leaves; and an x-no-y substantive in the last line (*taigendome*), which is practically a signature of the *Shinkokin* style. Just as Teika advocated, although the topic is a seasonal one,

---

70. See Chapter 2, notes 59 and 61, pp. 69 and 70.

the subtext is love: the Waiting Woman alone in her desolate bed visited only by nature. The judgment is laconic in the extreme, for this poem has more than just the image of the sleeping mat to recommend it.

By reputation (both in her own time and subsequently), Kunaikyō's work is thought to be on the reasoned, even dispassionate side, composed with the eye of a painter (supposedly a quality inherited from her maternal grandfather, a painter).[71] This poem certainly fits that characterization. The figure itself—a comparison of fallen maple leaves to a Chinese brocade—is not one Kunaikyō originated, although more often the poet will simply speak of brocade (*nisiki*), not Chinese brocade (*karanisiki*). The latter is treated by scholars as a pillow word for *tatu* ("sew," and of course any puns that may apply, such as "to rise") and similar, cloth-related words, though *siki* (to spread or drape) is not given as a companion word in most dictionaries.[72] Perhaps this is what struck the group—that she was using the word in a new way. Certainly she used it as more than a pillow word; she also took full advantage of its metaphorical possibilities and, by extending the metaphor, depicted a garden scene so deep in fallen leaves that the wind blows them about in billows, like folds of heavy cloth. The poem is missing, however, the sadness and pathos of Shunzei no Musume's poem, although the group at this contest obviously did not see "missing" as "lacking."

Now, one matchup between Teika and Ietaka:

Fallen Leaves, Round 10

Left, Teika, Tie

    Sore made no   Unable to wait
    yuki mo matiafezu   For the snow to come that far,
    momidiba no   Maple leaves fall
    furusato fukaki   Deep over the ancient village
    ato fa taetutu   Steadily wiping away its traces.

Right, Ietaka

    Mimuroyama   At Mount Mimuro
    kozuwe no nisiki   Brocade on the tree branches
    taenurasi   Seems to have torn off—

---

71. Ariyoshi's entry in the *Waka bungaku jiten* (p. 164) is typical.

72. *KKS* 1002 (XIX, Miscellaneous Forms), a *chōka* by Tsurayuki, uses the term this way, in a section of the poem cataloging the four seasons: *Karanisiki / Tatuta no yama no / momidiba o / mite nomi sinobu*)—"Chinese brocade / Stitched on Mount Tatsuta— / Maple leaves / Just seeing them makes me yearn."

Tatuta no kafa wo	Maple leaves that bury
udumu momidiba	The river Tatsuta.

Judgment: Although the word udumu *(bury) in the Right poem is lackluster, the overall structure* (sugata) *of the poem is nice; so a Tie is awarded.*

Neither of these poems would rank among its author's best, although the group at the contest found them at least equally "nice" (*yoroshi*). As he often did (and it was a device the Kyōgoku poets adopted), Teika played with prosaic diction in the first two lines ("Unable to wait for the snow to come that far"). Then, in a move reminiscent of his *fana mo momidi mo / nakarikeri* (I'm surprised that there are neither / Cherry blossoms nor maple leaves) poem, he upsets, even negates, the traditional waka view of a particular scene.[73] Here, his burial of the lonely village not in snow, as one would expect from the waka tradition, but in maple leaves, explicitly negates the snow convention. This is part of what is *neo* about the neo-Classicism of this age, and what is *shin* about *Shinkokinshū*—playing with the tradition and making it one's own, while exploiting the assumptions it has built into readers. Ietaka's poem is more conventional. Not only does it re-examine the "brocade of maple leaves in the Tatsuta River" figure, but it even employs *rasi* in a way that recalls *Kokinshū* diction. In fact, the poem alludes to a pair of anonymous *Kokinshū* poems that appear side-by-side in that collection:

Tatutagafa	In the Tatsuta River
momidi midarete	Maple leaves are flowing
nagarumeri	In confusion.
wataraba nisiki	If I were to cross the stream,
naka ya taenamu	I'd likely tear that leaf-brocade.
Tatutagafa	In the Tatsuta River
momidiba nagaru	Maple leaves flow.
kannabi no	At Mount Mimuro
Mimuro no yama ni	Of the sacred forests, it seems
sigure fururasi	Early winter rains are falling.[74]

---

73. The full poem, SKKS 363 (IV, Autumn 1), is one of the famous "Three Autumn Evening Poems" (*sanseki no uta*) that appear together in *Shinkokinshū*: Miwataseba / fana mo momidi mo / nakarikeri / ura no tomoya no / aki no yufugure—"As I survey the scene, / I'm surprised that there are neither / Cherry blossoms nor maple leaves— / Grass-thatched hut on the bay / In this autumn evening." A look at the *Kokka taikan* index shows that the vast majority of courtly poems beginning with the line "Miwataseba" describe either cherry blossoms or maple leaves.

74. KKS 283, 284 (V, Autumn 2).

Although his syntax (ending with a noun) is characteristic of the *Shinkokin* style, his only other new contribution to an old figure is the word "bury," for which he is criticized. However, the group praised the overall structure (*sugata*) of the poem, apparently appreciating the way in which he blended two allusions, using a pseudo-*Kokin* locution (the *rasi* to speculate as to a cause-and-effect relationship in some observed natural phenomenon) to contemporary effect. (I am less convinced than they were.) What this round does show about Ietaka is his skill at allusion, his fondness for "grand" (*take*) locations, and his preference for "objective" description.[75]

Unfortunately, Teika was apparently serious when he claimed in *Meigetsuki* that he took up the brush only half-heartedly when assigned to write the judgment comments for the Kasuga contest. However lively the discussions may have (must have?) been, most of the judgment remarks are, as in the examples above, no more than a line or so long and provide little detail. In fact, the judgments get shorter as the contest progresses, as if Teika were getting tired of writing. Nevertheless, a few rounds provide some insight into the standards being applied to the poems.

The first example shows some of the things the group was *not* looking for in a poem:

Round 9: Fallen Leaves

Left, Lady Echizen

Sasite yuku
miti mo sariafezu
Mikasayama
momidi zo nusa to
tirimagafikeru

Unable to enter
The road I'd aimed to travel down—
For here on Mount Mikasa
Maples leaves and prayer strips
Scatter, mingled in confusion.

Right, Lady Shimotsuke, Win

Siguretutu
sode mo fosiafezu
asibiki no
yama no ko no fa ni
arasi fuku koro

Winter rains keep falling,
And my sleeves cannot dry,
As through leaves on trees
In the foot-weary mountains
Storm winds blow.[76]

---

75. In his *Go-Toba-In no onkuden*, Go-Toba wrote that "one sees (in Ietaka's poetry) grandeur and noteworthy feeling" (*take mo ari, kokoro mo mezurashiku miyu*); see Hisamatsu and Nishio, *Karonshū nōgakuronshū*, p. 147.

76. *SKKS* 563 (VI, Winter).

Judgment: "(The road) I'd aimed to travel down" (sasite yuku) *is not exactly a perfect opening, and* "prayer strips scatter, mingled in confusion" (nusa to tirimagafu) *sounds old-fashioned. In the Right poem, the expression* "leaves on trees in the foot-weary mountains" (asibiki no yama no ko no fa) *has loftiness, and so the poem was awarded the Win.*

I confess I wonder why a reference to falling prayer strips and leaves is "old-fashioned" sounding whereas one to a brocade of maple leaves on the Tatsuta River is not, or why a reference to Kasuga Shrine on Mount Mikasa has no "loftiness" worth noting, whereas one to "foot-weary mountains" does. True, three poems in a row in *Kokinshū* use the figure of "prayer strips and maple leaves," but as we have seen, the figure of the maple-leaf brocade is no less thoroughly explored.[77] In fact, a *Kokinshū* travel poem by Michizane combines both images and is deemed as an example of *taketakashi* in *Teika jittei*.[78] Clearly, frequency of use in the past alone does not render an expression old-fashioned. But what does? Regarding the second problem, I am equally baffled. Not only is any shrine reference at least a candidate for *taketakashi* status, but this is the Kasuga Shrine itself that Echizen depicts. Furthermore, no mention of Mount Mikasa can escape the shadow of Abe no Nakamaro's (701–70) poem that opens the Travel chapter of *Kokinshū*, and which also graces Teika's *Kindai shūka*, the prototype for *Hyakunin isshu*:

Ama no fara	As I gaze
furisake mireba	Across the vast skies
Kasuga naru	Is that not the very moon
Mikasa no yama ni	I once saw emerging
idesi tuki kamo	From behind Mount Mikasa, at Kasuga?[79]

This poem seems the very essence of *take*. As mentioned in the discussion of *taketakashi* in Chapter 4, nighttime, an upward-looking line of sight, and a large scale were elements that *taketakaki* poems seem to share. However, recall that an allusion to Hitomaro's *Asibiki no* poem also helped Jien earn

---

77. The prayer strip and maple leaf image appears in *KKS* 298–300 (V, Autumn 2). As for the maple-leaf brocade image, in addition to *KKS* 283 cited above, it also appears in *KKS* 291, 296, and 297.

78. *Kono tabi fa / nusa mo toriafezu / tamukeyama / momidi no nisiki / kami no mani mani*— "On this trip I came / Unable to offer prayer strips / At the mountain shrine— / Instead this brocade of maples leaves / Might be to the gods' liking" (*KKS* 420 [IX, Travel]). It appears in the "Lofty Style" section of *Teika jittei* (Sasaki Nobutsuna, *Nihon kagaku taikei*, 4: 366).

79. *KKS* 406 (XI, Travel).

praise for his poem as *taketakaku* in the *Minasedono koi jūgoshu uta-awase*, and this may be what is behind the judgment that Shimotsuke's poem has "loftiness." In any case, the participants in the contest knew what they were looking for, and as long as some of their reasoning remains opaque, one needs to continue studying.

A final round shows two fine examples of the *Shinkokin* style. It is interesting how the group decides between them:

Round 5: Moon at Dawn

Left, Michiteru, Win

    Ama no gafa / The River of Heaven
    fayaki nagare wo / Its rapid flow
    yuku tuki no / Provides no anchoring place
    yodomu tomo naki / For the moon that rides along it,
    sinonome no sora / And into the dawning sky.

Right, Kintsugu

    Yasurafi no / Lingering,
    kage sadamaranu / Its light uncertain
    ama no to ni / In the sky above
    fonobono akuru / Which brightens slowly, faintly—
    sinonome no tuki / Moon at dawn.

Judgment: Although the Right poem possesses depth and charm, the Left poem shows a firm, forward-pressing diction that seems to make it a better poem, and so it was awarded the Win.

The "depth and charm" of Kintsugu's poem comes from its suggestion, although a nature poem, of a lover reluctantly leaving at dawn—he "lingers" (*yasurafi*), not wanting to leave, yet she fears he is "uncertain" (*sadamaranu*), but the time for parting grows nearer and nearer. The fourth line (*fonobono akuru*) also recalls the famous episode in *Ise monogatari* in which the lover returns one year later to the house, now empty, where he had last met his love and spends the night alone on the veranda gazing at the moon, before "returning in tears as the sky brightened slowly" (*fonobono akuru ni nakunaku kaerinikeri*).[80] A lovely poem, but on this night it could not compete with the force of Michiteru's piece. What the group liked is that the diction is as inevitable and forward-moving as the celestial motion it describes (not even the moon is a match for the grander cycles of heaven!).

---

80. Sakakura et al., *Taketori monogatari, Ise monogatari, Yamato monogatari*, pp. 112–13.

As noted above, one of the most important facts about the Kasuga contest is that fourteen of its poems were selected for *Shinkokinshū*. As Ariyoshi points out, given that twelve of the fourteen poems won their respective round (the other two tied) and that eight of the winning poems also earned letters of praise, this contest probably comes as close as any other event in reflecting the *Shinkokin* (or, perhaps more to the point, Go-Toba's) taste.[81] But we know that the classification process was well under way by this time, and it must have been difficult to fit these poems into the carefully integrated scheme of *Shinkokinshū*. Perhaps this explains why they tend to be clustered together. Seven of them appear in a row in the Winter chapter, and three more are grouped together in one of the Miscellaneous chapters.[82]

The Kasuga contest exhausted Teika. He stayed in bed as long as he could the next day and then went to the palace and received instructions on how to present the poems at the Kasuga Shrine, which he did two days later.[83]

One other poetry event in 1204 needs to be looked at. Now known as the *Kitano no miya no uta-awase*, its origins are obscure. Minegishi Yoshiaki claims that it was held at Kitano Shrine and sponsored by Emperor Tsuchimikado but cites no source for this.[84] Ariyoshi notes that Teika made mention of an impromptu, three-topic poetry "challenge" held after the formal presentation of the Kasuga contest poems and surmises that the poems from this event were subsequently put into contest form and submitted to Kitano Shrine and given the name *Kitano no miya no uta-awase*.[85] It is a plausible the-

---

81. Ariyoshi, *Shinkokin wakashū no kenkyū: kiban to kōsei*, pp. 223–24. He further argues that the two exceptions—the two Tie poems—are problematic. One was Yoshitsune's entry against Go-Toba in the Moon at Dawn round, and it was the only Tie Yoshitsune managed, against two losses. Ariyoshi argues, as I do below, that even group judgments favored imperial poets, and a Tie here, especially given the favorable comments made in the judgment itself, amounts to a Win. The other Tie, in the Fallen Leaves round, between Michitomo and Ariie, is also uncertain since the mark on the round has it a Tie, but the judgment remarks end with the comment "A Win is awarded to the . . . Right," that is, Ariie's poem. However, Ariyoshi and the editors of *Shinpen kokka taikan* (5: 1457) believe that a miscopy has occurred in the judgment remarks and the round is, in fact, a Tie, because both poems are equally good.

82. The first group are numbered 559–65 (VI, Winter), and the second set 1545–47 (XVI, Miscellaneous 1).

83. *Meigetsuki*, Genkyū 1/xi/11–13, 1: 387–88.

84. Minegishi, *Uta-awase no kenkyū*, p. 237.

85. Ariyoshi, *Wakabungaku jiten*, p. 137. This idea apparently came to Ariyoshi after he wrote his *Shinkokin wakashū no kenkyū; kiban to kōsei* since he makes no such speculation in that earlier volume.

sis. According to Teika, each poet submitted three poems, one on each of three topics, although he does not say how many people are involved. The texts of the Kitano contest have ten poets (all of whom participated in the Kasuga contest) and fifteen rounds, but since each poet submitted only three poems, the total works out.[86] The one problem I can see with this theory is that our texts of the Kitano contest show it to have been judged by a group (*shūgihan*), whereas in *Meigetsuki* Teika seems to say that Go-Toba had him judge the contest, although "reading the poems over and affixing the judgment marks" may simply mean that he recited the poems for the Retired Emperor and then affixed the judgment marks that the group had awarded. All in all, given the lack of evidence in *Meigetsuki* for any other contest around this time, Ariyoshi's theory seems tenable.

At any rate, the topics for the Kitano contest are Early Winter Rains, Hidden Love, and—an unusual one for such a contest—Travel. Of the four poems from this contest that were picked for *Shinkokinshū*, three are on Travel and are grouped together in the anthology.[87] Perhaps, as Ariyoshi speculates, the classification process had revealed a need for some contemporary poems on Travel, and Go-Toba ordered the topic.[88] One of the *Shinkokinshū* poems is by Ienaga:

Round 14: Travel

Left, Ariie

Nagamekosi	I watch it cross the sky—
tuki zo fedaturu	That moon that has emerged
miyako idete	From the capital I left behind—
ikufe no yama no	Shining on white snow
mine no sirayuki	Over how many mountain peaks.

Right, Ienaga, Win

Kefu fa mata	Again today,
siranu nofara ni	Over unknown fields and plains
yukikurenu	Have I come now at dusk—

---

86. The two readily available texts for the contest are GR 194 (12: 399–401), which is corrupt, and *Shinpen kokka taikan*, 5:201, pp. 519–20. The ten poets were Go-Toba (assuming *gyosei* refers to him, although Minegishi believes it means Tsuchimikado), Yoshitsune, Michitomo, Shimotsuke, Ariie, Teika, Ietaka, Masatsune, Ienaga, and Hideyoshi.

87. *SKKS* 954–956 (X, Travel).

88. Ariyoshi, *Shinkokin wakashū no kenkyū: kiban to kōsei*, p. 240.

| idure no yama ka | From beyond which mountaintop |
| tuki fa iduramu. | Will the moon emerge tonight?[89] |

Judgment: Although the Left poem is excellent, the Win must be awarded to the lines "from beyond which mountaintop."

Although Ariie's poem uses diction more typical of the *Shinkokin* style (and for that he was praised), the weariness, even confusion, suggested by Ienaga's "from beyond which mountaintop / will the moon emerge tonight?" wins the group's approval, presumably because it captures so well the feeling of a journey.

We have no record of who presented these poems to the Kitano Shrine or when. But with this, the year ended as far as public poetry events go. But private lives were another matter.

The honor of delivering the contest poems from the Kasuga event to Kasuga Shrine might have lingered with Teika longer, but on the 26th of the Eleventh Month he received bad news in a message from his brother Nariie. Teika himself had been quite ill for several weeks, but it seemed that now his father, Shunzei, was dangerously sick. Teika described his reaction:[90]

I was dumbfounded and rushed off to his house to tend to him. . . . When I arrived, he was demanding: "I want to go immediately to the Hosshō-ji Temple.[91] No one else must know about this. Get me there quickly."

His condition appeared fearfully bad. He was running a high fever, and the right half of his face was extremely swollen. They told me that right after he fell into this state, he stopped eating and drinking. Under the circumstances, it did not seem like a good idea to make him travel a long way, but it was difficult to counter his orders. . . .

Since I was unable to ride with him in the carriage, I returned home just before it

---

89. *SKKS* 956 (X, Travel).

90. The following sections are in *Meigetsuki*, 5: 390–94. In all the entries surrounding Shunzei's final illness and death, I am indebted to the readings and annotations suggested by Imagawa Fumio (*Meigetsukishō*, pp. 157–63), although I did not always follow the former, and because of his abridgements, he did not cover all the sections I deal with here. I also made reference to Ishida Yoshisada's readings and commentary in a section entitled "Shunzei Shūenki" (A journal of Shunzei's last days) in his *Shinkokin sekai to chūsei bungaku*, 2: 18–30.

91. Hosshō-ji (the modern pronunciation; it seems to have been pronounced Hōshō-ji in Shunzei's time), which still exists in the Higashiyama Ward of Kyoto, was the family temple for the Kujō branch of the Fujiwara. Kanezane's father, Tadamichi, retired there, as did Kanezane himself. As distant relatives and retainers of the Kujō house, the Mikohidari clan, Shunzei's branch, were also affiliated with it.

got light. I heard that he was to arrive at Hosshō-ji around mid-morning, and so I left my house and hurried over to his Kujō residence[92] to pick up my sister, Ken no Gozen, and together we went to Hosshō-ji. Since Father had just arrived, we went over to see him. The trip had indeed been hard on him, and he was hardly aware of his surroundings. With the help of one of his favored young servants, we lifted him down from the carriage. One of his ladies had also been in the carriage with Father and the young man. My sister and I together sat him up. The temple hall was quite dilapidated, and unbearably cold and drafty.... Finally the cold was too much for me to take in my own sick condition, and I had to leave. I spent the night at the Kujō residence and left father in the care of my sisters.[93]

Of course, Teika returned as soon as he could the next morning. Shunzei seemed a little better than the day before and wanted to talk. It turns out he was hoping to give Teika more instruction in waka! "But," Teika wrote, "He still could not eat or drink, and his face was still swollen." Visitors came, among them Michitomo and his estranged wife, Shunzei no Musume, who arrived together, much to Teika's surprise. After nightfall, Shunzei appeared to be very uncomfortable, but as Teika's own illness was plaguing him, he again took his leave and spent the night at the Kujō residence.[94]

The Meigetsuki entry for the 28th is as bleak as Shunzei's prospects:

It rained all day without stopping. In the morning, I went to Hosshō-ji. It was very depressing in the rain. Father's condition was the same. He was in a lot of pain today and seemed unable to eat. The prognosis was not good at all. He was in agony throughout the day. At nightfall, I once again left and stayed at the Kujō residence.[95]

On the 29th, Teika was summoned by Kanezane (how long since we have heard his name!) to the temple in which he now resided. Kanezane counseled him to take this opportunity to try and better understand the truth of Buddhism, and he also dispensed some practical advice on how to make Shunzei feel better. ("To ease his pain, take some hay and put it into a vessel, then add very hot water. Place his cushion on top and let it absorb the heat and steam. This is the best remedy. Give it a try.")[96]

---

92. This refers to Shunzei's house on Kujō Avenue, not to the residence of Yoshitsune and the Kujō branch.
93. *Meigetsuki*, Genkyū 1/xi/26, 1: 390.
94. Ibid., 1/xi/27, 1: 390.
95. Ibid., 1/xi/28, 1: 391.
96. Ibid., 1/xi/29, 1: 391. What I have translated as "some hay," is, literally in the original "that which horses eat" (*uma shoku suru mono*). I am not entirely sure it is not a euphemism for

When Teika arrived at Shunzei's sickroom, he learned that Shunzei had peevishly been demanding snow all day; he wanted to eat it because he was desperate for relief from his fever. They sent a servant out to the hills to find some. Later in the evening, Teika's half-brother, the priest Jōkai, arrived and gave Shunzei Buddhist vows. "I shall keep them always," Shunzei said firmly. As Teika and Jōkai were leaving (Teika was still suffering from his own discomforts and again spent the night at Kujō), the servant who had been sent out for snow arrived with some. Later in the night, a messenger awoke Teika with the news that Shunzei's cough had gotten much worse, and Teika wondered if letting him have the snow had not aggravated the cough. He nervously awaited dawn, when he could return to Shunzei's side.[97]

Finally that dawn did arrive (this citation includes a quote within a quote, which I have indented, as well as marginalia or parenthetical asides in the printed *Meigetsuki* text, which are shown here in parentheses):

Genkyū 1/xi/30. Weather fine. I had hoped to go to Father early in the morning, but before I could leave, a messenger arrived. I rushed off in great agitation. As I approached the temple, I could hear the *nenbutsu* being chanted loudly. I was told the end had since passed. When I entered the sickroom, I saw that his eyes were already closed and that the life force had passed from him. Ken no Gozen told me what had transpired:

> In the middle of the night, we gave him the snow he had been asking for. He was noticeably pleased and kept asking for more. He said, "What a relief this is! I can't tell you . . ." and he ate more. "What lovely stuff," he said. It made us all very nervous, and we hid the rest of the snow. Later on he woke us up and asked for more. He really had his heart set on it. Afterward, he fell asleep again. During this time, the priest never stopped reciting the *nenbutsu*.
>
> Toward dawn, father suddenly said, "I think it's time for me to die." Hearing this, I rushed to his side and asked, "Are you feeling worse?" He nodded. ("Then she asked him if he truly understood the 'Gateway of the Bodhisattva Sound-Observer (Kannon)' chapter of the *Lotus Sutra*, and he replied that he did, reciting some of it to her. His congestion had cleared up.")[98]

"that which horses have eaten." For that matter, I am not entirely certain horses ate *hay* in ancient Japan.

97. Ibid.

98. This refers to Chapter 25 of the *Lotus Sutra*, which Hurvitz (*Scripture of the Lotus Blossom of the Fine Dharma*, pp. 311–19) translates as "The Gateway to Everywhere of the Bodhi-

So I said to him, "Well, then, chant the *nenbutsu* and know that you will be reborn in the Western Paradise." He nodded again.

"Would you like to sit up?" I asked him, and his manner indicated that he would. So I summoned a young servant and asked him to pull father up to a sitting position. Although the young man came, he couldn't bring himself to touch father. "Help me up," father said.

In the meantime, I had returned to the other room. As the servant went to help father up, I heard your sister Enjū no Gozen mutter, "Look at his face." I hurried back into the room and saw that he was in terrible agony. I called the priest in and had him fervently chant the *nenbutsu*. Hearing the *nenbutsu*, he passed away with a peaceful look in his eyes.

As I listened to her, tears brought scant relief to my heart, and when I looked over at him and realized that life had already left him, I collapsed on the floor next to him.[99] The ladies all left the room, and with the help of the priest and the young servant, Nariyasu, we managed to place his body back up on the matting properly. (The mat was quite thick.) I brought the lamp over by his pillow, and again with the help of Nariyasu and the priest, we straightened his robes. (Apparently he had been wearing them loose and open. I did not look closely.)[100]

For the rest of the day, the family remained at Hosshō-ji, waiting for a messenger to return with Shunzei's last testament. But since he had taken ill so suddenly, they could not find any last requests, and they were left in a quandary as to how to handle the funeral. This caused them much concern.

At dawn the following morning, Teika and a few other people went to find a suitable burial site. They found the grave site of Teika's mother (and Shunzei's main wife), which had been marked by a circle of stones, and they decided that Shunzei would be laid to rest there, too. In the entry for xii/1,

---

sattva He Who Observes the Sounds of the World," or "The Gateway of the Bodhisattva Sound-Observer" for short. This chapter introduces the miraculous powers of the Bodhisattva Avalokiteśvara (Jpn. Kannon). For example, "If there is one who keeps the name of this bodhisattva He Who Observes the Sounds of the World, even if he should fall into a great fire, the fire would be unable to burn him, thanks to the imposing supernatural power of this bodhisattva" (p. 310). The reader is told that in times of peril, by "saying *Namo bodhisattvāya Avalokiteśvara* . . . by the mere calling upon his name, they shall forthwith gain deliverance" (p. 311). The similarities with Pure Land practices are obvious.

99. My reading of this sentence differs from Imagawa (*Meigetsukishō*, p. 160) here, but I am not sure either of us has it right.

100. *Meigetsuki*, Genkyū 1/xi/30, 1: 391–92.

Teika described the funeral in exhaustive, and surprisingly detached, detail, including the ritual preparation of the coffin (among other things, "the lid was put back on and nailed shut—ten nails, pounded in with a rock, just one stroke for each nail").[101] Anthropologists and historians have found this passage a gold mine of information about medieval funeral customs. The account ends with a jarring dryness: "This evening, we had been unhindered by wind and rain and were able to carry out things as planned. This made us happy, and we headed home."[102]

Other than the brief outburst of tears after hearing his sister recount Shunzei's last hours, Teika barely hinted at any emotion as he painstakingly recorded the funeral and mourning period over the next several weeks. Only the fact that he went into retreat and embarked on a round of sutra copying hints at how he felt.[103] Scholars have commented on his apparent detachment. Since elsewhere in the journal Teika proved himself to be quite capable of venting emotion even in *kanbun*, a second language for him, this detachment is not due, one assumes, to the idiom. (It should be noted, too, that this section of the diary contains more *kana* [in other words, explicit *wabun*] than virtually any other portion; this does imply that it was written more hastily. Still, even this part of the journal is predominantly *kanbun*.) Perhaps he was taking Kanezane's advice to heart and seeking a Buddhist truth in the event. Perhaps, because of Shunzei's advanced age, he had come to terms long before with the eventual loss. Maybe, as Ishida argues, he saw himself as chronicling the death of a poetry master and felt compelled for the sake of history to stand back and write dispassionately.[104] Perhaps he was, in modern parlance, "in denial." It is even possible that he had become somewhat estranged from Shunzei. After all, he had barely mentioned his father throughout the year's entries. Yet the fact that he took charge of the funeral suggests otherwise. I prefer to think that in the end Teika saved his emotions for his poetry and found solace in concentrating on every detail of the funeral. In fact, it was important that the funeral be properly chronicled, for the purpose of proving that it had been conducted in accordance with prece-

---

101. Ibid., 1/xii/1, 1: 392–94.
102. Ibid., 1: 394.
103. See, e.g., ibid., entries for Genkyū 1/xii/6, 9, 24 and 26, 1: 395, 397.
104. Ishida, *Shinkokin sekai to chūsei bungaku*, 2: 27. This is why Ishida entitles the section "Shunzei no shūenki," *shūenki* being a word that refers to the hagiographic account of a great person's death.

dent. (Yoshitsune's account of Shunzei's ninetieth-year celebration had been written in the same spirit.) Especially since there had been no last testament, the family was concerned that they do things right; Shunzei's soul, and reputation, depended on it.

It was up to Ienaga, then, to put the moving literary touches on Shunzei's passing, and once again he was up to the task:

(The ninetieth-year celebration for Shunzei had been held in) the 3rd Year of Kennin, but in winter of the following year came proof that every life must come to an end, for Shunzei passed away. Perhaps it was because he had devoted himself so singly to one thing that in the end, I hear, he died peacefully and with dignity. Ah, truly there have been few in the world as skilled in poetry as he. Indeed, once, when His Majesty had gone to Minase, he suddenly held a poetry contest with the intention of offering the resulting poems at the Wakamiya Shrine at Yahata.[105] His Highness judged the contest himself, and in one of his judgments, he wrote, "As the Lay Priest Shunzei said . . ." and cited some of Shunzei's writings. That is how much our sovereign respected Shunzei, and it seems to me quite an honor.

Still, everyone seems in accord that Shunzei's second son, Teika, is in no way inferior. And I agree, in terms of poetry, Teika is his father's equal. In the degree to which he has committed himself to the art and his level of achievement, who can see any difference between Teika and his father? In fact, we all wonder where our art would have been after Shunzei's death had it not been for his son Teika.

In the spring after Shunzei's death, because he was still in mourning, Teika could not respond to my good fortune in being promoted, but later he sent me this poem:

Siisiba ya	Oak-tree leaves—
yuki no siwore fa	Oak-dyed mourning sleeves withered,
musubofore	And left shriveled by winter snow;
faru no fikari wo	How was I to inquire about
ikaga tofubeki	The light that brightened your spring?[106]

---

105. This refers to a contest held in 1204 (Genkyū 1)/x/29, just a month before Shunzei's death (see above).

106. This translation is more explanatory than I normally prefer, but the poem relies on too much extraneous information to make sense by itself. The main "trick" of the poem is that oak leaves are used to make the dye for mourning clothes. On the surface, the poem says that snow has left the oak leaves shriveled and lifeless and not in a condition to appreciate the first light of spring. But the snow of winter points to the death in the previous winter of Shunzei, and the word *oak* suggests the leaves used to dye mourning robes, hence the second-level meaning that Teika himself, in oak-dyed mourning clothes, has been left dispirited by the death of his father and thus unable at the time to appreciate Ienaga's good fortune. (Of

My reply:

>   Sazona ge ni
>   tofanu fikazu wo
>   kazofete mo
>   oriuramesiki
>   siisiba no sode
>
>   True it is, I know,
>   No matter how many days passed
>   Without a note from you,
>   It was a sadness you could not brush away
>   From your oak-dyed mourning robes.

Whenever I write things like this, I am reminded of how unfortunate it is that Shunzei is no longer with us. Although he was old enough that such a thing was not unexpected, still parting is parting, and the feeling of loss is just the same. It is as Tsurayuki said so long ago: this world is one of separation, like the separate strands of twisted twine, and regret is inevitable.[107] More than anything, Shunzei must have regretted not being able to see the *Shinkokinshū* through to completion, and that probably made his crossing into the other world more difficult.

I recall lines from one of the poems in a 100-poem sequence Shunzei had submitted to His Majesty the year before: "How will it be when I have gone / Faded like dew in the evening!" And truly, I cannot help feeling "how desolate the garden seems" now.[108]

Unfortunately, Ienaga said nothing about Go-Toba's reaction, although it is clear from his remarks, not to mention the ninetieth-year celebration Go-Toba had sponsored the year before, that the retired sovereign held Shunzei in high esteem.

And so the 1st Year of Genkyū came to an end, without the man who not only represented the culmination of the great Heian waka tradition but also laid the groundwork for the poetic revolution that was even now in progress.

---

course, given his frustration about his own career, Teika probably had difficulty appreciating *any* promotion given to someone other than himself.)

107. Ienaga is making a tortured and not entirely accurate reference to a parting poem by Tsurayuki: *Ito ni yoru / mono naranaku ni / wakaredi no / kokorobosoku mo / omofoyuru kana*—"This road of parting / Is not like a single strand of thread / Before it's twisted into twine / And yet narrow and depressing / Is how it feels to me now" (*KKS* 415 [IX, Travel]; with the headnote "Composed on the road as he was traveling to the East"). Even Tsurayuki's original poem is a bit tortured.

108. Although Ienaga is vague on the point, the poem comes from the 100-poem sequence Shunzei submitted at the time of the so-called *Go-Toba in daisando hyakushu*, which became the basis for the *Sengohyakuban uta-awase*. This poem, which appears as the Right Poem in Round 695 (Autumn 3) of that contest (it was awarded a Tie), was also selected for *Shinkokinshū* (1559 [XVI, Miscellaneous 1]): *Arewataru / aki no nifa koso / afare nare / masite kienan / tuyu no yufugure*—"Desolate, it seems / The garden in autumn / How sad! / How will it be when I have gone / Faded like dew in the evening!"

EIGHT

Preparations Continue, Genkyū 2 (1205)

For Teika, the new year (Genkyū 2; 1205) started on a bleak note. Still in mourning for his father, he also began, on the 1st, ten days of rites to commemorate the thirteenth anniversary of his mother's death. The opening lines for the year in *Meigetsuki* say it all: "This year, we will not be putting out new blinds in our house, and all the curtains will be last year's, too. After all, who would be coming to visit that did not know our situation?"[1]

Despite the sadness that marked the end of 1204, for the rest of the court the new year got off to a more vigorous start with an elaborate event at the Kyōgoku Palace that excited a great deal of interest. It was the annual *chōkin*, or Emperor's New Year's visit to the Senior Retired Emperor (typically the emperor's father, as in this case).[2] In preparation for Emperor Tsuchimikado's call, Go-Toba went to great lengths to repair and spruce up the Kyōgoku Palace. In addition, he decided he was going to perform the *biwa* as part of the entertainment, and he drove the other members of the court to distraction practicing and making them practice with him.

The festivities were originally scheduled for the 13th, but according to Teika they were postponed because of (as far as he knew) a death on the

---

1. *Meigetsuki*, Genkyū 2/i/1, 1: 398.
2. Unless otherwise noted, the information about this imperial visit comes from Ienaga; see *IN*, pp. 190–203. Teika's account of this event is little more than a recitation of the names of those present, although he did note that six inches of snow had fallen. See *Meigetsuki*, Genkyū 2/i/19, 1: 402–3.

grounds of the Kyōgoku Palace, which rendered it ritually polluted.³ Ienaga's account of the visit reports that Go-Toba had memorized several difficult *biwa* pieces, which he performed splendidly. Indeed, his *biwa* instructor, Nijō Sadasuke (1163–1227), remarked at the time that Go-Toba would not be out of place performing at even the most formal of occasions. Leaving aside the hyperbole, Ienaga does remind us of an important fact: Go-Toba was getting older and wiser. He compared Go-Toba's performance on the *biwa* to one he had given nine years earlier on the flute and wrote: "At that time, since he was, after all, still young, he was not as dedicated to the art as he was later to become. On this occasion [the 1205 concert] because he was older and had many more life experiences in him, naturally he showed more depth."⁴ In the end, lineage was not, after all, everything—a surprising observation from Ienaga.

Then Ienaga offers a vision of the day's events as only he can:

The visit was on the 19th day of the First Month. It had snowed heavily, to the point that it made the parade of the guards in the courtyard rather difficult. It was quite dazzling to see them there lined up, struggling to brush the snow away. As musicians played softly in the garden, the attendant in charge of announcing the hour sounded his gong as if in harmony. I can even still see in my mind's eye the Minor Counselor brushing away snow with the handbell he was supposed to ring to announce the imperial presence. The Crown Prince was present, too; so we were witness to three generations of the imperial line. It seemed as though the majesty of the imperial house had never shone so brightly as it did this day.

The imperial performance began after sundown. Dancers, musicians, and others were crowded into the outer corridor (*hirobisashi*) creating a stir of excitement. The musicians:

His Majesty on the lute (*biwa*)
Prime Minister Yoshitsune on the Japanese koto (*wagon*)
Minister of the Left Iezane on the reed pipes (*shō*)
Major Captain of the Right Tadatsune on the thirteen-stringed koto (*sō*)
The Crown Prince's Steward Kintsugu beat time (*hyōshi*)
The Empress's Steward Sanenori on the flute (*fue*)
Consultant and Gentleman-in-Waiting Chikayoshi on flageolet (*hichiriki*)
Lord Arimasa sang the lyrics

---

3. *Meigetsuki*, Genkyū 2/i/12, 1: 402.
4. See *IN*, p. 193. The earlier performance was at a *chōkin* visit that Go-Toba, then emperor, paid on his mother, Shichijō no In, in Kenkyū 8 (1197)/iv/22; see *IN*, p. 195.

His Majesty had chosen only those recognized as the most talented on their respective instruments. The Nijō Middle Counselor Sadasuke, who had taught His Majesty the *biwa*, was rewarded by having his son, Kanenobu, granted the title of Biwa Master. He must have felt that all those years of devotion to his art were now bearing fruit. Yet to be truthful, Sadasuke's was not an old *biwa* family of standing, and there likely were more than a few people who resented the honor bestowed on him.[5]

Once again, Ienaga packed a great deal into a brief narrative. The opening passage is a brilliant (literally!) mix of sight and sound in counterpoint: a brightly lit, snow-covered parade of guards (the reader needs to supply the colorful uniforms, as Ienaga's reader would have) punctuated by music and gongs, echoed by the incidental tinkle of a handbell as its owner uses it to brush away the snow. The scene is dazzling, as it should be since at its center sit three members of the imperial line, Retired Emperor Go-Toba, Emperor Tsuchimikado, and Crown Prince Morinari, presently to become Emperor Juntoku. (It is not strictly accurate to call this "three generations" since Juntoku was Go-Toba's son, not Tsuchimikado's, but the Japanese term *yo* indicates a reign in this case.)

Then, quite suddenly, Ienaga "turns off the house lights," as it were, to prepare us for the concert to follow. The sounds in the garden earlier in the day had been incidental, yet somehow harmonious. They give way to a cacophonous commotion as onlookers ("onlisteners"?) crowd around to hear the imperial performance. In another clever turn, Ienaga wrote virtually nothing about the music itself (except who played what). Again he relied on the reader to provide it, although in fact, in the paragraphs preceding this passage (summarized above) he gave sufficient information about Go-Toba's ardent practicing and skills that the reader has plenty to build on.

He ended on an odd note, however, by describing the honor Go-Toba bestowed on his *biwa* teacher Sadasuke and then snatching that honor away by remarking that many people felt Sadasuke did not deserve it. We can take two things from this. First, it is a reminder that Go-Toba was interested more in talent than in family and that he would go out of his way to find and promote people skilled in the arts, regardless of whether they came from a lineage of repute. (In this one is reminded of Go-Shirakawa, whose fanatical devotion to *imayō* led him to ignore class boundaries in his pursuit

---

5. *IN*, pp. 197–98.

of that art.)[6] Second, that some resented Go-Toba's action hints at a phenomenon that would increasingly dominate the arts in medieval Japan, a phenomenon that runs counter to Go-Toba's attitude; namely, the notion that lineage *is* what counts and what should be rewarded. (As noted above in the matter of a political appointment, Go-Toba, too, had accepted this premise and had passed over Kamo no Chōmei for a shrine appointment and instead promoted the son of the family that had a traditional connection to that shrine. Here, however, art is the issue, not shrine management.)

In part of the passage not translated here, Ienaga also noted that in connection with this concert (whether before or after is not clear), Go-Toba brought out many vintage instruments and had even ordered Yoshitsune to bring several famed *biwa* from his family's treasure house at Uji. He had those in need of work restored. The neo-classical spirit that permeated Go-Toba's court probably helped keep many such arts alive, and of course it also manifested in the Mikohidari house, where, as noted earlier, Shunzei and Teika took much time and care collating and recopying ancient texts, a service that is still yielding dividends eight centuries later.

During this time, however, Teika was preoccupied with copying sutras rather than literary texts, and for several months *Meigetsuki* makes no mention of the classification of poems for *Shinkokinshū*, although we can assume it was continuing. Go-Toba, however, was growing impatient. On the 19th day of the Second Month, Teika arrived at the palace only to find Ienaga and several others in an uproar. Ienaga explained that Go-Toba, worried that they had fallen behind not only on the selection of poems but also on the editing and even the headnotes, wanted the Wakadokoro members to work every day.[7]

The stimulus was effective. For the next several days, Teika went to the Wakadokoro and worked all day (Ienaga often served the workers a cup of saké at the end of a hard day). On the 21st, Teika wrote, "Ietaka passed by

---

6. See Kim, *Songs to Make the Dust Dance*, p. 17.
7. *Meigetsuki*, Genkyū 2/ii/19, 1: 408. In entries during this period, the name Munenobu keeps appearing as someone working in the Wakadokoro alongside Ienaga. Taira Munenobu (1172–1232) was exiled in 1198 after a dispute with Kasuga Shrine but was brought back to Kyoto in 1201 and returned to his former rank in 1202. Although I have found no evidence to prove it, this sounds like Go-Toba's doing, and one imagines that Munenobu showed some poetic talent (perhaps a well-turned poem pleading for clemency?). He was invited to the *Shinkokinshū* presentation banquet, although he has no poems in the collection.

my front gate and stopped long enough to tell me I'd better get going right away to the Wakadokoro." Later that day, Fujiwara Chikatsune (1151–1210) showed Go-Toba the *mana* (that is, Chinese language) preface to *Shinkokinshū*. Go-Toba ordered him to show it to Yoshitsune, who suggested a few additions.[8] Yoshitsune himself had been assigned the *kana* preface.

The most specific mention we have that Go-Toba ordered the prefaces from these two men comes from the *Enkyō ryōkyō sochinjō* (Suits Between the Two Lords in the Enkyō Era), a document written about one century later by Nijō Tameyo (1250–1338) in which he disputed with Kyōgoku Tamekane (1254–1332) the particulars surrounding Emperor Fushimi's order making Tamekane the sole compiler of the imperial anthology that would become *Gyokuyōshū*. Tameyo claimed to be citing the *Meigetsuki* entry for Genkyū 2/vii/22 (translated below), in which Teika wrote that the two men had been assigned the respective prefaces and also talked about how *Shinkokinshū* got its name.[9] It is, or should be, chastening to anyone such as myself who would use such documents as *Meigetsuki* to reconstruct history that this purported entry to *Meigetsuki* cited by Tameyo does not appear in our extant texts of Teika's journal (including the *Meigetsuki shōshutsu*). There is some discussion of Yoshitsune's draft preface in the entry for iii/29, but this is quite different from the passage Tameyo cited.[10] Our extant *Meigetsuki* was passed down through Tameie and then his Reizei descendants, and there is evidence that at one point, the nun Abutsu (1222?–83), Tameie's last wife and the mother of Reizei Tamesuke (1263–1328), who founded the Reizei line, released forged documents when ordered by Retired Emperor Kameyama (1249–1305; r. 1259–74) to hand over the Mikohidari library to the Nijō house.[11] Perhaps what Tameyo was quoting comes from just such a forged work, or perhaps he or a subsequent copyist simply made a mistake. In any case, the disputes among Teika's descendants in the early fourteenth century undermined much of the careful bibliographic work Shunzei and Teika had done, as forgeries were introduced and particular copies were held

---

8. *Meigetsuki*, Genkyū 2/ii/20–21, 1: 408. Fujiwara Chikatsune served as tutor for both Go-Toba and Tsuchimikado, excelled in Chinese, and was considered by Kanezane to be the foremost Confucian scholar of his day.

9. Sasaki Nobutsuna, *Nihon kagaku taikei*, 4: 135. I am indebted for this reference to Gotō Shigeo, *Shinkokin wakashū kisōteki kenkyū*, pp. 144–45.

10. *Meigetsuki*, Genkyū 2/ii/29, 1: 416.

11. See Huey, *Kyōgoku Tamekane*, p. 28.

in secret. Textual lines for many works were considerably muddied at that time. *Meigetsuki* itself has suffered at the hands of centuries of copyists, making the new text discovered in the Reizei family library all the more valuable.[12]

In any case, the entry for ii/22 contains some interesting tidbits:

Genkyū 2/ii/22. Weather clear. At mid-morning I went to the Wakadokoro. Munenobu, Ienaga, Tomochika, and Hideyoshi were there, doing some cutting and pasting. Lord Yoshitsune stopped by. He opened up the sliding doors and watched us as we worked. He then left. Tomochika pulled out a lunchbox, in which he had some saké in a bamboo tube shaped to look like a scroll.[13] I left at sundown. Today we finished work on the Love poems and the Buddhist poems (*shakkyōka*). Since there were so many Miscellaneous poems to deal with, we decided to wait until more people showed up to help. We started work on the Shinto (*jingi*) poems.[14] But I explained to Ienaga that since I was ritually unclean [being still in mourning], I was extremely reluctant to take a hand in this chapter. There were a large number of poems attributed to gods, and it was very difficult to decide in what order these poems should be arranged. True, we had our instructions, but I felt we needed to look back through the ancient collections for examples to follow. Secretly I thought to myself that if we were simply to line up the god poems in order of the names of the gods themselves it could be a big mistake. So I kept out of it.[15]

Now that the pressure was on, the group worked surprisingly quickly and polished off six chapters (all the Love poems and the Buddhist poems) in one day. But after all, those sections were relatively easy to put together. The Miscellaneous poems in *Shinkokinshū* ended up taking three chapters, and because of the ambiguity of the category itself, the group felt it needed more time and manpower to tackle it. Most noteworthy, however, is the compilers' attitude toward the Shinto poems. Teika was diffident for personal

---

12. See note 11 to the Introduction, p. 5, for more information about this recently discovered text.

13. There is a marginal note in the text, in which the lunchbox is described as *sōshi fūryū*. I am guessing this means something along the lines of "stylish" or even "novel."

14. As noted above, for convenience I refer to *shakkyōka* as "Buddhist poems," though Morrell's "poems on Śākyamuni's Teachings" is more accurate. Similarly, I am rendering *jingika* as "Shinto poems." The term literally translates as "god poems," but as a genre it includes both poem attributed to gods, and poems about gods or poems written as petitions to them. When I use the term "god poems" in this study, I am referring to poems supposedly composed by the gods themselves.

15. *Meigetsuki*, Genkyū 2/ii/22, 1: 408.

reasons, but the whole group was hesitant, too, because they sincerely believed that a misstep in classification in this chapter could have grave consequences. No such concern was expressed with regard to the Buddhist poems. The power accorded to the Shinto poems, particularly those attributed to gods (what I have called "god poems" in the translation), was obviously closely tied to ritual, proper behavior, and even government. One is reminded that the ancient word for "government" was *matsurigoto* (originally, "the act of ritual offering"), which speaks of an intimate tie between ritual and politics. If this was an indigenous attitude, it was certainly reinforced by Confucianism, and the two became intertwined. Anecdotes like this remind us that notions of government in which ritual, art, and politics are tightly bound were still very much alive in Teika's time.

Although William LaFleur has demonstrated the important (he would say *defining*) role Buddhism played in shaping the medieval Japanese worldview, passages like this prove that Shinto notions also held enormous sway—long before they became ideological weapons in the hands of the Kokugakusha, Meiji "reformers," and twentieth-century militarists.[16] It is further interesting to note that despite the modern view that religious syncretism was the prevailing mode, Teika made a clear distinction between Buddhist and Shinto poems, and the workers at the Wakadokoro treated them as separate categories.

Within the poems and/or their headnotes, syncretism is still evident.[17] And hindsight may allow us to argue that Buddhist thought had implicitly permeated these belief systems (just as Taoist and Confucian thought, as well as Chinese folk practices, had permeated Buddhism itself and permanently altered it) so that they were what they were precisely because of it. Nevertheless, the Wakadokoro members themselves clearly made distinctions in their belief systems, and modified their behavior according to those distinctions. Their behavior, at least as recounted by Teika, toward poems

---

16. LaFleur, *The Karma of Words*, e.g., pp. ix–x. Arthur Thornhill (*Six Circles, One Dewdrop*, pp. 150–52) argues that Shinto did not mount an articulate challenge to what he calls "the Buddhist hegemony" until the mid-thirteenth century but notes that "debates" and efforts at syncretism emerge earlier, in the eleventh century.

17. For example, *SKKS* 1853 (XIX, Shinto Poems) is attributed to the *Shinto* god Tenma Tenjin (the *kami* manifestation of Sugawara Michizane), who speaks in a dream to a pilgrim at the *Buddhist* temple Anrakuji, where he was buried. And *SKKS* 1854 is attributed to one of the *Shinto* deities associated with Kasuga Shrine, composed when a new hall was being built at the adjacent *Buddhist* temple, Kōfuku-ji.

related to the *kami* showed an awe that simply did not obtain toward, say, Amida, because the gods seemed to have (and exercise) the power of life and death.

Toshiyori zuinō contains an anecdote that helps shed light on this attitude. Although Toshiyori mentioned poems associated with Buddhas and Bodhisattvas, he also wrote at length about poems associated with *kami*, including this story about Tsurayuki:

Once, riding on horseback through Izumi province, Ki no Tsurayuki passed by the shrine of the god Aridōshi. Since it was dark, he did not notice the shrine. Suddenly, his horse collapsed and died. Surprised at this turn of events, he noticed by the light of his torch the outlines of a *torii* gate. He asked aloud, "What god resides there?"

Someone replied, "He is called Aridōshi Myōjin, and he is easily offended. Perhaps you rode right past him still mounted on your horse?"

"Well, it being so dark, I had no way of knowing there was a god there, so I rode right past. What should I do now?" Tsurayuki summoned the shrine attendant and asked for advice.

The shrine attendant did not appear to be an ordinary person. "You rode right past me on horseback. What I should do is forgive you, since you did not realize what you were doing. Nonetheless, you are highly skilled in the way of poetry (*waka no michi*). If you can display your skills as you pass in front of me, I shall revive your horse. Thus speaks the god Aridōshi Myōjin!"

Tsurayuki immediately cleansed himself with water, composed a poem, wrote it on a slip of paper, and attached it to a pillar of the shrine. He then began to pray, and presently his horse rose up, shook itself off, and whinnied loudly. The shrine attendant said, "You have been forgiven," and the curse was lifted—or so one hears.

The poem:

Amagumo no	Since it was midnight
tatikasanareru	With heavy rain clouds
yofa nareba	Layered thick,
kami Aritohoshi	How was I to know as I passed
omofubeki kafa	That the god Aridōshi was there?[18]

It is fitting that this anecdote should involve Tsurayuki, since it is his *kana* preface to *Kokinshū* that formally articulates the importance of the gods to waka activities. Poetry, he claimed, "moves Heaven and Earth and elicits

---

18. Hashimoto et al., *Karonshū*, pp. 73–75. Sei Shōnagon also mentioned this story in the "Shrines" (Morris, Section 135) section of her *Pillow Book*, and it appears in somewhat different form in *Tsurayukishū* (*Shinpen kokka taikan*, 3:19, #830).

compassion from the unseen spirits and demons" (*ametsuchi wo ugokashi, me ni mienu onigami omo aware to omowase*), a sentiment echoed in slightly different form in the *mana* preface and derived ultimately from the Book of Odes (*Shi jing*).[19] In addition, Tsurayuki was (as far as extant records go) also the first in a line of waka scholars to credit the Shinto deity Susanoo no Mikoto with creating the first waka. This (as well as the remarks about the power of poetry to move the gods) became accepted as a truism by subsequent poet/scholars.[20]

In any case, the fear of death (after all, Aridōshi Myōjin can kill *and* resuscitate a horse) implicit in Teika's attitude toward the god poems was expressed explicitly a century later by Teika's descendants, Kyōgoku Tamekane and Nijō Tameyo, who, in their dispute over the compilation of the *Gyokuyōshū*, both acknowledged that violating the Way of Poetry could invite death and disaster. Furthermore, Retired Emperor Hanazono quoted Tameyo as having said of his own son, Tamefuji (1275–1324), "Tamefuji's poetry was rather unlike that of his ancestors. This is the reason for his unfortunate early death."[21]

Ipso facto, then, poems by and for the Shinto deities were to be handled carefully. Of course, there was added tension for the Wakadokoro members as they prepared *Shinkokinshū*. Go-Toba clearly favored Kumano Shrine, and presumably the compilers were concerned about making choices that the gods themselves would approve, while still respecting their patron's preferences.[22]

One also notices when reading the entries involving work in the Wakadokoro that one of the members, usually Ienaga, it seems, although here it is Tomochika, inevitably provided food and drink for the group. Obviously it was a custom, if not for all similar situations, at least for the Wakadokoro. In fact, Teika was chided on ii/20 for not having taken his turn as host the previous year (recall that he was ill and depressed and often skipped his duties in the Ninth and Tenth Months). So on the 23rd, Teika brought the feast. There is a kind of innocent glee in his account of his preparations, which take center stage in the midst of all the work on *Shinkokinshū*:

---

19. Ozawa, *Kokin wakashū*, pp. 49, 413.
20. For the Susanoo no Mikoto anecdote, see the *Kokinshū kana* preface (ibid., p. 50), and, for example, *Toshiyori zuinō* and *Korai fūteishō* in Hashimoto et al., *Karonshū*, pp. 43–44, 278.
21. See Huey, *Kyōgoku Tamekane*, pp. 164–66, and p. 156—the former is from the *Enkyō ryōkyō sochinjō*, discussed above, and the latter from *Hanazono tennō shinki*, Hanazono's diary.
22. Gotō Shigeo, *Shinkokin wakashū no kisōteki kenkyū*, p. 314–15.

Genkyū 2/ii/23. Weather clear. I had heard that there were to be Shinto rites at the Retired Emperor's palace today, so I had hoped to stay home, but about noon Ienaga announced that the rites were being postponed and that we should all show up for work. Ariie, Ietaka, and Munenobu were all at the Wakadokoro, cutting and pasting. . . .[23]

During that time I prepared food and drink, took it all to the Wakadokoro, and laid it out. When Ienaga and Kiyonori returned and saw everything, they started offering advice about the spread, telling me that we should leave it out until His Majesty had a chance to see it. I just kept silent, laying the comestibles out as carefully as I could.

Into a long, lidded box I had set out the repast as follows: I placed a tall earthenware bowl on a small, thinly planed tray. I lined the bowl with oak leaves, heaped *mirume* seaweed on it, then covered it with an oak leaf. On the oak leaf I inscribed the poem "this seaweed / with which the Sea God / adorns his head."[24] On another tray I drew a picture and placed a saké cup on it. Next to that was a wine bottle, the mouth of which I had covered with crimson "bird's egg" paper and which I had filled with chicken broth instead of saké.[25] Then I took a small portable food case, filled its lid with orange blossoms, and on the paper edging around its rim etched the poem "scent of sleeves of someone from my past" with a wooden stylus.[26] Under the orange-blossom-lined lid, I divided the inside of the case into three compartments and filled them with six varieties of sweets. I took another small portable food case

---

23. I omit here Teika's description of a series of social visits Go-Toba was paying that day.

24. This is from *Ise monogatari*, Episode 87, in which a lady offered her guests seaweed gathered from the shore that morning after a storm. She covered the delicacy with an oak leaf on which she had written the following poem: *Watatumi no / kazasi ni sasu to / ifafu mo mo / kimi ga tame nifa / osimazarikeri*—"This seaweed / With which the Sea God / Adorns his head / He now offers up to you / Quite without regret, it seems."

25. "Bird's egg" paper (*usuyō* or *tori no kogami*) was a high-quality paper made of *ganpi* (campion) bark, mulberry, and *mitsumata* (edgeworthia) bark. Smooth, finely textured, with a shiny surface, it came into vogue in the Kamakura period. It would seem that Teika, following the notion of *oyako* (parent/child, here chicken/egg) is playing off the name of the paper by putting chicken broth instead of saké into the bottle. *Oyakozuki* was also an alternative colloquial term for the First and Second Months of the year, and the action described here took place in the Second Month. Furthermore, the fact that the characters used to write *ganpi*, the bark from which the paper was made, literally mean "goose skin" might have added to the wordplay.

26. What I have called "portable food case" is a *hokai*, a kind of three-legged stand used to carry food from the preparation area to where it was being served.

The poem is *Satuki matu / fanatatibana no / ka wo kageba / mukasi no fito no / sode no ka zo suru*—"When I smell / The fragrance of orange blossoms in / This Fifth Month, long-awaited / What comes to me is the scent / Of sleeves of someone from my past" (*KKS* 139; III, Summer).

and lined its lid with *hijiki* seaweed and added the poem "a sleeve as our bedding."[27] Inside that case, I arranged six varieties of fish and fowl like the sweets. I placed a spray of wisteria blossoms in a blue-green porcelain saké bottle, the mouth of which I had left uncovered. (I secured it with string. The branch tendrils were quite long.) Then I filled the bottle with saké. Next I folded some heavy crepe paper (it had a design on the bottom) like a formal letter and placed chopsticks inside. On the outside of the paper I wrote the phrase "Musashi stirrups."[28] Around the outside edge of the tray, I arranged rice and then covered it with decorative rice cakes so that one could not see it. After I got all this arranged, I packed saké cups around it tightly and then set it out in a quiet corner and left it there. The whole idea was inspired by *The Tales of Ise*.

After dark, we finished the first section of Miscellaneous poems; then everyone went his separate way.[29]

This passage provides proof, if any more were needed, of the role that waka in general and *Ise monogatari* in particular, played in many arts. We can also see the basic elements of elegant play that make up *fūryū* or *suki*. It is particularly interesting that Teika made no mention at all in this entry of anyone actually ingesting this feast. He seems to have set it out for Go-Toba's aesthetic enjoyment. In any case, two days later he learns that Go-Toba had appreciated the spread.[30] If *Masukagami* is to be believed, Go-Toba had a special appreciation for elegant meals. In the "Odoronoshita" chapter, he serves some young courtiers a summer meal at Minase, comments on how the situation reminds him of a scene from *The Tale of Genji*, and rewards a quick-witted courtier who recognizes the allusion.[31]

---

27. These lines are from Episode 3 of *Ise monogatari* in which someone sends a bit of *hijiki* (*fiziki*), a kind of edible seaweed, to his lover, with this poem: *Omofi araba / mugura no yado ni / ne mo sinan / fizikimono nifa / sode wo situtu mo*—"If you love me / I should like to sleep with you / Even in a weed-choked hut / Using our sleeves / Like a bed of sea grasses." The verse puns on the two meanings of *hijiki*—the seaweed and bedding.

28. This is a reference to *Ise monogatari*, Episode 13, in which a man sends a letter to a woman he has been cheating on. On the outside of the letter, he writes the phrase *musasi abumi* (Musashi stirrups—a kind of stirrup made in the province of Musashi), which, because of pillow word associations, suggests that despite his unfaithfulness, he still loves her. Unlike the previous two allusions, there seems to be no direct connection between this one and the contents of the tray. Perhaps Teika's fashioning of a mock love letter is simply meant to call to mind the courtly elegance of Narihira's approach to love.

29. *Meigetsuki*, Genkyū 2/ii/23, 1: 408–9.

30. Ibid., 2/ii/25, 1: 409.

31. Iwasa et al., *Jinnō shōtōki Masukagami*, pp. 260–61.

The pressure to complete the project appeared to be taking its toll on the compilers. On the 26th of the Second Month, Teika wrote: "We went back over the last Miscellaneous book again, and we also made a little progress editing the first two Love books. People were in noticeably bad humor. The Love section needs to be especially fine, but there were so many poems to work with that we threw caution to the wind in our haste. Before we knew it, the day was over." Later in the same entry, Teika reported that Ienaga had received instructions from Go-Toba on how to handle the god poems in the Shinto section. The Retired Emperor, concerned that listing the poems following the rank-order of the gods would slight the Kumano deity, advised that the god poems be placed in seasonal order, and this is, in fact, how these poems end up being listed in *Shinkokinshū*, although only the first five of the total of thirteen contain season words.[32] Resorting to seasonal order absolved everyone of having to rank the gods and risk offending such among them who might be as touchy as Aridōshi Myōjin.

The next day, Go-Toba hinted even more strongly that he was growing impatient. Through Ienaga he asked the Wakadokoro members if there were anything he could look at yet. So they continued their editing.[33]

Later that evening, Teika's half-brother Takanobu died. Although a member of the Wakadokoro and a prolific poet, he is rarely mentioned in the *Meigetsuki* entries during this period and may have been ill for some time. However, Teika claimed that he was not even aware that Takanobu had been sick. Takanobu, like Kujō Kanezane, had become a disciple of Hōnen and had taken the tonsure three years earlier and the Buddhist name Kaishin. He turned his attention toward portraiture, for which he and his descendants became famous. Teika was told that Takanobu died most nobly, "chanting the *nenbutsu* in strong voice, dressed in white, holding on to the five-colored silk cord."[34] Perhaps because the project was near completion, Go-Toba did not replace Takanobu on the Wakadokoro.

Increasingly, Go-Toba seemed to be taking matters into his own hands. On the 2nd of the Third Month, he asked the Wakadokoro for a count of how many poems had been included from contemporary poets. As a count was being provided, Teika set about revising the headnotes in one of the books because, he muttered, "a certain person" (he did not name names, but

---

32. *Meigetsuki*, Genkyū 2/ii/26, 1: 409–10.
33. Ibid., 2/ii/27, 1: 410.
34. Ibid., 2/ii/28, 1: 410.

from later entries in *Meigetsuki*, as cited below, I would guess Michitomo) had made too many errors. Later in the day, Go-Toba announced that too many of the books began with poems by deceased writers. He asked that one poem each by Teika, Ietaka, and Shunzei no Musume be placed at the head of a book (*maki no tō*). Consequently, the compilers began the Autumn 2 book with a poem by Ietaka, the Love 2 book with one by Shunzei no Musume, and the Love 5 book with a Teika verse.[35] At this stage of the process, Teika reported that the collection contained more than forty of his poems and more than twenty of Ietaka's.[36] Since the *Shinkokinshū* as we know it has forty-six poems by Teika and forty-three by Ietaka, it appears that the process still had some way to go. Over the next few days, the Wakadokoro members set about revising the headnotes for the poems and preparing the list of contents (*mokuroku*) for the collection, which they sent along with a draft of the whole collection to Go-Toba. The Retired Emperor immediately sent back suggestions, and work continued.[37]

On the 9th day of the Third Month, Go-Toba, apparently still unsatisfied with the contemporary poetry in the collection, ordered that Teika submit twenty poems that he considered his best (*jisanka*). The sovereign did not intend, he said, to add any more poems to the anthology, but he wanted to make some substitutions.[38] The next day, through Ienaga, he asked for fifteen new poems, but Teika balked. "I can't come up with that many. I'll submit ten," the poet replied. He subsequently learned that two of the ten were added to the collection.[39]

---

35. Ienaga discussed Ietaka's poem in a passage cited below.
36. *Meigetsuki*, Genkyū 2/iii/2, 1: 410.
37. Ibid., 2/iii/2–8, 1: 410–11.
38. Ibid., 2/iii/9, 1: 411. It is not clear whether Go-Toba made the same request of anyone else.
39. Ibid., 2/iii/10, 1: 411. It is not entirely clear whether the two requests from Go-Toba were different (that is, the first order was for a selection of twenty pre-existing poems that Teika considered his best work, and the second for fifteen new poems), or whether the second request was just a reminder. Ariyoshi (*Shinkokin wakashū no kenkyū: kiban to kōsei*, p. 560) seems to think it is the latter, although I believe it is more likely the former, since on the 9th, Teika was asked to "*select* and submit twenty 'self-pride' poems" (*jisanka nijisshu erabisusumubeshi*—the term *jisanka* in other contexts usually refers to a selection of existing poems), whereas on the 10th he is told to "*write* and submit fifteen poems" (*uta jūgoshu kakisusumubeki yoshi*). There is still some ambiguity here since the verb in the second case is not *yomu* (to compose), which would be clearer, but rather *kaku* (to write), which might simply mean to "copy" the favorite poems.

While the Wakadokoro members were busy at the office, Go-Toba was equally busy outside it. Not all of his activities were quite so serious (he sponsored cockfights at the palace on the 3rd, went hunting on the 5th, and was entertained with dancing on the 13th and 14th as part of a festival). Yet he also visited the Iwashimizu and Kamo Shrines on the 12th and the Hie Shrine on the 13th, and these visits may have been for the purpose of seeking the gods' favor for the anthology since at Hie Go-Toba formally offered up thirty poems. (Masatsune was honored as the Imperial Messenger.)[40] Three of these imperial poems were subsequently selected for *Shinkokinshū*.[41]

The phenomenon of offering poems to the gods is the flip side of the compilers' fears regarding the god poems. As the Aridōshi Myōjin story demonstrates, poetry can *revive* as well as harm. It is beyond the scope of this book to attempt to chronicle the practice of offering waka to shrines, but several instances of it are cited here. (Go-Toba does it to obtain divine help for *Shinkokinshū*; Teika did it back at the time of the *Shōdo hyakushu* of 1200, when he realized how important that poetry submission could be to his career.[42] In addition, Teika and several others, as discussed in the next chapter, offer a formal petition to Sumiyoshi to ensure their success at the *Keishō jishin no uta-awase* in 1206. As noted below, Go-Toba also offers poems to Kitano Shrine to pray for rain.) In any case, on the 16th, Teika returned to the Wakadokoro and found that four of his poems had been removed, and two new ones (the verses mentioned on the 10th, above) added, giving him a total of 41 (five short of the number in the current version of the *Shinkokinshū*).[43]

The *Meigetsuki* entry for iii/18 contains several items of note.[44] In the first part of the entry, we see, yet more evidence of how prominent a role Go-Toba was playing in the process. (One can imagine how frustrating it sometimes must have been for the members to spend all day editing and working while Go-Toba was—to put it charitably—otherwise occupied, only to have the Retired Emperor undo their work later in the day.) First, he ordered that two more of his Hie poems be added and then asked that two of his

---

40. *Meigetsuki*, Genkyū 2/iii/3–14, 1: 410–12.
41. *SKKS* 2 (I, Spring 1), 581 and 614 (both VI, Winter). In the *Meigetsuki* entry for Genkyū 2/iii/16 (1: 412), Teika wrote that seven of Go-Toba's Hie poems were selected. Four of these must have been subsequently removed.
42. See Chapter 2, p. 60, and esp. note 30.
43. *Meigetsuki*, Genkyū 2/iii/16, 1: 412.
44. Ibid., 2/iii/18, 1: 412–13.

spring poems, one on the Yoshino Mountains and the other on "cherry blossom snow," be cut, presumably to keep the total constant. Teika objected to the latter request, arguing "these are two of His Majesty's finest poems and should not be taken out." Go-Toba relented, and both poems appear in the final collection.

The Yoshino Mountains poem comes first:

Miyosino no	On the peaks of Yoshino
takane no sakura	Cherry blossoms now
tirinikeri	Have begun to scatter!
arasi mo siroki	Storm winds, too, are white
faru no akebono	At dawn in spring.[45]

The "cherry blossom snow" poem was cited above and is the one Go-Toba sent to Yoshitsune when the latter was unable to join the sovereign and his courtiers in a cherry blossom–viewing excursion:[46]

Kefu dani mo	Only just today
nifa wo sakari to	The flowers in the garden bloomed
uturu fana	Full, then scattered—
kiezu fa ari tomo	Though they do not melt
yuki ka tomo miyo.	Please look on them as snow.[47]

The two poems, separated by just one verse in *Shinkokinshū* (a piece by Teika) are startlingly different in their effect. The Yoshino Mountains poem, which comes at the end of a series of six poems on mountain winds scattering cherry blossoms, is in the "lofty" (*take*) style associated with Go-Toba: grand in scale, unbounded, and primarily descriptive, although the antique setting of Yoshino and the nod, so prevalent in Shinkokin poetry, to Sei Shōnagon's "dawn in spring" ("In spring it is dawn, as the gradually whitening mountain ridge faintly brightens" are the opening lines of the *Pillow Book*) remind us that the poet is, after all, a neo-classicist, much concerned with waka's traditions. The second poem is much more clearly cut from Heian courtly cloth, with its intimate garden setting, snow seen as flakes rather

---

45. *SKKS* 133 (Spring 2). The headnote for this poem in the standard text of *Shinkokinshū* identifies it as a product of the *Saishōshitennō-in shōji* poems of the following year (discussed below). Either the extant version of *Meigetsuki* is wrong, or Go-Toba composed the poem in 1205 or earlier but chose to have it identified with the *Saishōshitennō-in* event.
46. See Chapter 6, pp. 226–30.
47. *SKKS* 135 (II, Spring 2).

than as a mass of white, and the slightest suggestion of love (as noted in the previous discussion of this poem, it alludes to a love poem by Narihira).

The second half of the entry for the 18th is worth quoting at length:

On the quiet, I took my son along with me and headed to Hosshō-ji.[48] (The circumstances were quite unsettling. I was dressed in pilgrim's white and was seeking a remedy for my failing eyes.) As I was at the northeast quadrant of my circumambulation of the temple, some young messengers came up to me and said, "Lords Tomochika and Ienaga are cross with you. You should be with them now." I replied through Tadahiro that I had some private business to attend to and would be along to the Shirakawa Villa shortly.

Just prior, I had heard that Ietaka, Masatsune, and Kiyonori had arrived at the West Gate in a roofed carriage. The two messengers came again, and this time there was no avoiding it, so I joined the party still dressed in my pilgrim whites. I was quite put out. The Awata Sanuki Governor Kanefusa was there in full mourning robes, viewing the cherry blossoms of Shirakawa, and this brought a great deal of criticism from those present. It was indeed shameful in the extreme.

The rest of us performed a circumambulation of the temple together, and then in the late afternoon sun, we sat down in a row underneath the flowers to the west of the nine-story pagoda and composed poems on three topics. The Priest Saiei was invited to join us, which he did.[49] After nightfall, our poems were read aloud (by Kiyonori) by the light of torches. And there was a bit of saké, too. Finally, we went our separate ways. I wonder if we'll be criticized for all this.[50]

No wonder Teika so often complained of being exhausted! He started the day at work in the office, had a run-in with his boss, sneaked away to take care of a medical matter, ran into his friends at a temple, and ended the day

---

48. Hosshō-ji (with the *masaru* character), founded in the eleventh century by Emperor Shirakawa and fallen into ruin by the middle of the fourteenth century, had as its main object of worship a statue of Dainichi Nyōrai (Vairocana), and was attached to the Shirakawa Villa (Shirakawa-dono). It is not to be confused with the other Hosshō-ji (with the *sei* ["gender"] character, and also read Hōshō-ji) frequently mentioned in *Meigetsuki*. This latter, discussed above in connection with Shunzei's death, was a Pure Land temple that had become the residence of tonsured scions of the Kujō house. This was where Kanezane lived between the time of his becoming a monk and his death in 1207. In this part of *Meigetsuki*, in fact, Teika refers to him as Hosshō-ji Dono (the Hosshō-ji Lord), although in later poetry collections he is often called Go-Hosshō-ji Dono (the Later Hosshō-ji Lord) to distinguish him from his father, Tadamichi, who also took his retired name from the same temple.

49. Saiei was Ienaga's brother. He had also joined the Wakadokoro poets two years earlier when they went cherry blossom viewing at the Palace; see Chapter 6, pp. 223–25.

50. *Meigetsuki*, Genkyū 2/iii/18, 1: 412–13.

drinking and singing under cherry blossoms. It must have been quite an education for young Tameie.

On the 20th, Teika received word that Go-Toba was planning a banquet (*kyōen*) to mark the completion of *Shinkokinshū*.[51] He was not at all happy about the idea. His main concern was that there was no precedent for such a thing. Go-Toba was obviously using as his model the banquets and attendant poems following lectures on the *Nihon shoki* that occurred periodically throughout the early Heian period. Participants at the banquets would compose poems making reference to the characters in *Nihon shoki*. The most famous of these banquets was held in the 6th year of Engi (906), and the fact that the Shinto Section of *Shinkokinshū*, which the Wakadokoro members had just completed and sent to Go-Toba, contained three poems from this event is seen by scholars as the germ of Go-Toba's idea to have a banquet for *Shinkokinshū*.[52] But Teika did not see this as adequate justification; he argued that the *Shinkokinshū* situation did not allow for the same type of banquet poems and could not be considered comparable. The Engi era was looked on as a kind of Golden Age of imperial rule, and some scholars have asserted that Go-Toba was hoping to imply a parallel between his own situation and that earlier time.[53] Given all the machinations we have seen so far, in the realms of both poetry and politics, there seems little doubt that by now Go-Toba was heading in a direction that would lead him to the Jōkyū War, and this reading has merit.

On the 22nd Teika went to visit Yoshitsune and learned that Go-Toba had requested the Minister to have a clean copy of *Shinkokinshū* and his *kana* preface ready by the 27th. He also wanted Yoshitsune to come up with topics for the banquet poems. Yoshitsune had protested, saying that the most he could manage would be a clean copy of the *kana* preface by that date. He had also questioned the need for poem topics. Clearly Yoshitsune, known as an expert in court precedent, was taking as dim a view as Teika toward the

---

51. For an excellent summary of the issues and Teika's position on them, as outlined in *Meigetsuki*, see Gotō Shigeo, *Shinkokin wakashū no kisōteki kenkyū*, pp. 128–33. See also *Meigetsuki*, Genkyū 2/iii/20–25, 1: 413–15.

52. For a text of the extant *Nihon shoki* poems, see *Nihongi kyōen waka*, ZGR 404, 15.1: 48–73. In this text, there are eighty-three poems by seventy-one poets. SKKS 1865–67 (XIX, Shinto) are from among these poems and are clearly identified as such in the headnote for #1865. It is also possible that Go-Toba was the one who added those poems as a kind of after-the-fact justification, but I know of no evidence one way or the other.

53. See, e.g., Gotō Shigeo, *Shinkokin wakashū no kisōteki kenkyū*, p. 128.

notion of a banquet. Later in the day, Teika heard a rumor that Go-Toba had abandoned the idea of having banquet poems composed for the occasion. Instead, there would be a formal reading of the first poem from each chapter, followed by a concert. Back at the Wakadokoro, Teika, Ietaka, and others tried to get as much done as they could; they recopied all the chapters and proofread over half of them.[54]

The next day, Teika learned that the banquet was being moved up to the 26th. Go-Toba had accepted that the *kana* preface and a full clean copy would not be ready by then and would have to be completed afterward. In the meantime, they would use the interim draft as the banquet text. Teika could not help wondering to himself about the reason for Go-Toba's haste, but he continued to do some last-minute editing of the collection.[55]

The forthrightness with which Yoshitsune rejected Go-Toba's request to complete his *Shinkokinshū*-related tasks demonstrates that the Retired Emperor was by no means omnipotent. As had emperors for centuries before him, he did need the support of the powerful families at the top of the aristocratic pyramid. He had helped the Kujō regain their position of preeminence, and Yoshitsune obviously felt comfortable there. Teika's *Meigetsuki* entry for the 24th is further proof, for on this day it is Yoshitsune, not Go-Toba, who "requests" (Teika takes it as an order) that a change be made in *Shinkokinshū*. Yoshitsune is concerned that there were no poems in the collection by the progenitor of what became the Kujō line, Fujiwara Morosuke (908–60, father of Kaneie, grandfather of Michinaga, and nine generations removed from Yoshitsune). "This," warned Yoshitsune, "could cause resentment."

Presumably, Yoshitsune was hinting that this slight might arouse Morosuke's vengeful spirit. But he was also concerned to see that his lineage got the respect it deserved. Teika, who was, after all, a family retainer of the Kujō house, passed the request/order on to Ienaga, and in the end one of Morosuke's poems was added.[56] In fact, all ten generations, including Morosuke on the one end and Yoshitsune on the other, are represented in *Shinkokinshū*. Since none of the previous three imperial anthologies (in reverse chronological order, *Senzaishū*, *Shikashū*, and *Kin'yōshū*) had included all the Kujō ancestors up to their respective dates, it would appear that the Kujō house, with the

---

54. *Meigetsuki*, Genkyū 2/iii/22, 1: 414.
55. Ibid., 2/iii/23, 1: 414.
56. *SKKS* 1180 (XIII, Love 3), a "morning after" love poem, as it turns out.

help of Go-Toba's political support and Yoshitsune's own enormous talent, had re-established itself at the very center of court politics and culture.

By now, the Wakadokoro members recognized the futility of trying to finish everything before the banquet, and after dealing with Yoshitsune's requested addition, Teika and his companions "took a look at one or two chapters, had a little food and drink, and then left."[57] Teika's state of mind by this time is pithily expressed in his entry for iii/25, the eve of the banquet: "I went to the Wakadokoro and spent the day clearing up matters. Toward evening, I left. I'm quite worn out. We haven't been able to see the collection as a whole yet. There are too many errors in it, and having so many people working on it actually makes things worse."[58]

On the night of the banquet, Teika decided not to attend, arguing that his being in mourning for his father prevented him from going, although one cannot escape the feeling that Teika did not want to go. Teika's diary entry for the day contains an ambiguous comment from Yoshitsune that may be interpreted as an order from Yoshitsune to Teika ("You must attend") or as Yoshitsune relaying to Teika the fact that Go-Toba has ordered *him* (Yoshitsune) to attend.[59] In any case, Teika stayed away. But in the entry for the next day, he wrote at great length about what he heard, and his account is not flattering. Teika had gone to Yoshitsune's home, where the Minister came home late after the banquet and went to bed. Later he recounted to Teika what had transpired.

After some hours, His Lordship awoke. It seems that His Majesty had said he could not compose any poems that night,[60] but the Minister had insisted, "That will not

---

57. *Meigetsuki*, Genkyū 2/iii/23, 1: 414–15.

58. Ibid., 2/iii/25, 1: 415.

59. See Gotō Shigeo, *Shinkokin wakashū no kisōteki kenkyū*, pp. 130–31, for a discussion of this problem. It arises because in *kanbun* Teika used the same honorifics for Yoshitsune as for Go-Toba, and when he quoted Yoshitsune in the diary, the latter also applied those same honorifics to the Retired Emperor when talking about him. So in the phrase "X ordered: 'you must attend the banquet,'—so it was ordered" (*ōsete iwaku, kyōen nao mairubeki yoshi ōseraruru*), the "X" could be Yoshitsune and the "you" could be Teika, or the "X" could be Go-Toba and the "you" could be Yoshitsune. In English, quotes and double quotes would resolve the ambiguity, but medieval *kanbun* does not provide that service.

60. Gotō Shigeo (*Shinkokin wakashū no kisōteki kenkyū*, p. 132) assumes that Go-Toba was basing his position on the fact that the imperial sponsors of the earlier poetry submissions connected to the *Nihon shoki* lectures, which were serving as Go-Toba's precedent for this event, had not themselves submitted poems.

do. Your Majesty must compose verse." His Majesty seems to have heeded the advice.

The Minister Yoshitsune was supposed to have composed two poems for the occasion but only produced one. In fact, it was not until after he had finished making a clean copy of the collection—it must have been about two in the morning—that he was able to leave for the event....[61]

The event took place at the Hiro Gosho (to the north of the Wakadokoro proper).[62] His Majesty's seat was set up at the north end of the room (partitioned off by two screens, running east/west). Two more screens were positioned running from there to the south end of the room. The higher-ranking lords were to sit in front of these screens, facing each other. The northwest corner was sectioned off by curtains of state. Infukumon-in and the Crown Prince watched from there.[63] His Lordship Yoshitsune and the former Prime Minister Yorizane (dressed in formal court robes and cap) took their places first, sat at the head of the rows, and waited there for quite a long time.

Ienaga sat just outside His Majesty's antechamber and from there relayed the imperial order summoning the assemblage to enter. Michiteru, of the Left Guards, and Michitomo, of the Right Guards, along with Takachika and Tsuneie, all dressed formally in *sokutai*, entered and took their seats.[64] At Minister Yorizane's instruction, they summoned Ienaga and Ariie to the front. Ariie took a position before the poem stand (*bundai*), which had a copy of *Shinkokinshū* placed on it, and a low, sculpted wood lampstand (*kiritōdai*) next to it. He began to read from the preface.[65] Then Lord Michitomo came up behind him and chanted the first four or five Spring poems from the collection. Afterward, the two returned to their seats.

Then each of the poets in the group offered his poem. Beginning with Tomochika, Hideyoshi, Kiyonori, Ienaga (who had a servant take his poem to the stand), Tadasada, Munenobu (Munenobu and Kiyonori had been given time off from their

---

61. There is a marginal note by Teika in the text here. It is discussed below.
62. The physical layout of the Wakadokoro and Hiro Gosho were discussed in Chapter 3, pp. 111–19.
63. Infukumon-in, the Princess Ryōshi, was a daughter of Go-Shirakawa. The Crown Prince Morinari, Go-Toba's son, was later to become the Emperor Juntoku.
64. Takachika is Fujiwara Takachika (?–1254), eldest son of Takafusa and his main wife, who was one of Kiyomori's daughters. He made a name for himself as a musician and had risen high as Major Counselor (*dainagon*), Second Rank, Senior, when he took the tonsure in 1227.
65. As happens with Ietaka and Ariie below, the first man apparently read the document quietly, in this case the preface and first few poems, checking for errors. The next man stood (or more likely sat) behind him and chanted the text out loud, after it has been confirmed by the first to be free of error. Thus together they seem to be performing the role of *kōji*, to which we have seen frequent reference in poetry contests.

duties that night), Masatsune, Chikafusa, Ietaka, Iechika, Yasusue, Tsunemichi, Ariie—one by one the gentlemen came forward.[66] His Lordship Yoshitsune did not leave his seat but had someone take his poem to the stand.

Then Ietaka was summoned forward to act as *kōji*. Ariie, at imperial command, intoned the poems out loud from behind him. Then the poets withdrew. (In both instances, the Former Prime Minister Yorizane had performed the role of *dokushi*.)

At this point, the musicians took their places. Gentlemen of the Fifth Rank brought in the instruments. Takanaka played the wooden rhythm sticks (*hyōshi*), the Grand Controller of the Right (*udaiben*) Kinsada played the lute (*biwa*), the thirteen-stringed koto (*sō*) was taken by Tsunemichi, the unfretted koto (*kin*) by Takamasa, and Lord Chikakane played the flute (*fue*). Morikane played the flageolet (*hichiriki*), and Lord Takachika played the reed pipes (*shō*). After the concert, His Majesty retired, and everyone else left. His Lordship Yoshitsune did not return to the Kujō residence until about noon.

Well, when all is said and done, what was the reason for this event? There was no precedent for it. It was too hastily conceived and therefore poorly planned. Not all the participants were proper poets. Whoever made the selections did not know what he was doing.[67]

After recording Yoshitsune's rather colorless account of the event, Teika could not resist expressing once again his own displeasure. In fact, in addition to his snide comments at the end, he added a long marginal note in which he complained bitterly that his title will be, in his mind, improperly recorded in the *Shinkokinshū* preface because he had resigned his office temporarily while in mourning for his father, and Go-Toba had not gotten around to restoring his appointment in time for the banquet. The rift between Go-Toba and Teika, which would eventually become unbridgeable, was already noticeable.

Not surprisingly, Ienaga, although hardly uncritical, has a rather warmer, vaguer recollection of the time leading up to the banquet and the banquet itself. Although he was writing memoirs, here as elsewhere in his diary he began a section as if it were in the present. However, his mistakes about the dates betray him:

---

66. I am omitting all the titles here but am including the list of names since it is interesting to note who was and was not there.

67. *Meigetsuki*, Genkyū 2/iii/27, 1: 415–16. The banquet poems themselves can be found in GR 178, 11: 423–26, under the heading *Shinkokin wakashū kyōen no waka*; and in *Shinpen kokka taikan*, 5:260, pp. 895–96.

Genkyū 2

Classification of the poems for *Shinkokin* was finished in the Fourth Month of this year.[68] His Majesty was impatient, however, and went ahead with the presentation banquet despite the copy being incomplete.[69]

From the Tenth Month of the previous year, the committee had been gathering at the Wakadokoro and from morning till sundown had worked to exhaustion, now copying, now editing—never resting.[70] And His Majesty had taken an active role in every step of the process, splitting hairs even down to the finest detail. As each of the five compilers had one by one submitted his selection of poems, His Majesty would carefully look everything over, marking this or that poem from among them as good enough for inclusion in the anthology. He then had Right Konoe Guardsman Kiyonori make a clean copy, which he inspected again and then yet again a third time. Truly, regardless of whether the writer was high-ranking or low, clever or slow, the quality of the poem came first. People of little account, even a priest from a mountain temple!—so long as they showed talent in the art of poetry, their work was not excluded. Thus, as the five compilers took the poems that His Majesty had designated and intently set about classifying them, the results were wide-ranging, indeed.

In total, there were 2,000 poems in the collection, and since His Majesty had looked them over so many times, he knew every one by heart, and it was a marvel how well he could recite them all. We had our doubts as to whether he really knew all the poems perfectly, and so he ordered us to test him: "Pick at random two or three of the chapters you have finished classifying, and read for me the first half of any poem, and I will tell you what the rest of the poem is." So we took a chapter and, hiding it from his eyes, read the beginnings of the poems. His Majesty completed each poem without mistake.

Perhaps this was to be expected. His Majesty was able to memorize poems that he had only seen two or three times. How much more deeply would he learn verses whose strengths and weaknesses he had pondered carefully after singling them out for possible inclusion in the anthology!

Since this was to be an anthology unprecedented in history, those poets who had assumed they would be included but who found themselves left out pulled every string they could. Or else they composed yet more poetry for consideration or composed flowery letters of appeal. Petitions fell upon his Majesty like rain.

---

68. The banquet, as noted above, was actually held in the Third Month.

69. As Teika noted in *Meigetsuki*, Yoshitsune had declared outright that he would not be able to finish the *kana* preface *and* complete the clean copy of the whole collection by the date set for the banquet. And in fact, he finished the clean copy the very night of the party and did not complete the *kana* preface until several days later.

70. Teika began talking about this work from the Seventh Month of Genkyū 1 (1204) rather than the Tenth.

During this time, the affairs of state were neglected. The only thing His Majesty cared about was the disposition of the anthology. Palace stewards and gentlemen in the Retired Emperor's service commented to each other about how much free time they had. One steward complained that there was nothing to do these days because nothing was happening. Troubled, His Majesty replied, "Right now, that sort of complaint falls on deaf ears, but after classification of the Shinkokinshū poems is finished, perhaps my hearing will improve," which I thought was rather an elegant reply. But none of us was inclined to lend an ear to the Retired Emperor's little joke at the time.[71]

Finally the classification process was nearing completion, and the Wakadokoro members were feeling a sense of sadness that each would soon be going his separate way. They held a poetry contest, dividing into teams of older and younger. The poems were judged by none other than the Retired Emperor himself. It was at this occasion that Lord Ietaka composed his verse "Is it because he is wet / that the stag bells, alone?," which was eventually added to Shinkokinshū.[72]

As a rule, in this collection, poems that displayed faults were not necessarily rejected. The quality of the poem took precedence. Part of the reason is that His Majesty was trying to recapture the essence of ancient poetry. For instance, there is this poem by Lord Ietaka, which has a fault:

Afu to mite	I dreamt we met
koto zo tomo naku	But it proved not to be the case
akenikeri	For now dawn breaks
fakana no yume no	And that empty dream, my only keepsake
wasuregatami ya	Of something impossible to forget.[73]

---

71. Ienaga is saying that at that time those at the Wakadokoro, who were being kept so busy by the project, had a difficult time finding humor in Go-Toba's obsession—although by the time he wrote his memoirs, he was able to take the wordplay one step further.

72. The full poem, which appears as the head verse (*maki no tō*) of the Autumn 2 book, is *Sita momidi / katu tiru yama no / yufusigure / nurete ya fitori / sika no nakuran*—"From the lower branches / Maple leaves scatter / In autumn showers on the mountain. / Is it because he's wet / That the lonely stag is belling?" (SKKS 437, V, Autumn 2). The headnote identifies this as having been written "on the topic of A Stag at Evening, at the Wakadokoro when the courtiers composed poems." This is the poem Teika referred to in his *Meigetsuki* entry for iii/2 above.

The wording in the last two lines is different in the standard Shinkokinshū version (*fitori sika no nakuran*—"the lonely stag is belling") and in Ienaga's diary, as well as several alternative textual lines of Shinkokinshū (*sika no fitori nakuran*—"the stag is belling, alone").

73. SKKS 1386 (XV, Love 5). (Line 3 in the standard *Shinkokinshū* text reads *akenu nari*—"it seems dawn has come.") Ietaka's poem alludes to KKS 635 (XII, Love 3) by Ono no Komachi: *Aki no yo mo / na nomi narikeri / afu to ifeba / koto zo tomo naku / akenuru mono wo*—"I now realize / It's not true what they say / About autumn nights / For hardly had we met / When

There must have been other examples, but I have written down only the one I can recall.

As for the banquet concert, the musicians were:[74]

Consultant and Right Grand Controller Kinsada, lute
Consultant Takachika
Jūsammi Chikataka (kane?), flute
Lord Tsunemichi, thirteen-stringed koto
Kage(Taka?)naka, rhythm sticks
Morikane, flageolet[75]

After the concert was over, each of the poets in attendance offered poems. Since some of these poets were not included in *Shinkokinshū* itself, there were people who nudged each other in criticism.[76] As for the concert itself, the *biwa* player, Kinsada, just could not seem to get in tune. How could someone who was considered such a master of that instrument have performed so poorly! After all, he had played in front of His Majesty several times before. If it had been his first time, he might have been nervous, but . . . This just wasn't right. Since the event itself was virtually without precedent, there were so many listeners packed into the garden that one could not see the ground underneath them. What must they have been saying to each other afterward? I understand that Kinsada was so dispirited by the experience that to this day no one has seen him so much as touch the *biwa*.[77]

As always, Ienaga gives us much to ponder. The bulk of the entry deals with the selection and classification process, and Ienaga's comments and anecdotes underscore what we have already learned from *Meigetsuki*—namely that it was a grueling process for the compilers (and other members of the

---

dawn now breaks, alas!" In interpreting this poem, commentators suggest that the "reputation" (*na*) of "autumn nights" is that they are long, but I am inclined to think Komachi is punning on the word *aki* ("to have one's fill"), and saying, in effect, "despite the fact that on an autumn (*aki*) night, one should be able to have one's fill (*aki*) of love, the term *aki* is just a name, with no meaning."

As for the "fault" in Ietaka's poem, Ishida and Satsukawa (*IN*, p. 219) can only surmise it is that *koto zo tomo naku* (it is really nothing) and *fakana* (empty) are synonymous and therefore display the fault known as *dōshinbyō* (literally, "the fault of identical sense").

74. The abruptness of the transition from the Ietaka anecdote to this sentence suggests to me that some part of Ienaga's diary might have been lost.

75. Again, the number of errors and omissions in this list (which I have shown using parentheses and question marks) suggests a corrupted text. See Teika's account above for a more complete list of the musicians.

76. As we have seen, Teika would have been one of the "nudgers" had he been there.

77. *IN*, pp. 211–23.

Wakadokoro, who evidently lent a good deal of support), and that Go-Toba took an active role in things. Ever so delicately, Ienaga hinted that perhaps it was too active a role. Affairs of state are neglected (one thinks of the opening of *Genji Monogatari* and in turn the Yang Guifei story, although Go-Toba's beguiling mistress was verse rather than woman), and the subjects themselves are getting restless and tired, unable even to appreciate an imperial jest.

When Ienaga turned to the banquet himself, his choice of topics is quite odd and again suggests an indirect criticism. He focused on the concert more than anything else, but what he recalled is that the *biwa* player, Fujiwara Kinsada, supposedly an accomplished one, played poorly that day and brought shame on himself—and by implication on the banquet itself. Twice Ienaga referred to others' criticism of (or at least skepticism toward) the event: first, people gossiped about the fact that some of the poets asked to contribute poems at the banquet were not good enough to have any of their work in the *Shinkokinshū* itself, and second, he wondered how the audience must have felt at Kinsada's clumsy performance.[78] He also remarked that "there are few precedents" for the event (*sono yo no koto tameshi sukunaki koto*—slightly softer than Teika's *zenrei ni arazu*, "having no precedent"), which cut both ways in the conservative imperial court. On the one hand, it is therefore risky and open to criticism, but on the other, it has the potential to be a historical first, which is what attracts the crowds to the garden. All in all, one senses that Ienaga shared Teika's jaundiced view of the whole banquet, but his forum, rank, and temperament did not permit him to express his views quite so clearly. By directing attention to the poor musical performance, he was able to belittle the entire banquet without directly attacking the poetic aspects that were so important to Go-Toba.

By some accounts, Go-Toba's banquet would seem to have been premature at best, and probably ill-advised in any case. The demands he made leading up to the event (a complete, clean copy of the collection and its prefaces) were hardly reasonable under the circumstances. His wavering even just days before the party about who would compose poems, whether there would be any at all, which parts of *Shinkokinshū* would be read out loud, and so on, must have been extremely annoying to those who were charged with organizing the proceedings. Ienaga, at least, allows us to take a charitable view of it all, though, in his depiction of Go-Toba as completely, even fa-

---

78. I agree with Ishida and Satsukawa (*IN*, p. 222) that Ienaga's remarks probably apply not just to the concert but to the entire event.

natically, devoted to the art of poetry. Go-Toba's fault, then, was that he "loved too much."

At any rate, it is indisputable that *Shinkokinshū* was *not* completed by the day of the banquet. In fact, Go-Toba was still quite dissatisfied and, soon after the party, embarked on a series of activities to further edit the collection and generate yet more and better poetry for it. Teika's diary entry for iii/28, the day after the banquet, provides some notable detail concerning the editing process:

28th. It rained all day, although toward nightfall the rain stopped and the sky cleared. Ienaga sent word that I was to go to the Wakadokoro. When I arrived, I found that he had brought along the banquet poems for us to copy. His Majesty had ordered us to have another look at the collection, and so I started going through it. In the Felicitations chapter, the poems on the First Day of the Rat (*ne no hi*) by Lords Kiyotada and Tsunenobu were too much alike, and I inserted several poems between them.[79] Likewise, among the Lament poems, two that I selected myself— one was Jōtōmon-in's reply poem to Izumi Shikibu, and the other was a poem by Suō no Naishi—were very similar.[80] When I reported these problems to His Majesty, his directive was that Tsunenobu's poem on the First Day of the Rat be taken out. However, the two Lament poems were not to be removed, but rather kept together where they were.[81]

Two points emerge here. First, in the context of association and progression within an anthology, it would seem that the line between "too much alike" and "complementary" is very fine. The first pair of poems that Teika referred to are:

Ne no fi site	It being the Day of the Rat
simeturu nobe no	Do not uproot the pretty little pine
fimekomatu	That stands in the sacred field!

---

79. On the first Day of the Rat in the New Year, the court would venture out to a specially designated area and pick young herbs and seedlings pines as part of a celebration for the long reign of the sovereign. Teika is apparently referring to poem #709 (in the current standard text of *Shinkokinshū*), by Fujiwara Kiyotada (d. 958), and #728, by Minamoto Tsunenobu (1016–97; he was Toshiyori's father). According to Gotō Shigeo (*Shinkokin wakashū no kisōteki kenkyū*, pp. 749, 751), Masatsune and Ietaka had selected Kiyotada's poem, and Teika had selected Tsunenobu's. Given that Go-Toba ordered the Tsunenobu poem to be removed (see below), it is possible that #728 is a different poem entirely, but I think not.

80. The poems in question here are numbered 776 and 777 in the current standard *Shinkokinshū*.

81. *Meigetsuki*, Genkyū 2/iii/28, 1: 416.

fikade ya tiyo no	Let us wait instead for its protective shade
kage wo matamasi	A thousand years hence.[82]
	—Fujiwara Kiyotada
Ne no fi suru	On this Day of the Rat
mikaki no uti no	Within the sacred fence
komatubara	A stand of seedling pines—
tiyo oba foka no	Can we see them as anything other than
mono to yafa miru	A sign of a thousand-year reign?[83]
	—Minamoto Tsunenobu

The similarities here are easy enough to see, yet the poem by Tsunenobu's rival, Fujiwara Michitoshi (1047–99), that immediately follows Tsunenobu's seems hardly less comparable.

Ne no fi suru	On this Day of the Rat
nobe no komatu wo	Let us transplant the seedling pine
utusiuwete	Away from the open fields
tosi no wo nagaku	So that the string of Our Majesty's years
kimi zo fikubeki	Might grow ever longer.[84]

Perhaps the point is that while the meaning of the three poems is almost the same, the first two also share structural features (*ne no fi suru*/*site*, modifier in the second line, modified noun in the third, ironic question with particle *ya* in the last section) as well as the word *tiyo* (a thousand-year reign or a thousand reigns) that make them "too much alike."

The exchange between Izumi Shikibu (976?–1027?) and Jōtōmon-in (Fujiwara Shōshi; 988–1074) laments the death of the former's daughter, Koshikibu no Naishi. Jōtōmon-in was the daughter of Michinaga and Empress (*chūgū*) of Emperor Ichijō and was served by Murasaki Shikibu, Izumi Shikibu, and Koshikibu no Naishi. The headnote explains the circumstances for the poetic exchange:

Koshikibu no Naishi had once appeared at court wearing a Chinese-style jacket with a design of dew on bush clover (*hagi*) woven into it. After the girl passed away, Jōtōmon-in inquired about the jacket, which Izumi Shikibu then sent to Her Majesty along with this poem:

---

82. *SKKS* 709 (VII, Felicitations).
83. *SKKS* 728 (VII, Felicitations).
84. *SKKS* 729 (VII, Felicitations). According to Gotō Shigeo (*Shinkokin wakashū no kisōteki kenkyū*, p. 751), this poem was selected by Teika and Ietaka.

Oku to misi	That dew which you saw
tuyu mo arikeri	Still remains here!
fakanakute	Fleeting indeed
kienisi fito wo	Was the girl who faded away—
nani ni tatofen	To what can we compare her?

—Izumi Shikibu

Omofiki ya	Could we have imagined it—
fakanaku okisi	That the fleeting dew fallen
sode no ufe no	On these sleeves
tuyu wo katami ni	Would someday become
kaken mono tofa	Our keepsake of her?[85]

—Jōtōmon-in

Izumi Shikibu's poem adheres to the exquisite logic (*kotowari*) of classical Japanese verse. If dew be the very essence of the "fleeting" (*fakanasa* [Hepburn *hakanasa*]), the phenomenon to which poets compare all things fleeting, especially human life, then what can one say about a child even more fleeting than dew? Jōtōmon-in transforms the article of clothing into a keepsake of the deceased and further notes that *any* dew—even the dew/tears she and Izumi Shikibu both shed on their sleeves—can also be in remembrance of the lost child.

Suō no Naishi (1068?–1108?) composed her poem lamenting the death of Retired Emperor Shirakawa's consort, Fujiwara Kenshi, when she saw some children collecting dew in the palace gardens on the 7th Day of the Seventh Month:

Asadifara	A field of sedge—
fakanaku okisi	The fleeting dew fallen
kusa no ufe no	On its grasses—
tuyu wo katami to	Did I ever imagine it would someday
omofikakeki ya	Be a keepsake of her?[86]

The similarities between Jōtōmon-in's poem and Suō no Naishi's are in some ways even more striking than those between Kiyotada's and Tsunenobu's, but in this case they are not enough to disqualify either poem. Yet, like Michitoshi's poem above, Suō no Naishi's verse describes a slightly different scene (in this case, an actual overgrown garden as opposed to an

---

85. *SKKS* 775–76 (VIII, Laments).
86. *SKKS* 777 (VIII, Laments).

imaginary garden scene depicted on a robe), which may have "saved" it from unacceptable redundancy. And one can hardly argue with Go-Toba's wish to keep the very moving exchange between the Empress and her lady.

The second interesting point about Teika's description of the editing process is that Go-Toba's recommendation was apparently ignored in the case of the Tsunenobu poem. However pervasive his influence was—and we have seen plenty of evidence that it was assertive—it was not absolute. Of course, it was dissatisfaction with the committee's *Shinkokinshū* that drove him to recompile it as the so-called Oki-bon during his Oki exile. But he himself eventually recognized the wisdom of his compilers on the point in question here, since he, too, seems to have left Tsunenobu's poem in his final version.[87]

For the next five years, editing continued off and on, and there are many entries in *Meigetsuki* like the one above. Teika was not always happy about the process, as his parenthetical asides in two well-known entries from 1207 reveal:

Jōgen 1 (1207)/ii/26. . . . Once again we were summoned to the Wakadokoro and given instructions regarding *Shinkokinshū*. (There seems no end to this!)

Jōgen 1 (1207)/xi/8. Weather fine. I went to the palace and, under His Majesty's orders, made yet more additions to *Shinkokinshū*. (We go back and forth all the time on which poems to include and which to remove.) Editing has become my profession, and this does nothing for my reputation.[88]

Japanese scholars have painstakingly chronicled this process, which some have called the "Editing Era" (*kiritsugi jidai*), and I will not dwell on the details here.[89] Besides, as always, Ienaga says it better than I could:

---

87. Like almost all ancient texts, the Oki-bon has survived only in numerous copies, many incomplete. It is virtually impossible to know exactly what Go-Toba himself did, but I am following Gotō (*Shinkokin wakashū no kisōteki kenkyū*, p, 941) here since he charts all the extant Oki-bon texts.

88. *Meigetsuki*, 2: 13, 47.

89. Ishida and Satsukawa (IN, pp. 225-28), for instance, cite a number of relevant *Meigetsuki* entries, although theirs is not an exhaustive list.

It was Kojima Yoshio (*Shinkokin wakashū no kenkyū, zokuhen*, pp. 69-74) who among modern scholars first articulated the process. Subsequent scholars have acknowledged and built on his work. For instance, Gotō Shigeo, *Shinkokin wakashū no kisōteki kenkyū*, devotes two lengthy chapters to the subject (pp. 167-376), although much of this involves detailed analysis of textual variants. However, in one section (pp. 168-202), he goes through each of the *Meigetsuki* entries referred to above one by one and discusses how the issues raised by Teika get played out in the "final version" (by now we should realize there is no such thing!) of *Shin-*

Well, following the banquet, there was no hurry about getting a clean copy (of *Shinkokinshū*) finished. For some time after, poems continued to be taken out and added. In fact, poems were even added from a Chinese and Japanese poem contest (*shiika-awase*) held after the presentation banquet.

Those whose poems were taken out of the collection complained bitterly. Just hearing them made me feel guilty. Some never imagined that such a thing could happen to them, and seeing the resolve [with which they set about to rectify the situation][90] was enough to soak the sleeves of even an outsider. I am sure that others felt as I did when they saw this going on. In any case, as long as the final clean copy had not been made, there was still hope, and these unfortunates left no shrine or temple unvisited as they went about offering prayers and petitions for their cause. Their fervor was quite touching.[91]

In fact, it was the clean copy Ienaga himself made in 1216 that is the basis for our modern texts of *Shinkokinshū*, although *Meigetsuki* makes no further mention of editing after 1210. The death of Yoshitsune in 1206 may have contributed to the delay since he was the one Go-Toba had originally asked to make the final copy. In any case, Ienaga's remarks about a Chinese and Japanese poem contest lead us to explore a few remaining public poetry events that contributed to *Shinkokinshū* as we know it today. There are also several private matters that will help to round out the picture.

In addition to his continual tinkering with the *Shinkokinshū* text he already had, Go-Toba evidently felt there was still something missing. Contemporary poets and styles were not yet adequately represented. To remedy this, he sponsored several large poetry events over the next few years in hopes of generating good work for the anthology. It was a pattern he had been following for more than five years.

The first of these was the Chinese and Japanese poem contest Ienaga mentions. Now known as the *Genkyū shiika-awase*, it was held on the 15th Day of the Sixth Month at Go-Toba's Itsutsuji Palace. Actually, it appears that the idea for the contest had originated with Yoshitsune several weeks earlier. In the *Meigetsuki* entry for iv/29, Teika said that after an evening of

---

kokinshū, although he is still interested primarily in textual matters and not in what all this might reveal about anyone's aesthetic vision.

90. The text is corrupt after the word *kokorozuyoku* (resolutely). I am following Ishida and Satsukawa's speculation (*IN*, pp. 224–25) as to what might be missing. It is at least clear that Ienaga was striving for two parallel sentences here ("hearing it made one feel guilty; seeing it moved one to tears").

91. *IN*, pp. 223–24.

composing and discussing Chinese verse at Yoshitsune's mansion, the Minister brought up the notion of having a contest of Chinese and Japanese verse and told Teika to set the topics and suggest participants. Teika did not think it a good idea and was not too thrilled by the way Yoshitsune dealt with it (in effect, Teika wrote, "After dumping this on us, His Lordship went to bed"). Nevertheless, he recorded his proposed topics (Spring Scenery at Waterside and Autumn Journey on a Mountain Path), which were the ones that were eventually used. Of the twenty names Teika listed as possible participants, all but two ended up in the actual event.[92]

Initially Yoshitsune had conceived of the contest as *his* private affair, but four days later Teika wrote: "Word of our Chinese/Japanese poetry contest has reached Go-Toba. Ienaga tells me that His Majesty wishes to try his hand . . . and evidently Ienaga wants to take part, too."[93] It was only a matter of time, then, before Go-Toba would begin to take control of the event. Indeed, on the 4th, when he learned that Yoshitsune would include him, Go-Toba asked (demanded?) that the event be postponed to give him time to prepare his poems. He further "recommended" that he be matched with Fujiwara Chikatsune (writer of the Chinese preface to *Shinkokinshū* and considered a master of Chinese poetry), although he believed he would lose.[94]

But all was not poetry parties and court activities. The world of urban crime was literally just outside the door. When Teika returned home that evening, he was not destined to have a restful sleep:

> I took a quick bath and lay down, but suddenly a thunderous commotion arose from Tadatsuna's house, which was next door to us on the south. I was quite startled and fearful. Someone was apparently trying to break into the house by force. I could see the light of pine torches through the latticed fence. It sounded as if someone were trying to break through the wall with a large club. The din might just as well have been coming from my own home! After a while, the noise stopped. I guess the intruders must have left. Tonight was the first time I had ever had to face such an awful thing. Truly, there's too much wrong with the world these days. Some time after the clamor had ceased, a temple bell began to ring for morning services, dispelling the spirits of the dead, but still I could not sleep.[95]

---

92. *Meigetsuki*, Genkyū 2/iv/29, 1: 422. Ariyoshi, *Shinkokin wakashū no kenkyū: kiban to kōsei*, pp. 242–44, provides a helpful summary of the various related *Meigetsuki* entries.
93. *Meigetsuki*, Genkyū 2/v/3, 1: 423.
94. Ibid.
95. Ibid.

Several days later, on the 10th day of the Fifth Month, Teika received a visit from Ienaga, who told him that Go-Toba wanted to have the Chinese/Japanese poetry contest at his palace and that since Go-Toba also wished to hear some lectures on Chinese poetry in preparation for the event, it should be postponed until the following month.[96] (Interestingly enough, though, Go-Toba spent the last part of the month at Minase, and Teika made no mention of any lectures there on Chinese poetry.)[97] On the 12th, Teika went to Yoshitsune's mansion to help plan the contest. He huffed that although *he* had been asked to make the arrangements, it was obvious that Yoshitsune already had made some decisions. However, Teika was able to persuade his patron that some of his contemplated matchups were not good ones, and Yoshitsune relented. Still, Teika was not at all pleased that he ended up being matched with Fujiwara Nagakane, perhaps because the latter was not particularly skilled, and he groused that he would not be able to write any good poems under the circumstances.[98]

The only other mention Teika made of the contest is the entry for the 13th day of the Sixth Month, where he complained of the debilitating summer heat, noted that in recent days he had been staying indoors (*chikkyo*), presumably because of his discomfort, and remarked that the contest had been scheduled for two days later. On the day of the contest, the only words entered in the *Meigetsuki* are, again, *chikkyo*, suggesting that Teika did not attend the actual event.[99]

We thus have no description of the night of the contest and now only incomplete textual evidence.[100] We do know that there were two topics chosen by Teika, thirty-eight participants, and seventy-six rounds. The Left Team, headed by Yoshitsune, composed Chinese verse (*shi*), and the Right Team, which included Go-Toba, Jien, Teika, and Ietaka, offered Japanese poems. The rounds were in fixed order, with each poet on the Left matched with the same poet on the Right for two consecutive rounds in each section (Spring and Autumn) for a total of four matchups for each pair. In the Spring section, the poets appeared in descending rank-order (starting with Yoshitsune on the Left versus Ietaka on the Right, with Go-Toba, using the

---

96. Ibid., 2/v/10, 1: 424.
97. Ibid., 2/v/22-29, 1: 424-25.
98. Ibid., 2/v/12, 1: 424.
99. Ibid., 2/vi/13 and 15, 1: 425.
100. For the cleanest extant text, see *Shinpen kokka taikan*, 5:203, pp. 523-26.

pseudonym of Chikasada, going last on his team); they then appeared in ascending order in the Autumn section (i.e., ABC, CBA), so that Yoshitsune, for example, started and ended the contest for his team.

Evidence that Chinese was still a privileged skill comes from the fact that the Left, or "Chinese," team was headed by a Chancellor / Prime Minister, followed by a Major Counselor (*dainagon*) and a Middle Counselor (*chūnagon*), whereas Ietaka, a former governor, just promoted to the Junior Fourth Rank, Lower, was the highest-ranking member of the Right team. This is somewhat misleading, since both Jien (who was "outside" the ranking system, but of the highest birth) and Go-Toba were on the Right team; still, it is quite noticeable that the waka poets are by and large a middle-ranking lot.

The contest was judged, but the extant texts do not record the name of the judge or the arguments. Judgment marks appear in most of the early rounds, but are missing entirely from the last thirteen rounds, as are the Chinese verses. The "score," although incomplete, shows seventeen Wins for the Left (Chinese verse) team, ten Wins for the Right (waka) team, twenty-two Ties, and twenty-seven rounds unmarked. The big "winners" on the waka team, with two marked wins each, were Ienaga, Dainagon no Tsubone,[101] Tango, and Masatsune—a noticeably low-ranking group. The Rokujō poets Yasusue and Rensei (Tomoie—although he was moving away from the Rokujō school) had a dismal record of four Losses, two Ties, and two rounds unmarked.

The topics (Spring Scenery at Waterside and Autumn Journey on a Mountain Path) were unusual for waka, and the Chinese air surrounding the event helped to produce some innovative verse. Eight of the poems from this event were added to *Shinkokinshū*.[102] Since only one of the rounds that contain poems added to *Shinkokinshū* shows judgment marks, we cannot tell whether these poems won or lost against the Chinese verses with which they were matched.[103] The one *Shinkokinshū* poem clearly marked as a winner was in Round Three of the Spring poems, by Michiteru:

---

101. I take this to refer to Shichijō-no-In no Dainagon, who was first discussed in Chapter 2, pp. 68–69, as one of the female poets Go-Toba "discovered." She also appeared, under the name Nyogo no Dainagon, in the *Kasuga no Yashiro uta-awase* of the year before (1204, see Chapter 7, pp. 275–87); there are three poems by her in *Shinkokinshū*.

102. See Ariyoshi, *Shinkokin wakashū no kenkyū: kiban to kōsei*, p. 540, for a list.

103. This includes four poems that appear in the portion of the text that shows judgment marks for the surrounding rounds and four poems that appear among the last thirteen rounds, all of which are missing both the Chinese verse and judgment marks.

> Misimae ya   At the banks of Mishima
> simo mo mada finu   Frost has not yet dissipated
> asi no fa ni   On reeds' tips—
> tunogumu fodo no   As though to bring them into ear
> farukaze zo fuku   A spring breeze blows.[104]

The Chinese poem it was matched with was by Fujiwara Yoshisuke:[105]

> North of the River Wei, dawn mist envelopes a file of geese.
> South of the Yangzi, spring willows enclose a fishing village.

Among the poems later appearing in *Shinkokinshū* is Go-Toba's Minase River verse, cited earlier in this book:

> Miwataseba   As I gaze out
> yamamoto kasumu   Over the Minase River, misted
> Minasegafa   At this mountain's base
> yufube fa aki to   I wonder why one ever thought
> nani omofikemu   That "evenings are for autumn."

Although, as noted above, no judgment marks remain for this round, it is probably safe to say Go-Toba's poem won over its Chinese verse match, not only because of Go-Toba's status but also because of the mundane nature of the opposing poem:

> North of the lake, south of the lake—mountains for a thousand miles.
> Coming off the lake, receding toward the lake—waves in countless folds.

Through the rest of the summer and fall, Teika mentioned several sessions of further editing and also noted that Go-Toba had solicited poems from him (and presumably others) to put together in contest form and dedicate to the Kitano Shrine as a prayer for rain.[106] In addition, he wrote at

---

104. *SKKS* 25 (I, Spring 1). Mishimae lay along the banks of the Yodo River north of present-day Osaka and was known for its reeds. This poem is an allusive variation on *GSIS* 42 (I, Spring 1), by Sone no Yoshitada: *Misimae ni / tunogumiwataru / asi no ne no / fitoyo no fodo ni / farumekinikeri*—"At the banks of Mishima / Reeds begin to sprout / All around / As though just overnight / Spring is now in the air."

105. Kujō Yoshisuke (1185–1218) was a younger half-brother of Yoshitsune (same father, Kanezane) and he rose as high as Minister of the Left, and Junior First Rank before his early death from smallpox. He was renowned as a Chinese scholar.

106. *Meigetsuki* entries referring to *Shinkokinshū* editing include Genkyū 2/*vii/24 and viii/2, 1: 430, 432–33; reference to the "rain contest" is found in the entry for Genkyū 2/vii/17, 1: 428. Poems 1669–71 in Go-Toba's personal collection appear with the headnote: "From a

length on Hōjō Tokimasa's (1138–1215) failed attempt to assassinate the Shogun Sanetomo. The latter entry conveys in some detail the increasingly tense relationship between the Court and the Bakufu and begins with the dramatic lines: "Weather clear. After cockcrow, a retainer came bursting into the house to announce: 'Warriors have gathered in front of the Retired Emperor's palace. There are colored banners everywhere!'"[107] There were no major poetry events during this period.

In the Tenth Month, Go-Toba commissioned a memorial service for Owari, the concubine who had died the year before.[108] He had a special hall built for the occasion at the Minase Villa. Ienaga, for one, was impressed by the fact that Go-Toba had still not come to terms with the loss. As he had the year before, Go-Toba exchanged a series of poems with Jien, lamenting the death of his beloved Owari. Ienaga dutifully recorded them, although unfortunately the text has been corrupted a bit over time. The extant text of his diary has only fifteen poems, but since two of Go-Toba's poems do not match any of Jien's and Jien's final poem does not match Go-Toba's, I suspect there were at least eighteen poems (nine each) in the original exchange. The poems as I think they should be matched appear in Appendix E (pp. 423–26).

Many of the poems in this exchange are quite extraordinary. The physical longing suggested in Go-Toba's poems of the year before (several of which used the rhetoric of love poetry) has given way to a deeper, more contemplative sorrow. As seen in his sixth poem in the sequence, he even allowed that his religion had begun to help him find solace—something he could not admit before:

Go-Toba's Poem

Mayofaresi	The mountain stream
yama no wogafa no	Which once was hindered
usugofori	By tenuous ice,
ima fa kakinagasu	Now flows free, rippling
nori no midunami	Waters of the Law.

---

poetry contest at Kitano Shrine in the Second Year of Genkyū, Seventh Month, 18th Day." The headnote includes a marginal notation that makes us want more: "Prayers for rain; topics provided at the contest; judged by the Regent; includes preface." Sadly, the contest text is lost.

107. *Meigetsuki*, Genkyū 2/*vii/26, 1: 430–32.

108. See Chapter 7, pp. 273–74, for a discussion of the exchange of poems between Go-Toba and Jien that was occasioned by Owari's death. See Appendix E, pp. 419–23, for the poems themselves.

Jien's Reply Poem
    Minasegafa
    tokinagasuran
    nori no midu
    yama no fiziri no
    satori narikeri

    That the Minase River
    Now flows freely,
    Like the Waters of the Law,
    Is surely because the mountain sage
    Has found enlightenment.

His last two poems are especially striking, even morbid, focusing on the smoke from the funeral pyre and the "corpse" (of course, there is none after cremation) lying under the moss and coupling these two images with, of all things, joy. These demonstrate with great force that his attachment to the physical body that was Owari had not completely faded away, although he no longer expressed his feelings in subtle, Waiting Woman figures:

Go-Toba's Poem
    Omofiiduru
    oritaku siba no
    yufukeburi
    musebu mo uresi
    wasuregatami ni

    When I recall her,
    Brushwood split and burned, its smoke
    At evening time may smother,
    Yet it brings me joy, a keepsake
    Of her, whom I cannot forget.

Jien's Reply Poem
    Omofiiduru
    oritaku siba to
    kiku karani
    tagufi sirarenu
    yufukeburi kana

    No sooner do I hear
    That brushwood split and burned
    Has brought you memories
    Than I realize how special
    That evening smoke must have been.[109]

Go-Toba's Poem
    Na fa kutinu
    koke no sita nimo
    uresi toya
    toburafu kane no
    oto wo kikuran

    Her name will not perish!
    And there, beneath evergreen moss
    She must be happy,
    Hearing the sound of the bell
    We ring in honor of her soul.

Jien's Reply Poem
    Kiku fito no
    kokoro fa sora ni
    narinu nari

    Her soul, which hears this
    Must now be soaring free—
    Such is the power

---

109. This pair of poems appears as *SKKS* 801–2 (VIII, Laments).

nodera no kane no	From the sound of the bell
oto zo kasikoki	At your rustic temple.

Jien's replies, likewise, were more indulgent than before. He seemed to feel that Go-Toba had in fact reached a higher level of spiritual understanding, and his tone was more gentle, acknowledging Go-Toba's sorrow instead of chiding him for it. Only his "Have a heart" (*kokoro are ya*) poem contains any hint of reproach. Although ostensibly he was chiding the wind, in his use of two expressions that point to ephemerality (*fakanaki* and *yosinaki*), he seemed to be reminding Go-Toba that nothing in this world can be relied on—even the things we use as keepsakes are themselves as fleeting as the things they are supposed to remind us of:

Go-Toba's Poem

Katami tote	Though I stare
sigururu sora wo	At rainy skies in hopes of finding
nagamete mo	Remembrances of her,
fakana no kumo no	How painful to see
ato no afare ya	Those clouds that do not last.

Jien's Reply Poem

Kokoro are ya	Have a heart,
katami yosinaki	O storm that sweeps away
kumo no ato	The fleeting beauty
fakanaki iro wo	Of clouds that were at best
farafu arasi fa	Undependable keepsakes!

And so for Go-Toba the year came to a close, on a quiet, melancholy note.

NINE

Finishing Touches,
Ken'ei and Beyond (1206–1208)

The first, and only, year of Ken'ei (1206) saw the passing of Kujō Yoshitsune. His death was sudden, and fittingly for such a complex man, rather mysterious. Unfortunately, *Meigetsuki* has no entries for the first four months of 1206, but there remain several other contemporary or near-contemporary accounts, including Ienaga's memoirs and Jien's remarks in *Gukanshō*. This incident provides another glimpse into medieval courtly discourse, in this case, how the death of an illustrious and well-liked person is framed and what language is used to describe it. To begin with, Ienaga:

What was it about that date—the 7th day of the Third Month, in the Third Year of Genkyū?—for that was day the Lord Regent faded away like a dream.[1] On the 6th he had been at the palace all day, performing his official duties. Around nightfall, he returned home, retired to his bedroom, and simply never woke up again.

Just before that, there had been a dazzling astrological event, and those who specialized in such things had reported to His Majesty that it was no ordinary phenomenon. Furthermore, on the 28th of that same month, the main shrine at Kumano had burned down.[2] These things coming at once had aroused His Majesty's

---

1. The year name (*nengō*) was not changed to Ken'ei until the 27th day of the Fourth Month, the forty-ninth day after Yoshitsune's death, an important point in the mourning period. Apparently, Yoshitsune's death had some bearing on the decision; see *DNS*, iv:8, pp. 965–73.

2. According to Ishida and Satsukawa (*IN*, pp. 268, 270–72), who cite *Gukanshō*, among other works, the "astrological event" to which Ienaga alluded was a conjunction of three planets, Venus, Jupiter, and Mars, which seems to have occurred around the 22nd of the Second

concern, and he had ordered continuous prayers and services at various sites. But it seems these prayers had no effect, for the Lord Regent's death was so contrary to what we think of as the laws of nature, and—I have to say it—so tragic.

On the morning of the 7th, His Lordship had stayed in bed later than usual, and when several of his maids went to wake him up, they discovered that his body was already cold. By noon the news had spread, and the air was filled with the noise of horses and carriages rushing to the scene. At that time, his main wife had been in retreat at Kasuga Shrine, and the household ladies were all sleeping in a separate part of the residence, so even if something untoward had happened to His Lordship, there would have been no one around to hear it. This was shamefully negligent and made the situation all the more heartbreaking.

Words could not do justice to the grief His Majesty felt. The stream of sympathizers—court nobles, lords, and their retainers—coming and going by horse and carriage from his Itsutsuji Palace looked for all the world like lines of ants on pilgrimage.[3] His Majesty's sorrow was completely understandable. Ever since His Lordship had been a Middle Captain of the Second Rank, he had kept close company with His Majesty, who was then but a child, and had paid no attention to the difference in their ages.[4] Thus His Majesty's fondness for Yoshitsune had grown quite deep, and so naturally His Majesty's sorrow at Yoshitsune's death was deep as well. People tiptoed around the palace, and His Majesty sank into a profound depression that was painful to see.[5] Hoping against hope, he summoned as many healers as he could find and ordered a great effusion of prayer, but to no effect. He sent messengers flying off to various mountain temples to arrange for sutra readings and offered countless horses and other treasures to numerous shrines, but still to no effect.

Month. The *Gukanshō* passage is translated below. See also *DNS*, iv:8, pp. 832–33, for descriptions of this event from two other early sources, Fujiwara Nagakane's *Sanchōki* and *Mon'yōki*, a record of the Shōren-in temple (a *monzeki*, or imperial temple) covering the years from 1110 to 1417, begun by Son'en Hosshinnō (1298–1356).

The Kumano Shrine was very special to Go-Toba and Go-Shirakawa, both of whom made numerous pilgrimages there. See *IN*, pp. 268, 271; and *DNS*, iv:8, pp. 843–45, for more information on the fire at Kumano.

3. Likening groups of pilgrims at Kumano Shrine to lines of ants (*ari no Kumano mairi*) was a metaphor that appears in numerous contemporary works. It came to be applied to lines of people in any circumstance, although presumably the mention of the Kumano Shrine earlier in the entry prompted Ienaga to use the figure here.

4. Ishida and Satsukawa (*IN*, p. 269) figure that the association between Yoshitsune and Go-Toba began around 1187, when the former was nineteen years old and the latter eight.

5. I have omitted an obscure expression in this sentence, used to modify the phrase "His Majesty sank into a deep depression," that has stumped even Ishida and Satsukawa. The phrase is *kotowamisi* (or *kotofamisi*), and although it may be a line from poetry, it does not appear anywhere in the *Kokka taikan*.

There is no way to describe how pitiful it was to see people leaving Yoshitsune's mansion late that afternoon and dejectedly going their various ways. Here, at his Nakamikado mansion, polished bright like a jewel or mirror, there was supposed to have been a "winding waters" banquet just a few days later.[6] That he did not live long enough to enjoy it—no words can express the pain![7]

Once again, Ienaga delivered a layered, poignant account. With subtle counterpoint, he moved back and forth from the private (Yoshitsune going to bed / not waking up / his cold body discovered by the maids) to the public (Yoshitsune "at the office" / crowds of mourners / religious services throughout the land) and even to the supernatural (astrological omens / the fire at Kumano). Yet, despite the fact that Yoshitsune was perhaps the most powerful civilian at court, the mourning, especially Go-Toba's, was personal. This is in stark contrast to Ienaga's entry for the death of Michichika, a public figure of comparable rank. There, Ienaga scarcely touched on Go-Toba's feelings, but cast the grieving in a wider, public context.[8] Here, we see Go-Toba, in neat parallel sentences that speak clearly of the complex web of medieval Japanese religious beliefs and practices, enlisting whatever aid he could in an attempt to revive the dead Yoshitsune. Then we see him fall into deep depression, remembering how Yoshitsune had been his friend since childhood—an "older brother" Go-Toba had always looked up to. Then Ienaga focused his lens one last time on Yoshitsune's mansion, as the mourners leave one by one.

In a brilliant twist, Ienaga bent the facts a bit to remind us one last time why Yoshitsune was so important to the Shinkokin world—not only because of his political deeds but also because he stood at the aesthetic heart of this tiny world of literati. His deep understanding of Chinese culture (at least as it was defined in late Heian Japan) and exquisite taste made it natural that his "polished, mirror-like" mansion should be the place where the annual "winding waters banquet" (a custom of Chinese origin) would be held. When he died, it was as if a light had gone out, and the banquet became an impossibility—or so Ienaga implied. We know from other sources that the banquet was to have been held on the 3th and had been postponed

---

6. A "winding waters banquet" (*gokusui no en*, or *kyokusui no en*) was a Chinese-inspired garden party held in late spring. Guests would take wine cups that were set floating in the garden stream and compose poetry.
7. *IN*, pp. 265–70.
8. See Chapter 4, p. 189.

till the 13th, *before* Yoshitsune's death, in response to the bad omen of the Kumano fire.[9] But surely truth is more important than fact here, and the truth is that Yoshitsune's death was a bitter loss to the poetry world (and the banquet would have been canceled if it had come to that).

Yoshitsune's uncle, Jien, had his own view of the tragic death:

(Yoshitsune) had built at Nakamikado Kyōgoku a mansion that surpassed all others. The garden was splendid, its trees and pond grand like a mountain landscape. And there he had hoped to hold, on the 13th day of the Third Month of Genkyū 3 [1206], the annual "winding waters" banquet, which had been postponed.[10] He had commissioned mother-of-pearl wine cups and other items, and everyone was waiting eagerly for the party. The Regent Yoshitsune had taken as his main wife the daughter of the Matsudono Regent Motofusa; so the Regent became the son-in-law of another Regent—a rare occurrence, indeed. Furthermore, given that his father was the Priestly Retired Chancellor Kanezane and his father-in-law a Priestly Retired Regent, Yoshitsune was extremely knowledgeable about court precedent and history. In addition, his expertise at Chinese and Japanese poetry was unprecedented. Naturally, then, everyone expected him to sponsor the "winding waters" banquet. Just when anticipation was highest and people had sharpened their poetry skills in preparation, Yoshitsune died in his sleep on the 7th Day of the Third Month, with no warning.

Words cannot begin to describe the effect this had on people. And it would be useless to try and relate the profound grief experienced by His Majesty Go-Toba. However, no one could bring His Lordship Yoshitsune back, and the Konoe Lord Motomichi's son, Iezane, who at that time was Minister of the Left and had held the post for an extended period, was named Chancellor/Regent (*kanpaku*).[11]

That same spring, there had been a very significant astrological event—the conjunction of the three planets[12]—and the official astrologers gave distressing predictions. At that time, the Archbishop Jien had just begun preparations for services to the Healing Buddha Yakushi at Go-Toba's Itsutsuji Palace. The conjunction, involving Venus, Jupiter, and Mars, occurred during those rites. For several evenings

---

9. *IN*, pp. 270, 272.

10. As noted above, the banquet, normally held on the 3rd Day of the Third Month, had been postponed because of the fire at Kumano.

11. In a footnote, Nakajima Etsuji (*Gukanshō*, p. 508) identifies "Konoedono" as Moto*fusa*, but Brown and Ishida (*The Future and the Past*, pp. 166-67) correctly identify him as Moto*michi*. All agree that the son in question is Iezane. Nakajima's identification is presumably a typographical error since on a subsequent page (p. 513) he shows a family tree that accurately depicts the information.

12. Nakajima (*Gukanshō*, p. 508n) lists Venus (*taihakusei*), Jupiter (*mokusei*), and Saturn (*dosei*) as the three planets, but the *Gukanshō* text itself says Venus, Jupiter, and Mars (*kasei*).

in a row, the three planets could be seen moving out of their normal spheres and approaching each other. Then it began to rain, obscuring the event. Then it cleared up again, and the conjunction was visible; but no sooner was it visible than the rains came again. For four or five days, it did not clear, which people took to be a good sign, but then the rains cleared up again, and there were the three planets, still conjoined. On the third day, it clouded over again, and from morning till evening it looked like rain. Perhaps because of the Archbishop's fervent prayers, a soaking rain fell that night, and the following morning the Archbishop predicted to His Majesty that the skies would clear. And indeed, when the weather cleared, one could see that the planets had moved away from each other, and the conjunction had passed.

But almost immediately thereafter, His Lordship Yoshitsune died. The official astrologer Haremitsu interpreted the event: "Undoubtedly this conjunction of the three planets presaged something grave for His Majesty. However, the fact that the planets eventually retreated to their proper spheres after having fought among themselves is because His Lordship Yoshitsune was taken in His Majesty's place." I also believe the vengeful ghost of Tadazane was probably involved in this at the time.[13]

Jien's account unfolds quite differently from Ienaga's, which is to be expected considering Jien's political agenda. He *began* where Ienaga *ended*, that is, with a nod to Yoshitsune's importance in the cultural activities of the court, but he tied that cultural accomplishment quite tightly to Yoshitsune's family background and marriage—in other words, to Yoshitsune's political standing. In contrast to Ienaga, Jien's description of the mourning period is quite brief and leads immediately to a discussion of the succession to Yoshitsune's post. Most interesting is the fact that just over half the account revolves around the astrological circumstances surrounding Yoshitsune's death and the political interpretation Jien claimed they were given by Go-Toba's advisors. The disorder among the planets is taken as a reflection of disorder in the realm (presumably a reference to the overthrow of the Shogun Sanetomo by Hōjō Tokimasa half a year before), which is resolved by Yoshitsune's "sacrifice." Jien then claimed for himself (although in the third person—he is "the Archbishop") success in causing the rains to lift so that the astrological omen could be properly read. The message here, as it is throughout *Gukanshō*, is that if Go-Toba would just listen to the Kujō house, he would be all right. This is underscored by the reference to Tadazane's

---

13. Nakajima, *Gukanshō*, pp. 508–513. I referred also to the translation of Brown and Ishida, *The Future and the Past*, pp. 166–67, although my interpretation of several passages differs from theirs.

"vengeful ghost"; Fujiwara Tadazane (1078–1162) was Yoshitsune's great-grandfather and progenitor of both the Kujō and the Konoe houses.

Both Go-Toba and Jien were deeply affected by Yoshitsune's death. As in the case of the concubine Owari, they turned to poetry for consolation. Ienaga recorded an exchange of forty-four poems between the retired emperor and Yoshitsune's uncle, the Tendai cleric, who apparently initiated the dialogue. (For a complete translation of the series, see Appendix E, pp. 427–36. Below I discuss some of the more compelling aspects of the exchange.)

This lengthy exchange provides much that is worthy of comment. One cannot help noticing immediately that Go-Toba assumed the role of philosopher and sought to console Jien, the Tendai priest. This is a reversal of the situation that we saw in the poetic exchange between these two over the death of Owari. However, Go-Toba's responses here are less detached, less "preachy," than those Jien gave before. On the other hand, Jien does seem truly stricken by this event—the mask of the sage has crumbled.

Their poems roam widely, although missing are verses cast in the "Waiting Woman" vein that Go-Toba used several times in lamenting the loss of Owari. One sees here nascent linked verse (*renga*—which was, in fact, already being practiced by these poets, although not in the form best known today) as the poems move from one topic to the next, unbounded by time and place. Although not as clean as a 100-poem sequence, nor as regulated as a linked-verse sequence from the Muromachi era, there is unmistakable direction in this exchange, be it a deliberate act on the part of the participants or an unconscious function of its discourse. There are recurring images and themes and, as might be expected from poets of this age, an awareness of the history of waka is never far from the surface. Even without a rigorous search for *honka* (foundation poems), I found numerous allusions.

The exchange begins in the reeds at Naniwa:

From Jien

Tu no kuni no	Reeds near the channel buoys,
Nanifa mo asi no	At Naniwa in Tsu,
mi wo tukusi	Are withered bare,
Koya uki koto no	A lonely hut at Koya revealed—
sirusi naruran	Surely a mark of the sad and frail.[14]

---

14. This translation is rather explanatory, but Jien's poem is thickly layered. The phrase *mi wo tukusi* does at least triple duty, suggesting the withered reeds, channel buoys, and Yoshitsune's death. The image of channel buoys—floating channel markers—is famous from *Genji*

Faru no yo no	"Awakened from
yume ni wodoroku	A spring night's dream"—
na nomi site	It's just an expression,
samenu fa fito no	For the feelings I have now
kokoro narikeri	Are of one not yet enlightened.

Go-Toba's reply

Tu no kuni no	"Left lonely, cutting reeds
asikarikeri na	In the province of Tsu,"
tanomikosi	How much sadder now to live
fito mo nagisa ni	When the one I long relied on
itodo sumiuki	Is on these shores no more.[15]
Ofokata no	That this sad world
ukiyo wo yume to	Is a dream—
siru fito no	There is virtually no one
nakereba koso fa	Who truly knows this.
sode wo fosurame	Perhaps that's why most sleeves soon dry.

One is reminded of Wani's "Naniwazu" poem, cited by Tsurayuki in his *kana* preface to *Kokinshū* and considered one of the progenitors of waka:

Nanifadu ni	In Naniwazu
saku ya ko no fana	They bloom, blossoms on the trees
fuyukomori	"From winter's sleep

(and many poems) and suggests someone at a loss, subject to the rise and fall of the waves (of fate). The notion of reed ears withering away to reveal a hidden hut at Koya (a place-name near Naniwa, in what is now Itami City) comes from SIS 223, by Minamoto Shigeyuki (d. 1000?): *Asi no fa ni / kakurete sumisi / Tu no kuni no / Koya mo arafa ni / fuyu fa kinikeri*—"The hut in which I lived / Hidden among the reeds / At Koya in the province of Tsu / Is now exposed— / Truly winter has come!" Ishida and Satsukawa (*IN*, p. 276) offer another take on *mi wo tukusi*: since it can also mean "throwing oneself into something to the point of exhaustion," they point to Yoshitsune's almost fanatical devotion to literature, and to his duty, as described in *Ienaga nikki* and *Gukanshō* (whose author was Jien himself)—recall that he "worked late at the office" the day he died—and wonder if Jien is saying this is one of the things that killed him.

There are other puns and *engo* (associated vocabulary) that challenge the translator: for example *mi wo tukusi* (channel buoy) / *sirusi* (marker); *uki* (floating) / *uki* (sad); Koya (a place-name) / *koya* (hut) / *koya* (a phrase meaning "like this)."

15. Go-Toba is alluding to a poem that appears among other places in *Yamato monogatari* (Episode 148; *Shinpen kokka taikan* 5:416, #249, p. 1316), *Shūishū* (#540; IX, Misc. 2), and eventually the Nō play *Asikari*. It is attributed to "a reed cutter": *Kimi nakute / asikarikeri to / omofu nimo / itodo Nanifa no / ura zo sumiuki*—"Now that you are gone / I am left to cut the reeds / Or so I thought— / But how sad it is living here / On the beach at Naniwa!"

ima fa farube to	Spring is now upon us," so
saku ya ko no fana.	They bloom, blossoms on the trees.[16]

Jien described reeds withered by winter to reveal a lonely hut, but Go-Toba, presumably mindful of Wani's poem, shifted the season to spring and used for the first of several times the image of waking from a spring night's dream (a phrase used to powerful effect in the opening lines of *Heike monogatari*).

The two poets then "travel" to Vulture Peak in India, reputed site of the Buddha's preaching of the Lotus Sutra, and they bring up notions of *mappō* (the corrupt "Latter Days of the Law," in which the Buddha's words, even if available, can no longer be understood), thus placing Yoshitsune's death into a larger framework:

Then, from Jien

Wasi no yama	Perhaps because we cannot see
tikaki fikari wo	The light that shines so close at hand
minu mama ni	From Vulture Peak,
naki mo madofinu	Those who are dead must wander,
aru mo madofinu	And those alive must wander, too.

Go-Toba's reply

Wasi no yama	The ancient moonlight
mukasi no tuki ya	From Vulture Peak
kasumuran	Seems misted over,
ukiyo ni madofu	How sorrowful it is for us
fito zo kanasiki	Left wandering in this sad world!

This is followed by several lament poems of a general nature still echoing the theme of the Buddhist Law and its impenetrability. Then Jien introduced the first of a number of poems that will contrast spring and autumn:

Then, from Jien

Sode no iro no	Were it autumn
tagufi mo aki fa	The scarlet of my dampened sleeves
arinamasi	Might find a match,
faru no kozuwe ni	But what am I to do
ware ikani sen	With the green leaves of spring?

---

16. Ozawa, *Kokin wakashū*, p. 51. The poem also appears as *KWR* 4032 and *Wakan rōeishū* 664. Wani, dates unknown but around the time of Emperor Ojin (ca. 300), came to Japan from the Kingdom of Paekche and was instrumental in introducing Confucianism to Japan.

Go-Toba's Reply

Kaminaduki	When I recall
kimi ni tugekosi	What His Lordship told you
omofi made	This past Tenth Month,
nafo wodorokasu	I am suddenly awakened
faru no yo no yume	From my spring night's dream.[17]

The time of Yoshitsune's death, and apparently of this exchange as well, is spring, but the tension between spring and autumn is an old Chinese antithetical opposition that was surely familiar to Yoshitsune, knowledgeable as he was of Chinese literature (as the passage from *Gukanshō* reminds us). It becomes something of a theme throughout this exchange. Go-Toba's response is a provocative poem that implies Yoshitsune had had some sort of premonition of his death in late autumn the year before; he again used the "spring night's dream" image to complete the autumn/spring opposition.

Jien's poem pairs the two seasons again, but then he moved the scene to Furu, a poetic place-name in ancient Yamato—its very name puns on the word for ancient (*furuki*). This speaks to Yoshitsune's expertise in ancient matters (again, the *Gukanshō* passage comes to mind), and Go-Toba followed suit, reminding us subtly that such expertise was not limited to artistic matters but was of importance to the governing of the nation, as well:

Then, from Jien

Faru no fana	In spring it was blossoms,
aki no tuki tote	In autumn, the moon
nagamesi wo	Upon which we used to gaze—
sono tomo ikani	Oh, how much I long
kofisikaruran	For that friend now!
Isonokami	That ancient road
Furuki miti koso	To Furu in Isonokami
kasuminure	Is now obscured in mist

---

17. This poem is opaque. Ishida and Satsukawa (*IN*, p. 278) speculate that it might refer to a letter or communication of some sort between Yoshitsune and Jien in the Tenth Month of the previous year, and which, when looked at in retrospect, seems to have presaged Yoshitsune's death. I have followed their interpretation here. In any case, Go-Toba was attempting to mirror the autumn/spring opposition that Jien sets out in his poem.

sirube fa nobe no	And the one who used to guide me
tuyu to kieniki	Is vanished like dew on the moors.[18]

Go-Toba's reply

Sono tomo no	It would seem
uti ni ya ware wo	That I, too, should be thought of
omofuran	As one of his friends,
kofisiki sode no	Might I show you the color of my sleeves,
iro wo misebaya	Stained with longing?[19]

Furumiti no	My guide
sirube fa tuyu to	To that ancient road
kiesi noni	Has vanished like dew,
fitori nokorite	And here I am, left alone,
sode nurasu koro	Wetting my sleeves with tears.

Jien then shifted the focus to Yoshitsune's garden, initiating a series of poems by both him and Go-Toba describing the garden as they imagine it will be in autumn—forlorn, without its master. They both made use of one of lament waka's most effective devices: the image of living flora planted by someone now dead. It is a theme played beautifully as far back as *Man'yōshū* and *Kokinshū*: the tension between nature, which is cyclical and ever-renewing, and man, whose life (*inochi*) is finite:[20]

---

18. Because there was a place named Furu in the region of Isonokami, in old Yamato, Isonokami came to be used as a pillow word for the word *furu*, which might means, variously "old," or "falling." As Jien had noted in the *Gukanshō* entry cited above, Yoshitsune was well versed in the "ancient ways," both in literature and court precedent.

19. Ishida and Satsukawa (*IN*, pp. 278–79) take this poem as addressed by Go-Toba to Yoshitsune, but I believe Go-Toba was addressing Jien. Much depends on how one interprets the third line, *omofuran*, which means something along the lines of "(one) seems to think / feel / long for." It can be taken as a first-person utterance, directed to Jien's poem, which said that he himself was one of Yoshitsune's friends, and saying something like "It seems you should think of me as one his friends, too—see, here, look at my sleeves, wet with tears!," which is the way I am taking it here, since the *ya . . . ran* combination in waka usually implies a speculation as to cause and effect (the tears on my sleeves must be because of my feelings for my departed friend). Ishida and Satsukawa read the *ran* as simply a softener, a mild conjecture: "I guess *Yoshitsune* thought of me as one of his friends—I wish I could show him my wet sleeves."

20. In *MYS* 196–98 (*NKBT* same), for example, Hitomaro masterfully played this song in his lament for the Princess Asuka. Her name puns on the word "tomorrow," and her temporary resting place is next to the Asuka River, which *will* know a tomorrow, even though the princess will not. Ki no Tsurayuki's *KKS* 851 (XVI, Laments), composed when he saw plum blossoms in the garden of a deceased friend, is another example: *Iro mo ka mo / mukasi no kosa*

Then, from Jien

    Fikiufesi / ike no ifane wo / nagamureba / ituka kodakaki / nifa no matukaze

    As I gaze where they were planted / Among the rocks / Along the pond— / When did they grow so tall? / Wind-blown pines in the garden.

    Ufeokisi / fitomoto susuki / kono aki fa / sigeki nobe toya / tare mo nagamen

    That single clump of plume grass / Which he had planted— / This autumn / All that anyone will see / Is a moor overgrown.

    Tatenamuru / isima no midu ni / tare sumite / aranu kage nimo / sode nurasuran

    By the waters / Among stones laid so carefully / Who lives now? / His face no longer reflected there, / And so, it seems, I wet my sleeves.

Go-Toba's reply

    Fikiufesi / ifane no matu ni / koto tofan / kodakaki kaze to / fito ya tanomesi

    To the pines he planted / Among the rocks / I would ask: / Was he hoping eventually to hear / The wind through your branches grown tall?

    Furusato no / fitomura susuki / aki kutomo / kari ni tatitofu / fito ya nakaran

    Though autumn comes / To that single patch of plume grass / At his home / There is no one here now / To tend it, or to visit.

    Nakikage yo / isima no midu ni / nokoru ya to / tofabaya fito no / ato no furusato

    A reflection no more!— / Does it still remain / In the waters among the stones? / I want to know, and so I come / Here to his old home.

---

ni / nifofedomo / uwekemu fito no / kage zo kofisiki—"Though they exude / A beauty and a fragrance / As insistent as before / How one misses the image / Of him who planted them!" See also the discussion of Masatsune's *ima fa tada* poem in Chapter 4, p. 177.

In their exchange of poems on plume grass (Jien's *uweokisi* and Go-Toba's *furusato no*), the two make allusion to a *Kokinshū* poem on this theme by Miharu no Arisuke (ca. 902), a retainer of Fujiwara Toshimoto (fl. 860-90), one of Yoshitsune's distant relatives.[21] Arisuke composed the poem one autumn night on seeing the desolate garden of the place where his late master had once lived:

Kimi ga uwesi	That single patch of plume grass
fitomura susuki	Which my lord planted
musi no ne no	Has now become a moor overrun
sigeki nobe tomo	By the hum of insects.
narinikeru kana[22]	

From Yoshitsune's garden, Jien's and Go-Toba's poems move to the site of his funeral and then to a lonely temple on the moors, whose bell awakes Go-Toba from his dawn dream (the third time he used this image):

Then came this poem from the Abbot's Quarters

Keburi tatu	The firewood
takigi mo ima fa	From which arose his smoke
tukinu tote	Has now burnt out,
kafereba kane no	And so, as I return home
kowe zo kanasiki	How sad the sound of the temple bell!

His Majesty's reply

Namida sofu	As if to add its own
kafesa ya sora mo	To your tears as you return home,
kumoriken	The sky clouds over—
nodera no kane no	A dream dispelled at daybreak
akatuki no yume	By the bell of the temple in the fields.

The mention of dawn (*akatuki*) elicits a moon poem from Jien (the moon lingering in the dawn sky is a venerable waka figure, eventually appropriated also to suggest the Buddha of the future, Maitreya)[23]—a moon that heads west, in the direction of Amida's Western Paradise, where Yoshitsune is now presumably residing. Jien, in his next poem, then placed the moon on the mountain's edge:

---

21. Toshimoto was the father of Kanesuke (877-933), influential poetic patron and aesthete.
22. *KKS* 853 (XVI, Laments).
23. See the discussion of Tomochika's *kore ya kono* poem in Chapter 3, pp. 127-29.

Again, from the Abbot Jien

    Fadukasi ya   How shameful
    kore wo uresi to   Those who find happiness
    omofu fito no   In this!
    kokoro wo terase   Please illuminate their hearts,
    yama no fa no tuki   Moon over the mountain's ridge!

This is a nod to Izumi Shikibu's death poem:

    Kuraki yori   Out of darkness
    kuraki miti ni zo   Into a darkened path
    irinubeki   I must now enter
    faruka ni terase   Illuminate the far reaches
    yama no fa no tuki   Moon over mountain's ridge![24]

The word *mountain* then triggered in him the memory of the fire at Kumano Shrine (he metonymically called it "that mountain to the south" in his next poem, translated below), which he had already anticipated three poems earlier in the *keburi tatu* ("smoke rising") verse. And he introduced the Fujiwara clan indirectly, through the figure of wisteria, which makes up the first character of their name, suggesting the fire was an ill omen for them. This image resurfaces a few poems later at the end of the exchange.

From Jien

    Ayasikarisi   The ominous smoke
    minami no yama no   That came from that mountain
    keburi kana   To the south,
    sono sirusi to ya   Might it not have been an omen
    kita no fudinami   For the northern branch of wisteria?[25]

Go-Toba's reply

    Kiesomesi   Because the smoke
    minami no yama no   From that mountain to the south
    keburi yuwe   Has begun to fade,

---

24. *SIS* 1342 (XX, Laments).

25. "Smoke from the mountain to the south" refers to the fire at Kumano Shrine on the 28th day of the Second Month (see above), and "northern branch of wisteria" refers to the Northern branch of the Fujiwara clan (the "fuji" element of the name means "wisteria"), which was the dominant branch and the one Yoshitsune belonged to.

nurenisi sode fa	We can expect our wetted sleeves
aki zo fosubeki	To dry by autumn.[26]

After several general lament poems, Go-Toba was prompted by Jien's mention of "(scarlet) tears" to reintroduce autumn imagery, this time scarlet maple leaves. They then exchanged several poems with imagery that alternates between autumn and winter. This back-and-forth play of time culminates in a pair of poems that alludes to two famous *Kokinshū* verses on the same theme:

From Jien

Omokage wo	Alas, what am I to do
ko fa ikani sen	About his ever-present image in
kinofu nado	my mind?
kefu wo kagiri to	Why is it that yesterday
katarazariken	He did not convey to me
	That today he would be gone?

Go-Toba's reply

Nakanaka ni	Whatever it is
kotosi ya koso fa	That has happened this year
sate okinu	Leave it as it is.
naresi mukasi wo	How can I ever forget
ikade wasuren	That past which was so sweet?

Jien's *omokage wo* refers to Narihira's deathbed poem, which also contrasts "yesterday" and "today":

Tufi ni yuku	Though I had often heard
miti to fa kanete	It was the road that all must travel
kikisikado	In the end,

---

26. This is the only poem in the series for which Ishida and Satsukawa offer no glosses at all. The words seem clear enough, but what the verse is suggesting is less obvious. A pat "time heals all wounds" does not seem enough. Kumano was an important spiritual place for Go-Toba, who may be arguing that the fire is out and the time of danger from its omen will pass by autumn. I wondered if perhaps Go-Toba were not promising something to Jien, a promotion or some such, but the closest I could find was his appointment of Yoshitsune's son, Michiie, who was thirteen at the time, to the post of Sakon'e Taishō, an honorary position that put him among the Emperor's personal bodyguards. This was an honor that Yoshitsune himself had been granted, but at the much later age of 20 in 1189, and it may well have been Go-Toba's way of sending assurances to the Kujō house.

| kinofu kefu to fa | Yesterday I did not imagine |
| omofazarisi wo | That it would be today![27] |

On the other hand, Go-Toba's *nakanaka ni*, with its pun on *kozo* ("last year") buried in the emphatic particle *koso*, plays off Jien's "yesterday/today" and makes sly reference to the poem by Ariwara no Motokata (fl. 890–905) that opens *Kokinshū*, which confuses "last year" with "this year":

Tosi no uti ni	Spring has come
faru fa kinikeri	While it's still the old year—
fitotose wo	As for this one year, then,
kozo to ya ifamu	Shall we say it is last year?
kotosi to ya ifamu	Or shall we say it is this year?

This allows the two poets to bring the season back to spring and end their exchange:

From Jien

Nagusamuru	Please become my means
tayori tomo nare	For communing with the departed—
Kasugayama	White clouds clinging
fana tiru mine ni	To the peak of Mount Kasuga
kakaru sirakumo	Where the blossoms have scattered.[28]

Go-Toba's reply

Ima fa tada	For now
fana tiru mine no	My own means will be
sirakumo ni	The rain that pours
sosogan ame yo	From those white clouds on the peak
tayori tomo nare	Where blossoms have scattered.

From Jien

Midorigo wo	For that toddler
ware to ware to ga	That you and your wife
naka ni mite	Looked after together
ikanaru koto wo	What sort of plans
omofiokiken	Must you have had?[29]

---

27. *KKS* 861 (XVII, Miscellaneous 1).

28. At the base of Mount Kasuga, in present-day Nara, stands Kasuga Shrine, the tutelary shrine for the Fujiwara clan, of which Yoshitsune was a member.

29. Ishida and Satsukawa (*IN*, p. 287) assume the "toddler" in this poem and the "seedling pine" in Go-Toba's reply refer to Yoshitsune's son Motoie, who was four years old at the time,

Go-Toba's reply

Midori naru	As for the future
futaba no matu no	Of the seedling pine
yukusuwe wo	That is still green,
nafo inisie no	Still better to entrust it
kami ni makase yo	To those ancient gods.

A symbolic year of mourning has now passed, and in the final poems they stand in front of Kasuga Shrine, tutelary shrine for the Fujiwara clan. They ponder the ancient past and the blessing of the gods, and in a domestic touch they conclude with a look at the young child (actually one of several) that Yoshitsune left behind—the future of the Kujō house, which Go-Toba counsels should be "entrusted to those ancient gods." It was a remarkable performance under the circumstances and one that belies Go-Toba's reputation as a dilettante who superficially jumped from one thing to the next.

Although the extant *Meigetsuki* has no entries for the first four months of the year, Teika was naturally not unmoved by the death of his friend and patron, as the following entries from his diary show. He seemed drawn to the Nakamikado residence each month as the moon neared full.

Ken'ei 1/v/12. Weather clear, the rising moon shone bright. Overcome by sad memories of the past, I went to the Nakamikado residence. As I gazed, now alone, at the garden under the moonlight, I was soon in tears. By the rarest of coincidences, I encountered a priest there performing services. I left very late.[30]

Ken'ei 1/vi/11. Weather clear. His Majesty has gone off to Kawakami.... Under the moonlight, I went to the Nakamikado residence and took a turn around the south garden. It seems that people have stolen the gold fittings from the bridge. I was deeply saddened by the desolation I saw before me.[31]

Here in *kanbun* dairy form is a poetic figure we have encountered before in Ienaga's description of Shikishi Naishinnō's Ōidono Villa a year after her death: a forlorn autumn garden gone to ruin after its master has died.[32]

And Teika also had a bittersweet evening with Kanezane, Yoshitsune's father, now himself ailing:

---

but it may refer to Michiie, to whom, as noted in note 26 above, Go-Toba granted an early promotion shortly after Yoshitsune's death. In either case, both poems are ostensibly addressed to Yoshitsune.

30. *Meigetsuki*, Ken'ei 1 (1206)/v/12, 1: 453.
31. Ibid., 1/vi/11, 1: 457.
32. See the opening section of Chapter 3, pp. 86–91.

Ken'ei 1/vi/27. Weather clear. Before sunrise I went to the Hosshō-ji Priest Kanezane's residence and was summoned to the south wing and invited within the blinds. His Lordship spoke to me with just a screen between us. His voice was extremely weak. He talked a lot about the late Minister, his son. Our tears could not be stopped.[33]

During this time, the editing on *Shinkokinshū* was continuing apace; the Wakadokoro members were as busy as ever. Numerous *Meigetsuki* entries during these months describe the process. One in particular shows that even posthumously Yoshitsune had a hand:

Ken'ei 1/vi/19. Weather clear. Then in mid-afternoon came a thunderstorm. The heavy rains stopped by evening.
During the day, there was a summons from the Retired Emperor. (Something about the poem count for *Shinkokinshū*. Kiyonori was His Majesty's delegate.) So I quickly headed to the Palace. They said that the Treasury Minister Ariie had also been called in, but he did not come. After the thunderstorm had passed, Kiyonori showed up. He brought with him five books of the *Shinkokinshū*, which he handed me. He told me that the late Regent Yoshitsune had left some notes about this part of the collection and that I needed to look it over with those opinions in mind and make my own recommendations.
In the Felicitations Section, there was a poem attributed to the Tsuchimikado Minister of the Right Morofusa, which was supposedly composed at the banquet following a poetry contest called the *Ippon Ryōshi naishinnōke no uta-awase*. Yoshitsune's notes questioned this, and so I looked into it. It turned out that the poetry contest in question was *Yūshi naishinnōke no uta-awase*. (This had been one of the Minamoto Lord Michitomo's selections. In fact, he got the date and the name wrong.)[34]
In the Laments Section, in a poem by the Chion-in Retired Priestly Former Prime Minister Tadazane, which was also selected by Michitomo, the headnote

---

33. *Meigetsuki*, Ken'ei 1/vi/27, 1: 461.
34. The poem Teika is talking about is now *SKKS* 713 (VII, Felicitations). It is attributed to Minamoto Morofusa (1008–77), and the headnote, as corrected by Teika, now reads: "A poem on Cherry Blossoms, from a poetry contest at the home of Princess Yūshi." Princess Yūshi (also known as Sukeko, 1038–1105) was Emperor Go-Suzaku's third daughter, and with the help of her grandfather, the powerful Regent and Chancellor Fujiwara Yorimichi (992–1074), she sponsored at least six poetry contests between 1041 and 1060; see *WBJ*, pp. 662–63, for details. Minemura (*Shinkokin wakashū* [1974], p. 226) says this poem is from a contest held in Eishō 5 (1050)/vi/5. There was apparently no such person as Ippon Ryōshi Naishinnō, and this poem is from the contest itself, not from the following banquet. But at least Michitomo got the name of the poet right!

read "Sent to Shinshōshō when Lady Ni-i passed away." Yoshitsune had put a query mark on "Lady Ni-i."[35] This is so careless! I cannot understand how someone could be so stupid. I suggested that the Record Keeper (*geki*) Moroshige should be consulted as to what was right here.[36]

Among the Love poems, there were two attributed to Saigyō, which Yoshitsune questioned. I indicated that if these attributions were wrong, they needed to be corrected.

In the Miscellaneous Section appeared an exchange of poems purportedly between Ise no Taifu and Middle Captain Masamitsu. Yoshitsune's notes questioned this since it could only have happened after Ise no Taifu entered the service of Jōtōmon-in.[37] Again, the Minamoto Lord was responsible for this attribution. I recommended that His Majesty's opinion prevail on this point.

---

35. There are actually two errors here. The first is the "Chio*n*-in" in "Chion-in Retired Priestly Former Prime Minister Tadazane," which should be "Chi*soku*-in." Fujiwara Tadazane (1078–1162) was Kanezane's grandfather. The second is "Lady *Ni*-i" (literally, "Lady Second Rank"), which is supposed to be Lady *Ichi*-i (Lady First Rank), i.e., Tadazane's wife, Minamoto Moroko. But according to Teika, Yoshitsune only queried the "Lady Ni-i" error. Imagawa's text of *Meigetsuki* (*Meigetsukishō*, p. 190) does not reproduce the "Chion-in" error but properly has "Chisoku-in" instead. So either the Kokusho Kankōkai text of *Meigetsuki* has a typographical error (or is reproducing an earlier copyist's mistake), and Imagawa took it upon himself to "correct" the text, or Imagawa simply made a mistake. However, it seems likely that either Yoshitsune or Teika would have commented if Michitomo had gotten Tadazane's title wrong, too, in addition to his wife's, and I believe the "Chisoku" got changed to "Chion" by some copyist along the way. Shinshōshō is the palace name of Minamoto Toshiyori's daughter (dates unknown), who was in the service of Emperor Toba's consort, Empress Taikenmon-in (1101–45). The poem in question is now *SKKS* 784 (VIII, Laments).

36. Nakahara Moroshige (1166–1221), like Teika a retainer of Kujō Kanezane, appears several times in *Meigetsuki*, the earliest appearance being Ken'ei 1 (1206)/vi/20, 1: 458, where he is referred to as Grand Record Keeper (*daigeki*), a position to which he was appointed in 1198.

37. The exchange is now *SKKS* 1502–3 (XVI, Miscellaneous 1). Ise no Taifu (fl. 1007–60) was one of the premier poets of her age and, in her younger years, served, as did Murasaki Shikibu, the Empress Jōtōmon-in (Fujiwara Shōshi). Fujiwara Masamitsu (956?–1014) was a lesser son from one of the branches of the Fujiwara that could provide Regents and Chancellors (*sekkanke*). In the current text of *Shinkokinshū*, he is identified in this poem exchange as a Consultant (*sangi*), which is a higher office, rather than a Middle Captain (*chūjō*), although the posts were often held simultaneously and called *saishō no chūjō* (*saishō* being another term for Consultant).

It is not clear what Yoshitsune and Teika are calling into question here. Commentators such as Minemura (*Shinkokin wakashū* [1974], p. 452), Kubota Jun (*Shinkokin wakashū*, 2: 171), and Kojima Yoshio (*Shinkokin wakashū*, pp. 314–15) focus on the fact that the headnote in the *Shinkokinshū* version of the poems differs from the one that appears in Ise no Taifu's personal collection. The headnote in the former says that Ise no Taifu initiated the playful exchange when she spied Masamitsu attempting to visit a court lady in secret, whereas the one in the

I left after nightfall but had to go back again later and did not leave again until after the late night roll call.[38]

Teika was not content to let the questions stand. The next day, apparently refreshed, he did some further research into the problems Yoshitsune had drawn attention to, and made some adjustments. He removed the dubious Saigyō poems, corrected the mistaken reference to "Lady Ni-i," and properly identified the poetry contest at Yūshi Naishinnō's residence. He wrote that Go-Toba ordered him to remove the reference to Masamitsu as a Middle Captain. Teika then groused a bit more about Michitomo's sloppy scholarship.[39] So even in death, Yoshitsune continued to affect the course of *Shinkokinshū*.

For another year or two after this, Go-Toba sponsored events that produced more poems for the final *Shinkokinshū*. Nonetheless, Yoshitsune's passing provides an opportunity (if arbitrary) to begin winding down this narrative, which began, in many ways, with his return to the center of Go-Toba's political and poetic world less than a decade earlier. However, even as

---

latter says that the exchange represented a game of what amounted to hide-and-seek between some court ladies and their "gentlemen callers," and that only one of the two oldest extant texts identifies Masamitsu (or in one case "Masamichi") as the other poet in the exchange. In other words, Michitomo seems not to have had a source for his headnote. But judging from Teika's comments in the entry for the following day, the issue seems to be that Yoshitsune and Teika did not believe Masamitsu was only a Middle Captain at the time the poems were composed. In any case, what we have in the current text of *Shinkokinshū* appears to be Michitomo's contribution, except that Masamitsu's title has been changed from *chūjō* to *sangi*.

Incidentally, there is a textual line of the *Ise no Taifushū* that does call Masamitsu a *chūjō*. It is the text marked "III" in the *Shikashū taisei* (vol. 2) and is a variant of the Shoryōbu line that is now considered the standard (marked "II" in *Shikashū taisei* and also the basis for the *Ise no Taifushū* that appears in *Shinpen kokka taikan*, 3:86). However, since this variant line also has marks at the tops of poems that appear in imperial anthologies (including ones subsequent to *Shinkokinshū*), it must be a later text and could not have been the one Michitomo was looking at, although its ancestor, no longer extant, might have been.

38. *Meigetsuki*, Ken'ei 1/vi/19, 1: 459. In the summer, the "late night roll call" (*meietsu* or *nadaimen*) would have been a little after 10:00 P.M.

39. Ibid., 1/vi/20, 1: 459. Gotō Shigeo (*Shinkokin wakashū no kisōteki kenkyū*, p. 180) reads this passage differently. He interprets the line *yamubeki no yoshi ōseraru* ("His Majesty ordered that it be discontinued") as referring to the whole exchange, but he then concedes that the exchange does, after all, appear in the various extant texts of *Shinkokinshū*. I believe Go-Toba was simply ordering them to remove the reference to *chūjō* since the line that precedes *yamubeki*, and presumably serves as the object that is to be discontinued is *Masamitsukyō chūjō ni haberikeru* ("When Lord Masamitsu was a Middle Captain"). And in fact that line does not appear in *Shinkokinshū*.

I step back somewhat from the journal-like approach of the previous chapters, I would be remiss if I did not examine in some detail three other poetry events that more or less put the finishing touches on *Shinkokinshū*. Although at least five other *Shinkokinshū* poems can be dated as from the second year of Jōgen (1208), all were by Go-Toba—four from two sequences he submitted to the Ise Shrine, and one from a contest he sponsored at the Sumiyoshi Shrine.[40] Thus for all intents and purposes, Go-Toba seems to have wrapped up his public campaign to generate verse for *Shinkokinshū* in 1207.

The first of these three events has become known as the *Keishō jishin no uta-awase* (Poetry Contest Between Lords and Their Retainers), which was a *kendai* contest held on the 25th Day of the Seventh Month of Ken'ei 1 (1206). The participants were a veritable who's-who of Go-Toba's poetry circle:

Left (Lords): Go-Toba, Tadatsune, Jien, Tadayoshi, Michiteru, Kintsune, Michitomo, Yoshihira, Sueyoshi, Shunzei no Musume

Right (Retainers): Ietaka, Ariie, Teika, Echizen, Hideyoshi, Tomochika, Tango, Yasusue, Narishige (Narimochi), Masatsune

The makeup of the team itself reveals some interesting points. First, Shunzei no Musume is on the Lords team and is the only female among them. (The other two women, Echizen and Tango, were on the Retainer team.) Her own family background should have placed her on the Retainer team, with her stepbrother Teika. Perhaps she was on the Lords team because she was married to Michitomo, also a Lord, although by this time they had been separated for several years.

Second, four of the twenty team members are either from the Rokujō school (Sueyoshi and Yasusue—I am not counting Tadayoshi, although he had earlier been a partisan of the Rokujō school, or Tomochika, whose father, Moromitsu, had been a Rokujō adherent, but whose own allegiance is unclear), or its patron line, the Tsuchimikado branch of the Minamoto (Michiteru and Michitomo). So Go-Toba was obviously still mindful of balancing the various factions in his group. (Another anecdote from *Meigetsuki* shows Go-Toba to be quite magnanimous on this point, in the hope of encouraging artistic output. On the 12th day of the Seventh Month, he sponsored a small poetry contest with ten participants, most of whom are

---

40. These are *SKKS* 236, 279, 1875 and 1876 (to Ise) and 1633 (to Sumiyoshi). The latter is considered the "newest" poem in the collection. See Ariyoshi, *Shinkokin wakashū no kenkyū: kiban to kōsei*, p. 541; and Minemura, *Shinkokin wakashū* (1974), p. 490.

virtually unknown. According to Teika, the Retired Emperor confided in him: "If these poets were to show their poetic 'skills' anywhere else, they would be laughed at, and so I have invited them here in hopes that in such a formal setting they might produce some good poems.")[41]

The Retainer team took the contest seriously. Is it too modern to think that the class boundaries so clearly drawn by the team formation may have had something to do with the fervor of the Retainers? Ariyoshi offers other suggestions. For one, since everyone knew the editing of *Shinkokinshū* was still going on, they may have seen this as another opportunity to get their work selected, a point Ienaga made in the passage cited in the preceding chapter from his memoirs.[42] Given that nine poems from this event were chosen for *Shinkokinshū* (see below), it seems that Go-Toba did, in fact, hope this contest would generate more material. Furthermore, since four members of the Retainer team (Ietaka, Ariie, Teika, and Masatsune) were *Shinkokinshū* compilers, and a fifth (Tomochika) was a Wakadokoro member involved in the day-to-day editing, professional pride may have played a role.[43] (By contrast, the Lords team included only one *Shinkokinshū* compiler, Michitomo—and we already know Teika's low opinion of *him*—and one Wakadokoro member, Jien, who was not especially active in the everyday work, as near as we can tell from *Meigetsuki*.)

In any case, the following well-known entry from *Meigetsuki* shows just how concerned the Retainer team was that it perform well:

Ken'ei 1/vii/13. . . . After the moon had come up, I went to the Wakadokoro. I joined Ariie, Ietaka, Masatsune, and Tomochika who were already there, deep in conference. We were secretly putting together a petition to the god of Sumiyoshi, promising our gratitude if we should be able to uphold our honor in the upcoming poetry contest. Lord Ariie wrote the petition on behalf of the five of us. Masatsune was to act as messenger and deliver the petition to the head priest of the shrine. Our offerings included sacred prayer wands (*heihaku*), a horse, a poetry contest record, a commissioned sutra reading, and a pilgrimage. This was all done in the greatest secrecy. We heard that Kiyonori was about to arrive, and so we hid everything away.

His Majesty had heard that the five of us were meeting; so he delivered poetry topics for us. Ariie had left before this, but the remaining four of us, plus Hideyoshi,

---

41. *Meigetsuki*, Ken'ei 1/vii/12, 1: 464.
42. See Chapter 8, p. 325.
43. A third explanation offered by Ariyoshi—namely, that Teika wanted to honor the memory of Yoshitsune by doing well—seems less compelling to me. For Ariyoshi's reasoning on all three points, see *Shinkokin wakashū no kenkyū: kiban to kōsei*, p. 256.

composed our verses. Deep into the night, His Majesty sent his poems over to us. Kiyonori was to collect all the poems together and recopy them since His Majesty had given orders that he wanted to see everything the next day. We were extremely grateful that His Majesty had heard of our gathering and sent topics to us.[44]

It is not clear whether the topics Go-Toba sent were for the upcoming poetry contest or whether they were meant for everyone's diversion. The gratitude could have been, then, either for the opportunity to get a headstart on things or for the fact that the Retired Emperor had taken note of them.[45] However, at some point, they did get the topics for the contest, and several nights later the group got together again to look at one another's poems. Teika fretted that all their poems lacked the right qualities. On the next day, Go-Toba sent word that he wanted the poems for the contest delivered to him. Teika complied promptly, but apparently others were slower.[46]

On the 20th, Teika had a look at the matchups for the contest, and Go-Toba also asked him to come to the Wakadokoro and look over the records for the impromptu contest that had been held several days before.[47] Go-Toba seemed to be concentrating a lot of energy on poetry during this period. Compared to some of his earlier entries, Teika's account of this contest, despite its obvious importance to him, is rather brief.

Ken'ei 1/vii/25. Weather partly cloudy. After nightfall, it began to rain. I went to the Wakadokoro and worked on *Shinkokinshū* as I had yesterday. I left in the evening and went to the palace. The Abbot Jien had also gone there. About 9:00 P.M., the poetry contest presentation and discussion (*hyōjō*) began. Michiteru was the only Lord there (although Jien was in attendance, too). His Majesty made his entrance following precedent. I was the Reader (*kōji*), and the lesser-ranked courtiers were seated behind me. After the discussions were finished, we composed some poetry extemporaneously, which we then arranged as a contest, recited to His Majesty, and judged. At daybreak, His Majesty retired, and I left.

To be in attendance and to be able to add my own opinions to the discussion at such a party, with priests and laymen, lords and lesser nobles—it was like the old days in every way! But there was just one person missing. As we all looked at one

---

44. *Meigetsuki*, Ken'ei 1/vii/13, 1: 464.
45. Ariyoshi (*Shinkokin wakashū no kenkyū: kiban to kōsei*, p. 562) argues that the topics mentioned in the *Meigetsuki* entry for the 10th are the ones for the *Keishō jishin* contest, but it is hard to tell since there were several other contests at this time, including one on the 12th (discussed below).
46. *Meigetsuki*, Ken'ei 1/vii/17 and 18, 1: 464–65.
47. Ibid., 1/vii/20, 1: 465.

another, who among us could not have felt the loss? But of all, surely I was the saddest, I was the one whose sleeves were the wettest with tears.[48]

From Teika's remarks at the end of the passage, it becomes obvious why his account is rather cursory. He was overcome by the occasion. Here was an event like so many others over the past few years, and yet something, someone, was missing. Imagawa believes that "one person" to be Jakuren, but surely Teika must be talking about Yoshitsune, who figured in virtually every contest and event during this period and whom Teika had been mourning (and mentioning in his diary) in the months since his death.[49] Without Jakuren, things had gone on, but without Yoshitsune, an era truly seems to have passed. (None of the scholars I looked at even mentions Shunzei as a possibility, maybe because almost two years had passed since his death. However, Teika's comment that he was surely the saddest in the group might point to Shunzei as the one whose lack they felt.)

What about the contest itself?[50] The extant text is virtually complete, with judgment marks as well as the judgments themselves, and this makes it especially valuable. As is generally the case with group judgments (*shūgihan*), the judgment does, when relevant (how frustrating that we cannot shout advice across time about what is "relevant"), record the gist of comments by each team about its own and the opposing poem, as well as the decision. Occasionally whoever transcribed the judgment added a comment. The discussions in this contest raise a few points about allusion, word choice, and the notion of *hon'i* but are disappointingly terse in most rounds.

There were three topics (Morning Flora, Moon by the Sea, Dusk on a Journey), with ten rounds for each topic. The order of the matchups was fixed, both in terms of opponent and in terms of the order of the round (for example, Go-Toba was always matched with Ietaka, and they competed in the first round of each of the three topics). I cannot discern a pattern in the matchups. They are neither consistently along patronage lines, which one might expect from the title of the contest, nor do they consistently cross those lines, as Go-Toba had deliberately arranged in the *Sengohyakuban utaawase*. For example, although Teika is matched with Jien, which is a natural

---

48. Ibid., 1/vii/25, 1: 465.
49. Imagawa, *Meigetsukishō*, p. 192. The editors of *DNS* (iv:9, p. 156), incidentally, assume it is Yoshitsune whom Teika is missing.
50. Complete texts can be found in *Shinpen kokka taikan*, 5:204, pp. 526–28; and *GR* 194, 12: 401–6.

combination because of Teika's service relationship to the Kujō house, Tomochika, of the Murakami Genji clan, is matched with Kintsune, of the Saionji branch of the Fujiwara. And there is no obvious reason for the pairing of Shunzei no Musume and Masatsune in the last rounds of each topic. I believe the teams are simply organized more or less by descending rank-order, and the matchups follow by coincidence.

In terms of results, the Left, or Lords, team won fully half of the rounds, and tied another eight, leaving the Right, or Retainers, team with only seven victories out of 30 rounds. This is an ironic mirror of the equally one-sided results of the *Rōnyaku gojisshu uta-awase* of 1201 (see Chapter 3, p. 95) in which the young upstarts on the Right team beat their elders two to one. In that contest, Go-Toba and Yoshitsune were on the "Young" team, which surely helped its cause. Here, Go-Toba headed the Left team, which, with Jien on it, was loaded with both clout and talent. If, as Teika says, few of the Lords were in attendance, their presence was still felt in the judging.

However, the Right team fared much better when it came to selecting poems from this contest for inclusion in *Shinkokinshū*. Six of the nine poems from this contest in that anthology come from the Right team, and these were chosen right away. It is evident that Go-Toba had high expectations for this contest, for on the very next day, he ordered Teika and others at the Wakadokoro to make preliminary selections from it for *Shinkokinshū*, add their comments, and send them to him. Within the day, he had reached his own conclusions, and Teika was gratified to learn that one of his poems had been chosen.[51] Actually, Teika calls the choice "unexpected" (*zongai*), which, given his perfectionism, may mean he did not think the poem was deserving. But since it was the only one of his three in the contest that did not lose (it tied), and the opposing poem by Jien was also selected, it seems likely that he was grateful rather than bemused. Individual results from the contest are hard to assess statistically since each poet submitted only three poems.[52] In

---

51. *Meigetsuki*, Ken'ei 1/vii/26, 1: 465–66.

52. Both Go-Toba and Jien won two of their rounds and tied the other (and this against top competition—Ietaka for the former and Teika for the latter), which was to be expected. In addition, Kintsune had a perfect record, and Michitomo and Sueyoshi (of the old Tsuchimikado/Rokujō axis we saw several years earlier) also had two wins. On the Right team, only Ariie and Masatsune had winning records, although the surprise would probably be Hideyoshi, a relatively minor player, not so much for his contest record (one Win, one Loss, one Tie) but for the fact that he alone had two of his poems selected for *Shinkokinshū* (Rounds 15 and 25 in the contest became *SKKS* 1556 and 960, respectively).

addition, poems that tied, or even lost, in the contest were chosen for *Shinkokinshū*. Thus, the score is not the story of this contest.

I have selected four rounds for discussion. For some reason, none of the poems in this contest resonated with me, but I will begin with two that came the closest and, since they were both included in *Shinkokinshū*, apparently attracted the compilers as well. The remaining three rounds are examined primarily for their judgments.[53]

Round 13: Moon by the Sea

Left, Jien, Tie

> Waka no ura ni
> tuki no desifo no
> sasu mama ni
> yoru naku turu no
> kowe zo kanasiki

> At Waka Bay,
> With moonlight emerging
> Over the incoming tide,
> The cry of a crane at night—
> How sad it sounds.

Right, Teika

> Mosifo kumu
> sode no tukikage
> onozukara
> yoso ni akasanu
> Suma no urabito[54]

> They dip the brine,
> Moonlight on their sleeves—
> As a matter of course
> They spend no nights without it,
> Dwellers on Suma's shore.

Judgment: Everyone agreed that both poems were especially fine.

Jien alluded to a poem by Yamabe Akahito:

> Waka no ura ni
> sifo mitikureba
> kata wo nami
> asibe wo sasite
> tazu nakiwataru.

> At Waka Bay
> As the tide comes flooding in
> Till tide pools disappear,
> Heading toward the reeds,
> Cranes fly crying overhead.[55]

Akahito's poem is actually an envoy (*hanka*) to a long poem (*chōka*) believed by the compilers of *Man'yōshū* to have been written to commemorate a visit

---

53. I am using the text in *Shinpen kokka taikan*, 5:204, pp. 526–28.
54. These poems appear side by side in *Shinkokinshū*: 1554–55 (XVI, Miscellaneous 1). They are followed by another poem from this same contest. Since they are set among several poems on the same or related topics, Go-Toba apparently set this particular topic for the contest precisely because he wanted poems to fill a gap in the collection.
55. *MYS* 924 (*NKBT* 919). The poem also appears as *KWR* 4353, attributed to Akahito but divorced from the *chōka* and other *hanka*.

Emperor Shōmu made to the province of Ki (where Waka Bay is located) in the Tenth Month of 724.[56] Since Jien more than likely knew the poem from *Kokin waka rokujō*, where it stands alone, separated from the *chōka*, under the category heading "Crane," we might downplay connections to sovereign-praising in the allusion, although the crane is a felicitous topic even if divorced from the *chōka* to Akahito's verse.

Although *Man'yōshū* scholarship was well under way by this time, there was still a considerable amount of ignorance about the collection, and such knowledge as people had was, as noted above, jealously guarded by the Rokujō family.[57] Most Heian and early Kamakura period poets knew the poems in *Man'yōshū* through the selections in *Kokin waka rokujō*, in which the verses were often stripped of their original context, had different wording, and were sometimes even attributed to a different poet. The facts that Jien's *honka* is found in *Kokin waka rokujō* and that in the *Man'yōshū* it is transcribed in a *kanbun/kana* mix, rather than a straight, phonetic *man'yōgana* (the latter style, applied mostly to poems by Yakamochi and the later Man'yō poets, was the first to be decoded by scholars) makes me think Jien knew this one poem only as an independent waka, rather than as an envoy for a felicitous poem about an imperial visit.[58] In any case, Jien's nighttime scene suggests a Love theme—the lonely, Waiting Woman—fulfilling Teika's contention that the best allusions are ones that change the category of the poem.

Teika's poem, too, hints at a Love theme. Its subject(s), with tears/brine on sleeves reflecting moonlight, stay up all night, as the Waiting Woman would. And no mention of Suma is possible without the image of Ariwara no Yukihira and the fictional Genji coming to mind. In fact, the Yukihira

---

56. This is not the place to get into who compiled *Man'yōshū*, or rather, which parts of *Man'yōshū* were compiled when, and by whom, and who wrote the headnotes and footnotes. In this case, there is a headnote that associates the poem with the visit by Emperor Shōmu and an endnote (*sachū*, literally "left note," because it appears to the left of a vertically written text) that says the text of the poem had no indications of the date, but that the editor(s) (early in the history of the text, not the modern editors of the NKBT edition) decided on the basis of a Ki province place-name mentioned in the *chōka* that the poems must have been written for that occasion. (Takaki et al., eds., *Man'yōshū 2*, NKBT 5, pp. 136–37.) For a recent discussion of how and when *Man'yōshū* was complied, see Gotō Toshio, *Man'yōshū seiritsu shinron*.

57. See Chapter 1, "The Politics of Allusion," pp. 17–23.

58. On the other hand, Kamens (*Utamakura*, pp. 207–8) argues that Akahito's *chōka* was in the minds of the *Shinkokin* poets, and that imperial presence was one of the primary associations of Waka no Ura as a place-name.

connection is noteworthy. There is his famous poem on Suma, where he has gone in self-imposed exile:

Wakuraba ni	If, by chance,
tofu fito araba	Anyone should ask,
Suma no ura ni	Just say this:
mosifo taretutu	That on the shores of Suma
wabu to kotafe yo.[59]	Dripping brine, I suffer.

Both this, and possibly Teika's poem, which is less self-pitying than Yukihira's because it focuses on the sad and forlorn lifestyle of the Suma folks, inspired the Nō play *Matsukaze*, which deals with two lonely sisters from Suma who dip brine for a living, and who, in a remarkable scene, discover deeper truths in the moon reflected on their sleeves and in their brine buckets.[60] Teika's poem allows this philosophical reading with its line *yoso ni akasanu* (something like "they do not let the night pass to day [thinking of the moonlight as something] strange or foreign to them"), which implies they are companions to the moon and perhaps ready to see it as a symbol of the Wheel of the Law, the Buddhist Truth.

The next round, with the same topic, is noteworthy for different reasons. The poems were seen as mediocre, but the arguments made by the teams and the comments added by the recorder of the judgments are amusing:

Round 14

Left, Tadayoshi, Tie

Uradutafu	From bay to bay
tuki fa Akasi no	Moonlight brightens, skies clear
sora farete	Over Akashi,
nami ni aki fuku	And waves in autumn always rise
Suma no sifokaze	Blown by Suma's salty winds.

Right, Echizen

Aki wo fete	Autumns pass
tosi mo tumori no	Years pile up, for the boatman,
urakaze ni	In breezes across the bay,

---

59. KKS 962 (XVIII, Miscellaneous 2), with a headnote that says Yukihira composed the poem while "lying low" (*komorifaberu*) in Suma "because of an incident" (*koto ni atarite*—a standard euphemism for some sort of political trouble).

60. Sanari, *Yōkyoku taikan*, 6: 2829–30. Or see Royall Tyler's translation in Keene, *20 Plays of the Nō Theater*, p. 25.

kumoranu tuki wo	This cloudless moon—
iku yo kafa min	How many nights will he see it?

Judgment: Each team showed bias toward its own poem in this round, and neither could make a very strong case. The Right team criticized the Left poem for mentioning too many place-names. "One cannot go wrong by sticking with just one place," they asserted, and asked which place the poet had in mind as the main location, but since he was not in attendance, there was no reply forthcoming. The Right team also argued that their poem was very auspicious, but the Left team countered that there was nothing auspicious about its opening lines.

The comments made by the recorder at the beginning of the judgment are very much to the point.[61] Neither poem is very good, but each team instinctively argued for its own (the recorder called it *katahiki*, "partisanship," "bias"). Yet the arguments are weak. Surely Tadayoshi is not the only poet ever to have mentioned more than one place-name in a poem, especially two places so closely yoked in *The Tale of Genji*, Suma and Akashi. In fact, Teika's preceding poem hints at the connection with his AKASanu Suma. However, with Teika's poem, there is no question where the focus is, and in this round, the Right team quite rightly pointed out that it is not so clear in Tadayoshi's poem. Still, since he was not present, Tadayoshi was unable to defend himself. The dispute over the Right poem was similarly lacking in substance. It was quite a stretch to defend Echizen's poem by saying it was "auspicious," presumably because of its use of the term *iku yo* ("how many nights/generations?"). The Left team's dry comment that the opening lines were anything but auspicious was on the mark.

The judgment in Round 16 discusses faults and also provides a tantalizingly brief look at *hon'i*, that allusive critical term that is usually defined as the "essence" of a topic:

Round 16

Left, Kintsune, Win

Nagameyaru	With my gaze, I follow it.
kokoro iduku ni	Where then,
kayofuran	Will my heart be carried?

---

61. It is not known who wrote these comments. In Round 11, the group seems to feel strongly that Jien's poem is better than his opponent, Go-Toba's, but the round ends up a draw. The recorder comments that this was "inappropriate" (*fushin*, which can also be interpreted as just plain "wrong"). This points to Go-Toba himself as the recorder, if we read this as a protestation. However, it could just as easily have been an indignant Teika.

Morokosi made mo	As far as distant China—
Suma no tukikage	Moonlight over Suma.

Right, Tomochika

Tuki no aki fa	In moonlit autumn
na nomi zo yoru no	The night is in name only.
mosifogusa	I rake, ceaselessly raking,
kaku kaki taete	Seaweed for salt kilns—
miru yume mo nasi	And no chance to dream.

Judgment: The Left team said, 'Seaweed for salt kilns' doesn't work here; and whether one 'rakes' it or 'is raking' it, it amounts to the same thing." The Right team argued that China was awfully far away from Suma, to which the Left team countered, "That feeling of distance is precisely the essence (hon'i) of the topic Autumn Moon!"

Although Teika eschewed the notion of using poems from recent collections as *honka* for allusions and also argued that when using the technique of *honkadori* one needed to change the category of the new poem, there is little doubt that Kintsune had the following poem from *Senzaishū* in mind:

Faruka naru	That which goes
Morokosi made mo	As far as distant China
yuku mono fa	Is the heart of one
aki no nezame no	Awake on an autumn night.
kokoro narikeri.[62]	

This speaks to that gray area between outright allusion and more generic intertext that Edward Kamens grapples with when discussing the use of *utamakura* (poetic place-names).[63]

Tomochika's poem also calls to mind an earlier poem without being an outright allusion. It is to the poem Genji wrote on the margin of one of Murasaki's letters after she died and before he burned them:

Kakitumete	Raked and gathered,
miru kafi mo nasi	There is no more reason to look
mosifogusa	at them,

---

62. *SZS* 302 (V, Autumn 2—the *maki no tō*, or first poem of the book), by Daini no Sanmi (fl. 1032-60). Her given name was Fujiwara Kenshi, and she was Murasaki Shikibu's daughter.

63. Kamens, *Utamakura*, pp. 23-62.

onazi kumowi no	These words, like seaweed for salt kilns.
kemuri tohonare	Let their smoke join that of hers,
	Distant, beyond the clouds.[64]

Poets frequently played with the homophones *kaku*, "to write," and *kaku*, "to rake," as "Genji" (Murasaki Shikibu) does here. Genji is looking at all the letters Murasaki had written him over the years, and the poem has the double sense (through the pun on *mosi*[o] and *moji* [words]) of describing seaweed to be burned for salt and the letters that he is about to burn. It is an achingly poignant moment in *The Tale of Genji*, and presumably Tomochika was hoping to borrow some of that feeling. However, his poem lacks any compelling double sense and is marred, the group agreed, by its awkward and unnecessary repetition of the verb "rake" in two forms.

Despite the fact that this contest gave him more poems for *Shinkokinshū*, Go-Toba apparently still felt something was missing. During the days just before and after the *Keishō* contest, he kept the Wakadokoro members extremely busy with editing chores.[65] Maybe this was what Tomochika's "seaweed gatherer" was complaining about.

There were several more poetry contests, including the impromptu one held the night of the 25th of the Seventh Month, after the poems for the *Keishō jishin no uta-awase* were presented, and another on the 28th. A total of eight (possibly ten) poems from these contests were placed in *Shinkokinshū*, and again they ended up clustered together in that anthology, suggesting that Go-Toba cooked the contests in order to produce certain types of poems. Unfortunately, complete texts for these contests no longer exist, and Teika's comments about them in *Meigetsuki* are too brief to be of use. What information we have comes from headnotes in *Shinkokinshū* and other house collections.[66]

---

64. See the "Maboroshi" chapter in *Genji monogatari* 4, NKBT 17, p. 215 (or the Seidensticker translation, "The Wizard" chapter, p. 734).

65. In just this short span, Teika mentioned going to the Wakadokoro or otherwise working on *Shinkokinshū* on the 20th, 24th, 25th, 27th, 28th, and 30th, as well as the 1st of the Eighth Month; see *Meigetsuki*, Ken'ei 1/vii/20–20 and viii/1, 1: 465–66.

66. For the impromptu contest on the night of the 25th, the topics were Hearing Geese at Dawn, Deer at a House in the Fields, and Love Deep in the Mountains. This information is from Go-Toba's personal collection; see *Shinpen kokka taikan*, 4:18, p. 144. The two selected poems from this contest appear next to each other among the Love poems in *Shinkokinshū*: #1316, by Ietaka, and #1317, by Hideyoshi (XIV, Love 4).

For the contest on the 28th, the topics were Longing for the Past, expressed by the image of Wind; Impermanence in the Rain; Love that has Forgotten. (This information also comes

One of these poems, on the topic Love that has Forgotten, from the contest on the 28th, is among Shunzei no Musume's best:

Tuyu farafu	Brushing away dewy tears,
nezame fa aki no	I lie awake this autumn night,
mukasi nite	As before, when he tired of me,
mifatenu yume ni	And in my dream, not realized,
nokoru omokage[67]	His lingering image...

Subsequently, Go-Toba seems to have perceived another lack, this time of poems in the *jukkai* ("expressing discontent," or, as Brower and Miner would have it "Personal Grievances") mode. *Jukkai* poems, in which the speaker bemoans his or her low lot in life or advancing age or life in general can be found in most collections, and there are even several well-known 100-poem sequences built around the notion.[68]

The mode was not always entirely serious:

Oiraku no	If I had known
komu to siriseba	Old age would come to call
kado sasite	I would have locked the door,

---

from Go-Toba's personal collection; see above.) Five poems were chosen from this contest for inclusion in *Shinkokinshū*; one appears in the Laments section, and the remaining four are in sequence among the Love poems, starting just four poems after the two verses taken from the contest on the 25th. The poems are *SKKS* 803, by Go-Toba (VIII, Laments); 1323, by Go-Toba; 1324, by Teika; 1325, by Ietaka; and 1326, by Shunzei no Musume (XIV, Love 4).

Gotō Shigeo (*Shinkokin wakashū no kisoteki kenkyū*, p. 184), presumably following Kojima Yoshio (*Shinkokin wakashū*, p. 326), where they are numbered 1564 and 1565, and based on the topics given in the headnote (the "longing and wind" topic), argues that two more poems from the contest on the 28th also appear in *Shinkokinshū*, although there is no corroborating evidence for this in various house collections. The poems in question are *SKKS* 1562, by Michiteru, and 1563, by Shunzei no Musume (XVI, Miscellaneous 1).

One other *Shinkokinshū* poem, an Autumn one by Ietaka, seems to be from a contest at around this time, but since its topic differs from any listed for the above two contests, we cannot be sure when it was composed. It is *SKKS* 389 (IV, Autumn 1). The topic, Moon by the Lake, is close to the first topic in the *Keishō jishin no uta-awase*, but this poem does not appear among Ietaka's poems from that contest. Ariyoshi, *Shinkokin wakashū no kenkyū: kiban to kōsei*, p. 541, argues it comes from a contest on the 28th, but he cites no evidence.

67. *SKKS* 1326 (XIV, Love 4).

68. See, e.g., the extended series in *Kokinshū* of poems lamenting old age (#890–905, XVII, Miscellaneous 1), or Shunzei's *Shunzeikyō jukkai hyakushu* (Lord Shunzei's One Hundred Poems of Personal Grievance), probably composed around 1140. See poems 102–201 in Shunzei's personal collection, compiled by the poet in 1178; *Shinpen kokka taikan*, 3:129, pp. 621–22. This sequence is also reproduced independently in GR 390.

nasi to kotafete	Said "no one's home!"
afazaramasi wo	And refused to meet it.[69]

But other examples are more poignant, such as this exchange between Narihira and his mother. The mother (speaking, it would seem, for all mothers everywhere) initiates the dialogue:

Oinureba	As one grows older
saranu wakare mo	People start to talk about
ari to ifeba	That inevitable parting,
iyoiyo mimaku	So more and more it is
fosiki kimi kana.	That I long to see you.
Yo no naka ni	Ah, in this world
saranu wakare no	Would that there were never
naku mo gana	Such "inevitable partings"—
tiyo motonageku	Or at least for the child's sake,
fito no ko no tame.[70]	That the parent lived a thousand years.

Ariwara no Yukihira (818–93) composed a more general, yet lovely, complaint when he saw the waterfall at Nunobiki, in present-day Kobe:

Kokitirasu	Let me gather up
taki no siratama	These jeweled droplets scattered
firofiokite	By the waterfall
yo no uki toki no	So that I may use them as tears
namida nizo karu	For times when the world seems sad.[71]

Of course, from our modern perspective, the mode walks a fine line between poignancy and self-indulgence. Perhaps that is why it became more and more prized as time went on. It was a risky genre. In *Shinkokinshū*, fully 69 of the 101 (or 103, depending on the text) poems in Book XVII (Miscellaneous 2) can be classified as *jukkai* poems.[72] Most of the poems in the next book, too, fall into that category. Among them are eight poems in sequence that were apparently solicited precisely for this section by Go-Toba. Teika

---

69. KKS 895 (XVII, Miscellaneous 1), Anonymous (though attributed in an "endnote" [*sachū*] to one of the "Three Old Men," otherwise unidentified).

70. KKS 900–901 (XVII, Miscellaneous 1). The headnote says Narihira's mother sent her poem because Narihira had not visited her in a long time. The exchange can also be found in *Ise monogatari*, Episode 84, although the mother and son are unidentified in that version.

71. KKS 922 (XVII, Miscellaneous 1).

72. Ariyoshi, *Shinkokin wakashū no kenkyū: kiban to kōsei*, p. 486.

claims to have composed and submitted his three poems (*jukkai sanshu*) on the 1st Day of the Eighth Month (1206), in the midst of all the other poetic and editing activities.[73] He may well have had a lot to complain about at this particular juncture. We do not know all the names of those included in Go-Toba's request, but the eight poems in *Shinkokinshū* are, in order of appearance, by Jien, Michitomo, Teika, Ietaka (three poems in a row), Masatsune, and Shunzei no Musume.

Their complaints are wide-ranging. Jien lamented his inability to really leave the world, even though he was a priest:

Yamazato ni	That mountain hermitage
tigirisi ifo ya	Where I had vowed to go
arenuran	Must now be in ruins,
mataren to dani	Though I never imagined
omofazarisi wo[74]	It would be waiting for me this long.

One cannot help being reminded of the fictional Genji, who frequently talked about his desire to renounce the world but never did. That Jien, four-time Head Abbot of the Tendai sect, could not break free of the political web his family name wove around him—who is to blame? (The question is *not* rhetorical.)

Michitomo's poem is a more general sigh, along the lines of Yukihira's Nunobiki Falls poem:

Sode ni oku	These tears upon my sleeves—
tuyu woba tuyu to	Although I try to hide them,
sinobedomo	Claiming they are just dew,
nareyuku tuki ya	That moon, which so often visits,
iro wo siruran[75]	Surely knows their true color.

The "true color" of his tears, of course, is scarlet—those bitter "tears of blood."

All three of Ietaka's efforts in this project were selected. One of them acknowledges the *Shinkokinshū* project itself and Ietaka's part in it:

Waka no ura ya	Ah, Poetry Bay!
okitu sifoafi ni	I am set afloat, a bubble,
ukabiiduru	In the riptides off its shore.

---

73. *Meigetsuki*, Ken'ei 1 (1206)/viii/1, 1: 466.
74. *SKKS* 1757 (XVIII, Miscellaneous 3).
75. Ibid., 1758.

afare waga mi no	Please tell helpless me
yorube sirase yo	What I can hold on to![76]

Not all the poems in this sequence fit, at first glance, the *jukkai* mode as it was practiced in earlier times. Indeed, Ietaka's comes very close to expressing gratitude rather than regret, at least according to some interpreters.[77] Consider how Ietaka has reworked the anonymous *Kokinshū honka* upon which his poem is based—or of which his poem is virtually a parody:

Watatumi no	The bubble that floats
okitu sifoafi ni	In the riptides offshore,
ukabu awa no	In the vast sea,
kienu mono kara	Does not vanish, and yet
yorukata mo nasi	It has nothing to hold onto, either.[78]

This redefining of categories, also noted by Edward Kamens in relation to *utamakura*, is one of the things that is "*shin*" about *Shinkokinshū*.[79] Teika's and Masatsune's poems in this sequence also initially *seem* even less clearly connected to the traditions of the genre. It is hard to see the "complaint" in them:

Kimi ga yo ni	If I had not encountered
afazu fa nani wo	My Lord's reign, how then
tama no wo no	Could this string of beads,
nagaku to made fa	My life, be so long—
osimarezi mi wo	However unappreciated it might be?[80]

—Teika

Kimi ga yo ni	That I could encounter
aferu bakari no	My Lord's reign is due
miti fa aredo	To the paths I have followed,
mi oba tanomazu	Yet I look ahead to an empty sky,
yukusuwe no sora	My lot in life unsettled.[81]

—Masatsune

---

76. Ibid., 1761.
77. See, e.g., Minemura's reading in *Shinkokin wakashū* (1974), p. 526. In Minemura's numbering system, the poem is #1759. He glosses it as essentially saying "Tell me what I need to do to live up to the honor of being involved in this important poetry project."
78. *KKS* 910 (XVII, Miscellaneous 1).
79. See Kamens, *Utamakura*, pp. 180, 288–89n20.
80. *SKKS* 1759 (XVIII, Miscellaneous 3).
81. Ibid., 1763.

However, as Ariyoshi points out, both poems—and Ietaka's as well, for that matter—imply a dissatisfaction with one's low station in life—a common stance in a *jukkai* poem.[82] Teika describes himself as someone whose loss no one would regret (*osimarezi mi*), and Masatsune argues—quite accurately—that it was his talent in the two "paths" (*miti*) of poetry and *kemari* that got him as far as he is, but that he has not been given the kind of rank (we'd call it "job security" in our day and age) that would allow him to face the future with confidence. Even Ietaka's "bubble afloat" might just as easily be "awash," given the demands Go-Toba was placing on the Wakadokoro members during this time.

What is striking is that Go-Toba must bear the brunt of these complaints, for he lay behind all of them. Yet Go-Toba was willing to include them in *Shinkokinshū*. (He did excise Teika's poem from his Oki-bon, but probably not because it was any more critical of him than the others.) Was Go-Toba magnanimous or just too stupid to see the implications of these verses? Neither; or maybe just a little of the former. I think to him, a good poem was a good poem—sometimes precisely because it suited the circumstances. This, as Robert Brower points out, is an aspect of Go-Toba's aesthetic vision that he articulated in his *Onkuden*.[83]

The evidence is strong that this sequence of poems was part of a vision Go-Toba had for this section.[84] The verses immediately preceding this group, starting with #1748 (or 1746 in some texts), are a series of four poems by Saigyō, then two by Jakuren, and three by Jien, all of which deal with themes of impermanence and renunciation of the world. They bear evidence of having been selected for *Shinkokinshū* by one or another of the compilers.

---

82. Ariyoshi, *Shinkokin wakashū no kenkyū: kiban to kōsei*, p. 497.

83. Brower ("Ex-Emperor Go-Toba's Secret Teachings," p. 12) paraphrases Go-Toba's attitude as he sees it: "'Why,' Go-Toba asks in effect, "cannot a poem be appreciated as much for the occasion that produced it as for any intrinsic merit? Why must there be only a single standard for judging poetic quality?'" One portion of the "Secret Teachings" in which Go-Toba expands on this point is his discussion of a cherry-blossom poem composed by Teika; see pp. 224–25.

84. The argument in this paragraph is based on information found in Gotō Shigeo's (*Shinkokin wakashū no kisōteki kenkyū*, pp. 864–66) detailed chart of compiler's marks found in the various texts of *Shinkokinshū*. Gotō's numbering is the same as Minemura's, which in this section of *Shinkokinshū* is two lower than the *Shinpen kokka taikan* edition. In other words, for example, Jien's *Yamazato no* poem is numbered 1757 in the *Shinpen kokka taikan*, but 1755 in Gotō's chart. (*Shinpen kokka taikan* actually lists both numbers above the poem, but 1757 is on the left and in bold type.)

However, poems 1755–62 bear no compiler's marks in any of the textual lines. I would argue that is because Go-Toba made these selections.[85] The sequence is bracketed on the other end by three poems from Yoshitsune, two of which (1763 and 1765—or 1765 and 1767) were likely selected by Masatsune, but one of which bears no marks. The first of these is especially poignant, considering Yoshitsune's recent death:

Ukisidumi	Will I rise or sink
kon yo fa sate mo	In the world to come?
ika nizo to	What will happen?
kokoro ni tofite	I ask my heart.
kotafekanenuru	It cannot answer.[86]

Bookended with poems by Saigyō, Jakuren, and Yoshitsune—all deceased but very much a part of Go-Toba's group in spirit—these *jukkai* poems, all by living members of the circle, stand out all the more.

Editing continued on *Shinkokinshū* for another year or so, but lest anyone think all was poetry in Go-Toba's court, Teika recorded that right after the flurry of poetic activity in the late Seventh and early Eighth Months, Go-Toba and the courtiers sponsored cockfights at Jōnan-ji temple near his Toba villa. (It was at Jōnangū, the Shinto shrine attached to this temple, that Go-Toba later gathered his anti-Bakufu forces at the time of the Jōkyū War.) Teika's bird won on the first day, and Go-Toba, as enthusiastic about this as about anything he did, ordered Teika to take the bird home, care for it, and bring it back the next day. The following day, the bird won two more rounds in what sounds from the description like an elimination tournament.

---

85. Gotō Shigeo (*Shinkokin wakashū no kisōteki kenkyū*, p. 467) sees the Edo period scholar Shimizu Hamaomi (1776–1824) as the first to take this line. He quotes Hamaomi: "From the evidence I've seen, I presume that those poems that do not bear the names of any of the five compilers must have been selected either by the Gokyōgoku Regent (Yoshitsune) or by the Retired Emperor (Go-Toba)." However, Gotō's review of scholarship dealing with the compilers' marks (ibid., pp. 464–93) reveals that because of the plethora of *Shinkokinshū* texts and textual lines, some of which show compilers' marks and some of which do not (with numerous permutations in between), it is risky to draw too many firm conclusions here. Still, after a mind-numbing parade of evidence, Gotō himself timidly puts forward the conclusion (pp. 595–96) that most of the unmarked poems were probably chosen by Go-Toba. He also allows for Yoshitsune's hand, but that is not relevant to the situation we are discussing here since Yoshitsune was dead by this time.

86. SKKS 1765 (XVIII, Miscellaneous 3). This also appears in the *Sengohyakuban uta-awase*, Round 1472 (Miscellaneous 2), in which it tied with a poem by Teika. Jien was the judge.

They (the courtiers, that is—one imagines the rooster got a respite) ended the evening with a linked verse (*renga*) session.[87]

This is not to say Go-Toba's attention was diverted from *Shinkokinshū* for long. For some time, he had been planning a new villa, on some land ceded to him by Jien. This villa was to be named the Saishōshitennō-in, the "Monastery of the Four Conquering Deva Kings." Like other imperial projects before it, this hall would need to be decorated with sliding doors (*shōji*), and Go-Toba ordered painters and his Wakadokoro poets to work together to create a series of *shōji* and poems that would celebrate the famous poetic places (*utamakura*) of the realm. Although Go-Toba commissioned both waka and Chinese verse for these paintings, I limit my discussion to the waka and their relation to *Shinkokinshū*.

Edward Kamens has discussed this project at length and sees it as an attempt on Go-Toba's part to marshal the cultural and religious forces at his disposal to create a kind of microcosmic representation of the imperial state as he wished it to be.[88] Since Ariyoshi Tamotsu also examines the event, and he and Kamens draw on a number of contemporary sources, including *Ienaga nikki* and *Meigetsuki*, I will not repeat the effort here.[89] In brief, in the Fourth Month of Jōgen 1 (1207) Go-Toba began planning his *shōji*/poem project.[90] He asked the Wakadokoro to come up with a short list of *meisho* (famous places) throughout Japan that would make suitable screen paintings, and about which appropriate waka could be written. Apparently, most of the burden fell on Teika (although we only have his word on that), and the *Meigetsuki* contains numerous references to the project.

Leaving aside for the moment the larger issues Kamens raises, even just from the standpoint of *Shinkokinshū*, the poems for this project are a valuable resource. With thirteen poems selected from this series, it is the eighth larg-

---

87. *Meigetsuki*, Ken'ei 1 (1206)/viii/8–9, 1: 468–69.
88. Kamens, *Utamakura*, chap. 4, "Saishōshitennōin Poems and Paintings" (pp. 168–221), is devoted entirely to this project.
89. Ariyoshi, *Shinkokin wakashū no kenkyū: kiban to kōsei*, pp. 257–78. On pp. 259–66, Ariyoshi neatly sets out the relevant *Meigetsuki* entries and then, after each one, gives a summary of its contents in modern Japanese.
90. Strictly speaking, the year was Ken'ei 2 until the 25th day of the Tenth Month, when it was changed to Jōgen 1 in response, according to *Inokuma kanpakuki*, to a smallpox epidemic and a series of floods (strangely enough, two big fires the month before did not seem to factor into the decision). However, following convention (for example, *Dai Nihon shiryō*, and our extent *Meigetsuki*) and for the sake of convenience, I am calling the year Jōgen 1. For details on the name change, see *DNS*, iv:9, pp. 790–91, 799–804.

est source of poems for the anthology and the largest among the post-banquet events. It was also the last public event that generated poems for *Shinkokinshū*, and since it had ten of the top poets of the day each writing forty-six poems on the same topics, it provides a unique window into the range of styles among Go-Toba's circle.[91]

The poets were Go-Toba, Jien, Michiteru, Shunzei no Musume, Ariie, Teika, Ietaka, Masatsune, Tomochika, and Hideyoshi.[92] Teika and Ariie submitted their poems on the 10th Day of the Sixth Month. Teika's did not come effortlessly. He had spent the day of the 7th discussing with the painter Mitsutoki some of the instructions Go-Toba had given. Go-Toba also announced he wanted the poems by the 10th. Teika was trying to juggle several demands, and on the following day, the stress bubbled to the surface:

Jōgen 1 (1207)/vi/8. Weather, partly cloudy. Suffering from nervous exhaustion, I took to my bed. I was quite depressed over the poems. (Was this really that important to me?) Mitsutoki came by, and I gave him further instructions on the paintings.... My sister Ken no Gozen also came to see me. I read to her my *shōji* poems. In my old age, I have lost hold of the family teachings. And I still miss the late Minister Yoshitsune! There's no one I can discuss things with.[93]

One hopes Ken no Gozen was not too offended by the idea that she was not useful as a sounding board, but there is no evidence that she shared her brother's passion for poetry. Nevertheless, he did finish his poems in time, as did Ariie:

Jōgen 1/vi/10. Weather clear. I had young Tameie come to see me.[94] Ariie informed me that he was taking his own *shōji* poems to the palace. Today we went out by ox-

---

91. Ariyoshi, *Shinkokin wakashū no kenkyū: kiban to kōsei*, p. 257. For a text of the poems submitted by the poets, see GR 178; or *Shinpen kokka taikan*, 5:261, pp. 896–905.

92. In *Meigetsuki* (Jōgen 1 [1207]/v/5, 2: 25), Michitomo is listed among the original participants, but there are no poems by him in the extant text of the event. According to *Meigetsuki*, he did appear in public on at least the 10th and 22nd of the Seventh Month, and it does not seem that he became too ill to participate. Perhaps he simply did not complete his charge on time or the poems he submitted were not up to standard and he was quietly dropped from the list. Or perhaps the *Meigetsuki* entry here is simply in error.

93. Ibid., 1/vi/8, 2: 31.

94. Teika uses the characters "little man" here, whom Imagawa (*Meigetsukishō*, p. 203, in a different entry) identifies as Tameie. However, in other entries, such as the one for the 22nd day of the Seventh Month, both the designations Tameie and "the little man" appear and it is not at all clear if it is the same person. Tameie would have been ten years old by the Japanese

cart. The ladies wanted to see the dog hunting at Uchino. At nightfall, I took my *shōji* poems to the palace. After His Majesty returned from the hunt—it was quite a long wait—I gave my poems to Kiyonori to give to His Majesty. He looked them over and sent them back to me. His response, conveyed through Kiyonori, was "As long as these are his best . . . ." Although he did not give me any detailed critique, even such an ordinary remark from His Majesty is an honor. Since I was not feeling well, I took my leave.[95]

If Teika was expecting a fanfare, he certainly did not get it. Go-Toba's remark literally translates as "Are these especially outstanding?" (*shushō ka* or *koto ni masareru ka*) and is rather ambiguous. It could be an ironic "Is this the best you can do?" or it could be a more solicitous "Are you satisfied with these? If so, then I am, too." Teika's reaction, too, could be ironic. Yet there is no evidence that he reworked any of the poems, and a number of them made the final cut. So it seems that basically Go-Toba was just too preoccupied to give a proper response. Still, in light of the agonizing Teika did over the poems, it must have been an unsatisfying moment for him.

Since others were apparently slower getting their poems done, the dedication ceremony was pushed back to the Eleventh Month.[96] This gave Go-Toba time to look the poems over carefully. Three months later, on the 24th day of the Ninth Month, he summoned everyone to the Wakadokoro:

Jōgen 1/ix/24. In response to a summons, I dragged my weary self off in the afternoon to the Wakadokoro. Ietaka was also there. His Majesty had more or less completed his inspection and marking of the *shōji* poems and had already selected poems for twenty-six of the places. But he was still uncertain about the remaining twenty. He passed a summary of his thoughts on the poems on to us, through Kiyonori, with instructions that we were supposed to make the other selections. People offered a few ideas. Then we moved to the main building and continued the discussion late into the night. Just before midnight, someone brought us three rolls of poems, which amounted to all the ones that had been submitted. His Majesty was pressing us to make our decisions. We looked everything over and continued to debate among ourselves.

Finally we came to some sort of consensus, but we suggested that more of His Majesty's fine poems be included than he had originally chosen. We also offered a few humble adjustments to some of the other selections His Majesty had made.

---

count. Teika had several sons after Tameie, and the most likely possibility here would be one named Kiyoie; see Kuroita, *Sonpi bunmyaku 1*, pp. 290–91.

95. *Meigetsuki*, Jōgen 1/vi/10, 2: 31.
96. Ibid., 1/vi/11–12, 2: 31.

Six or seven of my poems were chosen,[97] whereas those older than I, and my seniors in matters of poetry, were not so well treated.[98] Here I was, brooding about my low station in life and my foolish old age—did I deserve an honor like this? The very first sliding door on the south facade of the east quarter was to be the painting of Kasugano, the opening work of the series. But I was not confident about my poem, which had been chosen for this door, and I insisted that someone else's poem would be more appropriate here. Our discussions had gone on so long that Kiyonori announced it was already daybreak. We took our leave.[99]

The perfectionism shown here by Teika with regard to his own Kasuga poem was the kind of attitude that eventually caused a rift between Teika and Go-Toba.[100] In this case, at least, Go-Toba acquiesced, and one of Michitomo's poems ended up paired with the Kasuga painting.

But what of the poems from this event that were selected for *Shinkokinshū*? Can it be assumed that Go-Toba—and the others in the group, for that matter—would have an agenda here that was distinct from the program that apparently obtained for the *shōji* paintings? It is one thing to explore *utamakura* by means of paintings and poems in Go-Toba's monastery, whether or not there was a larger vision involving the assertion of imperial authority

---

97. The text is a bit garbled here, in what appears to be an inadvertent overlapping of lines by some copyist. One phrase says "six or seven," the next says "five or six." In any case, the final number selected was six.

98. The only ones older than Teika in the group were Jien, Ariie, and Ietaka (Tomochika's dates are unknown, but he was almost certainly younger than Teika). Jien had even more poems selected than Teika (ten), and Ietaka had six. On the other hand, Ariie, with whom Teika had consulted several times about the project and with whom he worked closely in the Wakadokoro (his name comes up often in *Meigetsuki* entries about work at the Wakadokoro) would seem to be the one Teika had in mind, since he had only two poems chosen. See Kamens, *Utamakura*, pp. 186–87, for a detailed chart showing the ten poets and which poems of each were selected.

99. *Meigetsuki*, Jōgen 1/x/24, 2: 42. I am not sure why Brower ("Ex-Emperor Go-Toba's Secret Teachings," p. 68n171) claims: "Since the text of Teika's diary happens to be completely missing for the year in which this event [i.e., the Saishōshitennō-in *shōji* poems] took place, there is no way of knowing what he might have written about it." I am citing the same *Meigetsuki* edition he claimed to be using. I would also modify Kamens's assertion (*Utamakura*, p. 195) that Teika was not at the dedication on Jōgen 1/xi/29. The *Meigetsuki* entry (2: 51–53) for that date is an exceptionally detailed description of the imperial progress to the monastery and the ceremonies involved, and it is clear that Teika played some role in it. However, it also seems he left early and was not included in the banquet that evening (at whose choice is not apparent), although he received lengthy secondhand reports, which he recorded in his diary.

100. For a detailed discussion of this issue, see Terashima, "Teika to Go-Toba-In."

Table 3
Shinkokinshū Poems from *Saishōshitennō-in shōji waka*

SKKS #	SKKS book	Poet	Place-name (*utamakura*)	Selected for screen?
133	II, Spring 2	Go-Toba	Yoshinoyama	yes
184	III, Summer	Masatsune	Asaka no numa	yes
259	III, Summer	Michiteru	Kiyomigaseki	yes
290	IV, Autumn 1	Hideyoshi	Takasago	yes
526	V, Autumn 2	Go-Toba	Suzukagawa	yes
636	VI, Winter	Go-Toba	Ujigawa	yes
637	VI, Winter	Jien	Ujigawa	no
649	VI, Winter	Hideyoshi	Narumi no ura	yes
650	VI, Winter	Michiteru	Narumi no ura	no
1577	XVI, Misc. 1	Ietaka	Abukumagawa	yes
1651	XVII, Misc. 2	Ariie	Nunobiki no taki	yes
1723	XVIII, Misc. 3	Teika	Ōyodo	yes
1900	XIX, Shinto	Jien	Oshioyama	yes

(as Kamens argues). But is that also relevant to *Shinkokinshū* at this, its final stage of compilation? In short, what kind of overlap is there between the poems that were selected for the *shōji* at Saishōshitennō-in, and those that were chosen for *Shinkokinshū*?

In fact, there is significant overlap in one sense, namely, that of the thirteen poems from this event that were included in *Shinkokinshū*, eleven were poems that also had been selected for the *shōji*. Of the ten poets who submitted *shōji* poems, only Shunzei no Musume and Tomochika failed to have any of those poems selected for the anthology. The *Shinkokinshū* selections are shown in Table 3.[101]

The question then arises whether the eleven overlapping poems were among the twenty-six poems Go-Toba had already decided on by the night of the 24th or from among the twenty he threw open for discussion; this we can probably never know. However, there is circumstantial evidence that points to the former case. Of the thirteen *Shinkokinshū* poems from this event, only three show compilers' marks, and even in those cases, not all textual

---

[101] For a view of similar information from the standpoint of the *shōji* poems rather than that of *Shinkokinshū*, see Kamens, *Utamakura*, pp. 181–84.

lines, least of all the main one, show marks.[102] Assuming, as I did earlier in the case of the poems from the *Keishō jishin no uta-awase*, that if no compiler is identified as the selector of a poem in *Shinkokinshū*, then Go-Toba was likely the one who made the choice, this seems to indicate that it was Go-Toba's vision that prevailed here.

But what was that vision? Unlike the *Keishō* contest or the *Jukkai sanshu*, the poems from the *Saishōshitennō-in shōji waka* do not, for the most part, appear in clusters. As seen in Table 3, they are spread throughout the collection. The only pattern I can discern in the placement of these poems is that in nine of the cases, the poem repeats an image or place-name in the previous poem, although in most instances the following poem does not continue the same image. For example, the Spring poem (*SKKS* 133) is about the mountains of Yoshino, as is the poem that precedes it, but the one that follows is about cherry trees in a garden. This is a very small point and at most suggests that Go-Toba was looking for a certain place-name or image to suit his "association and progression" scheme. However, although we can imagine him sponsoring an impromptu poetry contest with such-and-such topics to generate a poem or two that he could use, it seems hardly plausible that he would build a monastery and commission door paintings to do so. I am tempted to argue that the fact that this event yielded poems for *Shinkokinshū* was secondary to its larger purpose, and yet, to some degree, I see that larger purpose as precisely an exploration of poetic place-names (*utamakura*) quite apart from the political program Kamens argues for (although Kamens might well argue the two programs cannot be separated). In that sense, then, perhaps Go-Toba simply wanted more *utamakura* in the anthology, even if, as Kamens notes, the poems did not always explore those *utamakura* in conventional ways.[103] (Or maybe he just wanted a few more poems by particular poets.)

Let us look at four examples. First, one by Go-Toba, which was selected for the painting of Yoshino:

    Miyosino no   At lovely Yoshino,
    takane no sakura   On the peaks the cherry blossoms
    tirinikeri   Have all scattered,

---

102. Again, I have used the chart in Gotō Shigeo, *Shinkokin wakashū no kisōteki kenkyū*, pp. 670–890.

103. Kamens, *Utamakura*, pp. 180, 288–89n20.

> arasi mo siroki Even storm winds are white
> faru no akebono In spring's dawn![104]

Cherry blossoms and Yoshino form one of the most enduring associations in Japanese poetry, and in terms of image, Go-Toba was not breaking new ground here. However, he was giving a new twist to Sei Shōnagon's "four seasons." In her famous opening lines to *The Pillow Book*, Sei Shōnagon describes the time of day appropriate, in her mind, to each of the four seasons. Her notions became an intimate part of medieval waka—beyond allusion and into intertext. In *Shinkokinshū*, scores of poems end with the lines *faru no akebono* (spring dawn) or *aki no yufugure* (autumn evening), in accordance with the times of day Sei Shōnagon set out. But in *The Pillow Book*, Sei Shōnagon's dawn sky is whitening because of the rising sun (*Haru wa akebono, yōyō shiroku nariyuku yamagiwa sukoshi akarite*[105]—"In spring, dawn, as the gradually whitening mountain ridge barely brightens"), whereas Go-Toba's is white because of the cherry petals scattering in the wind.

One of Hideyoshi poems was chosen to accompany the painting of Takasago:

> Fuku kaze no   The wind that blows through it
> iro koso miene   Reveals no colors,
> Takasago no   But to the Onoe Pine
> Wonofe no matu ni At Takasago
> aki fa kinikeri   Ah, autumn has come![106]

There is some disagreement among scholars as to how to interpret the phrase *wonofe no matu* (*onoe no matsu* in Hepburn), since *onoe no* can be taken descriptively, simply meaning "at the top of the peak," which is the way Minemura reads it,[107] or as a reference to a specific pine tree, the Onoe Pine, an odd cross-breed of red and black pine that grows in the precincts of Onoe Shrine, in the present-day Kakogawa district of Hyōgo prefecture, which is also where Takasago is located.[108] I have followed the latter reading.

---

104. *SKKS* 133 (II, Spring 2).
105. Ikeda et al., *Makura no sōshi; Murasaki Shikibu nikki*, pp. 43–44.
106. *SKKS* 290 (IV, Autumn 1).
107. Minemura, *Shinkokin wakashū* (1974), p. 115.
108. See Ozawa Masao's (*Kokin wakashū*, pp. 128–29) reading of *KKS* 218 (IV, Autumn 1) for an example of this view. Yoshida et al., *Utamakura nayose*, 7: 112–18, lists a string of poems with the expression *takasago no onoe* in them; so the association was obviously quite strong for

Hideyoshi was also alluding to at least two poems. One is the opening poem of the first Autumn book of *Kokinshū*. Hideyoshi's use of allusion in this case is not a *honkadori* per se, but it is a poem that unquestionably lies behind Hideyoshi's conception:

Aki kinu to	Though my eyes
me nifa sayaka ni	Can see no evidence
mienedomo	That autumn has come,
kaze no oto ni zo	I find myself surprised
odorokarenuru	At the sound of the wind.[109]

In Hideyoshi's poem, too, there is no visual evidence for autumn, only the sound of the wind through pines (*matukaze*). The second allusion is a straightforward *honkadori* from a *Kokinshū* spring poem by Ōshikōchi no Mitsune (fl. 894–916):

Faru no yo no	On this spring night
yami fa ayanasi	The darkness is absolute;
ume no fana	And the plum blossoms—
iro koso miene	Their color cannot be seen,
ka yafa kakururu	But can their scent be hidden?[110]

Mitsune's poem, too, challenges the "reader" by opening the scene onto absolute darkness and forcing the mind to think in other senses. In Mitsune's poem, however, the evidence is to be detected by the nose rather than the ear, but in both poems, the point is that the beauty (*iro*) of nature operates through more than the visual sense.

The final example is a pair of poems, one by Go-Toba, the other by Jien. As we have seen, these two poets worked very well together. In this case, Go-Toba's poem was the one selected for the *shōji*, but Jien's was picked to follow it in *Shinkokinshū*. The poems were placed after a series of four verses by Yoshitsune, the last of which provides a thematic lead-in for Go-Toba's and Jien's poems:

Katasiki no	On the sleeves of my robe,
sode no kofori mo	Spread alone on half the bed,

---

poets. This still does not answer the question of whether, in the Heian and Kamakura periods, the poets were thinking "pines at the peak of Mount Takasago," or "the Onoe pine on Mount Takasago."

109. *KKS* 169 (IV, Autumn 1), by Fujiwara no Toshiyuki (d. 901?).
110. *KKS* 41 (I, Spring 1), by Ōshikōchi no Mitsune.

musubofore	Ice has crystallized, unmelting,
tokete nenu yo no	Restless through this sleepless night
yume zo mizikaki	How brief my dream!
	—Yoshitsune

Fasifime no	The maiden at the bridge,
katasikigoromo	Her robes spread alone on half
samusiro ni	Of the cold, narrow mat—
matu yo munasiki	Her night of waiting desolate,
Udi no akebono	Now Uji at dawn.
	—Go-Toba

Azirogi ni	The sound of waves
isayofu nami no	Lapping on weir pilings
oto fukete	Grows deeper with the night—
fitori ya nenuru	Do you sleep alone,
Udi no fasifime	Maiden at Uji Bridge?[111]
	—Jien

All three poems allude to this atmospheric anonymous *Kokinshū* love poem:

Samusiro ni	On the cold narrow mat
koromo katasiki	Does she spread her robe alone
koyofi moya	Once again tonight,
ware wo maturamu	And wait for me,
Udi no fasifime	Maiden at Uji Bridge?[112]

This provides an excellent opportunity to see how *Shinkokin* poets interacted with their literary past. To begin with, there is the place-name (*utamakura*) Uji. In *Man'yōshū* it was known for its river and, it seems, for warrior clans. The fixed expressions *mononofu no yaso udigafa* ("the Uji River and its eight thousand warrior clans") and *mononofu no udigafa* ("the Uji River where warriors are") appear here and there in that collection. In fact, as I will demonstrate below, Jien alluded to one of those very poems. Uji was also known for its fishing weirs and the crossing (*watari*) there.[113]

---

111. *SKKS* 635–37 (VI, Winter).
112. *KKS* 689 (XIV, Love 4).
113. See, e.g., MYS 3251 (NKBT 3237) for the expression *mononofu no udigafa*, MYS 3250–51 (NKBT 3236–37) for references to the Uji crossing, and MYS 266 (NKBT 264) for *mononofu no yaso udigafa*.

At some point, the generic "crossing," probably by boat, was replaced with a bridge. Bridges in ancient (and medieval) Japan were sometimes a place for prostitutes to attract customers. Takahashi Mushimaro wrote a disarming poem seemingly about one such professional, in which the speaker sees a women dressed in a red cloak making her way alone across the vermilion-lacquered bridge at Kōchi (in present-day Osaka), and wonders whether she has a man or whether she sleeps alone. He wants to find out, but "Ah, but I know not her home / the lady that I long for," he concludes. He ends with an envoy:

Öpöpasi no	Ah, if I had a house
tumë ni ipe araba	At the foot of the great bridge
uraganasiku	I would have her stay there,
pitöri yuku ko ni	That girl who walks alone
yado kasamasi wo	Looking so unhappy.[114]

I suspect that the original Maiden at the Uji Bridge (*udi no fasifime*) was just such a woman, and indeed, the *Kokinshū* poem cited above can certainly be read that way. But somewhere along the way, presumably in a process similar to the one in which the image of Izumi Shikibu gets transformed from passionate (if not promiscuous) court lady to Bodhisattva, the Maiden at the Uji Bridge becomes the Goddess of Uji Bridge, and this is how medieval commentators understood her.[115] Yet both Go-Toba's and Jien's poems

---

114. *MYS* 1746–47 (*NKBT* 1742–43), with the title "On Seeing a Maiden Walking Alone over the Great Bridge at Kōchi." The poem is actually "from the Mushimaro Collection," in *Man'yōshū*, and it is not certain whether Mushimaro himself wrote it. A charming translation of the poem and its envoy can be found in the Nippon gakujutsu shinkōkai translation of *Man'yōshū*, pp. 218–19.

115. Kiyosuke in his treatise *Ōgishō* (written sometime between 1124 and 1144) discussed the Maiden at Uji Bridge in a commentary on the *Kokinshū* poem cited above. He recounted a tale involving a husband kidnapped by the Undersea Dragon King and how his wives come looking for him one at a time and recite this poem to summon him. With little segue, Kiyosuke then concluded, analogizing from examples of other goddesses like Saohime and Tatsutahime, that the suffix *hime* (Lady) can be applied to goddesses and therefore Uji no Hashihime must be a goddess. See Sasaki Nobutsuna, *Nihon kagaku taikei*, 1: 332. The tale Kiyosuke told hardly seems relevant at all, and his remarks about the *hime* title are not compelling. However, his view of the situation seems to have prevailed, and still appears in modern commentaries (see following note).

For a discussion of Izumi Shikibu's transformation, see Marra, "The Buddhist Mythmaking of Defilement." That she came to be seen as "loose" on the mere evidence of her diary, which hardly depicts her as promiscuous, itself shows the power of the male-centered waka

can still be read as referring to a low-ranking lady, someone's mistress perhaps, even though scholars claim that it is the Uji River Goddess waiting for her male counterpart (a kind of earth-bound Tanabata).[116]

Jien's poem, in fact, is an allusive variation on a *Man'yōshū* poem said to have been written by Hitomaro as he was traveling to Ōmi and arrived at the banks of the Uji River—one of the poems mentioned above as a *locus classicus* for the expression *mononofu no yasoudigafa*:

Mononofu no	Like the waves
Yasoudigafa no	Lapping on weir pilings
aziroki ni	At the Uji River
isayofu nami no	Of eight thousand warrior clans
yukuwe sirazu mo	I know not where to go.[117]

Hitomaro's poem came to be read as a *mujō* poem, that is, a poem that expresses the notion of *mujō*, or impermanence, although the expression is somewhat anachronistic when applied to a late-seventh-century work.[118] This gives Jien two antecedents to draw on—the romantic/erotic/atmospheric Maiden at the Uji Bridge image and the more philosophical man-at-a-loss image.

But there is more. By the time of *Shinkokinshū*, no mention of Uji was innocent of resonance to the so-called Uji Chapters of *The Tale of Genji*. The storyline there depicts the convoluted and ultimately unhappy relationship among two men (Kaoru and Prince Niou) and three ladies (two sisters, Ōigimi and Nakanokimi, and their half-sister, Ukifune). The plot draws not only on the notion of a woman waiting at the Uji Bridge but also on a popular tale (versions of which are apparently common to north Asia), recounted in *Man'yōshū* and *Yamato monogatari*, of the Maiden Unai, who killed herself when two young warriors fought for her hand and died. So the three *Shinkokinshū* poems above take on yet another dimension, of unrequited love, disappointment, and finally, tragedy.

---

aesthetic that portrayed women poets like Ono no Komachi and Izumi Shikibu as victims of their own passion and discounted the possibility of aesthetic distance, at least as far as such poets were concerned.

116. See, e.g, Minemura, *Shinkokin wakashū* (1974), pp. 204–5, for this sort of reading.

117. *MYS* 266 (NKBT 264). As with Jien's earlier *Man'yōshū* allusion, this Hitomaro poem also appears in *Kokin waka rokujō* (1645, under the category *aziro*—weir), which is probably how Jien knew it.

118. Takagi et al., *Man'yōshū 1*, NKBT 4, pp. 154–55.

Yoshitsune doubled the *Genji* connection, for his poem is also an allusive variation of a verse Genji composed toward the end of the "Asagao" (Morning Glory) chapter, when he abruptly awakens from a dream of the dead Fujitsubo:

Tokete nenu	Restless sleep shattered,
nezame sabisiki	And now awake
fuyu no yo ni	This lonely winter night—
musuboreturu	How brief the dream
yume no mizikasa	That had crystallized![119]

And here, "crystallized" in these poems and the process of their production, is the Shinkokin world—complex discourse that builds its vision using pieces from *Man'yōshū* (or from *Man'yōshū* as mediated by Heian period collections), from *Kokinshū*, from folk tales, from *The Tale of Genji*, and from the layers of associations a single place-name can have. This is carried out with a rhetorical approach that often uses more nouns than verbs and combines them in ways that exploit the ambiguities inherent in Japanese syntax (in which predicates come at the end of the clause, but modifiers precede the modified). As soon as one thinks one has the reading nailed, one notices (or digs up—that is what scholars are for, after all!) another trick. It is a connoisseur's art, privileged by those who were privileged themselves, and thus an effective means for Go-Toba to help unify his court. Kamens's reading of the Saishōshitennō-in poems as a microcosmic map of Go-Toba's domain (or the domain he desired) seems apt for the *Shinkokinshū* project as a whole. In fact, the Saishōshitennō-in screen painting poems were the last of Go-Toba's *Shinkokinshū*-related poetry events and in that way, too, provided closure to his project.

---

119. Yamagishi Tokuhei, *Genji Monogatari* 2, NKBT 15, p. 270.

Conclusion

By 1208, *Shinkokinshū* as we know it today was virtually complete. Teika and Ietaka made several copies in the summer of 1209, but Go-Toba evidently ordered more adjustments.[1] Ienaga's clean copy, which is considered the "official" Wakadokoro version, was not produced until 1216. Unfortunately, the original does not survive, and there is some discrepancy among its descendants, but it is nonetheless the basis for modern editions.[2]

For a decade, from the late 1190s through 1208, Go-Toba had carefully, skillfully crafted the artistic consensus that produced this unique anthology, which, in part because it was produced by consensus, stands out from the imperial anthologies that precede it and those that follow. The standard view of Go-Toba—hot-headed, addicted to diversion, insensitive to those around him, and yet a genius in his way—is both belied and bolstered by what we know of the process surrounding compilation of *Shinkokinshū*. No dilettante would have had the patience to painstakingly piece together thirty 100-poem sequences into the *Sengohyakuban uta-awase*, for example, nor could he have so delicately balanced literary factions (led by such crabby personalities as Teika and Kenshō at that!) as well as political rivals. Go-Toba quietly, smoothly supplanted Michichika as the primary patron of poetry, yet the latter seemed hardly to have noticed and apparently died as convinced as ever that he was a central figure in the literary world of his day, no matter that we know better now. With equal acumen, the young retired

---

1. Ariyoshi, *Shinkokin wakashū no kenkyū: kiban to kōsei*, p. 565. For more details, see Gotō Shigeo, *Shinkokin wakashū no kisōteki kenkyū*, pp. 214–22.

2. Again, for full details, see Gotō Shigeo, *Shinkokin wakashū no kisōteki kenkyū*, pp. 378–404.

sovereign slowly but inexorably relegated the Rokujō school to the margins but kept a check on the new Mikohidari school by promoting (literally and figuratively) such figures as Asukai Masatsune and Fujiwara Hideyoshi. Yet if Teika, and even Go-Toba's faithful scribe Ienaga, are to be believed, all this was not produced without pain. Go-Toba pushed those around him hard. His whims—the compulsion to have a presentation banquet for the collection long before it was completed, for instance, and his constant pressure and heavy-handed suggestions for revision—must have been very difficult to bear.

Still, however important Go-Toba may have been to the process, there is no question that other remarkable names stand out during this period: Teika, of course, Yoshitsune, and Masatsune, as well as Ienaga, Ietaka, and Shunzei no Musume. They emerge not only as outstanding poets but also as distinct and powerful personalities.

Powerful, too, was the larger discourse engendered by waka itself. Not only did its production loom large over the court, but its language and vision permeated prose. Ienaga's diary is a record of waka in more ways than one. It chronicles, not always faithfully, the poems and poetic activities of the age. Even more faithfully, and perhaps in spite of itself, it chronicles how deeply waka had penetrated the courtly medieval discourse. Go-Toba and Jien played out their grief—the one for his lover, the other for his nephew—in a series of poems. Teika, Masatsune, Kunaikyō, Kamo no Chōmei, Jakuren—all built their careers on their verse. Ienaga mourned—without a single poem, but in no less a poetic way than Hitomaro himself—the death of the Princess Shikishi. In many ways, the lives of these people centered around waka—not just the verse form, but its figures and driving narrative. Even Teika's *kanbun* diary cannot escape this discourse: the meal he catered for the Wakadokoro is built on references to Ariwara no Narihira and *Ise Monogatari*.

Go-Toba himself rehearsed his grander political plans by orchestrating an anthology and furnishing a monastery with *shōji* paintings and poems. These became, in retrospect, signposts to his push to restore imperial rule. The monastery and its paintings have disappeared, but the anthology outlasted his worldly agenda. After his defeat in the Jōkyū War, Go-Toba took the tonsure in Jōkyū 3 (1221)/vii/8 and was exiled to Oki, where he died on 1239/ii/22. While there, he had plenty of time to pursue his vision of poetry, and he even edited, one last and far-reaching time, *Shinkokinshū*. But history had passed him by, and his Oki-bon version is now a series of asterisks in modern editions of the collection.

Once Go-Toba could no longer exert his charisma, the world of poetry began to harden around competing schools again. Teika himself turned his back on his former patron and, bowing before the political winds, erased all traces of him from the next imperial anthology, *Shinchokusenshū*.[3] After Teika's descendants, in the form of the Nijō house, gained pre-eminence in the waka world, for several centuries *Shinkokinshū* itself was viewed as an embarrassing anomaly; it was compiled, after all, by a *committee* rather than by the revered ancestor, Teika, alone. Worse yet, it was associated with the failures of Go-Toba, who, in turn, had declared his dislike of that same revered ancestor, Teika.

In fact, however, Go-Toba had been able to bring together, through enormous will, energy, effort, and sheer charismatic power, a bewildering array of talent and encourage them to a surge of poetic production that is probably unequaled in Japanese history. No one else could have done it. The other pretenders to this central position had quirks, enemies, flaws. Go-Toba clearly had these, too, but he also had the weight of imperial tradition behind him and the skill to use it. The result, *Shinkokinshū*, has outlasted any political program he, or anyone else at that time, could have dreamed of.

---

3. See Smits, "The Poet and the Politician"; and Huey, "Warrior Control over the Imperial Anthology." Mostow (*Pictures of the Heart*, p. 25) notes that Teika's exemplary collection *Hyakunin shūka* (1234?), arguably a forerunner of the more famous *Hyakunin isshu*, also contains no poems from either Go-Toba or Juntoku, and, contrary to the claims of its title, lists only 97 poets, rather than 100. However, in the so-called *Ogura hyakunin isshu* (1239), compiled after Go-Toba's death, Go-Toba and Juntoku appear as poets 99 and 100. This, too, appears to have been self-censorship on Teika's part.

Appendixes

APPENDIX A

Family Trees and Patronage Charts

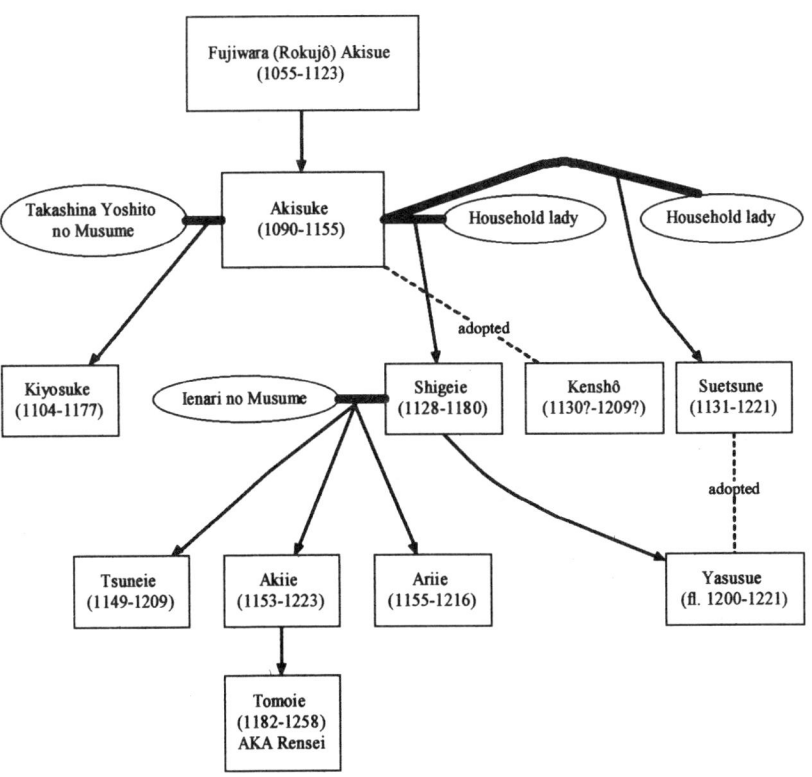

Fig. 3 Rokujō family tree through early 1200s

388 Appendix A

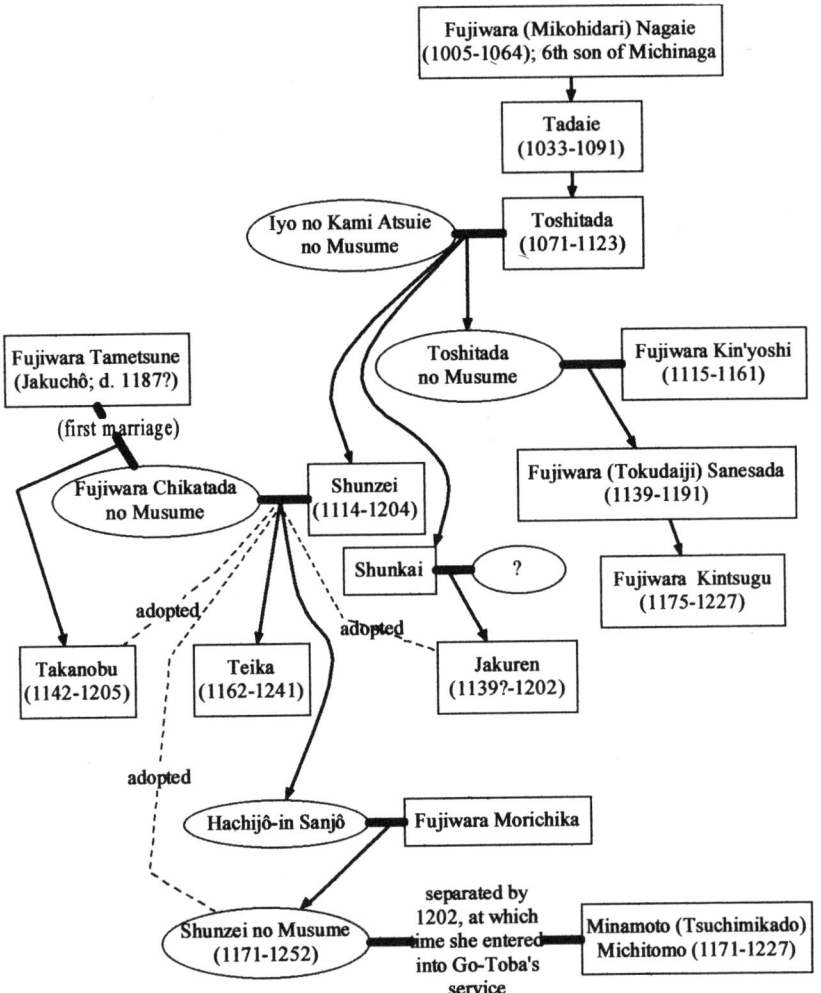

Fig. 4 Mikohidari family tree through early 1200s

Family Trees and Patronage Charts

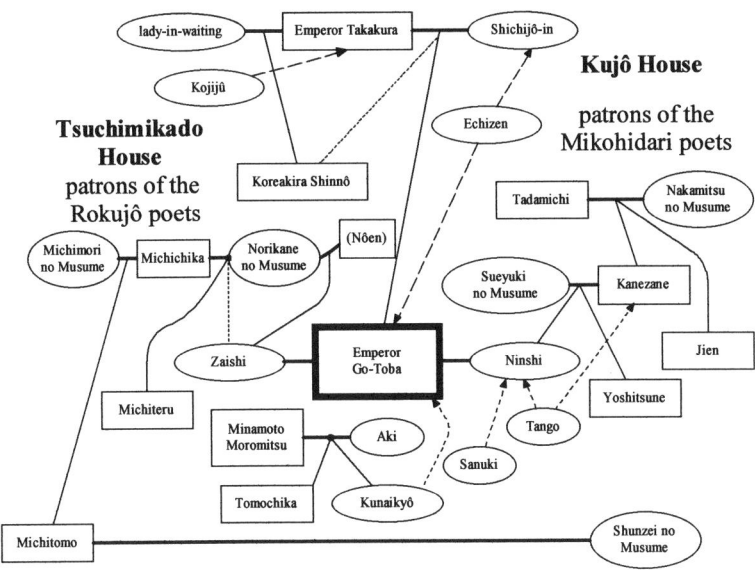

Fig. 5 Marriage and family ties in Go-Toba's poetry circle (─── marriage; ─── natural parent/child; ········ adoptive parent/child; ──▶ service)

APPENDIX B

Short Biographies of Principals

Most of the information here is derived from Ariyoshi's *Waka bungaku jiten*. Only such alternative names as are likely to be encountered in standard reference works or editions of collections are included.

Ariie, Fujiwara (Rokujō; 1155–1216); son of Junior Third Rank Shigeie (himself a son of Akisuke) and Senior Second Rank Fujiwara Ienari's Daughter (herself branched from Rokujō Akisue); nephew of Kiyosuke, Suetsune, and Kenshō. In 1202 he was appointed Lord-Secretary of the Treasury (Ōkurakyō) and, in 1208, rose to his father's rank of Junior Third Rank; took the tonsure in 1215. He participated in the major poetic events of both camps throughout the 1190s and took part in many of the more important poetic activities under Go-Toba; was both a Wakadokoro member and one of the *Shinkokinshū* compilers. Nineteen poems in *Shinkokinshū*.

Chōmei, Kamo (1155–1216); son of the Superintendent of the Lower Kamo Shrine, Nagatsugu, identity of mother now unknown. He made his public poetry debut in 1175 and had one poem in *Senzaishū*; studied poetry under Minamoto Shun'e (1113–91?; Toshiyori's son) and immortalized Shun'e's teachings in the treatise *Mumyōshō*. He was also skilled at *biwa* (lute). He became part of Go-Toba's poetry circle in 1200 and was named to the Wakadokoro but took the tonsure in 1204—evidently because Go-Toba denied him a shrine appointment he had coveted—and retired to Ōharayama (later moving to Hino). In 1211 he went to Kamakura to meet then-Shogun and poetry fan Sanetomo; returned to his hermitage in Hino and wrote his most famous essay, *Hōjōki* (Account of My Hut), the following year. Ten poems in *Shinkokinshū*.

Echizen (?–1248?); AKA Kayōmon-in Echizen; dates and parentage uncertain, but probably the daughter of one Ōnakatomi Kinchika, Chief Administrator (*shinkan*) of Ise Shrine. She was originally in the service of Shichijō-In (1157–1228), Takakura's consort and Go-Toba's biological mother, but Go-Toba invited her into his palace because of her poetic skills, and she came to serve his consort, Kayōmon-in. She made her poetic debut in the *Shōji ninen in shodo hyakushu* and appeared in many other events in this period. Seven poems in *Shinkokinshū*.

Go-Shirakawa, Emperor (1127–92; r. 1155–58); referred to as Go-Shirakawa no In in *Shinkokinshū*; seventy-seventh emperor, fourth son of Emperor Toba. Go-Shirakawa was better known for his interest in *imayō* (popular songs) and was responsible for the most important extant collection of them, *Ryōjin hishō*, for which he also provided important historical anecdotes and commentary. But he was also the sponsor of *Senzaishū*, compiled by Shunzei. In the world explored in this book, his impact was primarily as a politician trying to juggle the court and the Kamakura Bakufu; he and the partisans who survived him eventually helped bring about Kujō Kanezane's downfall. Four poems in *Shinkokinshū*.

Go-Toba, Emperor (1180–1239; r. 1183–98); referred to as Daijō Tennō in *Shinkokinshū*; eighty-second emperor, fourth son of Emperor Takakura, his mother was Fujiwara Nobutaka's daughter, who took the palace name Shichijō-In no Shokushi. He was handpicked at the age of four by his grandfather Go-Shirakawa (who ignored the normal succession order) to succeed the young Emperor Antoku, who had died at the Battle of Dan-no-ura. He began sponsoring poetry events after his abdication and commissioned *Shinkokinshū*, the eighth imperial anthology. Go-Toba was interested in many arts and diversions besides poetry, including *kemari* (kickball), horseback riding, *imayō*, and so on and was especially devoted to the Kumano Shrine, to which he journeyed more than twenty times during his early life. In 1221 he attempted to raise an army and topple the Kamakura Bakufu (the so-called Jōkyū War); after the attempt failed, he took the tonsure and was exiled to the island of Oki for the remainder of his life. In exile, he kept his hand in poetry by re-editing *Shinkokinshū* (producing the so-called Oki-bon version), composing poems of his own, and arranging the poems of others into *senka-awase*. Thirty-four poems in *Shinkokinshū*.

Hideyoshi, Fujiwara (1184–1240; given name also read as Hidetō, the reading Ariyoshi Tamotsu prefers); more commonly known by his priestly name of Nyogan; son of Fujiwara Hidemune and Minamoto Mitsumoto's Daughter. He was originally one of Michichika's retainers, but entered Go-Toba's service when he was sixteen. Go-Toba especially favored him, appointing him to the Wakadokoro, and he was active in virtually all the major events of the era. He took the tonsure and the name Nyogan after the Jōkyū Disturbance, in which he lost many of his family members. Seventeen poems in *Shinkokinshū*.

Ienaga, Minamoto (Daigo; 1173?–1234); son of Minamoto Tokinaga; identity of mother now unknown. He entered Go-Toba's service in 1196; held minor administrative offices and rose to the rank of Junior Fourth Upper. He was named Chief Recorder (*kaikō*) to the Wakadokoro in 1201 and provided administrative supervision for the process of collecting and editing poems for *Shinkokinshū*; calligraphed the so-called Ienaga-bon version of that collection in 1216, which is considered the basis for the standard text; was moderately active in Go-Toba's poetry activities, including *Sengohyakuban uta-awase*. He remained loyal to Go-Toba and resigned his public office after the Jōkyū War. He lived a quiet life until his death. His memoirs, *Minamoto Ienaga no nikki*, focus on the years surrounding *Shinkokinshū*. Three poems in *Shinkokinshū*.

Ietaka, Fujiwara (1158–1237); AKA Karyū and Mibu no Nihon; son of Senior Second Rank Fujiwara Mitsutaka and Fujiwara Sanekane's Daughter. He rose to the Junior Second Rank in 1235, took the tonsure the following year, and then died the year after that. He began to attract attention as a poet in the 1180s and had four poems in *Senzaishū*; grew close to the Mikohidari poets in the 1190s and was part of the *Roppyakuban uta-awase*. He became an integral part of Go-Toba's poetry circle in the early 1200s and was appointed to the Wakadokoro and the *Shinkokinshū* selection committee; he remained close to Teika and Go-Toba throughout his life and was one of the pivotal poets of his age. His house collection, *Gyokuginshū*, is better known as *Minishū* (from the initial syllables of his nickname, *Mi*bu no *Ni*hon). Forty-three poems in *Shinkokinshū*.

Jakuren (1139?–1202); AKA Shōsuke Nyūdō; secular name, Fujiwara Sadanaga; son of the Ajari Shunkai (one of Shunzei's brothers); mother now not known. He was adopted at a young age by Shunzei and in 1172 took the tonsure. In the 1170s, he made several journeys throughout Japan, and in the early 1190s he made a trip to Izumo and Kantō. Throughout, he continued to participate in poetry activities; allied himself with Shunzei, Teika, and the Mikohidari school, and became part of Go-Toba's circle in the early 1200s (Ienaga says Go-Toba brought him out of retirement); participated in all the major poetry events and was named both a Wakadokoro member and one of the *Shinkokinshū* compilers, although he died before its completion. Thirty-five poems in *Shinkokinshū*.

Jien (1155–1225) AKA Jichin; sixth son of Fujiwara Tadamichi and Fujiwara Nakamitsu's Daughter; the younger brother of Kujō Kanazane and uncle of Kujō Yoshitsune. He entered religious life in 1165, taking the priestly name Dōkai; with help from his family connections, he rose quickly in the clerical hierarchy, achieving the high rank of *hōin* in 1181, whereupon he changed his priestly name to Jien. He was named Chief Abbot of the Tendai Sect (*Tendai zasu*) in 1192, a post that he held and resigned four times over the next two decades; he first resigned in 1196, when his brother Kanezane was forced to resign all his offices; Go-Toba reappointed him to the Tendai post in 1203. After Kanezane and Yoshitsune died, he became the most important member of the Kujō house; declined to support Go-Toba in the Jōkyū War and wrote the history *Gukanshō* in an effort to discourage a restoration movement. He began to attract notice as a poet in the mid-1180s and had nine poems in *Senzaishū*; was friends with Saigyō; in the 1190s helped Kanezane sponsor poetic activities; from the time of the *Shōji ninen in shodo hyakushu* became a key member of Go-Toba's poetry group and was a contributor and judge for the *Sengohyakuban uta-awase*; was named to the Wakadokoro in 1201. Ninety-two poems in *Shinkokinshū* (second in number to Saigyō's ninety-four).

Kanemune, Fujiwara (1163–1242); son of Fujiwara Tadachika and Fujiwara Mitsufusa's Daughter. He rose to Senior Second Rank, Provisional Major Counselor. He had his first work published in *Senzaishū*; participated in the *Roppyakuban uta-awase*; then became part of Go-Toba's group in the early 1200s; competed in the *Sengohyakuban uta-awase*. Two poems in *Shinkokinshū*.

Kanezane, Fujiwara (Kujō; 1149–1207; AKA Go-Hōshōjidono); son of Fujiwara Tadamichi and Fujiwara Nakamitsu's Daughter; elder brother of Jien and father of Yoshitsune. He became Regent (*sesshō*) and head of his clan in 1186; named Chancellor (*daijō daijin*) in 1190 and Chancellor/Regent (*kanpaku*) in 1191; toppled in a palace coup led by Minamoto Michichika in 1196 and spent the rest of his life in retirement, taking the tonsure (with Hōnen presiding) in 1202, upon the death of his wife. He initially became interested in poetry in the 1170s and studied with the Rokujō school, but grew closer to Shunzei and Teika (perhaps because of his son's friendship with the latter) in the 1180s; became an important patron of the Mikohidari school; supported Go-Toba's poetry group and even participated quietly in some events. Eleven poems in *Shinkokinshū*.

Kenshō (1130–1209); biological parents now not known; adopted son of Fujiwara (Rokujō) Akisuke. Kenshō entered the priesthood at a young age, starting out at the Tendai headquarters on Mount Hiei, but later moving to the Iwasimizu Shrine before finally ending up affiliated with Ninna-ji. A staunch supporter of the Rokujō school, he wrote a well-known criticism of Shunzei's judgments for the *Roppyakuban uta-awase* known as the *Roppyakuban chinjō*; took part in *Sengohyakuban uta-awase* and several other events sponsored by Go-Toba, but seemed out of place among the innovators that dominated Go-Toba's circle. Two poems in *Shinkokinshū*.

Kintsugu, Fujiwara (Tokudaiji; 1175–1227); fourth son of Fujiwara Sanesada and Jōsaimon-in no Bingo. He rose to the rank of Junior First, his highest office being Minister of the Left. His father had been a highly regarded poet, with close ties to Shunzei and the poets patronized by the Kujō house; Kintsugu first appeared as a poet in the late 1190s; participated in the *Sengohyakuban uta-awase*. Five poems in *Shinkokinshū*.

Kintsune, Fujiwara (Saionji; 1171–1244); son of the Ōmiya Palace Minister Sanemune and Fujiwara Motoie's Daughter; married Ichijō Yoshiyasu's Daughter. He himself rose to the position of Chancellor in 1222 and the Junior First Rank the following year; although he served in Go-Toba's court during the time covered in this book, his marriage ties drew him closer to the Bakufu, and he opposed Go-Toba at the time of the Jōkyū War. The younger brother of Teika's wife, he was close to Teika and was active in poetry events from contests in late 1200 until at least the 1230s. Ten poems in *Shinkokinshū*.

Kojijū (fl. 1161–1203); daughter of Ki no Mitsukiyo and Hanazono Sadaijinke no Kodaishin (herself a poet who had participated in the *Kyūan hyakushu*). She served in the court of Retired Emperors Nijō and Takakura; took the tonsure in 1179 (she was believed to be in her late fifties at that time). She took part in many poetry activities in the 1180s and 1190s; became part of Go-Toba's group and was involved in, among other events, the *Shodo hyakushu*, and *Sengohyakuban uta-awase*. Seven poems in *Shinkokinshū*.

Koreakira Shinnō (Prince Koreakira; 1179–1221); third son of Emperor Takakura, his mother was Taira Yoshinori's Daughter; older brother of Go-Toba, adopted by Go-Toba's birth mother (Shichijō-In Shokushi) in 1195. He became a monk in 1211. He participated in Go-Toba's poetry activities from the time of the *Shōji ninen in shodo hyakushu* and sponsored events of his own; was part of *Sengohyakuban uta-awase*. Six poems in *Shinkokinshū*.

Kunaikyō (1185?–1205?); daughter of Minamoto Moromitsu and Aki (a lady-in-waiting in Retired Emperor Go-Shirakawa's court); younger sister of Tomochika; her paternal grandfather was a famous painter, and her mother was said to be a talented *biwa* player. She first appeared in Go-Toba's group in 1200, participating in the *Shōji ninen in dainido hyakushu*, the *Sengohyakuban uta-awase*, and numerous other events until her death in late 1204 or 1205. Kamo no Chōmei spoke of her and Shunzei no Musume as the two most talented women poets of the time. Fifteen poems in *Shinkokinshū*.

Masatsune, Fujiwara (Asukai; 1170–1221); Son of Junior Fourth Rank Lower Yoritsune and Fujiwara Akimasa's Daughter; took the clan name Asukai (the clan was renowned for several centuries thereafter as experts in poetry and *kemari*). In 1189, his father was exiled to Izu for being allied with Minamoto Yoshitsune; sometime after that, Masatsune moved to Kamakura and trained the Shogun Yoriie (1182–1204; Yoritomo's eldest son, Shogun 1202–3) in *kemari*; Go-Toba summoned him back to Kyoto in 1197, and he became a central figure in the poetry activities of the age; was both a Wakadokoro member and a *Shinkokinshū* compiler; promoted to Junior Third Rank in 1218. His personal poetry collection is known as *Asukaishū*, and he was also the author of a *kemari* treatise. Twenty-two poems in *Shinkokinshū*.

Michichika, Minamoto (Murakami/Tsuchimikado; 1149–1202); referred to as the Tsuchimikado Naidaijin in *Shinkokinshū*; son of Minamoto Masamichi and Fujiwara Yukikane's Daughter (herself a lady-in-waiting for Princess Hachijō-in, daughter of Emperor Toba). He began his court career in 1158 and eventually rose to Senior Second Rank, Palace Minister; a skillful politician, he adopted the daughter (Zaishi) of his main wife's previous marriage and sent her to the palace as one of Go-Toba's consorts (where she became the mother of Emperor Tsuchimikado); for a time in the late 1190s he eclipsed Kujō Kanezane and his son Yoshitsune as the most powerful politician at court, but Go-Toba reined him in somewhat from 1200 on. He studied poetry under Rokujō Suetsune and was an avid, if not the most skilled, poet; he sponsored and participated in many events, was appointed to the Wakadokoro, and was asked to help judge the *Sengohyakuban uta-awase*, but died before he could do so. Six poems in *Shinkokinshū*.

Michiteru, Minamoto (Tsuchimikado; 1187–1248); third son of Minamoto (Tsuchimikado) Michichika, his mother was Norikane's Daughter; younger brother of Michitomo (one of the *Shinkokinshū* compilers). Since his mother was Michichika's main wife, he had the more stellar official career, rising to Senior First Rank and Chancellor. His poetic debut was apparently the 100-poem sequence that became *Sengohyakuban uta-awase*. Fourteen poems in *Shinkokinshū*.

Michitomo, Minamoto (Tsuchimikado; 1171–1227); son of Minamoto (Tsuchimikado) Michichika and Taira Norimori's Daughter (or possibly Michimori's Daughter). He eventually rose as high as Senior Second Rank, Major Counselor (*dainagon*), but in 1201 was just a Senior Fourth Rank, Middle Captain. He married Shunzei no Musume in 1190, but they separated in the early 1200s. He was active in some of Go-Toba's poetry activities and was appointed to the Wakadokoro and the *Shinkokinshū* selection committee (possibly as a nod toward the power of the Tsuchimikado clan). Although an important member of Go-Toba's circle, among the compilers he had the fewest number of poems selected for *Shinkokinshū*—seventeen.

Moromitsu, Minamoto (Murakami; 1130?–1203?); AKA Shōren; son of Minamoto Moroyori and Fujiwara Yoshizane's Daughter. He was adopted by Fujiwara Yorinaga, who backed the losing side in the Hōgen Disturbance of 1156; this kept Moromitsu from rising much in rank (he rose to only Senior Fifth Lower, with a post in the city government). Originally close to the Rokujō poets, he became part of Go-Toba's circle, submitted poems for the *Shōji ninen in shodo hyakushu*, and was named a judge for the *Sengohyakuban uta-awase* (although he was not asked to submit poems). He was given the priestly name Shōren after taking the tonsure late in his life; he was the father of Tomochika and Kunaikyō. Three poems in *Shinkokinshū*.

Norimitsu, Fujiwara (1154–1213); son of Fujiwara Norikane and Minamoto Toshishige's Daughter. He reached the Junior Third Rank in 1201 and rose to Provisional Middle Counselor (*gonchūnagon*) in 1203. He took the tonsure in 1207. He was the brother of Kyō no Sanmi (or Kyō no Sanpin), who had been Go-Toba's nurse, who herself married Fujiwara Yorizane (Prime Minister during part of the era described here); she wielded considerable influence in the palace. Two poems in *Shinkokinshū*.

Sanefusa, Fujiwara (1147–1225; AKA [Sanjō] Nyūdō Sadaijin); third son of Kinnori; his mother was Fujiwara Kiyotaka's Daughter. He rose to Senior Second Rank in 1171 and was appointed Minister of the Left (*sadaijin*) in 1190; he took the tonsure in 1196 due to what he feared was a terminal illness (it was not). He was active in poetry contests in the 1180s and 1190s and also participated in the *Shōji ninen in shodo hyakushu* before fading from the poetic scene; more or less allied with the Rokujō school. Four poems in *Shinkokinshū*.

Sanuki (1141?–1217?); referred to as Nijō no In no Sanuki in *Shinkokinshū*; daughter of Minamoto Yorimasa and Fujiwara Tomozane's Daughter. She began her poetry career in the service of Emperor Nijō; married Fujiwara Shigeyori after Nijō died; later entered the service of Fujiwara Ninshi (AKA Gishūmon-in; Kanezane's daughter and one-time consort to Go-Toba) but resigned in 1196, after Ninshi's abrupt departure from the Palace, and took the tonsure. She was subsequently active in Go-Toba's poetry group, participating in *Shōji ninen in shodo hyakushu* and *Sengohyakuban uta-awase* among other events. Sixteen poems in *Shinkokinshū*.

Shikishi Naishinnō (1152?–1201); AKA Shokushi Naishinnō, Kaya no Saiin, Ōi no Mikado no Saiin; daughter of Emperor Go-Shirakawa and Fujiwara Suenari's Daughter, Takakura Sanmi no Seishi; full sister of Shukaku Hosshinnō, and half-sister of Emperor Takakura (who had a different mother). She was appointed Kamo Priestess (Kamo no Saiin) in 1159, but resigned ten years later due to illness. She took the tonsure in 1194; very little is known about her life, but Ienaga's depiction of her living a lonely, solitary existence—as well as the popular story that she had an affair with Teika—have become widely accepted, whether accurate or not. An early disciple of Shunzei, she had nine poems in his *Senzaishū*, and is believed to have been the sponsor of his treatise *Korai fūteishō* (1197, rev. 1201). From 1181, she was also close to Teika. She participated in the *Shōji ninen in shodo hyakushu*. Forty-nine poems in *Shinkokinshū* (fifth highest among poets in that collection).

Shōren, see *Moromitsu*

Shukaku Hosshinnō (1150–1202); AKA Kita no In Omuro; second son of Go-Shirakawa; his mother was Takakura Sanmi no Seishi; full brother of Shikishi Naishinnō. He entered Ninna-ji as a layman in 1156 and took the tonsure there in 1160, eventually becoming its Chief Administrative Officer (*sōhōmu*) in 1195. He began sponsoring poetic activities at Ninna-ji from the late 1170s, culminating in 1198 when his monks joined with the likes of Shunzei, Teika, Kenshō, and others to compose the *Shukaku Hosshinō no ie no gojisshu* (Fifty Poems at the Residence of Priest-Prince Shukaku); was eventually eclipsed by Go-Toba as a poetry patron. Five poems in *Shinkokinshū*.

Shunzei (Toshinari), Fujiwara (Mikohidari; 1114–1204); AKA Akihiro, Shakua; son of Fujiwara Toshitada and Fujiwara Atsuie's Daughter. After his father's death in 1123, he was adopted by Hamuro Akiyori and took the name Akihiro, but he returned to his main family in 1167 and took the name Toshinari (Shunzei). He was the father of Teika and foster father to both Jakuren and Shunzei no Musume. He reached his highest rank (Senior Third) in 1167, and his highest office, Master of the Grand Empress's Household (*kōtai gōgū no daibu*), in 1172; a serious illness led him to take the tonsure in 1176 (some sources say 1175). He was active in poetry from the age of eighteen; he was part of Retired Emperor Sutoku's poetry circle and was asked to categorize the two rounds of 100-poem sequences that make up the *Kyūan hyakushu*. By the 1170s he was frequently called on as a judge for poetry contests, and he eventually attracted the patronage of Kujō Kanezane, who studied poetry under him. Go-Shirakawa commissioned him to compile the seventh imperial anthology, *Senzaishū*, in 1184, and he submitted the collection in 1188. By this time, he was at the center of poetry in Japan, rivaled only by members of the Rokujō house, and wrote his famous treatise *Korai fūteishō* (1197). Probably through his connections with the Kujō house, he became a key member of Go-Toba's poetry group. He died a year after Go-Toba honored him with an elaborate ninetieth-year celebration. Seventy-two poems in *Shinkokinshū* (fourth highest of any poet).

Shunzei(kyō) no Musume (1171?–1252?); AKA Koshibe no Zenni, Saga no Zenni, Nakanoin no Ni; her father was Fujiwara no Moriyori (a low-ranking guardsman); her mother was Shunzei's daughter, Hachijō-in Sanjō; raised from youth by Shunzei (perhaps because her father had been implicated in the Shishigatani plot of 1177). In 1190 she was married to Minamoto Michitomo, but after they had two children, they separated in the early 1200s, and she went into formal service with Go-Toba in 1202. She became a nun in 1213 and moved out to Saga in the early 1230s. After Teika's death in 1241, she moved to Harima province, where she died ten or so years later. She became part of Go-Toba's poetry circle in 1201 and subsequently also associated with Juntoku's poetry group; she also composed with Tameie and remained active in poetry activities even after moving to Harima (she submitted a sequence in the *Hōji hyakushu* of 1248); Chōmei ranked her with Kunaikyō as the best women poets of the age. Twenty-nine poems in *Shinkokinshū*.

Suetsune, Fujiwara (Rokujō; 1131–1221); son of Akisuke, but of a different mother from Kiyosuke (1104–77, Suetsune's older half-brother and head of the Rokujō school till his death). He rose to Senior Third Rank, Consultant; took the tonsure in 1201. A staunch supporter of the Rokujō school, he originally participated in various activities sponsored by the Kujō house in the 1180s and 1190s, but was bitterly opposed to the Mikohidari school and tried to block Teika's participation in the *Shōji ninen in shodo hyakushu*; represented the Rokujō in some of Go-Toba's poetry activities, including *Sengohyakuban uta-awase* (where he was asked to judge, but not to submit poems). One poem in *Shinkokinshū*.

Sueyoshi (Fujiwara; 1153–1211); son of Fujiwara Toshimori and Minamoto Masakane's Daughter; great-great-grandson of Rokujō Akisue. Originally in the service of Go-Shirakawa, he made his poetry debut in a Rokujō-sponsored contest in the early 1170s and had work selected for *Senzaishū*. He eventually rose to the Senior Third Rank; took the tonsure in 1207. He represented the Rokujō school in several of Go-Toba's events, including *Sengohyakuban uta-awase*. Three poems in *Shinkokinshū*.

Tadatsune, Fujiwara (1173–1229); eldest son of Kiyomasa; his mother was one of Taira Kiyomori's daughters. He rose to Senior Second Rank, Minister of the Right. He participated in many of the poetry events of the early 1200s but usually in the background; was more or less associated with the Mikohidari school. Three poems in *Shinkokinshū*.

Tadayoshi, Fujiwara (1164–1225); son of Fujiwara Motozane (and thus a nephew of Kujō Kanezane) and Rokujō Akisuke's daughter. He reached Senior Second Rank and the position of Major Counselor (*dainagon*). Although his mother was from the Rokujō poetry family, Tadayoshi (perhaps because his father was from the Kujō house) apparently steered clear of poetic factions; he was active in many of Go-Toba's poetry events, and was one of the judges for the *Sengohyakuban uta-awase*. Five poems in *Shinkokinshū*.

Takafusa, Fujiwara (1148–1209); eldest son of Fujiwara Takesue and Fujiwara Tadataka's Daughter; rose to the Senior Second Rank, Provisional Major Counselor (*gondainagon*) before taking the tonsure in 1206; married one of Taira Kiyomori's daughters; active in poetry events from the 1170s; participated in, among other events, the *Shodo hyakushu*, but had only two poems in *Shinkokinshū*.

Takanobu, Fujiwara (1142–1205); eldest son of Fujiwara Tametsune and Fujiwara Chikatada's Daughter. His father (more commonly known by his priestly name Jakuchō) was an early critic of the Rokujō style in the mid-1100s; his mother married Shunzei after Tametsune took the tonsure, and Takanobu grew up with Teika and the others in Shunzei's clan. He rose to Senior Fourth Rank Lower; was for a time one of Lady Daibu's (Kenreimon'in Ukyō no Daibu) lovers. He took the tonsure in 1202 as a disciple of Hōnen, founder of the Pure Land sect. He was active in poetry events of all kinds from the 1160s and was named by Go-Toba to the Wakadokoro; also believed to have been an accomplished portrait painter. Three poems in *Shinkokinshū*.

Tango (1113?–1208?); AKA Gishūmon-in no Tango, Sesshōke no Tango, Kotoura no Tango; not to be confused with Tango no Tsubone (see pp. 28–29); daughter of Minamoto Yoriyuki (who was son of Yorimasa [pro-Go-Shirakawa in Hōgen, pro-Heike in Heiji, but eventually supported the Minamoto and died at Uji, fighting with Prince Mochihito] and who committed suicide for his role in Hōgen Disturbance); mother unknown. She first served in the home of Kujō Kanezane and then followed his daughter Ninshi (Gishūmon-in) to court when she became one of Go-Toba's consorts. She took the tonsure in 1201 at the death of Kanezane's main wife. She was active in poetry from 1175; participated in a number of poetic events in the early 1200s, including the *Sengohyakuban uta-awase*. Nine poems in *Shinkokinshū*.

Teika (Sadaie), Fujiwara (Mikohidari; 1162–1241; AKA Kyōgoku Chūnagon); son of Fujiwara Shunzei and Fujiwara Chikatada's Daughter (herself AKA Bifukumon-in no Kaga). He eventually rose to the Senior Second Rank (in 1227) and Provisional Middle Counselor (*gonchūnagon*); took the tonsure in 1233. He began to attract notice as a poet in the early 1180s; became a retainer of the Kujō house in 1186 and explored innovative approaches to poetry with his patrons, Yoshitsune and Jien, earning the disdain of the Rokujō school in the process. Go-Toba began to favor him from the time of the *Shōji ninen in shodo hyakushu*, and he participated in almost all the major events of the era; was a poet and judge in the *Sengohyakuban uta-awase*; named to the Wakadokoro and selected as a *Shinkokinshū* compiler. As Go-Toba continued to tinker with the *Shinkokinshū* after its initial completion, relations between him and Teika grew hostile, and Teika stayed out of Go-Toba's restoration efforts in the Jōkyū War. In the 1220s, Teika became more interested in renga and virtually stopped writing waka for public consumption after taking the tonsure in 1233. However, he did agree to be the sole compiler for the ninth imperial anthology, *Shinchokusenshū* (completed in 1235), for which he selected no poems by Go-Toba. He spent his last years collecting and copying classical literary works and writing treatises; his library became a crucial link to the past for scholars, and much of it survives today in the Reizei family's Shiguretei collection. Forty-six poems in *Shinkokinshū*.

Tomochika, Minamoto (fl. 1200–1262); second son of Minamoto Moromitsu (Shōren), mother now not known; elder brother of Kunaikyō (uncertain if they had the same mother). He rose to Junior Fourth Rank Upper, Lesser Captain of the Left Guards. He participated in many of Go-Toba's important poetry events, including *Sengohyakuban uta-awase* and the *Saishōshitennōin shōji waka*; was named to the Wakadokoro; remained active in poetry at least through 1262. Seven poems in *Shinkokinshū*.

Tsuneie, Fujiwara (Rokujō; 1149–1209); eldest son of Shigeie and Ienari's Daughter. He rose to Senior Third Rank in 1198; took the tonsure in 1208. He was active in poetry from the mid-1170s; loyal to the Rokujō style; participated in *Shodo hyakushu*. Two poems in *Shinkokinshū*.

Yasusue, Fujiwara (Rokujō; 1171–?); the son of Shigeie (mother uncertain); adopted by his uncle Suetsune. He rose to Junior Third Rank and held a minor post in the guards. He represented the Rokujō school in a number of Go-Toba-sponsored activities, including *Sengohyakuban uta-awase*, and seems to have been recognized by Go-Toba's group as a more accomplished poet than his adoptive father. Three poems in *Shinkokinshū*.

Yoshitsune, Fujiwara (Kujō; 1169–1206; AKA Nakamikado no Sesshō; Go-Kyōgoku-dono); second son of Kanezane, his mother was Fujiwara Sueyuki's Daughter; nephew to Jien. When his elder brother died in 1188, he became heir to the Kujō house. He went into seclusion in 1196 for several years when Kanezane was forced into retirement, but was rehabilitated by Go-Toba thereafter; was named Regent (*sesshō*) in 1202; rose to the Junior First Rank and was named Chancellor (*daijō daijin*) in 1204; died suddenly in 1206. He began serious study of Japanese and Chinese poetry at the age of thirteen and had seven poems selected for *Senzaishū* (before he was twenty); became an important patron of poetry, particularly the Mikohidari school, from the early 1190s, and continued sponsoring events, especially *shiika* (Chinese and Japanese verse) activities until he died. From the time of the *Shōji ninen in shodo hyakushu*, he became a central figure in Go-Toba's poetry group, participating in virtually every event until his death; was both a judge and contributor of poems to *Sengohyakuban uta-awase*; was a member of the Wakadokoro and wrote the *kana* preface to *Shinkokinshū*. Seventy-nine poems in *Shinkokinshū* (third after Saigyō and Jien).

APPENDIX C

'Shōji ninen Shunzeikyō no waji sōjō'

With regard to Your Majesty's recent commission of 100-poem sequences, there are a few remarks I would like to offer, although I fear I will not be able to express myself clearly.[1] To begin with, the fact that Your Majesty has commissioned the sequences at all shows a respect for the Way of Poetry as it was in the past and is commendable indeed. Since poetry has been part of the lifeblood of this land since the Age of the Gods, it has helped to govern our society, and since there are so many instances of its efficacy, I find your project auspicious and praiseworthy.

Man'yōshū was compiled during the reign of Emperor Shōmu, he who had constructed Tōdai-ji temple in Nara.[2] Then, in our present capital, during the Engi era interest in the Way of Poetry was revived.[3] In this light,

---

1. I am translating from the annotated text that appears in Hisamatsu, *Karonshū I*, pp. 271–76, with endnotes on pp. 421–22. Although Hisamatsu was the chief editor of the volume and wrote the introduction, this particular section was edited and annotated by Inoue Muneo; hence I have used his name in relevant footnotes.

2. Shōmu reigned from 724 to 749. *Man'yō* scholarship was still evolving in Shunzei's time, and, as Inoue notes, there were conflicting theories of when *Man'yōshū* had been compiled. Here we have Shunzei's view. Although the various theories fixed the compilation date earlier than we now believe to have been the case, all of them implicitly recognize that ideologically it was part of the effort of the Yamato kings to establish their line as pre-eminent. In that sense, Shunzei's rhetorical coupling of *Man'yōshū* with Tōdai-ji is right on the mark. Both were public works projects that sought to establish the ruler's legitimacy.

3. The Engi era (901–23), during Emperor Daigo's reign, saw the compilation of *Kokinshū*, which is what Shunzei is referring to here. Again, he was implicitly describing an ideology, too, since the Engi era came to be seen as a Golden Age, a fountainhead of cultural precedents, when emperors ruled and reigned "as they were supposed to." As above, this ideological undertone is no accident. Shunzei has already reminded us of the importance of poetry for governing society (*yo no naka o osamari*), a notion made explicit in both prefaces of *Kokinshū*.

Your Majesty's intentions are most estimable. Now, if you commission 100-poem sequences, it would be most desirable if you could ensure that the largest possible number of good poems results, so that the event can be noteworthy not only in its own time but through the ages as well. In principle, then, talented poets ought to be included in the commission. Yet it appears that only older poets have been invited to participate in this activity, with the result that some who are not qualified have been included.[4] Forgive me, but no matter how I look at it, it seems strange.

During the 100-poem sequences of the past, no attention was paid to whether the poets were old or young. At the time of the *Horikawa hyakushu*, Kunizane, Moroyori, and Morotoki were all in their thirties.[5] Toshiyori and Mototoshi were in their fifties.[6] And Lord Masafusa was sixty.[7] The first three were not very old, but because they were good poets, they participated. Age had nothing to do with it.

Furthermore, at the time of the *Sutoku-in hyakushu*,[8] the Minister of the Right Kin'yoshi was in his thirties.[9] And as for this old priest, well, I was hardly of any consequence at the time, but I, too, was invited to take part from the very start even though I was just thirty. At the beginning of that year,[10] in addition to himself His Majesty Emperor Sutoku asked thirteen others to participate: noble Lords Kin'yuki, Kin'yoshi, Yukimune, Norinaga,

---

4. Shunzei's actual words are a little stronger here, although difficult to work into a smooth translation. What I have called "some who are not qualified," he describes more literally as "those who compose what is contrary to poetry" (Hisamatsu, *Karonshū I*, p. 271).

5. Minamoto Kunizane (1069–1111), Minamoto Moroyori (1068–1139), and Minamoto Morotoki (1077–1136), the latter two brothers, were of the Murakami Genji branch of the family, among the highest ranks of the aristocracy, and therefore not perfect analogies for Teika's situation. Strictly speaking, Morotoki was actually in his late twenties at the time of the sequences.

6. Minamoto Toshiyori (1055–1129) and Fujiwara Mototoshi (1060–1142) were bitter rivals. Three-quarters of a century later, in Shunzei's time, the family names were different, but the rivalries no less intense.

7. Ōe Masafusa (1041–1111).

8. More commonly known as the *Kyūan hyakushu*, these sequences, commissioned by Retired Emperor Sutoku from fourteen poets, were probably completed and submitted by 1150. But due to the death of several of the original participants, the commission was extended; hence Shunzei's remark below that he had been involved from the beginning. After the poems were finished, Shunzei was ordered to work on classifying them for formal presentation, but the Hōgen Disturbance interrupted the project, and it was never fully completed.

9. Fujiwara Kin'yoshi (1115–61).

10. Although there is some uncertainty about the timing of the *Kyūan hyakushu*, since Shunzei turned thirty in Kōji 2 (1143), that is probably the year to which he referred here.

and Akisuke,[11] Lords Tadamori and Chikataka,[12] followed by the Priest Kakuga, myself, and Ladies Horikawa, Hyōe, Aki, and Kodaishin. But the formal presentation of our poems was delayed, and three of the original number—Kin'yuki, Yukimune, and Kakuga—passed away in the interim, and so three new poets were asked to replace them: Takasue, Kiyosuke, and Sanekiyo.[13] So in this case, too, the Emperor placed no restrictions with regard to age.

It is true that there are what we call "Elders Parties," participation in which *is* limited to those of advanced age,[14] but for 100-poem sequences age limits have not been an issue. Besides, Teika is almost forty anyway. With regard to his skills in poetry, I have complete confidence in him; so after I am dead, whatever Your Majesty wishes him to do in matters of poetry—be it as a judge[15] or an anthologizer—I believe he will accept the charge when it is given and will carry it out as requested. So the fact that he has not been included in the 100-poem sequence commission this time causes me unimaginable grief and consternation.

All in all, the reason he is capable of rendering judgments and selecting poems for an anthology is because he is so good at composing poetry himself.

---

11. Shunzei refers to these five as *kyō* (aristocrats of the Third rank or above).

12. These two are *ason* according to Shunzei. Although not as precise a term as *kyō*, in this context it means aristocrats between the Fifth and Third rank.

13. Of these three "replacements," Takasue was twenty-seven, and Kiyosuke forty-seven; Sanekiyo's age is not known. Inoue (Hisamatsu, *Karonshū I*, p. 272) notes that Shunzei's memory was faulty as to who replaced whom and when, but since the details have no bearing on this book, I omit them. Also, except for Akisuke, Kiyosuke, and Shunzei himself, none of the other poets listed is of consequence to the line of inquiry pursued in this study, and so I have omitted biographies for them. Inoue provides short biographical sketches of each of them on pp. 421–22 of *Karonshū I*.

14. *Shōshikai*, or *shōshie*, were poetry gatherings to which only poets of advanced age were invited. The characters used to write *shōshi* might, by stretching, be literally translated as "long in the tooth," teeth being as far back as the *Book of Rites* a figure for age since their cycle matches a person's physical aging process. The term is one of respect, not derision. *Shōshikai* gatherings go back to Tang China (the earliest recorded one being sponsored by Bo Juyi in 845) and were quickly adopted by Japan, where the earliest known one was in 877. Inoue (Hisamatsu, *Karonshū I*, p. 272) remarks that two especially well-known *shōshikai* parties occurred in 1131 and 1172; hence Shunzei's reference here to the practice would not be especially obscure.

15. Inoue rightly says this refers both to acting as a judge at contests and to evaluating and marking (*gatten*) poems submitted as part of a sequence (in fact, this is just what Teika did for others, such as Shikishi Naishinnō, at the time of the *Shōji ninen in shodo hyakushu*).

Nowadays, those who call themselves poets (*utayomi*) are all just mediocre.[16] The poems they compose are an affront to the ears. Their diction is verbose and of dubious quality, whereas Teika composes wonderfully, adopting an innovative manner of expression (*sugata*),[17] a relaxed attitude toward vocabulary, and a determination not to imitate older poems.[18] As for the others who call themselves poets, when they do manage despite themselves to come up with a good poem, it is in the manner of some older poem. But more often, they just compose in awkward, ordinary diction and resent Teika's style, calling it names and going around speaking ill of him to other people.[19]

As a rule, if those poets whom [Suetsune et al.] call their artistic forefathers had really understood the nature of poetry, they would have been able to evaluate and select poems, but since their very basis for judging good or bad in poetry was evidently flawed, everything they did was detrimental to the way of poetry. Take, for instance, Norinaga, who made a private collection of the poems that came to his attention and called it *Shūi kokin*.[20] At that time Kiyo-

---

16. The text describes these would-be poets as *chū no mono* (using the *hiragana chi + u*), which is difficult to interpret here. Inoue thinks it means something like "lacking substance" (that is, the *chū* that means "space"), but I have opted for a more obvious reading, the *chū* that means "middle." In any case, Shunzei is definitely being pejorative here, as is clear from what follows.

17. Among the various meanings of *sugata*—the most common of which has to do with the overall effect of the poem both in terms of its diction and its emotional content—is a relatively limited one, that is, the tone of the diction used in a poem (e.g., elevated, elegant, etc.). I am following Inoue in assuming this is the meaning that applies here, since Shunzei in the previous sentence mentioned diction issues with regard to the mediocre poets with whom he is comparing Teika.

18. It is interesting that the words Shunzei used to praise Teika could just as easily be used to condemn him. In particular, what I have translated as "a relaxed attitude toward vocabulary" (*kotobazukai iichirashi*) might as easily be rendered "he uses language recklessly." It is only the context that makes Shunzei's attitude clear.

19. The phrase "calling it names" (*betsu no azana nado na o tsukete*) probably points, as Inoue says, to the fact that Teika's poetry was often dismissed by conservative critics as *Daruma uta*, a reference to the deliberately incomprehensible (or at least alogical) utterances used in Zen Buddhism (whose patriarch, Bodhidharma, was called Daruma in Japanese) to shock the rational mind into seeing the world differently. Of course, in the hyperconservative world of waka, the term is pejorative. At court during this period, the Zen sect was looked on with some skepticism by most, and certainly none of Teika's rivals would ever suggest that his poems might have some spiritual efficacy. As Inoue states (Hisamatsu, *Karonshū I*, p. 273), this whole sentence is unclear; my interpretation of it differs somewhat from his.

20. Norinaga is Fujiwara Norinaga (1109–78?), one of the more fascinating, and little-studied, characters in waka history. After a promising court career under Emperor Sutoku, in which he rose to the Senior Third Rank and participated in the landmark *Kyūan hyakushu*, he

suke was his friend and stood at his side as he prepared the collection.[21] What they produced together contained some awkward bits indeed.

To begin with, for instance, they took the poem "It neither shines / Nor yet is clouded over / On this spring night . . ." and assuming that it referred to a summer night, placed it in the Summer section.[22] It was in reference to this very poem that the lady Naishi no Kami came to be called "Oborozukiyo" on a night in the Second Month in the "Hana no En" chapter of *The Tale of Genji*.[23] But neither Norinaga nor Kiyosuke seems to have read *Genji*. Even less are they familiar with the work known as *Monjū* (Ch. *Wenji*). Therein is a poem by Bo Juyi with the following lines to which this waka refers: "Neither brightening nor darkening, the misty moon / Neither warm nor cold the constant breeze."[24] But not knowing about either of these sources, they recorded the (third) line as "On this summer night" and placed

---

got caught on the wrong side in the Hōgen Disturbance, took the tonsure, and was then exiled. Pardoned in 1162, he returned to the poetic scene and remained active as a participant, sponsor, and judge in various well-known contests at least until 1178. Among the several writings credited to him is *Shūi kokinshō*, date unknown and text now mostly lost, which was conceived as a critique of *Shikashū* (see *WBJ*, p. 439). There is a problem here in that *Shikashū* was compiled by Kiyosuke's father, and since Kiyosuke is on record elsewhere defending *Shikashū* against attack (namely, his *Bokutekiki*, another fragmentary document from the late Heian period; see *WBJ*, p. 440), it seems unlikely that he would help Norinaga in his endeavor. And Inoue notes that there is no other evidence linking Kiyosuke to Norinaga's project.

21. Fujiwara (Rokujō) Kiyosuke (1104–77), was perhaps Shunzei's bitterest rival, even though both served as poetic advisers to Kujō Kanezane. Shunzei's distaste aside, others, among them Go-Toba, had at least modest praise for his work, and even Teika called him one of the Kindai Rokkasen (Six Poetic Sages of Our Times) in his *Kindai shūka*, a treatise prepared for the Shogun Sanetomo and admittedly not representative of Teika's most sophisticated poetic theory.

22. The poem, by Ōe no Chisato (fl. 894–903), is a *kudai waka*, that is, a waka poem using part of a Chinese verse as topic. See below for Shunzei's discussion of the topic verse for Ōe's poem. The whole waka is *Teri mo sezu / kumori mo fatenu / faru no yo no / oborodukiyo ni / siku mono zo naki*—"It neither shines / nor yet is clouded over / On this spring night / Truly nothing can compare / To this mist-enfolded moon." The poem originally comes from the *Ōe Chisatoshū*, and a few years after Shunzei's letter, it was anthologized as *SKKS* 55 (I, Spring 1).

23. For an English translation of the incident, see Seidensticker, trans., *The Tale of Genji*, Chapter 10, "The Festival of the Cherry Blossoms," pp. 151–52. The lady in question was a sister of Genji's enemy Kokiden and was promised to the emperor. Genji's illicit relationship with her was the immediate cause for his exile. The main point here, though, is that the incident unequivocally occurred in the spring. As noted earlier, this episode was one which Shunzei frequently cited.

24. The lines are from a poem called "Feeling Nostalgic on a Spring Night at Jialing," found in Bo Juyi's *Hakushi Monjū*.

the poem in the Summer section. This was a lamentable slip on the part of both Norinaga and Kiyosuke.

Or take Lord Akisuke, who compiled *Shikashū*. Although he did produce some skillful work, such as "When I see the moon / Settled among the reeds," as he got older he began to favor nonsense poems (*zare-uta*).[25] Because he paid too much attention to the flood of advice he was getting from the know-it-alls around him, *Shikashū* ended up full of just such nonsense poetry.[26] This is why the late Hachijō Prime Minister Saneyuki dismissed the collection, saying "This anthology was poorly put together. I would like to try and fix it up." He was sent poems for this purpose by others and even by Retired Emperor Sutoku, but his son, the late Minister Kinnori, argued against it, saying that to attack the *Shikashū* so directly would bring unnecessary shame on people. His Majesty agreed that this would not be desirable and strictly forbade the project, and I hear Saneyuki ended up abandoning it.

Or let us talk about Kiyosuke. He presented a collection of his family's verse called *Shokushikashū* to Retired Emperor Nijō and asked His Majesty to designate it an imperial anthology, but the request was refused.[27]

The late Minister of the Left turned Monk, Sanesada, complained about the results: "He put only poor poems of mine in the collection and ignored all of my good ones." Accordingly, he demanded that Kiyosuke "remove not only all of my poems but all the works of my forefathers in the Kan'in family as well." Kiyosuke replied that perhaps he should therefore also remove all my poems and those of my forefathers, since our house was directly related to Sanesada's. "That's not what I asked," said Sanesada. "You are deliberately being difficult. My family's poems should be taken out, right now!"

---

25. The poem, composed by Akisuke when he was out of favor with Retired Emperor Shirakawa, appears as SKS 347 (IX, Miscellaneous 1): *Nanifae no / asima ni yadoru / tuki mireba / waga mi fitotu mo / sizumazarikeri*—"When I see the moon / Settled among the reeds / At Naniwa Inlet / I realize that I, too / Am following a downward course."

26. This sentence is obscure, and I have rendered it quite freely, although more or less following Inoue's suggested gloss (Hisamatsu, *Karonshū I*, p. 422). I suspect textual corruption, but given the remarks that surround this sentence, Shunzei's overall attitude is clear: Akisuke had talent when he was young but got sidetracked.

27. The expression Shunzei uses here is *Shokushikashū to mōsu uchigiki*. An *uchigiki* (literally, "[something] heard") was a kind of family poetry collection, including poems by generations of a clan, in this case, the Rokujō house. By using the term, Shunzei was criticizing Kiyosuke's partisanship, but in truth the collection was intended as an imperial anthology and includes poems from many non-Rokujō poets. Furthermore, there is evidence that the reason it was never designated a *chokusenshū* was not so much that Retired Emperor Nijō disapproved of it as that he died before final editing was completed.

Kiyosuke, although he left in the collection poems by the Grand Counselor Nagaie, progenitor of our Mikohidari branch, removed works from members of the Kan'in family. This resulted in a pitiful collection indeed! Generally speaking, a true anthology would contain more than just the works the compiler was familiar with.

This brings us to Suetsune. The thought that this man is influential in judging poetry contests these days is disgraceful indeed from the standpoint of the Way of Poetry.[28] He truly knows nothing, and the way he distorts what has been handed down from the past is just as disgraceful for the whole world. For example, in this instance, he is purposely misleading about past precedents when he discusses the number of people who should be involved in Your Majesty's proposed 100-poem sequence project. In point of fact, judging from past practice, Your Majesty's current commission should include several more people....[29]

---

28. I am following Inoue (Hisamatsu, *Karonshū I*, p. 275) here in assuming that *omowaji* (shall not think) should be *omowaku* (to think that), as it appears in a variant text.

29. I am omitting two sentences here that seem hopelessly corrupt. Shunzei appears to be arguing against a suggestion evidently made by Suetsune that "a *hyakushu* at the time of Horikawa" (*Horikawa-in no ontoki no hyakushu*) and another "at the time of Sutoku-in" (*Sutoku-in no ontoki no* [*tameshi*]) were suitable precedents to establish the proper number of poets for this occasion. It is clear from Inoue's notes (Hisamatsu, *Karonshū I*, p. 422) that he is assuming that *Horikawa hyakushu* refers to the so-called *Tarō hyakushu* or *Shodo hyakushu*, that is, the main commission, which included from fourteen to sixteen poets depending on which text one follows. He further assumes that the reference to the *Sutoku-in hyakushu* must be to the *Kyūan Hyakushu* (1150–52), which involved fourteen poets. (Ariyoshi, *Shinkokin wakashū no kenkyū: kiban to kōsei*, pp. 72–73, seems to be making the same assumption.) Given these assumptions, Inoue tries gamely to make sense of the sentences in Shunzei's letter, but his various suggestions seem to miss the point. His interpretations have Shunzei arguing against using these two events as precedents, but in fact the number of poets commissioned in them should lend weight to Shunzei's argument that Go-Toba's current commission needs to be expanded. (Ariyoshi, *Shinkokin wakashū no kenkyū: kiban to kōsei*, p. 74—see also Chapter 2 of this study—has argued persuasively that Go-Toba's original invitation was only to eight or nine poets.) Furthermore, Shunzei clearly used them as precedents himself earlier in the letter.

There is another possibility: maybe Inoue is looking at the wrong *hyakushu*. Perhaps in a document no longer extant, or in an oral argument that came to Shunzei's attention, Suetsune had raised different precedents. For example, Suetsune may have referred to the so-called *Horikawa jirō hyakushu* (or *Horikawa kodo hyakushu*), presented in 1116 as a memorial to the late Emperor Horikawa (and following the topics set forth in the *Horikawa hyakushu*), which involved only seven people. And the reference to a "*hyakushu* at the time of Sutoku-in" may in fact be about the so-called *Sutoku tennō shodo hyakushu*, by extant accounts a small and casual event (matching Shunzei's characterization *sata nimo oyobazu*, which can be interpreted, as Inoue does, to mean "private, unofficial"). If Suetsune had made these his justification for a

I understand that Lord Takafusa has also made this argument.[30] For that matter, Ietaka has served His Majesty skillfully as a poet. I submit that it would be a very good thing for poetry to add two or three people to the commission.

And of course in that case, Teika should certainly be invited to participate. He can always be counted on to contribute excellent verse to Your Majesty—an extremely important consideration for this 100-poem sequence. I am not suggesting these poets out of mere paternal feeling. I sincerely feel it would be beneficial to the world of poetry and to Your Majesty to include them.

For that matter, there are among Your Majesty's ladies those whom it might be beneficial for Your Majesty to address concerning this project. You really ought to ask them as well.[31] Although it is with great trepidation that I broach this, given the precedents, I believe Your Majesty ought to increase the number of poets in the commission. It is with the utmost humility that I seek to convey this view to you, and I apologize for having rambled on so long.

Your humble servant

Waka no ura no	The crane that cries
asibe wo sasite	As it heads toward the reeds
naku tadu mo	By Poetry Bay—
nado ka kumowi ni	Why can it not return
kaferazarubeki	To that place beyond the clouds?

---

small *hyakushu* commission, then Shunzei's argument makes sense, since he is saying that both these events were atypical and not deserving to be true precedents. This would in turn fit with his earlier assertion that the better-known *Horikawa hyakushu* and *Kyūan hyakushu*, which he cited at the beginning of his letter, are the proper precedents to follow. In any case, the passage is too ambiguous to translate reliably, but one thing is clear: Shunzei is attacking Suetsune's position.

30. In other words, Takafusa would like to be named to the group, too, and Shunzei agrees that he belongs there.

31. My translation of this portion is tentative. Inoue (Hisamatsu, *Karonshū I*, pp. 275, 422) argues that since Shunzei was writing his petition in Japanese instead of Chinese, he was appealing to Go-Toba's ladies to speak on his behalf. But he admits this is something of a stretch, and he cites with tentative approval Ariyoshi's argument (*Shinkokin wakashū no kenkyū: kiban to kōsei*, p. 72) that Shunzei is petitioning *on behalf* of the ladies (in which case the "crane" could be taken as plural "cranes"). I am following the latter, although either interpretation is hard to fit to the text, which is rather opaque at this point.

APPENDIX D

Details of the *'Sengohyakuban uta-awase'*

Table D.1
Teams in the *Sengohyakuban uta-awase*

Left	Right
L1 Go-Toba (N)	R1 Koreakira Shinnō (N)
L2 Fujiwara Yoshitsune (KP)	R2 Minamoto Michichika (TP)
L3 Jien (KP)	R3 Fujiwara Tadayoshi (R)
L4 Fujiwara Kintsugu (M)	R4 Fujiwara Kanemune (R)
L5 Fujiwara (Saionji) Kintsune (M)	R5 Minamoto Michiteru (TP)
L6 Fujiwara Sueyoshi (R)	R6 Fujiwara Shunzei (M)
L7 Kunaikyō (N)	R7 Shunzei no Musume (M)
L8 Sanuki (M)	R8 Tango (M)
L9 Kojijū (R)	R9 Echizen (N)
L10 Fujiwara Takanobu (M)	R10 Fujiwara Teika (M)
L11 Fujiwara Ariie ([R]/M)	R11 Minamoto Michitomo (TP)
L12 Fujiwara Yasusue (R)	R12 Fujiwara Ietaka (M)
L13 Fujiwara Yoshihira (KP)	R13 Fujiwara (Asukai) Masatsune (N)
L14 Minamoto Tomochika (N)	R14 Jakuren (M)
L15 Kenshō (R)	R15 Minamoto Ienaga (N)

KEY: N = Neutral; TP = Tsuchimikado patron (of Rokujō school); KP = Kujō patron (of Mikohidari school); R = Rokujō poet; M = Mikohidari poet

NOTE: Ariie (by birth) and Kunaikyō and Tomochika (through their father's poetic training) were related to the Rokujō house/school, but their poetic practice had more in common with the Mikohidari school.

Table D.2
Arrangement of Rounds in the *Sengohyakuban uta-awase*
(to be read vertically down the columns, which continue on facing page)

1. L1–R1	46. L1–R4	91. L1–R7	136. L1–R10	181. L1–R13	
2. L2–R2	47. L2–R5	92. L2–R8	137. L2–R11	182. L2–R14	
3. L3–R3	48. L3–R6	93. L3–R9	138. L3–R12	183. L3–R15	
4. L4–R4	49. L4–R7	94. L4–R10	139. L4–R13	184. L4–R1	
5. L5–R5	50. L5–R8	95. L5–R11	140. L5–R1	185. L5–R2	
6. L6–R6	51. L6–R9	96. L6–R12	141. L6–R15	186. L6–R3	
7. L7–R7	52. L7–R10	97. L7–R13	142. L7–R1	187. L7–R4	
8. L8–R8	53. L8–R11	98. L8–R14	143. L8–R2	188. L8–R5	
9. L9–R9	54. L9–R12	99. L9–R15	144. L9–R3	189. L9–R6	
10. L10–R10	55. L10–R13	100. L10–R1	145. L10–R4	190. L10–R7	
11. L11–R11	56. L11–R14	101. L11–R2	146. L11–R5	191. L11–R8	
12. L12–R12	57. L12–R15	102. L12–R3	147. L12–R6	192. L12–R9	
13. L13–R13	58. L13–R1	103. L13–R4	148. L13–R7	193. L13–R10	
14. L14–R14	59. L14–R2	104. L14–R5	149. L14–R8	194. L14–R11	
15. L15–R15	60. L15–R3	105. L15–R6	150. L15–R9	195. L15–R12	
16. L1–R2	61. L1–R5	106. L1–R8	151. L1–R11	196. L1–R14	
17. L2–R3	62. L2–R6	107. L2–R9	152. L2–R12	197. L2–R15	
18. L3–R4	63. L3–R7	108. L3–R10	153. L3–R13	198. L3–R1	
19. L4–R5	64. L4–R8	109. L4–R11	154. L4–R14	199. L4–R2	
20. L5–R6	65. L5–R9	110. L5–R12	155. L5–R15	200. L5–R3	
21. L6–R7	66. L6–R10	111. L6–R13	156. L6–R1	201. L6–R4	
22. L7–R8	67. L7–R11	112. L7–R14	157. L7–R2	202. L7–R5	
23. L8–R9	68. L8–R12	113. L8–R15	158. L8–R3	203. L8–R6	
24. L9–R10	69. L9–R13	114. L9–R1	159. L9–R4	204. L9–R7	
25. L10–R11	70. L10–R14	115. L10–R2	160. L10–R5	205. L10–R8	
26. L11–R12	71. L11–R15	116. L11–R3	161. L11–R6	206. L11–R9	
27. L12–R13	72. L12–R1	117. L12–R4	162. L12–R7	207. L12–R10	
28. L13–R14	73. L13–R2	118. L13–R5	163. L13–R8	208. L13–R11	
29. L14–R15	74. L14–R3	119. L14–R6	164. L14–R9	209. L14–R12	
30. L15–R1	75. L15–R4	120. L15–R7	165. L15–R10	210. L15–R13	
31. L1–R3	76. L1–R6	121. L1–R9	166. L1–R12	211. L1–R15	
32. L2–R4	77. L2–R7	122. L2–R10	167. L2–R13	212. L2–R1	
33. L3–R5	78. L3–R8	123. L3–R11	168. L3–R14	213. L3–R2	
34. L4–R6	79. L4–R9	124. L4–R12	169. L4–R15	214. L4–R3	
35. L5–R7	80. L5–R10	125. L5–R13	170. L5–R1	215. L5–R4	
36. L6–R8	81. L6–R11	126. L6–R14	171. L6–R2	216. L6–R5	
37. L7–R9	82. L7–R12	127. L7–R15	172. L7–R3	217. L7–R6	
38. L8–R10	83. L8–R13	128. L8–R1	173. L8–R4	218. L8–R7	

Details of the 'Sengohyakuban uta-awase' 415

Table D.2, cont.

39. L9–R11	84. L9–R14	129. L9–R2	174. L9–R5	219. L9–R8
40. L10–R12	85. L10–R15	130. L10–R3	175. L10–R6	220. L10–R9
41. L11–R13	86. L11–R1	131. L11–R4	176. L11–R7	221. L11–R10
42. L12–R14	87. L12–R2	132. L12–R5	177. L12–R8	222. L12–R11
43. L13–R15	88. L13–R3	133. L13–R6	178. L13–R9	223. L13–R12
44. L14–R1	89. L14–R4	134. L14–R7	179. L14–R10	224. L14–R13
45. L15–R2	90. L15–R5	135. L15–R8	180. L15–R11	225. L15–R14

The above cycle repeated five more times through Round no. 1,350; it then ran for another 150 rounds (through Kenshō vs. Echizen, L15–R9), for a total of 6 2/3 repetitions.

Table D.3
Participants in *Sengohyakuban uta-awase* Ranked by Number of Winning Poems

Name and affiliation	Win/Loss/Tie	Related activities
1. Go-Toba (P)	66\11\13	J
2. SHUNZEI (M)	49\18\23	J, WD
3. YOSHITSUNE (PK)	48\21\21	J, WD
4. JIEN (PK)	42\23\25	J, WD
5. Michichika (PT)	40\22\28	J, WD
6. JAKUREN (M)	40\27\23	WD, SKKS
7. IETAKA (M)	39\26\25	WD, SKKS
8. SHUNZEI NO MUSUME (M)	38\27\25	
9. TEIKA (M)	36\31\23	J, WD, SKKS
10. *Tadayoshi* (R)	35\29\26	J
11. *Ariie* ([R]/M)	34\26\30	WD, SKKS
12. SANUKI (M)	32\26\32	
13. MASATSUNE (M)	32\30\28	WD, SKKS
14. Prince Koreakira (P)	31\29\30	
15. *Kunaikyō* (N)	30\26\34	
16. *Michitomo* (PT)	29\20\41	WD, SKKS
17. *Ienaga* (I)	29\40\21	WD (*kaikō*)
18. *Echizen* (I)	28\32\30	
19. *Yasusue* (R)	27\40\23	
20. *Michiteru* (PT)	26\25\39	
21. YOSHIHIRA (PK)	25\31\34	
22. KINTSUGU (M)	25\32\33	
23. KINTSUNE (M)	25\35\30	
24. *Kanemune* (R)	25\44\21	
25. TANGO (M)	21\35\34	
26. *Tomochika* (N)	21\39\30	WD
27. *Sueyoshi* (R)	18\48\24	
28. TAKANOBU (M)	16\41\33	WD (later)
29. *Kojijū* (R)	14\49\27	
30. *Kenshō* (R)	11\51\28	

KEY: P = Imperial patron; PK = Kujō (Fujiwara) House patron; PT = Tsuchimikado (Minamoto) House patron; I = Imperial retainer; K = retainer of the Kujō House; T = retainer of the Tsuchimikado House; M = Mikohidari poet; R = Rokujō poet.

Normal print = neutral; ALL CAPS = Kujō/Mikohidari; *italics* = Tsuchimikado/Rokujō.

J = *Sengohyakuban uta-awase* judge; WD = member of the Wakadokoro; SKKS = *Shinkokinshū* compiler.

NOTE: My total count for this contest differs slightly from that given by Ariyoshi in his *Shinkokin wakashū no kenkyū: kiban to kōsei*, p. 210.

Table D.4
Judgments by Judge and Faction

Wins	Tadayoshi	Shunzei	Michichika	Yoshitsune	Go-Toba	Teika	Suetsune	Moromitsu	Kenshō	Jien
Wins to T/(R)	20	28	x	20	21	28	26	23	34	25
Wins to R	11	18	x	11	14	16	16	10	20	14
Wins to K/(M)	59	47	x	51	60	51	50	46	53	54
Wins to M	45	32	x	43	41	38	38	34	38	47
Wins to Neutral	27	25	x	34	20	26	25	26	25	29
Ties	44	50	x	45	49	45	49	55	38	42
Wins to Ptr.	23	25	x	17	26	25	22	25	29	18

KEY: K = Kujō; M = Mikohidari; R = Rokujō; T = Tsuchimikado; Ptr. = patron
SOURCE: calculated from the text in Ariyoshi, *Sengohyakuban uta-awase no kōhon to sono kenkyū*.

Table D.5
Details of Judgments in Rounds Matching Kujō/Mikohidari Poets Against Tsuchimikado/Rokujō Poets

Judge	M/K win over R/T	R/T win over M/K	M win over R	M win over T	K win over R	K win over T	R win over M	R win over K	T win over M	T win over K
Tadayoshi	23	8	12	2	5	4	3	0	4	1
Shunzei	14	12	10	1	2	1	6	1	5	0
Yoshitsune (Michichika)	22	8	15	2	4	1	1	2	1	4
Go-Toba	24	6	12	3	4	5	3	0	2	1
Teika	17	13	11	2	2	2	7	0	5	1
Suetsune	14	11	10	1	3	0	4	2	4	1
Moromitsu	15	8	11	1	3	0	1	0	5	2
Kenshō	14	14	10	2	0	2	8	0	4	2
Jien	17	11	10	3	1	3	3	2	3	3

KEY: K= Kujō; M = Mikohidari; R = Rokujō; T = Tsuchimikado
SOURCE: Calculated from the text in Ariyoshi, *Sengohyakuban uta-awase no kōhon to sono kenkyū*.

APPENDIX E

Three Poetry Exchanges Between Go-Toba and Jien

When Go-Toba's favorite concubine, Owari, died in the Seventh Month of 1204, Go-Toba sought solace in an exchange of a set of ten poems with Jien. All twenty poems appear below.[1]

Go-Toba's poem

    Nani to naku   Hoping somehow
    nagusamu ya tote   That I might find solace
    kitaredomo   I came here, and yet
    sigure zo masaru   Winter rain teardrops fall
    fuyu no yamazato   Harder in this mountain village.

Jien's reply poem

    Toni kakuni   Though this way or that
    nagusamade simo   You find no solace,
    ikaga sen   What can you do?
    munasiki sora no   It's a lonely mountain village
    fuyu no yamazato   Under an uncertain winter sky.

---

1. For this and the next exchange below, the extant text of *Ienaga nikki* groups all of Go-Toba's poems together, followed by all of Jien's, and this is likely how the exchanges were made (that is, as sequences, rather than one poem at a time). However, I have matched the poems with one another so that their dialogic nature can be more clearly seen.

Go-Toba's poem

    Ofozora ni
    ofofu bakari no
    sode nare ya
    nurureba tuki no
    nururu gafo naru

    Is it that my sleeves
    Are broad enough to cover
    The great sky?
    For when they dampen it appears
    That the moon's face dampens, too.

Jien's reply poem

    Tufi ni nafo
    uresisa tutume
    nururu sode
    ofofan sora no
    tuki mo sayakeku

    Those wet sleeves—
    May they someday
    Envelop happiness
    So in the sky that they cover
    The moon might shine clear.

Go-Toba's poem

    Kore fa yo no
    sazo narafi zo to
    omofedomo
    nageku kokoro zo
    musuboforetutu

    "This is the world,
    The way things really are"—
    So I tell myself.
    Yet my grieving heart
    Keeps aching away.

Jien's reply poem

    Musuboruru
    kimi ga kokoro no
    toku bakari
    sazona narafi wo
    koko nite zo siru

    All it would take
    To soothe the aching heart
    Of my lord
    Is true knowledge that this death
    Is indeed the way of the world.

Go-Toba's poem

    Nagekazi to
    omofitorinisi
    kokoro nifa
    kafarazu nagara
    nururu sode kana

    I told myself
    I must not grieve,
    And this resolve
    Remains unchanged,
    Yet still my sleeves are wet.

Three Poetry Exchanges Between Go-Toba and Jien

Jien's reply poem

    Omofazi to   This feeling that you feel
    omofu omofi fa   You should not feel—
    sore nagara   As long as it is there,
    nururan sode yo   What can I do
    ware ika ni sen   About your still-wet sleeves?

Go-Toba's poem

    Wasurenan   I must forget her,
    nakanaka ima fa to   I who am plagued by the thought
    omofitutu   That she might yet soon return!
    suguru tukifi no   But still this world is full of regrets
    uramesi no yo ya   As days and months pass by.[2]

Jien's reply poem

    Kore made mo   I would have you
    kofuru waga mi wo   Shift the burden to me,
    tanomanan   Who also cared for her,
    kimi fa wasureyo   So that you can forget her now
    ware fa wasurezi   And I can guard her memory.

Go-Toba's poem

    Sekikafesi   I get along now,
    sirazu gafo nite   Suppressing my sorrow,
    suguru mi wo   Wearing an unconcerned look.
    nasakenasi to ya   People must see me
    fito no miruran   As utterly unfeeling.

Jien's reply poem

    Nasakenasi to   Surely none will see you
    miru fito mo arazi   As utterly unfeeling,
    Minasegafa   When they glimpse your sleeves,
    seze ni moreyuku   Drenched by rapids
    sode no kesiki wo   Like those of the Minase River.

---

2. Go-Toba is alluding to an anonymous *Shūishū* poem (#800, XIII, Love 3, with the headnote "Sent to a woman who had said to him, 'I'm sure you will not be visiting me tonight.'"): *Wasurenamu / ima fa tofazi to / omofitutu / nuru yo simo koro / yume ni miekere*— "I try to forget you / And though it's true I had resolved / Not to visit you then, / When I fell asleep last night / I saw you in a dream!"

Go-Toba's poem

Itu made ka	How long would I have stared
sigururu yama no	At early winter rain clouds
mine no kumo	Round the mountain peak
sode yori foka ni	And seen them as unconnected
utinagameken	To tears upon my sleeves?

Jien's reply poem

Kimi ga sode	Surely no winter shower
ima mo nurubeki	Could dampen once again
sigure kafa	My Lord's sleeves—
to omofu karani	No sooner do I think that,
farenu ofozora	Than I see a sky yet clouded over.

Go-Toba's poem

Ofozora wo	To the vast skies I direct
uramite mo yo no	Resentment, yet it avails me not,
kafinaki ni	In a world where all is vain.
ikanika subeki	What then should I do,
ariake no tuki	Lingering moon at dawn?

Jien's reply poem

Sayakesi na	Shining brightly, isn't it?
uramifatubeki	If the vast skies were really the place
sora naraba	To direct your resentment,
kumori koso seme	Then it would surely be clouded over,
ariake no tuki	This lingering moon at dawn.

Go-Toba's poem

Sode no ufe ni	"Does the moon reside
nurureba tuki no	On your sleeves, too,
yadoru ka to	Since they are damp?"—
sifo kumu ura no	This I would ask of the fisherwomen
ama ni tofabaya	Who dip brine along the shore.³

---

3. I disagree with Ishida and Satsukawa here (*IN*, p. 164). They interpret the sleeves in the first line as belonging to Go-Toba ("I would ask the fisherwomen if the moon resides on *my* sleeves"), which makes no sense to me. How would the fisherwomen know the answer? I think Go-Toba is asking them if the moon resides in *their* sleeves, too, although I am troubled by the lack of a "mo." Jien's reply seems to support my reading, since he says Go-Toba's sleeves are damp from *sigure*, whereas the fisherwomen's are damp from brine.

Three Poetry Exchanges Between Go-Toba and Jien

Jien's reply poem

 Kawakanan
 sigure ni nururu
 yofa no tuki
 sifo kumu ama no
 sode ni yudurite

Would that they might dry,
Sleeves wet from a fall of winter tears,
By transferring their late night moon
To the sleeves of fisherwomen
Who dip brine.

Go-Toba's poem

 Nani to mata
 wasurete suguru
 sode no ufe ni
 nurete sigure no
 wodorokasuran

Why is it
That once again my sleeves,
Which had forgotten,
Are dampened with winter rains,
Calling forth old tears?

Jien's reply poem

 Odorokasu
 sode no sigure no
 yume no yo wo
 samuru kokoro ni
 omofiafase yo

A world of dreams
Where rain on sleeves
Calls forth old tears—
May your heart come to know
That it is nothing more than that!

☙

In 1205, on the one-year anniversary of Owari's death, Go-Toba and Jien again exchanged poems.

Go-Toba's poem

 Ko no fa tiru
 okuyamazato ni
 sumafi site
 kokoro ni mono wo
 omofu koro kana

I make my home
Deep in the mountains
Where leaves fall—
And here I am
My heart full of memories.

Jien's reply poem

 Nagamuran
 onazi sora yori
 sigure kite
 yamazato naranu
 sode mo nurekeru

From that very sky
That you must be gazing at
Winter rains have come
To dampen even the sleeves
Of one who is not in the mountains.

Go-Toba's poem
    Kimi narade　　　　　　　If not to you,
    tare nika tuge no　　　　　To whom could I confess
    womakura no　　　　　　These nighttime longings,
    kakaru namida no　　　　　And how my tears flow
    yoru no omofi wo　　　　　On the boxwood pillow?

Jien's reply poem
(the text of this poem has been lost)[4]

Go-Toba's poem
    Katami tote　　　　　　　Though I stare
    sigururu sora wo　　　　　At rainy skies in hopes of finding
    nagamete mo　　　　　　Remembrances of her,
    fakana no kumo no　　　　How painful to see
    ato no afare ya　　　　　　Those clouds that do not last.

Jien's reply poem
    Kokoro are ya　　　　　　Have a heart,
    katami yosinaki　　　　　　O storm that sweeps away
    kumo no ato　　　　　　　The fleeting beauty
    fakanaki iro wo　　　　　　Of clouds that were at best
    farafu arasi fa　　　　　　　Undependable keepsakes!

Go-Toba's poem
    Ikani sen　　　　　　　　What can I do?
    kozo fa kinofu to　　　　　I long for her as if last year
    sinobarete　　　　　　　　Were only yesterday,
    namida ni kumoru　　　　　And now clouded with my tears
    yamaorosi no sora　　　　　Windswept mountain skies.

[I believe Jien's reply poem is missing here]

---

4. This note is in the received text itself.

Go-Toba's poem

    Yamazato ni
    sumu kafi araba
    fito sirenu
    nageki wo farafe
    mine no kogarasi

If there were benefit
From living in this mountain refuge,
Let it be that withering winds
From off the peak might blow away
This sorrow that none can understand.

Jien's reply poem

    Kaze mo ina
    kimi ga yamakage
    sigeredomo
    moto yori naki fa
    nageki narikeri

Though winds
May buffet Our Lord
In his mountain fastness,
It is due to his protection
That his subjects know not sorrow.

Go-Toba's poem

    Mayofaresi
    yama no wogafa no
    usugofori
    ima fa kakinagasu
    nori no midunami

The mountain stream
Which once was hindered
By tenuous ice,
Now flows free, rippling
Waters of the Law.

Jien's reply poem

    Minasegafa
    tokinagasuran
    nori no midu
    yama no fiziri no
    satori narikeri

That the Minase River
Now flows freely,
Like the Waters of the Law,
Is surely because the mountain sage
Has found enlightenment.

Go-Toba's poem

    Omofiiduru
    oritaku siba no
    yufukeburi
    musebu mo uresi
    wasuregatami ni

When I recall her,
Brushwood split and burned,
    its smoke
At evening time may smother,
Yet it brings me joy, a keepsake
Of her, whom I cannot forget.

Jien's reply poem

    Omofiiduru   No sooner do I hear
    oritaku siba to   That brushwood split and burned
    kiku karani   Has brought you memories
    tagufi sirarenu   Than I realize how special
    yufukeburi kana   That evening smoke must have been.[5]

Go-Toba's poem

    Na fa kutinu   Her name will not perish!
    koke no sita nimo   And there, beneath evergreen moss
    uresi toya   She must be happy,
    toburafu kane no   Hearing the sound of the bell
    oto wo kikuran   We ring in honor of her soul.

Jien's reply poem

    Kiku fito no   Her soul, which hears this
    kokoro fa sora ni   Must now be soaring free—
    narinu nari   Such is the power
    nodera no kane no   From the sound of the bell
    oto zo kasikoki   At your rustic temple.

[I believe a poem by Go-Toba is missing here]

Jien's reply poem

    Yasukaranu   How uncertain
    mi tozo narinuru   I've come to feel,
    afigataki   I who now dwell
    nori ni afu mi no   Away from others,
    yamada moru koro   And seek the precious Law.

---

5. This pair of poems appears as *SKKS* 801–2 (VIII, Laments).

☙

When Jien's nephew, Kujō Yoshitsune, died in the Third Month of 1206, Jien and Go-Toba conducted the following lengthy exchange of poems:[6]

From Jien

    Tu no kuni no   Reeds near the channel buoys,
    Nanifa mo asi no   At Naniwa in Tsu,
    mi wo tukusi   Are withered bare,
    Koya uki koto no   A lonely hut at Koya revealed—
    sirusi naruran   Surely a mark of the sad and frail.[7]

    Faru no yo no   "Awakened from
    yume ni wodoroku   A spring night's dream"—
    na nomi site   It's just an expression,
    samenu fa fito no   For the feelings I have now
    kokoro narikeri   Are of one not yet enlightened.

Go-Toba's reply

    Tu no kuni no   "Left lonely, cutting reeds
    asikarikeri na   In the province of Tsu,"
    tanomikosi   How much sadder now to live
    fito mo nagisa ni   When the one I long relied on
    itodo sumiuki   Is on these shores no more.[8]

---

6. Some of the poems vary according to textual line. I am following the texts as they appear in the main body of Ishida and Satsukawa (*IN*, pp. 272–87), rather than the emendations suggested by those two scholars in their notes. Also, unlike the Owari exchanges above, the extant *Ienaga nikki* texts give this exchange as a series of one, two, or three poems at a time, and I have left that format intact in my translation.

7. See Chapter 9, note 14, p. 338, for a discussion of some of the rhetorical elements of this poem.

8. See Chapter 9, note 15, p. 339, for information about the foundation poem (*honka*) for this poem.

Ofokata no
ukiyo wo yume to
siru fito no
nakereba koso fa
sode wo fosurame

That this sad world
Is a dream—
There is virtually no one
Who truly knows this.
Perhaps that's why most sleeves
soon dry.

Then, from Jien

Wasi no yama
tikaki fikari wo
minu mama ni
naki mo madofinu
aru mo madofinu

So long as we cannot see
The light that shines so close at hand
From Vulture Peak,
Those who are dead must wander,
And those alive must wander, too.

Go-Toba's reply

Wasi no yama
mukasi no tuki ya
kasumuran
ukiyo ni madofu
fito zo kanasiki

The ancient moonlight
From Vulture Peak
Seems misted over,
How sorrowful it is for us
Left wandering in this sad world!

Then, from Jien

Kore zo kono
yo no kotofari to
omofedomo
tagufinaki nifa
ne wo nomi zo naku

Although I realized
That just this sort of thing
Is the way of the world,
I cannot help sobbing
At its untimeliness.

Kari no miti wo
fukaku satoranu
fito fa mina
asamasi to nomi
omofunarikeri

No one truly understands
That our time on the road of life
Is temporary,
For all seem to be taking
This passing rather lightly.

Go-Toba's reply

Katagata ni
sode zo nureyuku
ofokata no
yo no kotofari wo
siru ni tukete mo

At this and that
My sleeves keep growing damper
Even though I know
That thus is the way of the world
For all such things.

Nori no miti wo	A heart that truly understands
satoru kokoro fa	The way of the Law
sika ya aran	Must be like yours.
nafo Udiyama no	But for me here in sad Uji,
uramesi no yo ya	It is a bitter world indeed.

Then, from Jien

Sode no iro no	Were it autumn
tagufi mo aki fa	The scarlet of my dampened sleeves
arinamasi	Might find a match,
faru no kozuwe ni	But what am I to do
ware ikani sen	With the green leaves of spring?

Go-Toba's reply

Kaminaduki	When I recall
kimi ni tugekosi	What His Lordship told you
omofi made	This past Tenth Month,
nafo wodorokasu	I am suddenly awakened
faru no yo no yume	From my spring night's dream.[9]

Then, from Jien

Faru no fana	In spring it was blossoms,
aki no tuki tote	In autumn, the moon
nagamesi wo	Upon which we used to gaze—
sono tomo ikani	Oh, how much I long
kofisikaruran	For that friend now!

Isonokami	That ancient road
Furuki miti koso	To Furu in Isonokami
kasuminure	Is now obscured in mist
sirube fa nobe no	And the one who used to guide me
tuyu to kieniki	Is vanished like dew on the moors.[10]

---

9. See Chapter 9, note 17, p. 341, for a discussion of interpretations of this poem.
10. See Chapter 9, note 18, p. 342, for a discussion of the pillow word *Isonokami*.

Go-Toba's reply

    Sono tomo no
    uti ni ya ware wo
    omofuran
    koisiki sode no
    iro wo misebaya

    It would seem
    That I, too, should be thought of
    As one of his friends,
    Might I show you the color of
      my sleeves,
    Stained with longing?[11]

    Furumiti no
    sirube fa tuyu to
    kiesi noni
    fitori nokorite
    sode nurasu koro

    My guide
    To that ancient road
    Has vanished like dew,
    And here I am, left alone,
    Wetting my sleeves with tears.

Then, from Jien

    Fikiufesi
    ike no ifane wo
    nagamureba
    ituka kodakaki
    nifa no matukaze

    As I gaze where they were planted
    Among the rocks
    Along the pond—
    When did they grow so tall?
    Wind-blown pines in the garden.

    Ufeokisi
    fitomoto susuki
    kono aki fa
    sigeki nobe toya
    tare mo nagamen

    That single clump of plume grass
    Which he had planted—
    This autumn
    All that anyone will see
    Is a moor overgrown.

    Tatenamuru
    isima no midu ni
    tare sumite
    aranu kage nimo
    sode nurasuran

    By the waters
    Among stones laid so carefully
    Who lives now?
    His face no longer reflected there,
    And so, it seems, I wet my sleeves.

---

11. Ishida and Satsukawa (*IN*, pp. 278–79) take this poem as addressed by Go-Toba to Yoshitsune, but I believe Go-Toba is addressing Jien. See Chapter 9, note 19, p. 342, for a discussion of the issues.

Three Poetry Exchanges Between Go-Toba and Jien

Go-Toba's reply

 Fikiufesi   To the pines he planted
 ifane no matu ni   Among the rocks
 koto tofan   I would ask:
 kodakaki kaze to   Was he hoping eventually to hear
 fito ya tanomesi   The wind through your branches
             grown tall?

 Furusato no   Though autumn comes
 fitomura susuki   To that single patch of plume grass
 aki kutomo   At his home
 kari ni tatitofu   There is no one here now
 fito ya nakaran   To tend it, or to visit.

 Nakikage yo   A reflection no more!—
 isima no midu ni   Does it still remain
 nokoru ya to   In the waters among the stones?
 tofabaya fito no   I want to know, and so I come
 ato no furusato   Here to his old home.

Then again came this poem from the Abbot's Quarters

 Keburi tatu   The firewood
 takigi mo ima fa   From which arose his smoke
 tukinu tote   Has now burnt out,
 kafereba kane no   And so, as I return home,
 kowe zo kanasiki   How sad the sound of the temple bell!

His Majesty's reply

 Namida sofu   As if to add its own
 kafesa ya sora mo   To your tears as you return home,
 kumoriken   The sky clouds over—
 nodera no kane no   A dream dispelled at daybreak
 akatuki no yume   By the bell of the temple in the fields.

Then from Jien

    Nisi fe yuku   To that very moon
    tuki koso ima fa   Which now is headed west
    kotoduten   I would entrust a message,
    kumoru namida wo   As I wipe away repeatedly
    uti farafitutu   The tears that cloud my eyes....[12]

Go-Toba's reply

    Nisi fe yuku   Whenever I see
    tuki miru tabi ni   That moon which now is headed west
    omofiiden   I shall recall
    kimi mo namida wo   How you, too, are struggling
    farafiwabu ya to   To wipe away the tears.

Again, from the Abbot Jien

    Fadukasi ya   How shameful
    kore wo uresi to   Those who find happiness
    omofu fito no   In this!
    kokoro wo terase   Please illuminate their hearts,
    yama no fa no tuki   Moon over the mountain's ridge!

Go-Toba's reply

    Sikasuga ni   That may well be,
    (tare wo uresi to   Yet who could find happiness here?
    tukikage no   Still, there are those
    sasite) yadoranu   On whose sleeves the moonlight
    sode fa aritomo   Will find no lodging.[13]

---

12. The moon is heading in the direction of the Western Paradise, where Yoshitsune is presumably to be reborn.

13. For this pair of poems, my interpretation differs radically from that of Ishida and Satsukawa (*IN*, p. 285). For Jien's poem, their gloss, which can only work if one takes the *no* after *omofu fito* as a subject marker (and even then it's a stretch), is "How splendid is Your Majesty's heart! The moon on the mountain's edge has illuminated Your Majesty's heart so that you are able to find happiness in the Regent's death by seeing it as an opportunity for enlightenment (*satori*). I wish I could be shown this, too." I read the *no* as the one that designates, as in *hito no kokoro* (a person's heart), and I see the poem as a swipe at Yoshitsune's enemies. (Recall that the Kujō position at the top of the ladder was by no means undisputed.)

Go-Toba's poem is more problematic since the text is corrupt. Ishida and Satsukawa reconstruct it as *Sikasuga ni / kore wo uresi to / tukikage no / sarade yadoranu / sode fa aredomo*, which they concede still does not make sense. Their gloss is: "Though the Regent's death was indeed

From Jien

    Ayasikarisi
    minami no yama no
    keburi kana
    sono sirusi to ya
    kita no fudinami

The ominous smoke
That came from that mountain
To the south,
Might it not have been an omen
For the northern branch of wisteria?[14]

Go-Toba's reply

    Kiesomesi
    minami no yama no
    keburi yuwe
    nurenisi sode fa
    aki zo fosubeki

Because the smoke
From that mountain to the south
Has begun to fade,
We can expect our wetted sleeves
To dry by autumn.[15]

From Jien

    Yo ni sumeba
    omofisiranu ni
    narifatenu
    oturu namida fa
    mata kafi mo nasi

Since I remain alive
I must have ended up
An unfeeling one, indeed.
The tears that I shed
Are still to no avail.

    Yo no naka wo
    asaku omofeba
    tae mo senu
    fukaki kokoro fa
    siru fito mo nasi

Since most people
Have such shallow feelings
There is no one who understands
This profound emotion
Impossible to bear.[16]

---

sad, for me it brought happiness since it became the opportunity for my enlightenment (*satori*), even if the moon on the mountain's edge did not illuminate my sleeves." I have opted for a version that incorporates the two main textual alternatives as noted in Ishida and Satsukawa (*IN*, p. 280) and that seems to respond to Jien's accusation better, though my reading, too, does not quite hang together grammatically. The reason the moonlight will find no lodging on those sleeves is that the wearers are not shedding any tears to reflect it.

    14. See Chapter 9, note 25, p. 345, for a discussion of the reference to "Smoke from the mountain to the south."

    15. See Chapter 9, note 26, p. 346, for a discussion of possible interpretations of this poem.

    16. The line *tae mo senu* might mean either "cannot bear" or "endless." I am following Ishida and Satsukawa (*IN*, p. 286) in reading it as the former, because that seems to be how Go-Toba took it in his reply poem.

Go-Toba's reply

Yo ni tare ka	Who in the world
omofisirazu to	Would ever describe you
kakete ifan	As one unfeeling?
namida no iro fa	The scarlet of your tears
yoso no sode made	Reaches to other sleeves.

Yo no naka wo	Those scarlet maple leaves
aki mo tafenisi	Have withstood the vicissitudes
momidiba no	Of autumn in this world.
fukaki wo sasofu	How sad that the wind takes
kaze zo kanasiki	now them
	When their hue is at its deepest.

From Jien

Kono aki fa	This autumn
mukasi wo kofuru	Due to tears of longing
namida yuwe	For the past,
tuki wo dani minu	I shall be one
mi toya narinan	Who cannot even see the moon.

Yuki furaba	If snow should fall
koto tofu ato ya	I shall recall with longing
omofiiden	The footprints left from his visit
kienokorubeki	Even though I myself
mi ni fa aranedo	May not last without melting away.

Go-Toba's reply

Aki mo nafo	"Even in autumn,
aki wo kofisi to	Still more one longs for autumn,"
ifiokisi	He used to say.
sono koto no fa ya	Now you must be recalling
omofiidubeki	Those very words.

Yuki furaba	If snow should fall
madu omofiiden	The first thing I shall recall
kimi ga yado ni	Is your sleeves wet with tears
ato naki ato ni	For his footprints
sode nurasuran	Now no more.

Three Poetry Exchanges Between Go-Toba and Jien

From Jien

    Omokage wo
    ko fa ikani sen
    kinofu nado
    kefu wo kagiri to
    katarazariken

Alas, what am I to do
About his ever-present image in
    my mind?
Why is it that yesterday
He did not convey to me
That today he would be gone?

Go-Toba's reply

    Nakanaka ni
    kotosi ya koso fa
    sate okinu
    naresi mukasi wo
    ikade wasuren

Whatever it is
That has happened this year
Leave it as it is.
How can I ever forget
That past that was so sweet?[17]

From Jien

    Nagusamuru
    tayori tomo nare
    Kasugayama
    fana tiru mine ni
    kakaru sirakumo

Please become my means
For communing with the departed—
White clouds clinging
To the peak of Mount Kasuga
Where the blossoms have scattered.[18]

Go-Toba's reply

    Ima fa tada
    fana tiru mine no
    sirakumo ni
    sosogan ame yo
    tayori tomo nare

For now
My own means will be
The rain that pours
From those white clouds on the peak
Where blossoms have scattered.

---

17. Go-Toba's poem actually contains an embedded pun (the emphatic particle *koso* is also *kozo*, "last year") which yields a "this year / last year" opposition that plays off Jien's "yesterday/today."

18. At the base of Mount Kasuga, in present-day Nara, stands the Kasuga Shrine, the tutelary shrine for the Fujiwara clan, of which Yoshitsune was a member.

From Jien
>   Midorigo wo
>   ware to ware to ga
>   naka ni mite
>   ikanaru koto wo
>   omofiokiken

>   For that toddler
>   That you and your wife
>   Looked after together
>   What sort of plans
>   Must you have had?[19]

Go-Toba's reply
>   Midori naru
>   futaba no matu no
>   yukusuwe wo
>   nafo inisie no
>   kami ni makase yo

>   As for the future
>   Of the seedling pine
>   That is still green,
>   Still better to entrust it
>   To those ancient gods.

---

19. See Chapter 9, note 29, p. 347, for a discussion of the "toddler" reference.

APPENDIX F

'Shinkokinshū' Time Line

The process of commissioning, compiling, and presenting an imperial anthology is rarely a smooth one. *Shinkokinshū* was no exception. Many steps were involved in Go-Toba's struggle to forge a consensus among his courtiers and generate poetry for the collection. The major events are listed below (more details on each can be found through the Subject Index, pp. 463–80).[1]

1200 (Shōji 2)/vii/15—Go-Toba commissioned a set of 100-poem sequences from twenty-three poets (*Shōji ninen in shodo hyakushu*). The idea was initially suggested by the Rokujō poet Suetsune, but after hearing Shunzei's complaints, Go-Toba expanded the list of names involved in the commission be-

---

1. Between Shōji 2 (1200) and Jōgen 2 (1208), Ariyoshi (*Shinkokin wakashū no kenkyū: kiban to kōsei*, pp. 538–41) lists a total of forty-seven poetry events, including contests, parties, and poem sequences, that contributed poems to *Shinkokinshū*. His entire list of sources for *Shinkokinshū* covers every event he could identify from the *Kanpyō no ōntoki Kisainomiya no uta-awase* of Kanpyō 5 (893), from which five poems were drawn, down to the *Sumiyoshi uta-awase* of Jōgen 2 (1208), from which one poem was taken (see pp. 533–41). He also gives a detailed time line from Kenkyū 1 (1190) through Jōgen 3 (1209) of every verifiable poetry-related event and the location of relevant texts or supporting documents (although these citations are not as complete as they might be; see pp. 542–65). Ariyoshi also gives, on pp. 44–49, a list of nineteen events, starting in Bunji 6 (1190) and ending in Jōgen 1 (1207), that contributed five or more poems to *Shinkokinshū*.

My own much shorter list of important events, which appears here, started from a different set of assumptions from Ariyoshi's, although there is, of course, much overlap. I was primarily interested in identifying those events that were sponsored by Go-Toba and illustrate his effort to mediate among contending factions. My list of events include some that contributed no poems to *Shinkokinshū*, and conversely, I exclude some of Ariyoshi's forty-seven events because they were essentially private or narrow in focus or because their details were too hard to verify.

yond Suetsune's elite group to include younger, more innovative poets. The sequences were formally presented on Shōji 2 (1200)/xi/22. The event became the second largest source of poems for *Shinkokinshū*.

1200 (Shōji 2)/xi?—Go-Toba commissioned a second set of 100-poem sequences from eleven mostly lesser-known poets (*Shōji ninen in dainido hyakushu*) in an apparent step toward establishing himself as the main supporter of poetic activity.

1201 (Kennin 1)/ii/16, 18—In an ironic twist on the conservative Rokujō faction's privileging of its senior members, Go-Toba sponsored the *Rōnyaku gojisshu uta-awase*, ostensibly pitting "old" (*rō*) and "young" (*nyaku*) poets against each other. In reality, even the "old" team, which included Teika, was made up of progressives, and the event was a showcase for new poets of several styles.

1201 (Kennin 1)/iii/29—Go-Toba sponsored the *Shingū senka-awase*, in which he first commissioned ten-poem sequences from twenty-six poets and then had work groups of master poets make blind selections of seventy-two poems from the 260 submitted. Subsequently, all twenty-six poets met and discussed the selected poems, arranged in contest format, and Shunzei made final judgments. Participants came from all poetic and political factions.

1201 (Kennin 1)/iv/30—By holding the *Kennin gannen shigatsu sanjūnichi Tobadono eigu uta-awase* in his Toba palace, Go-Toba replaced Minamoto (Tsuchimikado) Michichika as the sponsor of the monthly *eigu* contests. These contests, honoring the early eighth-century poet Hitomaro, had become an important fixture of the literary scene, and by appropriating their sponsorship, Go-Toba further positioned himself as the main patron of poetry at court.

1201 (Kennin 1)/vi—Go-Toba commissioned a third set of 100-poem sequences (*Go-Toba-in daisando hyakushu*) from thirty poets. This would become the basis for the *Sengohyakuban uta-awase* discussed below.

1201 (Kennin 1)/vii/27—Go-Toba established a new Wakadokoro with eleven members. They would provide research and editing support for the imperial anthology (what we now call *Shinkokinshū*) that he was apparently already planning, and six among them would be named compilers for that anthology. He also conceived of the Wakadokoro as the locus of poetic activity and immediately sponsored two important contests there, both judged by Shunzei (the *Kennin gannen hachigatsu mikka eigu uta-awase* of viii/3, which was the first of many *eigu* events there, and the *Kennin gannen hachigatsu jūgoya senka-awase* of viii/15, a contest of selected poems that involved group discussions). These were followed by the *Sentō kudai gojisshu* in which six poets composed fifty poems each and then discussed and marked one another's poems, seminar-style. These activities exemplified Go-Toba's approach to poetic composition and evaluation.

1201 (Kennin 1)/xi/3—Go-Toba issued the commission for *Shinkokinshū* and named six compilers: Minamoto (Tsuchimikado) Michitomo, Fujiwara Ariie, Fujiwara (Mikohidari) Teika, Fujiwara Ietaka, Fujiwara (Asukai) Masatsune, and the priest Jakuren (who died less than a year later, before the project was completed).

1201 (Kennin 1)/xi/3–1203 (Kennin 3), iv/20—Compilers selected poems for the collection.

1202 (Kennin 2)/iii/22—Go-Toba sponsored the *Santai waka*, inviting nine poets to compose on six topics in three different styles—further evidence of his seminar-like approach to the study of poetry. Seven poets (Kujō Yoshitsune, Jien, Teika, Ietaka, Jakuren, Kamo no Chōmei, and Go-Toba himself) accepted the challenge.

1202 (Kennin 2)/ix/13—On one of his many visits to his villa at Minase, at which poetry activities inevitably took place, Go-Toba sponsored a loosely structured poetry contest (*Minasedono koi jūgoshu uta-awase*) with ten of his favorite innovative poets. The theme was "Love," and he summoned the nearly ninety-year-old Shunzei all the way from the city to judge the works. Some of the poems from this event were subsequently reworked into two selected-poem contests (*senka-awase*), and fifteen of its poems were included in *Shinkokinshū*.

1202 (Kennin 2)/ix/6—Go-Toba assigned ten poets to judge the 3,000 poems that had been generated by his *Daisando hyakushu* of the previous year. He had subsequently reworked the poems into a poetry contest of 1,500 rounds. The final version of this contest, with judgments, was completed late in 1202 or early 1203, and is now known as the *Sengohyakuban uta-awase*. Ninety of its poems were added to *Shinkokinshū*, making it the single most important source for that anthology.

1203 (Kennin 3)/iv/20—Teika presented a first clean draft of prospective *Shinkokinshū* poems to Go-Toba.

1203 (Kennin 3)/iv–1204 (Genkyū 1)/vi—Go-Toba prepared his own editorial suggestions for the *Shinkokinshū* draft the Wakadokoro had submitted him.

1203 (Kennin 3)/xi/23—Go-Toba hosted a ninetieth-anniversary celebration for Shunzei—a rare honor for someone of such modest rank and a clear indication of the high regard Go-Toba had for poetic talent.

1204 (Genkyū 1)/vii/22—After having spent a year making his own changes to the *Shinkokinshū* draft, Go-Toba ordered the classification (*burui*) process to begin, and the compilers started sorting the poems into appropriate sections and ordering them.

1204 (Genkyū 1)/xi/10—Apparently hoping to generate more contemporary poems of a specific type and topic for *Shinkokinshū*, Go-Toba organized the *Kasuga no Yashiro no uta-awase*, with thirty poets in forty-five rounds. The poets were matched by skill, and the contest, judged by the group, was very competitive. Soon after, fourteen of its poems were chosen for *Shinkokinshū*.

1205 (Genkyū 2)/iii/26—Go-Toba prematurely sponsored a presentation banquet for the *Shinkokinshū*, although neither the anthology nor its prefaces were done yet, and many later revisions in fact occurred.

1205 (Genkyū 2), iii/28–1210 (Jōgen 4), ix—A series of revisions and additions took place during which more than sixty poems were added, mostly from poetry events held for the purpose of producing more poems for the collection.

1205 (Genkyū 2)/vi/15—Go-Toba sponsored his first mixed Chinese/Japanese poetry contest, the *Genkyū shiika-awase*. Eight of its Japanese poems were added to *Shinkokinshū*.

1206 (Ken'ei 1)/vii/25—Perhaps playfully, Go-Toba matched the ruling elite against their retainers in the *Keishō jishin no uta-awase*, a contest involving most of the important poets of the day, including remnants of the conservative Rokujō/Tsuchimikado faction. The "retainer" team, which included Teika, took the event seriously, and although they "lost" the contest in terms of score, six of the nine poems selected from this contest for inclusion in *Shinkokinshū* were from their team.

1207 (Ken'ei 2/Jōgen 1)/iv—Go-Toba commissioned screen paintings and poems for his new monastery, the Saishōshitennō-in. Ten poets were asked to compose poems related to each of forty-six famous poetic place-names as decided upon by members of the Wakadokoro. In the Ninth Month, at a gathering at the Wakadokoro, one poem for each screen was selected from among the 460 poems submitted. Furthermore, thirteen poems from the group (not in all cases ones selected for the screens) were also added to *Shinkokinshū*. This was the last major event from which poems were drawn for that anthology.

1216 (Kenpō 4)/xii/26—Minamoto Ienaga completed a clean copy of *Shinkokinshū* that is the basis for most current texts. However, see the following entry.

1221 (Jōkyū 3)/vii/13–1235 (Katei 1)/ii—Go-Toba continued to edit and revise the collection during his Oki exile, taking out 360 poems and producing the so-called Oki-bon text.

Reference Matter

Works Cited

Unless otherwise noted, Japanese publishers are located in Tokyo.

Amino Yoshihiko. *Chūsei no hinin to yūjo*. Akashi shoten, 1994.
Aoki Kengō. *Fujiwara Yoshitsune zenkashū to sono kenkyū*. Kasama shoin, 1976.
Ariyoshi Tamotsu. *Sengohyakuban uta-awase no kōhon to sono kenkyū*. Kazama shobō, 1968.
———. *Shinkokin wakashū no kenkyū: kiban to kōsei*. Sanseidō, 1968.
———. *Shinkokin wakashū no kenkyū: zokuhen*. Kasama shoin, 1996.
———. *Wakabungaku jiten*. Ōfūsha, 1982.
Bentley, John R. "The Creation of Hitomaro, a Poetic Sage." In *The Life of Language, the Language of Life: Selected Papers from the First College-wide Conference for Students in Languages, Linguistics and Literature*, ed. Dina Yoshimi and Marilyn Plumlee, pp. 153–58. Honolulu: University of Hawai'i at Mānoa, Second Language Teaching and Curriculum Center, 1998.
Bialock, David. "Voice, Text, and the Question of Poetic Borrowing in Late Classical Poetry." *HJAS* 54, no. 1 (July 1994): 181–231.
Borgen, Robert. *Sugawara no Michizane and the Early Heian Court*. 2d ed. Honolulu: University of Hawaii Press, 1994.
Brower, Robert H. "'Ex-Emperor Go-Toba's Secret Teachings': *Go-Toba no in gokuden*." *HJAS* 32 (1972): 5–70.
Brower, Robert H., and Earl Miner. *Fujiwara Teika's Superior Poems of Our Time: A Thirteenth Century Poetic Treatise and Sequence*. Stanford: Stanford University Press, 1967.
———. *Japanese Court Poetry*. Stanford: Stanford University Press, 1961.
Brown, Delmar, and Ishida Ichirō. *The Future and the Past*. Berkeley: University of California Press, 1979.

Bundy, Roselee. "*Santai waka*: Six Poems in Three Modes." 2 pts. *MN* 49, no. 2 (Summer 1994): 197–227; no. 3 (Autumn 1994): 261–86.

Ch'en, Kenneth. *Buddhism in China*. Princeton: Princeton University Press, 1964.

Chūsei uta-awase kenkyūkai, ed. *Chūsei uta-awase denbon shomoku*. Meiji shoin, 1991.

Cranston, Edwin A. "'Mystery and Depth' in Japanese Poetry." In *The Distant Isle*, ed. Hare et al. (q.v.), pp. 65–104.

Friday, Karl F. *Hired Swords: The Rise of Private Warrior Power in Early Japan*. Stanford: Stanford University Press, 1992.

Fujihira Haruo. *Karon no kenkyū*. Perikansha, 1988.

———. *Shinkokin kafū no keisei*. Meiji shoin, 1969.

———. *Shinkokin to sono zengo*. Kasama shoin, 1983.

Fukuda Hideichi and Inoue Muneo. *Chūsei uta-awaseshū to kenkyū*, vol. 1. Mikan kokubun shiryō kankōkai, 1968.

Goble, Andrew. *Kenmu: Go-Daigo's Revolution*. Cambridge, Mass.: Harvard University, Council on East Asian Studies, 1996.

Goff, Janet. "Nō and Its Antecedents: 'Journey to the Western Provinces.'" In *The Distant Isle*, ed. Hare et al. (q.v.), pp. 165–81.

Gomi Fumihiko and Meigetsuki kenkyūkai, eds. "*Meigetsuki* Kennin ninen hachigatsu o yomu." *Meigetsuki kenkyū* 1 (Nov. 1996): 2–36.

———. "*Meigetsuki*, Kennin ninen shichigatsu o yomu." *Bungaku* n.s. 6, no. 4 (Fall 1995): 2–31.

Goodwin, Janet R. "Shadows of Transgression: Heian and Kamakura Constructions of Prostitution." *MN* 55, no. 3 (Autumn 2000): 327–68.

Gotō Shigeo. *Shinkokin wakashū no kisōteki kenkyū*. Hanawa shobō, 1968.

Gotō Toshio. *Man'yōshū seiritsu shinron*. Ōfūsha, 1986.

Hagitani Boku, ed. *Heianchō uta-awase taisei*. 10 vols. Dōhōsha, 1987.

Hagitani Boku and Taniyama Shigeru, eds. *Uta-awaseshū*. NKBT 74. Iwanami shoten, 1977.

Hall, John W. "Kyoto as Historical Background." In *Medieval Japan: Essays in Institutional History*, ed. Hall and Mass (q.v.), pp. 3–38.

Hall, John W., and Jeffrey Mass, eds. *Medieval Japan: Essays in Institutional History*. New Haven: Yale University Press, 1974.

Hare, Thomas. "Reading Kamo no Chōmei." *HJAS* 44, no. 1 (June 1989): 163–228.

———. "A Separate Piece: Proprietary Claims and Intertextuality in Rokujō Plays." in *The Distant Isle*, ed. Hare et al. (q.v.), pp. 183–203.

Hare, Thomas; Robert Borgen; and Sharalyn Orbaugh, eds. *The Distant Isle: Studies and Translations of Japanese Literature in Honor of Robert H. Brower*. Ann Arbor: University of Michigan, Center for Japanese Studies, 1996.

Harries, Phillip. *The Poetic Memoirs of Lady Daibu*. Stanford: Stanford University Press, 1980.

Hashimoto Fumio, Ariyoshi Tamotsu, and Fujihira Haruo, eds. *Karonshū*. NKBZ 50. Shōgakukan, 1980.
Higuchi Yoshimaro. "Kennin gannen sentō kudai gojisshu to sono seiritsu." *Aichi gakugeidai kenkyū hōkoku* 12 (3/1963).
Higuchi Yoshimaro et al., eds. *Chūsei wakashū: Kamakurahen*. SNKBT 46. Iwanami shoten, 1991.
Hirota Akiko. "Ex-Emperor Go-Toba: A Study in Personality, Politics and Poetry." Ph.D. diss., University of California at Los Angeles, 1989.
Hisamatsu Sen'ichi. *Biographical Dictionary of Japanese Literature*. New York: Kodansha, 1976.
Hisamatsu Sen'ichi, ed. *Chūsei no kajin II*. Nihon kajin kōza 4. Kōbundō, 1962.
———. *Karonshū I*. Chūsei no bungaku 1. Miyai shoten, 1971.
Hisamatsu Sen'ichi and Nishio Minoru, eds. *Karonshū nōgakuronshū*. NKBT 65. Iwanami shoten, 1981.
Hisamatsu Sen'ichi, Matsuda Takeo, Sekine Yoshiko, and Aoki Takako, eds. *Heian Kamakura shikashū*. NKBT 80. Iwanami shoten, 1964.
Huey, Robert. "*Fushimi-in Nijūban Uta-awase.*" MN 48, no. 2 (Summer 1993): 167–203.
———. "The Kingyoku Poetry Contest." MN 42, no. 3 (Autumn 1987): 299–330.
———. *Kyōgoku Tamekane: Poetry and Politics in Late Kamakura Japan*. Stanford: Stanford University Press, 1989.
———. "The Medievalization of Poetic Practice." HJAS 50, no. 2 (Dec. 1990): 651–68.
———. Review of Steven Carter, *The Road to Komatsubara*. HJAS 50, no. 1 (June 1990): 352–77.
———. "Warrior Control over the Imperial Anthology." In *The Origins of Japan's Medieval World: Courtiers, Clerics, Warriors, and Peasants in the Fourteenth Century*, ed. Jeffrey Mass, pp. 170–91. Stanford: Stanford University Press, 1997.
Hurst, G. Cameron, III. *Insei: Abdicated Sovereigns in the Politics of Late Heian Japan, 1086–1185*. New York: Columbia University Press, 1976.
———. "The Kōbu Polity: Court-Bakufu Relations in Kamakura Japan." In *Court and Bakufu in Japan*, ed. Mass (q.v.), pp. 3–28.
———. "The Structure of the Heian Court: Some Thoughts on the Nature of 'Familial Authority' in Heian Japan." In *Medieval Japan*, ed. Hall and Mass (q.v.), pp. 39–59.
Hurvitz, Leon, trans. *Scripture of the Lotus Blossom of the Fine Dharma (The Lotus Sutra)*. New York: Columbia University Press, 1976.
Ienaga Kaori. "Kennin gannen no Go-Toba In kadan: *Rōnyaku gojisshu uta-awase, Shingū senka-awase* o chūshin ni." *Bungaku* n.s. 6, no. 4 (Fall 1995): 54–63.
Ikeda Kikan, Kishigami Shinji, and Akiyama Ken, eds. *Makura no sōshi; Murasaki Shikibu nikki*. NKBT 19. Iwanami shoten, 1958.

Imagawa Fumio. *Meigetsuki jinmei sakuin*. Hatsune shobō, 1972.

———. *Meigetsukishō*. Kawaide shobō shinsha, 1986.

Inagaki Hisao and Harold Stewart, trans. *The Three Pure Land Sutras*. Kyoto: Nagata bunshodo, 1994.

Inoue Muneo. *Heian koki kajinden no kenkyū*. Kasama shoin, 1978.

Inoue Muneo and Matsuno Yōichi, "Shōji ninen Shunzeikyō waji sōjō honkoku to kaisetsu." *Waka bungaku kenkyū* 15 (1963): 19–22.

Inukai Kiyoshi et al. *Waka daijiten*. Meiji shoin, 1986.

Ishida Yoshisada. *Shinkokin sekai to chūsei bungaku*. 2 vols. Kitazawa tosho shuppan, 1972.

Ishida Yoshisada and Satsukawa Shūji. *Minamoto Ienaga no nikki zenchūkai*. Yūseidō, 1968.

Iwasa Masashi, Tokieda Motoki, and Kidō Saizō, eds. *Jinnō shōtōki Masukagami*. NKBT 87. Iwanami shoten, 1965.

Kamens, Edward. *The Buddhist Poetry of the Great Kamo Priestess: Daisaiin Senshi and Hosshin Wakashū*. Ann Arbor: University of Michigan, Center for Japanese Studies, 1990.

———. Review of Robert Huey, *Kyōgoku Tamekane*. *JJS* 17, no. 2 (1991): 377–81.

———. *Utamakura, Allusion, and Intertextuality in Traditional Japanese Poetry*. New Haven: Yale University Press, 1997.

Katano Tatsurō and Matsuno Yōichi, eds. *Senzai wakashū*. SNKBT 10. Iwanami shoten, 1993.

Katō, Hilda. "The *Mumyōshō* of Kamo no Chōmei and Its Significance in Japanese Literature." 2 pts. *MN* 23, nos. 3 and 4 (1968): pp. 321–430.

Keene, Donald, ed. *Anthology of Japanese Literature: From the Earliest Era to the Mid-Nineteenth Century*. New York: Grove Press, 1955.

———. *20 Plays of the Nō Theater*. New York: Columbia University Press, 1970.

Kim, Yung-hee. "The Female Entertainment Tradition in Medieval Japan: The Case of Asobi." *Theater Journal* 40, no. 2 (May 1988): 205–16.

———. *Songs to Make the Dust Dance: The Ryōjin hishō of Twelfth Century Japan*. Berkeley: University of California Press, 1994.

Koehn, Joni. "Gender and Narrativity in Japanese Literature: Images of Ono no Komachi." *Literary Studies East and West* 9 (1994): 141–47.

Kojima Yoshio, ed. *Shinkokin wakashū*. Asahi shinbunsha, 1960.

———. *Shinkokin wakashū no kenkyū*. Hoshino shoten, 1944. (This and the following book by Kojima were reissued as *Zōho Shinkokin wakashū no kenkyū*, 2 vols., Kenkyū sōsho 134 [Izumi shoten, 1993].)

———. *Shinkokin wakashū no kenkyū, zokuhen*. Shin Nihon tosho, 1946. (This and the preceding book by Kojima were reissued as *Zōho Shinkokin wakashū no kenkyū*, 2 vols., Kenkyū sōsho 134 [Izumi shoten, 1993].)

Kokushi daijiten henshū iinkai, ed. *Kokushi daijiten*. Yoshikawa Kōbunkan, 1990.
Kokusho kankōkai, ed. *Gyokuyō*. 3 vols. Kokusho kankōkai, 1907.
———. *Meigetsuki*. 3 vols. Kokusho kankōkai, 1911.
Konishi Jin'ichi. "Association and Progression: Principles of Integration in Anthologies and Sequences of Japanese Court Poetry, A.D. 900-1350." Trans. Robert H. Brower and Earl Miner. *HJAS* 21 (1958): 67-127.
———. *A History of Japanese Literature*. 3 vols. Trans. Aileen Gatten and Nicholas Teele; ed. Earl Miner. Princeton: Princeton University Press, 1984- .
Kubota Jun. *Shinkokin kajin no kenkyū*. Tōkyō daigaku shuppankai, 1973.
Kubota Jun, ed. *Ronshū chūsei no bungaku*, vols. 1 and 2 (Poetry [*inbunhen*] and Prose [*sanbunhen*]). Meiji shoin, 1994.
———. *Shinkokin wakashū*. 2 vols. Shinchōsha, 1979.
Kubota Jun and Matsuno Yōichi, eds. *Senzai wakashū*. Kasama shoin, 1969.
Kubota Shōichirō, Fujihira Haruo, and Yamaji Heishirō, eds. *Waka kanshō jiten*. Tōkyōdō, 1970.
Kubota Utsuho, ed. *Shinkokin wakashū*. 2 vols. Tōkyōdō, 1932.
Kunaichō shoryōbu, ed. *Katsuranomiyabon sōsho*. 19 vols. Nara: Yōtokusha, 1957.
Kurano Kenji and Takeda Yūkichi, eds. *Kojiki Norito*. NKBT 1. Iwanami shoten, 1958.
Kuroita Katsumi, ed. *Sonpi Bunmyaku 1*. Kokushi taikei 58. Yoshikawa Kōbunkan, 1961.
LaFleur, William. *The Karma of Words: Buddhism and the Literary Arts in Medieval Japan*. Berkeley: University of California Press, 1983.
Marra, Michele. "The Buddhist Mythmaking of Defilement: Sacred Courtesans in Medieval Japan." *JAS* 52, no. 1 (Feb. 1993): 49-65.
———. *Representations of Power: The Literary Politics of Medieval Japan*. Honolulu: University of Hawai'i Press, 1993.
Martin, Samuel. *The Japanese Language Through Time*. New Haven: Yale University Press, 1987.
Marumo Takesige. *Chūsei no tabibitotachi*. Rokkō shuppan, 1987.
Maruya Saiichi. *Go-Toba In*. Nihon shijinsen 10. Chikuma shobō, 1973.
Mass, Jeffrey. *The Development of Kamakura Rule, 1180-1250*. Stanford: Stanford University Press, 1979.
———. "The Early Bakufu and Feudalism." In *Court and Bakufu in Japan*, ed. Mass (q.v.), pp. 123-42.
———. *The Kamakura Bakufu: A Study in Documents*. Stanford: Stanford University Press, 1976.
Mass, Jeffrey, ed. *Court and Bakufu in Japan*. Stanford: Stanford University Press, 1982.

———. *The Origins of Japan's Medieval World: Courtiers, Clerics, Warriors, and Peasants in the Fourteenth Century*. Stanford: Stanford University Press, 1997.
Matisoff, Susan. *The Legend of Semimaru: Blind Musician of Japan*. New York: Columbia University Press, 1978.
Mikkyō gakkai. *Mikkyō daijiten*. 6 vols. Hōkōkan, 1931, 1965.
Minamoto Ienaga nikki kenkyūkai, ed. *Minamoto Ienaga nikki: kōi, kenkyū, sōsakuin*. Kazama shobō, 1985.
Minegishi Yoshiaki. *Uta-awase no kenkyū*. Sanseidō, 1969.
Minegishi Yoshiaki, ed. *Uta-awaseshū*. Nihon koten zensho, unnumbered volume. Asahi shinbunsha, 1952.
Minemura Fumihito, ed. *Shinkokin wakashū*. NKBZ 26. Shōgakukan, 1974.
———. *Shinkokin wakashū*. Nihon no koten 35. Shōgakukan, 1983.
Miner, Earl. *Introduction to Japanese Court Poetry*. Stanford: Stanford University Press, 1968.
———. *Japanese Poetic Diaries*. Berkeley: University of California Press, 1969.
Miner, Earl; Hiroko Odagiri; and Robert E. Morrell. *The Princeton Companion to Classical Japanese Literature*. Princeton: Princeton University Press, 1985.
Mitani Eiichi and Sekine Yoshiko, eds. *Sagoromo monogatari*. NKBT 79. Iwanami shoten, 1965.
Morrell, Robert E. "The *Shinkokinshū*: 'Poems on Śākyamuni's Teachings' (*Shakkyōka*)." In *The Distant Isle*, ed. Hare et al. (q.v.), pp. 281–320.
Morris, Ivan. *The World of the Shining Prince*. London: Oxford University Press, 1964.
Morris, Mark. "Waka and Form, Waka and History." *HJAS* 46, no. 2 (1986): 551–610.
Mostow, Joshua S. *Pictures of the Heart: The Hyakunin Isshu in Word and Image*. Honolulu: University of Hawai'i Press, 1996.
Nakahara, Gladys, "Songs of *Ryōjin hishō*." Ph.D. diss., University of Hawai'i, 1999.
Nakajima Etsuji. *Gukanshō zenchūkai*. Yūseidō, 1969.
Nakanishi Susumu. *Kokin rokujō no Man'yōka*. Musashino shoin, 1964.
Nihon bungaku daijiten henshū iinkai, ed. *Nihon bungaku daijiten*. 6 vols. Iwanami shoten, 1984.
Nihon tosho sentaa, ed. *Man'yōshū sengakushō, Man'yōshū meibutsukō ta nihen*. Man'yōshū kochūshaku taisei. Seishinsha, 1978.
Nippon gakujutsu shinkōkai, trans. *Man'yōshū*. New York: Columbia University Press, 1965.
Nishiki Hitoshi. "Inseiki uta-awase no kōzō to hōhō—'ke' kara 'hare' e no wakashikan no hihan." In *Higi to shite no waka—kōi to ba*, ed. Watanabe Yasuaki, pp. 39–54. Yūseidō, 1995.
Ōae Akira. *Gyokuyō jikō sakuin*. Kazama shobō, 1991.
Ogami Hachirū, ed. *Shinkokin wakashū*. 2 vols. Meiji shoin, 1953.

Okada, H. Richard. *Figures of Resistance: Language, Poetry, and Narrating in "The Tale of Genji" and Other Mid-Heian Texts.* Durham, N.C.: Duke University Press, 1991.
Ōno Susumu, Satake Akihiro, and Maeda Kingoro, eds. *Iwanami kogo jiten.* Iwanami shoten, 1974.
Ono Yasuhiro et al. *Nihon shūkyō jiten.* Kōbundō, 1985.
Ōsone Shōsuke and Horiuchi Hideaki, eds. *Wakan rōeishū.* Shinchōsha, 1983.
Ōsone Shōsuke and Kubota Jun et al., eds. *Kenkyū shiryō Nihon koten bungaku,* vol. 6, *Waka.* Meiji shoin, 1983.
Ozawa Masao, ed. *Kokin wakashū. NKBZ* 7. Shōgakukan, 1971.
Piggott, Joan R. "Hierarchy and Economics in Early Medieval Tōdaiji." In *Court and Bakufu in Japan,* ed. Mass (q.v.), pp. 45–91.
Pollack, David. *Fracture of Meaning: Japan's Synthesis of China from the Eighth Through the Eighteenth Centuries.* Princeton: Princeton University Press, 1986.
Sakakura Atsuyoshi, Ōtsu Yūichi, Chikushima Yutaka, Abe Toshiko, and Imai Gen'e, eds. *Taketori monogatari, Ise monogatari, Yamato monogatari. NKBT* 9. Iwanami shoten, 1958.
Saku Setsu. *Kanshi taikan,* vol. 4. Ida shoten, 1943.
Sanari Kentaro. *Yōkyoku taikan,* vol. 6. Meiji shoin, 1994.
Sansom, George. *A History of Japan to 1334.* Stanford: Stanford University Press, 1958.
Sasaki Nobutsuna, ed. *Nihon kagaku taikei.* Kazama shobō, 1989.
Sasaki Takahiro. "Go-Toba In kadan seiritsuki ni okeru ichimondai—*Shōji ninen jūgatsu tsuitachi uta-awase* no daisakusetsu o megutte." *Kokubungaku kenkyū shiryōkan kiyō* 22 (1996): 107–42.
Satō, Hiroaki. "Lineation of Tanka in English Translation." *MN* 42, no. 3 (Autumn 1987): 345–56.
———. *String of Beads: Complete Poems of Princess Shikishi.* Honolulu: University of Hawai'i Press, 1993.
Seidensticker, Edward G., trans. *The Tale of Genji.* 2 vols. New York: Alfred A. Knopf, 1976.
Shinkokinshū o yomu tame no kenkyū jiten. Special issue of *Kokubungaku kaishaku to kyōzai no kenkyū* 35, no. 14 (Dec. 1990).
Shinpen kokka taikan henshu iinkai, ed. *Shinpen kokka taikan.* 20 vols. Kadokawa shoten, 1983–92.
Shirane, Haruo. "Lyricism and Intertextuality: An Approach to Shunzei's Poetics." *HJAS* 50, no. 1 (June 1990): 71–85.
Smits, Ivo. "The Poet and the Politician: Teika and Compilation of the *Shinchokusenshū.*" *MN* 53, no. 4 (Winter 1998): 427–72.
———. *The Pursuit of Loneliness: Chinese and Japanese Nature Poetry in Medieval Japan, ca. 1050–1150.* Stuttgart: Steinner, 1995.

Suzuki Tomotaro, Kawaguchi Hisao, Endō Yoshimoto, and Nishishita Kyōichi, eds. *Tosa nikki, Kagerō nikki, Izumi shikibu nikki, Sarashina nikki*. NKBT 20. Iwanami shoten, 1958.

Taga Munehaya. *Gyokuyō sakuin*. Yoshikawa kōbunkan, 1974.

———. *Jien*. Yoshikawa kōbunkan, 1959.

Taga Munehaya, ed. *Kōhon shūgyokushū*. Yoshikawa kōbunkan, 1970.

Takagi Ichinosuke, Gomi Tomohide, and Ōno Susumu, eds. *Man'yōshū*. 4 vols. NKBT 4–7. Iwanami shoten, 1957–62.

Takeuchi Rizō. *Ritsuryōsei to kizoku seikan*. 2 vols. Ochanomizu shobō, 1957.

Tanaka Yutaka and Akase Shingo, eds. *Shinkokin wakashū*. SNKBT 11. Iwanami shoten, 1992.

Taniyama Shigeru. *Shinkokin jidai no uta-awase to kadan*. Kadokawa shoten, 1983.

Teramoto Naohiko. *Genji monogatari juyōshi ronkō*. Kazama shobō, 1970.

Terashima Tsuneyo. "Teika to Go-Toba In: Saishōshitennōin shōji waka o megutte." *Bungaku* n.s. 6, no. 4 (Fall 1995): 43–53.

Thornhill, Arthur H., III. *Six Circles, One Dewdrop*. Princeton: Princeton University Press, 1993.

Tōkyō daigaku shiryō hensanjo, ed. *Shiryō sōran*, vols. 4–5, *Kamakura jidai*. Tōkyō daigaku shuppankai, 1965.

Tōkyō teikoku daigaku bunka daigaku shiryō hensangakari, comp. *Dai Nihon shiryō*. Tōkyō teikoku daigaku, 1906.

Tsugita Kasumi. "Tamekane no bungaku no mondaiten." *Bungaku* 8 (1963): 15–20.

Tsuji Hikosaburō. *Fujiwara Teika Meigetsuki no kenkyū*. Yoshikawa kōbunkan, 1977.

Uwayokote Masataka. *Kamakura jidai seijishi kenkyū*. Yoshikawa kōbunkan, 1991.

Wada Hidematsu and Satō Kyū, eds. *Masukagami yōkai*. Meiji shoin, 1943.

Wakabungakukai, ed. *Ronshū: waka to retorikku*. Wakabungaku no sekai 10. Kasama shoin, 1986.

Wakashi kenkyūkai, eds. *Shikashū taisei*. 8 vols. Meiji shoin, 1975.

Watanabe Yasuaki. "'Furumaeru' sugata o megutte—Shunzei karon to setsuwa no setten." In *Higi to shite no waka—kōi to ba*, ed. Watanabe Yasuaki, pp. 101–20. Yūseidō, 1995.

Yamagishi Tokuhei, ed. *Genji monogatari*. 5 vols. NKBT 14–18. Iwanami shoten, 1958–64.

Yamazaki Toshio. "Fujiwara Ietaka." In *Chūsei no kajin II*, ed. Hisamatsu (q.v.), pp. 79–135.

Yasuda Motohisa. *Kamakura Muromachi jinmei jiten*. Shinjinbutsu ōraisha, 1985.

Yoshida Kōichi, Kansaku Kōichi, and Tachibana Ritsu, eds. *Utamakura nayose*. 8 vols. Koten bunko, 1974.

Index of First Lines

Afu koto wo, 265
Afu to mite, 318
Akatuki no,
    sigi no fanegaki, 170n78
    Takano no yama ni, 129
    toko fa kusaba no, 219
Aki fa nafo, 211
Aki fa tuki, 129
Aki kinu to, 376
Aki mo nafo, 434
Aki no yo mo, 318n73
Aki wo fete, 359–60
Amagumo no, 303
Ama no fara, 285
Ama no gafa, 286
Amatukaze
    kumo no kayofidi, 228
    sibasi fukitodi yo, 227
Arewataru, 295n108
Asadifara, 323
Asadifu ni, 211
Asato akete, 74
Asibiki no, 184, 253
Asi no fa ni, 339n14
Asitadu fa, 61
Asitadu no, 61
Atanari to, 229

Ayasikarisi, 345, 433
Azirogi ni, 377

Fadukasi ya, 345, 432
Fana min to, 182n102
Farafubeki, 233
Faru aki no, 214
Faru goto ni, 182
Faruka naru, 361
Faru no fana, 341, 429
Faru no yo no
    yami fa ayanasi, 376
    yume ni wodoroku, 339, 427
Fasifime no, 377
Fatuaki no, 241n51
Fatuseyama, 127
Fikiufesi
    ifane no matu ni, 343, 431
    ike no ifane wo, 343, 430
Fima siramu, 74
Fitori nuru, 219
Fototogisu, 186
Fudigoromo, 236
Fukakusa no
    nobe no sakura si, 88n7
    sato no tukikage, 209
    yado ni narinuru, 175n

Fukikureba, 181
Fuku kaze no, 375
Furumiti no, 342, 430
Furusato no, 343, 431
Fuyu no kite, 277
Fuyu no yume to, 205

Ikade ware, 218
Ikani sen, 424
Iku yo fenu, 160
Ima fa tada
    fana tiru mine no, 347, 435
    konu yo amata ni, 177, 180
Iriyarade, 278
Iro mo ka mo, 342–43n20
Isonokami, 429
Ito ni yoru, 295n107
Itu made ka, 422
Iza ikani, 212

Kage kiyoki
    fana no kagami to, 202
    fana no tokoro fa, 201
Kagiri araba, 236–37
Kakitumete, 361–62
Kakusitutu, 233
Kame no wo no
    taki no siratama, 255
    yama no ifane wo, 255n92
Kaminaduki, 341, 429
Karakoromo
    fi mo yufugure no, 217
    susono no kaze ya, 240–41
Karanisiki, 282n72
Kari no miti wo, 428
Kasugayama, 278
Katagata ni, 428
Katami tote, 332, 424
Katasiki no, 376–77
Kawakanan, 423

Kayofikosi, 173–74
Kaze kayofu, 199
Kaze mo ina, 425
Kaze no oto ni, 207
Keburi tatu, 344, 431
Kefu dani mo, 228, 310
Kefu fa mata, 288–89
Kefu kozu fa, 229
Kefu made fa, 254
Kefu nomi to, 224n9
Kesa mireba, 229n20
Kiesomesi, 345–46, 433
Kiku fito no, 331–32, 426
Kiku ya ika ni, 177, 180
Kimi ga fen, 79n87
Kimi ga sode, 422
Kimi ga uwesi, 344
Kimi ga yo fa
    futaba no matu no, 216
    koke no ifafo ya, 251
Kimi ga yo ni
    afazu fa nani wo, 366
    aferu bakari no, 366
    kasumi wo wakesi, 62
Kimi nakute, 339n15
Kimi narade, 424
Kimi ya kosi, xvi$n$6
Ko no fa tiru, 423
Kokitirasu, 364
Kokoro are ya, 332, 424
Kokoro etu, 217n51
Kono aki fa, 434
Kono tabi fa, 285n78
Kono tuwe fa, 251
Kore fa yo na, 420
Kore made mo
    kofuru waga mi wo, 421
    miti aru miyo no, 262
Kore wo miru, 233
Kore ya kono, 127

Index of First Lines

Kore zo kono
  mukasi Nagara no, 262
  yo no kotofari to, 428
Koyofi simo, 263
Kozuwe nifa, 224
Kuma mo naku, 134
Kumo wo nomi, 277
Kumorekasi, 68
Kuraki yo no, 209
Kuraki yori, 210n34, 345
Kusa no ifo, 220

Madoromade, 129
Mayofaresi, 330, 425
Midori naru, 348, 436
Midorigo wo, 347, 436
Mikumano no, 216
Mimuroyama, 282–83
Minasegafa, 331, 425
Mine no tuki, 209
Misimae ni, 329n104
Misimae ya, 329
Mitinoku fa, 266
Miwataseba
  fana mo momidi mo, 283n73
  yamamoto kasumu, 156, 329
Miyosino no, 310, 374–75
Momotose no, 249–50
Mononofu no, 379
Mosifo kumu, 357
Mosiogusa, 116
Mukasi ima, 89n13
Murasame no, 237
Musuboruru, 420

Nadefaten, 252
Na fa kutinu, 331, 426
Nagamekosi, 288
Nagamesi ya, 170
Nagameturu, 88n6

Nagameyaru, 360–61
Nagamuran, 423
Nagarafete
  kesa ya uresiki, 249
  kesa zo uresiki, 250n82
Nagekazi to, 420
Nagusamuru, 347, 435
Nakanaka ni, 346, 435
Nakikage yo, 343, 431
Nakiwataru, 169
Namida safe, 170
Namida sofu, 344, 431
Nanifadu ni, 339–40
Nanifae no, 410n25
Nani to mata, 423
Nani to naku
  kikeba namida zo, 278–79
  nagusamu ya tote, 273, 419
Nasakenasi to, 421
Ne no fi site, 321–22
Ne no fi suru
  mikaki no uti no, 322
  nobe no komatu wo, 322
Nisi fe yuku
  tuki koso ima fa, 432
  tuki miru tabi ni, 432
Nori no miti wo, 429

Odorokasu, 423
Ofokata no, 339, 428
Ofozora ni, 420
Ofozora wo, 422
Oinureba, 364
Oiraku no, 363–64
Oku to misi, 323
Omofazi to, 421
Omofi araba, 306n27
Omofiiduru
  oritaku siba no, 331, 425
  oritaku siba to, 331, 426

Omofiiru, 174
Omofiki ya, 323
Omofitutu
   fenikeru tosi no, 160
   fenikeru tosi wo, 161
Omokage wo, 346, 435
Öpöpasi no, 378
Ore to ifaba, 224
Ozasafara
   kafaranu iro no, 190
   kaze matu tuyu no, 190

Sakura saku, 252
Samusiro ni, 267, 377
Samusiro ya, 267
Sasanami no, 131n109
Sasite yuku, 284
Sasofarenu, 228
Sato fa arenu, 153–54
Satuki matu, 305n26
Sayakesi na, 422
Sazona ge ni
   kore mo yosinaki, 67
   tofanu fikazu wo, 295
Sekikafesi, 421
Sifodi yori, 207
Siguretutu, 284
Siisiba ya, 294
Sikasuga ni, 432
Sikisima ya, 205
Sirotafe no
   sode no wakare fa, 180–81
   sode no wakare ni, 177, 178, 180
Sita momidi, 318n72
Sitamoe ni, 136
Sode ni oku, 365
Sode no iro no, 340, 429
Sode no ufe ni, 422
Sono tomo no, 342, 430
Sore made no, 282

Suma no ura, 159
Sumiwabinu, 232
Sumiyosi no, 234
Suzusisa fa, 242
Suzusisa wo, 206

Tadunubeki, 175n
Tamakifaru, 165
Tamakura no, 154n29
Tanometutu, 183
Tatenamuru, 343, 430
Tatinoboru, 191
Tatutagafa
   momidi midarete, 283
   momidiba nagaru, 283
Teri mo sezu
   kumo mo kakaranu, 201
   kumori mo fatenu, 202, 409n22
Tirimagafu, 281
Tofu fito mo, 211
Tokete nenu, 206n25, 380
Toko no simo, 174
Toni kakuni, 273, 419
Tosi no uti ni, 182n101, 347
Tosi wo fete
   miyuki ni naresi, 224
   sumikosi sato wo, 175n, 210n34
Tufi ni nafo, 420
Tufi ni yuku, 346–47
Tukifatesi, 214
Tuki no aki fa, 361
Tuki wo nafo, 136
Tuki yosuru, 220
Tuki zo moru, 281
Tumoriyuku, 117
Tu no kuni no
   asikarikeri na, 339, 427
   Nanifa mo asi no, 338, 427
Tu no kuni ya, 159
Tuyu farafu, 363

Ufeokisi, 343, 430
Ukikoto no, 207
Ukisidumi, 368
Ume ga ka wo, 199
Uradutafu, 359
Uresiku mo, 116–17
Utifafete, 217
Utifarafu, 211–12
Uturiyuku, 278

Waga ifo fa, 263n17
Waga kimi no, 117
Waga yado no, 219
Wagimoko ga
  koromo no suso wo, 241
  sode fukikafesu, 240
  yufitesi fimo wo, 218n52
Waka no ura ni
  sifo mitikureba, 58n24, 357
  tuki no desifo no, 357
Waka no ura no, 58, 412
Waka no ura ya, 365–66
Wakaredi wo, 165
Wakuraba ni, 159n42, 359
Warenagara, 278
Wasi no yama
  mukasi no tuki ya, 340, 428
  tikaki fikari wo, 340, 428
Wasuraruru, 265
Wasurenamu, 421n2
Wasurenan, 421
Wasurezu yo, 170
Watatumi no
  kazasi ni sasu to, 305n24
  okitu sifoafi ni, 366
Wotomera ga, 161
Woyamada ni, 253–54

Yagumo tatu, 205
Yama fukaku, 233
Yamabuki fa, 227
Yamabuki no, 227
Yamakage ya, 179, 180
Yamazato ni
  sumu kafi araba, 425
  tigirisi ifo ya, 365
Yaso yorodu, 252
Yasukaranu, 426
Yasurafi no, 286
Yo mo sugara
  Fira no yamakaze, 131
  fitori miyama no, 232
  ura kogu fune fa, 131
Yo ni sumeba, 433
Yo ni tare ka, 434
Yo no naka fa, 89–90n13
Yo no naka ni
  furinuru mono fa, 264
  saranu wakare no, 364
Yo no naka wo
  aki mo tafenisi, 434
  asaku omofeba, 433
Yorodu yo to, 216
Yo ya fukuru, 212–13
Yufudati fa, 238
Yuki furaba
  koto tofu ato ya, 434
  madu omofiidenu, 434
Yukinayamu, 213n41
Yuku fotaru
  kumo no ufe made, 159n43
  nare mo yami nifa, 157
Yuma ka to yo, 153
Yume fa Suma mo, 220

Index of Poets

Abe no Nakamaro, 285
Anonymous (*Gosenshū*), 161
Anonymous (Hitomaro?), 186
Anonymous (*Ise monogatari*), 305n24, 306n27
Anonymous (Ise Vestal), xvin6
Anonymous (*Kokinshū*), 89–90n13, 170n78, 182, 219, 227, 229, 264, 265, 267, 283, 305n26, 363–64, 366, 377
Anonymous (*Komachishū*), 266
Anonymous (*Kokin waka rokujō*), 241n51
Anonymous (*Kin'yōshū*), 229n20
Anonymous (*Man'yōshū*), 131n109, 180–89
Anonymous (*Sagoromo monogatari*), 175n
Anonymous (*Shūishū*), 154n29, 421n2
Anonymous (*Yamato monogatari*, "a reed cutter"), 339n15
Ariwara no Motokata, 182n101, 347
Ariwara no Narihira, 159n43, 175n, 210n34, 229, 346–47, 364
Ariwara no Yukihira, 159n42, 359, 364

Chikamoto, 219
Chikasada, *see* Emperor Go-Toba

Daini no Sanmi, 361

Echizen, 67, 284, 359–60
Emperor Fushimi, 89n13
Emperor Go-Toba, 156, 159, 160, 190, 207, 209, 216, 227, 228, 234, 240, 252, 273, 310, 329–32, 339–48, 374–75, 377, 419–36

Fujiwara (Rokujō) Akisuke, 410n25
Fujiwara (Rokujō) Ariie, 242, 249–50, 254, 278, 288
Fujiwara Hideyoshi, 117, 375
Fujiwara Ietaka, 170, 174, 212, 217, 236–37, 278, 282–83, 318n72, 365–66
Fujiwara Kanemune, 207
Fujiwara Kintsugu, 218, 286
Fujiwara Kintsune, 240–41, 360–61
Fujiwara Kiyotada, 321–22
Fujiwara (Asukai) Masatsune, 165, 170, 177, 180, 255, 262, 278, 366
Fujiwara Michitoshi, 322
Fujiwara Mototoshi, 211
Fujiwara Sadanaga, 61
Fujiwara Shunzei, 58, 61, 190, 207, 236, 251, 295n108, 412
Fujiwara Sueyoshi, 212
Fujiwara Tadatsune, 277
Fujiwara Tadayoshi, 74, 220, 359

Fujiwara Takanobu, 116–17
Fujiwara Teika, 62, 157, 159, 160, 165, 174, 177, 178, 180, 191, 213n41, 224, 267, 282, 283n73, 294, 357, 366
Fujiwara Toshiyuki, 376
Fujiwara (Rokujō) Yasusue, 278
Fujiwara (Kujō) Yoshitsune, 205, 211, 228, 253–54, 263, 368, 376

Henjō (Yoshimine no Munesada), 228
Hitomaro, 161, 183, 184, 216, 253, 379
Hitomaro (?; Kasa no Kanamura?), 218n52
Hōribe Narimochi, 277

Izumi Shikibu, 210n34, 323, 345

Jakuren, 129, 153–54
Jien, 129, 179, 180, 220, 273, 331–32, 338–47, 357, 365, 377, 419–36
Jōtōmon-in, 323

Kamitsuke no Mineo, 88n7
Kamo no Chōmei, 117, 127, 232, 233
Kasa no Kanamura (?; Hitomaro?), 218n52
Kenshō, 199, 206
Ki no Koreoka, 255n92
Ki no Tomonori, 181
Ki no Tsurayuki, 282n72, 295n107, 303, 342–43n20
Kisen Hōshi, 263n17
Kojijū, 209
Kunaikyō, 129, 136, 177, 180, 249, 250n82, 281

Michitsuna no Haha, 175n
Miharu no Arisuke, 344

Minamoto no Arihito, 202
Minamoto Ienaga, 116, 216, 233, 237, 252, 262, 295
Minamoto (Tsuchimikado) Michichika, 74, 131, 214
Minamoto (Tsuchimikado) Michiteru, 286, 329
Minamoto (Tsuchimikado) Michitomo, 209, 219, 365
Minamoto Shigeyuki, 339n14
Minamoto Tomochika, 127, 134, 214, 220, 361
Minamoto Tsunenobu, 322
Murasaki Shikibu, 206n25, 211–12, 361–62, 380

Nakahara no Muneyasu, 224
Narihira's Mother, 364

Ōe no Chisato, 202, 409n22
Ōe no Yoshitoki, 182n102
Ono no Komachi, 318n73
Ōshikōchi no Mitsune, 224n9, 241, 376

Sagami, 79n87
Saiei, 224
Sakanoue no Korenori, 265
Sanuki, 201, 217
Shikishi Naishinnō, 88n6
Shimotsuke, 284
Shunzei no Musume, 136, 153, 169, 173–74, 199, 201, 211, 281, 363
Sone no Yoshitada, 329n104
Sosei, 227
Sugawara no Michizane, 285n78
Suō no Naishi, 323
Susanoo no Mikoto, 205

Taira Kagemitsu, 238
Takahashi Mushimaro, 378
Takakura-dono, 68
Tango, 131, 278–79
Tsuchimikado Mikushigedono, 217n51

Wani, 339–40

Yamabe Akahito, 58n24, 357
Yoshimine no Munesada, *see* Henjō

Subject Index

100-poem sequences, see *hyakushu uta*

Abe no Nakamaro, 285
Abutsu, 300
Akahito, see Yamabe Akahito
Akashi, 360
Aki, 389
Akihiro, see Fujiwara Shunzei
Akishino gesseishū, 95n20, 110n55
Akisue, see Fujiwara (Rokujō) Akisue
Akisuke, see Fujiwara (Rokujō) Akisuke
Amida's Pure Land, see Western Paradise
Aridōshi Shrine, 303
Ariie, see Fujiwara (Rokujō) Ariie
Arima Hot Springs, 238–39
Ariwara no Motokata, 182n101, 347
Ariwara no Narihira, xvin6, 21, 130, 154, 159n43, 253n88, 364, 382; as source for allusion, 175, 210n34, 229
Ariwara no Yukihira, 159–60, 358–59, 364
Ariyoshi Tamotsu, 8, 10; on *Shinkokinshū*, 53, 106–7, 437n1; on various poetry events, 55–56, 73n67, 98, 137, 173n83, 353

Association and Progression, 106, 107n46
astrological omens, 39n65, 45, 333, 336–37
Asukai house, 18n4, 48–49, 66
Asukai Masatsune, see Fujiwara (Asukai) Masatsune
Azuma Kagami, 7

Banquets, feasts, see Theme meals
Bentley, John, 132n110
Bialock, David, xvii, 42n75
biwa (lute), 297–98, 391
Bo Juyi, 28, 57, 202, 407n14, 409
Book of Odes (*Shi jing*), 304
Borgen, Robert, 203
Brower, Robert, 7–8, 10n21; and Earl Miner, 41n75, 185, 186
Buddhist poems (*shakkyōka*; *shakkyō no uta*), 2, 128, 301–2
Bundy, Roselee, 185n108
byōbue no uta (*byōbu uta*; screen painting poems), 12, 243, 245, 246, 252–55
Byōdō-in, 259–60

canon, in traditional Japan, 1, 22
chakutō waka, 117–18n75

Chikasada, see Emperor Go-Toba
chōkin (Emperor's New Year's visit to the Retired Emperor), 296
chokusenshū (imperial anthology), xiv, 1n2, 3, 11–12, 141, 219
Chōmei, see Kamo no Chōmei
concerts, 296–98, 316, 319–20
courtesans, 100. See also yūjo
Crown Prince Morinari, see Emperor Juntoku

dai (poetic topic), xix, 78–79n87, 102n37, 135, 167
Daijō Tennō, see Emperor Go-Toba
Dainagon-dono (Lady Dainagon), 68–69, 280
Dai Nihon shiryō, 6
dai'ei (composing poetry on topics), 123, 127–28
Daruma uta, 408n19
Denki, 6. See also Fujiwara (Kujō) Yoshitsune
dokushi (Recorder), 114

Echizen, 67–68, 389, 392; and poetry contests, 92, 95n21, 96, 99, 102n37, 108, 122, 123, 124, 135, 144–45, 150, 280, 284–85, 352, 359–60, 413, 416; and other poetry activities, 65, 66, 72
Eguchi, 100, 101n32, 156–57, 158, 168n73, 238–39
Eifukumon-in, 71n63
Eiga no taigai, 212
eigu/eigu contest, see Hitomaro eigu

Elders Parties (shōshikai or shōshie), 407
Emperor Daigo, 405n3
Emperor Fushimi, 300
Emperor Go-Daigo, 2
Emperor Go-Shirakawa, 23–29 passim, 35, 37, 48, 392; and literary activities, 19, 31, 32, 298
Emperor Go-Toba, 2n3, 3–4, 10, 11, 21, 53, 198, 382, 389, 392; and residences, xiv, 187–88; and Kumano and other shrines, 234, 304, 307, 309, 346n26; and Wakadokoro, 111, 119, 307; and Oki exile, 281, 382–83, 392. See also Go-Toba-in onkuden; Oki-bon; Wakadokoro
—court politics, post–Genpei War, 24n16, 25, 29, 30, 37–41 passim, 49, 55; abdicates, 9, 46–47; builds political and artistic consensus at court, 9, 10, 51, 53, 72, 97, 113–14, 141, 155, 187, 191–92, 381; promotes new talent, 48–49, 65–72 passim, 119, 121–22, 135, 140, 147, 352–53
—and poetry contests, 15, 75–76, 133; appropriates sponsorship of Hitomaro eigu contests, 109–10, 140, 438; and contests in Shōji 2 (1200) 73, 76, 81; and contests in Kennin 1 (1201), 84, 91–93, 96, 102–8 passim, 121–26 passim, 135; and contests in Kennin 2 (1202), 145, 150–51, 153, 155, 158–61, 166–69, 173, 178–79; and contests after Kennin 2 (1202), 235–36, 239–41, 275–80, 326–29, 354, 356; and Sengohyakuban uta-awase, 194–96, 208–10, 216, 413, 416–18; uses pseudonym Chikasada, 150, 153, 159–60, 168, 328. See also individual contests by name
—and other poetry activities, 83; sponsor of public poetry activities, 12, 108, 120, 193–94, 351, 437–41; and the three hyakushu of 1200–1201, 55, 57–58, 65–66, 110–11, 194, 405–12; and Shunzei's ninetieth-year celebration,

243–46, 250, 252–53, 440; and various other public poetry activities, 91, 135–37, 142, 145–46, 369–79; and poetry exchanges, 228–30, 273–74, 330–32, 338–48, 419–36
—and *Shinkokinshū*, 300, 310–14 *passim*, 380, 381; plans and commissions, 138, 141, 439; active role in selection and editing of, 96–97, 107–8, 178, 235, 237, 257, 309–10, 317–21 *passim*, 324, 362, 440; solicits contemporary poems for, 308, 363–68. See also *Shinkokinshū*
—leisure activities, 50–51, 100–101, 168, 296–99, 392; and Minase Villa, 155–58, 166, 269, 275, 306; and excursions, 226–30, 258–64 *passim*, 267, 309, 368–69
—and various courtier/poets, 98, 134, 231–33, 284n75, 393, 394; and Teika, 7–8, 61–63, 114, 149, 190, 225, 402; and other Mikohidari family members, 136n120, 162, 234, 294–95; and Yoshitsune, 43, 140, 334–35, 403; and his concubine Owari, 272–74, 330; and other royals, 37, 48, 396. See also under individuals by name
Emperor Hanazono, 304
Emperor Horikawa, 13
Emperor Juntoku, 37, 297–98 (as Crown Prince Morinari), 383n3, 400
Emperor Kameyama, 300
Emperor Kazan, 3n8
Emperor Murakami, 111
Emperor Shirakawa, 14, 18
Emperor Shōmu, 405
Emperor Sutoku, 13, 19, 399, 406–7
Emperor Takakura, 70, 389, 396
Emperor Toba, 36, 392

Emperor Tsuchimikado, 9, 10, 30, 37, 38n63, 41, 42, 45–46 (as Crown Prince Tamehito), 287, 296–98
en (or *yōen*; ethereal, elegant beauty, charm), 22, 201, 206
Engi era, 26, 27, 312, 405
engo (associative vocabulary), 217–18
Enjū no Gozen, 292
Enkyō ryōkyō sochinjō (Suits Between the Two Lords in the Enkyō Era), 300

Flower-viewing parties of 1203, 222–30
Fujiwara clan, xv, 7
Fujiwara (Rokujō) Akisue, 18–19, 83, 387, 407, 410
Fujiwara (Rokujō) Akisuke, 57, 387
Fujiwara (Rokujō) Ariie, 192, 204, 242–43, 276–79 *passim*, 387, 391; and poetry contests, 33, 102n37, 108n50, 122, 124n93, 145, 150–51, 166–69, 280, 352, 413, 416; and other poetry events, 143, 148, 372n98; and Shunzei's ninetieth-year celebration, 248–50, 254–55; and Wakadokoro, 111–12, 115; as *Shinkokinshū* compiler, 138, 139, 176, 275, 439
Fujiwara Chikatsune, 300, 326
Fujiwara Hideyoshi (AKA Hidetō; Nyogan), 382, 393; and poetry activities, 124n93, 150n24, 280, 352, 375–76; and Wakadokoro, 112, 116–17, 119, 143, 269
Fujiwara (Matsudono) Iefusa, 33
Fujiwara Iehira, 280
Fujiwara Ietaka, 124–25, 236–37, 311, 382, 393; and poetry contests, 33, 73, 92–96 *passim*, 102n37–104, 108, 145, 150–51, 166, 168–71, 174–76, 352; and *Sengohyakuban uta-awase*, 213, 218, 413, 416; and *Kasuga no Yashiro no uta-*

awase, 278–84 passim; and other poetry activities, 55, 57–58, 146, 148, 412; appointed to Wakadokoro, 111–12, 115; and *Shinkokinshū*, 138, 176, 178–79n94, 308, 365, 367, 439

Fujiwara (Konoe) Iezane, 6, 187–88, 297, 336. See also *Inokuma kanpakuki*

Fujiwara Kanefusa, 43–44, 311

Fujiwara Kanemune, 113, 142–43, 208, 394; and poetry contests, 33, 102n37, 103, 150n24, 151, 413, 416

Fujiwara (Kujō) Kanezane, 6, 142, 144, 289n91, 311, 336, 348–49, 389, 394–95; and Mikohidari house, 31, 290, 399; and court politics after the Genpei War, 24–30 passim, 38–47 passim; and poetry activities, 19, 31–32, 33, 36, 54, 84, 204, 409n21. See also *Gyokuyō*

Fujiwara Kinsada, 319–20

Fujiwara Kintō, xvn6, 15, 84

Fujiwara Kintsugu, 286, 388, 395; and poetry contests, 102n37, 107n47, 142–43, 150n24, 151, 153, 166, 168–69, 413, 416

Fujiwara Kintsune, 56, 139, 142–43, 395; and poetry contests, 76n79–78, 82, 102n37–106 passim, 109, 124n93, 150n24, 240–41, 280, 352, 360–61, 413, 416

Fujiwara Kin'yoshi, 388, 406

Fujiwara (Rokujō) Kiyosuke, 19, 21, 57, 132n112, 378n115, 387, 407–11 passim

Fujiwara Kiyotada, 321–22

Fujiwara (Asukai) Masatsune, 165, 382, 396; and Go-Toba, 48, 98, 140, 262, 264, 309; and *Rōnyaku gojisshu uta-awase*, 92, 96, 97–99; and *Shingū senka-awase*, 102n37–104, 106n45; and *Kennin gannen hachigatsu jūgoya senka-awase*, 124–26, 133; and contests at Minase in 1202, 166–68, 170, 177–84 passim; and *Kasuga no Yashiro no uta-awase*, 276, 278, 279; and poetry contests, 73, 76n79, 78, 122, 135, 145, 280, 352, 353, 413, 416; and other poetry activities, 65, 66, 72, 91, 143, 148, 223, 225, 254–55, 311, 366–67; and Wakadokoro, 111–12, 115; as *Shinkokinshū* compiler, 138–39, 176, 439

Fujiwara Michinaga, 25

Fujiwara Michitoshi, 322

Fujiwara Morofusa, 349

Fujiwara (Konoe) Motomichi, 24, 28, 45

Fujiwara Morosuke, 313

Fujiwara Mototoshi, 18, 114n66, 406

Fujiwara Motozane, 24

Fujiwara (Asukai) Munenaga, 82

Fujiwara Nagakane, 6, 39, 44n83, 327

Fujiwara (Mikohidari) Nariie, 57n20, 191, 249, 289

Fujiwara Narikiyo, 280

Fujiwara Nobuzane (AKA Takazane), 65, 66, 76n79, 78

Fujiwara Norimitsu, 58, 65, 66, 76n79–78, 102n37, 103, 104n40, 108, 143, 397–98

Fujiwara Norinaga, 57, 406, 408–10

Fujiwara Sanefusa, 32, 38n65, 55, 58, 398

Fujiwara Sanesada, 32, 388, 410

Fujiwara (Mikohidari) Shunzei, 17, 53, 115, 236, 398, 399; and *Senzaishū*, 11n23, 19, 56, 392; and rivalry with Rokujō school, 19, 35, 405–12 passim; and literary scholarship, xvn6, 20, 132, 299–300; and respect for *Genji monogatari*, 17–23, 172, 272; and family ties, 61, 163, 190, 388, 393; and the *Shōji sōjō*, 57–58, 405–12; and

Sengohyakuban uta-awase, 194–202 *passim*, 413, 416–18; as judge in other poetry contests (before 1200), 9, 19–20, 33–34, 35, 53n11, 56, 80n93, (1200 and after), 70, 76–80, 104–5, 126, 133, 166–69, 173, 178, 240, 438, 439; as participant in other poetry contests, 84, 102n37–107n47 *passim*, 108, 122, 124n93, 125, 140, 145, 150, 280; and other poetry activities, 13n28, 32, 55–56, 58, 62, 64, 136, 363n68, 437; and appointment to the Wakadokoro, 111–12, 115; and ninetieth-year celebration, 92n18, 240, 243–55 *passim*, 440; death and funeral, 164, 289–95, 355. See also *Shunzeikyō kujū no gaki*

Fujiwara (Rokujō) Suetsune, 32, 35, 113, 139, 144, 155, 387, 400; and *Shōji ninen in shodo hyakushu*, 55–56, 58, 92, 108, 114, 411, 437–48; and poetry contests, 33, 54, 194, 214, 417–18

Fujiwara Sueyoshi, 148, 352, 400, 413, 416

Fujiwara Sukeie, 167

Fujiwara (Kujō) Tadamichi, 24, 389, 394

Fujiwara Tadasada, 280

Fujiwara Tadatsune, 246, 277, 279–81, 297, 400

Fujiwara Tadayoshi, 58, 113, 143, 400–401; and poetry contests, 73–76n79 *passim*, 79, 84, 92, 95n21, 96–97, 102n37–103, 121, 123, 124, 150n24, 153, 280, 352, 359–60; and *Sengohyakuban uta-awase*, 194–200 *passim*, 220–21, 413, 416–18

Fujiwara Tadazane, 337–38, 349

Fujiwara Takafusa, 57–58, 142–43, 150n24, 151, 153, 401, 412

Fujiwara Takanobu, 307, 388, 401; and poetry contests, 33, 73, 76n79, 78, 102n37, 108, 124n93, 150n24, 151, 413, 416; and other poetry activities, 32, 55, 58, 143; and Wakadokoro, 112, 116, 191

Fujiwara Takanori, 76n79, 78

Fujiwara Takasuke, 81

Fujiwara (Mikohidari) Tameie, 11n23, 138–39, 140, 155, 191, 234, 300, 311–12, 370, 400

Fujiwara (Mikohidari) Teika, 11n23, 45, 175, 204, 401–2; and family, 140, 155, 162–63, 249, 289–93, 296, 388, 408; mentors other poets, 62–63, 83; health problems, 139, 155, 234–36, 239, 271–72, 290, 291, 327, 370; banned from palace, 56, 60–62; trouble getting promoted, 140, 189–91, 257–59; and the Wakadokoro, 111–15 *passim*, 117n75, 119, 304–6; excursions/leisure activities, 157, 238–39, 259–60, 270, 311–12, 368; and *honkadori*, xvii, 210, 212, 361; and respect for Heian classical literature, 22, 172, 270, 299, 300
— and relationships at court: with Go-Toba, 7, 157–58, 382, 383, 402; with Kanezane and Yoshitsune, 49, 155, 348–49; with Rokujō/Tsuchimikado adversaries, 48, 54, 409n21; with Shikishi Naishinnō, 86–87, 398; with Ietaka, 280–83, 393; and Jakuren's death 163–65; and others, 48, 53, 395
— and poetry contests: as Reader (*kōji*), 145, 148, 151, 155, 167, 245, 260, 275, 354; and contests through Shōji 2 (1200), 33–34, 73, 76n79, 77–83 *passim*; and contests in Kennin 1 (1201),

84, 92–96 passim, 102n37–108 passim, 121–27 passim, 133, 140; and contests in Kennin 2 (1202), 145, 150–51, 155, 158–61, 166–69 passim, 173, 174, 177–82; and contests after Kennin 2 (1202), 276, 280, 283, 287, 325–27, 351–60 passim; and Sengohyakuban uta-awase, 194, 197, 210–14, 215, 413, 416–18
—other poetry activities, 32, 135–37, 142–48 passim, 223, 224–26, 370–72; and the *hyakushu* for Shōji 2 (1200), 57–64 passim, 110, 114, 196n3, 407, 412
—and *Shinkokinshū*, 235; appointed as compiler of, 138, 439; and selection and editing process, 165, 176, 235, 275, 299–300, 307, 321–23, 324, 349–51; ordered by Go-Toba to compose more poems for, 308, 364–67 passim; poems placed prominently by Go-Toba, 178, 179n94, 308; opposes Go-Toba's presentation banquet, 312–16 passim
—*Meigetsuki*, on various poetry contests, 77–80, 124, 150–51, 166–67, 194, 275–76, 353–55; on other poetry activities, 56, 142–45, 148, 155, 370; on activities at the Wakadokoro, 268–69, 304–6; on *Shinkokinshū*, 138, 314–16, 321, 324, 349–51; on excursions and leisure activities, 157, 238, 260, 270, 311; on his family, 140, 155, 162–63, 289–93; on his health, 155, 271–72, 290, 291, 370; on the death of various people, 48, 163–64, 289–93, 348, 349; on court life, 268–69, 269–70, 326; on his enemies, 48, 409n21; on his stalled career, 140, 258. *See also main entry for Meigetsuki*

Fujiwara (Rokujō) Tomoie (AKA Rensei), 242, 328, 387
Fujiwara Toshimoto, 344
Fujiwara Tsunefusa, 35–36
Fujiwara (Rokujō) Tsuneie, 33, 55–56, 58, 139, 387, 402
Fujiwara (Rokujō) Yasusue, 113, 387, 402; and poetry contests, 82, 102n37, 124, 150, 276–80 passim, 328, 352, 413, 416
Fujiwara Yorimichi, 215, 349n34
Fujiwara Yorizane, 271, 398
Fujiwara (Kujō) Yoshihira, 280, 352, 413, 416
Fujiwara (Kujō) Yoshisuke, 329
Fujiwara (Kujō) Yoshitsune, 6, 49, 59, 299, 341, 342n18, 382, 389, 402–3; and Go-Toba, 9–10, 43, 140, 228–30, 334; and Mikohidari house, 19–20, 155, 243, 248–51, 270, 370; court career, 25, 30, 40, 42–43, 45n87, 51–52, 54, 60, 257; as sponsor of waka activities, 31, 32–34, 54; as patron of Chinese literature and culture, 32n45, 83, 204–6, 242–43, 335–36, 341; and poetry contests (to 1201), 20, 32n45, 73–75, 81, 84, 92, 96, 102n37–106 passim, 121–22, 204, (from 1202), 124n93, 125–26, 150–51, 153, 166–69, 173, 280, 325–27; and Sengohyakuban uta-awase, 194, 196, 202–3, 206–8, 215, 413, 416–18; and other poetry activities, 32, 58, 62–64, 110n55, 135–37, 146, 148, 196n3, 246, 253–54; and Wakadokoro, 111–15 passim, 123; and *Shinkokinshū*, 176, 300, 312–14, 317n69, 349–51, 376–80; hosts court excursion to Uji, 259–60, 263, 266; death of, 164n56, 325, 333–49, 355, 427–36. *See also Shunzeikyō kujū no gaki*

Fujiwara (Ichijō) Yoshiyasu, 25, 43
Fujiwara Yukiyoshi, 280
fūryū, 259, 306
Fushimi-in nijūban uta-awase, 210n35

gatten (marking of poems), 135n118, 136, 146n15, 407n15
Genji monogatari (*The Tale of Genji*), 22, 90n15, 379; as intertext and source for allusion, 46n96, 128, 158, 160, 205–6, 211, 213–14, 221, 272–73, 360–62, 380; importance to Mikohidari aesthetic, 17–23, 57, 172, 409. *See also* Murasaki Shikibu
Genkyū shiika-awase, 156, 325–29, 440
Genpei War, 1, 18, 21, 23, 24, 32, 35, 41
Gishūmon-in, *see* Ninshi
Go-Hōshōjidono (or Go-Hosshōjidono), *see* Fujiwara (Kujō) Kanezane
Go-Toba-in daisando hyakushu, 110–11, 194, 196n3, 438, 439
Go-Toba-in no Shimotsuke (Lady Shimotsuke; AKA Shinano), 275, 277n59, 280, 284–86
Go-Toba-in onkuden, 6, 7, 225, 284n79, 367
Goble, Andrew, 1–2
Gomi Fumihiko, 5n11
Gosenshū, 111, 123, 161
Goshūishū, 2, 3, 116n72
Gotō Shigeo, 8
Gukanshō, 48, 162, 394. *See also under* Jien
Gyokuginshū, 393
Gyokuyō, 6, 26–28, 40, 43, 46
Gyokuyōshū, 213, 300, 304

Hachijō-in, 68
Hakushi (identity unknown), 150n24

Hakushi monjū, 57n22, 409
Hall, John, xiii
Haremitsu, 164, 337
hare no uta (poem appropriate for public occasions), 199
Heike monogatari (*Tales of the Heike*), 48, 101n33, 340
Henjō (AKA Yoshimine no Munesada), 228
Hepburn romanization system, xvin8, xviii–xix
Hidetō, *see* Fujiwara Hideyoshi
Hie Shrine, 140, 309
Higuchi Yoshimaro, 137
Hiro Gosho, 111n58, 115, 119, 315
Hirota Akiko, 10n21, 48
Hitomaro, *see* Kakinomoto no Hitomaro
Hitomaru *eigu* (Hitomaro veneration), 19, 83, 108–9, 110, 121, 134, 139, 145, 150–53, 189, 438, 439. *See also* individual contests by name
Hōgen Disturbance, 18, 24n16, 24n18, 26n27, 397, 409n20
Hōji hyakushu, 400
Hōjō Tokimasa, 330, 337
hōjōe ("liberation" festival), 245
Hōjōki, 126, 391
Hōnen, 144n5, 307, 395, 401
hon'i, 158, 360–61
honkadori, xvii, 2, 3, 17, 19–20, 130, 200, 206, 214, 220, 241, 273, 376; and Teika, 210, 212, 361
honzetsu, 17, 128, 206
Hōribe Narimochi (AKA Narishige), 277, 280, 352
Horikawa hyakushu, 13, 57, 72, 406, 411n29, 412
Hosshō-ji (built by Emperor Shirakawa), 311

Hosshō-ji temple (also read Hōshō-ji; built by Fujiwara Tadahira), 289–90, 292, 311n48
house collections (kashū), 11
Hyakunin isshu, 132n111, 184
hyakushu (no uta) (100-poem sequence), xiv, 12–13, 193–94. See also individual hyakushu by name
hyōjō (hyōtei; group discussion of entries at a poetry contest), 104. See also under uta-awase/shūgihan

Ienaga, see Minamoto Ienaga
Ienaga-bon (1216 copy of Shinkokinshū), 325, 381, 393
Ienaga nikki, see under Minamoto Ienaga
Ietaka, see Fujiwara Ietaka
Ima kagami, 202
imayō, 100–101n32, 392
imperial anthology, see chokusenshū
Infukumon-in no Daisuke, 67
Inokuma kanpakuki, 47n97, 187–88, 369n90. See also Fujiwara (Konoe) Iezane
insei (retired emperor system), xiii, 18, 29n36
Ise monogatari (Tales of Ise), xvin6, 175, 253n88; as intertext and source for allusion, 22, 229, 286, 305n24, 305n26, 306, 382
Ise Shrine, 352
Ishida Yoshida, 8, 62n31, 110
Itsutsuji Palace, 271, 275, 325, 336
Iwashimizu Hachiman Shrine, 238, 245, 309, 395
Iwashimizu Wakamiya Shrine, 274
Izumi Shikibu, 210n34, 321–23, 345, 378

Jakuren, 20, 128, 146, 382, 388; biographical information, 71–72, 163–64, 355, 393–94; and Rōnyaku gojisshu uta-awase, 92, 95n21, 96; and Shingū senka-awase, 102n37–104, 105n44, 106; and other poetry contests, 33, 84, 108, 122, 124n93, 125, 145, 150–54 passim, 413, 416; and other poetry activities, 55, 58, 73, 136, 146, 148; and Wakadokoro and Shinkokinshū, 111–12, 115, 138, 439
Japanese phonology, xvi–xix, 184–85n106
ji-amari, xvii
Jichin, see Jien
Jien, 24n18, 49, 382, 389, 394
—court career: Kenkyū no seihen, 37–43 passim; as Tendai zasu, 30, 100, 161–62; career revived by Go-Toba, 51–52, 257; appointed to Wakadokoro, 111–12, 115, 116
—Gukanshō, 7; on the Kenkyū no seihen, 38–41; on Michichika's death, 188; on Yoshitsune's death, 336–38
—poetry contests, 33; with Yoshitsune, 32n45, 204n19; and Shingū senka-awase, 102n37, 103, 104n40, 105n44, 107n47; and Kennin gannen hachigatsu jūgoya senka-awase, 124, 126, 129–30, 133; and Jōnan Temple eigu contest of Kennin 2/v/26, 150, 151, 153; and Sengohyakuban uta-awase, 194, 196, 220–21, 413, 416–18; and contests at Minase, 166–69, 173, 179, 180, 184–86; and other contests, 73, 81, 82, 84, 92, 95–96, 108, 121–22, 145, 280, 352, 357–58
—other poetry activities: 55, 58, 64, 65, 135–37, 146, 148, 365, 376–79; poetry exchanges with Go-Toba, 273–74, 330–32, 338–48, 419–36

jige (courtiers of the Fifth Rank or below), 119, 147
jingika (or *jingi no uta*), see Shinto poems
Jishū sannen jūgatsu jūhachinichi udaijin Kanezane no ie no uta-awase, 172
Jōkaku, 132n112
Jōkyū War, 4, 42, 55, 312, 368, 382, 392–95 passim, 402
Jōnan Temple *eigu* contest of Kennin 2/v/26, 150–54
Jōtōmon-in (Fujiwara Shōshi), 321–23, 350
Jukkai no uta ("Personal Grievance" poems), 363–68
Jūnigatsu nijūhachinichi Iwashimizu no Yashiro no uta-awase, 139–40

Kaen renjo no kotogaki, 213
Kagerō nikki, 175
Kakinomoto no Hitomaro, 19, 253n88, 264, 268; as source for allusion, 160–61, 183, 184, 216, 253. See also Hitomaro *eigu*
kakushidai (hidden topic), 167
Kamakura Bakufu, 1, 21, 23–25, 37n62, 41; and relations with the Heian Court, 30, 42, 46, 244, 330, 392
Kamens, Edward, 2n4, 361, 369, 372–73, 374, 380
Kamo no Chōmei, 382, 391; and *Mumyōshō*, 6, 126; on Kunaikyō and Shunzei no Musume, 70n61, 281, 396, 400; on the *Santai waka*, 146–47; and poetry contests, 76n79, 78, 81, 83, 102n37, 107n47, 124n93, 126–29, 135, 150; and other poetry activities, 65, 66, 143, 146–48, 155n30, 223; and Go-Toba, 127, 230–33, 299; and Wakadokoro, 112, 116–17, 119, 231
Kamo no Sueyasu, 65, 66, 102n37

Kamo Shrine, 231–32, 309
Kaneakira Shinnō, 132n110
Kanemune, see Fujiwara Kanemune
Kanezane, see Fujiwara (Kujō) Kanezane
Kan'in family, 410–11
Kanpaku sadaijin Yorimichi uta-awase, 215
Kanpyō Era, 130
kanshi (Chinese poems), 12n25
Kanzaki, 100, 101n32, 157, 168n73, 238
Kaō ninen jūgatsu kokonoka Sumiyoshi no Yashiro no uta-awase, 15
Karyū, see Fujiwara Ietaka
Kasuga no Yashiro no uta-awase, 275–87 passim, 440
Kasuga Shrine, 285, 347n28, 348
Kayōmon-in (Go-Toba's consort), 392
Keishō jishin no uta-awase, 123, 309, 352–62, 440
Ken no Gozen, 290–92, 370
Kenkyū no seihen, 37–43, 162n52, 394, 395, 397, 403
Kenkyū rokunen shōgatsu hatsuka minbukyō no ie no uta-awase, 35
Kenmu Restoration, 2
Kennin gannen hachigatsu jūgoya senka-awase, 123–36 passim, 439
Kennin gannen hachigatsu mikka eigu uta-awase, 121–23, 439
Kennin gannen kugatsu jūsannichi wakadokoro eigu uta-awase, 134–35, 147
Kennin gannen nigatsu yōka jisshu waka, 91
Kennin gannen sangatsu jūrokunichi eigu uta-awase, 108–9
Kennin gannen shigatsu sanjūnichi Tobadono eigu uta-awase, 110, 438
Kennin ninen kugatsu nijūrokunichi Wakamiya senka-awase, 173–87

Kennin sannen rokugatsu jūrokunichi Wakadokoro eigu uta-awase, 235–37
Kennin sannen shichigatsu jūgonichi Hachiman Wakamiya senka-awase, 238–42
Kenreimon-in Ukyō no Daibu, 243, 250, 255, 401
Kenreimon-in ukyō no daibushū, 243, 250
Kenshō, xvn6, 21, 34, 53, 54, 113, 144, 155, 199, 201, 387, 395; and classical scholarship, 19, 20, 21, 132; and *Sengohyakuban uta-awase*, 207–8, 215, 413, 416; as judge in *Sengohyakuban uta-awase*, 194, 197–98, 218–20, 417–18
Ki no Tokibumi, 111n57
Ki no Tomonori, 181
Ki no Tsurayuki, 3, 21, 70–71n62, 132n110, 295, 303–4
Kindai shūka, 132n111, 210, 409n21
Kinkage, 124n93
Kintsugu, see Fujiwara Kintsugu
Kintsune, see Fujiwara Kintsune
Kin'yōshū, 3, 229
Kisen Hōshi, 263, 266
Kitano no miya no uta-awase, 287–88
Kitano Shrine, 60, 235, 287–89, 309, 329, 330n106
Kiyonori (aide and copyist for Go-Toba), 97n24, 311, 317, 349, 353–54, 371
Kokinshū, xvii, 1, 3, 12, 21, 42, 160, 175, 182, 212, 363n68; and prefaces, 201n10, 303–4, 405n3; as intertext and source for allusion, 170n78, 205, 220, 227, 228, 243, 251n85, 255, 263, 265, 267, 283, 285, 342–47 *passim*, 366, 376–80 *passim*
Kōbō Daishi, 128–29
kōji (Reader), 114
Kojijū, 113, 389, 395–96; and poetry activities, 58, 122–27 *passim*, 413, 416

Kojima Yoshio, 8, 324n89
Kokin waka rokujō, as mediating collection for *Man'yōshū* poems, xviii, 20, 131n109, 132, 161, 184n105, 357n55, 358; as source for allusions, 216n48, 241n51
Konishi Jin'ichi, 106
Konoe house, 7, 24
Korai fūteishō, xvn6, 200, 205, 398, 399
Koreakira Shinnō, 389, 396; and poetry activities, 58, 194, 413, 416
Koshibe no Zenni, see Shunzei no Musume
kotowari (Ch. li; [governing/operating] principle), 182, 323
Kōya-san (Mt. Kōya), 128
Kubota Jun, 4, 8, 59–60, 63
kudai waka (waka based on Chinese verse), 203, 409n22
Kujō (Fujiwara) house, xv, 4, 49, 51, 289, 389; and political fortunes, 9, 43, 49, 51, 337; revived by Go-Toba, 52, 257; as patrons of Mikohidari house, 34, 103; and poetry activities, 112, 194, 197, 313; and *Sengohyakuban uta-awase*, 413, 416–18. *See also individual family members by name*
Kujō Kanezane, see Fujiwara (Kujō) Kanezane
Kujō Yoshitsune, see Fujiwara (Kujō) Yoshitsune
Kumano Shrine, 334nn2–3; and Go-Toba, 261, 304, 392; destroyed by fire, 333, 336, 345, 346n26
Kunaikyō, 192, 382, 389, 396; brought to court by Go-Toba, 68, 140; and Shunzei no Musume, 69n59, 280–82; and *Shōji ninen in dainido hyakushu*, 65, 66, 72; and *Rōnyaku gojisshu uta-awase*, 92, 96, 99; and *Kennin*

gannen hachigatsu jūgoya senka-awase, 124–26, 129–30; and contests at Minase, 166, 168–69, 177, 179–80, 183; and *Sengohyakuban uta-awase*, 215, 413, 416; and other poetry contests, 102n37, 107n47, 108, 122, 135, 140, 144, 150, 280, 282; and other poetry activities, 135–37, 248–50
kyō (poetic device), xv, 215–16, 279n65
Kyōgoku Palace, 89, 91, 187–88, 296–98; and Wakadokoro activities, 111n58, 222, 234, 245, 256
Kyōgoku school, xvii, 71, 129–30, 210, 213, 214, 283
Kyōgoku Tamekane, 57n20, 130, 300, 304
Kyōgoku Tameko, 71n63
Kyūan gannen rokugatsu jūhachinichi uemon no kami Ienari no ie no uta-awase, 171
Kyūan hyakushu, 13–14, 72, 399, 406–7, 411–12n29

Lofty (*taketakaki*) style, 149n21, 184–86, 285–86, 310
Lotus Sutra, 291, 340

Maiden at Uji Bridge (*Uji no hashihime*), 263, 267–68, 377–79
Maiden Unai, 379
Maigetsushō, 185
man'yōgana, 131, 358
Man'yōshū, xx, 1, 3, 11, 14, 42, 184; early scholarship on, xviii, 19, 20n7, 132, 405; as intertext or source for allusion, 131, 160, 181, 216–17n48, 357, 377–80 passim. *See also under Kokin waka rokujō*
mappō, 340

Masatsune, *see* Fujiwara (Asukai) Masatsune
Mass, Jeffrey, 37n62
Masukagami, 7, 38n63, 155–56, 208, 306
Matsukaze (Nō play), 359
Meigetsuki, 5, 7, 8, 14, 40, 100–101, 230, 300–301, 333, 382. *See also Meigetsuki* subheading *under* Fujiwara (Mikohidari) Teika
Meigetsuki shōshutsu, 5n11, 300
Michichika, *see* Minamoto (Tsuchimikado) Michichika
Michiteru, *see* Minamoto (Tsuchimikado) Michiteru
Michitomo, *see* Minamoto (Tsuchimikado) Michitomo
Michitsuna no Haha, 175
migyōsho (letter of praise), 276–79
Miharu no Arisuke, 344
Mikawa no Naishi, 67, 69
Mikohidari house, xv, 4n10, 18n4, 51, 289n91, 388
Mikohidari school, 4, 17, 21, 33, 54, 172, 215; and rivalry with Rokujō school, 53, 108, 218, 400; growing influence of, 64, 92, 112–13, 192, 382; and *Sengohyakuban uta-awase*, 194, 197–98, 218, 413, 416–18; and Kujō patrons, 34, 49, 395, 403; and affiliated poets, 393, 394, 400. *See also* Fujiwara (Mikohidari) Shunzei; Fujiwara (Mikohidari) Teika
Minamoto clan, xv
Minamoto Ienaga, 158, 277n59, 311, 393; as Chief Recorder (*kaikō*) for the Wakadokoro, 5, 112, 116; and Wakadokoro activities, 143, 268, 299; on the death of Go-Toba's concubine Owari, 272–73, 330

—and poetry activities: contests, 102n37, 124n93, 150, 237–38, 280, 413, 416; other poetry activities, 65, 66, 91; and *Shinkokinshū*, 325, 381, 393
—*Ienaga nikki*, 5, 393; characteristics of, 46n96, 66n45, 120, 230, 264–66, 382; description of poetry events, 134, 276–79; on Go-Toba, 46, 50–51, 60, 67–72 *passim*, 261–68; on parties, 223–28 *passim*, 243, 249–52, 297–98; on other courtier/poets, 61n31, 190, 230–33, 294; on Wakadokoro and *Shinkokinshū*, 115–19, 138, 316–20, 325; on the death of various courtiers, 87–91, 164, 188–89, 294–95, 330, 333–35

Minamoto (Tsuchimikado) Michichika, 59, 138, 139, 142–44, 157–58, 163, 187, 389, 396–97; as Rokujō patron, 19, 35; rise at court, 28–29, 31n40, 38–48 *passim*, 51, 162n52; as sponsor of poetry events, 83–84, 108–9, 120, 189; supplanted by Go-Toba as poetry patron, 140, 381, 397, 438; and *Shōji ninen in shodo hyakushu*, 55, 56, 58, 64, 84, 92, 114; and *Kennin gannen hachigatsu jūgoya senka-awase*, 124–26, 130–33; and *Sengohyakuban uta-awase*, 194–97 *passim*, 202–3, 215, 413, 416–18; and other poetry contests, 73, 74–75, 76n79–80, 84, 102n37–105, 106n45, 121–22, 140, 145, 150–53 *passim*, 158, 167, 168; appointed to Wakadokoro, 111–12, 115; sudden death of, 188–89, 276, 335

Minamoto (Tsuchimikado) Michiteru, 187–88, 389, 397; and poetry activities, 143, 150, 280, 286, 352, 413, 416

Minamoto (Tsuchimikado) Michitomo, 59, 389, 397; and Shunzei no Musume, 162–63, 290, 388; and *Shingū senka-awase*, 102n37, 104, 105n44, 106n45; and *Sengohyakuban uta-awase*, 210, 413, 416; and other poetry contests, 76n79, 77–78, 124, 145, 150–51, 276, 280, 352; and other poetry activities, 91, 143–44, 365; and appointment to Wakadokoro, 111–12, 115; as *Shinkokinshū* compiler, 138, 176, 235, 308, 349–51, 439

Minamoto Moromitsu (AKA Shōren), 71, 72n66, 112, 389, 397; and poetry activities, 55, 58, 122, 194, 215–18, 417–18

Minamoto Muneyori, 187

Minamoto no Arihito, 202

Minamoto no Ienaga nikki, see under Minamoto Ienaga

Minamoto Sanetomo (Shogun), 132n111, 244, 257, 330, 337, 391, 409n21

Minamoto Shitagō, 111n57, 132n110

Minamoto Shun'e, 126, 391

Minamoto Tomochika, 215, 389, 402; and Go-Toba, 71–72, 79n88; and *Sengohyakuban uta-awase*, 214, 220–21, 413, 416; and other poetry contests, 76n79, 78, 81, 102n37, 108, 124–29, 134, 150n24, 151, 280, 352, 361–62; and other poetry activities, 65, 66, 91, 143; and leisure activities, 223, 301, 304, 311; appointed to Wakadokoro, 111–12, 115

Minamoto Toshiyori, 2, 13, 18, 406. See also *Toshiyori zuinō*

Minamoto Tsunenobu, 2, 321–22

Minamoto Yoriie (Shogun), 244, 257, 396

Minamoto Yoritomo (Shogun), 21, 23–25, 30, 37, 39, 41, 45, 47–48

Minamoto Yoshitsune, 24

Minasedono koi jūgoshu uta-awase, 166–87 passim, 439. See also *Minase Sakuranomiya jūgoban uta-awase*; *Kennin ninen kugatsu nijūrokunichi Wakamiya senka-awase*
Minase Sakuranomiya jūgoban uta-awase, 173–87
Minase tsuridono rokushu uta-awase, 155, 158–61
Minase Villa, 163–64, 439; described in *Masukagami*, 155–56, 306; and *yūjo*, 156–58, 167n66, 267; as site for poetry activities, 156–57, 161, 275; Go-Toba visits, 258–59, 268, 274–75, 327; Go-Toba mourns Owari at, 272–73, 274, 330. See also various poetry events at Minase by name
Minegishi Yoshiaki, 34
Miner, Earl, 264. See also under Brower, Robert
Minishū, 236, 393
Mitsutoki (head painter for *Saishōshitennō-in shōji waka*), 370
Monogatari nihyakuban uta-awase, 175
Moromitsu, see Minamoto Moromitsu
Mostow, Joshua, xvii, 107n46
Mt. Hiei, 244, 268–70
Mumyōshō, 6, 126, 391. See also Kamo no Chōmei
Murasaki Shikibu, 21, 160, 172, 205. See also *Genji monogatari*
musubidai (compound topic), 158

Nagafusa, 142, 163, 194
Nagara Bridge, 260–66
Nakahara Morishige, 350
"Naniwazu" poem, 339–40
Nankaigyofu hokuzanshōkyaku hyakuban uta-awase, 32n45, 204–6
Narihira, see Ariwara no Narihira

Narishige, see Hōribe Narimochi
Nashitsubo no Gonin (Pear Jar Five), 111, 132
New Sandaishū (*Shinsandaishū*), 11, 113n63
Nihon shoki lectures, 312, 314n60
Nijō house (descendants of Mikohidari house), 10, 383
Nijō Palace, 111, 115, 187; burned down again, 255, 256
Nijō Sadasuke, 297, 298
Nijō school, xvii, 213
Nijō Tamefuji, 304
Nijō Tameyo, 300, 304
Nin'an ninen hachigatsu taikō taigōgū no suke Tsunemori no ie no uta-awase, 171
Ninna-ji, 52–53, 395, 399
Ninshi (AKA Gishūmon-in; daughter of Kujō Kanezane), 25, 33–34n49, 36–40 passim, 45, 162n52, 389, 398, 401. See also *Kenkyū no seihen*
Nobuhiro (identity unknown), 58
Nōen, 38, 389
Norimitsu, see Fujiwara Norimitsu
Nyogan, see Fujiwara Hideyoshi

Ōe no Chisato, 202, 203, 409n22
Ōe no Yoshitoki, 182n102
Ōgishō, 378n115
Ōidono, 88–90
Oki-bon (version of *Shinkokinshū* edited by Go-Toba), 53, 96, 107, 176, 324, 367, 382–83, 392
Omuro senka-awase, 53
Ono no Komachi, 21, 201n10
oriku (acrostic poems), 167, 245
Ōshikōchi no Mitsune, 224, 241, 376
Ōtomo Tabito, 14
Ōtomo Yakamochi, 3, 253n88
Owari (Go-Toba's concubine), 272, 277, 330–31, 338, 419–26

parallelism, xv, xvi
Pear Jar Five (*Nashitsubo no Gonin*), 111, 132
Pillow Book, The, see Sei Shōnagon
poems as offerings to shrines or temples, 60, 274, 287, 309, 329, 352
poetry contests, *see uta-awase*
poetry parties (*kakai, utakai*), 12, 14
Pollack, David, 203
Prince Tamehito, *see* Emperor Tsuchimikado
pseudonyms in poetry contests, 133

Reizei house, 300–301, 402
Reizei Tamesuke, 300
Rensei, *see* Fujiwara (Rokujō) Tomoie
Rokujō Akisue, *see* Fujiwara (Rokujō) Akisue
Rokujō Akisuke, *see* Fujiwara (Rokujō) Akisuke
Rokujō Ariie, *see* Fujiwara (Rokujō) Ariie
Rokujō house, xv, 4n10, 32, 51, 139, 358, 387. See also *individual family members by name*
Rokujō sadaijin no ie no uta-awase, 219
Rokujō school, 4, 18, 35, 53, 54, 64, 112–13, 171, 352, 398, 400; and rivalry with Mikohidari school, 9, 35, 53, 218, 402; and poetics, 20–21, 132; and role in *Sengohyakuban uta-awase*, 194, 197, 198, 218, 413, 416–18; and other poetry contests, 20, 34, 124; declining influence of, 10, 99, 113, 192, 382
Rokujō Suetsune, *see* Fujiwara (Rokujō) Suetsune
Rokujō Tsuneie, *see* Fujiwara (Rokujō) Tsuneie
Rokujō Yasusue, *see* Fujiwara (Rokujō) Yasusue

Rōnyaku gojisshu uta-awase, 55, 91–100 passim, 108, 123, 133, 153, 356, 438
Roppyakuban chinjō, 20, 34, 395
Roppyakuban uta-awase, 9, 15, 32–35, 52, 72, 393, 394
Ryōjin hishō, 392

Sadaie, *see* Fujiwara (Mikohidari) Teika
Sagami, 76n79, 99
Sagoromo monogatari, 22, 175
Saiei (Ienaga's brother), 223–25, 311
Saigyō, 9, 100n32, 220, 239, 394
Saishōshitennō-in shōji waka, 310n45, 369–80, 402
Saitō inshi hyakushu, 204–5
Sanbyakurokujūban uta-awase, 54, 84–85
Sanefusa, *see* Fujiwara Sanefusa
Sanetomo, *see* Minamoto Sanetomo
Sansom, Sir George, 25, 41–42
Santai waka, 146–49, 155, 439
Sanuki (AKA Nijō no In no Sanuki), 58, 62, 67, 99, 389, 398; and *Sengohyakuban uta-awase*, 201–2, 217, 413, 416; and other poetry contests, 76n79, 78, 102n37, 106n45, 122, 124n93, 127
Sasaki Takahiro, 81n97
Satsukawa Shūji, 8
screen painting poems, *see byōbue no uta*
Sei Shōnagon (and *The Pillow Book*), 120, 156n32, 172, 375
Seiashō, 7, 34n50
sekkanke, 7n15, 187
Semimaru, 221
Sengaku, 20n7
Sengohyakuban uta-awase, 10, 15, 21, 70, 75, 93n19, 97, 113, 193–221, 355, 413–18, 439; and *Go-Toba-in daisando hyakushu*, 82, 110–11, 438. See also under *individual poets by name*

Sentō kudai gojisshu, 135–38, 439
Senzaishū, 116n72, 205; and Mikohidari aesthetic vision, 2, 11, 19; and Shunzei as sole compiler, 3, 113, 399; and Kyūan hyakushu, 14, 72; sponsored by Go-Shirakawa, 31, 32, 392; as source for allusion, 128, 202, 361. See also Appendix B for poets with connections to this collection
Shakkyōka, see Buddhist poems
Shakua, see Fujiwara (Mikohidari) Shunzei
Shichijō no In, 67, 68, 389, 392
Shiguretei library, 301, 402
shiika (Chinese and Japanese verse), 33, 403
shiika-awase, 242–43, 325
Shikashū, 3, 13, 57, 72, 211, 409n20, 410
Shikishi Naishinnō (also Shokushi Naishinnō), 52, 58, 64n41, 69–70, 84, 382, 398; illness and death of, 86–91, 164, 165
Shimizu Hamaomi, 368n85
Shinchokusenshū, 11, 113, 172, 242n52, 383, 402
Shingū senka-awase, 84, 101–8, 124, 125, 134, 136, 438
Shinkokinshū, 1, 2–4, 8–13 passim, 51, 113, 308, 352, 381, 383, 391–403 (poets), 437–41 (time line). See also Oki-bon
—and poetry contests: before 1201, 33–34, 35, 74; in 1201 (Kennin 1), 93n19, 96–99, 105n42–109 passim, 121, 134, 140; in 1202 (Kennin 2), 145, 153; Minase contests: 161, 169, 173, 176, 178; in 1203 (Kennin 3), 194, 195, 210, 277–79, 287, 288; after Shinkokinshū presentation banquet, 328, 329, 353, 356–57, 362–63

—and other poetry activities, 64, 65, 136–38, 144, 149, 228, 252–55, 363–80 passim
—and prefaces, 300, 326, 403
—and compilers, 18, 71, 99, 138, 439
—and compilation process; selection, 8n18, 165, 234, 439–40; classification of poems (burui), 268–71, 275, 287, 299, 300, 317–18, 440; editing, 301, 305–9, 313, 314, 321–25, 329, 349–51, 354, 368
—and presentation banquet, 312–20, 440
—and Ienaga copy, 325, 381
—and neo-classicism, 41, 366, 375
—and Shinto poems in, 301–4, 307
—stylistic characteristics, 17, 154–55, 170–72, 175–76, 187, 200, 210, 212, 238, 243, 279–86 passim, 380
Shinsan (identity uncertain), 108–9n50
Shinsen Man'yōshū, 203
Shinto, 302–3
Shinto poems (jingika, jingi no uta), 2, 301–3
shirabyōshi (white-suited dancers), 101, 158, 166n66, 168n73, 258–59
Shitennōji, 238–39, 259
Shodo hyakushu, see Shōji ninen in shodo hyakushu
Shōji ninen in dainido hyakushu, 65–66, 72, 147, 193, 396, 438
Shōji ninen in shodo hyakushu, 10, 66, 84, 92, 108, 113, 114, 193, 405–12, 437–38; and events surrounding, 55–59, 63–64; and Teika, 60, 62–64, 402; and Shikishi Naishinnō, 64n41, 87–88. See also under individual poets in Appendix B; Shōji sōjō
Shōji ninen jūgatsu tsuitachi uta-awase, 81–83

Shōji ninen kugatsu sanjūnichi nijūyoban uta-awase, 78–81, 99
Shōji ninen sentō jūnin uta-awase, 73–75
Shōji sōjō (*Shōji ninen Shunzeikyō no waji sōjō*), 35n54, 55n15, 200, 405–12
Shōka (proof poem), 20
Shokugosenshū, 11
Shokushi Naishinnō, *see* Shikishi Naishinnō
Shokushikashū, 57, 410–11
Shōren, *see* Minamoto Moromitsu
Shūi gusō, 225
Shūishū, 3n8, 123, 154, 184n105, 251n85
Shukaku Hosshinnō, 52–53, 58, 72, 399
Shukaku Hosshinnō no ie no gojisshu, 53, 399
Shunzei, *see* Fujiwara (Mikohidari) Shunzei
Shunzei no Musume (or Shunzeikyō no Musume), 162–63, 382, 388, 389, 399–400; and Go-Toba, 68–69, 136n120, 140, 162–63, 190; and Kunaikyō, 69n58, 280–82; and Minamoto Michitomo, 162–63, 290; and the 1202 Minase contests, 166–71 *passim*, 174–76; and *Sengohyakuban uta-awase*, 200–202, 413, 416; and other poetry contests, 109, 124–26, 150, 153–54, 280–82, 352; and other poetry activities, 135–36, 144; and *Shinkokinshū*, 178–79n94, 308
Shunzeikyō jukkai hyakushu, 363n68
Shunzeikyō kujū no gaki, 243, 248–50
Smits, Ivo, 203, 242
Sone no Yoshitada, 13
Suetsune, *see* Fujiwara (Rokujō) Suetsune
Sueyoshi, *see* Fujiwara Sueyoshi
sugata, 408
Sugawara Michizane, 203

suki (connoisseurship), 168, 306
Suma, 160, 358–59, 360
Sumiyoshi no Kami, 165
Sumiyoshi Shrine, 46, 352, 353
Suō no Naishi, 323–24
Susanoo no Mikoto (and the earliest waka poem), 205, 304
Sutoku-in hyakushu, *see* *Kyūan hyakushu*

Tadatsune, *see* Fujiwara Tadatsune
Tadayoshi, *see* Fujiwara Tadayoshi
taigendome (substantive final), 155, 171–72, 176, 187, 200, 210, 238, 243, 281
Taira Kagemitsu, 237–38
Taira Kiyomori, 24n16, 28, 30
Taira Munenobu, 299n7
Takafusa, *see* Fujiwara Takafusa
Takahashi Mushimaro, 267, 378
Takakura-dono, 68, 280
Takanobu, *see* Fujiwara Takanobu
Takazane, *see* Fujiwara Nobuzane
take/taketakaki, *see* Lofty style
Tale of Genji, The, *see* *Genji monogatari*
Tameie, *see* Fujiwara (Mikohidari) Tameie
Tanabata, 265
Tango (AKA Gishūmon-in no Tango, Sesshōke no Tango), 58, 63, 67, 389, 401; and poetry contests, 102n37, 106, 107n47, 122, 124, 130–31, 276–80 *passim*, 352, 413, 416
Tango no Tsubone (Takashina Eishi), 26n24, 28–29, 37n62, 401
Taniyama Shigeru, 73n67, 109
Teika, *see* Fujiwara (Mikohidari) Teika
Teika jittei, 185–86, 285
Teika Karyū ryōkyō senka-awase, 75, 281
Teramoto Naohiko, 22n12–13, 23
Theme meals, 268–69, 301, 304–6
Toba Palace, 150, 258–59, 438

Tomochika, see Minamoto Tomochika
Ton'a, 5n11, 7, 34n50
Tō no chūjō Minamoto Akifusa no ie no uta-awase, 219n55
Tosa nikki, 46n96
Toshinari, see Fujiwara (Mikohidari) Shunzei
Toshiyori zuinō, 205, 303
Tsuchimikado (Minamoto) house, 4, 9–10, 35, 49, 51, 112, 194, 389, 396–97; and poetry events, 124, 194, 352
Tsuchimikado Michichika, see Minamoto (Tsuchimikado) Michichika
Tsuchimikado Michiteru, see Minamoto (Tsuchimikado) Michiteru
Tsuchimikado Michitomo, see Minamoto (Tsuchimikado) Michitomo
Tsuneie, see Fujiwara (Rokujō) Tsuneie
Tsurayuki, see Ki no Tsurayuki

Uji: and court excursion to, 259–69, 266; and associations in poetry, 265–66, 377, 379. See also Maiden at Uji Bridge
Uji no hashihime, see Maiden at Uji Bridge
uta-awase (poetry contest), 12, 14–15, 241–42, 219; shūgihan (group-judged) contests, 14, 82, 104n41, 109, 151, 289, 355; tōza (impromptu) contests, 15, 65, 76, 82, 91; senka-awase (contest of selected poems), 34, 75, 79n89, 84, 91, 94–95, 239–40, 392, 439. See also individual contests by name
utakai (kakai, poetry party), 12, 14
utamakura (poetic place-names), 12n26, 207, 369, 372, 374, 377
Uwayokote Masataka, 25, 37n62, 41n74, 43

Waiting Woman topic, 102n37, 175, 183, 186, 218, 274, 331, 358
waka: structure of, xv–xvi
Wakadokoro, 5, 18, 114, 134, 164, 223, 382, 393; Go-Toba re-establishes, 111–12, 438–39; membership of, 71, 99, 112, 115–16, 195, 396–97, 401–3; layout and furnishings of, 115, 119, 262–65; as site for work on Shinkokinshū, 117–19, 268–70, 275, 299–304 passim, 307, 314, 324; as site for poetry activities, 118–20, 123, 135, 142–45, 148, 260, 277, 318, 369, 371; as new site for Hitomaro eigu contests, 121–22, 145, 189; relocations of, 222, 234, 271; as site of Shunzei's ninetieth-year celebration, 243, 246, 248; theme meals served by members of, 268–69, 301, 304–6
Waka ichijishō, 132n112
Waka iroha, 132n112
Wakamiya Shrine, 238, 294
Wakan rōeishū, 128, 203, 226
Waka shogakushō, 132n112
Wani, 339–40
Western Paradise, 90, 344
Winding Waters Banquet (gokusui no en; kyokusui no en), 335–36

Yamabe Akahito, 253n88, 357–58
Yamato monogatari, 379
Yasusue, see Fujiwara (Rokujō) Yasusue
Yoritomo, see Minamoto Yoritomo
yoriudo (Wakadokoro members), 111, 114, 119. See also under Wakadokoro
Yoshimine no Munesada, see Henjō
Yoshitada hyakushu, 13
Yoshitsune, see Fujiwara (Kujō) Yoshitsune

Yoshitsune Jichin hyakuban uta-awase, see *Nankaigyofu hokuzanshōkyaku hyakuban uta-awase*
Yoshitsune no ie no nijūban uta-awase, 54
yū (elegance), 21
yūgen, 130, 206
yūjo, 101n34, 156–58, 166–67n66, 238–39, 267

Yukihira, *see* Ariwara no Yukihira
Yūshi Naishinnō, 349n34

Zaishi (adopted daughter of Michichika), 37–38, 162n52, 389, 396
zekku (Ch. *jueju*) verse form, 203, 206

Harvard East Asian Monographs
(* out-of-print)

*1. Liang Fang-chung, *The Single-Whip Method of Taxation in China*
*2. Harold C. Hinton, *The Grain Tribute System of China, 1845–1911*
3. Ellsworth C. Carlson, *The Kaiping Mines, 1877–1912*
*4. Chao Kuo-chün, *Agrarian Policies of Mainland China: A Documentary Study, 1949–1956*
*5. Edgar Snow, *Random Notes on Red China, 1936–1945*
*6. Edwin George Beal, Jr., *The Origin of Likin, 1835–1864*
7. Chao Kuo-chün, *Economic Planning and Organization in Mainland China: A Documentary Study, 1949–1957*
*8. John K. Fairbank, *Ching Documents: An Introductory Syllabus*
*9. Helen Yin and Yi-chang Yin, *Economic Statistics of Mainland China, 1949–1957*
*10. Wolfgang Franke, *The Reform and Abolition of the Traditional Chinese Examination System*
11. Albert Feuerwerker and S. Cheng, *Chinese Communist Studies of Modern Chinese History*
12. C. John Stanley, *Late Ching Finance: Hu Kuang-yung as an Innovator*
13. S. M. Meng, *The Tsungli Yamen: Its Organization and Functions*
*14. Ssu-yü Teng, *Historiography of the Taiping Rebellion*
15. Chun-Jo Liu, *Controversies in Modern Chinese Intellectual History: An Analytic Bibliography of Periodical Articles, Mainly of the May Fourth and Post–May Fourth Era*
*16. Edward J. M. Rhoads, *The Chinese Red Army, 1927–1963: An Annotated Bibliography*
17. Andrew J. Nathan, *A History of the China International Famine Relief Commission*
*18. Frank H. H. King (ed.) and Prescott Clarke, *A Research Guide to China-Coast Newspapers, 1822–1911*
19. Ellis Joffe, *Party and Army: Professionalism and Political Control in the Chinese Officer Corps, 1949–1964*
*20. Toshio G. Tsukahira, *Feudal Control in Tokugawa Japan: The Sankin Kōtai System*
21. Kwang-Ching Liu, ed., *American Missionaries in China: Papers from Harvard Seminars*
22. George Moseley, *A Sino-Soviet Cultural Frontier: The Ili Kazakh Autonomous Chou*

Harvard East Asian Monographs

23. Carl F. Nathan, *Plague Prevention and Politics in Manchuria, 1910–1931*
*24. Adrian Arthur Bennett, *John Fryer: The Introduction of Western Science and Technology into Nineteenth-Century China*
25. Donald J. Friedman, *The Road from Isolation: The Campaign of the American Committee for Non-Participation in Japanese Aggression, 1938–1941*
*26. Edward LeFevour, *Western Enterprise in Late Ching China: A Selective Survey of Jardine, Matheson and Company's Operations, 1842–1895*
27. Charles Neuhauser, *Third World Politics: China and the Afro-Asian People's Solidarity Organization, 1957–1967*
28. Kungtu C. Sun, assisted by Ralph W. Huenemann, *The Economic Development of Manchuria in the First Half of the Twentieth Century*
*29. Shahid Javed Burki, *A Study of Chinese Communes, 1965*
30. John Carter Vincent, *The Extraterritorial System in China: Final Phase*
31. Madeleine Chi, *China Diplomacy, 1914–1918*
*32. Clifton Jackson Phillips, *Protestant America and the Pagan World: The First Half Century of the American Board of Commissioners for Foreign Missions, 1810–1860*
33. James Pusey, *Wu Han: Attacking the Present through the Past*
34. Ying-wan Cheng, *Postal Communication in China and Its Modernization, 1860–1896*
35. Tuvia Blumenthal, *Saving in Postwar Japan*
36. Peter Frost, *The Bakumatsu Currency Crisis*
37. Stephen C. Lockwood, *Augustine Heard and Company, 1858–1862*
38. Robert R. Campbell, *James Duncan Campbell: A Memoir by His Son*
39. Jerome Alan Cohen, ed., *The Dynamics of China's Foreign Relations*
40. V. V. Vishnyakova-Akimova, *Two Years in Revolutionary China, 1925–1927*, tr. Steven L. Levine
*41. Meron Medzini, *French Policy in Japan during the Closing Years of the Tokugawa Regime*
42. Ezra Vogel, Margie Sargent, Vivienne B. Shue, Thomas Jay Mathews, and Deborah S. Davis, *The Cultural Revolution in the Provinces*
*43. Sidney A. Forsythe, *An American Missionary Community in China, 1895–1905*
*44. Benjamin I. Schwartz, ed., *Reflections on the May Fourth Movement.: A Symposium*
*45. Ching Young Choe, *The Rule of the Taewŏngun, 1864–1873: Restoration in Yi Korea*
46. W. P. J. Hall, *A Bibliographical Guide to Japanese Research on the Chinese Economy, 1958–1970*
47. Jack J. Gerson, *Horatio Nelson Lay and Sino-British Relations, 1854–1864*
48. Paul Richard Bohr, *Famine and the Missionary: Timothy Richard as Relief Administrator and Advocate of National Reform*
49. Endymion Wilkinson, *The History of Imperial China: A Research Guide*
50. Britten Dean, *China and Great Britain: The Diplomacy of Commercial Relations, 1860–1864*
51. Ellsworth C. Carlson, *The Foochow Missionaries, 1847–1880*

Harvard East Asian Monographs

52. Yeh-chien Wang, *An Estimate of the Land-Tax Collection in China, 1753 and 1908*
53. Richard M. Pfeffer, *Understanding Business Contracts in China, 1949–1963*
54. Han-sheng Chuan and Richard Kraus, *Mid-Ch'ing Rice Markets and Trade: An Essay in Price History*
55. Ranbir Vohra, *Lao She and the Chinese Revolution*
56. Liang-lin Hsiao, *China's Foreign Trade Statistics, 1864–1949*
*57. Lee-hsia Hsu Ting, *Government Control of the Press in Modern China, 1900–1949*
58. Edward W. Wagner, *The Literati Purges: Political Conflict in Early Yi Korea*
*59. Joungwon A. Kim, *Divided Korea: The Politics of Development, 1945–1972*
*60. Noriko Kamachi, John K. Fairbank, and Chūzō Ichiko, *Japanese Studies of Modern China Since 1953: A Bibliographical Guide to Historical and Social-Science Research on the Nineteenth and Twentieth Centuries, Supplementary Volume for 1953–1969*
61. Donald A. Gibbs and Yun-chen Li, *A Bibliography of Studies and Translations of Modern Chinese Literature, 1918–1942*
62. Robert H. Silin, *Leadership and Values: The Organization of Large-Scale Taiwanese Enterprises*
63. David Pong, *A Critical Guide to the Kwangtung Provincial Archives Deposited at the Public Record Office of London*
*64. Fred W. Drake, *China Charts the World: Hsu Chi-yü and His Geography of 1848*
*65. William A. Brown and Urgrunge Onon, translators and annotators, *History of the Mongolian People's Republic*
66. Edward L. Farmer, *Early Ming Government: The Evolution of Dual Capitals*
*67. Ralph C. Croizier, *Koxinga and Chinese Nationalism: History, Myth, and the Hero*
*68. William J. Tyler, tr., *The Psychological World of Natsume Sōseki*, by Doi Takeo
69. Eric Widmer, *The Russian Ecclesiastical Mission in Peking during the Eighteenth Century*
*70. Charlton M. Lewis, *Prologue to the Chinese Revolution: The Transformation of Ideas and Institutions in Hunan Province, 1891–1907*
71. Preston Torbert, *The Ch'ing Imperial Household Department: A Study of Its Organization and Principal Functions, 1662–1796*
72. Paul A. Cohen and John E. Schrecker, eds., *Reform in Nineteenth-Century China*
73. Jon Sigurdson, *Rural Industrialism in China*
74. Kang Chao, *The Development of Cotton Textile Production in China*
75. Valentin Rabe, *The Home Base of American China Missions, 1880–1920*
*76. Sarasin Viraphol, *Tribute and Profit: Sino-Siamese Trade, 1652–1853*
77. Ch'i-ch'ing Hsiao, *The Military Establishment of the Yuan Dynasty*
78. Meishi Tsai, *Contemporary Chinese Novels and Short Stories, 1949–1974: An Annotated Bibliography*
*79. Wellington K. K. Chan, *Merchants, Mandarins and Modern Enterprise in Late Ch'ing China*

Harvard East Asian Monographs

80. Endymion Wilkinson, *Landlord and Labor in Late Imperial China: Case Studies from Shandong by Jing Su and Luo Lun*
*81. Barry Keenan, *The Dewey Experiment in China: Educational Reform and Political Power in the Early Republic*
*82. George A. Hayden, *Crime and Punishment in Medieval Chinese Drama: Three Judge Pao Plays*
*83. Sang-Chul Suh, *Growth and Structural Changes in the Korean Economy, 1910–1940*
84. J. W. Dower, *Empire and Aftermath: Yoshida Shigeru and the Japanese Experience, 1878–1954*
85. Martin Collcutt, *Five Mountains: The Rinzai Zen Monastic Institution in Medieval Japan*
86. Kwang Suk Kim and Michael Roemer, *Growth and Structural Transformation*
87. Anne O. Krueger, *The Developmental Role of the Foreign Sector and Aid*
*88. Edwin S. Mills and Byung-Nak Song, *Urbanization and Urban Problems*
89. Sung Hwan Ban, Pal Yong Moon, and Dwight H. Perkins, *Rural Development*
*90. Noel F. McGinn, Donald R. Snodgrass, Yung Bong Kim, Shin-Bok Kim, and Quee-Young Kim, *Education and Development in Korea*
91. Leroy P. Jones and Il SaKong, *Government, Business, and Entrepreneurship in Economic Development: The Korean Case*
92. Edward S. Mason, Dwight H. Perkins, Kwang Suk Kim, David C. Cole, Mahn Je Kim et al., *The Economic and Social Modernization of the Republic of Korea*
93. Robert Repetto, Tai Hwan Kwon, Son-Ung Kim, Dae Young Kim, John E. Sloboda, and Peter J. Donaldson, *Economic Development, Population Policy, and Demographic Transition in the Republic of Korea*
94. Parks M. Coble, Jr., *The Shanghai Capitalists and the Nationalist Government, 1927–1937*
95. Noriko Kamachi, *Reform in China: Huang Tsun-hsien and the Japanese Model*
96. Richard Wich, *Sino-Soviet Crisis Politics: A Study of Political Change and Communication*
97. Lillian M. Li, *China's Silk Trade: Traditional Industry in the Modern World, 1842–1937*
98. R. David Arkush, *Fei Xiaotong and Sociology in Revolutionary China*
*99. Kenneth Alan Grossberg, *Japan's Renaissance: The Politics of the Muromachi Bakufu*
100. James Reeve Pusey, *China and Charles Darwin*
101. Hoyt Cleveland Tillman, *Utilitarian Confucianism: Chen Liang's Challenge to Chu Hsi*
102. Thomas A. Stanley, *Ōsugi Sakae, Anarchist in Taishō Japan: The Creativity of the Ego*
103. Jonathan K. Ocko, *Bureaucratic Reform in Provincial China: Ting Jih-ch'ang in Restoration Kiangsu, 1867–1870*
104. James Reed, *The Missionary Mind and American East Asia Policy, 1911–1915*
105. Neil L. Waters, *Japan's Local Pragmatists: The Transition from Bakumatsu to Meiji in the Kawasaki Region*
106. David C. Cole and Yung Chul Park, *Financial Development in Korea, 1945–1978*

Harvard East Asian Monographs

107. Roy Bahl, Chuk Kyo Kim, and Chong Kee Park, *Public Finances during the Korean Modernization Process*
108. William D. Wray, *Mitsubishi and the N.Y.K, 1870–1914: Business Strategy in the Japanese Shipping Industry*
109. Ralph William Huenemann, *The Dragon and the Iron Horse: The Economics of Railroads in China, 1876–1937*
110. Benjamin A. Elman, *From Philosophy to Philology: Intellectual and Social Aspects of Change in Late Imperial China*
111. Jane Kate Leonard, *Wei Yüan and China's Rediscovery of the Maritime World*
112. Luke S. K. Kwong, *A Mosaic of the Hundred Days:. Personalities, Politics, and Ideas of 1898*
113. John E. Wills, Jr., *Embassies and Illusions: Dutch and Portuguese Envoys to K'ang-hsi, 1666–1687*
114. Joshua A. Fogel, *Politics and Sinology: The Case of Naitō Konan (1866–1934)*
*115. Jeffrey C. Kinkley, ed., *After Mao: Chinese Literature and Society, 1978– 1981*
116. C. Andrew Gerstle, *Circles of Fantasy: Convention in the Plays of Chikamatsu*
117. Andrew Gordon, *The Evolution of Labor Relations in Japan: Heavy Industry, 1853–1955*
*118. Daniel K. Gardner, *Chu Hsi and the "Ta Hsueh": Neo-Confucian Reflection on the Confucian Canon*
119. Christine Guth Kanda, *Shinzō: Hachiman Imagery and Its Development*
*120. Robert Borgen, *Sugawara no Michizane and the Early Heian Court*
121. Chang-tai Hung, *Going to the People: Chinese Intellectual and Folk Literature, 1918–1937*
*122. Michael A. Cusumano, *The Japanese Automobile Industry: Technology and Management at Nissan and Toyota*
123. Richard von Glahn, *The Country of Streams and Grottoes: Expansion, Settlement, and the Civilizing of the Sichuan Frontier in Song Times*
124. Steven D. Carter, *The Road to Komatsubara: A Classical Reading of the Renga Hyakuin*
125. Katherine F. Bruner, John K. Fairbank, and Richard T. Smith, *Entering China's Service: Robert Hart's Journals, 1854–1863*
126. Bob Tadashi Wakabayashi, *Anti-Foreignism and Western Learning in Early-Modern Japan: The "New Theses" of 1825*
127. Atsuko Hirai, *Individualism and Socialism: The Life and Thought of Kawai Eijirō (1891–1944)*
128. Ellen Widmer, *The Margins of Utopia: "Shui-hu hou-chuan" and the Literature of Ming Loyalism*
129. R. Kent Guy, *The Emperor's Four Treasuries: Scholars and the State in the Late Chien-lung Era*
130. Peter C. Perdue, *Exhausting the Earth: State and Peasant in Hunan, 1500–1850*
131. Susan Chan Egan, *A Latterday Confucian: Reminiscences of William Hung (1893–1980)*
132. James T. C. Liu, *China Turning Inward: Intellectual-Political Changes in the Early Twelfth Century*

Harvard East Asian Monographs

133. Paul A. Cohen, *Between Tradition and Modernity: Wang T'ao and Reform in Late Ching China*
134. Kate Wildman Nakai, *Shogunal Politics: Arai Hakuseki and the Premises of Tokugawa Rule*
135. Parks M. Coble, *Facing Japan: Chinese Politics and Japanese Imperialism, 1931–1937*
136. Jon L. Saari, *Legacies of Childhood: Growing Up Chinese in a Time of Crisis, 1890–1920*
137. Susan Downing Videen, *Tales of Heichū*
138. Heinz Morioka and Miyoko Sasaki, *Rakugo: The Popular Narrative Art of Japan*
139. Joshua A. Fogel, *Nakae Ushikichi in China: The Mourning of Spirit*
140. Alexander Barton Woodside, *Vietnam and the Chinese Model: A Comparative Study of Vietnamese and Chinese Government in the First Half of the Nineteenth Century*
141. George Elision, *Deus Destroyed: The Image of Christianity in Early Modern Japan*
142. William D. Wray, ed., *Managing Industrial Enterprise: Cases from Japan's Prewar Experience*
143. T'ung-tsu Ch'ü, *Local Government in China under the Ching*
144. Marie Anchordoguy, *Computers, Inc.: Japan's Challenge to IBM*
145. Barbara Molony, *Technology and Investment: The Prewar Japanese Chemical Industry*
146. Mary Elizabeth Berry, *Hideyoshi*
147. Laura E. Hein, *Fueling Growth: The Energy Revolution and Economic Policy in Postwar Japan*
148. Wen-hsin Yeh, *The Alienated Academy: Culture and Politics in Republican China, 1919–1937*
149. Dru C. Gladney, *Muslim Chinese: Ethnic Nationalism in the People's Republic*
150. Merle Goldman and Paul A. Cohen, eds., *Ideas Across Cultures: Essays on Chinese Thought in Honor of Benjamin L Schwartz*
151. James Polachek, *The Inner Opium War*
152. Gail Lee Bernstein, *Japanese Marxist: A Portrait of Kawakami Hajime, 1879–1946*
153. Lloyd E. Eastman, *The Abortive Revolution: China under Nationalist Rule, 1927–1937*
154. Mark Mason, *American Multinationals and Japan: The Political Economy of Japanese Capital Controls, 1899–1980*
155. Richard J. Smith, John K. Fairbank, and Katherine F. Bruner, *Robert Hart and China's Early Modernization: His Journals, 1863–1866*
156. George J. Tanabe, Jr., *Myōe the Dreamkeeper: Fantasy and Knowledge in Kamakura Buddhism*
157. William Wayne Farris, *Heavenly Warriors: The Evolution of Japan's Military, 500–1300*
158. Yu-ming Shaw, *An American Missionary in China: John Leighton Stuart and Chinese-American Relations*
159. James B. Palais, *Politics and Policy in Traditional Korea*
160. Douglas Reynolds, *China, 1898–1912: The Xinzheng Revolution and Japan*
161. Roger Thompson, *China's Local Councils in the Age of Constitutional Reform*
162. William Johnston, *The Modern Epidemic: History of Tuberculosis in Japan*

Harvard East Asian Monographs

163. Constantine Nomikos Vaporis, *Breaking Barriers: Travel and the State in Early Modern Japan*
164. Irmela Hijiya-Kirschnereit, *Rituals of Self-Revelation: Shishōsetsu as Literary Genre and Socio-Cultural Phenomenon*
165. James C. Baxter, *The Meiji Unification through the Lens of Ishikawa Prefecture*
166. Thomas R. H. Havens, *Architects of Affluence: The Tsutsumi Family and the Seibu-Saison Enterprises in Twentieth-Century Japan*
167. Anthony Hood Chambers, *The Secret Window: Ideal Worlds in Tanizaki's Fiction*
168. Steven J. Ericson, *The Sound of the Whistle: Railroads and the State in Meiji Japan*
169. Andrew Edmund Goble, *Kenmu: Go-Daigo's Revolution*
170. Denise Potrzeba Lett, *In Pursuit of Status: The Making of South Korea's "New" Urban Middle Class*
171. Mimi Hall Yiengpruksawan, *Hiraizumi: Buddhist Art and Regional Politics in Twelfth-Century Japan*
172. Charles Shirō Inouye, *The Similitude of Blossoms: A Critical Biography of Izumi Kyōka (1873–1939), Japanese Novelist and Playwright*
173. Aviad E. Raz, *Riding the Black Ship: Japan and Tokyo Disneyland*
174. Deborah J. Milly, *Poverty, Equality, and Growth: The Politics of Economic Need in Postwar Japan*
175. See Heng Teow, *Japan's Cultural Policy Toward China, 1918–1931: A Comparative Perspective*
176. Michael A. Fuller, *An Introduction to Literary Chinese*
177. Frederick R. Dickinson, *War and National Reinvention: Japan in the Great War, 1914–1919*
178. John Solt, *Shredding the Tapestry of Meaning: The Poetry and Poetics of Kitasono Katue (1902–1978)*
179. Edward Pratt, *Japan's Protoindustrial Elite: The Economic Foundations of the Gōnō*
180. Atsuko Sakaki, *Recontextualizing Texts: Narrative Performance in Modern Japanese Fiction*
181. Soon-Won Park, *Colonial Industrialization and Labor in Korea: The Onoda Cement Factory*
182. JaHyun Kim Haboush and Martina Deuchler, *Culture and the State in Late Chosŏn Korea*
183. John W. Chaffee, *Branches of Heaven: A History of the Imperial Clan of Sung China*
184. Gi-Wook Shin and Michael Robinson, eds., *Colonial Modernity in Korea*
185. Nam-lin Hur, *Prayer and Play in Late Tokugawa Japan: Asakusa Sensōji and Edo Society*
186. Kristin Stapleton, *Civilizing Chengdu: Chinese Urban Reform, 1895–1937*
187. Hyung Il Pai, *Constructing "Korean" Origins: A Critical Review of Archaeology, Historiography, and Racial Myth in Korean State-Formation Theories*
188. Brian D. Ruppert, *Jewel in the Ashes: Buddha Relics and Power in Early Medieval Japan*
189. Susan Daruvala, *Zhou Zuoren and an Alternative Chinese Response to Modernity*

Harvard East Asian Monographs

190. James Z. Lee, *The Political Economy of a Frontier: Southwest China, 1250–1850*
191. Kerry Smith, *A Time of Crisis: Japan, the Great Depression, and Rural Revitalization*
192. Michael Lewis, *Becoming Apart: National Power and Local Politics in Toyama, 1868–1945*
193. William C. Kirby, Man-houng Lin, James Chin Shih, and David A. Pietz, eds., *State and Economy in Republican China: A Handbook for Scholars*
194. Timothy S. George, *Minamata: Pollution and the Struggle for Democracy in Postwar Japan*
195. Billy K. L. So, *Prosperity, Region, and Institutions in Maritime China: The South Fukien Pattern, 946–1368*
196. Yoshihisa Tak Matsusaka, *The Making of Japanese Manchuria, 1904–1932*
197. Maram Epstein, *Competing Discourses: Orthodoxy, Authenticity, and Engendered Meanings in Late Imperial Chinese Fiction*
198. Curtis J. Milhaupt, J. Mark Ramseyer, and Michael K. Young, eds. and comps., *Japanese Law in Context: Readings in Society, the Economy, and Politics*
199. Haruo Iguchi, *Unfinished Business: Ayukawa Yoshisuke and U.S.-Japan Relations, 1937–1952*
200. Scott Pearce, Audrey Spiro, and Patricia Ebrey, *Culture and Power in the Reconstitution of the Chinese Realm, 200–600*
201. Terry Kawashima, *Writing Margins: The Textual Construction of Gender in Heian and Kamakura Japan*
202. Martin W. Huang, *Desire and Fictional Narrative in Late Imperial China*
203. Robert S. Ross and Jiang Changbin, eds., *Re-examining the Cold War: U.S.-China Diplomacy, 1954–1973*
204. Guanhua Wang, *In Search of Justice: The 1905–1906 Chinese Anti-American Boycott*
205. David Schaberg, *A Patterned Past: Form and Thought in Early Chinese Historiography*
206. Christine Yano, *Tears of Longing: Nostalgia and the Nation in Japanese Popular Song*
207. Milena Doleželová-Velingerová and Oldřich Král, with Graham Sanders, eds., *The Appropriation of Cultural Capital: China's May Fourth Project*
208. Robert N. Huey, *The Making of 'Shinkokinshū'*

OHIO UNIVERSITY LIBRARY
Please return this book as soon as you have finished with it. In order to avoid a fine it must be returned by the latest date stamped below. All books are subject to recall after two weeks or immediately if needed for reserve.

CF